THE PUBLICATIONS

OF THE

𝕾𝖊𝖑𝖉𝖊𝖓 𝕾𝖔𝖈𝖎𝖊𝖙𝖞

περὶ παντὸς τὴν ἐλευθερίαν

VOLUME CXXIX

FOR THE YEAR 2012

THE RIGHTS AND LIBERTIES OF THE ENGLISH CHURCH

READINGS FROM THE PRE-REFORMATION INNS OF COURT

EDITED FOR
THE SELDEN SOCIETY
BY

MARGARET McGLYNN

Associate Professor of History
University of Western Ontario

LONDON
SELDEN SOCIETY
2015

ISBN 978 0 85423 221 5

Printed in the UK by Henry Ling Ltd,
at the Dorset Press, Dorchester, DT1 1HD

CONTENTS

PART III: OTHER TEXTS ON THE COMMON LAW AND THE CHURCH

PREFACE

As even a quick glance through the Selden Society volumes will indicate, editions tend to be lengthy labours and to draw on a wide range of expertise and support, and this one is no exception. As with most Selden Society volumes in recent years, my first debt of gratitude is to Professor Sir John Baker, for his practical help, generous encouragement, and quiet patience, as well as for comments on earlier drafts of this work. While anyone working in the field of late-medieval or early-modern English law is indebted to his enormous contributions to the field, his work on readings has been foundational, and his massive volume of *Readers and Readings in the Inns of Court and Chancery* has made this work possible. I am also most grateful for the careful and detailed feedback I received from Dr Neil Jones as well as for his patience, a quality high on the list of requirements for the Literary Director of the Society. Their combined wisdom and expertise has greatly improved this edition, though any remaining errors are mine.

This project began while I was teaching at Wellesley College and has concluded at the University of Western Ontario, and I am grateful to both institutions for providing financial support for my research, as well as congenial work environments. This research was also supported by the Social Sciences and Humanities Research Council of Canada. While the financial support from all three institutions was necessary and very much appreciated, this work would have been impossible without the help and support of friends and colleagues. I would especially like to thank Donald Logan, who read an early version of the Edward Hall reading many years ago and encouraged me to continue with the project, R. H. Helmholz, Bruce O'Brien, Mario Longtin, Debra Nousek and Christopher Mackay.

The manucript readings edited in this volume have often travelled far and wide before they reached the safe havens in which they now rest. I would like to thank the Bodleian Library, Oxford, the British Library, Harvard Law School, the John Rylands Library at the University of Manchester, the London Metropolitan Archives, Northwestern University School of Law, the Masters of the Bench of Gray's Inn, the Master and Fellows of University College, Oxford, the Philadelphia Free Library, the Syndics of Cambridge University Library and Mr Anthony Taussig for allowing me access to their collections, and in particular Joel Sartorius, Godfrey Waller, Audrey Chapuis and Theresa Thom for all their help. Thanks are due also to the Stenton Fund of the British Academy which made a generous subvention towards this volume.

Finally, I thank Niamh and Ardith, who have never known a world in which their parents were not working on an edition, and Richard, who makes all things possible.

M. McG.

MANUSCRIPTS

WESTMINSTER I
Reading A: *Ub* = University College, Oxford, MS. 163, fos 77–79v
Reading B: *Hb* = CUL MS. Hh.2.6, fos 101–105
Reading C: *Ib* = CUL MS. Ii 5.43, fos 75–77v
Reading D: *Hk* = BL MS. Hargrave 87, fos 302–306v
Reading E: *Eb* = CUL MS. Ee.5.22, fos 115–121
Reading F: *N* = Northwestern University, Newcastle, MS. fos 92–93v
Reading G: *Q* = CUL MS. Ee.2.26, fos 92–93
Reading H: *J* = John Rylands MS. GB 133 Eng MS. 288, fos 60v–61v
Reading J: *Cb* = Gray's Inn MS. 25, fos 121–124
Reading K: *B* = Bodleian MS. Tanner 428, fos 1–14v

MAGNA CARTA
Reading 1: *Ra* = Bodleian MS. Rawlinson C294, fo. 1
        T = Taussig MS. 82.5.5 (a), fo. 79
Reading 2: *U* = University College, Oxford, MS. 163, fos 1–3
        E = CUL MS. Ee.5.22, fos 18–19v
        H = CUL MS. Hh.2.6, fos 1–3
        Pa = Philadelphia Free Library MS. LC 14.12, fo. 1
        Ga = Guildhall Library MS. 86, fos 17–17v
        I = CUL MS. Ii.5.43, fos 25–25v
        [*Rb* = Bodleian MS. Rawlinson C294, fo. 199]
Reading 3: *L* = BL MS. Lansdowne 1138, fos 1–2
Reading 4: *HLSb* = Harvard Law School MS. 13, pp. 7–8
Reading 5: *HLSc* = Harvard Law School MS. 13, pp. 379–382
Reading 6: *Hg* = BL MS. Hargrave 87, fos 195–198v
        Pb = Philadelphia Free Library MS. LC 14.12, fos 236–237v
        HLSa = Harvard Law School MS. 88, fos 1–3
Reading 7: *S* = CUL MS. Ee.3.46, fos 56–65v
Reading 8: *C* = Gray's Inn MS. 25, fos 20–20v
Reading 9: *G* = CUL MS. Gg.6.18, fos 3–5v
        Gb = London Metropolitan Archives CLC/270/MS00086, fos 14–16v
Reading 10: *Hl* = BL MS. Harley 4990, fos 146–61

HALL
Ha = BL MS. Hargrave 88, fos 74–78v
Hr = BL MS. Hargrave 92, fos 57–62v

ABBREVIATIONS

Baker, *Men of Court*	*The Men of Court 1440 to 1550*, J. H. Baker. ed., 2 vols. (18 Selden Soc. Suppl. Series), (London, 2012)
Baker, *OHLE*	Sir John Baker, *Oxford History of the Laws of England*, vol. 6, *1483–1558* (Oxford, 2003)
Baker and Milsom	Sir John Baker, *Baker and Milsom, Sources of English Legal History: Private Law to 1750*, 2nd ed. (Oxford, 2010)
BL	British Library
Bracton	*Bracton on the Laws and Customs of England*, G. E. Woodbine ed., S. E. Thorne trans. (Cambridge, Mass., 1968–77)
Bray, *Tudor Church Reform*	Gerald R. Bray ed., *Tudor Church Reform: The Henrician Canons of 1535 and the* Reformatio Legum Ecclesiasticarum (Woodbridge, 2000)
CUL	Cambridge University Library
Cal. Pat. Rolls	*Calendar of the Patent Rolls*
Caryll, reports	*Reports of Cases by John Caryll*, J. H. Baker ed. (115 and 116 Selden Soc.), (London, 1998, 1999)
Dig.	*The Digest of Justinian*, Theodor Mommsen and Paul Krueger eds., Alan Watson, trans., 4 vols. (Philadelphia,1985)
Early Treatises	B. H. Putnam, *Early Treatises on the Practices of the Justices of the Peace in the Fifteenth and Sixteenth Centuries* (Oxford, 1974)
Exchequer Chamber	*Select Cases in the Exchequer Chamber*, M. Hemmant ed. (51 and 64 Selden Soc.), (London, 1933, 1945)
Fitzherbert	Sir Anthony Fitzherbert, *La graunde abridgement …* (London: Richard Tottell, 1577) [STC/226:16]
Gabel, *Benefit of Clergy*	Leona C. Gabel, *Benefit of Clergy in England in the Later Middle Ages* (Northampton, Mass., 1929)
Glanvill	*The Treatise on the Laws and Customs of the Realm of England commonly called Glanvill*, G. D. G. Hall ed., with a guide to further reading by M. T. Clanchy (Oxford, 1993)
Helmholz, *Ius Commune*	R. H. Helmholz, *The* Ius Commune *in England* (Oxford, 2001)

Legal Profession	J. H. Baker, *The Legal Profession and the Common Law* (London, 1986)
L&P	*Letters and Papers, Foreign and Domestic, of the Reign of Henry VIII, 1509–1547*, J. S. Brewer et al. eds, 21 vols. (London, 1862–1932)
Lib. Ass.	*Le Livre des Assises et Pleas del' Corone* [*Liber Assisarum*] (London, 1679)
Littleton, *Tenures*	*Littleton's Tenures in English*, E. Wambaugh ed. (Washington, D.C., 1903)
McGlynn, *Royal Prerogative*	Margaret McGlynn, *The Royal Prerogative and the Learning of the Inns of Court* (Cambridge, 2003)
Perkins, *Profitable Booke*	John Perkins, *Here beginneth a verie profit-able booke of Master John Perkins fellovve of the inner Temple treating of the lawes of this realme...* (London: Richard Tottel, 1555) [STC (2nd ed.)/19633]
Port, *Notebook*	*The Notebook of Sir John Port*, J. H. Baker ed. (102 Selden Soc.), (London, 1986)
Register	William Rastell, *Registrum Omnium Brevium tam Originalium quam Iudicialiam* (London, 1531) [STC 20836]
Readers and Readings	*Readers and Readings in the Inns of Court and Chancery*, J. H. Baker ed. (13 Selden Soc. Suppl. Series) (London, 2001)
Reports, Hen. VIII	*Reports of Cases from the Time of King Henry VIII*, J. H. Baker ed., 2 vols. (120 and 121 Selden Soc.), (London, 2003, 2004).
Spelman, reports	*The Reports of Sir John Spelman*, J. H. Baker ed., 2 vols. (93 and 94 Selden Soc.), (London, 1976, 1977).
Spelman, *Quo Warranto*	*John Spelman's Reading on Quo Warranto*, J. H. Baker ed., (113 Selden Soc.), (London, 1997)
SR	*Statutes of the Realm*, 11 vols. (London, 1810–22)
Statham	*Statham's Abridgment of the Law*, M. Klingelsmith ed. (Boston, Mass., 1915) (repr. Clark, NJ, 2007)
Thorne, *Moots*	*Readings and Moots at the Inns of Court in the Fifteenth Century*, S. E. Thorne ed., vol. 1 (71 Selden Soc.), (London, 1952)
Wilkins, *Concilia*	David Wilkins, *Concilia Magnae Britanniae et Hiberniae*, 4 vols. (London, 1737).
YB	Year Books

INTRODUCTION

Twenty-one of the twenty-two texts in this volume are editions of manuscript readings, given at one of the four inns of court between about 1430 and 1540.[1] Readings were lecture series delivered as part of the educational programme of the inns; the readers were fairly senior lawyers, usually men who had held the status of utter barrister within the inn for a decade or more. Readings were held twice a year, in the Lent and Autumn vacations, with the Lent vacation usually going to the senior or double reader, who would have delivered his first reading some five to ten years earlier.[2] They were the high point of the educational cycle, particularly the Lent reading, and were regularly attended, not only by the students but by judges and serjeants who might return to their old inns for the occasion. Each reader chose a statutory text on which to base his exposition of the law, and moved through the text explaining the logic of the law and demonstrating its operation through examples and cases. His audience, from junior utter barristers through to the serjeants and judges, might argue his cases, and the whole exercise was designed to test the knowledge, ingenuity and logic of both reader and audience. The manuscript readings which survive are usually notes taken at these learning exercises, probably by students, and are often anonymous. In most cases the readings are not attributed to any particular reader, and they are generally undated. They are also written in a truncated and technical law French, heavily abbreviated in both form and content, and paleographically challenging – in short, thoroughly unappealing. Why then are they worthy of study?

In the introduction to his edition of Spelman's reading on *Quo Warranto*, Baker points out that much of the interest of that volume derives from the light it throws on the ways in which the law was taught and transmitted in the inns of court. Two distinct manuscript traditions survive for that reading: one represents the reader's exposition of the law, and the other the disputation, the putting and arguing of cases related (sometimes quite distantly) to the topic under discussion. As Baker notes, though each lecture seems to have involved both exposition and disputation, it is not entirely clear whether the two were separate or intermingled; discussion may have followed as each point was made, or a complete lecture may have

---

[1] The single exception is explained below, p. xli.
[2] This sequence was sometimes interrupted by a call of serjeants, for the serjeants-elect were expected to deliver a third reading in their home inn as part of their elevation to the coif. Serjeants' readings were usually gala affairs.

been followed by a discussion session.[3] Surviving manuscript readings make it
apparent that for the most part the note-takers had no interest in maintaining a
tidy distinction between lecture and argued cases, as exposition and argument are
jumbled together, often in no apparent order.[4] Their interest was primarily, if not
solely, in content. Keeping the distinction between lecture and cases in mind is
often helpful in sorting out the untidy jumble, however, and in this introduction
I have used this distinction to help break the readings in this volume down into
manageable components.[5]

Because they are far less orderly than the surviving manuscripts of Spelman's
reading, the readings on the Statutes of Westminster I and Magna Carta allow us
to see the process of legal education from a different perspective. Thorne's pio-
neering work suggested a system of readings in which the readers worked their
way through the major statutes from Magna Carta onwards in an orderly cycle
lasting ten to fifteen years.[6] Subsequent work, mostly by Baker, has demonstrated
that the cycle was rather less orderly, and, especially from the late fifteenth century on, could be interrupted by readings on much more recent statutes.[7] As well
as working to elucidate the process of legal education, Putnam, Thorne, and
Baker also edited readings, usually readings which were significant because of
their content, or their reader, or both.[8] Although all of these scholars were clear
that the readers depended on the work of their predecessors, and that their work
was in turn used by their successors, most of the texts they edited – Marowe on
keeping the peace, Constable on *Prerogativa Regis*, Spelman on *Quo Warranto*,
for example – are clearer and more coherent than many of the surviving reading
texts.[9] These readings provide valuable information on the development of the
law in this period, and in the ongoing campaign to draw attention to readings
and their value as sources, this was a logical and useful choice. The readings on
Westminster I and Magna Carta in this volume, on the other hand, demonstrate

---

[3] Spelman, *Quo Warranto*, pp. xi–xiii.

[4] None of the manuscript readings in this volume can be confidently identified as autographs, so we are
dealing with notes taken by auditors with all the issues of transmission that implies. As will become
clear, many of the surviving manuscripts have also been copied at least once, so we are often looking at
texts with a number of layers of transmission. For purposes of clarity the original auditor is referred to
as the note-taker, and all subsequent copiers as scribes.

[5] Some of the readings, generally the later ones, are already divided into lectures, either explicitly with
numbers or words in the margins, or implicitly with breaks and text from the statute.

[6] Thorne, *Moots*, pp. ix–xviii. For general background on legal education in this period see: J. H. Baker,
'Learning Exercises in the Medieval Inns of Court and Chancery', in *Legal Profession*, pp. 7–23;
J. H. Baker, 'The Inns of Court in 1388', in *Legal Profession*, pp. 3–6; S. E. Thorne, 'The Early History of
the Inns of Court with Special Reference to Gray's Inn', in S. E. Thorne, *Essays in English Legal History*
(1985), pp. 137–154; A. W. B. Simpson, 'The Early Constitution of the Inns of Court', *Cambridge Law
Journal* 28 (1970), pp. 241–256; McGlynn, *The Royal Prerogative*, pp. 15–22.

[7] See *Readers and Readings*, pp. 3–4.

[8] *Early Treatises*; S. E. Thorne ed., *Prerogativa Regis: Tertia Lectura Roberti Constable de Lyncolnis Inne
Anno 11 H. 7* (New Haven, Conn., 1949); Thorne, *Moots*; *Readings and Moots at the Inns of Court in the
Fifteenth Century*, vol. 2, S. E. Thorne and J. H. Baker eds. (105 Selden Soc.) (London, 1990); Spelman,
Quo Warranto. G. O. Sayles also edited 'A Fifteenth-Century Law Reading in English', in G. O. Sayles,
Scripta Diversa (1982), pp. 301–312. This reading deals with the opening chapters of Magna Carta in a
clear, brisk and brief exposition.

[9] See Spelman, *Quo Warranto*, pp. xvi–xviii, for an exposition of Spelman's sources, for example.

the full range of coherence and incoherence of the readings. While some of them, for example Readings A and D (on Westminster I) and 2, 3, and 9 (on Magna Carta) stand alone as fairly coherent expositions of their topics, others are rather less orderly. Partly because of this disorder, they demonstrate the ways in which these various manuscripts are connected and thus allow us further insight into the construction of a reading, while reminding us that some manuscript 'readings' most probably had only a tenuous relationship with any particular learning exercise.

The choice of subject matter for this volume was driven by two separate yet connected concerns. The first, as already suggested, was to better understand these manuscripts as a product of, and thus an insight into, the process of legal education. The second was to see what the common lawyers were teaching on the general subject of the Church in the century or so leading up to the Reformation. The two most obvious places to look for this were Westminster I chapters one to three and Magna Carta chapter one.[10] There is some overlap in the material that the readers discuss under these two texts. Westminster I is more clearly defined: chapter one deals with extortions against religious houses (though it is often not included in these readings) and chapter two is a foundation text for the common law of benefit of clergy. Chapter three deals with escapes, and while it is not specifically related to the Church the readers often discuss the escapes of clerks convict or attaint, and escapes from bishops' prisons or sanctuary under this heading, presumably because of its proximity and thematic connection to chapter two. Magna Carta chapter one, the confirmation of the liberties of the Church, prompts discussions of grants to the Church, sanctuary and benefit of clergy, villein priests and monks, tithes, and cognizance of pleas in virtually every reading, with a smattering of other topics, such as fifteenths and tenths, and oblations, obventions and mortuaries. Though benefit of clergy is the most obvious topic on which the two texts overlap, the various readers tend to treat it differently because it appears in two different contexts. Between the two sets of texts these readings cover a good deal of Church-related material, though always, obviously, from the perspective of the common law.

The depth of these expositions varies substantially. Only one of the readings on Magna Carta deals solely with chapter one: all of the rest cover multiple chapters, ranging from two to all thirty-seven.[11] Similarly, two texts deal solely with chapter one of Westminster I, but most treatments omit it, and many deal with much more of the statute.[12] Naturally, the depth and the accuracy of the lectures vary substantially for this reason, and it is entirely likely that some of the readers, or the note-takers, were only marginally interested in the material on

---

[10] *SR*, i. 26–28 and *SR*, i. 114 respectively. The 1297 confirmation of Magna Carta has been used as that was the standard version in this period.

[11] Snede is the only one to deal purely with chapter one. It is unfortunate that his reading is both heavily damaged and not very good.

[12] One of these is Reading H, which is a very brief treatment, the other is Reading K, which is a translation of one version of Marowe's reading on Westminster I, c. 1, though both the original and the translation wander into a consideration of 1 Ric. II, c. 15 (*SR*, ii. 5).

the Church. By divorcing the lectures on these chapters from the rest of a longer reading we lose the benefit of some context and completeness. Nevertheless, given the hodgepodge nature of these statutes, this loss is more than made up for by the coherence of the subject matter in these excerpts. And it is worth keeping in mind that even if some readers were not particularly interested in or knowledgeable about the law relating to the Church, this was what the students at the inns were exposed to. Studying the very best readings allows us to see what the best lawyers understood the law to be, but examining the full range of readings exposes us to a much more varied and variable transmission of the law. Before expanding on this theme, it will be helpful to consider the various manuscripts briefly.

READINGS ON WESTMINSTER I

I have chosen to edit readings which deal with chapters one to three of the statute, although most of the surviving readings do not cover all three chapters. Unlike the readings on Magna Carta, all of the readings survive in only a single manuscript. This makes the task of editing somewhat easier, but raises different questions about the circulation of this material.

Reading A

Reading A, *Ub*, is in a fifteenth-century manuscript, which also contains two readings on Magna Carta, including one of the versions of Reading 2. This reading covers chapters two and three.[13] It probably dates from shortly before 1430: it refers to the statute 8 Hen. VI, c. 6 as 'the new statute', but seems to be unaware of 2 Hen. VI, c. 21, which made an escape by one detained for high treason, treason.[14] It is likely that the reference to 8 Hen. VI, c. 6 was a later addition to the original text, though it does not appear as an interjection in the text. The sections of the reading which deal with chapters two and three are fairly brief, but they are clear and well-organized. There are no case references, and the lectures are simple expositions of the law. The reader does use a number of maxims from the civil and canon law: he points out that 'a benefit cannot be conferred on someone who is unwilling', that 'literacy does not make a clerk, nor habit a monk, but the tonsure' and that 'the church closes her bosom to no-one returning'.[15] The maxims originate in the *Digest*, the *Liber Extra* and the *Codex* respectively, but the second is probably known to the reader via a year book case, and the last is presented as a 'text in the pleas of the Crown'.[16] It is not clear whether the reader is aware of the origins of the various maxims, and even if he was aware, there is no suggestion that his familiarity with either civil or canon law runs deep.

---

[13] The reading as a whole covers thirteen chapters of the statute in twenty-four folios. *Readers and Readings*, p. 591.
[14] 8 Hen. VI, c. 6 (*SR*, ii. 242–243); 2 Hen. VI, c. 21 (*SR*, ii. 226–227).
[15] Reading A, below, pp. 1, 2.
[16] *Dig.* 50.17.69; *Liber Extra*, 3.31.13; *Codex* 1.1.8.35. Reading A, below, p. 2.

The reading opens with the most basic statement that the ordinary must claim the clerk, then goes on to define who is a clerk; what is a felony; how benefit of clergy interacts with other ways of avoiding death, such as sanctuary, approving and abjuring; the test for clergy; and the implications of bigamy. The reading then has a brief section on sanctuary, which is striking, because the statute says nothing about this topic. Sanctuary and benefit of clergy were usually handled together in readings on Magna Carta, as we shall see, and it seems likely that either the reader or his audience assumed that the discussion of one meant a discussion of the other. The reading gets back to the statute with purgation and forfeiture, and concludes with a brief consideration of late claims, errors and pardons. Its handling of chapter three is similarly efficient, with only a single mention of the ordinary's fine for an escaped clerk in the midst of the lecture.

Reading B

This reading is in *Hb*, a fifteenth-century manuscript which also has one of the versions of Reading 2. Baker suggests that it is from Gray's Inn *c.* 1450/60.[17] This reading also begins with chapter two, and deals with six chapters in fifteen folios. Reference is made to one case, from 8 Edw. II, while the latest statutory reference is to 4 Hen. IV, c. 3.[18] One possible clue to the date of this reading is the argument that the felon used to be able to plead his clergy without answering to the felony, but that it is better for him to answer and demand over. This sounds like class C of the benefit of clergy pleas as categorised by Leona Gabel: she argues that this process was used for a limited time at the end of the reign of Edward I, and only in the Middlesex gaol delivery, but her division of pleas into classes A, B, and C seems to be overly schematised when compared with the discussions in the year books and the readings.[19] Again, the reading is fairly clear, with the reader opening with the purpose of the statute, asserting that the clerk must claim the privilege, and moving on to the test; the order of pleading; for which crimes it may be claimed; an indictment for felony and treason; purgation; the difference between clerks convict and attaint; forfeiture; traverse; appeal; and escape. Under chapter three there is only the briefest mention of both sanctuary and the escape of clerks. The reading seems to be almost completely lecture, with little in the way of case references. There are a number of statute references, but they are generally incomplete, usually referring only to Edward with a space left for the king (III) and the year to be filled in. The manuscript does seem to have been used, however, since there are marginal notes in at least two hands pointing to important elements of the lectures. This text also has fairly large spaces left at the end of each lecture to allow for further notes to be added. This is fairly common in the manuscripts of readings, and we will see in some of the later manuscripts how those spaces were filled.

---

[17] *Readers and Readings*, p. 417.
[18] *SR*, ii. 133.
[19] Gabel, *Benefit of Clergy*, pp. 48–49.

Reading C

The next reading is in *Ib*, also a mid-fifteenth-century manuscript, which also has one of the texts of Reading 2 on Magna Carta. This reading begins with chapter two of Westminster I, running all the way to chapter forty-seven in seventeen folios.[20] Like Reading A there are no case references, but here there are three statute references to Edward I, and a fourth to Edward III. This reading seems to be a little later than Reading B, since the reader asserts that a felon cannot claim his clergy until after he has pleaded to the felony, a proposition later associated with Prysot C.J.C.P.[21] Here the assertion is noted, but not argued, suggesting a date probably in the 1460s or 1470s. Once again the reading is fairly organised, running quickly through the purpose of the statute; the delivery to the ordinary; the kinds of felony involved; the test; bigamy; the difference between clerks convict and attaint; error; and purgation. Under chapter three, this reading mentions escape from sanctuary, briefly, and the escape of a clerk convict in a little more detail.

Given that Readings A, B and C all come from volumes which also contain versions of Reading 2, it is tempting to speculate that the two readings might have travelled together. However, this does not seem likely: Readings A and B come from manuscripts with related versions of Reading 2, but there are few similarities between them, perhaps even fewer than we might imagine being imposed by the material. Reading C has one of the variant versions of Reading 2, but given that Readings C and 2 are in different hands, it seems fairly clear that they all travelled independently to their current locations.

Reading D: Thomas Kebell

The fourth reading, *Hk*, is in a fifteenth-century hand, but added into a sixteenth-century manuscript. BL MS. Hargrave 87 is probably the largest surviving volume of manuscript readings, and, not surprisingly, also has a reading on Magna Carta chapter one, in this case one of the texts of Reading 3. This is the only one of the Westminster I readings with a known author, and was given by Thomas Kebell of the Inner Temple. Again there are few case or statute references to help with dating. Baker dates it to *c.* 1460–75: in his treatment of chapter three Kebell mentions the statute 1 Edw. IV, c. 2, but the later end of Baker's range seems more likely since Kebell also refers to a case from 1468, which he describes as being argued 'lately'.[22] Ives suggested that this was Kebell's second reading, given in about 1472, and while his assumption of a strict cycle of readings is now generally accepted to be problematic, this date is certainly still possible.[23]

Kebell's reading was also extant in an Inner Temple manuscript which disappeared during the Second World War. Bertha Putnam, in her study and

[20] *Readers and Readings*, p. 427.
[21] See J. H. Baker, 'Some Early Newgate Reports', in C. Stebbings ed., *Law Reporting in Britain* (1995), p. 48. The case usually given is YB Mich. 3 Hen. VII, fo. 12, pl. 10.
[22] *Readers and Readings*, p. 325. *SR*, ii. 389–391; YB Pas. 8 Edw. IV, fo. 3, pl. 6. See Reading D, p. 30.
[23] E. W. Ives, *The Common Lawyers of pre-Reformation England* (Cambridge, 1983), pp. 48–49. See also *Readers and Readings*, p. 66.

edition of Thomas Marowe's 1503 reading on Westminster I chapter one, looked briefly at this manuscript.[24] She comments that Kebell's reading was 'altogether different from other early readings on this statute, which ordinarily treat almost exclusively of abuses in houses of religion'.[25] Putnam claims that Kebell

> begins with a brief discussion of the peace of the Church, shows the difference between statute and common law, and describes the remedies afforded by the writ *De vi laica removenda*. He then takes as his main subject the question as to who were responsible for enforcing the statutes on the peace, and gives a long list of officials … One is forced to believe that Marowe was thoroughly familiar with Keble's sections on surety of peace, riot, rout and assembly, escapes, and gaoler by inheritance.[26]

This does indeed seem to closely anticipate Marowe's treatment, but it only vaguely relates to *Hk*. In the Hargrave manuscript Kebell's chapter one opens with a brief paragraph on *vi laica removenda*, carries on with two paragraphs on the remedies for religious houses which have suffered extortions and a paragraph on the officers of the peace, and concludes with a lengthier section on sureties. There are some slight thematic similarities with Marowe's first lecture, but nothing substantial. In lecture two Marowe moves on to the peace of the bodies of spiritual persons, which could lead us into benefit of clergy, but he quickly veers off into a discussion of 1 Ric. II, c. 15, on the arrest of religious persons, and that becomes his text for the rest of this lecture, before he returns to the keeping of the peace in later lectures.[27] *Hk*, on the other hand, goes on to chapter two of Westminster I and the familiar discussion of benefit of clergy. Given Putnam's description, it is probable that the actual lectures dealt with the justices of the peace in much more detail, and the note-taker of the Hargrave version was simply less interested in this material. The loss of manuscripts is always frustrating, but it would have been particularly useful to have two versions of a known reading which differ so substantially and which could have been related to a later reading on the same topic. Both readings circulated with Kebell's name attached, which raises interesting questions about the problems of attributing authorship to the surviving texts: if two note-takers could come away with such substantially different versions of a lecture series which circulated under the name of a known and respected reader, it makes any statement that anonymous reading texts are definitively unrelated rather more uncertain.

Once into chapter two, Kebell follows the usual pattern of material for benefit of clergy. He opens with a brief overview which explains what crimes the privilege applies to; abjurers; the reading test; when the privilege is refused; the

---

[24] *Early Treatises*, pp. 154–155.

[25] Ibid., 184, 185, n. 1. Putnam dates Kebell's reading to shortly before 1486, which would make it his third: ibid., 179.

[26] Ibid., pp. 184–185. *Hk* is Putnam's manuscript K, which she labels as a 'fragment only': ibid., p. 179 n. 3.

[27] Ibid., p. 295. The statute is *SR*, ii, 5. Reading K, p. 60 below, is a later translation of an abridged version of Marowe's reading.

forfeitures that apply to those convicted; and the remedies of purgation and pardon. His treatment of the material is a little more detailed than that of the earlier readers, and generally more useful. His treatment of chapter three makes only a brief mention of the escapes of clerks convict, but spends an unusually long time on sanctuary.

Reading E

This reading is in a fifteenth-century manuscript, *Eb*, which also contains a reading on Magna Carta chapter one, in this case a version of Reading 2. This is a lengthy reading, taking up fifty-six folios, but since it deals with thirty-two chapters of the statute its treatment of each section is not substantially more detailed than the other readings.[28]

This is only the second reading to consider chapter one of the statute, and unlike Kebell, this reader deals in some detail with religious houses. He opens by pointing out the mischief which occasioned the statute, and then discusses sureties and damages, as Kebell had done. From there, however, he moves on to describe what counts as extortion, takes a brief detour into founders' rights, and then goes to the process for claiming relief under the statute, pointing out that by the equity of the statute any lord or common person can use this statute, but that the remedy under the common law is better than the remedy under the statute. He ends the lecture with a discussion of public places and services.

Once the reading moves into the discussion of chapter two, the structure of this text becomes a bit more complex. It quickly becomes apparent that the reading is related to Reading A, though it is not a direct copy: it borrows about two-thirds of Reading A's lecture on chapter two, and the borrowed material is about a quarter of the text in Reading E. The pattern is much the same in chapter three, where the opening page comes quite directly from Reading A, but only a handful of lines in the following six pages are in the earlier lecture.[29]

The discussion of chapter two opens with the usual brief survey of the mischief behind the statute and then moves on to a discussion of clerks attaint and convict. The reading gives four ways in which a clerk may be attainted (outlawry, confession, abjuration and judgment) and their implications for purgation, and then four ways in which a clerk may be convicted, which all deal with the issue of jurisdiction and the process of claiming clergy. It is somewhat surprising that the first three methods are Gabel's classes A, C and B, with no suggestion of any chronological or geographical distinction between them, while the fourth is when the felon is arraigned and stays mute.[30] The reader sums up

---

[28] *Readers and Readings*, pp. 405–406.
[29] Reading E has two of the same maxims as Reading A, but both seem to come directly from the earlier reading. See Reading E, pp. 36–37, below, cf. Reading A, pp. 37–38, below.
[30] See Gabel, *Benefit of Clergy*, pp. 31–49. Gabel suggests that pleas of class A tended to be earlier, class B were mid fourteenth to fifteenth-century, and class C were confined to Middlesex in the reign of Edward I. If this were the case it seems unlikely that the reader would treat them quite so evenly, and the paucity of surviving gaol delivery records may account for Gabel's findings.

this section by pointing out that neither a clerk convict nor a clerk attaint may maintain a personal action or be sued in one.

The next section examines the cases for which benefit of clergy can be claimed, how it can be combined with sanctuary or abjuration (the first addition from Reading A) and the exception of bigamy. There is a brief interjection of material on sanctuary and approvers from Reading A and then the lecture goes on to provide the definition of a clerk, which focuses mainly on tonsure. It then deals with the ordinary's role, and approvers again, before the longest interjection from Reading A. This points out that if the ordinary accepts a felon when he is not a clerk the ordinary shall lose his temporalities, and then discusses the court's responsibility for the test; sanctuary; purgation; appellors, and the process of due purgation. There is a brief diversion into escapes, and then the reading returns to material from Reading A with a discussion of the rights of the wife of a clerk convict via Sybil Belknap's case, and the implications if a clerk is attainted erroneously.[31] The text ends with additions which discuss what happens when the ordinary refuses a clerk generally or specially, and the need for bigamy to be judged by the ordinary.

In its discussion of chapter three the text draws on Reading A primarily in the opening, but it has only a few short comments relevant to the Church. It notes that if a clerk escapes from the ordinary the ordinary shall pay £100 'as it is done today', rather than forfeiting his temporalities as it had said should happen when the ordinary accepts a supposed clerk. It also points out that the vill shall be amerced if a felon escapes from sanctuary and mentions the escape of a clerk attaint from Westminster, none of which come from Reading A.

This raises the question of whether Reading E is indeed a distinct text, or whether it is simply a longer version of Reading A, but on balance the latter seems unlikely. Reading A is not really integrated into the text, and the sections taken from it are occasionally jarring. Reader E generally tends to be quite systematic in his exposition, dividing clerks attaint and clerks convict into four groups, for example, and summing up his discussion of them before moving on. The material brought in from Reading A, on the other hand, while it usually adds to the substance of the discussion, does not seem to be added in the most useful or obvious spot. For example, Reading E has a lengthy discussion of the role of tonsure in the identification of a clerk, immediately followed by a discussion of the need for the ordinary to be present in court. This would be a logical place to discuss the literacy test, but the text moves on to approvers first, then adds material from Reading A on what happens if the ordinary accepts one who is clearly not a clerk, before getting to the literacy test.

Manuscript texts of readings are generally not models of organization, and this is a fairly typical state of affairs, but it means that we need to think more carefully about the levels of construction in the text. There are a number of references in

---

[31] YB Mich. 1 Hen. IV, fo. 1, pl. 2 reports that the king sued Sibyl Belknap in the Common Pleas without naming her husband, who was then in exile in Gascony, and Gascoigne C.J.K.B. accepted the action. See Reading A, p. 4, n. 1, below.

Reading E from late in the reign of Henry VI, suggesting that the reading was originally written down some time after 1456 with space left in the manuscript for later additions. The same scribe, or someone else, added in the material from Reading A after this date, not always very smoothly, and may have added other notes or comments. The Reading E scribe copied all of that material without distinguishing between the two (or more) texts and later added his own notes: there is a blank folio and a half at the end of the lecture on chapter one for such additional material, while the half folio left blank at the end of the lectures on chapters two and three seems to have been filled by the same hand as the main text, though at a different time. The notes at the end of chapters two and three refer three times to points made by the justices 'recently', suggesting that the compiler was adding material from contemporary cases as they were argued.[32] Two of the three 'recent' examples date from 1467 and 1469, but if the identification to *The Carrier's Case* on folio 143 is accepted, the scribe was still making additions in 1474.[33] We cannot date 'Reading E' to a particular year or a particular reader, because the text as it exists is effectively a palimpsest, and a reminder that these texts grew organically and idiosyncratically as they were used. The process is somewhat visible in this version, but it is likely that many surviving reading texts are the product of a similar process.

Reading F

This is certainly the case with Reading F, which survives in *N*, a fifteenth-century volume with some sixteenth-century additions. This reading deals with eight chapters of the statute in ten folios.[34] It begins with chapter two, and the text of the lecture on that chapter covers a page and a half, with the bottom half of the page taken up with two sixteenth-century additions. The lecture on chapter three is a little shorter, and has just a couple of lines in the later hand. There are also marginal notations in three different hands, so this reading appears to have been fairly well used.

Reading F opens, as usual, with a discussion of the mischief behind the statute, the problem of due purgation, and notes that it is a prohibition against the ordinary, and that a contempt lies on it. It also points out that the statute is to be understood of clerks convict and not clerks attaint, presumably because the reader thinks that clerks attaint cannot purge themselves. From there it points out that the felon must answer to the felony before he can have benefit of clergy (a point it makes again later), and notes those who may not claim the privilege. It spends a little time on the ordinary's obligation to be in court and quickly runs through the crimes the privilege can be claimed for; forfeitures; and what happens if one who has claimed his privilege is arraigned for treason. It then turns to due purgation; to the difference between clerks convict and attaint; and finishes with a discussion of error.

---

[32] See below pp. 41, 45. The third 'recent' case, regarding bigamy, has not been identified, below, p. 41.

[33] *The Carrier's Case* is in the discussion of chapter 20 of Westminster I and is not included in this edition. See *Readers and Readings*, p. 406; Thorne, *Moots*, pp. lvi-lvii.

[34] See *Readers and Readings*, p. 549.

Below the main body of the text are two blocks of notes in a sixteenth-century hand, both of which are drawn from Reading A or E. The first deals with attainder by false oath, erroneous outlawry and the escape of a pardoned felon. The second opens with the statement that a man cannot have his clergy unless he asks for it, and goes on to argue that a man cannot be called a clerk unless he has a tonsure.[35] It then notes that one who takes his clergy shall not be handed over to the ordinary until after the inquisition, and ends with the rights of the wife of a clerk convict. The notes are closer to the text in A than in E, but it is striking that at least two students thought these passages worth copying.

Reading F's treatment of chapter three is brief, and it has no discussion of sanctuary or the escapes of clerks convict or attaint. There is one brief sixteenth-century note at the end of the lecture, but it does not appear to come from Reading A or E. There are no case or statute references in Reading F, which focuses more on the lecture part of the readings than the disputation. The owner of this text was presumably more interested in exposition than argument, but again, the variety of added notes drawn from the earlier readings and the marginal notations make it clear that this text was constructed over time, and was used by a variety of students.

Reading G

Reading G is in a fifteenth-century manuscript, *Q*, which is mostly made up of year books. It deals with chapters two and three in three pages, and the material on chapter three takes up less than one page, breaking off abruptly at the bottom of folio 93.[36]

The reading opens with the usual discussion on mischief, and makes the same point as the previous reading that the statute must be understood of a clerk convict, though it elaborates that a clerk attaint shall not have his purgation. It argues that the clerk must answer before he can have his test and then lays out for which crimes the privilege can be claimed. Next it moves to who cannot claim the privilege, focusing mainly on bigamy, but with mention of bastardy and villeiny. Then it deals with the ordinary's obligation to be in court in person or by deputy, following Readings E and F in the statement that if two deputies appear and one refuses the clerk while the other accepts him, he will be accepted by them *in favorem vitae*. It then moves on to what happens if the ordinary and the justices disagree about whether the felon is a clerk and to the distinction between a clerk convict and a clerk attaint. Finally it mentions due purgation and escapes from the bishop's prison.

There is nothing in this reading to date it specifically, and only those brief mentions which link it to Readings E and F. Overall it seems to date from the later part of the fifteenth century.

---

[35] This material appears in Reading E, but it has been separated, and changed somewhat.

[36] See *Readers and Readings*, p. 394.

Reading H

This is in a fifteenth-century manuscript, *J*, containing a variety of legal texts: treatises, year books, moots, and moot cases, along with some readings.[37] This reading deals only with chapter one of Westminster I, on abbeys. It opens with a statement of the mischief and the process for suing on the statute. It then moves on to an abbot's grants, and which ones will bind his successor; founders' rights; and the difference between a fine, ransom and amercement. As usual, there are no case or statute references to help date it, and because fewer of the readings deal with chapter one than chapters two and three, there is less to compare it to, but its treatment of this material seems to be unique.

Reading J

This manuscript, *Cb*, dates from the early sixteenth century, and belonged to Robert Chaloner of Gray's Inn. It contains mostly readings, possibly including Chaloner's own on Magna Carta, and some reports of cases, all in a very challenging hand.[38] The reading on Westminster I deals with chapters one to twenty-nine and thirty-one to forty-nine over fifty folios, but the material on chapters one to three is very brief. Chapter one of the statute is quoted in full, but there is no lecture at all, and the three following pages are blank, suggesting again that the scribe expected further material to be added later. Chapter two is also quoted in full, and then the text makes a series of very short and disconnected points on purgation, examination and forfeiture.[39] If this is indeed a reading, then the order of the points is unusually mixed up, since a discussion of examination usually precedes purgation and forfeiture. One of the points is introduced with the tag 'at a moot it was said…' suggesting that rather than representing an entire reading, this material was gathered from a number of sources. Much of it may come from readings, but most likely not the same one. In Chaloner's manuscript the text is continuous, but as we can see with other texts, including another reading in this manuscript, it is entirely possible that he copied another student's disconnected references into one continuous block of text.[40]

Unlike the other readings on Westminster I this text has a lot of case references, mostly to the reigns of Henry VI and Edward IV, and it also seems to refer to the statute 4 Hen. VII, c. 13.[41] Baker notes that later in the text there are references to Fyneux and Brudenell although he suggests that they are probably additions.[42] If this text is not a reading *per se*, but a collection of points on the topic, it is not possible to assign a date to it, but the material seems to have been gathered in the last decade of the fifteenth century and the beginning of the

[37] See ibid., p. 561.
[38] See below p. xxxv, and *Readers and Readings*, p. 470.
[39] There is also a blank page following this material.
[40] Reading 8 below, p. xxxv.
[41] Chaloner owned at least a manuscript year book of Edward IV: Baker, *Men of Court*, i. 451. He may have supplemented his notes through private study, or the case references may have been added by the earlier note-taker, possibly his father, who may also have owned the year book originally.
[42] *Readers and Readings*, p. 470. Brudenell was unlikely to comment in a Gray's Inn reading.

sixteenth before being copied by Chaloner. John Chaloner, probably Robert's father, read in Gray's Inn in 1493, and it is tempting to speculate that the material might have originally been collected by him before being passed to the next generation.[43]

Reading K

The final text in the series on Westminster I is in *B*. This is an octavo late sixteenth- or early seventeenth-century manuscript, and the reading text is in English. The entire volume deals with Westminster I, c. 1 in 101 folios, but only folios 1 to 14 deal with the peace of the Church.

This a translation of Marowe's 1503 reading, but of the version preserved in BL MS. Hargrave 87, fos 262–265v, labelled F by Putnam, which bears only a limited resemblance to the A text she edited.[44] Putnam argues that A and F were the two texts closest in date to Marowe's reading, suggesting that F was copied around 1505.[45] The text is only about half the length of A but Putnam argues, based on a paragraph by paragraph comparison, that the brevity is due to the omission of explanation and illustration rather than content and she labels it 'a condensation performed on the whole with great skill'.[46] *B* is Putnam's manuscript L which she describes as 'a fairly literal and intelligent translation into English of the F version'.[47]

Reading K has been compared with the Hargrave version of Marowe and the comparison confirms that while this is not the French original used by Reading K, it is very close. The translation is generally fairly fluid, but the translator has mis-read some words in the manuscript, and has adapted the text to the needs of the post-Reformation Church. In a discussion of the writ *vi laica removenda*, for example, where Reading K explains that 'the sheriff has power to remove the lay power, but not spiritual persons', the original text continues 'such as recluses and other such'.[48] It is not clear whether these changes were made by the translator, or were already in the manuscript that the translator used. For example, the Hargrave version shows signs of post-Reformation changes: in a discussion of certificates of restoration, it argues that 'the certificate shall be made by the bishop himself or by the archbishop or by the guardian of the spiritualities during a vacancy, but it is otherwise of the pope, for he shall not make this certificate'.[49] A later hand has scratched out 'pope' and replaced it with 'bishop of Rome' while in Reading K the sentence simply ends at 'during a vacancy'.[50] This change is not surprising

---

[43] Baker, *Men of Court*, i. 450–451; *Readers and Readings*, p. 27.

[44] *Readers and Readings*, p. 265; *Early Treatises*, pp. 155–157.

[45] *Early Treatises*, p. 157. Putnam bases this dating on the changing of some stock dates in the text, but the erasure of Henry VIII and correction to Henry VII in the title suggests that this version was copied some time after 1509, though perhaps from a fairly recent copy.

[46] Ibid.

[47] Ibid., p. 158. This version of Marowe's reading does not bear any resemblance to Kebell's.

[48] BL MS. Harg. 87, fo. 261; Reading K, p. 60, below.

[49] BL MS. Harg. 87, fo. 261.

[50] Reading K, p. 60, below.

but Reading K also removes pre-Conquest references. In the introduction, for example, 'the laws of Canute' in the Hargrave version are replaced by a rather vague 'book'.[51] In lecture two Reading K refers to 1 Ric. II, c. 15 in the heading, and this is in fact the focus of the text, but the Hargrave version notes that this is the second lecture on Westminster I, c. 1. It has been noted that the late fifteenth- and early sixteenth-century readers largely still felt obliged to read on the 'old' statutes, explaining Marowe's choice of Westminster I as the base text for a reading on the justices of the peace.[52] His late sixteenth-century translator seems to be working in a rather different tradition, which left him freer to recognise the reader's actual texts rather than his ostensible ones, but also inclined him to remove pre-Conquest and pre-Reformation content.

READINGS ON MAGNA CARTA

Reading 1

The first text survives in two manuscripts, *Ra* and *T*, and *Ra* has been chosen as the base text. It is the shortest of the readings, with only a brief exposition of the statute, followed by two cases. In the exposition the reader makes only the most fundamental points: he begins by asserting that God is not an acceptable donee, and moves on to the distinction between rights and liberties of the Church. He identifies the rights of the Church as benefit of clergy and cognizance of pleas pertaining to the Church, and the liberties as when a cleric has a market or other thing granted by the king. Both of these first two paragraphs also appear in Reading 2, though there they are not consecutive, as the opening paragraph of Reading 1 is paragraph 2, and the second paragraph is paragraph 7.

The discussion of cases returns to benefit of clergy and sanctuary in its opening, though the first case deals only with abjuration, and the consequences when an abjured man on his way out of the country is imprisoned and escapes. This is a fairly standard question, and seems to be based on a case in Statham, though there the abjurer was not sent to prison.[53] The second case seems to deal with usury, but is quite obscure. It is also in a different hand from the rest of the text, and in the same hand as the marginal notes, so it is clearly a later addition.

---

[51] Ibid., p. 94.

[52] *Early Treatises*, pp. 167, 45–46. This tradition could already be breached in the final decade of the fifteenth century: Gregory Adgore of the Inner Temple read on 1 Ric. III, c. 1 in 1489/90, but there is no evidence of a reading on another 'new' statute in the Inner Temple until Thomas Audley read on 4 Hen. VII, c. 17 in 1526 (*Readers and Readings*, pp. 69, 78). The early evidence for Gray's Inn is slender, but the first clear example of a reading on a 'new' statute there is John Petit on 1 Hen. VII, c. 1 in 1518 (ibid., p. 31). George Treherne may have tackled 11 Hen. VII, c. 8 in Lincoln's Inn in 1520 and John Densell took on 4 Hen. VII, c. 24 in the same inn in 1530 (ibid., pp. 117, 119). Edmund Knightly provides the earliest evidence for reading on a 'new' statute in the Middle Temple, 1 Ric. III, c. 1 in 1523 (ibid., p. 153). It should be stressed that there are many, many gaps in our knowledge of the topics tackled by the readers in this period, but the vast majority of the surviving reading material from the fifteenth and early sixteenth centuries deals with the 'old' statutes.

[53] Statham, *Corone*, 27.

Reading 1 is thus rather truncated, and not terribly informative, but it, or the text on which it is based, seems to have circulated, since it is clearly related to Reading 2.

Reading 2

Reading 2 survives in six manuscripts, the most of any reading on the topic. It also seems to be closely connected with two others, *Rb* and Reading 3.[54] None of the surviving manuscripts appears to represent an original text: *U* has been chosen as the base text for the edition, since it seems to come closest to a complete reading. *E* and *H* are very similar to *U*, and to each other, but all of them seem to be copies of a lost original rather than directly related to each other. The three remaining manuscripts, *Pa*, *Ga* and *I* are shorter versions of the text, each containing a substantial portion of the reading, each overlapping substantially with the others, but none of them directly copying another. *Pa*, while relatively short, is probably the most logically organised of all the versions of this reading, for it omits much of the confusion in the longer version, partly by omitting all the discussion of cases. It is tempting to see in *Pa* a stripped-down version of the actual lectures, as it moves smoothly through grants, villein priests (in a single sentence), and the rights and liberties of the Church, with little elaboration or back-tracking. *Ga* is a longer version than *Pa* and does include cases, but it omits the second, lengthier, run at the liberties of the Church in *U* and thus does not discuss benefit of clergy and sanctuary or tithes. *I* has virtually everything in the longer version, but is the most muddled of any of them, going from grants, to benefit of clergy, to grants, to villein priests, and back to grants in the first couple of pages.

Following Baker's arguments that most readings incorporate a combination of lecture and disputation material, it is possible to disentangle the various threads of Reading 2. It opens with a general introductory paragraph on the origin of Magna Carta. The next paragraph continues lecture one, ostensibly treating the words *to God*, and repeats paragraph one of Reading 1.[55] This sets the ground for a lecture on grants, but the reading quickly moves on to *that the Church shall be free*, probably lecture two, which deals with villein priests and monks, and is followed by a number of cases. Lecture three deals with the rights and liberties of the Church, and is essentially the same as paragraph two of Reading 1. This material from Reading 1 is followed by an extended group of cases relating to grants which probably should have followed lecture one. *Pa* is the only manuscript to omit this section of cases, and it is tempting to speculate that it was brought in from another source relatively early in the circulation of this material. However, since *Pa* is simply not interested in case materials, it is just as likely that it was

---

[54] *Rb* has not been included in this edition: its brief text contains nothing that does not appear in other readings, and while its content is close to the Reading 2 tradition, it has not been possible to determine any direct connection.

[55] The readers typically use a phrase from the statute to ground their reading and to move from one lecture topic to the next. These phrases have been given in italics throughout the volume.

misplaced at some point in the copying. The reading then returns to rights and liberties with a new, short section of lecture, which outlines the Church's rights (cognizance of pleas) and liberties (undefined) and goes on to give cases outlining the Church's privileges: benefit of clergy, sanctuary and tithes. Again, it is tempting to see this second run at rights and liberties as a later addition, but it appears in *Pa* as well as *U*, so it seems likely that it is original. This raises the possibility that the first mention of rights and liberties is an interjection, but that material is also in Reading 1. *Pa* omits this paragraph, but, together with all the other manuscripts, has the first paragraph from Reading 1, so it seems logical to assume that this material was original, or added at a very early stage. Given how little we know about the ways in which the reading actually took place, it is just as likely that the reader wandered off course in an earlier lecture and came back to the topic with a more extensive and coherent treatment on a later day. Lecture four deals with the rights of bondmen, but there are no cases, and the reading ends with two brief unrelated points, either from the final discussion, or jotted down out of order.

It has not seemed worth trying to construct a formal stemma for the edition of Reading 2, since it is clear that the lawyers who copied these texts were not unduly concerned with reproducing their copy text exactly: it is common to find clauses reversed, or one turn of phrase replaced by another, while the substance and most of the wording remains intact. These were not literary texts, and there was no particular value attached to the literal prose of the readings. While this was a pragmatic approach, it makes the job of the editor rather more complicated, or perhaps simpler. All that can be said with confidence is that these six manuscripts are all products of the same reading, that they represent six of the ways in which it was amended and abridged by the legal profession, and that it is reasonable to assume that they are the survivors of a larger field of interpretation.

Some sense of the range of that field can be garnered from the marginal notations within the manuscripts. Five of the six manuscripts have marginal notations, with *Pa* being the only exception. *E* and *I* both have notations in two different hands, while *H* has four different hands. Some of the notations are not terribly illuminating: the first commentator in *I*, for example, simply marked 'nota' five times, 'nota diversitatem' once, and 'vide statutum' once. Many of the marginal notes are simply subject headings, such as 'droit del esglise' or 'privelege.' Some add a little more; the commentator in *Ga* added case references, as did one of the commentators in *H*: marginal notations like these could be absorbed into the text of the reading by subsequent scribes. While individual manuscripts provide slim pickings, taken together the marginal notes can be revealing, for they suggest the topics of particular interest to readers. Thus, for example, the reader argues that when a villein is made a priest, his lord may still seize him; this point is made in almost all the readings, though it might seem to have had little relevance by this time.[56] The commentators in *H* (hand 3), *E*, and *Ga* all note the passage however,

---

[56] See Readings 4, 5, 6, 7, 8, 9.

suggesting that it continued to be of interest. Similarly, both *H* (hand 1) and *Ga* respond to the argument that while a lord can seize a villein who enters a religious house before he is professed, after profession he can only have an action of trespass and damages: *H* notes in the margin that 'a man can seize the goods of an abbot or priest but not of a parson who is his villein'; while *Ga* adds one of its three case references. The introduction to the material on benefit of clergy attracts a good deal of attention too, with *H* (hand 1), both *E*s and *U* noting the statement that a man claiming benefit of clergy will be delivered to the ordinary, though this might seem to be the most basic of points. The *H* annotators are particularly expansive and most likely to add substance, while the *I* and *U* annotators are most reticent, but taken together the marginal notes can both add to the information in the text, and add some information about how it was read by different lawyers. In this case they suggest that the lectures provided very basic instruction.

There are no case references within the text itself, and only two statute references, both to old statutes (Westminster II and 25 Edw. III). The marginal references date between 11 Hen. IV and 11 Hen. VII (1409–96). The reading is thus entirely self-contained, making it quite difficult to date.

As for content, after a very brief treatment of grants, the reading gets down to business with the statement that *the Church shall be free*, which it interprets to mean both that the Church shall be free of all secular charges, and that no unfree man shall take orders. It only pursues the second of these points, which it immediately contradicts by presenting cases which discuss a lord's rights over his villein in orders.

There is a brief interjection on the distinction between the rights and liberties of the Church, which is followed by cases demonstrating the proper forms of granting to the Church. The reading then returns to the discussion of the rights of the Church, not based on grants, but on the Church's rights as an institution – marriage, wills, tithes, oblations, and mortuaries. It also notes that different churches will have different liberties, pointing to Westminster as a clear example of this, and states the privilege of benefit of clergy (which it notes is more generous in the common law than in the canon law) and of sanctuary, before moving into the discussion of cases.

Regarding benefit of clergy, the reader notes that the ordinary must be present for delivery, and discusses what should be done if he is not, and what the roles of the ordinary and the judges are. On sanctuary it deals with the fugitive's right to food, to commit another felony while in sanctuary, and to stay in sanctuary after his allotted forty days are up. It also deals with the process of abjuration, noting, as Reading 1 did, that an abjurer who did not leave the country could be arrested and executed.[57]

The reading points out that the Church can also have liberties to have fairs or markets, but that these liberties come from the king's grant, and 'not of their own right', in which cases the king may enter and put the Church out if they

---

[57] Statham, *Corone*, 27.

are misused. It notes that some churches will also have special liberties, such as
Westminster or Beverley in the case of sanctuary, but argues that these are not
of the king's grant, and so even if they are misused the king cannot seize them.
The nature of these claims to sanctuary came up numerous times in the fifteenth
century. The first case to suggest that the king could not grant this kind of sanctuary appeared in 1399, but an anonymous late fifteenth-century reading on Magna
Carta chapter nine (the liberties of London) states it without hesitation.[58] On the
other hand Townshend J.C.P. argued vigorously that the king could grant a sanctuary in *Stafford's Case*, suggesting that this reading pre-dates the reign of Henry
VII.[59]

Next the reading looks briefly at jurisdiction over tithes and the liberties of
bondmen, and concludes with a couple of notes, presumably from the discussions, on benefit of clergy and the feoffment of monks.

Reading 3

The introduction to this reading in *L* is virtually identical with Reading 2, and
most particularly with the version in *Pa*. This could be simply the use of a fairly
formulaic opening, but Reading 3 follows Reading 2 more closely than coinci-
dence would allow. The opening of lecture one, on grants, is virtually identical to
that from Reading 2, but in Reading 3 it is immediately followed by a group of
cases on grants, and while there are some similarities between the cases and the
delayed discussion of grants in the previous reading, they are clearly different.
Lecture two in Reading 3 deals with the rights and liberties of the Church, and
again the language of the lecture is virtually identical to that from lecture two
and the second part of lecture three of Reading 2, but the cases here are quite different, as the reader goes into an extended exposition of tithes. The third lecture
in Reading 3 is on the liberties of the Church. Here the lecture material is original, and the cases, on sanctuary and benefit of clergy, also do not appear in the
earlier texts.

The reader opens with the fairly standard discussion of the problems of making grants *to God and the Church*, but he focuses mainly on the latter. He makes
the point that grants cannot be made to the material church 'such as the walls and
the windows', demonstrating that the Church is the parson and parishioners or
abbot and convent. He also, briefly, shows that for any gift to be good there must
be a capable donor and donee. After covering this material briefly, he elaborates
in a fairly extensive discussion of good grants, dealing with a mayor and commonalty, a borough, a convent, and, briefly, an alien.

The reading really hits its stride with the discussion of jurisdiction, however.
At this point the text leaves Reading 2 behind, and introduces statute and case
references. Its focus is primarily on tithe cases, and the jurisdiction of the king's
court. It opens with the standard interpretation that in the case of a tithe dispute

---

[58] YB Mich. 1 Hen IV, fo. 4, pl. 6; Spelman, *Quo Warranto*, p. 4.
[59] YB Trin. 1 Hen. VII, fo. 25, pl. 1. Townshend's argument seems to have been directed to a particular
short-term purpose and was not supported by the other justices.

between two parsons, jurisdiction is clearly with the court Christian, but quickly moves on to the problem of cases involving a covenant between two parsons; a parson impounding alleged tithe grain along with the horse and wagon carrying it; parish boundaries; and the right of the court to hear a dispute over mortuaries, because the statute only restricts cases regarding tithes. In all these circumstances the reading finds in favour of the common law jurisdiction. In the final case, where an abbot brings an action of trespass against a prior and the prior justifies the removal of corn as his tithe, the reading explains that the case must be removed to the court Christian, since tithes had emerged as the issue at stake, though a little later it specifies that in a case like this the plaintiff cannot simply aver that the grain is a lay chattel, but must show special matter.[60] The cases involved in this discussion range from 38 Edw. III to 5 Hen. V (1364–1418), with the majority (six cases) clustering between 38 and 43 Edw. III (1364–70), one from Richard II, one from Henry IV, and two from Henry V.

The final section of the reading deals with sanctuary, but it is quite a cursory treatment. Its focus again is on jurisdiction, with the note that only the pope may make a sanctuary, and the concern with how sanctuary can be proved: should the felon's word be enough, must there be a record, or should the lord be compelled to come and prove it? The reading cites Waw's case of 1429, and the process in that case, where a writ was issued to the abbot, seems to have become standard.[61] For benefit of clergy, another standard topic under this text, there is simply a final sentence pointing to the *Ordinacio pro clero*.[62]

It seems fairly clear that these first three texts are related, but it is not clear what that relationship is. Reading 1 could be an abridgment of Reading 2, or, perhaps more likely, of a longer reading that the lecturer of Reading 2 had access to, but it is too short to allow a definitive conclusion. Reading 2 and Reading 3 could be different versions of the same lecture, but this seems unlikely given the difference in the cases provided. It is possible that different note-takers with different interests might note different cases on the same topic, and this would explain the cases on grants in lecture one, but it seems less likely that the reader would dispute cases on both villeins in orders and on tithes in lecture two, with neither version noting any of the other cases (but compare Reading D above). Reading 3's lecture two incorporates Reading 2's lecture two and part of its lecture three, while the material for lecture three of Reading 3 differs from lecture three of Reading 2. Given this confusion, the most likely explanations seem to be that the lecturers of Reading 2 and Reading 3 had access to a longer version of Reading 1 which they both used for their lecture material (though dividing it in different places) while supplying their own cases, or that Reading 1 and Reading 3 are both based on a version of Reading 2. Given the difficulties of dating all three manuscripts, either explanation is possible, or, given the ways in which

---

[60] There is no case reference here, but the discussion echoes closely the arguments made in YB Mich. 13 Ric. II (Ames Ser.), p. 34, pl. 2.

[61] See p. 81, below.

[62] The reference in the reading is 25 Edw. III, c. 8 *de cleris*, but properly 25 Edw. III stat. 6, c. 4 (*SR*, i. 325).

the readings on Westminster I were compiled, it is entirely possible that they share a common core which different scribes then supplemented for their own purposes.

Reading 4

Reading 4 survives in only one manuscript, *HLSb*. Unlike the other readings, it is laid out as a set of cases. There is a brief historical introduction, and then the reading gives the text of the statute, followed by a series of cases on each topic. It follows a similar progression to the previous readers, from grants (to monks, a dean and chapter, and of wardship), to villein priests and monks, to sanctuary, ending with a brief case on grants to corporations.

There are no explicit case references in this reading, and only a few statute references, to the 1297 confirmation of Magna Carta, and to 50 Edw. III, c. 5 and 1 Ric. II, c. 15, which both deal with the arrest of priests during divine service.[63] It is likely that some of the cases given as examples here are taken from the year books: for example, the reading gives a case of an abjurer being imprisoned on the way to his port which is reminiscent of the example in Reading 1, and also possibly from Statham.[64] It is possible that other cases in the reading also come from the year books or abridgments, but given their generic nature, it is just as likely that they are not based on any specific case, but simply standard examples to cover in the course of a lecture on this topic.

Reading 5

Reading 5 is in the same manuscript as Reading 4, *HLSc*, but is virtually the opposite of the previous reading. Here there are primarily lectures, with little evidence of the disputation of cases. The reading has no introduction but launches into its first lecture, arguing that *the English Church* is properly understood as its clergy and those who serve it. Lecture two, based on *shall be free*, deals with villein priests, and lecture three, based on *rights entire*, with jurisdictional issues. Here the reader mentions two obvious places where canon and common law differ: the issue of *privilegium fori* as compared to the English benefit of clergy; and bastardy. He also briefly treats cognizance of pleas. Lecture four, *liberties inviolate*, covers sanctuary and benefit of clergy, and concludes with a brief disputation.

The only explicit reference to a statute in the reading is to Merton chapter nine, (though there is an oblique reference to *Pro Clero* in the discussion of bishops' temporalities), and there are no obvious case references. In the section on benefit of clergy the reader comments that the privilege can only be claimed after verdict, at which point the felon is in danger of his life. By the end of the fifteenth century this position was associated with Prysot C.J.C.P., and thus dates from somewhere in the middle of the fifteenth century.[65]

---

[63] *SR*, i. 398; *SR*, ii. 5.

[64] Statham, *Corone*, 27.

[65] J. H. Baker, 'Some Early Newgate Reports', in C. Stebbings ed., *Law Reporting in Britain* (1995), p. 48. See above, Reading C, p. xviii.

Reading 6

Reading 6 survives in multiple manuscripts: *Pb*, *Hg* and *HLSa*. The differences between the three versions are fairly minimal, and they are clearly all versions of the same reading, but *Hg* has been chosen as the base text, since it is very close to *HLSa* and fairly close to *Pb*, but those two manuscripts differ more, with *Pb* tending to omit small sections of text. Although the orthography and grammar of the three manuscripts differ, the differences in content are small, mostly small additions or omissions to the sense.

This reading can be dated more precisely than some of the earlier texts. There are numerous case references dating from 20 Edw. III to 22 Edw. IV (1346–1482). The statute references are to older statutes, Marlborough and 50 Edw. III, but there is also a reference to 4 Hen. IV, c. 12. References to 'the time of' Edward IV confirm a date after 1483 and Baker dates *Pb* before 1509.[66] *HLSa* has the name 'Hervye' prominently at the top, and ends 'finis lecturae secundum Hervy, lectorem Templi Interioris'. Baker conjectures that this may refer to Humphrey Harvey, a bencher of the Inner Temple.[67]

Reading 6 is almost entirely cases, with only the briefest of introductions to each topic. In lecture one the reader opens with grants, as usual. Under the freedom of the Church he discusses villein monks, as in Reading 2, and also the Church's freedom from temporal dues, such as fifteenths and tenths and views of frankpledge. In lecture two he deals with tithes and cognizance of pleas under *rights entire* and sanctuary, for the most part, under *liberties inviolate*, though he also mentions clerics' right to avoid temporal office and service in leets.

Reading 7

Reading 7 is in a single manuscript, *S*, but this is by far the most challenging of the manuscripts. It is out of its binding, very faded and crumbling at the edges. The manuscript is badly damaged down the outside and in the bottom corner, and conjectural readings in these areas are presented in italics. Some parts of the manuscript are completely unintelligible, and this is represented by ellipses in the text. As a result the text is rather piecemeal but worth pursing nonetheless, for a number of reasons. It is the first of the readings on Magna Carta with a known author, Richard Snede of the Inner Temple, delivered in Lent 1511.[68] It is also the longest reading on the topic, with the whole of the reading devoted to chapter one of the statute. Snede deals with grants in great detail, devoting lectures one to six to the phrase, *we have granted to God*. He then moves to *the English Church*. Under this heading he tackles the privileges of the Church: lecture seven is on sanctuary and lectures eight and nine on benefit of clergy, though Snede divides

---

[66] *Readers and Readings*, p. 558. He dates the other two manuscripts to the early sixteenth century: ibid., 324, 481.

[67] *HLSa* fo. 1, 3v. Baker, *Men of Court*, i. 828, 820, updating *Readers and Readings*, p. 481, where he suggested John Harvey.

[68] This was Snede's first reading, although the Lent reading was generally given to a double reader. Snede was elected to read in the previous Autumn vacation, but was displaced by a call of serjeants. Baker, *Men of Court*, ii. 1423.

them oddly, focusing in lecture eight on the clergy's immunity from arrest, and in lecture nine on benefit of clergy proper, though he seems to see it as a lay privilege.[69] Lecture ten covers fifteenths and tenths, though quite briefly. Snede opens lecture eleven by explaining that having dealt with the privileges of the Church, he will now move on to the rights of the Church, and he spends the rest of that lecture on tithes. Lecture twelve deals with oblations, obventions, and mortuaries, and lecture thirteen with cognizance of pleas, covering a range of smaller issues. There is a note at the end of the reading that there were originally two more lectures – another one on ecclesiastical courts and one on villeins, based on *free men* – but that the scribe had chosen not to copy them because of their 'turpitude'.[70]

Since we have the name of the reader in this case, dating is not a problem, but Snede's text has an unusual pattern of case and statute references. His introduction gives a very brief history of Magna Carta, complete with some statute references. There are no explicit case references in the first two lectures, but in the third there are a couple of references to cases from Henry VI and Richard II.[71] Case references remain rare, however, with one in lecture six, and one in lecture seven.[72] In lectures six and seven there are also two explicit references to statements made by 'the reader' though the note-taker seemed unconvinced by one and argued with the other.[73]

Once Snede starts deeper into the material on the privileges of the Church, the number of references increases. Lecture eight (freedom from arrest) has three statute references, lecture nine (benefit of clergy) has eight statute references and one case reference, and lecture ten (fifteenths and tenths) has two statute references in little more than a page. Lecture eleven (tithes) has five statute references, five year book cases, and one reference each to the *Register* and to *Bracton*.[74] The number of references falls off in lectures twelve and thirteen, though there is a handful. This pattern suggests that the material on benefit of clergy, fifteenths and tenths and tithes was of most interest to the note-taker, since it seems unlikely that Snede himself would have presented such differing material. It is clear that there is a good deal of disputation material in this reading, and the lectures serve primarily as brief introductions to the examples. It is possible that there were more case references in the manuscript which are simply illegible, but it seems unlikely that this would change the overall balance through the reading.

---

[69] Reading 7, p. 114, below.

[70] Reading 7, p. 127, below.

[71] Lecture three also has a reference to 'Malat', presumably Baldwin Malet, who gave his first reading in the Inner Temple in the autumn of the following year. Baker, *Men of Court*, ii. 1052–1053.

[72] Lecture seven also has a reference to Sheffield, presumably Robert Sheffield who was a reader and governor of the Inner Temple. Baker, *Men of Court*, ii. 1389.

[73] Reading 7, pp. 109, 110, below. There is little evidence about the note-taker or scribe in the text, though his disagreements with the reader's points and his final comment suggest that he was not impressed with the reading. His use of the Middle English letter yogh in lectures five, six, seven and eleven may also indicate that he was relatively old, since this was an unusual orthography by the early sixteenth century.

[74] This is fairly unusual, but Reading 6 also made reference to the *Register*, suggesting perhaps that these two Inner Temple readings have some connection. While both referred to prohibitions in tithe cases, however, they refer to different writs, and their other *Register* references are to different subject matter.

Reading 8

This reading survives only in the Chaloner manuscript at Gray's Inn, one of the most palaeographically challenging of all the manuscripts which contain readings. The manuscript (*C*) belonged to Robert Chaloner, and Baker suggested that it might be Chaloner's own reading, given in Lent 1522.[75] Besides the technical difficulties of the manuscript, this text is further complicated by the fact that it appears to be slightly out of order, and this disorder further suggests that Chaloner was more likely to have been the scribe than the reader.

Written across the top of the first page (folio 20) of the reading is an invocation to Mary and Jesus, with a short sentence on the history of Magna Carta squeezed into a corner of the page. Under the title, the reading proper begins with *we have granted to God*, and the usual lecture on grants, though this is a modest paragraph compared with Snede's exposition. Lecture two covers villein priests and sanctuary, briefly (based on *free*). Lecture three promises cognizance of pleas, but actually deals with tithes, much as Snede had done, though this treatment is so brief that there is clearly a great deal missing and the original lecture may well have dealt with both. Lecture four discusses sanctuary and benefit of clergy, and is the only section of the reading with disputation of cases, at some length: the text mentions points made by John Hales, whose second reading in Gray's Inn was in Lent 1520, and Fyneux C.J., whose participation in *Pauncefote* v. *Savage* in 1519 presumably made his comments on the subject of sanctuary of particular value.[76] About halfway down folio 20v there is a proper introductory section with the usual background to the statute and, in this case, a brief section on the interpretation of statutes. This section begins on a new line (the first such break since the beginning of the text), but when it comes to an end the scribe runs right into a brief consideration of *the English Church*, which appears to be the beginning of a different lecture one. This complicates any assumption that this reading was given by Chaloner himself, since it seems apparent that the introduction was mislaid when the scribe began copying, and added in when he found it again, an error that the reader would be unlikely to make with his own text. It is possible that this reading represents two different treatments, one with no introduction and another with only an introduction, but even if this is the case, it still seems unlikely that either are the scribe's own text.

Reading 8 has no explicit case references, and only two statute references. Whether this originated as one reading or two, the case material makes it likely that a date around 1522 is still appropriate for most of the content.

Reading 9

Reading 9 survives in two manuscripts, *Gb* and *G*, and *Gb* has been chosen as the base text. This reading is something of a puzzle. It is preceded by a relatively long

---

[75] See *Readers and Readings*, pp. 32, 469. Chaloner was elected to read in autumn 1521, but there was no reading because of plague. Baker has since noted that since the text contains remarks by judges who died in 1520, that this is Chaloner's own reading is less likely.

[76] Baker, *Men of Court*, i. 802; Caryll, reports, ii. 704–713.

historical introduction on the origins of Magna Carta and its various confirma-tions.[77] After a blank folio the reading proper begins, as usual, with a discussion of grants. There is virtually no lecture material here, but the topic is heavily pep-pered with case references, many of them from the reigns of Henry VII and one from 12 Hen. VIII. When the reader moves on to consider *for us and our heirs* he stays with the topic of grants, and there are three more case references, from the reigns of Henry IV, Edward IV and Henry VII. On *shall be free*, this reading, like the earlier ones, discusses villein priests, and here the text incorporates material from *Britton*, Littleton, and Fitzherbert, as well as a couple of case references. Topic four is based on *Church*, but continues the discussion of *shall be free*, and here the reading argues that the word extends to colleges, hospitals and sanctuar-ies, among other places, and that those in major and minor orders are entitled to the privileges of the Church.[78] In this topic there are a couple of case refer-ences, one from Fitzherbert's *Abridgement*, and one from Henry VII. The last three topics, cognizance of pleas, villeins, and liberties, are dealt with much more briefly, and without any case references.[79] Baker suggested that this is a copy of a fifteenth-century reading with case references added, and this would explain the flurry of references at the beginning, which then dwindle as the text progresses.[80] The only problem is that if the cases were removed from the first topic there would be no lecture left. It is more likely that a later student was using a brief set of reading notes as the framework for assembling a body of reference material on the topic, and ran out of time or interest as he worked his way through the material, ending up with just the brief lectures for the later topics. This would also explain the treatise references in topics one and two, and not elsewhere. If this is a working composite, it throws some light on the ways in which earlier reading texts could be used as a framework within which a student could assem-ble his own collection of sources. We have seen that it was not uncommon for a scribe to leave space in a manuscript to add more material on the various subjects as he gathered them, but this scribe seems to have been replacing the early read-ing with layers of case, statute, and treatise material as he found them, or at least copying the work of someone who had.

Reading 10

Reading 10 also survives in a single manuscript, *Hl*. This is one of the longer treatments of chapter one, if not quite as long as Snede's (it deals only with

---

[77] Baker suggests that this is a separate item, and not part of the reading. *Readers and Readings*, pp. 474, 414. This is entirely possible, since this reading is followed by *Ga*, one of the abridged versions of Reading 2. The same historical introduction also appears in the version in *G*, however, with no break in the text, suggesting that the two were seen as either companion pieces or parts of the same reading.

[78] This arose as a topic of discussion at the end of the fifteenth century, and it comes up a number of times in the course of *Standish's Case*: Caryll, reports, ii. 684–686. Benefit of clergy was not removed from minor orders until 23 Hen. VIII, c. 1 (*SR*, iii. 362–363).

[79] There is one statute reference, to 9 Edw. II, *Articuli cleri* (*SR*, i. 171–174).

[80] *Readers and Readings*, p. 474. Baker is currently working on *G* and now believes this reading dates from the 1550s but relies heavily on early reading material. This argument will be elaborated in his Selden Society volume, *Selected Readings and Commentaries on Magna Carta, 1400–1604*.

chapters one and two). It is also unusual in having an introduction in English. This introduction provides the background to the making of Magna Carta, but in rather more detail than the earlier readings, with rather more editorialising, and supported by rather more citations, not only from *Bracton*, but from Horace (via *Bracton*) and Cicero. The inclusion of these citations suggests that the reader was trying to adorn his text in humanist fashion, but his classical learning did not run deep. Once into the body of the text there are few references. In lecture seven the reader refers to Jerome and Cyprian, though again his references are not entirely accurate, and he seems to refer to 23 Hen. VIII, c. 1.[81] The reader also refers to the statute of Carlisle (35 Edw. I) and to the *Register* in lecture nine, and gives two statute references (50 Edw. III, c. 5 and 1 Ric. II, c. 14) in lecture eleven, a reference to the Fourth Lateran Council in chapter twelve, and three statute references in lecture thirteen.[82] There are no explicit case references, though some of the reader's examples probably come from year book cases, such as Townshend's peculiar argument regarding the king's ability to grant sanctuary for treason in *Stafford's Case*, used in lecture eight.[83]

Like most of the readings, Reading 10 is undated and anonymous. The statute reference to Henry VIII suggests that the reading belongs to the early 1530s, but a slip in the manuscript, where the scribe has written 'Edward the sixte' for Edward I, suggests that it might be slightly later.[84] The reader has also included a couple of sentences from Sir John Fortescue's *De Laudibus Legum Angliae*, first published *c.* 1545, in his introduction, though unlike his other authorities, this one is unattributed.[85] The scribal slip and the use of Fortescue suggest that the reading dates from the late 1540s, but the reader's translation adapts Fortescue for his own purposes and thus cannot be definitively connected to the printed text, while some of the arguments made in the reading are quite conservative for such a late date. The *De Legibus* was circulating in legal circles before its publication; it was cited by Rastell in his edition of the *Liber Assisarum* in 1513 and by Christopher St German in *Doctor and Student* in 1530.[86] Once again a composite process of authorship and transmission allows for a more complex dating, with a reader in the 1530s adapting and translating Fortescue either from memory or manuscript and a scribe in the 1540s momentarily confusing his Edwards.

The reading proper begins, as usual, with grants to God and the Church, and as with Snede, this material takes up the first six lectures. At lecture seven the reading moves on to *the English Church*, where the reader identifies his subject as the clergy, rather than the laity, buildings or revenues.[87] The actual subject matter of the lecture is rather miscellaneous. Lecture eight deals with

---

[81] This reading is divided into lectures in the manuscript.
[82] The reference to Lateran IV in lecture thirteen probably comes via *De Bigamis*, 4 Edw. I, c. 5 (*SR*, i. 43).
[83] YB Trin. 1 Hen. VII, fo. 25, pl. 1. Reading 10, p. 149, below.
[84] See below, pp. 140.
[85] See below, p. 138.
[86] Sir John Fortescue, *De Laudibus Legum Anglie*, S. B. Chrimes ed. (Cambridge, 1949), p. cv.
[87] This is mildly reminiscent of lecture one of Reading 3, but there is only a passing similarity.

sanctuary. Lecture nine seems to discuss the complaints of the clergy more generally, and its focus is on asserting the king's position as governor of the spirituality. Though Baker asserts that this argument is unlikely to have been made in public before 1534, the reader is quite conservative: he claims that the king has that position 'by the course of the common law', which would seem to separate it from the later statutory provisions, and he points to examples before the making of Magna Carta, and in the reign of Edward I.[88] This claim seems to fit into a much longer tradition of argument about the king's (and thereby the common law's) role in defining secular control over such issues as sanctuary and benefit of clergy, particularly as they had developed since *Standish's Case* and *Pauncefote* v. *Savage*, rather than alluding to the sweeping changes that would come.[89] After making this point, there is a brief discussion of election, presentation, tithes, excommunication and benefit of clergy from this perspective.

Lecture ten seems to be missing. At the beginning of lecture eleven the reader says that he discussed how the clergy should be free in their persons, and this material was covered in lecture nine, though very briefly. It is possible therefore that the remaining lectures are misnumbered, or that the note-taker or scribe was not particularly interested in this material and so compressed the reader's material. If this is the case it is particularly striking that the note-taker was concerned to keep the comments on the king's role as governor of the spirituality. Lecture eleven then goes on to freedom in person, goods, lands, trials, and elections, mostly dealing with the places where the clergy are not compelled to answer to the temporal law. Lecture twelve picks up with cognizance of pleas, and again, like Snede, mostly talks about tithes, though there is a brief mention of contracts and wills. Lecture thirteen deals with benefit of clergy. Lecture fourteen opens with a discussion of the difference between rights and liberties which may be a summing up of lectures twelve and thirteen before moving on, either because the reader has realised that he never made that point explicitly, or because it arose out of discussion. Having established what liberties are, the lecture then focuses on how they may be lost.

Though we do not know to what extent the text we have reflects the reader's choices rather than the original note-taker's or the scribe's, the decision to provide what we might think of as 'authoritative' references, whether to statute, treatise, theologian or philosopher, rather than the more experiential references to year book cases, makes this reading stand out from the run of earlier lectures.

READINGS AS SOURCES FOR LEGAL EDUCATION

Having now worked through ten reading texts on Westminster I chapters one to three and ten on Magna Carta chapter one, it is worth returning to the question of what these texts tell us about the process of legal education. It is clear that many

---

[88] *Readers and Readings*, p. 289.
[89] Caryll, reports, ii. 683–692, pl. 505; Caryll, reports, ii. 704–713, pl. 513; Port, *Notebook*, 41–42, pl. 40, 41; reports, *Hen. VIII*, i. 191, pl. 263.

texts we call 'readings' are in fact composite texts built up via multiple layers of copying and possibly over multiple generations, whether generations of a family, of an inn, or, more broadly, of students of the law. Some of the surviving manuscripts allow us to glimpse the various stages in the process or to speculate about how it might have worked, and these traces are common enough that it seems likely that many other texts developed organically in much the same way, even if their compilers produced a tidier result.

This should change the way we think about the readings in a number of ways. Firstly, it makes the prospect of attaching names and dates to many surviving 'readings' unlikely in the extreme, since even those readings which are clearly focused on a named statute are not necessarily the product of a particular person speaking in a particular place and at a particular time. Secondly, as a result of this the 'readings' are difficult to use as an index to change in the law since one text can hold several generations' worth of opinion, which might well be contradictory, without feeling any obligation to note that fact. This is frustrating for historians whose focus is the establishment and elucidation of the timing and the pace of change, but it does demonstrate that this did not seem to be of central importance to the note-takers, scribes and translators of these documents. Thirdly, since named 'readings' seem to be the exception rather than the rule, we need to think about how and why certain texts seem to have travelled as a unit and under a particular name. The most obvious reason is that the individual reader's name gave the material authority, and the readings by Kebell and Marowe in this volume support that theory. On the other hand, the readings of many eminent lawyers of the period have been lost, or at least separated from their authors, which implies that some combination of name and content was required to keep the two together – is it possible that Thomas More's readings, for example, were just not very good? We also have surviving readings attached to not very eminent lawyers, such as the Harvey named in Reading 6. Kebell's reading complicates even this suggestion, however, since we know that at least two very different versions of his text circulated: the one which provided the basis for Marowe's later reading, and the one which survives. We have no way of knowing at which point the two versions were distilled from the learning exercise, or whether their relationship was known to the legal community at the time, or even whether this would have been a point of any interest.

If readings produced by a single learning exercise are the exception rather than the rule, should we simply give up on the idea of connecting people to texts? The biggest benefit of a name and a date, of course, is context. Knowing who gave a particular lecture immediately allows us to fill in what was going on around him, and, if we are lucky, gives us a hook on which to hang other reading texts, both earlier and later. Of course this may be more pious hope than reality – the single named reading on Magna Carta, Snede's, gives us little help in dating those that came before, or after. Equally unhelpfully, the reading most clearly based on Kebell's reading on Westminster I, Marowe's, is also a named and dated reading, but one which covers very different material from that in the surviving version

of Kebell's lectures. A good named reading might also give us a bench-mark for how the law on a particular topic was understood by an eminent lawyer at a given moment, but given that lawyers were prone to disagree, even good readings can provide us with more questions than answers about when and why the law changed.[90]

Thinking about all the various elements that might be operating in a given text can make them a great deal easier to navigate, however. Manuscript texts of readings are often challenging to use: the hands can be bad, the orthography is peculiar, there is little in the way of guidance to the contents beyond the occasional marginal note, and analysing the brief, often inscrutable and contradictory points made in them can be challenging. Knowing that the material originates either in a lecture or a disputation process, while being aware of the possible various layers of accumulated learning, helps sort through the various strata of any given text. Knowing that rather than looking at a reasonably coherent and consistent exposition of a topic given by one man, at one inn, during one learning vacation, you are likely to be reading a kind of commonplace book makes some 'readings' make much more sense. Of course this is not the case for all readings, but it is important to keep in mind that these texts cover a fairly broad spectrum, extending from relatively coherent expositions of their stated topic (whether named or not), to collections of cases or examples more or less on the topic without any further exposition, with a wide variety of possibilities in between.

While it is possible to see the more coherent readings, especially those which circulated fairly widely, as a type of textbook introduction to the various topics at hand, thinking about them as commonplace books moves them rather more in the direction of yearbooks or abridgments. It raises similar questions about the purpose and structure of each collection, and the role of cases as sources of law. Rather than collecting by term or by topic, students might choose to use the statute as a framework for gathering relevant examples and cases, providing another learning approach. Again, there is a good deal of variety within the readings, with some leaning much more heavily on case material than others, and some subsuming case material within the examples. The main way in which the readings differ from year books or abridgments, of course, is that actual cases generally seem to have played a fairly small role in their exposition of the law. It is striking, for example, that very few stock cases seem to have emerged for these topics. There are a handful of cases that appear in more than one reading, but only a couple that appear in more than two. Not only does each lecturer, note-taker or scribe seem to have compiled his own collection, this compilation does not seem to have been central to either the teaching or the learning process. While this says something about the independence and industry of law students, it also suggests that the law on these topics remained remarkably fluid, at least through to the reign of Henry VIII, when circumstances

---

[90] See, for example, McGlynn, *The Royal Prerogative*, pp. 73–149, which discusses the readings given by Thomas Frowyk and Robert Constable on *Prerogativa Regis* as serjeants-elect in 1495.

forced some definition. As will be argued elsewhere, however, the changes of Henry's reign drew upon the traditions of the readings more than has been recognised.

OTHER TEXTS

Certen considerations ...

The next text in the collection is not a reading, but its subject matter makes it an appropriate addition to this volume. Again surviving in a single manuscript, BL MS. Cotton Cleo F. ii, fos 241–245v, the text is headed in a later hand, 'Certain considerations why the spiritual jurisdiction would be abrogated and repelled, or reformed at least' and dated, in the same hand, to the time of Henry VIII. It appears to be part of the lengthy process of reforming the canon law after the break with Rome.

The position of canon law in England was first called into question with the submission of the clergy in 1532, and in 1534 the Act of Submission provided that the king might appoint a commission of thirty-two (sixteen parliamentary laymen and sixteen clergy) to examine the existing body of canon law and produce a recommendation as to which canons were to be retained.[91] The commission was never appointed, but there is evidence that a small group was trying to produce a working draft in 1534 and 1535. The group was headed by Thomas Thirlby, one of the king's chaplains, who wrote to Cromwell in July 1534 that they were at work on the matter but needed help from men learned in the laws of God and the realm.[92] They had approached Christopher St German, probably the best known polemicist arguing for the extension of common law in matters ecclesiastical, but he had several times refused the commission.

However, another prominent common lawyer, Richard Pollard, agreed to work on the project, and in 1535 he wrote to Cromwell that he and others had 'communed with Drs Thyrleby and Olyver and others of the Arches, respecting divers articles which they ministered to us'.[93] Pollard complained that the canonists' articles 'were all in general and not special' and told Cromwell that they had asked the canonists to 'devise a certainty of all such crimes and offences as they think ecclesiastical judges have had jurisdiction heretofore', whereupon the lawyers would meet again, and the common lawyers would 'show them our minds'. Pollard's mind appears to have been already made up, since he concludes that 'we think it advisable that the temporal judges should hereafter have jurisdiction of all such crimes etc. as the ecclesiastical have heretofore had, and then there would be but one law in the realm, which I think would be better'.

Pollard presumably had not said as much to the canonists, but this anonymous text suggests what he might have said. It follows the headings of the Henrician Canons fairly closely, though it does not contain all the material in the draft

---

[91] F. D. Logan, 'The Henrician Canons', *Bulletin of the Institute of Historical Research* 47 (1974), p. 100.
[92] *L&P*, vii, no. 1008.
[93] Ibid., ix, no. 119.

code.[94] The text has a running header 'In Criminibus', and there are individual section headings, mostly in Latin, beginning with 'Private Heresies' (c. 1 of the Henrician Canons) and moving on through 'Simony' (c. 3), 'Adultery, incest, fornication and concubinage' (c. 4), 'Sins against nature', 'Usury', 'Falseness' (c. 5), 'Perjury and breach of faith' (c. 6), 'Sacrilege, divination by augurs, idolatry and blasphemy' (cc. 7–8), 'Sacrilege', 'Defamation and abuse' (c. 9), 'Placing violent hands upon clerks ...', 'Benevolences', 'Matrimony' (c. 22), 'Tithes...' (c. 24), and 'Oblations, obventions ...' (cc. 27–28). It attempts to suggest ways in which issues which traditionally belonged to the ecclesiastical courts might be handled in the secular courts, arguing, for example, that reparations, dilapidations and churchwardens' accounts 'stand in the nature of an action of waste or account' while 'if a man knows my servant carnally within my house and gets her with child, I shall have an action of trespass against him'.[95]

The text begins with the air of a treatise, but as it proceeds it becomes apparent that it has been initiated by a set of questions, as on the topic 'Benevolences' the author struggles to give an answer to what he thinks the questioner is asking, and concludes 'And if you mean any other thing we desire you to declare it to us.'[96] This comment, or a variation on it, becomes more and more common as the text proceeds, and by the time he has reached oblations and obventions the author seems to throw up his hands, telling his anonymous questioner 'In these we desire to know of you what jurisdiction you think the clergy should have by reason of their terms. And then we shall further show our minds to thee as we shall see cause and also to the residue of the articles.'[97] This fits quite well with the process Pollard outlined, whereby the canonists sent a list of subject headings to the common lawyers for their comment and the common lawyers discovered, apparently with some annoyance, that while they could articulate their desire for one law, producing it was rather more complicated.[98]

The introduction to this text opens with the assertion that all spiritual laws are, and always have been, against the royal prerogative and moreover have deprived the common law system of fines, amercements and forfeitures, as well as sovereignty. The author of the report is clearly a reformer, who hopes that a revision of the law 'would cause the clergy better to remember their bounden duty to God and the people, which is to edify the people with good preaching and teaching of the true word of God'.[99] He goes on to complain about the inequities in the canonical

[94] The Henrician Canons were the draft version of a new canon law prepared in late 1535 or early 1536. See Bray, *Tudor Church Reform*, pp. xxvi–xxix.

[95] *Certen considerations*, pp. 160, 162, below.   [96] Ibid., p. 164, below.   [97] Ibid., p. 166, below.

[98] *Certen considerations* does leave some topics clearly in the competence of the spiritual courts, such as simony, sacrilege, blasphemy and idolatry. In the autumn of 1535, with Richard Gwent now in charge, the canonists produced the Henrician Canons, but they proceeded no further. In 1536 another statute allowed the king to appoint the same kind of commission, which would have the authority to work on the project until April 1539 (27 Hen. VIII, c. 15, *SR*, iii. 548–549). This commission was also still-born, and by the end of the decade the English Church was no closer to a revised canon law than it had been in 1532. Bray argues that this was not surprising, since 'things were moving so fast by 1536 that any attempt to codify the existing situation would have been out of date almost before it was written ... the years 1536–1540 were not a time for reaching the sort of long-term conclusions which an official version of the canon law would have entailed' (Bray, *Tudor Church Reform*, xxix).

[99] *Certen considerations*, p. 159, below.

system, where ecclesiastical judges punish offenders but then also force them to go to confession, and where they rule on profits of the clergy and violence against clergy, in which they cannot be impartial judges. He points out that the topics of the canon law could easily be handled at common law or that statutes could be passed to cover them. And he complains about the approach of the ecclesiastical courts which seek to get the parties to a suit to come to an agreement, since in the case of such agreement the wronged party cannot then sue in the king's court and the king loses his advantages. The author shows no awareness of the different function of the ecclesiastical court, its concern to reconcile and instruct. Instead he complains both about the ecclesiastical judges' lack of knowledge of the common law and the ways in which their law contravenes the common law.

Having set the tone for the piece, the author then moves into the body of the report. There are spaces, usually about 6 to 7 cm, left between many of the topics, implying that the author planned to come back and write more later. The entries vary in length and tone, and there are some topics on which the author has little to say: on simony, for example, he notes that it belongs to the spiritual jurisdiction, but that 'if it were brought by parliament to the king's court we think it were well done, for we never saw correction done on that behalf, and yet many have offended therein, as we think'.[1] On usury he points out that there are four articles in the bill he was given but that penalties were set in the reign of Henry VII and 'if some other were so likewise it were well done, so we think'.[2] 'Falseness' seems to have befuddled the author, for he retorts that actions on false returns belong at the common law and the only suits for falseness at the canon law are for perjury and breaking faith, which are elsewhere on the list, and so he asks that if there are any other such issues 'we desire that you declare them to us'.[3] He seems to be unaware that this was intended to deal with forgery, which would have led him nicely back to the common law. Perjury, divination, idolatry and blasphemy also get short shrift, as do oblations and obventions, the last title.

On other topics the author provides a fuller reply, and the answer is generally the same: the statutes of Henry VII and Henry VIII have provided remedies for some of these problems, and statutes can provide remedies for the problems that remain. For example, the author starts out with some confidence on heresy, pointing out that the ordinaries had always examined heresy until the statute of 25 Hen. VIII, since which time examination was by a commission appointed by the king.[4] Under adultery, incest, fornication and concubinage, he accepts that these have customarily been examined by the clergy, but points out that a brothel can be dealt with as a common nuisance and common law remedies could be adapted for other sexual offences. He cannot help but add, apropos of his concern for the partiality of ecclesiastical judges, that 'great partiality has been seen in such things when clerks have gone unpunished in their greater

---

[1] Ibid., p. 162, below.
[2] Ibid., p. 162, below.
[3] Ibid., p. 163, below.
[4] 25 Hen. VIII, c. 14 (*SR*, iii. 454–455).

offences and poor men have been greviously handled in lesser offences'.[5] Sins against nature are also handled with some confidence, as he points to the statute against buggery of 25 Hen. VIII and argues that the church courts cannot handle any felony since they would prejudice the process at the common law.[6] Under usury he also points to a statute, 11 Hen. VII, c. 8.[7] These latter topics were not included in the draft of the Henrician Canons, and it is possible that the confidence of the common law response on these points suggested that this was indeed material better handled at the common law, or at least material on which the common law had decided to assert itself. At this point the common lawyer starts to falter, however, as falseness, perjury and sacrilege all require him to ask for more information.

The longest section of the report deals with laying violent hands on clerks and benefit of clergy, which seems to exercise the author considerably. He argues against the remedy in *sub qua forma* for the same reasons he has given above, that the procedure in the ecclesiastical court threatens procedure in the king's court. His knowledge of benefit of clergy is shaky, since he argues that the ordinary may not punish clerks for treason, murder, rape, felony or trespass, but only for adultery or fleshly incontinency, as provided in 1 Hen. VII, c. 4.[8] Furthermore, he argues that the ecclesiastical courts may not proceed to correct sin in a case where the principal matter belongs in the king's court, since if the witnesses lied in the ecclesiastical court this would cause confusion in the common law court. He may simply be ignoring the whole field of benefit of clergy because it already falls within the common law in practical terms, or because he sees the episcopal punishment of clerks after judgment or verdict as something quite apart from his problem of episcopal jurisdiction over sin, but it remains a striking omission.

There seems to be a section missing under benevolences, since the heading here is a query, and the beginning of the topic seems to be missing. The author handles marriage with aplomb, making similar points about the conflict of the laws as he did in the introduction, but again asking for more information. Tithes he also approaches with some confidence, pointing out some situations in which tithe suits belong in the king's court, and noting that there are so many variants when the case should be heard in the Chancery or the Exchequer that it would be tedious to list them all. The report ends abruptly with oblations and obventions, which the author does not even attempt to deal with, asking instead for more information from his source, at which time he will respond further.

Overall the text seems to be a far from complete response to the queries of the canonists, even in the areas which it attempts, and it is more interested in pointing out the value of statute law than in providing a thoughtful analysis of the ways in which canon and common law interacted, or could be made to interact. It is

---

[5] *Certen considerations*, p. 162, below.
[6] 25 Hen. VIII, c. 6 (*SR*, iii. 441).
[7] 11 Hen. VII, c. 8 (*SR*, ii. 574).
[8] 1 Hen. VII, c. 4 (*SR*, ii. 500–501).

very much a product of its moment, with the vast majority of the statutes it refers to coming from 25 Hen. VIII, and it reflects an attempt to turn a political aim of 1534 into a long-term legal process. It demonstrates how challenging it was for even a determined and effective common lawyer to amalgamate a codified system of law like the canon law with the sprawling complexity of the common law, and reveals the even greater difficulty of moving beyond this technical problem to also encompass the differing aims of the two systems. It does seem to have had some impact – it may have at least contributed to the omission of usury and sodomy from the Henrician Canons – but overall it cannot have been terribly useful to the broader programme of re-writing the canon law, though it does provide some insight into the possible legislative programme of the common lawyers.

Edward Hall's Reading

The final text in the collection is Edward Hall's reading, given in Gray's Inn at Lent 1541. Hall is, of course, best known as the author of the massive chronicle, which Betteridge describes as 'one of the first historical attempts to make sense of the Henrician Reformation'.[9] Hall was born in London in the late 1490s, and attended Eton and King's College, Cambridge, before moving to Gray's Inn.[10] In 1529 he was elected a member of the reformation parliament, one of a substantial number of lawyers in the house.[11] As his legal career developed he was appointed common serjeant of London in 1533, and in the autumn of the same year he gave his first reading in Gray's Inn.[12] In July 1533 Hall was retained as counsel in a rather lurid murder case which may have brought him to Cromwell's attention.[13] In 1535 he went on to become undersheriff of London with a letter of support from the king.[14] As well as being a member of one of the most important parliaments of the period and a successful lawyer in both academic and administrative circles, Hall's interest in history, for which he is best known, linked him with the London literary scene. He was friends with the printer Richard Grafton, who completed his *Chronicle* after his death, and he was also familiar with John Foxe, who in turn linked him to John Bale.[15] These men, of course, were not

[9] Thomas Betteridge, *Tudor Histories of the English Reformation* (Aldershot, 1999), p. 55.

[10] R. Treswell, *Visitation of Shropshire* (London, 1889), p. 208; *Eton College Register 1441–1698*, Sir Wasey Sterry ed. (Eton, 1943), p. 154; J. & J. A. Venn eds., *Alumni Cantabrigienses*, 10 vols. (Cambridge, 1922–54), ii. 285. For a summary of Hall's biography, see Baker, *Men of Court*, i. 804–805.

[11] *L&P*, iv. 6043 [2]. Hall sat in Parliament for both Bridgenorth and Much Wenlock in Shropshire, maintaining his connection with his father's home county. S. E. Lehmberg, *The Reformation Parliament* (Cambridge, 1970), pp. 24–25.

[12] C. L. Kingsford ed., *Two London Chronicles* (1910), p. 7.

[13] *L&P*, vi. 741.

[14] Pollard cites the city records to this effect: A. J. Pollard, 'Edward Hall's Will and Chronicle', *Bulletin of the Institute of Historical Research* 9 (1932), p. 174; for Hall's office see C. L. Kingsford ed., *Two London Chronicles* (1910), p. 10; John Stow, *A Survey of London*, C. L. Kingsford ed., 2 vols (Oxford, 1908), i. 260–261.

[15] Foxe mentions Hall's composition of the *Chronicle*, and Foxe's story of providing Hall with Bale's version of the Oldcastle rebellion is frequently used in discussions both of Hall's historiography and the date of the completion of the text. Foxe also claims to have the original copy of the chronicle in which Hall had made the changes. John Foxe, *Acts and Monuments of John Foxe*, Stephen Reed Cattley ed., 8 vols. (1838), iii. 377–378.

simply literary figures but proponents of religious reform who were themselves connected with men like Cromwell and Thomas Audley.[16] Though Hall was not a figure of national standing he was an important man in the capital: as Richard Grafton describes him in his preface to the *Chronicle*, Hall 'though not to al men, yet to many [was] very wel knowen'.[17] From the early 1530s he was centrally placed to watch the unfolding of the English reformation; although he had little effect on events, he was connected both to the men who did and to the men who recorded them. Indeed Stow argues that Hall's *Chronicle* came directly from this milieu, as he was 'stired vp by men of Authoritie' to write it.[18]

Given this context, it is not entirely surprising that Hall chose to lecture 'on the statute of Holy Church', but it is surprising that the statute he chose was 2 Hen. IV, c. 1.[19] By the 1520s and 1530s it was becoming more common to read on new statutes, but this was still an odd choice for Hall. It did not have the authority of an ancient statute or the relevance of a more recent one. There were no previous readings on it and none afterwards.[20] And it is, to all intents and purposes, a fairly generic statute, of the kind which can be found at the beginning of most parliaments: it confirms the rights and liberties of the Church, Magna Carta and the Charter of the Forest, and all good statutes not revoked. Given that it was neither old, new, distinguished, innovative or obviously relevant to the topic at hand, why did Hall choose this text?

The answer, to a large extent, lies in Hall's alter ego as an historian. Since his chronicle establishes Henry IV as the beginning of the story that ends with the triumphant Henry VIII, it is not surprising to see him turning to that reign to provide a foundation for his reading. On first glance Henry IV's first parliament might seem like a neater starting point, but that parliament was absorbed with the legal consequences of Henry's usurpation and Richard's deposition, a series of events which Hall probably did not want to evoke. Henry's second parliament, in contrast, focused rather more on setting the tone for the rest of the reign. It was clearly intended to promote law and order: the parliament was opened by Thirning C.J.C.P., rather than by one of the bishops, as was normal. The beginning of the opening speech usually made reference to the standard confirmation elements, but Thirning's speech is far closer to the text of the statute that was passed than normal, suggesting that this was a programme which had been thought through and was being presented through the mouth of the chief justice rather than the Church.[21]

[16] MacCulloch comments on Grafton's connections with both Cranmer and Cromwell: D. MacCulloch, *Cranmer* (New Haven, Conn., 1996), p. 196, while Foxe relates the story of Grafton's falling foul of Bonner after the fall of Cromwell and his subsequent rescue by Chancellor Audley: Foxe, *Acts and Monuments*, v. 414.

[17] R. Grafton, 'To the reader', in Edward Hall, *Chronicle* (1548).

[18] T. Dibdin ed., *Typographical Antiquities* (1816), iii. 425.

[19] *SR*, ii. 120.

[20] Only three statutes from Henry IV's reign ever had readings based on them, all of which are unique.

[21] C. Given-Wilson ed., 'Henry IV: Parliament of 1401, Text and Translation', in *The Parliament Rolls of Medieval England*, C. Given-Wilson et al. eds., item 2. [CD-ROM Scholarly Digital Editions] (Leicester, 2005).

2 Hen. IV, c. 1 also allowed Hall to disguise the novelty of his subject matter. Magna Carta was the standard text to use when discussing the Church, but Hall's reading as it stands does not deal with grants to the Church, sanctuary, benefit of clergy or tithes, and mentions only two topics which sometimes appear in readings on Magna Carta, probate and defamation.[22] Though much of Hall's reading is missing, he has clearly introduced a substantial amount of new material, and seems to have left out many of the standard topics. His choice to leave Magna Carta for a more recent text seems to signal his plan to deal with current issues, but his decision to use a confirmation statute both echoes the confirmatory nature of Magna Carta chapter one, and evokes Magna Carta itself.[23]

It is also worth considering the more immediate context in which Hall spoke. We know that the attempt to re-write canon law had been ongoing and unsuccessful through the period of Cromwell's ascendancy, and that presumably provided some impetus. However, the period of Hall's own readership was rather turbulent. Elected in spring 1539 with the expectation that he would read in the following Lent, he was pushed back a year by the call of serjeants of 1540 and did not read until Lent 1541. In the intervening period he was responsible for the removal of an image of Thomas Becket from a window of the Gray's Inn chapel in May 1539, sat in the parliament which passed the Act of Six Articles in June 1539, was perhaps one of the readers lectured in Star Chamber by the lord chancellor on his duty to expound the law without 'subtle practice, imagination, or deceit' in February 1540, saw the execution of Cromwell in July 1540, and sat on a commission in London to enforce the Act of Six Articles in January 1541.[24]

Under these circumstances, why did he choose to lecture on the Church? If Hall had been an ardent reformer, perhaps planning a more radical reading a year earlier under Cromwell's eye, we might expect him to retire the subject for something a little safer. His choice to take on 'Holy Church' in those circumstances, with that text, suggests instead that Hall was trying to present a model where the process of integrating new legislation into the common law could proceed along with the process of integrating the canon law into the common law. Rather than a new codification which might be out of date as it was being printed, canon law could be functionally incorporated through the process of reading, in the same way that new statute law was incorporated in the common law. It could take its place as part of the king's law, as the spiritual courts were taking their place as part of the king's jurisdiction. This is a very different approach to the problem than the one taken by the author of *Certen considerations*, but one more likely to be productive, as it uses the traditions of legal teaching and learning to absorb the

---

[22] And only the introduction to a lecture on the latter. Readings 6, 7 and 9 mention defamation briefly (pp. 92, 124, 137, below), but only in the context of jurisdiction. Readings 6, 7, and 9 also mention probate of wills, generally in the same context (p. 93, 125–126, 137, below).

[23] This is the reverse of a more typical situation where readers took on a new statute, but re-used material from older lectures on a standard statute. See, for example, Spelman, *Quo Warranto*, pp. xix–xx.

[24] William Dugdale, *Origines Juridiciales* (1666), p. 283; Hall, *Chronicle*, p. 837; Spelman, reports, ii. 351.

flood of material coming from Parliament and to begin to work through the new problems posed by the royal supremacy.

Hall's reading as it survives is incomplete. There are two manuscripts, *Ha* and *Hr*, and *Ha* has been chosen as the base text. The first lecture opens with the text 'the holy Church has this right', and goes on to talk about the proper election of bishops; the profession of religious; the capacity of religious to sue at common law; the difference between the rights of dereigned and suppressed religious; and their right to marry. Lecture two opens with the statement 'Before I have shown you how the clergy claim as their right to have the probate of wills if a man makes a will', but this material does not appear in lecture one as it survives. In *Hr* there are seven blank pages left between lecture one and two, presumably with the intention of adding in the missing text. Lecture two goes on to deal with intestacy, the ordinary's role in sequestration, and where legatees without remedy at the spiritual law may turn to the common law or Chancery. The next lecture is numbered eight, and in *Hr* three and a half pages are left blank between lecture two and lecture eight. The text given for the lecture, however, is 'the Church should have its right' which is the opening of the statute. In the missing lectures Hall had apparently 'shown juridical law and the law of the prophets which the clergy claim to have' suggesting that much of the reading focused on the nature of the Church's claim to jurisdiction and the ways jurisdiction worked in practice. He went on in lecture eight to show 'another law which they claim to punish overt sin and this is in three principal points, namely usury, perjury and defamation'.[25] He opens with a fairly extensive treatment of usury and the distinction between usury at the common law and the canon law, and begins his treatment of perjury, but the lecture trails away before he can get to defamation.

Hall's references are almost all unique. The reading has only four case references, and only one of them appears in another reading.[26] His reference to *Capell's Case* is quite contemporary, but all of the other cases are much older. Hall's statutory references are also unusually recent: of the twelve, seven date from 1530 or later and another two from the reign of Henry VII. This reinforces the argument that Hall's primary concern is to deal with contemporary issues and to speed up the process of integrating this new material into the body of common legal knowledge.

The text as it survives raises many of the same questions as the other readings. It is more obviously truncated than most of the other readings, with five lectures ostensibly missing, but it also demonstrates the ways in which even a reduced reading might circulate. The scribe of *Hr* presumably copied a truncated version, but left gaps in his transcription in the hopes of filling them, either from another version of the text, or perhaps more generally with other relevant material, since the gaps he left do not seem to be substantial enough to accommodate all the missing text. The scribe of *Ha* either copied a truncated text, but was

---

[25] Hall's Reading, p. 176, below.
[26] Fitzherbert, *Devise*, 27 appears also in Reading 9.

less concerned about recovering the missing material, or truncated it himself. In either case, it is clear that multiple versions were in circulation, and that the scribes were comfortable adapting the texts they found to their own needs and expected to integrate the material further as they moved along. It would obviously be very nice to know what was in the missing material in rather more detail and to have some sense of why it was dropped. Given the timing and subject matter of the reading some speculation that Hall had raised controversial or dangerous ideas is hard to resist, but it is worth keeping in mind that most of the reading texts that we have examined, even those that can be clearly associated with a given reading, represent only a small proportion of what was said during their learning exercise. The editing that occurs seems for the most part to be driven by the interests of the note-takers and scribes, and there is no reason to assume that the violence done to Hall's text, though more obvious, is any different in nature or purpose than the more diffuse abridgements and amalgamations in the earlier texts.

CONCLUSION

The choice of subject matter for this volume was driven by two separate, yet connected concerns. The first, as already suggested, was to better understand these manuscripts as a product of, and thus an insight into, the process of legal education. An examination of these manuscripts demonstrates that the surviving reading texts are complex products of a complex learning system and that they may represent a variety of different experiences of that system. Some of the note-takers and scribes who produced these texts were very good law students, both diligent and able, and some were probably neither. We may work on the assumption that bad notes would probably not have circulated, or not very far, but it is fairly clear that some bad things must have happened to some good notes along the way. In all fairness, the quality of the readings as they were delivered must have varied quite widely also, and it is entirely likely that able and diligent students found themselves trying, on some occasions, to spin gold from dross.

Recognition of these circumstances makes elaborating on the second reason for this collection, to see what the common lawyers were teaching on the general subject of the Church in the century or so leading up to the Reformation, rather more challenging. Having tried to draw some preliminary conclusions for this introduction on the subjects of sanctuary and benefit of clergy, it quickly became clear that the material in the readings bears very little resemblance to the standard interpretations in the historiography of those two subjects. Benefit of clergy and sanctuary will be examined elsewhere, in order to give them the space that the complexity and interest of the material deserves, and hopefully in due course all of this material will be worked through, but this is not the place for it.

A third concern has developed while working through the material, and that is the broader question of the role of the readings in the development of legal understanding. Milsom's *A Natural History of the Common Law* raised again the question of what drives and directs change in the law. In it he argues, in numerous

contexts, that no-one directed the law, that 'the minds behind … change were those of countless individual lawyers through the centuries, each concerned not with "the law" as such but with a small immediate predicament of his client'.[27] He suggests that developments that historians see as significant were rarely intended, and generally not recognized as novelties until they were well-advanced.[28] It is relatively easy to object to this suggestion, and to point to moments of substantial and intentional change, most obviously in the reigns of Henry II and Edward I, for example. This, however, does not seem to be Milsom's point, since he is largely concerned with the bigger picture of long-term change. He accepts the role of legislation in promoting change, but for him the interesting thing is what happens once the legislation is passed, since 'the legislator … had a specific mischief in mind when he prescribed his remedy, but he had no control once it was launched. There was nobody to monitor the use made of his creature, nobody able to veto an "improper" application. There was no propriety.'[29] This was probably true for much of the period that Milsom is concerned with, but by the fifteenth century it seems fair to say that the inns played an important role both in the process of vetoing 'improper' applications and in validating acceptable ones through their various learning exercises.[30] Neither the evolutionary model of development nor the great leaps forward of major statutory change can stand alone, but they are connected, integrated, prompted and sometimes defeated by the actions and opinions of individual lawyers working within a common profession and adhering, more or less, eventually, to a common learning. The reading texts, messy, obscure and challenging as many of them are, probably take us as close as we can get to that process in action.

THIS EDITION

Given the inherent variety in orthography, grammar and format in these texts, it seemed wise to employ a relatively light editorial hand. To comply with Selden Society practice, i/j, u/v and c/t have been normalized to modern usage. Capitalisation and punctuation have also been modernized throughout. In readings with multiple manuscripts the orthography of the base text has been used and variants have not been noted. Deletions and interlineations have been indicated with < > and editorial emendations with [ ], while marginal headings which have been brought into the body of the text are indicated with { }.

Marginal notations in the manuscripts are noted in the French text, along with omissions and textual problems. Case, statute and treatise references are given in the notes to the translation. When the text of the reading statute is used as the basis for the lecture or to introduce the next topic, it has been given in italics in both the original and the translation. Since it is often integrated into the sentence

---

[27] S. F. C. Milsom, *A Natural History of the Common Law* (New York, 2003), p. 27. He is returning to arguments that he made first in *Historical Foundations of the Common Law* (1969).
[28] Milsom, *Natural History*, p. 50.
[29] Ibid., 93.
[30] But see ibid., 79.

this serves to distinguish it from the rest of the text without disturbing the flow of the passage.[31]

The French of the readings can be challenging at the best of times: these were oral exercises on which notes were taken in law French (a language which existed only to serve the law) by native English speakers, and the process often seems to challenge their grasp of grammar. For example, subject/verb agreement often leaves much to be desired, as does the consistency of verb tense and number. These problems were compounded by the compilation process that many of these texts went through. In most cases the basic meaning of the passage remains clear, in many cases it is retrievable, and in some it can only be conjectured. In all cases the English translation strives to provide a clear rendition of the sense while remaining as close as possible to the original.

---

[31] In his edition of the English reading on Magna Carta Sayles noted that the reader mis-quoted the statute, but this is very common throughout the readings, presumably because the readers were not working with standardised texts (G. O. Sayles, 'A Fifteenth-Century Law Reading in English', *Law Quarterly Review* 96 (1980), pp. 569–580. Reprinted in G. O. Sayles, *Scripta Diversa* (1982), pp. 301–312). The readers often seem to be working from memory rather than from a written text when they discuss both statutes and cases. When the readers venture further afield the mis-quotes become far more striking. See Reading 10, and Hall, below, pp. 138, 148, 177.

PART I

READINGS ON WESTMINSTER I, cc. 1–3

READING A

WESTMINSTER I {,CHAPTER 2}

[*fo. 77*] *Pur vew est ensement que quant un clerk est pris* etc. Cest estatute de Marlebryg capitulo xxviij°[1] Si Clericus etc. et auxi aferma le comen ley, quar le comen ley fuist si un home soit endite et arain et il luy prist a son clerge, si le ordinarij volet luy receyver nient contristeaunt que il fuist clerke il averoit sicom lou il fuist clerke, et cest sub suo periculo quod incumbit, mez si ne soit pur haut treason, quar la il navera sa clergie. Lestatute est si lordinare luy demanda quil serra delivere sicome il fuist use en auncien temps, mez cet[2] ne serra entend sinon que cestui que le ordinare demanda son clerge et ceo est le cause pur ceo que la invito non datur beneficium ubi petenti et pur ceo etc.

Le statute est *quant un clerke* etc.: que serra dit clerk? Et null peut estre dit clerke sinon cestui que avera tonsour quar litteratura non facit clericum, nec habetus monecum, sed tonsura etc., quar si un home port un action de dette ou de trespass envers un auter per condition de clerke lou il ne avoit tonsour, le bref abatera pur ceo que ceo est faux addition. Et sil ne aver tonsour per le regeuste de la ley sil fuist endite de felonie et trove gilte il serroit morte, mez est sic per prescription quil aver le benefite de son clerge que il ne serra mort etc. Si un home que est endite est un prest et ne aver tonsour, per le regeuste de la ley il serroit mort nient contresteaunt que il luy prest a son clerge, mez pur ceo que le custome est auter etc.

Lestatute est *si soite demande pur* [ret][3] *de felonie* etc. Sunt divers maners de felon, quar felony peut estre petit treason, si come un home tua son maister ou si un monke tua son abotte, cest petit treason et en cest avera son clerge. Si le roy graunt a un segnior que il avera toz lez terres de sez tenauntz sils soient atteints de felonie de petit treson, <coment>[d] come si le tenant tua son maister pur ceo que est sicome felon etc. Mez de burnyng il navera son clerge pur ceo que est haut treason fait per novell estatute. Si un monke tua son abbott ou fait petit treason et soit endit, il avera son clerge nient contresteaunt quil avoit fait forfaite al esglis, et en meme le maner sil entra en auter esglis il avera le benefite quar

---

[1] A reading on Marlborough in the same volume and same hand immediately before this reading has this numbering.
[2] This word looks as if it has been written over ceo, but the scribe uses this form elsewhere.
[3] MS. reads recet.

READING A

WESTMINSTER I, CHAPTER 2

It is provided also that when a clerk is taken etc. The statute of Marlborough c. 28 says 'If a clerk' etc. and also affirms the common law, for at the common law if a man was indicted and arraigned and he took his clergy, if the ordinary wished to receive him notwithstanding that he was [not] a clerk, he would have him as if he were a clerk, and this is at the peril that befalls him, as long as it was not for high treason, for there he shall not have his clergy.[1] The statute is that if the ordinary demands him, [the clerk] shall be delivered as it was done in olden times, but this shall only be understood where the one whom the ordinary demands [prays] his clergy: and the reason is, because 'a benefit cannot be conferred on someone who is unwilling' and therefore, etc.[2]

The statute is *when a clerk* etc.: who shall be called a clerk? And no-one can be called a clerk unless he has a tonsure, for 'literacy does not make a clerk, nor habit a monk, but the tonsure' etc.,[3] for if a man brings an action of debt or trespass against another as a clerk where he does not have a tonsure, the writ shall abate because this is a false addition. And if he does not have a tonsure, by the rigour of the law if he is indicted of felony and found guilty he shall be put to death, but by prescription he shall have the benefit of his clergy so that he shall not be put to death etc. If a man who is indicted is a priest and does not have the tonsure, by the rigour of the law he shall be put to death, notwithstanding that he took his clergy, but because the custom is otherwise, etc.

The statute is *if he is demanded as guilty of felony* etc. There are various kinds of felonies, for felony may be petty treason, as when a man kills his master or a monk kills his abbot: this is petty treason and for this he shall have his clergy. If the king grants to a lord that he shall have all the lands of his tenants if they are attainted of felony [or] of petty treason, as when the tenant kills his master, [he shall have them] because this is only a felony etc. But he shall not have his clergy for arson, because this is made high treason by the new statute.[4] If a monk kills his abbot or commits petty treason and is indicted, he shall have his clergy notwithstanding that he has made a forfeit to the church, and in the same manner if he enters another church he shall have the benefit [of sanctuary], for

---

[1] 52 Hen. III, *rectius*, c. 27 (*SR*, i. 25).

[2] *Dig*. 50.17.69. This also appears in Reading E, p. 38, and Reading F, p. 49, below.

[3] A version of this maxim appears in YB 26 Lib. Ass., fo. 122, pl. 19, 'literatura non facit Clericum, nisi haberet sacram tonsuram'. It may have developed from a statement in the *Liber Extra*, 3. 31. 13: 'monachum non faciat habitus, sed professio regularis'. Another version appears in YB Mich. 11 Hen. IV, fo. 31, pl. [57] 'quia habitus non facit monachum', per Thirning, and Mich. 11 Edw. IV, *Exchequer Chamber* 2: 190, per Catesby. It also appears in Reading E, pp. 37–38, and Reading F, p. 49, below.

[4] 8 Hen. VI, c. 6 (*SR*, ii. 242–243).

est un texte en les plees de le coron que [nemini redeunti claudit ecclesia gremium].[1]

Si un home soit clerke convicte ou atteint et il escapa et prist un esglis son keper poet luy prendre hors de le esglis pur ceo que le ley suppose quil est tout temps deinz le kepyng de le [*fo. 77v*] clerge et pur ceo etc. Mez [si][2] fait un felony apres le escape et prist un esglise, il avera le benefite de le esglise pur ceo que il pur cell felony serroit mort, nient contresteaunt quil averoit le benefite de son clerge adevaunt et null peut luy prendre hors de le esglise.

Item si un home soit prover et il tua un home il ne serra prest saunz dispensation de le pape, mez nient contresteaunt il avera son clerge et le cause est que un home avera son clerge lou il ne aver tonsour, pur ceo que il peut estre un prest nient contristeaunt que il ad cest wave etc.

Item si un home abjure le terre sicom pur felon ou petit treason sil revient et prist un esglis, ou prist luy a son clerge, pur ceo quil peut aver adevaunt, et auxi le cause est pur ceo que nemini redeunti etc. Mes pur haut treason sil reveyne il navera, pur ceo quil ne purroit aver adevaunt.

Item si un feme soit arayne il navera son clerge, [nient] contristant ele aver litterater sufficient, pur ceo que ele ne peut estre prist.

Lestatute est que le ordinare aver sil voet sub periculo quod incumbit et le cort avera un assay si soit clerke ou non et le ordinary peut luy resseyver nient contresteaunt quil nest clerke, mez sil luy resseyva lou il nest clerke et ceo est trove devaunt lez justices de Banke le Roye, oue devaunt justices de oier et determener, le ordinarie peut aver travers a cel office, et si cest soit trove encontre le ordinarie il ne perdre sez temporalties et ceux justices ount power auxibien de enquerere de tiels fattes cum les justices en heire averount quaunt eux fuerunt deinz le terre etc.

Item si un home soit arreine et <le ordinarie>[d] il dit quil est clerke et le ordinare [n]est presente et les jugis mittent devaunt luy un lyver et il ne saver leger, le cort ne aga[r]de que execution serra fait, mes ils mittent proces pur le ordinare devaunt que le ordinare vient, quar si lordinare voet luy resceyver il avera sub suo periculo etc. Si le ordinare ne voet rescever un que est clerke il nest null remedie don envers le ordinare pur luy, mes si ceo soit presente et trove il perdra sez temporalties etc.

Item si bigamy soit allegg en un home ceo serra trie per le evesque et si le evesque certefia que il est bigamus il ne serra reguler pur cell et pur ceo etc.

---

[1] MS. reads nemi undenti clausit ecclesia gremium.
[2] MS. reads sic.

it is a text in the pleas of the Crown that 'the church closes her bosom to no-one returning'.[1]

If a man is a clerk convict or attaint and he escapes and takes sanctuary in a church, his keeper may take him out of the church, because the law supposes that he is always within the keeping of the clergy, and therefore etc. But if he commits a felony after the escape and takes sanctuary in a church, he shall have the benefit of the church because he shall be put to death for this felony, notwithstanding that he would have the benefit of his clergy before, and no-one may take him out of the church.

Item, if a man is an approver and he kills a man, he shall not be a priest without a dispensation from the pope, but he shall have his clergy nevertheless, and the reason is that a man shall have his clergy where he does not have a tonsure, because he could be a priest notwithstanding that he has waived this etc.

Item, if a man abjures the land as for felony or petty treason, if he returns and takes sanctuary in a church, or takes his clergy, [this is allowed] because he could have had it before, and also the reason is because 'to no-one returning' etc. But for high treason, if he returns he shall not have it, because he could not have it before.

Item, if a woman is arraigned she shall not have her clergy, even if she is sufficiently lettered, because she cannot be a priest.

The statute is that the ordinary shall have [the clerk] if he wants him, at the peril that befalls, and the court shall have a test whether he is a clerk or not, and the ordinary may receive him notwithstanding that he is not a clerk: but if he receives him where he is not a clerk and this is found before the justices of the King's Bench, or before justices of oyer and terminer, the ordinary may have a traverse of this office, and if it is found against the ordinary he shall not lose his temporalities, and those justices have power also to enquire of such matters as the justices in eyre had when they were in the land etc.[2]

Item, if a man is arraigned and he says that he is a clerk, and the ordinary is not present, and the judges put a book before him and he does not know how to read, the court shall not award execution, but they shall send process to the ordinary before the ordinary comes, for if the ordinary wishes to receive him, he shall have him at his peril etc. If the ordinary does not wish to receive one who is a clerk, there is no remedy given against the ordinary for him, but if this is presented and found, he shall lose his temporalities etc.

Item, if bigamy is alleged in a man, this shall be tried by the bishop, and if the bishop certifies that he is a bigamist he shall not be regular for this [benefit] and therefore [he shall not have it] etc.[3]

---

[1] This tag probably comes from the *Codex* 1.1.8.35 'quia gremium suum numquam redeuntibus claudit ecclesia'. A version of it also appears in YB Mich. 9 Hen. V, p. 23, pl. 29. Ralph V. Rogers, *Year Books of the Reign of King Henry the Fifth* (Würzburg, 1948). It also appears in Reading E, pp. 36–37, below.

[2] This is presumably a reference to 25 Edw. III, stat. 6, c. 6 *Pro Clero* (*SR*, i. 326).

[3] This seems to mean 'irregular' in the sense of being out of conformity with Church doctrine or ineligible for ordination. It consistently appears as 'regular' in the readings. See below Reading C, p. 16, Reading E, pp. 37, 38, Reading G, p. 53, Reading Two, p. 75, and Reading Seven, pp. 113, 124. Cf. Baker, *OHLE*, pp. 533–534.

Item si un home avoit pris un esglis pur certeine felon et est pris hors del esglise et arrein devaunt justices, il est bon plee pur luy adire que il avoit pris un esglise et fuist pris hors et fuist en tiell ville et en tiell conte et pledera ouster all felony et sic pria quil peut estre restore all esglis. Les justices agarderont un venire facias al vile lou il dit quil fuist pris, et si soit trove per lenquest que [*fo. 78*] il fuist pris hors, il serra restore et si nemi ils agarderont venire facias pur enquerer sil soit culpabull ou nemi, et si soit trove culpabull execution serra fait sur luy sil ne soit quil soit clerke etc. Et le feloni et le pris hors de le esglis serra enquire per xij homez etc.

Item si le partie soit arein in un conte et il dit quil fuist pris hors dun esglis que est en auter conte, lez justices agardont venire facias en le conte ou leglis est, sicome il fuist en meme le conte etc.

In ascun cas un certificat serra directe al vicar generall et en ascun cas all metropolitan: il serrra direct al vicar generall come si le evesque soit outer le meir, et si le vicar certifia quil est bastard ou bigamus le entre serra que le ordinare cet certifia, pur ceo quil nest sicome servaunt al ordinare etc., pur ceo etc. Et il serra direct al metropolitan cum si le evesque soit morte etc. le certificate est void.

Le statute va ouster que le roye eux amonesta quils ne serrount deliveres saunz due purgation ceux que sount convictez et ceux que sount atteintez in null maner, mes sil suffra un que est clerke atteint de faire son purgation nest remedy don envers lordinarie etc.

Si un que est apprewe luy prest a son clergee [*sic*] il ne serra <deverl>^d dilivere al ordinare devaunt que un enquest de office est pris, et si un enquest de office est pris et luy trova nient culpable, il alera aquite et ne serra delivere all ordinare, et si soit trove culpabull il serra dilivere a le ordinare et toutz sez biens serront forfaitz a roye.

Lestatute est *en null manere lez deliverent saunz due purgation* et proclamation serra fait en iiij ou en v contes ajoinant, et si ascun voet venir et dire que un tiele ne dever faire sa purgation per la ley de seint esglis, un poet venir et dire quil tua son auncester et il tiendra de averer per provez de xij prodomz il averement [*sic*].

Item si un home soit convicte ou atteinte lou il ne dever fair sa purgation, si le ordinare suffra defaire lour purgation ne serra enquere si le purgation fuist du ou non, quar per metropolitan ne serra certifie, et le enqueste de layez homez ne enquerent null auter sinon que sil avoit fait purgation ou non, mes si le purgation soit due [ou] nemi, quar ceo ne gist en lour notis.

Est clerke convicte et clerke atteint, clerke convicte perdra toutz sez bienz et nemi sa terre, et sil soit seisi de certeine terre ou sa feme est seisi et disseisi le action serra port en son nome et en le nome de feme et nemi en le nome de feme soule, pur ceo que per cest conviction nade il perduz null

Item, if a man takes sanctuary in a church for a certain felony and is taken out of the church and arraigned before justices, it is a good plea for him to say that he had taken sanctuary in a church and was taken out and was in such a vill and such a county, and to plead over to the felony and thus pray that he might be restored to the church. The justices shall award a *venire facias* to the vill where he says that he was taken, and if it is found by the inquest that he was taken out he shall be restored, and if not they shall award a *venire facias* to enquire if he is guilty or not, and if he is found guilty execution shall be made on him unless he is a clerk etc. And the felony and the removal from the church shall be enquired of by twelve men etc.

Item, if the party is arraigned in one county and he says that he was taken out of a church in another county, the justices shall award a *venire facias* in the county where the church is, as if it were in the same county etc.[1]

In some cases a certificate shall be directed to the vicar general and in some cases to the metropolitan: it shall be directed to the vicar general when the bishop is overseas, and if the vicar certifies that he is a bastard or bigamist the entry shall be that the ordinary certified this, because [the vicar] is only a servant to the ordinary etc. for this, etc. And it shall be directed to the metropolitan [in the event] the bishop is dead etc. [If the vicar general certifies after the bishop is dead] the certificate is void.

The statute says further that the king admonishes them that they shall not deliver without due purgation those who are convicted and those who are attainted in any manner, but if they allow one who is a clerk attaint to make his purgation, there is no remedy given against the ordinary etc.

If one who is an approver takes his clergy he shall not be delivered to the ordinary before an inquest of office is taken, and if an inquest of office is taken and finds him not guilty he shall go quit and shall not be delivered to the ordinary, and if he is found guilty he shall be delivered to the ordinary and all his goods shall be forfeit to the king.

The statute is *in no manner shall they be delivered without due purgation*, and proclamation shall be made in four or five counties adjoining, and if anyone wishes to come and say that such a one should not make his purgation by the law of Holy Church, one may come and say that he killed his ancestor and he shall be held to aver his claim by the proofs of twelve good men.

Item, if a man is convicted or attainted where he should not make his purgation, if the ordinary allows [him] to make purgation it shall not be inquired if the purgation was due or not, for this shall not be certified by the metropolitan, and the inquest of lay men shall not inquire of anything except whether he made purgation or not, but not whether the purgation was due or not, for this does not lie in their notice.

There is a clerk convict and a clerk attaint, the clerk convict shall lose all his goods and not his land, and if he is seised of certain land or his wife is seised and disseised the action shall be brought in his name and in the name of his wife, and not in the name of his wife alone, because by this conviction he did not lose any

---

[1] This was not dealt with by statute until 4 Hen. VIII, c. 2 (*SR*, iii. 49).

tere et pur ceo etc., et [*fo. 78v*] cest action trench en le realte. Clerke atteinte perdra tout, et le roy avera annum diem et vastum etc., mes si ne soit dez terrez de sa feme, quar la feme peut prendre de le roy et tener de luy per fee ferm, et si ele soit disseisi ele avera action en son nom tamen pur ceo que <per>[i] le atteindre <l>[d] son baron ad perd tout etc. Ecce modo mirum quod femina etc.[1]

Item si un dit devaunt lez justicez que il ne voet luy rescever a sa clerge et puis est trove culpable il poet luy prendre a son clerge nient contresteaunt quil aver refuse adevaunt pur ceo que nemini [redeunti][2] etc.

Item si jugement soit done sur un home il poet luy prendere a son clerge ou si ceux que avoient <que>[d] luy pur faire execution de ly voilent luy reducer devaunt lez justicez il peut luy prendere quar [nemini] [redeunti][3] etc.

Item si un home soit clerke atteynte, nient contristient quil soit atteynt sur un faux serement il navera attient pur ceo que lez jurors diont presise et nemi sur lour consciens etc.

Item si un home soit atteint per erronious proces de utlagary de felony et est mort, son heire avera bref de error pur ceo que est aperd son enheritaunce et sil reversa il avera sez terrez hors de mayn le roy.

Si le roy pardon un que est clerke convicte ou atteint et le ordinare luy suffra de escapere le roy navera escape pur ceo quil est pardon per sez lettrez <per>[d] patentes et le ordinare peut monstrer lez lettrez patentes etc. Furunt legez in simul.

{CHAPTER 3}

Purvew est ensement que null rienz desormez soit demande ne leve per viconte etc. Per le comen ley le viconte avoit power en son counte denquerer des escapes, mes naver power de agarder null proces vers null home pur enquerer de cest escape. Mes il dever per le comen ley quaunt un presentment fuit fait devaunt luy, il dever mitter devaunt lez justices en eir et eux agarderont proces et enquirent si ceo fuist escape cum il fuist presente ou nemi, et sil fuist trove devaunt eux un escape le viconte dever lever fele [*sic*] escape. Mez lez vicontes voillent [*fo. 79*] prend un enquest sicom justices en heir nient contristeaunt quil fuist encontre le comen ley, et auxi agard proces vers les jurrors pur venir et pur enquerer de cele escape, et pur ceo cest estatut voet que le viconte ne dever lever null escape devaunt quil soit trove que est un escape devaunt justices en eire, et cet que desormes le viconte etc.

Le segnior de un segniore aver power a le comen ley pur enquerer et a cest jour ad en son lete de escapes, mes il ne avoit power al comen ley, ne ad a cest jour, pur trier lez escapes nient pluis que le viconte etc.

---

[1] Ecce modo mirum, quod femina fert breve regis, non nominando virum conjunctum robore legis.
[2] MS. reads rudenti.
[3] MS. reads rudenti.

land and therefore etc., and this action touches on realty. A clerk attaint shall lose all and the king shall have year, day and waste etc. but not in the lands of his wife, for the wife may hold them of the king and hold them of him by fee farm, and if she is disseised she shall have an action in her name alone, because by the attainder her husband has lost everything etc. 'Look, indeed it is a wonder that a woman' etc.[1]

Item, if one says before the justices that he does not wish to claim his clergy and then is found guilty, he may take his clergy notwithstanding that he refused it before, because 'to no-one returning' etc.

Item, if judgment is given on a man he may take his clergy, or if those who have him to make execution on him wish to bring him before the justices again, he may take it, for '[to no-one] returning' etc.

Item, if a man is a clerk attaint, notwithstanding that he is attainted on a false oath, he shall not be attainted because the jurors spoke falsely and not by their conscience etc.

Item, if a man is attainted by erroneous process of outlawry for felony and is put to death, his heir shall have a writ of error because he has lost his inheritance, and if he reverses [the outlawry] he shall have his lands out of the king's hands.

If the king pardons one who is a clerk convict or attaint and the ordinary allows him to escape the king shall not have the escape, because the clerk is pardoned by his letters patent, and the ordinary may show the letters patent etc. There were readings at the same time.[2]

CHAPTER 3

It is provided also that nothing shall henceforth be demanded or levied by the sheriff etc. By the common law the sheriff had power in his county to inquire concerning escapes but did not have power to award process against any man to enquire of this escape. But by the common law when a presentment was made before him he should send it before the justices in eyre and they should award process and enquire if this was an escape as it was presented or not, and if it was found [to be] an escape before them, the sheriff should levy [a fine for] the escape. But the sheriffs wished to take an inquest just like the justices in eyre, notwithstanding that it was against the common law, and also to award process against the jurors to come and to enquire concerning this escape, and therefore this statute wills that the sheriff should not levy any [fine for an] escape before it is found that it is an escape before the justices in eyre, and thus henceforth the sheriff etc.

The lord of a lordship has power at the common law to enquire and nowadays has escapes in his leet; but he did not, and does not, have the power at the common law to try escapes, any more than the sheriff etc.

[1] 'Look, indeed, it is a wonder that a woman brings the king's writ without naming her husband, who by law is united to her.' It is reported in YB Mich. 1 Hen. IV, fo. 1, pl. 2 that the king sued Sibyl Belknap in the Common Pleas without naming her husband, who was then in exile in Gascony, and Gascoigne C.J.K.B. accepted the suit. This verse is not there, but per Markham when the case is cited in YB Mich. 2 Hen. IV, fo. 7, pl. 26. It appears other times through the fifteenth century: YB Mich. 11 Hen. IV, fo. 7, pl. 16; YB Pas. 5 Edw. IV, Long Quinto, fo. 17; YB Mich. 5 Edw. IV, Long Quinto, fo. 68, and is cited by Coke: Co. Litt. 132b. It also appears in Reading E, p. 40, and Reading F, p. 49, below.

[2] Conjectural emendation.

Lestatut voet que le viconte ne ad null power de lever le escape devaunt que lescape soit trie devaunt justices arrauntes. Item fuit auter justices que avoient power all comen ley de triere un escape si come justices en heire, et ount auxi graunt power en tout a cest jour, si come justices de banke le roy et lez justices de oier et determiner ount auxi graunt power de trier un escape si come justices en [heire]¹ ou justices de banke le roy.

Item si le partie soit pris pur escape per le viconte lou le escape nest trie devaunt lez justicez en heire ou devaunt lez justicez de oier et determiner, le partie le quell escape est pris naver generall action de trespass, mes il avera son action de trespass sur cest estatut pur ceo que le estatute est un prohibition en luy meme et pur ceo etc. Et si le viconte soit convicte de cell endroiterell pris il rendra al partie le escape arereman et ouster damages, nient contristeaunt que damages ne sont expressez deinz lestatute, pur ceo que damages fuerit all comen ley en action de trespass et ouster ceo le viconte serra charge all roy pur cell escape etc.

A cet jour ne sont justices en cest terre mez sont in Wales et la eux ount auxi graunt power com ils averont deinz cell terre, mez lez justicez de banke le roye ne ount power, ne null justicez, pur arain un que est pris pur felony saunz ceo quil est devaunt eux per originall ou le record de le coronere.

Item un home que est pris pur felonie, si il escape hors de le gaole le gaoler perdre c s., mez pur un que est clerke convicte ou atteint sil escapa le ordinare ferra un escape a le volunte de le roye, mes le common custom est ceo.

Item si un home soit arest pur suspecion per un viconte, baill[iff], ou per auter sicome un cunstapill que aver power de luy arester, sil escape il perdra c s., mes si un home arest un auter pur suspecion et il nad null power de luy arester, sicom quil nest constabill ne bailliff, et ce quil ad areste escape luy, il ne perdra null escape pur ceo quil ne aver power etc.

Item si un home est en prison pur haut treason et il escape nest haut treason nient contristeaunt quil est eins pur haut treason, mes est felonie et si soit acquite de la treason il serra arein de le felonie.

Item si [fo. 79v] un home escape et le gailor fait fresch suit et luy reprent, il ne perdra null escape pur ceo que la leie supposa que il fuist tout temps en son garde. Mes si un home escapa et le gaillor ne fait fresch suite, nient contristeaunt quil apres reprente arermain il perdra un escape etc.

Item si un home soit commite all prison et le gaillor suffra luy de alere suth un de les kepers auxi long que il ad animum eundi et redeundi, nest escape et ne serra dit felonie pur ceo que le ley supposa luy de estre tout temps en gard. Mes si il escapa voluntarie le gailor perdra un escape et est felony, et si le gaillor suf-fra luy de escape est felonie et le gaillor, si ceo soit trove, serra mort, et meme le ley est des borowe.

Item si un home feru un auter et est mys en prison pur ceo, sill escapa en le vi le home et le home morust apres de cell stroke, le gaillor perdra un escape pur ceo quil avera relation a le jour que le partie fuist fere etc.

---

¹ MS. reads breve.

The statute wills that the sheriff should have no power to levy [a fine for] the escape before the escape is tried before justices in eyre. Item, there were other justices who had as much power at the common law to try an escape as justices in eyre, and who have as great power in all things today, such as the justices of the King's Bench; and the justices of oyer and terminer have as great power to try an escape as justices in eyre or justices of the King's Bench.

Item, if the party is taken for an escape by the sheriff where the escape is not tried before the justices in eyre or before the justices of oyer and terminer, the party from whom the [fine for the] escape is taken shall not have a general action of trespass, but he shall have his action of trespass on this statute, because the statute is a prohibition in itself and therefore etc. And if the sheriff is convicted of this unlawful taking he shall render [the fine for] the escape to the party again and damages on top of this, notwithstanding that damages are not expressed within the statute, because damages were at the common law in an action of trespass, and on top of this the sheriff shall be charge[able] to the king for this escape etc.

Today there are no justices [in eyre] in this country, but there are in Wales and there they have as great power as they had within this country, but the justices of the King's Bench do not have power, nor do any justices, to arraign one who is taken for felony unless he is before them by original [writ], or the record of the coroner.

Item, if a man who is taken for felony escapes out of the gaol the gaoler shall lose 100s, but if one who is a clerk convict or attaint escapes, the ordinary shall make [a fine for] an escape at the will of the king, but the common custom is this.

Item, if a man is arrested on suspicion by a sheriff, bailiff, or by another such as a constable who has power to arrest him, if he escapes [the officer] shall lose 100s: but if a man arrests another on suspicion and he has no power to arrest him, as he is not a constable or a bailiff, and the one he has arrested escapes from him, he shall lose nothing [for the] escape because he has no power etc.

Item, if a man is in prison for high treason and he escapes, this is not high treason notwithstanding that he is in for high treason, but it is a felony, and if he is acquitted of the treason he shall be arraigned for the felony.[1]

Item, if a man escapes and the gaoler makes fresh suit and takes him he shall lose nothing [for the] escape because the law presumes that he was always in his custody. But if a man escapes and the gaoler does not make fresh suit, even if he takes him again he shall lose [a fine for] an escape etc.

Item, if a man is commited to the prison and the gaoler allows him to go [out] under one of the keepers so long as he has the intention of going and returning, this is not an escape and shall not be called a felony because the law presumes that he was in custody all the time. But if he escapes voluntarily the gaoler shall lose [a fine for] an escape and it is a felony, and if the gaoler allows him to escape it is a felony and the gaoler, if this is found, shall be put to death, and the law is the same of pledges.

Item, if one man strikes another and is put in prison for this, if he escaped while the man was alive and the man dies afterwards from this stroke, the gaoler shall lose [a fine for] an escape because it relates to the day that the party was struck etc.

---

[1] 2 Hen. VI, c. 21 (*SR*, iii. 226–227) made an escape for high treason, treason.

READING B

[WESTMINSTER I, CHAPTER 2]

[*fo. 101*] *Purview est ensement que quaunt clerk est* etc.[1] Cest estatut strecche en ij braunchez et quaunt al primer braunche, nest que confirmation de comen ley et ceo prove lez parolz de cell queux voient que *quaunt clerk est demande per lordinarie quil a luy soit livere solonc le privilege de seint esglise solonc le costom avaunt ceux hourez use.* Mez devaunt le fesaunce del ij braunche de cest estatut si clerk ust este delivere al ordinarie coment quil fuit endite devaunt, unquore il voile luy lesser aler alarge saunz faire due purgation, quel fuit mischevous. Et pur ceo ore est purview per cest estatut que en tiel cas clerk issint comyse al ordinarie ne serra lesse daler alarge saunz faire purgation etc. Lez parolz en le ij^{de} braunche sont *solonc le foy que a luy doient*: issint est destre entend que ceo fuit promyse fait al roy quel est ore pris pur ley sur lour agrement al temps del fesaunce de cest estatut. Cest estatut serra entend dez clerkes convicte et nient dez clerkes atteinte, quar deux null purgation fuit suffre destre al comen ley, ne unquore nest.

Lez parols destatut sont *purview est ensement* etc. et *soit demande per lordinarie*. Lez parolx ne serront issint prisez que si clerk soit demande per lordinarie que il serra a luy delivere. Quar si home soit enprison pur suspecion de felonie, ou endite de felonie, et lordinarie voile dire que un tiel quest enprison est clerk et prie quil peut estre livere a luy, lordinarie ne luy avera quar il ne luy demandera devaunt que son vie soit myse en juperdie.[2] Et coment que lordinarie luy demande come clerk et quil peut [*fo. 101v*] estre delivere a luy, il navera son prier sinon que le clerk ceo voet prier: come si lenquest luy trove coupable et lordinarie conust bien que il est clerk, unquore sil ne voile luy prender a son clergie lordinarie ne luy avera; come si home fue a seint esglise et ne voile prier daver le tuition et lez privilegez de seint esglise, il serra pris hors dicell. Auxi en cas sur son areignement sil ne voile rien parler il serra mys a mort et avera jugement de forte et dure. Et coment que lez justicez luy conustre clerk, si lordinarie ne voile luy resceiver il ne serra a luy livere. Et auxi sil meme ne voet ceo prier, coment que lez justicez sachont luy clerk, il ne serra delivere al ordinarie.

Covient al ordinarie que voile aver tiel clerk a luy deliver daver lez lettrez levesque de meme le dioces quar autrement le clerk ne serra a luy livere, quar si soit per commaundement nest dascun effect.[3] Et issint covient al ordinarie daver evydent prove per lez lettrez del evesque quil est ordinarie quar autrement un puissoit luy demander que nest ordinarie etc.

---

[1] Fo. 100 has Westm' primer as a heading, with 'capitulo primo' in the margin. Fo. 100v is blank. The text on fo. 101 begins half-way down the page.

[2] In margin: que le ordynary peut demandez un clerk (hand 2).

[3] In margin: que serra dit sufficient deputie al ordinary a demandez un clerk etc. (hand 2).

READING B

WESTMINSTER I, CHAPTER 2

It is provided also that when a clerk is etc. This statute spreads in two branches: the first branch is only a confirmation of the common law and the words of the statute, which are that *when a clerk is demanded by the ordinary, that he shall be delivered to him according to the privilege of Holy Church according to the custom used before now*, prove it. But before the making of the second branch of this statute if a clerk was delivered to the ordinary, even if he was already indicted, still the ordinary could let him go at large without due purgation, which was mischievous. And because of this it is now provided by this statute that in such a case a clerk thus committed to the ordinary shall not be allowed to go at large without purgation etc. The words in the second branch are *according to the faith which they owe to him*: this is to be understood that this was a promise made to the king, which is now taken as law by their agreement at the time of the making of this statute. This statute shall be understood of clerks convict and not of clerks attaint, for no purgation was allowed to them at the common law or is now allowed.

The words of the statute are *it is provided also* etc. and *if he is demanded by the ordinary*. The words shall not be so taken that if a clerk is demanded by the ordinary, he shall be delivered to him. For if a man is imprisoned on suspicion of felony, or indicted of felony, and the ordinary wishes to say that the one who is imprisoned is a clerk and to ask that he may be delivered to him, the ordinary shall not have him for he shall not demand him before his life is put in jeopardy. And even though the ordinary demands him as a clerk, and that he may be delivered to him, he shall not have his request unless the clerk wishes to make this request: for example, if the inquest finds him guilty and the ordinary knows well that he is a clerk, still if [the clerk] does not wish to take his clergy the ordinary shall not have him; or, for example, if a man flees to the Holy Church and does not wish to ask to have the protection and the privileges of the Holy Church, he shall be taken out. Also, if he will not speak on his arraignment he shall be put to death and shall have judgment of [*peine*] *forte et dure*. And even though the justices know he is a clerk, if the ordinary will not receive him he shall not be delivered to him. And also if he himself will not ask this, even if the justices know he is a clerk, he shall not be delivered to the ordinary.

The ordinary who wishes to have a clerk delivered to him must have letters from the bishop of the same diocese, for otherwise the clerk shall not be delivered to him, for if it is by commandment it is not of any effect. And thus the ordinary must have evident proof by the bishop's letters that he is the ordinary, for otherwise one who is not the ordinary could demand [the clerk] etc.

Si un come clerk demande lordinarie, soit il que il lie bien ou male ceo serra en le jugement del ordinarie de luy prender ou nemi. Mez sil parle latyn et sur ceo lordinarie luy voile resceivere unquore il ne serra livere a luy, quar peut estre quil ne conust ascun lettre en le lyvere coment quil de custom parle latyn, et issint ceo gist en le jugement dez justicez. Et coment que il ad tonsure et corone clerk, unquore sil ne lie il ne serra livere al ordinarie.

Donques est a veier a quel seisine il avera son clergie et le benefice de cell. Si home areigne de felonie sur appell ou enditement al primez, il peut prier le benefice de son clergie et demander lordinarie saunz respondre al felonie et sur ceo ne serra mys a fort et dure, quar per ceo quil luy prist a son clergie la court est mys del jurisdiction. Et auxi a cel temps son vie est mys en juperdie. Mez pluis meillour est pur luy a respondre al felonie et demander ouster que quel chose que lenquest dit, quil est clerk, quar si sur ceo il soit acquite del felonie il serra dismisse. Et coment que il soit trove coupable unquore il peut prier le benefice de son clergie. Et auxi ceo quil dit que, quel chose que lenquest trove, quil est clerk. Unquore peut aver ceux chateux pur favoure de son vie est don per lestatut de Edw. [III] anno [25][1] pro clero capitulo [4][2] que clerk convicte de petit treson, come si moigne tue son soveraigne, servaunt son maister, et autrez semblable come clyppyng et wasshyng dargent, serra committe al ordinarie, quar en ceux casez reles de toutz maners appelles dez felonies en appell est bon barr.

Et le segnior avera leschete dascun felonie coment que home soit trove coupable et voile demander lordinarie et avera son clergie: il ceo ne avera come de petit larcenye come de vj d. ou xij d. pur ceo que cel felonie ne requira mort. Mez en tiel cas lez justicez recordent cest mater, et si apres soit trove quil emble taunt que peut ovesque le some precedent amounte a xiij d., cest darrein mater ovesque lauter mater devaunt causeront luy destre mort, coment sil ust estre trove en primez quil [ad] viij d. dez bienz un home et taunt dez bienz dauter home, ceo causeroit luy destre [fo. 102] mys a mort et issint en ceux ambideux casez il luy peut prender a son clergie. Home peut aver appell de petit larcyne come de xij d. mez sur cel lappelle ne gaga batayll pur ceo, come est dit devaunt, mort de ceo ne peut ensuer, et unquore si soit trove ovesque lappellaunt il avera sez bienz areremayn. Mez si apres il soit appell demblements dez bienz amountaunt a vj d. ouster lauter some, la il peut gage bataill pur ceo que sil soit trove coupable de ceo il serra mort. Auxi en cest cas darrein il avera bref de conspiracie.

Si home soit endite de emblements de several biens come de xx chosez several al value de xx s. in gros et est trove quil est coupable de prender de xix chosez et nient del <lie>[d] xx[ti] shoce, ore sur cest mater trove il ne serra mort pur ceo que peut estre que toutz lez xix shocez ne amountont sinon al value de xij d. et que le xx[ti] shoce de quel il est trove nient coupable vaut xx s., et issint adonques serroit enconter reson quil serroit mort. Et auxi non constat ex certitudine curiae le value de chescun chose, et lenquest ad bien fait quar

---

[1] Blank in MS.
[2] Blank in MS.

If one claiming to be a clerk demands the ordinary, whether he reads well or badly, it shall be in the judgement of the ordinary to take him or not. But if he speaks Latin and the ordinary wishes to receive him thereupon still he shall not be delivered to him, for it may be that he does not know any letter in the book even though he is accustomed to speak Latin, and thus this lies in the judgment of the justices. And even though he has the tonsure and crown of a clerk, still if he does not read he shall not be delivered to the ordinary.

Now it is to be seen at what season he shall have his clergy and the benefit of this. If a man was arraigned of felony on appeal or indictment before now, he could pray the benefit of his clergy and demand the ordinary without responding to the felony, and on this he was not put to the [*peine*] *forte et dure*, for because he took his clergy the court was ousted from jurisdiction. And also at that time his life was put in jeopardy. But it is much better for him to respond to the felony and demand over that whatever the inquest says he is a clerk, for if he is acquitted of the felony thereupon he shall be dismissed. And even if he is found guilty, still he can pray the benefit of his clergy. And also that he shall say that, whatever the inquest finds, he is a clerk. And that he may have those things in favour of his life is given by the statute of 25 Edw. III *pro clero* c. 4,[1] that a clerk convicted of petty treason (as, for example, when a monk kills his superior, a servant his master and other similar things, such as clipping and washing money) shall be committed to the ordinary, for in these cases a release of all manner of appeals of felonies is a good bar in an appeal.

The lord shall have the escheat for any felony even if the man is found guilty and wishes to demand the ordinary and have his clergy: he shall not have this for petty larceny of 6d. or 12d., because this felony does not require death. But in such a case the justices shall record this matter, and if afterwards it is found that he stole something which, with the preceding sum, amounts to 13d., this latter matter with the previous matter shall cause him to be put to death, as if it had been found first that he had 8d. of the goods of one man and as much of the goods of another man, this would cause him to be put to death, and thus in these two cases he may take his clergy. A man may have an appeal of petty larceny for 12d. but on this the appellee shall not wage battle because, as was said before, death may not follow on this, and yet if it is found for the appellant he shall have his goods again. But if afterwards he is appealed of theft of goods worth 6d. above the other sum, there he may wage battle because if he is found guilty of this he shall be put to death. Also in this latter case he shall have a writ of conspiracy.

If a man is indicted of the theft of several goods such as twenty items worth 20s. altogether, and it is found that he is guilty of taking nineteen things and not the twentieth thing, now on this matter found he shall not be put to death, because it might be that all the nineteen things only amount to the value of 12d. and that the twentieth thing, of which he was found not guilty, was worth 20s. and thus it would be against reason that he should be put to death. And also the value of each thing is not certainly known by the court, and the inquest has done well, for

---

[1] 25 Edw. III, stat. 6, c. 4 (*SR*, i. 325).

lour charge est de trover generalment coupable ou nient coupable et nemi de trovere chescun chose de quel value. Et issint nest semble al action de trespass, quar la ils assesserount le value de chescun chose etc., mez unquore tiel enditement est bon pur le roy et le partie responder a cell, quar en cas quil soit trove coupable de tout, il serra mort. Mez si appell soit pris en tiel maner il abatera pur le noun certeinte del value de chescun choce, mez en le cas avaunt reherce, sur tiel enditement lez justicez voient comitter luy al prison areremayn et enquerer de luy meillour et peraventor luy endite de novel. Si home soit areigne sur enditement quil duissoit emble biens a le value de xij d. et lenquest dit que lez bienz dez queux il est endite amount a le value de[1] xx s. lour verdit est voide quar lenquest nad pluis afair sinon de luy trove coupable ou nient coupable etc. Nec via versa, come adire lou il est endite quil prist bienz al value de xx s. que lez biens ne vailent que xij d. causa qua supra et issint ils nenquergent de la value.

Si un soit endite de felonie et auxi de treson, si primerment soit areigne sur le felonie et est trove coupable et luy prent a son clergie et lordinarie luy resceive, il ne serra puis areigne de le treson quar il est hors del poiar dez laiez mayns et auxi en favour de son vie.

Si home soit appell de felonie ou endite de felonie et puis soit delivere al ordinarie, coment que lestatut soit que lou tiel clerk soit *endite de tiel recte per solempne enquest dez prodez homez*, si lordinarie luy lesse aler saunz fair purgation, il nest plee pur luy sur action pris sur cest estatut a dire quun de sez enditorz fuit endite, excomenge, ou utlage, ou tiel semble, etc. Mez est bon plee pur cestui quest endite sur le areignment adire quun de sez enditors fuit atteint, ou excomenge, ou tiel semble, etc.

Lestatut voet *saunz fair dewe purgation.* Si present soit que lordinarie lessa clerk convicte daler alarge saunz fair due purgation et issue sur ceo soit pris per lordinarie, cest mater serra remitte a le ley de seint esglise et ceo serra enquise [*fo. 102v*] per le metropolitan. Mez si issue soit pris sur purgation generalment et nient sur due purgation,[2] ceo serra trove per le pays. Clerk convicte de petit treson ou que soit comyn laron ne ferra son purgation mez solonc le forme de constitution provyncyll icy devise anno iiij^{to} H[en.] iiij^{ti} ca^o iij^o. Et la le dit estatut voet que ne ferra purgation etc. sauns etc. en especiall cas etc.: vide statutum etc.

Nota que clerk convicte est cestui que luy prent a son clergie[3] devaunt jugement don, quar tout quil soy prist a son clergie devaunt lenquest pris ou puis lenquest pris, unquore il nest que clerk convicte. Mez si apres verdit le jugement soit don quil serra pendu, unquor si longement come il est devaunt lez justices,[4] il peut aver le benefice de son clergie in favorem vite. Et issint quaunt le jugement est issint don quil serra mort, si il apres pria son clergie il est clerk atteint. Si un fait abjuration et puis revient et est pris, la il avera son clergie mez il ne ferra son purgation pur ceo quun foitz quaunt il abjura, et pur <ceo>^{i} <son>^{d}

[1] In margin: verdit (hand 3).
[2] In margin: que ferra son purgation et que nemi (hand 2).
[3] In margin: clerk convict (hand 3).
[4] In margin: clerk atteint (hand 3).

their charge is to find generally guilty or not guilty, and not to find the value of each thing. And thus it is not like the action of trespass, for there they assess the value of each thing etc., but still such an indictment is good for the king and the party shall respond to this, for in the case where he is found guilty of all, he shall be put to death. But if an appeal is taken in such a manner it shall abate for the non-certainty of the value of each thing, but in the case rehearsed before, on such an indictment the justices shall commit him to prison again and inquire further of him, and perhaps indict him anew. If a man is arraigned on an indictment that he stole goods to the value of 12d. and the inquest says that the goods for which he was indicted amount to the value of 20s. their verdict is void, for the inquest has nothing more to do except to find him guilty or not guilty etc. Nor vice versa, as to say that where he is indicted for goods to the value of 20s. that the goods were worth only 12d., as above, and thus they should not inquire of the value.

If one is indicted of felony and also of treason, if he is first arraigned on the felony and is found guilty, and takes his clergy and the ordinary receives him, he shall not then be arraigned on the treason because he is out of the power of the lay hands, and also in favour of his life.

If a man is appealed of felony or indicted of felony and then is delivered to the ordinary, even though the statute is that where such a clerk is *indicted of such offences by the solemn inquest of good men*, if the ordinary allows him to go at large without making purgation, it is not a plea for him to say on an action taken on this statute that one of his indictors was indicted, excommunicated, outlawed or such a thing etc. But it is a good plea for one who is indicted to say on arraignment that one of his indictors was attainted or excommunicated or such a thing etc.

The statute says *without due purgation*. If it is presented that the ordinary allowed a clerk convict to go at large without due purgation, and issue was taken on this by the ordinary, this matter shall be remitted to the law of the Holy Church and this shall be inquired into by the metropolitan. But if the issue is taken on purgation generally and not on due purgation, this shall be found by the country. A clerk convicted of petty treason or one who is a common thief shall only make his purgation according to the form of the provincial constitution devised here in 4 Hen. IV, c. 3.[1] And there the said statute wills that he shall not make purgation etc. without etc. in a special case etc.: see the statute etc.

Note that a clerk convict is one who took his clergy before judgment was given, for whether he took his clergy before the inquest was held or after the inquest, still he is only a clerk convict. But if it is after verdict, [and] the judgment is given that he shall be hanged, still as long as he is before the justices he can have the benefit of his clergy *in favorem vitae*. And thus when the judgment is thus given that he shall be put to death, if he afterwards takes his clergy he is a clerk attaint. If one abjures and then returns and is taken, there he shall have his clergy but he shall not make his purgation because he once abjured, and therefore

---

[1] 4 Hen. IV, c. 3 (*SR*, ii. 133). The statute refers to a provincial constitution to be made based on a letter of Simon Islip, archbishop of Canterbury. Islip's letter of March 1351 is Wilkins, *Concilia*, iii. 13-14, and the provincial constitution of 21 October 1402 is Wilkins, *Concilia*, iii. 271-272.

sur son confession il apres ne ferra purgation. Quere: sil soit utlage sil ferra purgation apres etc.

Clerk atteint forfera toutz sez biens et terrez queux il avoit jour del felonie fait[1] ou unques puis. Et clerk convicte forfera sez biens en meme le manere mez il ne forfera sez terrez et tenementz, <queux il avoit jour del utlagerie>[d]. Mez sur utlagerie de felonie home forfera sinon toutz sez terrez et toutz queux il aver jour de utlagarie pronounce et nemi del jour de felonie suppose. Et le cas est pur ceo que le contempt cause le <fof>[d] forfetour et lutlagarie et peut estre quil nest coupable etc., mez en lauter cas est trove per verdit etc. scilicet de ij enquestez, scilicet de lenditement et de lareignement.

Si home soit trove coupable sur enditement sur quel il est atteint, cestui quest estraunger avera travers a ceo si come adire quil ne fist le felonie. Come si home est atteint et sur ceo leschetor voile entre en le terre pur le roy, le tenant del terre [porte][2] assize, leschetor dit quun tiel fuit seisi etc. et fuit atteint et pled tout le mater en certein: lauter dirra que puis le felonie suppose que le dit home que fuit atteint luy enfeoffa etc.[3] per force de quel il fuit seisi etc. saunz ceo quil fist le felonie. Et issint ceo mittera en triell areremayn quar il nad autre remedie, quar atteint ne peut il aver, ne bref derror, ne per auter voie estre eide, pur ceo quil nest partie ne prive etc. En meme le maner il luy eidre en bref deschete vers le segnior ou sil voile confesser le felonie, unquore cestui quest estraunge mittera ceo en triel areremayn come devant.

Si iij homez suont iij severalz appells devers un home de robberie et quaunt al un appel il est trove coupable et prie son clergie, la serra delivere alordinarie et lautrez ij averont lour biens areremayn quar ceo ad regard as toutz appellys, mez sil soit vencu per bataill per un dez appellauntz ou soyt atteint al suyt dun et penduz, la ils ne averont lour biens areremayn et serra pris sicome il ust deie en quel cas ils ne averont lez bienz areremayn quar est indifferent [fo. 103] sil soit mort a lour suet ou nemi. Quere: et en cest cas il nad regard a toutz etc.

Si clerk atteint soit lesse daler alarge, la il serra pris et puis peut aver son clergie et la lordinarie responder del eschape, mez de clerk convicte autrement est, quar ne serra unques enquis de luy.

Si clerk soit committe al ordinarie le quel tue son gardens il apres navera son clergie. Et ceo ad estre adjuge etc.

Si home soit <conpd>[d] condempne a un auter en cest somme et puis soit committe al ordinarie et fait son purgation, le ordinarie ne serra charge de cel condempnation etc. Quere: etc

---

[1] In margin: forfeture de et (hand 2).
[2] MS. reads porter.
[3] In margin: ou chose unfoitz trye serra auterfoitz mis en triell (hand 2).

on his confession he shall afterwards not make purgation. Query: if he is out-lawed can he can make purgation afterwards etc.?

A clerk attaint shall forfeit all the goods and lands which he had on the day he committed the felony or anytime afterwards. And a clerk convict shall forfeit his goods in the same manner, but he shall not forfeit his lands and tenements. But on outlawry for felony a man shall forfeit only all his lands and all that he had on the day the outlawry was pronounced, and not on the day of the presumed felony. And the reason is because the contempt caused the forfeiture and the outlawry and it is possible he is not guilty etc., but in the other case it is found by verdict etc., namely by two inquests, namely of indictment and of arraignment.

If a man is found guilty on indictment on which he is attainted, a stranger shall have a traverse on this, such as to say that he did not commit the felony. For example, when a man is attainted and on this the escheator wishes to enter in the land for the king, the tenant of the land brings an assize, the escheator says that such a one was seised etc. and was attainted and pleads all the matter in certain: the other shall say that after the supposed felony the man who was attainted enfeoffed him etc., by force of which he was seised etc., without that he com-mitted the felony. Thus this matter is sent to trial again for [the stranger] has no other remedy, for he cannot have attaint, nor a writ of error, nor can he be helped in any other way, because he is neither party nor privy etc. In the same manner it shall help him in a writ of escheat against the lord, or if he wishes to confess the felony, still the stranger shall send this to trial again as before.

If three men sue three separate appeals against one man for robbery, and on the first appeal he is found guilty and takes his clergy, there he shall be delivered to the ordinary and the other two shall have their goods again for this applies to all the appeals: but if he is defeated in battle by one of the appellants, or is attainted at the suit of one and hanged, there they shall not have their goods again and it shall be taken as if he had died, in which case they shall not have their goods again, for it is indifferent if he dies at their suit or not. Query: and in this case there is no regard to all etc.

If a clerk attaint is let go at large, in this case he shall be taken and afterwards he can have his clergy, and there the ordinary shall answer for the escape, but it is otherwise of a clerk convict, for it shall never be inquired of him.

If a clerk is committed to the ordinary and kills his keepers, he shall not have his clergy afterwards. And this was adjudged etc.[1]

If a man is condemned to another in [a certain] sum, and then is committed to the ordinary and makes his purgation, the ordinary shall not be charged for this condemnation etc. Query etc.

---

[1] This seems to refer to Fitzherbert, *Corone*, 419, from the eyre of Kent of 8 Edw II. A similar example also appears in Fitzherbert, *Corone*, 250 (Pas. 22 Edw. III). Spelman notes that in 1314 it was argued that if a clerk convict kills his warder he shall not have the privilege of a clerk: Spelman, reports, i. 63, pl. 49.

{CHAPTER 3}

Purview est ensement que null riens soit demande deshormes etc. Devaunt le fesaunce de cest estatut, si ascun home ust estre arest pur suspeccion de felonie et ust eschape, le viconte voileit fair leve pur cel eschape devaunt ceo quil fuit prente ou adjuge eschape devaunt lez justicez errauntes queux fuer a cel temps, quar fuit certeinte del eschape cestui que fuit arestue pur suspeccion de felonie, scilicet c s., et puis leschape duun que fuit atteint c li. Et coment que lez justicez errauntes ussent sur due presentement fait devaunt eux adjuge eschape sur celuy dez queux bienz le visconte devaunt ust fait leve, unquore pur ceo que le vis-conte ceo voilloit <concelle>ᵈ conceler entaunt que lez <ditz>ⁱ justicez de ceo ne ussent ewe conusaunz, ilz voillent agarder de fair <que lez ditz justicez>ᵈ auter leve de cez bienz areremayn, quel fuit mischevous, pur que per le ordinaunce de cest estatut est ore *purvieu que null rienz desormes soit demande pur pur [sic] eschape de laron ne leve per le visconte ne per auter devaunt que ceo soit trove et adjuge eschape per lez justices errauntes*, et que fait enquore cest serra punye come lestatut fait [*fo. 103v*] mention etc.: vide statutum.

Devaunt cest estatut, al comen ley le partie averoit action de trespass vers le visconte sur le prisel de sez biens pur le leve del eschape quar il de ceo ne fuit juge, quar il fuit arbitrable solonc le discreteon dez ditez justices. Et coment que lez justices ussent adjuge un eschape et sur ceo ils ussent lemitte le certeinte pur cel, unquore le visconte ne ferroit leve de ceo saunz bref ou sufficient garrant de ceo fair. Si le partie ust deliver al visconte biens pur leschape de son bon volunte a satisfier pur leschape lou le visconte navoit garrant per bref de fair leve, et puis le visconte ne ust contenter pur leschape, la naveroit action de trespass mez action de dette, come si home delivere a un auter certenz deners a deliver a un auter et il eux ne deliver oustre, le baillour avera action de dette ou accompt. Si le visconte, per bref a luy directe, face leve pur leschape et puis fait auter leve pur meme leschape, le partie navera action de trespass pur ceo quil ad auctorite per bref, mez il avera action de dette ou disceit a son election, mez le meillour est lac-tion de disceit, quar per cel il recovera tout son dette areremayn et auxi damages pur le disceit et per le bref de dette sinon tauntsolement le dette.

Lez parols sont *que null rienz* etc. *soit demande*. Quant a cest parol *demande* ne fait mater, quar per cel le partie nad prejudice, mez sil soit pris et leve devaunt que soit adjuge le partie avera action sur cest estatut etc.

Donques est a veier queux serront justicez dajuge eschape lou a cest jour ne sont justices errauntes et jeo entend que justices de peas ne ount poiar den-querer deschape pur ceo que ils ont lour poiar per commission coment que de ascunz chosez ils ount poiar denquerer per diverce statutes: ils ont poiar a oier et terminer felonies en lour countes dez homez devaunt eux endites, et issint ils ount generall poiar en tout lour countes en auters divers pointes etc. Mez justices de gaole deliverer nount tiel poiar mez ad deliberandum prisones in

CHAPTER 3

It is provided that nothing shall be demanded from henceforth etc. Before the making of this statute, if any man had been arrested on suspicion of felony and had escaped, the sheriff could make a levy for [a fine for] this escape before it was taken or adjudged as an escape before the justices in eyre at that time, for there was certainty [in the fine for] the escape of one who was arrested for suspicion of felony, that is 100s, and [the fine] after the escape of one who was attainted [was] £100. And even though the justices in eyre used to judge escapes on the one on whose goods the sheriff had previously made a levy on due presentment made before them, still, because the sheriff wished to conceal his levy so that the said justices did not have cognizance, [the justices] then wished to award another levy on his goods again, which was mischievous: wherefore by the ordinance of this statute it is now *provided that nothing shall from henceforth be demanded for the escape of a thief nor levied by the sheriff, nor by another, until it is found and adjudged an escape by the justices in eyre*, and that this shall be punished as the statute says etc.: see the statute.

Before this statute, at the common law the party would have an action of trespass against the sheriff upon the taking of his goods for the levy of [the fine for] the escape, for the sheriff was not a judge of this, for it was dealt with according to the discretion of the said justices. And even if the justices had adjudged an escape, and upon it had delimited the certainty [of the fine] for this, still the sheriff should not levy concerning this without a writ or sufficient warrant to do this. If the party had delivered goods to the sheriff [for the fine] for the escape of his free will, to make satisfaction for the escape, where the sheriff did not have a warrant by writ to make a levy, and then the sheriff was not content for the escape, there [the party] should not have an action of trespass, but an action of debt, as for example when a man delivers to another certain money to deliver to another and he does not deliver them over, the baillor shall have an action of debt or account. If the sheriff, by a writ directed to him, makes a levy [for the fine] for the escape and then makes another levy for the same escape, the party shall not have an action of trespass because he has the authority by the writ, but he shall have action of debt or deceit at his choice: but the action of deceit is better, for by this he shall recover all his debt again and also damages for the deceit, and by the writ of debt he shall only have the debt.

The words are *that nothing* etc. *shall be demanded*. As to this word *demanded* it does not matter, for by this the party is not prejudiced, but if [a fine] is taken and levied before it is adjudged the party shall have action on this statute etc.

Now we shall see who shall be justices to judge an escape since there are no justices in eyre today, and I understand that justices of the peace do not have power to inquire of escapes, because they have their power by commission, even though they have power to inquire of other things by divers statutes: they have power to hear and determine felonies in their counties of men indicted before them, and thus they have general power in all their counties in other divers points. But justices of gaol delivery do not have such power, except 'to deliver prisoners

gaola existentes. Et issint tout lour poiar est compris deinz lour commissionz. Auxi justices de gaole deliverer nount poiar de prender presentementes del eschape et justices de gaole deliverer unquore per estatut de anno [4] Edw. [III,] capitulo [10] vel [...]¹ ount poiar de punier viscontes et gaolers queux ne ount resceuz gentz enditez, appellys, ou trovez ove maynor amesnez per constablez et villez etc. Auxi justices dassize ou nisi prius per lestatut de Edw. [III] de anno [4], capitulo [11]² ount poiar a trover meintenaunce, mez justices errauntez averont pluis poiar a cel temps etc. come a trier eschapys et auterz etc. Justices de bank le roy purront enquerer de leschapys, auxi peut un commission especial estre directe a certeins personz de enquerrer de toutz eschapys.

Et nota que le presentement de leschape covient destre certain, scilicet quun tiel fuit tiel jour et an et lieu per un tiel arestu pur suspeccion de felonie et surmitter le felonie et que a tiel jour et an il luy lessa aler, et ceo covient destre presente certeinement pur le fyn de ceo quel est arbitrable solonc le discreton dez justices accordaunt al mater certain compris deins le presentement, et sur cest presentement un pone per vadium issera vers cestui que suffra leschape. Et quaunt [fo. 104] il vient il responder a cest presentement de leschape et il peut dire que fist null tiel felonie fait, mez ne dirra quil (cestui que escapa) ne fuit coupable mez il peut dire quil ne eschap pas, ou quil ne fuit en son gard, et ceo covient destre entend sur eschape dun quest pris et areste pur suspeccion de felonie, come de maynor ou tiel semblable, lou auxi covient al enquest de presenter en certain le mater de suspeccion, come a presenter que tiel jour, an, et lieu un tiel fuit robbe dez tiels biens et que cestui eschapa fuit pris et areste pur suspeccion de le dit robberie et que puis tiel jour et an il eschapa, soit il per lagremement le partie ou non, hors de son gard.

En meme le maner si un endite de felone eschapa, lenquest presenta tout le certeinte del mater compris deinz lenditement, come adire que cestui que eschapa fuit endite de ceo, que il tiel jour, an, et lieu, certain bienz dun tiel a tiel value felonisment prist et inporter sur le enditement, puis il fuit pris et amesne a cestui sur que leschape est presente et en son gard esteant il luy lessa aler etc. Et unquore il remanit de record quun tiel est endite ne pur quaunt ceux del enquest presenter le certeinte, auxibien de le felonie de cestui que eschapa, come de cestui que luy lessa deschaper, sibien sur enditement de felonie come sur suspeccion. Et cestui envers que le process est fait pur le dit eschape peut dire que lendite ne fuit mye en son gard, ou que [il] ne eschape mye, mez il ne peut dire que nul tiel felonie fuit fait, pur ceo que cestui que eschapa est endite de felonie quel estoit de record, le contrarie de quel il ne avera.

Autferment est en lauter cas lou cestui que eschapa fuit en gard sinon pur suspeccion de felonie quel serra trie per le pais. Et pur ceo sur lenditement de

---

¹ All supplied material fills blanks left in MS.
² Blanks left in MS. for [4] and [11].

from gaol'. And thus all their power is comprised in their commissions. Also justices of gaol delivery do not have the power to take presentments of escape, and yet justices of gaol delivery by the statute of 4 Edw. III, c. 10 or [ ][1] have the power to punish sheriffs and gaolers who do not receive persons indicted, appealed, or found with a mainor [when they are] brought by the constables and vills etc.[2] Also justices of assize or *nisi prius* by the statute of 4 Edw. III, c. 11 have power to find maintenance, but justices in eyre have more power now etc., as to try escapes and other things etc.[3] Justices of the King's Bench can inquire of escapes, and a special commission can be directed to certain persons to inquire of all escapes.

And note that the presentment of the escape must be certain, namely that such a one was on such a day and year and place arrested on suspicion of felony by such a one, and [that he] committed the felony, and that at such a day and year he let him go, and this must be presented with certainty, for the fine on this is variable according to the discretion of the justices, according to the certain matter contained in the presentment, and on this presentment a *pone per vadium* shall issue against him who allows the escape. And when he comes he shall respond to this presentment of the escape, and he may say that no such felony was committed, but he shall not say that the one who escaped was not guilty, but he may say that he did not escape, or that he was not in his custody, and this must be understood of the escape of one who is taken and arrested on suspicion of felony, when there is mainour or suchlike, where also the inquest must present with certainty the matter of suspicion, such as to present that on such a day, year, and place, such a one was robbed of such goods and that the one who escaped was taken and arrested on suspicion of the said robbery and that afterwards, on such a day and year, he escaped, whether by the agreement of the party or not, out of his custody.

In the same manner if one indicted of felony escapes, the inquest shall present all the certainty of the matter contained in the indictment, as to say that the one who escaped was indicted on this that he, on such a day, year, and place, feloniously took certain goods of such a value and was brought on the indictment, then he was taken and brought to the one who is presented for the escape and was in his custody until he allowed him to go etc. And yet it remains of record that such a one is indicted by what those of the inquest presented as certainty, both the felony of the one who escaped, and the felony of the one who let him escape, both on indictment of felony and on suspicion. And the one against whom the process is brought for the said escape may say that the indictee was never in his custody, or that he never escaped, but he may not say that no such felony was committed, because the escapee is indicted of a felony which is of record, and he shall not aver the contrary.

It is otherwise in the other case where the one who escaped was only in custody on suspicion of felony, which shall be tried by the country. And for this on

---

[1] Left blank in MS., not supplied.
[2] 4 Edw. III, c. 10 (*SR*, i. 264).
[3] 4 Edw. III, c. 11 (ibid.).

felonie le visconte ou gard peut dire null tiel record, quel serra trie per le record, scilicet per lenditement, et lauters deux issues, scilicet que ne fuit en son gard, ou que ne eschape mye, serront triez per le pais.

Si constable arrest un pur suspeccion de felonie et puis il eschape hors de gard il respondera pur leschape et ouster ceo le constable luy arrest lou ne fuit ascun suspeccion fait il respondera et serra charge a lauter en bref de faux enprison-ment. Si soit command per visconte quil ferra examination dun quest atteint de felonie quel eschapa, la sur leschape vers luy presente sur cest certeinte, que ces-tui que fuit atteint fuit commise a luy de fair de luy examination, il ne dire quil ne fuit en son gard pur ceo que le contrarie de ceo aperist de record. Mez unquore il dirra que null tiel record, quel serra trie come devaunt est dit per mater de record. Et coment que aperist per mater de record que il est eschape, unquore ceo ne serra trie per le record mez covient destre enquis per presentement sur originall. Et tout soit que aperist devaunt certeinz justices <nient poiar dajuger cel>[d] sur le livere dun tiel al visconte quel est eschape, unquore memez lez justices nount power dajuge cel eschape coment quil soit de record, mez ceo covient estre pre-sente devaunt lez justices de bank le roy, ou devaunt certain personys per special commission a cel enquerrer assignez. Et bon plee pur le visconte, [fo. 104v] sur tiel eschape vers luy presente, a dire que cestui que suppose que eschap morust en prison, ou quil est unquore en prisone, saunz ceo quil eschapa, et issint de responder al eschapement.

Si lez justicez de bank le roy command a le marchall de meme le bank de amesne certeinz homez queux sont comprisez en lour kalendar, et le marchall ne eux amesna, unquore lez justicez avauntditez ne ceo ajuger eschape, coment que eux ont power de prender presentement dez eschapez devaunt eux, devaunt ceo que soit presente pur eschape devaunt eux.[1] Mez en tiel cas lou le marchall ne amesna ceux comprisez deinz le calendar devaunt lez justicez il ferra fyn. Et issint ne serra pris eschape, coment que soit de record, devaunt quil vient einz per triel ou presentement.

Si soit presente quun tiel fuit committe al viconte de tiel <etc>[d] jour a tiel jour [sic] et que mesne il eschapa, coment que le visconte surmitter quil aperuist al jour quil devoit apperer, unquore covient a luy de responder al eschape quar lap-peraunce ne respond al eschape, nient pluis que serra lou il lessa un a meinpris que nest maynpernable, quar il nad power a ceo fair.

Si soit presente que le visconte felonice permisit ipsum evadere ceo nest sufficient mater del eschape mez sil soit quod felonice et voluntarie permisit evadere ceo est eschape et felony etc.[2] Mez voluntarie permisit saunz felonice nest eschape de felony. Et pur ceo covient deux joindre ove un copulatif come voluntarie et felonice etc.,[3] ou auterment nest felonie nient pluis que si home soit endite come accessorie suppose quod felonice idem receptavit ceo nest felonie

---

[1] In margin: Escape (hand 2).
[2] In margin: ou lescape serra dit felony en le viconte et ou nemi (hand 2).
[3] In margin: enditement (hand 2).

the indictment of felony the sheriff or keeper may say no such record, which shall be tried by the record (that is, by the indictment), and the other two issues (namely that he was not in his custody, or that he did not escape) shall be tried by the country.

If a constable arrests one on suspicion of felony and then he escapes out of custody, [the constable] shall answer for the escape, and moreover [if] the constable arrests him where there was no suspicion, he shall answer and shall be charged by the other in a writ of false imprisonment. If he were commanded by the sheriff to examine one who is attainted of felony who escapes, there on the escape presented against him on this certainty (that the one who was attainted was committed to him to make an examination of him), he shall not say that he was not in his custody, because the contrary appears of record. But still he shall say that there is no such record, which shall be tried, as before is said, by matter of record. And even though it appears by matter of record that he has escaped, still this shall not be tried by the record, but it must be inquired of by presentment on the original [writ]. And although it appears before certain justices on the delivery of such a one to the sheriff that it is an escape, still the same justices do not have the power to judge this escape, even though it is of record, but this must be presented before the justices of the King's Bench, or before certain persons assigned to inquire of this by special commission. And it is a good plea for the sheriff, when such an escape is presented against him, to say that the one who is supposed to have escaped died in prison, or that he is still in prison, without that he escaped, and thus to answer for the escape.

If the justices of King's Bench command the marshal of the same bench to bring certain men who are contained in their calendar, and the marshal does not bring them, still the aforesaid justices shall not judge this as an escape, even though they have the power to take presentment of escapes before them, until this is presented as an escape before them. But in such a case where the marshal does not bring those contained in the calendar before the justices, he shall make a fine. And thus it shall not be taken as an escape, even though it is of record, until it comes before them by trial or presentment.

If it is presented that such a one was committed to the sheriff on such a day and that he has since escaped, even though the sheriff submits that he appeared on the day that he should have appeared, still he must answer to the escape, for the appearance is not an answer to the escape, any more than it shall be where he alllows one to mainprise who is not mainpernable, for he does not have power to do this.

If it is presented that the sheriff 'feloniously allowed him to escape' this is not sufficient matter for the escape, but if it is that he 'feloniously and voluntarily allowed him to escape', this is escape and felony etc. But 'voluntarily allowed' without 'feloniously' is not a felonious escape. And for this two must be joined with a copulative, such as 'voluntarily and feloniously' etc., or otherwise it is not felony, notwithstanding that if a man is indicted as a supposed accessory because 'he feloniously received someone' this is not a felony

saunz dire pluis sciens idem quandam feloniam fecisse felonice receptavit et donques est bon.

Le visconte sur tiel eschape ut supra peut dire a luy discharge que il pursua leschape, luy esteant tout temps en son view, pur que il luy reprist saunz ceo que il eschape en auter maner, mez sil fuit hors de son view, coment quil luy veia apres et luy reprist, unquore ceo est eschape. Auxi est bon plee pur le visconte, sur process vers luy agarde, de responder al eschape a dire que per vertue dun bref il prist cestui que eschape et tiel jour, an, et lieu, certeinz persons a luy fieront rescus, pur ceo que nest ascun certeinte davisement issint que a ches-cun temps que ascun bref serroit a luy directe, quil duissoit prender le poiar del comitatus. Mez auterment est quaunt il ad avisement, come sil soit engard et puis eschape per rescuz, quar ceo <li>ᵈ ne luy excusera.¹ Ou sil eschape per ascun engine le viconte serra charge del eschape, mez si auter home que visconte arrest un home quel de luy est rescue il ne dischargera per le rescuz a luy fait mez il responder del eschape, quar il nad garrant a ceo fair etc.

Si un constable arrest un home pur suspeccion de felonie et luy amesna a un vile et pria eux del vile de luy aider et ils ne voilent issit quil eschape, le vile serra charge de leschape et nemi le constable. En meme le maner si home soit robbe et pursua le felon tanque al prochin vile et la fait huy et crye accordaunt al estatut de Wynchestre et le felon eschape, le vile serra charge de leschapc.² Auxi cn meme le maner si home ad pris [fo. 105] un esglise pur son tuition, si il eschape deinz xl jours la vile serra charge de ceo etc. Si un constable amesna a un gaiole un home quel estoit en un vile et luy amesna al gardein quel ne voile luy resceiver, le viconte ou gard serra charge deschape et nient le constable ou le vile. Et la sur eschape presente vers le viconte ou gardein il ne dirra quil ne fuit en son gard, pur ceo quil fuit amesne a luy, mez il peut dire que null tiel felonie fuit fait, ou quil ne eschape, ou quil est unquore en son gard. Si un que nest constable amesne un al gaiole et le viconte ou gardein luy resceive et puis il eschape, la le partie avera bref de faux emprisonment envers le viconte ou gardein si null felonie fuit fait, et auxi il respondera del eschape, quar il nest tenu de rescevere ascun home a luy amesne per estraunge saunz maynour.³ Mez si un estraunger que nest constable amesne un al viconte ou gardein ovesque maynor, sil eschape il respondera del eschape mez nemi al bref de faux emprisonment, pur ceo que maynor fuit amesne ovesque cestui que eschapa. Mez en cel cas lestraunge que luy areste, si null felo-nie fuit fait, respondera et serra charge en bref de faux emprisonment. Mez si un constable amesna un al gaoler, coment que ne soit ovesque maynour, unquore le gaoler est tenu de luy resceyvere et pur ceo, coment que puis soit trove que le constable luy areste saunz cause dascun suspeccion, le partie navera remedie vers le gaoler mez vers le constable. Mez unquore il respondera al eschape etc.

---

¹ In margin: ou le rescue dun prisoner excuser le viconte de escape et ou nemi (hand 2).
² In margin: ou le visconte serra charge descape (hand 2).
³ In margin: dyversite ou un est amesne al gaole per estranger que nest officer ove le maynor et ou sans le maynour (hand 2).

without saying further 'knowing the same to have feloniously committed a felony he received [someone]' and then it is good.

The sheriff on such an escape, as above, may say for his discharge that he pursued the escapee, having him always in view, by which he re-took him, without that he escaped in another manner, but if he was out of his view, even if he saw him afterwards and re-took him, still this is an escape. Also it is a good plea for the sheriff, on a process against him, to answer to the escape by saying that by virtue of a writ he took the one who escaped and on such a day, year and place certain people rescued him, because there is no certainty of advisement, such that at every time that any writ was directed at him, that he should take the *posse comitatus*. But it is otherwise when the sheriff has advisement, as if he is in custody and then escapes by a rescue, for this shall not excuse him. Or if he escapes by any trick the sheriff shall be charged for the escape, but if another man than the sheriff arrests a man who is rescued from him, he is not discharged by the rescue made from him, but he shall answer for the escape, for he had no warrant to do this etc.

If a constable arrests a man on suspicion of felony and brings him to a vill and asks those of the vill to help him and they do not wish to do so, so that he escapes, the vill shall be charged for the escape and not the constable. In the same manner, if a man is robbed and pursues the felon to the next vill and there makes the hue and cry according to the statute of Winchester and the felon escapes, the vill shall be charged for the escape.[1] Also in the same manner if a man has taken to a church for his protection, if he escapes within 40 days the vill shall be charged for this etc. If a constable leads to a gaol a man who was in a vill and brings him to the keeper who does not want to receive him, the sheriff or keeper shall be charged with the escape and not the constable or the vill. And there, on an escape presented against the sheriff or keeper, [the keeper] shall not say that [the man] was not in his custody, because he was brought to him, but he may say that no such felony was committed, or that [the man] did not escape, or that he is still in his custody. If one who is not a constable brings one to the gaol and the sheriff or keeper receives him and then he escapes, there the party shall have a writ of false imprisonment against the sheriff or keeper if no felony was committed, and also [the keeper] shall answer for the escape, for he is not bound to receive any man brought to him by a stranger without mainour. But if a stranger who is not the constable brings one to the sheriff or keeper with mainor, if he escapes [the keeper] shall answer for the escape, but not to a writ of false imprisonment, because mainor was brought with the one who escaped. But in this case the stranger who arrests him shall answer if no felony was committed, and shall be charged in a writ of false imprisonment. But if a constable brings one to the gaoler, even if he is not with mainour, still the gaoler is bound to receive him and thus, even though it is afterwards found that the constable arrested him without cause of any suspicion, the party shall not have remedy against the gaoler, but against the constable. But still [the gaoler] shall answer for the escape etc.

---

[1] 13 Edw. I, cc. 1, 2 (*SR*, i. 96).

Si un evesque lessa clerk atteint eschape il respondera del eschape coment que ne serroit mort, mez coment que il lessa un quest convicte de eschape, la ne respondera al eschape mez serra puny solonc le forme del estatut precedent.

Si home soit endite de petit larcyn puis eschapa, la serra c s., mez si apres soit pris et endite dauter petit larcyn que amount a tout xij d. et puis eschape, ore est felonie etc. Et auxi <meme> [i] ceo que luy less aler eschape serra adjuge et pris come felonie etc.

Premisse de cest estatut le partie en ascun cas avoit remedie al comen ley, scilicet action de trespass, mez sil voile avera remedie sur cest estatut covient a luy de prender son action sur lestatut, et coment que lestatut voet que *celuy que face leve de tiel eschape* etc. *rendra a celuy ou a ceux* etc., *ataunt quil ad recu et auxi au roy ataunt* unquore coment que le partie sue et recovera, le roy navera avauntage per son suyte. En meme le manere <si> [d] coment que soit presente pur le roy le partie de ceo navera avauntage et issint ils [averont] [1] severals <avowrez> [d] recoverez per severalz mesnez, scilicet le roy per presentement et le partie per action concewe sur cest estatut, et issint ambideux recoverent. Et nest semble al decies tantum, quar per le suist dune estrange le roy avera avantage etc.

---

[1] MS. reads overont.

If a bishop allows a clerk attaint to escape he shall answer for the escape even though [the clerk] would not be put to death, but if he allows one who is convict to escape, there he shall not answer for the escape but shall be punished according to the form of the preceding statute.

If a man is indicted of petty larceny and then escapes, there [the fine] shall be 100s., but if he is afterwards taken and indicted of another petty larceny which amounts in total to 12d. and then escapes, now it is a felony etc. And also in the same way the one who allowed him to escape shall be judged and it shall be taken as a felony etc.

The premise of this statute [is that] the party in any case shall have a remedy at the common law (that is, an action of trespass), but if he wishes to have a remedy on this statute, he must take his action on the statute and even though the statute wills that *one who makes a levy for such an escape* etc. *shall restore to him or to them* etc., *as much as he has received, and as much also to the king*, still even if the party sues and recovers, the king shall not have advantage by his suit. In the same manner even if it is presented for the king, the party shall not have advantage of this, and thus they shall have separate recoveries by separate means, that is, the king by presentment and the party by action founded on this statute and thus both shall recover. And it is not like *decies tantum*, for by the suit of a stranger the king shall have advantage etc.

READING C

[WESTMINSTER I, CHAPTER 2]

[fo. 75] Purveu est ensement que quaunt clerk est pris etc. Al comen ley quaunt clerk atteynt fuit commit al ordinarie il fuit a luy livere per ceux parols 'saunz ascun purgation fait' et issint le ley est unquor, mez clerk convicte fuit livere generalment al ordinarie saunz rien parler dascun purgation per que lez ordinarez en taunt[1] quilz navoient expressement en charge[2] deux garder tanque ils fier purgation, voudrent souffrerr eux daler a large ou ils voudrount. Et coment que le ley fuit quilz ne duissent isser en tiel cas mez lou ils aver fait lour purgation, come il appiert per le statut, unquore devaunt cest statut sils furent le contrarie null peyn fuit ordeyne vers lordinarez, per que cest estatut voet que en tiel cas ils ferra liverez al ordinarie solonque le custom avaunt cez heurs use, cest generalment saunz mention fait de purgation, mez il aieynt en le statut que *le roy amonist lez prelatez et lour amoynt en la foy quils luy devoient quils ne deliveront ceux enditez* etc. *saunz due purgation*, le quell est a entendre que sils font le contrarie de ceo quils [chier][3] al roy en un contempt et ceo est le remedie de le statut.

Et nota que fuit reherce sur le letter que *quaunt clerk est pris* etc. et *est demande per son ordinarie* etc. Coment que lordinarie voill vener et demander un tiell endite per cas que il est clerk et cestui quest endite ne soy prent a son clerge, en cest cas il ne serra mye livere al ordinarie per son demande, quar il poet estre que il nest culpable de felonie et doncques il serra prejudice a luy destre committe al ordinarie, per que lestatut serra entend lou il soy prent <a son clerge>[d] meme al benefite de son clergie, et sur ceo lordinarie luy demande que donques il serra livere solonque etc.

Et nota que pur chescun felonie que demande execution de mort home avera benefite de son clergie, tout soit il pur enfrender ou robber deglis, mez le ley est auter. Si home soit endite pur petit larcene, quil ne demande execution du mort, ou en cas quil soit trove quil tua un home soi defend, en quell cas le roy luy ferra grace per le statut, en ambedeux casez avauntditz, pur ce que execution du mort ne gist come il apert il navera benefite de son clergie ne per demande lordinarie ne per son demande demesne.

Et nota que si un home soit endite de felony per nomme de clerk ou preste, tout quil soy prent a son clergie il ne serra my livere al ordinarie saunz examination unquor il appert per enditement que il est clerk ou preste.

Et nota que lez enditez ne soi prender pas a lour clergie devant quilz ount pled al felonie ou confesse le felonie, quar si un voill rien dire al felonie mez soi

---

[1] First letter scratched out and replaced.
[2] MS. reads cherge.
[3] MS. reads chirr.

READING C

WESTMINSTER I, CHAPTER 2

It is provided also that when a clerk is taken etc. At the common law when a clerk attaint was committed to the ordinary he was delivered to him by these words 'without any purgation made', and this is the law now, but a clerk convict was delivered generally to the ordinary without saying anything of any purgation, because the ordinaries, inasmuch as they did not expressly have the charge of keeping them until they made purgation, wished to allow them to go at large as they wished. And even though the law was that they should only go in such a case when they had made their purgation, as it appears by the statute, still before this statute if it was done to the contrary no penalty was ordained against the ordinary: for which reason this statute wills that in such a case they shall make delivery to the ordinary according to the custom used before now, that is generally, without mention made of purgation, but it has in the statute that *the king admonished the prelates and enjoined them in the faith that they owed him that they would not deliver those indicted* etc. *without due purgation*, which is to be understood that if they did the contrary of this that they shall fall in a contempt to the king, and this is the remedy of the statute.

And note that the statute says that *when a clerk is taken* etc. *and he is demanded by his ordinary* etc. Even if the ordinary wishes to come and demand one indicted in this way because he is a clerk, and the one who is indicted does not wish to take his clergy, in this case he shall not be delivered to the ordinary at all on his demand, for it may be that he is not guilty of felony and then it would be prejudicial for him to be committed to the ordinary, so the statute shall be understood that he himself should claim the benefit of his clergy and on this the ordinary shall demand him so that then he shall be delivered according etc.

And note that for each felony which demands the death penalty a man shall have benefit of his clergy, even if it is for breaking into or robbing a church, but the law is otherwise. If a man is indicted for petty larceny (which does not demand the death penalty), or if it is found that he killed a man in self-defence (in which case the king shall pardon him by the statute), in both cases aforesaid it appears that he shall not have benefit of clergy, either by the ordinary's demand or by his own, because the death penalty does not lie.[1]

And note that if a man is indicted of felony by the name of clerk or priest, if he takes his clergy he shall not be delivered to the ordinary without examination, even though it appears by the indictment that he is a clerk or priest.

And note that those indicted cannot take their clergy before they have pleaded to the felony or confessed the felony, for if one wishes to say nothing to the felony but to

---

[1] 6 Edw. I, c. 9 (*SR*, i. 49).

prender a son clergie il serra pris come mewet et mys a penaunce de fort et dur per le statut de Westminster primer ca°[12][1] etc. Mez home poet bien prender luy a son clergie quaunt il ad pled et devaunt que lenquest serra charge, et il avera apres ceo quil ad dit quil est clerk toutz cez challenges peremptorie et auters challenges si come il avera sil ust rien dit de son clergie.

Et nota que si lordinarie luy refus lou il ad lie bien et sufficient il serra charge de luy prender ne voet comparer quaunt il est demande pur examination fair, il serra amercie.[2] Et cestui que soi prent a son clergie doit lier sur un livere et sil lie [*fo. 75v*] sufficientment il serra gard tanque a auter jour que lordinarie veign et donques il serra livere al ordinarie, quar il ne serra reson de luy metter <en>[i] execution de vie, ne prejudice le benefite deleglis per defaut lordinarie. Et nota que si lordinarie luy refus lou il ad lie bien et sufficiement, il serra charge de luy prender sur un peyn et il serra savement gard tanque lordinarie luy voill prender, per le reson suysdit.

Et nota que fuit dit que en ley spirituall il est bon exception de luy ouster de son clergie a dire quil est bastard, ou veilleyn, ou regular, per cas il ad tue un home en taunt que en ceux cases il ne poet estre fait prest, ne auter benefice prender del eglis, unquore en nostre ley tot soit que lordinarie jure ascun tiel exception et luy refus per tiel cases il ne serra allowe mez serra chace de luy prender come en le cas prochain avaunt.

Et nota que si tiel clerk soit examine et ne lie poynt, tout voill lordinarie luy prender il ne serra a luy livere, mez sil ne soit bien lier mez speleer ou lier un parol et nemi auter il serra en le discretion lordinarie de luy accepter pur un clerk ou non.

Et issint nota que en toutz casez de felonie lou il est daver execution de mort sil se prent a son clergie et lie bien et sufficientment il serra livere al ordinarie nient obstante ascun exception forsque exception de bigame quell est don per statut de bigamis acordant a le spirituell ley etc. Et cest bigame sera tout temps allegge quaunt il ad confesse le felonie ou est trove culpable et se prent a son clargie et nemi devaunt, quar al plee de rien culpable et soy prent a son clergie, unquor bigame ne serra allegge devaunt quil soit trove culpable quar il poet estre quil ne serra trove culpable en <etc.>[i]

Et nota que lordinarie, quaunt il est demande en tiel cas, poet comparer per son depute ou per son commissare et sil apiert per depute il [faut][3] que le depute eit prest lez letterz lordinarie provaunt que il est depute, mez null poet apperer

---

[1] Blank in MS.
[2] In margin: cell reson issint <sur>[i] trahe ne wante.
[3] MS. reads tout.

take his clergy, he shall be taken as mute and put to the penance of [*peine*] *fort et dure* by the statute of Westminster I, c. 12 etc.[1] But a man may well take his clergy when he has pleaded and before the inquest is charged, and after he has said that he is a clerk he shall have all his peremptory challenges and other challenges just as if he had said nothing about his clergy.

And note that if the ordinary refuses him where he has read well and sufficiently he shall be charged to take him, and if he will not appear when he is demanded to carry out an examination he shall be amerced. And one who takes his clergy must read from a book, and if he reads sufficiently he shall be kept until the day the ordinary comes and then he shall be delivered to the ordinary, for it is not reasonable that he should be put in execution of his life or prejudiced in his benefit of clergy by default of the ordinary. And note that if the ordinary refuses him when he has read well and sufficiently, he shall be charged to take him on a penalty, and [the clerk] shall be safely kept until the ordinary wishes to take him, for the reason above.[2]

And note that it was said that in the spiritual law it is a good exception to deny him his clergy by saying that he is a bastard, or a villein, or regular,[3] or perhaps has killed a man, insomuch as in those cases he could not be made a priest or take any other benefice in the church, yet in our law even if the ordinary swears any to such exception and refuses him for such reasons, it shall not be allowed, but he shall be compelled to take him as in the case above.

And note that if such a clerk is examined and cannot read at all but the ordinary wishes to take him, he shall not be delivered to him, but if he does not read well but spells or reads one word and not another it shall be in the discretion of the ordinary to accept him as a clerk or not.[4]

And thus note that in all cases of felony where he shall have the death penalty, if he takes his clergy and reads well and sufficiently he shall be delivered to the ordinary, notwithstanding any exception except the exception of bigamy, which is given by the statute *De Bigamis* according to the spiritual law etc.[5] And this bigamy shall always be alleged when he has confessed the felony or is found guilty and takes his clergy and not before, on the plea of not guilty and taking his clergy: bigamy shall not be alleged before he is found guilty for it might be that he is not found guilty.

And note that the ordinary, when he is demanded in such a case, may appear by his deputy or his commissary, and if he appears by deputy, the deputy must have ready letters from the ordinary proving that he is the deputy, but none may

---

[1] 3 Edw. I, c. 12 (*SR*, i. 29).

[2] This may be a reference to YB Trin. 34 Hen. VI, fo. 49, pl. 16.

[3] This seems to mean 'irregular' in the sense of being out of conformity with Church doctrine or ineligible for ordination. It consistently appears as 'regular' in the readings. See above Reading A, p. 2, and below Reading E, pp. 37, 38, Reading G, p. 53, Reading Two, p. 75, and Reading Seven, pp. 113, 124.

[4] By 1469 the judges seem to be arguing that if the ordinary chose to claim such a man he would pay a fine and the felon would still be hanged, though the argument was still made that only a fine would apply: see YB Trin. 9 Edw. IV, fo. 28, pl. 41.

[5] 4 Edw. I, c. 5 (*SR*, i. 43).

come depute a son depute etc., quar cestui que nest forsque ne poet fair auter depute.

Et nota que si un home soit delyvere al ordinarie per cas dun felonie et puis il est surmys quil est endite de treson, il ne serra mye mys de responder al treson, pur ceo que lordinarie fuist seisi de luy devaunt etc., et ils luy poient aver arraine de ceo devaunt. Et au tiel ley est si home soit arreyne dun felonie et est utlage pur auter felonie, sil soit livere al ordinarie per case del felonie pur quell il est arraine il ne serra mys a responder al utlage apres pur la cas avauntdit. Meme le ley est dun abjuration etc.

Et nota que clerk atteint est tout d<i>ⁱez lou un est atteint per jugment ou per confession et puis soy prent a son clergie: per jugement, come sil soit utlage de felonie ou soit atteint per verdit et jugement sur <ceo>ⁱ <son>^d don et puis se prent a son clergie etc.; per confession, come il soit devenu approver, ou confess devaunt le coroner et abjur le roialme, ou conust devaunt lez justicez de deliveraunce. En toutz ceux casez sil se prent a son clergie apres tiel confession ou tiel jugement il est clerk atteint, et cel clerk [forfitera]¹ toutz sez terrez et biens. Clerk convict est lou il se prent a son clergie devaunt tiel confession ou tiel jugement, soit il devaunt verdit ou apres, et cel clerk forfitera toutz sez bienz et serra disable [fo. 76] a [suer]² ascun action mez per son purgation il serra enable et restore a le ley.

Et nota que si home soit utlage de felonie et mesne perenter le felonie supra et lutlagerie il eneff un estranger et le segnior porter bref [deschete]³ vers lestranger, il poet pleder quil yad error en lutlagerie et unquor cestui que luy eneff navera unques cel matter per voie de plee, mez serra mys a son bref derror. Et en meme le cas si cestui quest utlage ne fuist mys coupable de felony, lestranger dirra en bref deschete pur maintener <de>^d de sa possession que lutlagie ne fuit mye coupable etc., et unquor lutlagie meme ne lavera.

Et nota que si clerk atteynt ou convicte soit condempne a ascun en dett ou damages, il navera unquore execution pur quil est delivere al ordinarie einz est saunz remedie.

Et nota que si clerk, puis quil est livere a lordinarie, va a large saunz ascun purgation fait, et soit pris et examine devaunt justices et il dit quil ad fait son purgation, bref issera a meme lordinarie de certifier sil ad fait purgation ou non, et sil certifie que il ad fait purgation donquez il serra delivere. Et lez justices poient enquererr si lordinarie ad souffre ascun tiel aler a large saunz due purgation fait, et si trove soit, lordinarie serra mys a respondere quar cell mater gist bien en notice de laies gentez per le fesaunce de certen proclamations, et per le verdit dez xij clerks que luy doient acquitter, et per auters semblablez que sount requis a ceo que le purgation soiet duement fait.

Et nota que per le spirituell ley si un soit comen laron il ne ferra purgation, mez en nostre ley si tiel fait purgation il est assez bon sil ne soit

---

¹ MS. reads forfater.
² MS. reads fuer.
³ MS. reads desch ater.

appear as deputy to his deputy etc. for one who is only [a deputy] may not make another deputy.

And note that if a man is delivered to the ordinary because of a felony and then it is surmised that he is indicted of treason, he shall never be made to answer to the treason, because the ordinary was seised of him before etc., and they were able to arraign him on this before. And it is the same law if a man is arraigned of one felony and is outlawed for another felony, if he is delivered to the ordinary because of the felony for which he is arraigned, he shall not be put to answer to the outlawry afterwards, for the reason aforesaid. The law is the same of an abjuration etc.

And note that a clerk attaint is always where one is attainted by judgment or by confession and then takes his clergy: by judgment, as where he is outlawed for felony or is attainted by verdict and judgment is given on this, and then he takes his clergy etc.; by confession, as when he becomes an approver, or confesses before the coroner and abjures the realm, or confesses before the justices of [gaol] delivery. In all these cases if he takes his clergy after such a confession or such a judgment he is a clerk attaint, and such a clerk shall forfeit all his lands and goods. A clerk convict is where he takes his clergy before such a confession or judgment, whether it is before verdict or after, and such a clerk shall forfeit all his goods and shall be disabled from suing any action, but by his purgation he shall be enabled and restored to the law.

And note that if a man is outlawed of felony, and between the felony and the outlawry he enfeoffs a stranger and the lord brings a writ of escheat against the stranger, [the stranger] may plead that there was an error in the outlawry, and yet the one who enfeoffed him shall never have this matter by way of plea, but shall be put to his writ of error. And in the same case if the one who is outlawed was not guilty of the felony, the stranger shall say in the writ of escheat to maintain his possession that the outlaw was not guilty etc., and still the outlaw himself shall not have it.

And note that if a clerk attaint or convict is condemned to anyone in debt or damages, still he shall not have execution because he is delivered to the ordinary, and thus [the plaintiff] is without remedy.

And note that if a clerk, after he is delivered to the ordinary, goes at large without any purgation made, and is taken and examined before the justices, and he says that he has made his purgation, a writ shall issue to the same ordinary to certify whether he has made his purgation or not, and if [the ordinary] certifies that he has made purgation, then [the clerk] shall be delivered. And the justices can inquire if the ordinary has suffered any such to go at large without due purgation made, and if it is found [that he has], the ordinary shall be put to answer, for this matter lies well in the notice of laymen through the making of certain proclamations, and through the verdict of the twelve clerks who ought to have acquitted him, and through other such things which are requisite for the purgation to be duly made.

And note that by the spiritual law if one is a common thief he shall not make purgation, but in our law if such a one makes purgation it is good enough if he is not

clerke atteynt. Et nota que si un soit clerk atteynt et livere al ordinarie et puis il est pris et examine, en cest cas il est null plee a dire que il ad fait sa purgation, mez il se poet prender a sa clergie arere, et auterment il serra mys en execution et <pus> [d] puis issera scire facias vers lordinarie a responder al roy de contempt.

Et nota que pur graunt treson home ne prender benefite de sa clergie. Et pur petit treson fuit meme le ley al comen ley, mez il est orden per le statut de que en cas de petit treson home se prender a sa clergie etc.

[CHAPTER 3]

[*fo. 76v*] *Purveu est ensement que nul fine desormes* etc. Al comen ley lez vicontes en lour counte tourns voudriont enquerer deschapes deinz meme le counte faitz per office et per auters que avoient ascun prison en lour gard, et quaunt tiels eschapes fuerent presentz ils voudriont lez ajuge et lever le fyne deux pur leschape lou lez ditz viconte[s] ne fuerent sufficientment appris en ley dajugger lequell serra en ley dit un eschape et quell non, et auxi lou il est un eschape en ascun cas le fyn serra plus graundz que en auter le quel ne fuist en conusaunce dez viconte nient appris en le ley, per que cest estatut voet et ordeyne que nul viconte ne auter *ne leve tiel fyne pur eschape de laron ou felon iesque que leschap soit ajuge per justice errauntez et sil fait auterment quil rendra al partie taunt come il ad paie et al Roy a taunt* et cest le remedie per lestatut.

Et cest statut ne serra dit voide coment que ils ne sount a cest jour justices errauntez dajuger leschape, quar ceux que ount lour power le devoient adjuger, scilicet dez maters de corone ount lez justicez <ount lez justicez> [d] du bank le roy lour power, et ensement justices de gaole deliverer lez queux ambideux poient ajugger leschape. Et auxi justices per especiall commission denquerer deschapes ount poier sil soit compris en lour commission que ils doient ajuge eschapez, mez auterment ils nount power ne auctorite forsque denquerer.

Et en cas quaunt prisoners sount mesne en le gard le viconte devaunt justices de gaole deliverer, ou en le gard le marchal en bank le roy, lez clerk dez justicez fount un kalandar de record lour noms, et si ascun dez prisoners remaynont en le gard le viconte ou le marchal de record a auter jour quaunt il mesne cez prisoners al barr devaunt <devaunt> [d] eux, et lez noms lez prisoners lies et est trove per record quil fail dascun deux que apperer a lauter jour et il ne excuse luy per mort del prisoner, ou per cas quil est remove hors del prison per bref ou auter [semblable],[1] il serra ajuge un eschape et ceo est appelle eschape de record.

Et nota que le cours de fyn deschape fuit al comen ley et unquor est pur un prisoner nient atteint c s., et pur un felon atteint c li., et nient contriteant il est arbitrarie.

---

[1] MS. reads semblawe.

a clerk attaint. And note that if one is a clerk attaint and is delivered to the ordinary, and then he is taken and examined, in this case it is no plea to say that he has made his purgation but he may take his clergy again, and otherwise he is put in execution and then a *scire facias* shall issue against the ordinary to answer to the king for contempt.

And note that for high treason a man shall not have benefit of clergy. And for petty treason the law was the same at the common law, but it is ordained by the statute that in the case of petty treason a man may take his clergy etc.[1]

CHAPTER 3

It is provided also that no fine henceforth etc. At the common law sheriffs in their county tourns could inquire into escapes within the same county by office and for others who had any prisoner in their keeping, and when such escapes were presented they were able to judge them and to levy the fine for the escape [even] where the said sheriffs were not sufficiently informed in the law to judge what shall be called an escape in the law, and what shall not, and also where there is an escape in one case the fine shall be greater than in another, which was not in the cognizance of the sheriff uninformed in the law: for which reason this statute wills and ordains that no sheriff nor any other *shall levy any such fine for the escape of a thief or felon until the escape is judged by justices in eyre, and if he does otherwise that he shall restore to the party as much as he has paid, and as much to the king*, and this is the remedy by statute.

And this statute shall not be said to be void even though there are no justices in eyre today to judge the escape, for those who have their power ought to judge it; that is the justices of the King's Bench have their power in matters of the Crown, and also the justices of gaol delivery are able to judge escapes. And also justices by special commission to inquire into escapes have the power if it is contained in their commission that they ought to judge escapes, but otherwise they only have the power and authority to inquire.

And in the case when prisoners are brought in the sheriff's keeping before the justices of gaol delivery, or in the marshal's keeping in the King's Bench, the justices' clerk shall make a calendar to record their names, and if the sheriff or the marshal brings any of the prisoners remaining in his keeping by the record from another day to the bar before the justices, and the names of the prisoners are read and it is found by record that he does not produce some of those who appeared on the other day, and he is not excused by the death of the prisoner or because he is removed from the prison by a writ or other such thing, it shall be adjudged an escape and this is called an escape of record.

And note that the course of a fine for escape was at the common law, and for a prisoner who is not attainted it is 100 shillings, and for an attainted felon £100 and notwithstanding it is arbitrary.

---

[1] 25 Edw. III, stat. 6, c. 4 (*SR*, i. 325).

Et nota que cest estatut <est>[i] a entendre dez eschapez per necligens et nemi voluntare eschapez, quar pur voluntare eschapez pur un felony il ne ferra fyne mez il avera jugement de vie et de membrez, tout soit le prisonere coupable ou nemi, si le gard de prisoner soit atteint de voluntare eschap, quar donquez il serra pris come accessorie al felony.

Item si un viconte ou un constable arest un home pur suspeccion de felony ou ascun auter home arrest un pur suspecion de felonie et puis luy suffer deschaper saunz proclamation fait et deliveraunce per course de ley, il serra ajuge un eschap auxi bien en officer come en auter home. Et pur ceo quaunt ascun tiel est arest il serra deliverer al prochine gaole pur la demurer son deliveraunce. Mez si le viconte ou gardeyn del prisonere refus ascun tiel prisonere areste per le constable, sil porter ove luy ascun del viell ou il fuit arrester de testimoignere le case de suspecion, adonques le constable est charge del prisoner et leschap serra ajuge sur le viconte ou gardeyn del prison, quar il nest oblige de luy garder forsque al temps quil luy ad comys al prochine gaole. Mez si un auter person que nest pas officer luy arester pur suspecion et luy amesne al [fo. 77] prochine gaole, et le viconte ou le gardeyn luy refus, et il ne port mye ove luy le maynur, cesty que luy prist luy garderent a son peraill, mez sil port le maynur ove luy le viconte ou gardeyn luy prenderent sur peyn deschap, come en le cas avauntdit etc.

Et nota que si un constable arest un pur suspecion et luy amesne al vill, et puis il eschape, que tout le vill serra charge de eschaper. Meme la ley est quaunt un ad pris lesglise en un vill per case de felonie fait: sil eschape tout la [vill] serra charge de leschape, et le fyne pur leschape serra leve de toutz lour biens ou ascun deux per luy per le roy.

Et nota que si un felonie soit fait en un hundred ou un vill, et huy et cry est freschement fait apres le felonie, et ils luy suffier deschaper, il serra ajuge vers vill ou hundred si come la cas est un eschape, si come est done per lestatut de Wynton un action en tiel cas vers eux pur le partie que est [rob].[1]

Et nota que si le viconte ou gardeyn suffre un felon deschaper et luy happe arrer et luy ad prist al jour del deliveraunce, il ne serra ajuge un eschape tout fuit il a un foitz un eschap. Et en cas que le viconte lesse un tiel laron ou felon a maynpris et il gard son jour devaunt lez justices per record, il ne peut estre ajuge un eschape sur luy pur ceo que il ad le prisonere prist la. Et sil soit endicte generalment de ceo que il suffre un tiel, son prisonere, eschaper, il doit monstrer quil est de record quil luy aver prist a son jour long temps puis que leschape est suppose, et per cest mater il soy eidera, mez sil soit enditte per especial endittement scilicet que il lessa a maynpris un tiell que fuit en son gard pur son felonie, ore en cest enditement il ne se peut eider quar il covient covient [sic] responder a cest special matter, quar il ne list a luy de lesser un tiel felon a maynpris et issint per tiel voie il serra ajuge un eschape. Meme la ley est quaunt le viconte ad pris un per capias utlagatum et luy lessa a

---

[1] MS. reads roberie.

And note that this statute is to be understood of escapes through negligence and not of voluntary escapes since for voluntary escapes for a felony he shall not make a fine, but if the prisoner's keeper is attainted of a voluntary escape he shall have judgment of life and members whether the prisoner is guilty or not, for then he shall be taken as an accessory to the felony.

Item if a sheriff or a constable arrests a man on suspicion of felony, or any other man arrests one on suspicion of felony, and then allows him to escape without a proclamation made and deliverance by course of law, it shall be adjudged an escape as well in the officer as in the other man. Therefore when any such one is arrested he shall be delivered to the nearest gaol to await his deliverance there. But if the sheriff or keeper of the prison refuses any such prisoner arrested by the constable, if he brings with him anyone from the vill where he was arrested to witness the cause of suspicion, then the constable is charged with the prisoner and the escape shall be judged on the sheriff or keeper of the prison, for [the constable] is only obliged to keep him until he commits him to the nearest gaol. But if another person who is not an officer arrests him on suspicion and brings him to the nearest gaol, and the sheriff or keeper refuses him, and he does not bring the mainour with him, the one who took him shall guard him at his peril, but if he brings the mainour with him, the sheriff or keeper shall take him on pain of escape, as in the case aforesaid etc.

And note that if a constable arrests one on suspicion and brings him to the vill and then he escapes, all the vill shall be charged with the escape. The law is the same when one has taken sanctuary in a vill because he committed a felony: if he escapes all the vill shall be charged with the escape, and the fine for the escape shall be levied on all their goods or any of them through him for the king.

And note that if a felony is committed in a hundred or a vill, and the hue and cry is raised immediately after the felony, and they allow him to escape, it shall be judged against the vill or the hundred (as in the case of an escape) as an action in such a case for the party who is robbed is given against them [the vill or the hundred] by the statute of Winchester.[1]

And note that if the sheriff or keeper allows a felon to escape and gets hold of him again and brings him on the day of delivery, it shall not be judged an escape, although it was once an escape. And in the case where the sheriff allows such a thief or felon to mainprise and he keeps his day before the justices by record, it cannot be judged an escape in him, because he has the prisoner ready there. And if he is indicted generally that he allowed such a one, his prisoner, to escape, he must show, if it is of record, that he had brought him on his day a long time after the supposed escape and by this matter he helps himself, but if he is indicted in a special indictment, namely that he allowed such a one who was in his keeping for this felony to mainprise, now in this indictment he cannot help himself for he must answer to this special matter, for it is not lawful for him to allow such a felon to mainprise and thus in this way it shall be judged an escape. The law is the same when the sheriff has taken one by *capias utlagatum* and allowed him to

---

[1] 13 Edw. I, cc. 1, 2 (*SR*, i. 96).

maynpris, et puis il gard son jour: sil soit endite de se generalment il se eidera, et si specialment il covient responder a la matter special si come en la cas avaunt reherce et sur meme la pyne etc.

Et nota que a un que est en prison pur petit larcyne fait eschape le viconte ou gard serra charge deschap tout soit que pur ceo il ne serra mort, mez sil soit lesse a maynpris et puis gard son jour, le viconte ne serra charge deschape, ne per general enditement, ne per special, pur ceo que il est resplevisable etc.

Et nota que pur eschape de clerk convict levesque ne serra charge deschape, quar il est en le cas destre prochine avaunt reherce, mez pur clerk atteint il paier eschap.

Et nota que lordinarie ne peut dire de luy excuser pur eschap de clerk atteint que il ne fuit unquez en son gard lou il est present que il fuit en son gard per matter de record, mez il peut dire nul tiel record, ou quil ad luy en son prison. Et si plede issint que il luy ad en son prison, bref issera al viconte daler al prison et sercher sil soit la, et certifier al court, et sil soit certifie quil soit la donquez il alera quite ou autrement il serra ajuge eschap. Mez sil soit que le prisonere est en lieu specialment privilage si come Westminster, issint que lofficer le roy ne peut entrer, donquez la dit matter serra trie per pays. Et en cas que le viconte ad en gard tiel prisoner per matter de record il avera meme la manere de pleder si come lordinarie ad en la cas suisdit. Et en cest cas le coronere [*fo. 77v*] ferra le serche.

Et nota que soit que ascun eschap soit adjuge, unquor le viconte ne le peut levere devaunt quil <est>[d] soit special garaunt et comaundement de le levere.

Et nota que la partie que avera laction sur cest statut covient reherce en son counte tant un tiel prisonere que fuit en son gard demesne eschapa, per quell cas le viconte prist taunt dargent de luy pur leschape enconter la forme de lestatut, quar quil ne fuit en gard meme le pleyntiff il peut aver action de trespass: issint il pria al comen ley.

Et nota que si le partie ne voill mye suer, coment que lestatut don *al roy a taunt*, le roy navera unques riens, quar nul action est don forsque pur la partie.

mainprise and then he keeps his day: if he is indicted on this generally he may help himself, and if specially he must respond to the special matter as in the case rehearsed above, and on the same penalty etc.

And note that if one who is in prison for petty larceny makes an escape the sheriff or keeper shall be charged with the escape even though he shall not die for this, but if he is allowed to mainprise and then keeps his day, the sheriff shall not be charged with the escape, either by general indictment or special, because he is repleviable etc.

And note that for the escape of a clerk convict the bishop shall not be charged for an escape, for it is within the case rehearsed above, but for a clerk attaint he shall pay [for] the escape.

And note that the ordinary cannot excuse himself for the escape of a clerk attaint by saying that he was never in his keeping, whereas it is presented that he was in his keeping by matter of record, but he may say 'no such record' or that he has him in his prison. And if he pleads thus, that he has him in his prison, a writ shall issue to the sheriff to go to the prison and search if he is there and to certify to the court, and if it is certified that he is there then [the ordinary] shall go quit, or otherwise it shall be adjudged an escape. But if the prisoner is in a specially privileged place, such as Westminster [abbey], so that the king's officer cannot enter, then the said matter shall be tried by the country.[1] And in the case where the sheriff has such a prisoner in custody by matter of record he shall have the same manner of pleading as the ordinary has in the case above. And in this case the coroner shall carry out the search.

And note that if any escape is adjudged, still the sheriff cannot levy before there is a special warrant and commandment to levy it.

And note that the party who shall have the action on this statute must rehearse in his count how such a prisoner who was in his own keeping escaped, and why the sheriff took so much money from him for the escape against the form of the statute, for if the prisoner was not in the keeping of the same plaintiff, he could have an action of trespass: thus he shall plead at the common law.

And note that if the party does not wish to sue, even though the statute gives *as much to the king*, still the king shall have nothing, for no action is given except for the party.

---

[1] This may be a reference to YB 21 Lib. Ass. fo. 79, pl. 12, though there is no mention in the case of the matter being tried by the country.

READING D

KEYBELL LECTOR

WESTMINSTER PRIMER, C. 1

[*fo. 302*] *In primis le roy voit et commaunde que le peas del terre et seint esglise soit bein gard*. Cest estatute est affirmans del comen ley del terre, scilicet auxibien dell peas del <esglise>[i] come dell terre, quar si le peas dell esglise soit disturbe, come si induction dell parson soit disturbe, ou le visitation dell ordinarie, vi laica removenda fuit all comen ley. Et ceo est aschun foitz originall et cest quaunt tiell disturbance est certifie en le chauncerie per lordinarie, et aschun foitz judiciall, si come home rec[over] p[re]s[entation] et eit bref all evesque et le present[ation] est disturbe, il avera bref de vi laica removenda hors dez rollez dez justicez. Et issint appert que al comen ley le disturbance de seint esglise fuit punishable per le comen ley et or est affirme per le comen ley et per cest estatute.

Et per cest estatute lez extortions et oppressions faitz sur lez persons de seint esglise et dez auterz, come de gisers en lour measons cum daver maynger et boyer encounter lour volunte, sont auxi inhibetz et oustez per cest estatute, et ceo affirme le comen ley. Et encounter tiells [mesfesors][1] est un action doner a eux que eux sentent grevez, et pur recovery vers lez ditz [mesfesors][2] nosmez en cest estatute double damages si lez parties volent suer ceo. Et si nemi, donquez le roy eit le suit et cest a entendre per enditement ou per action sur cest estatute, le roy puit eslier. Et le proces sur cest enditement est attachement que serra entend per lez [capias][3] en taunt que un distress est pursuant et le distraint conteignera le space duun moys retorne en le court le roy ove luy et sil ne veigne a cell temps donquez auter distraint per que eux serra distreynez a venir a auter jour conteignera le space de vj semayne et sil ne veigne la, donquez soit il attaint per son defaulte et la partie greve recover cez double damages.

Ceux parolx serra entend lou le bref est sue vers eux pur ceo que lez parolx sount *quilz serront distreyntez* etc., et per lequite de ceux parolx si le partie soit attaint sur lenditement per confession, verdit, ou per fesaunce del fyn, le partie greve recover cez double damages et si le partie greve soit mort, lez executorz averont execution de cez damages, et si un abbe soit greve et le partie attaint de ceo, et labbe devi, son successor avera execution, mez en ceux casez il covient de suer execution per un scire facias entaunt que eux sont auterz personez que ne fuer my parties etc. Vide le letter de cest estatute quar il est playn etc.

---

[1] MS. reads meffesorz.
[2] MS. reads meffesors.
[3] MS. reads chnez.

KEBELL READER

WESTMINSTER I, CHAPTER 1

First the king wills and commands that the peace of the land and the Holy Church shall be well kept. This statute is an affirmation of the common law of the land, namely the peace of the Church as well as of the land, for if the peace of the Church is disturbed, for example if the induction of a parson is disturbed, or the visitation of the ordinary, *vi laica removenda* was at the common law. And this is sometimes original, and this is when such a disturbance is certified in the chancery by the ordinary, and sometimes it is judicial, as when a man recovers his presentation and has a writ to the bishop and the presentation is disturbed, he shall have a writ of *vi laica removenda* out of the rolls of the justices. And thus it appears that at the common law the disturbance of the Holy Church was punishable by the common law, and now it is affirmed by the common law and by this statute.

And by this statute the extortions and oppressions made on the persons of the Holy Church and others, such as staying in their houses so as to have food and drink against their will, are also inhibited and ousted by this statute, and this affirms the common law. An action is given to those who feel themselves aggrieved against these wrongdoers, and double damages against the said wrongdoers named in this statute if the parties wish to sue it. And if [they do] not [wish to sue], then the king has the suit and this is to be understood by indictment or by action on this statute at his choice. And the process on this indictment is an attachment which shall be understood by the *capias*, inasmuch as a distress follows and he must return to the king's court within a month (by the date specified in the distress), and if he does not come at this time then another distress issues by which he shall be distrained to come at another day within six weeks, and if he still does not come, then he shall be attainted for his default and the aggrieved party shall recover his double damages.

These words shall be understood where the writ is sued against them because the words are *that they shall be distrained* etc., and by the equity of these words if the party is attainted on the indictment by confession, verdict, or by making a fine, the aggrieved party shall recover his double damages, and if the aggrieved party is dead the executors shall have execution of his damages, and if an abbot is aggrieved and the party is attainted of this, and the abbot dies, his successor shall have execution, but in these cases they must sue execution by a *scire facias* inasmuch as they are other persons who were not parties etc. See the letter of the statute for it is plain etc.

In primez est a voier as queux personz le commaundment de cest estatute extende. Pro quo modo notandum est quil extende a chescun home quaunt a ij ententez: lun entent est a cheschun pur amendance dell payn denprisonment que est don a eux que enfrent le paez, lauter est le comaundment le roy extende a chescun home pur lettyng deux que voillent enfrendre. Mez sont auterz personz as queux le conservation del peas [*fo. 302v*] appertient plus especialment, come a le chaunceler, justicez luun banck et lauter, lez baronz del escheker queux ont poier de prender <de prender>[1] suerte del pees, et leez justicez del pees. Auxi ilz ont power de recorde affraiez devaunt eux sedente curia et assess lez trespassors al fyn, et lez justices del assize, nisi prius et doyer et termyner ont tiell pouer de recorder lez affraiez devaunt eux, et lez misfesours denprisoner et assess fyn sur eux a que nell lez parties naveront traverse pur ceo que toutz lez justicez avaunt-ditz sont justicez de record. Le viconte, eschetor, ou coroner poront committer lez affrayours devaunt eux en prison, mez nemi de assess et de record fynez, pur ceo quilz ne sont justicez de record, mez lez parties serront enditez de cest affray et donquez ferra fyn. Suitors de le court baron ne purront enprisoner aschun home pur affray devaunt eux. Un cunstable sil soit present al affray il peut enpris-oner le partie, et sil face fresche suyt nyent obstant quil ne soit present, mez il ne peut enprison un home devaunt le affray ne appris etc., mez al temps del affray ou freschment apres cest affray come devaunt est dit etc.

Et lez justicez poient prender suerte de pees ex officio et auxi al request del partie. Le cunstable prendra suerte solement ex officio et cest per obligation. Et notandum est queux personz purront prender suerte de pees et vers queux enfan-ttz deinz age <age>[d] peut aver, et vers enfaunt peut estre demand et en tiell cas lenfant serra jure. Feme vers son baron, et moign vers son soverign, et villen vers son segnior, de maym ou de mordre mez nemi de baterie, pur ceo que le segnior peut chasticer son villen.

Home atteint per praemunire facias navera suerte pur ceo quil est hors del pro-tection le roy et le statute de provisoribus. Dit que soit fait de luy come enmy le roy. Enmy le roy navera suerte mez enmy que est per savecondit avera suerte pur ceo endempnyte en taunt que le roy ad pris luy en son savegard. Home mute peut aver suerte de peas et il peut responde per signez. Et null home peut aver suerte sinon pur luy meme, quar feme ne peut aver suerte pur son baron nec econtra. Chescun dez eux prendra suerte pur luy meme et chescun vers lauter et auxi semble est de moigne et labbe etc. Et notandum [est] del suerte pro quo modo est que le suerte serra pris solonque le discretion dez justicez, quare poient prender suerte per reconysans de luy meme, ou per auter, ou per reconisans de luy meme et lauterz, ou il peut prender suerte per un gage ou plege doyer ou dargent, mez si suerte de pees soit fait per un enfant ou moigne professe ou feme conter eux ne purr fair reconisans, einz auterez ceo ferront pur luy. Et nota que suerte de pees ne serra unques pris sinon pur choce que touch le person dun home sicome dassaut, baterie,

---

[1] Words repeated by dittography.

First we must see to what persons the commandment of this statute extends. In a certain way, it is to be noted that it extends to every man in two ways: one way is to everyone to amend the penalty of imprisonment which is given to those who break the peace, the other is that the king's commandment extends to every man to stop those who wish to break [the peace]. But there are other people to whom the conservation of the peace appertains more specially, such as the chancellor, justices of both benches, the barons of the exchequer (who have power to take surety for the peace), and the justices of the peace. Also, they have power to record affrays before them *sedente curia* and to assess the trespassers' fine, and the justices of assize, *nisi prius* and oyer and terminer have such a power to record the affrays before them, and to imprison the wrongdoers and to assess a fine on them, which none of the parties shall traverse, because all the justices aforesaid are justices of record. The sheriff, escheator, or coroner may commit the affrayers before them to prison, but not assess or record fines, because they are not justices of record, but the parties shall be indicted on this affray and then they shall make a fine. Suitors of the court baron may not imprison any man for an affray before them. A constable may imprison the party if he is present at an affray, or if he makes fresh suit even if he was not present [at the affray], but he may not imprison a man before the affray or afterwards etc., but only at the time of the affray or immediately after this affray as is said before etc.

And the justices may take sureties for the peace *ex officio* and also at the request of the party. The constable shall take surety only *ex officio* and this is by bond. And it is noted which people may take sureties of the peace and against whom infants within age may have it, and what may be demanded against an infant, and in which case the infant shall be sworn. A wife [may have a surety] against her husband, and a monk against his superior, and a villein against his lord for maiming or murder, but not for battery, because the lord may chastise his villein.

A man attaint by *praemunire facias* shall not have surety because he is out of the protection of the king and the statute of provisors.[1] It is said that it would be done with him as with an enemy of the king. The king's enemy shall not have surety, but an enemy who is under safe-conduct shall have surety by this indemnity, inasmuch as the king has given him his safeguard. A mute man may have surety of the peace and he may answer by signs. And no man may have surety except for himself, for a wife may not have surety for her husband nor vice versa. Each of them shall take surety for himself and each against the other, and so it seems for a monk and his abbot etc. And it is to be noted concerning surety that in a certain way the surety shall be taken according to discretion of the justices, for they may take surety on one's own recognizance, or [the recognizance] of another, or on one's own recognizance and the other's, or he may take surety by a gage or pledge of gold or of silver, but if a surety of the peace is made by a child or a professed monk or a wife, they may not make it on their own recognizance, but others shall make it for them. And note that a surety of the peace shall only be made on something that touches the person of a man, such as assault, battery,

---

[1] 25 Edw. III, stat. 4 (*SR*, i. 316–318).

rappe, emprisonment et huius, sinon de un choce, scilicet de incendio domorum et le cause est que cest defendaunt le person dun home et cest de forfetur del reconisans pur suerte de peas.

Si home soit lye al pees et appris il fait trespass et cest contra pacem uncore ceo nest forfetur de reconisans. Meme le ley est sil face entry ove force pur ceo que le suerte est prise soulement pur le chocez touchuntez le person: sicome soit lie al suerte [fo. 303] de pees econtra A et cunctum populum domini regis et fer-yst un alien enmie ou alien per saveconduct, il nad forfet son reconisans pur ceo quil nest my de populo domini regis. Mez pur offences touchuntes le person dun home come baterie et huiusmodi, il ad forfet etc.

Le suerte serra discharge si lez suertez deviount et donques lez justicez purront compeller luy de trover auter suerte. Meme le ley est lou le suerte del peas est forfet per lenfrender del pees. Et siun trovera suerte vers A et cunc-tum populum domini regis tanque a certen jour, A peut reless cel suerte a cest jour, mez si null jour soit limite A ne peut reless mez le roy solement. Si lez justicez ex officio preignent le suerte lez justicez ne purrent ceo reless ne null home sinon le roy, si come ad trove suerte en le banck le roy ou aillours per reconisans et il purchez supersedias del chauncere, le suerte est determine et ale, mez si un fait obligation al cunstable pur suerte de pees per tiel supersedias loblige nest my discharge pur ceo que le partie nest pas lie directe al roy. Quere tamen si un fait reconisans pur suerte del pees et le roy luy pardoner toutz dettes etc.,[1] et apres il enfrent le peas, il ad forfet son reconisans nient obstante le par-don, pur ceo quil ne fuit accrue al roy al temps del pardon. Si le princypall soit attaint del enfrender del pees cez suertez, silz sont liez severalment, ne serront estoppez ne concludez adire quil ne enfreint le pees mez auter est silz sount liez joyntement etc.

Patrons del abbeis sont ceux que sont estrayngez al sanck dez founders, et founders sont ceux que continuont en sanck.

Entre per force poet estre dit per un home soul. Riottes, rowttes, ou semblez sont cum multitudine gentium come de ij al meyns etc.

[CHAPTER 2]

[fo. 303v] *Purvew est ensement que quant clerk est prise pur reite de felonie* etc. Tout cest estatute est en le affirmaunce del comen ley et voit que *quant clerk est prise* etc. Ceo est a entendre quant il est arraign de felonie quar il navera avauntage de ceo devaunt quil soit arraigne. Lordinarie luy avera sil luy demande solonque le auncien custom. Et le roy comaund ouster per meme lestatut en affir-maunce del comen ley si clerk soit lyver all ordinary quil ne luy lyvera sauns due purgation fair etc.

---

[1] In margin: Quar sil pardon discharge recognizsans al peais nient forfet al temps.

rape, imprisonment and such things, except for one thing, that is of the burning of houses, and the reason is that this protects one's person, and this is concerning forfeiture of a recognizance for surety of the peace.

If a man is bound to the peace and afterwards he commits a trespass and this is against the peace, still this is not a forfeiture of the recognizance. The law is the same if he makes an entry with force because the surety is taken only for things touching the person: as when he is bound to the surety of the peace against 'A and all the people of the lord king', and he kills an alien enemy or an alien under safe-conduct, he has not forfeited his recognizance because [the alien] is not one of the lord king's people. But for offences touching one's person, such as battery and such things, he has forfeited etc.

The surety shall be discharged if the sureties die and then the justices may compel him to find another surety. The law is the same where the surety of the peace is forfeit by breaking the peace. And if one finds surety against 'A and all the people of the lord king' until a certain day, A may release the surety on that day, but if no day is fixed A may not release him, but only the king. If the justices take the surety *ex officio* the justices may not release him, nor anyone except the king, as when he has found surety in the King's Bench or elsewhere by recognizance and he purchases a *supersedeas* from the chancery, the surety is determined and gone, but if one makes an obligation to the constable for a surety of the peace by such a *supersedeas* the obligee is not discharged because the party is not directly bound to the king. Query, however, if one makes a recognizance for a surety of the peace and the king pardons him all debts etc. and afterwards he breaks the peace, has he forfeited his recognizance notwithstanding the pardon because it had not accrued to the king at the time of the pardon? If the principal is attainted for breaking the peace, his sureties, if they are bound separately, shall not be estopped or concluded from saying that he did not break the peace, but it is otherwise if they were bound jointly etc.

Patrons of abbeys are those who are strangers to the blood of the founders, and founders are those who continue the blood.

One man alone may make an entry by force. Riots, routs or such things are 'with a multitude of people' as with at least two etc.

CHAPTER 2

It is provided also that when a clerk is taken for guilty of felony etc. All this statute is in affirmation of the common law and wills that *when a clerk is taken* etc. This is to be understood when he is arraigned of felony, for he shall not have advantage of this before he is arraigned. The ordinary shall have him if he demands him according to the ancient custom. And the king commands further by the same statute in affirmation of the common law that if a clerk is delivered to the ordinary that [the ordinary] shall not deliver him without due purgation made etc.

In primez est avoier lou le clerk avera son clerge, en queux cases et en queux nemi. En petit treson, come si un servaunt tua son maistre ou moign son sov-erigne, si le servaunt ou le moigne sont clerkes ilz averont son clerge et cest expressement per lestatute anno xxv E[dw.] iij. En graunt treson nemi, sinon en esspeciall casez come si un occist leigne fitz le roy, ou un ocist lez justicez sedeauntz pur le roy, en queux cases si ascun appell soit suez pur lour mortez en lez appellez ilz averont avauntage de lour clerge, mez sur enditementes de ceo al suit le roy nemi.

Si un soit soit [*sic*] arraign quil ad emble vj d. il navera son clergie mez si le enditement soit depredatus fuit vj d. il avera son clergie et ceo est a entendre per ceux parols depredatus fuit quil prent lez deniers del person ove manace etc. Sil soit trove culpable quil emble biens al value de vj d. et apres il est arraigne sur auter enditement deinz meme le court quil emble auter vj d., il avera avauntage de son clergie. Deux homes sont enditez quilz ount emble xx d., lun luy prent a son clergie sur son arraignment et est comys all ordinarie apres, lauter est arr-aigne et il pleda all felone et don en evidence que lez bienz que fueront suppose destre embleez ne fuer forquez al value de vj d., et cest fuit trove, il serra dismys et lauter que fuit comys al ordinarie navera de ceo avauntage.

Si lun soit endite de plusors felonez il serra arraigne de toutz ensemble et ceo est done per novell estatute, et le cause fuit dell estatute quilz voillent vexer un home que fuit endite et [ussoit][1] temporall emprisonement apres ceo quil aver pris son clergie. Si un soit endite de felonie et de treson sil preigne son clergie quaunt al felone, unquor il serra mys al prison tanque il ad respondue al treson. Si un clerk soit convycte et comitte al ordinare et apres il est endite de treson il serra remaund cienz destre arraignez de ceo.

Si clerke soit abjure le reyalme et apres reveigne et est pris et arraigne il avera avauntage de son clergie. Loppinion en auncien temps quil ne avera son clergie devaunt ceo que le roy luy pardon son entre en le terre, mez ore loppinion est al contrarie.

Home est enprison pur felonye et le jaylor luy suffre destre erudite issint quil avoit bien lie per lenformation quil ad en le gaile per le sufferauns del gayler, il avera avauntage de son clergie mez le gailor ferra fyn et cest un comen inquisi-tion sur lez defautez dell gaioler.

Si batell soit joyn perenter un approver et lappelle, chescun deuz peut aver son clergie et home aver son clergie apres verdit et auxi apres jugement.

---

[1] MS. reads issint.

First we must see where the clerk shall have his clergy, in which cases [yes] and in which no. They shall have their clergy in petty treason, as when a servant kills his master or a monk his superior, if the servant or the monk are clerks and this is expressly by the statute of 25 Edw. III.[1] In high treason [they shall] not, except in special cases such as where one kills the king's eldest son, or kills the justices sitting for the king: in these cases if any appeal is sued for their death, they shall have the advantage of their clergy in the appeal, but not on indictments for this at the suit of the king.

If one is arraigned for stealing 6d. he shall not have his clergy, but if the indictment was *depredatus fuit* 6d. he shall have his clergy and it is to be understood by these words *depredatus fuit* that he took the money from the person with menace etc. If he is found guilty of stealing goods to the value of 6d. and afterwards he is arraigned on another indictment within the same court for stealing another 6d., he shall have benefit of his clergy. Two men are indicted for stealing 20d., one of them takes his clergy on his arraignment and is committed to the ordinary afterwards, the other is arraigned and pleads to the felony and gives in evidence that the goods that were supposedly stolen were only worth 6d., and this is found, he shall be dismissed and the other who was committed to the ordinary shall not have the benefit of this.

If one is indicted of many felonies he shall be arraigned on them all together, and this is given by a recent statute, and the reason for the statute was that they wished to vex a man who was indicted and make use of temporal imprisonment after he had taken his clergy.[2] If one is indicted of felony and of treason, if he takes his clergy on the felony still he shall be put in prison until he has answered to the treason. If a clerk is convicted and committed to the ordinary and afterwards he is indicted for treason, he shall be remanded here, [in this court], to be arraigned on this.

If a clerk abjures the realm and afterwards returns and is taken and arraigned, he shall have benefit of his clergy. The opinion in past times was that he should not have his clergy before the king pardoned him for his entry into the land, but now the opinion is the contrary.[3]

If a man is imprisoned for felony and the gaoler suffers him to be taught enough so that he can read by the teaching he had in gaol by the sufferance of the gaoler, he shall have advantage of his clergy but the gaoler shall make a fine and this is a common inquisition on the defaults of the gaoler.

If battle is joined between an approver and the appellee, each of them may have his clergy, and a man shall have his clergy after verdict and also after judgment.

---

[1] 25 Edw. III, stat. 5, c. 2 (*SR*, i. 319–320) defines petty treason, but it makes no comment on benefit of clergy. 25 Edw. III, stat. 6, c. 4 *Pro Clero* generally affirms benefit of clergy, but makes no mention of petty treason (*SR*, i. 325).

[2] 1 Edw. IV, c. 2 (*SR*, ii. 389–391). There is no mention of benefit of clergy in the statute, or any suggestion that this was the impetus for the statute.

[3] In YB Trin. 9 Edw. IV, fo. 28, pl. 41 a felon who had previously abjured tried to claim clergy when his charter of pardon for the crime was disallowed because it did not mention abjuration. While this does not exactly fit Kebell's point, it suggests that the need for a pardon for the entry had been reasserted relatively recently.

Lestatut dit *sil soit demande per lordinary lie son lyver* etc. Nient obstante ceux parols si le ordinarie luy demand et le felon ne voil pas avauntage de son clergie il navera pur ceo quil meme navera avauntage sil ne voile ceo demande. Si lordinary claym un clerke que ne [*fo. 304*] lie come clerke, il ad estre opinion et ajuge en temps E[dw.] le ij^{de} quil ne unquez avera avauntage pur claym aschun clerk apres, mez ceo nest ley pur ceo que cest claym nest my don al ordinary come auters frauchez quar il don a luy en droit de seint esglice. Si lordinary claym un destre clerk que nest my clerk il ne luy avera et il ferra fyn pur son mysclaymer, et sil refuce un clerk que lie come clerk il ferra fyn et le clerk serra tout temps repris tanque lordinary luy accepte. Si lordinary refuce un clerk et apres il luy accept, il ferra fyn pur son primer refusal.

Lordinary est levesque de meme le diocese ou etc., ou le vicar generall quaunt levesque est hors del royalme, ou le garden espiritualtez quant levesque est mort. Et il serra attendaunt a chescun session generall mez nemi a chescun especiall sessionz come sount deinz lez fraunchez ou all nisi prius. Et en ceux especiall sessionz si aschun clerke demand lavauntage de son lyver il serra remaunde al chescun generall sessions et le recorde de ceo claym devaunt eux le triell.

Si un soit clerk ou nemi est per lexamynation dez justicez et ilz luy assign-ount son lyver et nient obstante que le comen use soit quun sawter est assigne a eux, uncore gist en discrecion dez justicez dassigner tiell lyver come ils plerront, issint quil soit legible et nemi blynde ou malement escripte. Home mute arraign pur felonie quest clerk sil [poit]^1 escrier il aver avauntage de son clergie. Et auxi si home soit blynde et arreygn, sil savoit parler laten per erudition et nemi per naturall elocution come lez Italians fount, il aver avauntage de son clergie et uncore en ceux cases ilz ne legunt ut clerici. Et le cause est pur ceo que lez actez de parler laten presuppose que eux savont lier et sont plus noble et digne que est soulement de lier etc. Si clerk blynd demande son clergie et dit quil savoit bien lier, sil avoit sez ogles mez il ne savoit my parler laten, ceo serra trie per le pays come le nonablement del clerk en quare impedit, ou si tenant en action dit que lez terrez sount seisiez en le mayn le roy, leschetor, sil soit present, serra examine, et sil ne soit present serra trie per laction, et issint pris especiall le triell variant a divers temps.

Si lordinary soit arraign de felony le metropolyton est son ordinary que nest my lie dattendre a lez generall sessions, mez en cest cas lez justicez escrierent a luy pur rescever etc. En le marschacie lavauntage del clergie nest forsque solonque le ley syvyle etc. Si un home ad fraunchese pur rescever lez clerks convyctez et atteyntez uncore eux serra delyver tauntsolement al ordinare. Labbe de Westm' est ordinare deinz W[estminster], et sil soit arreign et luy prist a son clergie le metropolyton luy avera et nemi levesque de lordinare uncore il est en le diocese de Londres mez

---

^1 MS. reads soit.

The statute says that if *he is demanded by the ordinary to read his book* etc. Despite these words, if the ordinary demands him and the felon does not wish to have advantage of his clergy, he shall not have it, because he shall not have advantage if he does not wish to demand it. If the ordinary claims a clerk who does not read as a clerk, it has been the opinion and [was] ajudged in the time of Edw. II that he shall never have advantage to claim any clerk afterwards, but this is not law, because this claim is never given to the ordinary like other franchises, for it is given to him in right of the Holy Church.[1] If the ordinary claims one to be clerk who is not a clerk, he shall not have him, and he shall make a fine for his mis-claim, and if he refuses a clerk who reads as a clerk he shall make a fine, and the clerk shall always be taken again until the ordinary accepts him. If the ordinary refuses a clerk and afterwards he accepts him, he shall make a fine for his first refusal.[2]

The ordinary is the bishop of the same diocese where etc., or the vicar-general when the bishop is out of the realm, or the guardian in spiritualities when the bishop is dead. And he shall attend at every general session, but not at every special session, like those within franchises, or at *nisi prius*. And in these special sessions if any clerk demands the advantage of his book, he shall be remanded to any general sessions and the record of this claim [shall be] before them at the trial.

[It is decided] by the examination of the justices whether a man is a clerk or not and they shall assign him his book, and notwithstanding that the common use is that a psalter is assigned to him, still it lies in the discretion of the justices to assign whatever book pleases them, as long as it is legible and not faded or badly written. A mute man arraigned for felony who is a clerk shall have advantage of his clergy if he can write. And also if a man is blind and is arraigned, if he knows how to speak Latin by learning, and not by natural speech like the Italians do, he shall have advantage of his clergy, and yet in these cases they do not 'read as clerks'. And the reason is because the act of speaking Latin presupposes that they know how to read and this is nobler and more worthy than it is simply to read etc. If a blind clerk demands his clergy and says that he knows how to read well, if he had his eyes, but he does not know how to speak Latin, this shall be tried by the jury, like the non-ability of a clerk in *quare impedit*, or if a tenant in an action says that the lands are seized into the king's hands, the escheator, if he is present, shall be examined, and if he is not present it shall be tried by the action, and thus the special trial varies at different times.

If the ordinary is arraigned for felony the metropolitan is his ordinary: [the metropolitan] is not bound to attend at the general sessions, but in this case the justices shall write to him to receive [the ordinary as a clerk]. In the Marshalsea the advantage of clergy is only according to the civil law etc. If a man has a franchise to receive clerks convict and attaint, still they shall be delivered only to the ordinary. The abbot of Westminster is ordinary within Westminster, and if he is arraigned and takes his clergy the metropolitan shall have him and not the bishop of the ordinary, for even though it is within the diocese of London, but not of the

---

[1] Fitzherbert, *Corone*, 233. Mich. 20 Edw. II.
[2] This is probably also a reference to YB Trin. 9 Edw. IV, fo. 28, pl. 41.

nemi de diocese de londres. Si un abbe claym son comoyn il ne luy aver sinon quil soit son ordinary.

Et si un clerk demande son lyver il ceo aver mayntenant saunz pleder al felonie et lez purront ex officio adeprimez enquer del felon ou ilz purront luy examyner adeprimez et donquez ex officio enquerer del felonie et tout est [*fo. 304v*] un, et si le clerk demande son clergie et pleder de rien culpable lenquest que est pris nest forsque dofficio, sil soit clerk lordinarie peut fair son attorney. Et en tiell casez lou lordinary meme ferra fyn pur son misfessauns demesne, la il ferra fyn pur le misfeasauns de son attorney. Et sil fait ij son attornez le refusell lun est le refusell de ambideux, lordinary ferra fyn. Et sil fait ij son attornez conjunctim et divisim, la si lun refuce le clerk lauter peut luy prender et est bon.

Si un clerk ad enfrent le prison, ou ad emble bienz del esglise (que est sacrilege), ou il faut tonsure ou vesturam clericali [*sic*], est rule, et est tenuz per toutz lez justicez, que ceux casez ne outeront luy del privalage etc. Ou si lordinary luy refuce generalment ou especialment ceo nest cause pur luy ouster de son clergie si lez justicez veient que il est clerk, quar lordinary pur ceo refuce ferra fyn. Depopulatores viarum nest cause de luy ouster etc., ne adire que il est herytyke pur ceo que ceo nient obstante il peut estre abjur, mez adire que il est convicte del heresye est bon cause etc. Mayhym ou bastardie nest mye cause mez bigamy est et cest pur ceo quod privavit eos omni juri ecclesiastici.

Si lordinary meme voyll allegge bygamye cest bon cause, uncore le clerk serra tanque il meme apres ad ceo certyfie per proces hors de son cort. Si un home espouce un feme deinz age que all annos nubiles dysasent et apres il marie auter feme, il nest my bigamus. Si un hier port appell et allegge bygamye et devaunt ceo soit certyfie il morust, son heir navera bref de certifier pur ceo que lappell est abater. Si un soit bigamus et le pape dispence ove luy et don privelage de son clergie, lestatute est que eux ne serront delyverez sauns due purgation, anno iiij H[en.] iiij^ti. Larchyvesquez de Canterbyrie graunt que null arett de petit treson ou de graunt felonye uncore serra rescever a lour purgation uncore cest voide. Si toutz lez prelatez voylent fayr constitution provinciall serra void pur ceo que eux ne poient chaunger le ley del terre.

Clerke convicte est commis al ordinary sauns ascun sauns aschun [*sic*] jugement don sur luy, il perdre sez bienz et nemi terrez. Clerke attaint est quaunt il

diocese of London.[1] If an abbot claims his co-monk he shall not have him unless he is his ordinary.

And if a clerk demands his book he shall have this forthwith without pleading to the felony, and they may first enquire concerning the felony *ex officio*, or they may examine him first and then enquire concerning the felony *ex officio* and it is all the same, and if the clerk demands his clergy and pleads not guilty the inquest which is taken is only by office, [and] if he is a clerk the ordinary may make his attorney. And in such cases, where the ordinary himself shall make a fine for his own misfeasance, there he shall make a fine for the misfeasance of his attorney. And if he makes two attorneys, the refusal of one is the refusal of both, [and] the ordinary shall make a fine. And if he makes two his attorneys 'jointly and severally', there if one refuses the clerk the other may take him, and it is good.

If a clerk has broken the prison, or stolen goods from the church (which is sacrilege), or he does not have a tonsure or clerical dress, it is the rule and it is held by all the justices that these cases shall not oust him from the privilege etc. Or if the ordinary refuses him generally or specially, this is not a reason to oust him from his clergy if the justices see that he is a clerk, for the ordinary shall make a fine for this refusal. '*Depopulatores viarum*' is not a reason to oust him etc., nor to say that he is a heretic, because this notwithstanding he may abjure, but to say that he is convicted of heresy is a good reason etc.[2] Being maimed or a bastard is not a reason, but bigamy is, and this is because [the statute *de Bigamis*] deprived them of all ecclesiastical rights.[3]

If the ordinary himself wishes to allege bigamy this is a good reason [to refuse benefit of clergy], yet the clerk shall be [kept] until he himself [the bishop] afterwards certifies this by process out of his court. If a man marries a woman within age who does not agree at the age of consent and afterwards he marries another woman, he is not a bigamist. If an heir brings an appeal and alleges bigamy and before this is certified he dies, his heir shall not have a writ to certify this, because the appeal is abated. If one is a bigamist and the pope dispenses him and gives him the privilege of his clergy, the statute is that he shall not be delivered without due purgation: 4 Hen. IV.[4] [If] the archbishop of Canterbury grants that no-one arrested for petty treason or for grand felony shall be received to their purgation, this is void. If all the prelates wish to make a provincial constitution this shall be void because they cannot change the law of the land.[5]

If a clerk convict is committed to the ordinary without any judgment given on him he shall lose his goods and not his lands. A clerk attaint is when he

---

[1] This distinction was also made for other franchises. In YB Mich. 15 Edw. IV, fo. 15, pl. 20 Bryan notes that St Martin le Grand is 'in and not of' London.

[2] 4 Hen. IV c. 2 (*SR*, ii. 132–133) provided that the words 'insidiatores viarum et depopulatores agrorum' (highway robbers and pillagers of fields) should not be used in indictments etc. The language comes from the canon law: *Decretales Gregorii IX*, 3.49.6. See Helmholz, *Ius Commune*, 34. This point is also raised in Readings Seven and Nine below, pp. 116, 136.

[3] This is a paraphrase of the language of the statute, 4 Edw. I, c. 5 (*SR*, i. 43).

[4] 4 Hen. IV, c. 3 (*SR*, ii. 133).

[5] This is presumably a reference to the constitution made on 21 October 1402 and refered to in the statute above: Wilkins, *Concilia*, iii. 271–272.

commys al ordinarye apres jugement don sur verdyt ou objuration ou utlagarie, et il perdra sez beinz et terrez: per abjuration del royalme, per utlagarie, per confescion, ou si soit provour, le clerk serra ouster de son purgation, mez per verdyt trove nemi, pur ceo que nient obstante quun enquest ad trove luy culpable, uncore poit estre quilz disont faux. Et sic vide que clerk convycte peut estre oust de son purgation, et cestui quest attaint peut fair son purgation.

En aschun casez deux sont remedyez et enablementes a cestui que est commys al ordinary: lun le purgation sil peut ceo fair, lauter le pardon le roy sil soit attaint al suit le roy, et per pardon le roy et per partie quaunt est en appell. Et quaunt il port aschun action si disablement soit allege envers luy il peut luy enableler solonque le matter per pardon le roy, et si fuit delyver per purgation donquez il covient jure lez lettrez le esvesque desouth son seall son tesmoign ou auterment il ne serra respond etc.

[CHAPTER 3]

[fo. 305] *Purvew est ensement que null rien soit leve*. Item semble devaunt cest estatute que lez viconte[s] voillent assess eschapez dez constablez et gailers ou dauterz, et auxi de lour gailor demesne et fair le fyn nient [obstante] que loffens fuit en eux et <pur ceo que>[d] en auters plus, et pur ceo le remedie appert que null fyn serra assess devaunt le venaunt dez justicez en heir. Et pur ceo que ne sont justicez en eyre, justicez de banke ont lour power et plus, et eux poient assess, ou justicez [doier][1] et termyner et justicez de gayole delyvereux a cest jour poient fair lasseser dez eschapez. Justicez de peas nont power pur assesser le fyn, mez si leschape soit voluntarie et felony donques eux poient enquerer de ceo et cest pur ceo que ont power pur enquerer de felonie. En torne del viconte ilz [enqueront][2] deschapes, mez le viconte <le v>[d] ne assess le fyn come appert per lestatute anno primo E[dw.] iiij[ti], mez lez justicez come devaunt.

Donquez est avoier quest eschape. Eschape presuppose ij choicez scilicet prisell et deliverer, aschun foitz finable et aschun foitz felonye. Eschape encounter le volunte finable soit le person treytor ou felon. Quaunt un prisoner est pursuite issint que ne soit hors del viewe, ceo nest aschape. Si le jailer don lycens a son prisoner tanque a certen voy sil ne ala hors son lymytation nest eschape, mez sil ala hors de lez boundez cest eschape en le gaylor nient obstante que il revenit mayntenaunt, pur ceo que un foytz fuit eschape. En appell bref est directe all viconte, il prent le prisoner, il eschape et devaunt le jour return le viconte luy ad pris areremayn, uncore cest eschape envers le roy et envers le partie nemi, pur ceo que son suyt nest delaye. Home ad fait divers felonyez eschape, un fyn serra fait al roy et nemi divers pur ceo que ne fuit forsque un neclygens en le jayler, mez le fyn serra le plus. Appell port per ij chescun de eux aver son remedie envers le viconte et le roy auxint.

---

[1] MS. reads doorr.
[2] MS. reads enqueys.

is committed to the ordinary after judgment given by verdict, or abjuration, or outlawry, and he shall lose his goods and lands: by abjuration of the realm, by outlawry, by confession or if he is an approver, the clerk shall be ousted from his purgation, but by verdict found not, because notwithstanding that an inquest found him guilty still it might be that they spoke falsely. And thus see that a clerk convict might be ousted from his purgation, and the one who is attainted might make his purgation.

In some cases there are two remedies and enablements to one who is committed to the ordinary: one is purgation, if he can make this; the other is by the king's pardon if he is attainted at the king's suit, and by the king's pardon and by the party when it is by appeal. And when he brings any action, if disability is alleged against him he may enable himself according to the matter by the king's pardon, and if he was delivered by purgation then he must swear the bishop's letters under the witness of his seal, or otherwise he shall not be answered etc.

CHAPTER 3

It is provided that nothing shall be levied. Item it seems that before this statute the sheriffs could assess escapes of constables and gaolers or of others and also of their own gaoler and make the fine, notwithstanding that the offence was more theirs and others' and for this the remedy appears that no fine shall be assessed before the coming of the justices in eyre. And because there are no justices in eyre, justices of the Bench have their power and more, and they can assess [fines], or justices of oyer and terminer and justices of gaol delivery nowadays can make assessments for escape. Justices of the peace do not have power to assess the fine, but if the escape was voluntary and felonious then they can enquire of this, and this is because they have power to enquire of felony. In the sheriff's tourn they enquire concerning escapes, but the sheriff shall not assess the fine, as appears by the statute 1 Edw. IV, but the justices as before.[1]

Now we must see what is an escape. An escape presupposes two things, namely taking and delivery, sometimes finable and sometimes felonious. Escape against the will is finable whether the person is a traitor or felon. When a prisoner is pursued so that he is not out of view, this is not an escape. If the gaoler gives a licence to his prisoner up to a certain road, if he does not go past his limitation it is not an escape, but if he goes out of bounds this is an escape in the gaoler, notwithstanding that he returned immediately, because he had once escaped. In an appeal a writ is directed to the sheriff, he takes the prisoner, he escapes, and before the return day the sheriff has taken him again: this is still an escape against the king, and not against the party because his suit is not delayed. A man who has committed several felonies escapes, one fine shall be made to the king and not several, because it was only one negligence in the gaoler, but the fine shall be heavier. An appeal is brought by two people, each of them shall have his remedy against the sheriff, and the king [shall have his remedy] also.

[1] 1 Edw. IV, c. 2 (*SR*, ii. 389–391).

Clerke fait son purgation lou ne ferra de ley, est eschape en [levesque].[1] Home endite de eresye et delyver al evesque pur luy examiner, sil depart de levesque est eschape. Mes si [levesque][2] per son autoryte demesne et il eschape donques null fyn. Si un vient all sessionz come attorney lordinary et eit prisoners et eux suffre deschaper et lordinarie nest unques luy fyst son attorney, uncore levesque respond pur eux.

Le viconte lessa home a mainpris que nest mainpurnable, cest eschape voluntare mez nest felony sil navoit conisauns al contrarie. Prisoner penduz et apres <revyve>[i] <reigne>[d] le gaylor ferra fyn, est eschape, mez sil revyve per miracle nulla sequatur pena. Home abjure le royalme et apres soit delyver all cunstable come usont de vyle en vile: sil ala deux nest eschape quar lour office de pur son gard que null rien a luy soit fait.

Fynez pur eschapez nont certen mez apres le discrescion dez justicez et solonque le matter et person. Eschape pur un que est prise pur suspecion de felone est use c s., home attaint ou convicte c marc, en direz pur un provour x li., pur un que avoit abjur le royne x marc, et sil soit graunt serra per que molt [fo. 305v] damages peut avener donques plus.

Viconte morust devaunt quil ad amesne prisonerz al gayle et il eschape null fyn. Si le gaylor ad le custody en fee il respondra pur leschape, mez si le viconte ad le ruyle dell gayle et face son depute, il meme respondra pur chescun eschape. Le gailor que ad le gayle per enheritans devi et apres son mort, devaunt aschun possession ewe per leir, lez laronz eschapont: leir ferra fyn sil agre de aver son offyce maintenant, mez sil refuce cel enheritans nemi. Si alienz frengent le prison et ilz eschapont le gayler ne serra punisch, mez si auters font ceo il serra nient obstante quil ne peut eux resister. Auxi si le prisone per tempest soit debruse null punysment envers le gaylor pur eschape, si le roy reparera le meason. Mez est felony pur lez prisoners de aler de cest terre et deinz lestatute de frangentibus prisonam. Et si auter person que nest prisoner et frent le prison, uncore est felony pur eux daler hors del prison.

A ore est dit de gailors en fait que ont custodie per enheritans ou per lour acceptans demesne a ceo est avenuz, que ascuns sont fait per ley, come un que prent lesglice le vyle est tenuz de luy garder per cors de le ley. Si le vile luy lessomus aler ilz ferront fyn pur leschape, et si le vile ne soit sufficient le hundred, et si hundred ne soit sufficient le countie. Uncore le vill ne serra charge devaunt que il ad puplice et ad dit a partie quil est felon, quar devaunt ilz nont aschun conisauns et issint null eschape.

Item eschapez pur laronz sont en comen esglice et nemi en sentwariez come en sent Martyns yn Londrez quar la ilz poient aler et null

---

[1] MS. reads lesveque.
[2] MS. reads levsque.

[If] a clerk makes his purgation where he should not in law, this is an escape in the bishop. A man is indicted of heresy and delivered to the bishop to examine, if he leaves the bishop this is an escape. But if the bishop by his own authority [brings him in for examination] and he escapes, then no fine. If one comes to the sessions as attorney for the ordinary and has prisoners and allows them to escape, and the ordinary had never made him his attorney, still the bishop shall answer for them.

The sheriff lets a man to mainprise who is not mainpernable, this is a voluntary escape, but it is not a felony if he did not know to the contrary. A prisoner is hanged and afterwards revives the gaoler shall make a fine [for this] is an escape, but if he revives by a miracle 'no penalty shall follow'. A man abjures the realm and afterwards is delivered to the constable, as is done, [to take him] from vill to vill: if he goes from them it is not an escape, for their office is to protect him, so that nothing shall be done to him by anyone.

Fines for escapes are not certain, but at the discretion of the justices and according to the matter and the person. An escape by one who is taken on suspicion of felony is usually 100s., a man attainted or convicted, 100 marks, it is said £10 for an approver, 10 marks for one who has abjured the realm, and if he is great so that greater damages may befall, then [the justices may assess] more.

[If] the sheriff dies before he has brought the prisoner to the gaol and [the prisoner] escapes, no fine. If the gaoler has the custody in fee he shall answer for the escape, but if the sheriff has the rule of the gaol and makes his deputy, he shall answer for each escape himself. The gaoler who has the gaol by inheritance dies and after his death, before any possession was had by the heir, the thieves escape: the heir shall make a fine if he agrees to have his office immediately, but if he refuses this inheritance, [he shall] not. If aliens break the prison and they escape the gaoler shall not be punished, but if others do this he shall notwithstanding that he cannot resist them. Also if the prison is broken open by a storm, there is no punishment for the gaoler for the escape if the king [is responsible for] repairing the building.[1] But it is a felony for the prisoners to leave the country, and [this is] in the statute *de frangentibus prisonam*.[2] And if there is another person who is not a prisoner and he breaks the prison, still it is a felony for them to go out of the prison.

Now it is said of gaolers in fact who have custody by inheritance, or who have come to this by their own acceptance, that some are made by law: as when one takes sanctuary the vill is bound to guard him by the course of law. If the vill allows him to go, they shall make a fine for the escape, and if the vill is not sufficient, the hundred, and if the hundred is not sufficient, the county. Still the vill shall not be charged before it has declared and said to the party that he is a felon, for before this they have no cognizance and thus there is no escape.

Item, escapes for thieves are in common churches and not in [private] sanctuaries, as in St Martin's in London, for there they may go and there is no

---

[1] See *Combe* v. *Gargrave* (1455): *The Case of the Marshalsea. Baker and Milsom*, 261–262.
[2] 23 Edw. I (*SR*, i. 113). The statute makes no mention of prisoners leaving the country.

punishment pur leschape. Item sil prent meason de sent John, que ad use de garder prisonerz, le townschype est charge ove luy sur payn dischape hospital. Iij esglysez en un vile et laron aschape daschunz de lez esglisez, tout le vill serra charge quar le fyn est uncore assess de villata. Et si lesglise soit en un countie et le vile en auter uncore le ville serra charge et eux que trovent laschape ont power denquerer de tout le matter (que le ville luy suffre deschape, nient obstante que lesglise soit en auter countie), pur ceo que est choce que depende sur leschape. Iij villz en un parich et iij esglices, tout le parisch ne serra charge forsque solement le ville tamen. Si le ville extende en deux countez, sil prent lesglice en lun countie uncore tout le ville serra charge. Si iij esglices en un ville et le laron eschape dun esglice en auter deinz meme le ville, uncore nest eschape pur ceo quun mesne instravit sur que fuit entitle devaunt quil entra en auter esglice. Eglice sauns aschun pariche, cum le ville est distroie, uncore leglice et le chyrchyard [ferra][1] tuition daschun laron et sil eschape null fyn pur ceo que le terre nest charge, einz lez personz scilicet villata et pur ceo que ne sont aschunz personz deinz meme leglice ou pariche etc.

Si consolidation soit fait de ij esglices en un et que tout lobservauns et dyvyne servyce serra celebre en un esglice, uncore lauter esglice [ferra][2] tuition a laronz. Si un novell chapel ferrez ou hospitall soit found en un [fo. 306] ville et ad toutz lez servicez divynez de babtister et sacerfyce en toutz poyntes, cest lyeu ferra tuition a laron et uncore le vill ne serra charge deux garder pur ceo que le vill ne serra aschun disavauntage de ceux chocez purchez per particular personz.

Si laron soit en mure et cloce, sil eschape ilz ferra fyn et est eschape en eux pur ceo que eux ont le custodie de luy et null auter person, et est pur eux ease pur issint fair mez uncore eux sont chargez. Si home prent prisoner hors de sentwayre et ducent luy toward le gayole et luy amesnent araremayne eux ne ferra fyn pur ceo que eux reforment ceo que eux male fier devaunt, mez silz luy liverer al gayle et le gaylor luy restore est eschape.

Si un home ad arrest un auter pur suspecion de felonie et ad loiall cause de ceo fair, il ne peut my luy suffre aler <a>[d] nient obstante quil soit a certen quil nest culpable, pur ceo quil nest juge ne conust le ley. Mez si il luy arest pur felony saunz color il luy peut suffre daler et nest eschape pur ceo que ceo fuit de son tort demesne et navoit aschun cause, mez est punysment per faux emprisonement.

Si eschape soit present en un lete nest traversable et null chose que est fynable. Si le gaylor present et est un del unquest que font presentment que le jaylor ad lesse un prisoner deschaper et le jaylor meme est un delenquest il ne dirra le contrare apres pur ceo que il fuit un deux que present.

---

[1] MS. reads serra.
[2] MS. reads serra.

punishment for the escape. Item, if he takes the house of St John, which is used to keep prisoners, the township is charged with him on a penalty if he should escape the hospital. [If there are] three churches in a vill and the thief escapes from any of the churches, all the vill shall be charged, for the fine is assessed *de villata*. And if the church is in one county and the vill in another, still the vill shall be charged, and those who find the escape have the power to enquire of all the matter (that the vill allowed him to escape, notwithstanding that the church is in another county), because this is something that depends on the escape. [If there are] three vills in a parish and three churches, all the parish shall not be charged but only the vill, however. If the vill extends into two counties, if he takes the church in one county, still all the vill shall be charged. If there are three churches in one vill and the thief escapes from one church into another within the same vill, yet this is not an escape because one intervened between, upon which he was entitled before he entered the other church. [If there is] a church without any parish, such as where the vill is destroyed, still the church and the churchyard shall give protection to any thief, and if he escapes there shall be no fine because the land is not charged but rather the people, that is the vill, and because there are no people within the same church or parish etc.

If two churches are consolidated into one, and all the observances and divine service are celebrated in one church, the other church shall still give protection to the thief. If a new chapel is made or hospital is founded in a vill and it has all the divine services of baptizing and sacrificing[1] in all points, this place shall give protection to a thief, and yet the vill shall not be charged to guard them, because the vill shall not be at any disadvantage from those things purchased by particular persons.

If a thief is immured and closed in, if he escapes they shall make a fine and it is an escape in them because they had the custody of him, and no-one else, and it is for their benefit to do this, but they are still charged. If a man takes a prisoner out of sanctuary and leads him towards the gaol and brings him back again [to the sanctuary], he shall not make a fine, because he is correcting that which he did badly before, but if they deliver him to the gaol and the gaoler restores him, this is an escape.

If a man arrests another on suspicion of felony and has legal cause to do this, he may not let him go notwithstanding that he is certain that he is not guilty, because he is not a judge and does not understand the law. But if he arrests him for felony without reason he may allow him to go, and this is not an escape because this was his own fault and he did not have any cause, but there is punishment for false imprisonment.

If an escape is presented in a leet it is not traversable and nothing which is finable. If the gaoler presents and is a member of the inquest which makes the presentment that the gaoler has allowed a prisoner to escape, and the gaoler himself is one of the inquest, he shall not say to the contrary afterwards, because he was one of those who presented.

---

[1] That is, celebrating Mass.

Si home soit endite pur eschape et pur utlage il navera traverse al eschape si soit fynable, mez ferra fyn. Eschape voluntary est felonye si soit fait ove entent felonius, auterment nemi. Sil lesse prisoner aler a ceo entent quil ne serra pend ne arreign pur un felony cest felony en luy, mez ignoranz eschape nest felony, forsque fynable, come sil suffre un home pur a meynpris que nest maynpurnable cest voluntary eschape, et uncore nest que fynable et null felonye. Et issint est desvesque que suffre un de fair son purgation que ne duist de ley fair.

Ad este question si home pris pur suspicion de felony, sil luy suffre le prisoner daler voluntarie si soit felony ou nemi, et ad estre tenuz en daren jourz que nest felonye, pur ceo que nest aschun choce certen en son person.

Si home soit wounded quil ne peut viver per comen entent et le partie soit areste, sil luy suffre daschaper voluntariement son entent peut faier ceo felonye et null fyne quar si sount entent soit que il aler pur ceo que il ne serra pendu pur ceo, donques est felonye. Mez sil <suss>[d] suppose que le dit home voiet viver ou que il duist per le ley luy suffre aler tanque le dit home soit mort, donquez nest felony einz eschape voluntare et fynable.

Traitor eschape voluntarie le jailor est traytor enconter son volunte fynable. Home <endite pur>[i] eschape <pur>[d] voluntarie dun laron, ad estre question sil serra areigne devaunt que lauter felon que est eschape soit attaint ou nemi, et il dit que le eschape est novell felonie [fo. 306v] et serra areign devaunt etc.

Laron en lesglice le towneshyp luy suffre deschape voluntarie, nest felony quare tout le vill ont le custodie de luy et cest chose corporat ne peut estre felony et pur ceo est fynable et null felony. Si home frent le prison que nest en prison et lez laronz eschapont est felony en le prisoners et uncore eux ne frenderont le prison mez eux covient pur garder son lieu quest a eux lymyte sur payn de felonye, quar si le huys soit overt ilz ne duyssent departer, si eux fount est felonye en eux etc.

Home endite et est arrest per le viconte et sil eschape de le viconte est nul felonye en le <vic>[d] prisoner pur ceo que quaunt est en gard per le viconte il est en prison per le ley. Quaunt home est mure et frent le mure et ala avaunt nest felony en luy, ne si auter luy lesser daler, nest felony. Prisoner en le prison pur felony et il frent le prison apres pardon fait a luy de son felonye, cest frendre nest felonye en luy pur ceo que donques nest felon. Si home frent lez apres quaunt est einz pur felonye, cest [felony][1] en luy pur ceo quil frent son prison. Mez si home soit en stockez en le gayle et frent lez apres nest felony quar le meacon est savegard.

Si cestui que est en prison pur felony et purchez loffice de jayler de cestui que ad cest offyce en fee ou si le fitz soit en prison et le per devi loffyce a luy discend, uncore sil departe nest eschape pur ceo que eschape est de jaylor, et il ne peut eschaper de luy meme et pur ceo nest eschape. Mez le departure de luy est felony et pur ceo quil ne peut licence luy meme daler hors

---

[1] MS. reads noll felony.

If a man is indicted for an escape and for outlawry, he shall not have a traverse for the escape if it is finable, but shall make a fine. A voluntary escape is a felony if it was made with a felonious intent, otherwise not. If he allows a prisoner to go with the intention that he should not be hanged nor arraigned for a felony, this is a felony in him, but an ignorant escape is not a felony, just finable, as if he allows a man to go on mainprise who is not mainpernable this is a voluntary escape, and still it is only finable and is not a felony. And it is the same of a bishop who allows one to make his purgation who should not make it under the law.

There was a question if a man was taken on suspicion of felony, if [the gaoler] allowed the prisoner to go voluntarily, if it was a felony or not, and it has been held lately that it is not a felony because there is nothing certain in his person.[1]

If a man is wounded so that it is generally believed that he cannot live and the party is arrested, if he allows him to escape voluntarily his intent may make this a felony and not finable, for if his intent is that he goes so that he shall not be hanged for this, then it is a felony. But if he supposes that the said man will live, or that according to the law he should allow him to go until the said man is dead, then it is not a felony but a voluntary escape and finable.

[If a] traitor escapes voluntarily the gaoler is a traitor, [if] against his will, [it is] finable. A man [is] indicted for the voluntary escape of a thief, it has been a question if he should be arraigned before the other felon who escaped is attainted or not, and [the reader] says that the escape is a new felony and he shall be arraigned before etc.

A thief [is] in the church [and] the township allows him to escape voluntarily this is not a felony, for all the vill has the custody of him and this corporate thing cannot be a felony and for this reason it is finable and no felony. If a man breaks the prison who is not in prison and the thieves escape it is a felony in the prisoners, and yet they did not break the prison, but they must keep themselves within the place limited for them on pain of felony, for if the door is open they may not leave, [and] if they do it is a felony in them etc.

A man [is] indicted and arrested by the sheriff and if he escapes from the sheriff it is no felony in the prisoner because when he is in the custody of the sheriff he is in prison by the law. When a man is immured and breaks the wall and goes forth this is not a felony in him, nor is it a felony if another allows him to go. A prisoner [is] in the prison for felony and he breaks the prison after a pardon is given to him for his felony, this breach is not a felony in him because then he is not a felon. If a man breaks the [prison] after he is in for felony, this is a felony in him because he broke his prison. But if a man is in stocks in the gaol and breaks them afterwards, this is not a felony because the house is safeguarded.

If someone who is in prison for felony buys the office of gaoler from someone who has the office in fee, or if the son is in prison when his father dies and the office descends to him, still if he leaves it is not an escape because an escape is from the gaoler, and he cannot escape from himself and therefore it is not an escape. But his departure is a felony because he cannot license himself to go out

---

[1] YB Pas. 8 Edw. IV, fo. 3, pl. 6 per Catesby, but Billing makes a different argument.

de prison et donques nad il auctorite daler et pur ceo est felonye. Quere quar semble quaunt le jayler peut don lycens a son prisoner aler et nest eschape, donques
quaunt il meme est jayler son lycence est enplie en luy meme et issint jesque le
lycens en luy meme est voide, uncore il est escuasable.

Ij homez sont jaylers, lun suffre son prisoner daler voluntarie, est felony en luy
et eschape neclygent en lauter, est fynable. Si feme espouce un prisoner que est
en le jayle, uncore son baron est desouth son obediens et sil ala de le jale encounter le volunte le feme est felony, et issint si le villen ad le custodie de son segnior.
A et B sont enditez et en le jayle et lenheritance dell jayle discend a eux deux et
A suffre B deschape et B suffre A deschape, est double felony en ambideux et
chescun de eux ferra fyn pur ceo que chescun deux ad lauter en custodie.

Lestatute dit *rendra a cely ou a ceux* taunt come il est ust. *Rendra*: ceo serra
per voie daction. Le partie sur cest estatute peut aver action et sil et sil [*sic*] soit
convicte al suit del partie il ferra fyn ove le roy ataunt a taunt [*sic*] come il rendra
a partie, per lez parolz de cest estatute, et issint le roy avera son remedie per le
suit le partie, ou auterment le roy serra eide per enditement etc.

Eschape presuppose ij chosez scilicet prisell et delyverie.

of the prison and therefore he does not have the authority to go and therefore it is a felony. Query, for it seems that the gaoler can give licence to his prisoner to go and it is not an escape, then when he himself is the gaoler his licence is implied in himself and thus the licence in itself is void, yet it is excusable.

Two men are gaolers, one allows his prisoner to go voluntarily, it is a felony in him and a negligent escape in the other, which is finable. If a woman [gaoler] marries a prisoner who is in the gaol, now her husband is under her obedience, and if he goes out of the gaol against the will of his wife it is a felony, and the same if a villein has the custody of his lord. A and B are indicted and are in the gaol and the inheritance of the gaol descends to them both, and A allows B to escape and B allows A to escape, it is a double felony in them both, and each of them shall make a fine because each of them had the other in custody.

The statute says *shall restore to him or to them* as it is used. *Restore*: this shall be by way of [the party's] action. On this statute he can have an action, and if he is convicted at the suit of the party he shall make a fine with the king of as much as he restores to the party, by the words of this statute, and thus the king shall have his remedy by the party's suit or otherwise the king shall be helped by indictment etc.

An escape presupposes two things, viz. taking and delivery.

READING E

WESTMINSTER PRIMER, C. 1

[*fo.115*] *Pur ceo que nostre segnior le Roy* etc. Le myschif devaunt le fesaunce de cest estatut fuit que quaunt segniors, vicontes, et auterz homez voillent vener a abbeis, priorys, et auterz measonz de religion et la aver manger et boyer et sur charite le meason que labbe ne peut fair lez chocez quil fuit lie a fair per son foundation, si come en lightz, obites et hospitalite et auterz chosez et auxi quil ne peut aver commoynz accord a son foundation, et labbe navera envers eux nul auter remedy si non generall action de trespas. Et pur ceo cest estatut voet quil avera speciall action sur lestatut et recovera dowble damagez, et le defendant ferra fyn al roy.

Donquez lestatut voet *In primis voet le roy et commaund que la pees* etc. Ceo fuit al comen ley devaunt le fesaunz de cest estatut, mez donquez est a voir queux homez poient prender suerte del peeas et quel nemi. Al comen ley devaunt le fesaunce de cest estatut un constable voile arrester home al pees, mez il ne peut fair a cell temps si non que homez soient pugnantez et en son viewe donquez il peut eux arrester pur garder le peez etc. Et asconz diont que viconte[s] poient prender suerte del pees en lour tournz, mez jeo entend que non si non quilz ont un supplicant, et silz ont un supplicant ils poient arrester un home al pees et <porter>^d <amener>ⁱ luy en le chauncerie et illonquez il trouver suerte. Et auxi justices del peas poient fair warantez al viconte pur arrester home al pees et le viconte peut luy arrest. Et le maire, come en Loundre, de vile peut accepter suerte del peas del home. Et lez justicez del bank le Roy et <lez baronz>^d del comen bank et lez baronz del escheker sedent en cur poient fair home arrester al pees.

Donquez jeo entenk que home peut trover suerte tanque a certen jour ou imperpetuell suerte etc. En bank le roy ou en le chauncerie home peut trover suerte imperpetuell et si apres cell suerte trove il soit arrest aremayn al pees, il peut aver un supersedeas hors del chauncerie et luy discharge.

Donquez lestatut parla ouster *Purveu est ensement que lez abbeis et lez mesonz de religion* etc. Donquez pur le mischief que jeo parla adevaunt, cest estatut voet que le roy avera le suyte et que lez justicez per special commission doient enquerr de tielx gentz, et sil soit endite process serra fait al suyte le roy et le partie avera dowble damages, quar sils soient graunt segniors que labbe ou le prior ne audont suer, donques ils serront indite a le suyte le roy etc. Lestatut parla ouster que nul face batterie etc.

Donquez si un abbe prie un home vener a son meason pur un <die>^d <jour>ⁱ ou ij <diez>^d <jours>ⁱ et il voill estre illonquez ij auterz diez, labbe avera cest action pur lez auterz dies, mez nemi pur lez ij primer dies. Et si le sexten voile causer

READING E

WESTMINSTER I, C. 1

Because our lord the king etc. The mischief before the making of this statute was that when lords, sheriffs, and other men wished to go to abbeys, priories and other religious houses and eat and drink there on the charity of the house, so that the abbot was not able to do the things which he was bound to do by [the conditions of] his foundation, such as lights, obits, hospitality and other things, and also that he could not have co-monks according to his foundation, the abbot had no remedy against them except a general action of trespass. And therefore this statute wills that he shall have a special action on the statute and shall recover double damages, and the defendant shall make a fine to the king.

Then the statute wills *first the king wills and commands that the peace* etc. This was at the common law before the making of this statute, but now we must see which men may take surety for the peace and which not. At the common law before the making of this statute a constable could arrest a man for the peace, but he cannot do it now unless the men are fighting in his sight, and then he can arrest them to keep the peace etc. And others say that the sheriffs may take surety for the peace in their tourn, but I do not think so unless there is a supplicant, and if there is a supplicant they can arrest a man for the peace and bring him into the Chancery and there he shall find surety. And also justices of the peace may make warrants to the sheriff to arrest a man for the peace and the sheriff may arrest him. And the mayor of a vill such as London may accept surety of the peace from a man. And the justices of the King's Bench and of the Common Pleas, and the barons of the Exchequer, sitting in court may have a man arrested for the peace.

Next, I understand that a man may find surety until a certain day, or perpetual surety etc. In the King's Bench or Chancery a man may find perpetual surety, and if after he finds this surety he is arrested again for the peace, he may have a *supersedeas* out of the Chancery to discharge him.

Then the statute says further *it is provided also that the abbeys and the houses of religion* etc. Then, because of the mischief about which I spoke before, this statute wills that the king shall have the suit and that the justices by a special commission should inquire concerning such people, and if one is indicted process shall be made on the king's suit and the party shall have double damages, for if they are greater lords than the abbot or the prior [the abbot or prior] will not dare to sue, therefore the lords shall be indicted at the king's suit etc. The statute says further that no-one shall commit battery etc.

Then if an abbot asks a man to come to his house for a day or two days and he wishes to stay there for two more days, the abbot shall have this action for the other days, but not for the first two days. And if the sexton wishes to cause

ascun home vener a son meason et quaunt il vient il batuz un de sez servauntes ou il <enblea>[i] furez un pece dargent ou dauter chose, labbe avera cest action nient obstante quil prie luy vener. Et en meme le maner si home lessa terre a auter pur terme de vie, sil veign sur le terre a voir si ascun wast soit fait, il navera action. Mez sil maynor le terre il avera action. Ou si le segnior veign sur le terre pur distreigner et distreign, le tenant navera action. Mez sil vend le distreint il avera action quar la ley supposer quil vient sur le terre al entent de distreyner et vendr le distreint, que nest droitrell. Et en meme le maner si home veign al abbe et batuz le servaunt etc.

Donquez si home veign al abbe tempore vacacionis que avera [*fo. 115v*] le action, quar le prior ne peut avera action pur ceo quil nest person capax. Et pur ceo jeo entenk que son successor avera action <si come il avera>[i] de bonis asportatis tempore predecessoris. Mez si un prior soit fait abbe, ou si labbe soit fait evesque, son successor navera action pur ceo quil ne voill aver ascun avauntage en son temps demesne.

Donquez jeo entenk que si le roy soit foundor dun abbe come en droit de son coron quil avera lez temporalitez tempore vacationis si non quil ad graunt ceo al covent per charter, come a Seynt Albonz il ad un certeyn som dargent pur ceo. Mez si auter, come un parson, soit foundor dun abbe, il navera ceo. Et le roy avera del abbe ou il est foundor come en droit de son Corown un corodie pur son valect et un reasonable pension pur son clerk. Mez jeo entenk que il navera le corodie apres le deces de chescun abbe, mez apres le decese de chescun valect il ceo avera. Mez il avera le pension apres le disces de chescun abbe et ceo est le diversite enter ceux casez. Et auxi le roy avera auter choses del abbe ou il est foundor, come al Abynton, il avera cez coursours troves et en auterz placez auxi etc.

Donquez lestatut parla ouster *Et ceux que viendront encontre cest estatut* etc. Donquez jeo pose quun abbe sue cest action et demande jugement pur recovery et apres release al defendant, en cest cas le roy navera fyn. Mez sil soit endite al suyte le roy et de ceo atteynt et labbe release, unquor le roy avera son fyn pur ceo quil fuit atteynt a son suite et suis vide etc. Donquez en ascun cas cest action faut, come si un abbe et un auter estrange home ont un maner en comen et un home vient encontre cest estatut, ore lestraunger et labbe naveront cest action mez generall action de trespass etc. Et nota que si un soit endite al suet le roy sur cest estatut et puis de ceo il soit attaint etc., labbe ou prior etc. recovere sez double damagez envers luy come est dit etc. per un scire facias etc.

some man to come to his house and when he comes he beats one of [the abbot's] servants or he steals a piece of silver or something else, the abbot shall have this action notwithstanding that he asked him to come. And in the same manner if a man leases land to another for term of life, if he comes on the land to see if any waste was committed, [the tenant] shall not have an action. But if [the lessor] cultivates the land [the tenant] shall have an action. Or if the lord comes on the land to distrain and he distrains, the tenant shall not have an action. But if he sells the distraint the tenant shall have an action, for the law supposes that he came on the land with the intent of distraining and he sold the distraint, which is not lawful. And in the same manner if a man comes to the abbey and beats the servant etc.

Now, if a man comes to the abbey *tempore vacationis* who shall have the action? For the prior cannot have the action because he is not a capable person. And thus I think that his successor shall have the action, just as he shall have for goods carried away in the time of his predecessor. But if a prior is made abbot, or if an abbot is made a bishop, his successor shall not have an action because he will not have any advantage in his own time.

Now, I understand that if the king is founder of an abbey as in right of his crown that he shall have the temporalities *tempore vacationis* unless he has granted this by charter to the convent, as with St Albans, [where] he has a certain sum of money for this.[1] But if another, such as a parson, is the founder of an abbey he shall not have this. And the king shall have a corody for his manservant and a reasonable pension for his clerk from an abbey where he is founder as in right of his Crown. But I think that he shall not have the corody after the decease of each abbot, but after the decease of each manservant. But he shall have the pension after the decease of each abbot, and this is the difference between these cases. And also the king shall have other things of the abbot where he is founder, as at Abingdon, [where] he shall have his chargers provided for, and in other places also etc.[2]

Now, the statute says further *and those who go against the statute* etc. Now suppose that an abbot sues this action and demands judgment by recovery and afterwards releases to the defendant, in this case the king shall not have a fine. But if [the defendant] is indicted at the king's suit and attainted of this and the abbot releases, still the king shall have his fine because he was attainted at his suit, and see above etc. Now, in another case this action fails, as when an abbot and another unconnected man have a manor in common and a man comes against this statute, now the stranger and the abbot shall not have this action but shall have a general action of trespass etc. And note that if one is indicted at the king's suit under this statute and then he is attainted of this etc., the abbot or the prior etc. shall recover double damages against him, as is said etc., by a *scire facias* etc.

---

[1] *Cal. Pat. Rolls Edw. I* (1292–1301), iii. 604. The abbey paid 1,000 marks per annum during the vacancy for the privilege.
[2] *Cal. Close Rolls Edw. I* (1288–1296), iii. 507.

Et nota que coment que lestatut ne parla forsque dez measonz de religionz etc., unquor chescun auter segnior ou comen person quest greve encountre le purviance de cest estatut serra eide per lequite del estatut, pur ceo que cest estatut est forsque en affirmans de le comen ley, et pur ceo il serra pris large. Et unquor, come il appiert, le remedy que fuit al comen ley devaunt cest estatut per action de trespass generalment don mellior proces pur le partie pleintif que ceo est don, quar en un general action de trespas proces dutlagerie gist, mez le proces sur cest estatut nest forsque un atteynt et ij distreints et si le viconte return nihil le partie <ne>[i] avera forsque petit remedy: vide statutum. Et auxi sont diverse queux ne sont my deinz le cas destatut, come le foundor dun meason ou lez patronz, auxi tielx lieuz queux devoient trover hospitaliter. Mez chescun auter person, forsque le roy meme, est deinz le cas del estatut, auxibien lez justicez et lez conselers le roy come auterz comen personz.

Auxi si un comen [hostiler][1] soit, jeo chacera luy de moy herbeger et javera quecunque soit la destre vend pur mon argent, ou si un come carriar soit, jeo luy chace de carriar mez bienz etc., ou si un comen [ferrey][2] soit et jeo soit impedite ou hurt en son defaute, jeo avera bon action envers luy. Et issint jeo avera vers chescun tiel occupier en queux le comen ley don a moy conge dentre, nient contristeant que ceo soit encontre <nient>[d] le bon volunte cestui que gard le occupation en meason: issint jeo entre en un <vute>[d] taverne ou alehous et ceux que jeo prender la de vend javera pas mez deners, et la partie navera action envers <moy>[i] pur mon entre, et pur ceo que <comen>[i] ley done <a>[i] moy entre per comen droit, si ne soit issint que jeo face ascun choce que serra encounter le ley, come de <prender>[d] [fo. 116] furez un pece dargent, ou de frender un fenestre, ou ascun tiel choce que est encounter ley, quar donquez le taverner avera bon action de trespas envers <luy>[d] <moy>[i] et recovera sez damagez eiant regard a le primer entre, pur ceo que le ley entend que mon entre fuit torcious a adeprimez.

Come en cas un auter semblez cause, si jeo veign per un forest et [mes][3] <canez>[d] <cheines>[i] per cas avoit pursuer un dere <savage>[i] devaunt quil veignont ale forest, et quaunt ilz veignont al forest le dere <savagee>[i] entre et [mes][4] canez auxi et jeo pursue mez canez et entre le forest, come ley don moy conge, et al mon primer entre jeo fle mon cornu iij foitz pur le forster et il ne vient, jeo meme purrai pursuer mez canez et eux reprender per le comen ley. Mez si mez canez occident ascun fer, ou font ascun tiel trespas en le forest apres mon entre, mon entre serra entend adeprimes torcious, et sur laction sue envers moy lez damagez serra taxez eiant regards a mon primer entre, et issint serra fait en chescun tiel cas lou le commencement soit loiall et le fin torcious.

Mez auterment serra serra [sic] lou un home avoit un private licence, come si jeo don a vous licence pur succider j arbour en mon soile, vous poiez bien entre et succider cest arbour, mez si vous succider ij arborez, javera bon action de trespas

[1] MS. reads hospite.
[2] MS. reads verrey.
[3] MS. reads moys.
[4] MS. reads moys.

And note that even though the statute only speaks of houses of religion etc., still every other lord or common person who is aggrieved against the provision of this statute shall be helped by the equity of the statute, because this statute is only in affirmation of the common law and because of this it shall be taken widely. And yet, as it appears, the remedy at the common law before this statute by the action of trespass generally gives a better process for the party plaintiff than is given here, for in a general action of trespass the process for outlawry lies, but the process on this statute is only an attaint and two distraints, and if the sheriff returns Nihil the party shall only have a small remedy: see the statute. And also there are many who are not within the case of the statute, such as the founder of a house or the patrons, [and] also places which must provide hospitality. But every other person, except the king himself, is within the case of the statute, the justices and counsellors of the king as well as other common people.

Also if there is a common innkeeper, I shall compel him to lodge me, and I shall have for my money whatever is there to be sold, or if one is there as a carrier, I shall compel him to carry my goods etc., or if there is a common ferry, and I am delayed or hurt by his default, I shall have a good action against him. And I shall have this against every such occupier in which the common law gives me permission to enter, even if this is against the good will of the one who keeps the occupation of the house: thus [if] I enter in a tavern or alehouse, and those whom I take there to sell, I shall not have my money, and the party shall not have action against me for my entry, because common law gives me entry by common right, as long as I do not do anything against the law, such as steal a piece of silver, or break a window or any such thing which is against the law, for then the taverner shall have a good action of trespass against me and shall recover his damages having regard to the first entry, because the law understands that my entry was tortious from the beginning.

In another similar case, if I go through a forest and my dogs had perhaps pursued a wild deer before they went in the forest, and when they came to the forest the wild deer entered and my dogs also and I follow my dogs and enter the forest, as the law allows, and at my first entry I blow my horn three times for the forester and he does not come, I may chase my dogs and take them again by the common law. But if my dogs kill any wild animal or commit any such trespass in the forest after my entry, my entry shall be understood as tortious from the beginning, and on the action sued against me the damages shall be assessed having regard to my first entry, and it shall be done this way in every such case where the beginning is legal and the end tortious.[1]

But it shall be otherwise where a man has a private licence, as where I give you a licence to cut down one tree in my soil, you may well enter and cut down this tree, but if you cut down two trees, I shall have a good action of trespass

---

[1] See *Anon.* (1439) *Baker and Milsom*, pp. 367–368. The full case is YB Mich. 18 Hen. VI, fos 21–22, pl. 6.

envers vous pur le succider de cest ij^{de} arbor. <mez>^d Et lez damagez naveront regardez a le primer entre, mez apres le primer arbour succise etc. Et issint vide le diversite lou le comen <ley>^i don a un home un entre et lou il avoit un private licence etc.[1]

[CHAPTER 2]

[fo. 117][2] *Purveu est ensement que quaunt clerk* etc. Le mischief devaunt le fesaunce de cest estatut fuit que quaunt homez fuerent enditez de felony et arreyntez et apres prieront lour clerge et lordinarie eux accepter, que lordinarie voill eux delivere saunz ascun purgation fait. Donquez per cest estatut est remedie quil ne mettera eux aler saunz due purgation fait, et sil fait auterment il ferra fyn al roye.

Donquez est a voier queux sont clerkez atteynt et queux sont clerkes convicte. Jeo entenk que home peut estre <un clerk>^i attaint en iiij casez, scilicet: un, si home soit utlage de felony per process en court le roy. Auter est si home confesse le felony: son confession demesne serra plus [fort][3] encounter luy que sil soit atteynt per xij homez, <le tercia>^d quar peut estre que xij homez ne voillent dire le verite. Le tierce est si un home fait felony et prist lesglise et confesse le felony et pria coroner et abjure le realme. Le quarte est lou un home fait felony et sur ceo est endite et sur ceo arreign et pled de rien coulpable etc., et lenquest dit que il est coulpable, sur quell verdit jugement est don, et apres il pria son clergie.

Et nota que lou un est clerk atteynt per son confession demesne, ou abjure del roialme, il ne ferra unquor son purgation. Mez soloncque ascunz lou il est attaint per process dutlagarie en court le roy il ferra son purgation, pur ceo que cest disobediaunce nest cy graunt mez quil peut ceo fair: tamen quere, quar solonc ascunz il ne ferra son purgation en cest cas. Auxi lou il est atteynt per xij homez il ferra son purgation, quar le surment de xxiiij clerkes serra pluis credebill que le suerment de xij homez queux per cas ne voillent dire le verite. Et <pur ceo>^d nota que en chescun cas avauntdit il forfera toutz sez terrez et tenementez et auxi sez bienz et chateux et issint ferra chescun home quest atteint de felony.

Clerk convicte, come jeo entenk, peut estre en iiij maners: un est lou un home est endite de felony et sur ceo il est arreign et il dit que il est clerke et pria son clergie et rienz responder al felony, mez son plee devaunt va al jurisdiction del court, en quell cas le court prender un enquest de office denquerere sil soit culpable ou nemi del felony, et si lenquest trove quil soit culpable il perdre sez bienz et chateux et lez issuez de sez terrez durant le temps quil est convicte scilicet tanque il ad fait son purgation. Et si trove soit per lenquest quil nest pas culpable, unquore il serra commicte all ordinarie, et le cas est pur ceo que il nad pled my directment all felony, mez il ne forfeter my sez bienz ne chateux etc.

---

[1] Bottom half of the page blank.
[2] In margin: ca [2].
[3] MS. reads foit.

against you for cutting down the second tree. And the damages shall not apply to the first entry, but after the first tree is cut down etc. And thus see the difference where the common law gives a man an entry and where he shall have a private licence etc.

CHAPTER 2

It is provided also that when a clerk etc. The mischief before the making of this statute was that when men were indicted of felony and arraigned and afterwards pleaded their clergy and the ordinary accepted them, that the ordinary wished to deliver them without any purgation. Now, this statute provides the remedy that he shall not let them go without due purgation made, and if he does otherwise he shall make a fine to the king.

Now we must see who are clerks attaint and who are clerks convict. I understand that a man can be a clerk attaint in four cases, namely: one, if a man is outlawed for felony by a process in the king's court. Another is if a man confesses a felony: his own confession shall be stronger against him than if he were attainted by a jury, for a jury may perhaps not tell the truth. The third is if a man commits a felony and takes sanctuary, and confesses the felony and asks for the coroner, and abjures the realm. The fourth is where a man commits a felony and is indicted and arraigned on this and pleads not guilty etc., and the inquest says that he is guilty, on which verdict judgment is given, and afterwards he asks for his clergy.

And note that where one is a clerk attaint by his own confession, or abjures the realm, he shall not make his purgation later. But according to some, where he is attainted by a process of outlawry in the king's court he shall make his purgation, because this disobedience is not so great that he should not be able to do it: however query, for according to others he shall not make his purgation in this case. Also, where he is attainted by a jury he shall make his purgation, for the oath of twenty-four clerks shall be more credible than the oath of twelve men who perhaps will not tell the truth. And note that in each case aforesaid he shall forfeit all his lands and tenements and also his goods and chattels, and so it shall be done for every man who is attainted of felony.

A clerk convict, as I understand, can be in four ways: one is where a man is indicted of felony and arraigned on this, and he says that he is a clerk and prays his clergy and does not respond to the felony, but his plea before goes to the jurisdiction of the court, in which case the court shall take an inquest by office to enquire if he is guilty or not of the felony, and if the inquest finds that he is guilty he shall lose his goods and chattels and the issues of his lands for the time he is convict, that is, until he has made his purgation. And if it is found by the inquest that he is not guilty, still he shall be committed to the ordinary, and the reason is because he never pleaded directly to the felony, but he shall not forfeit his goods or chattels at all etc.

Auter est lou il est arreign sur le felony et il pled de rienz culpable et sur ceo mitter luy sur le pays et devaunt que le enquest don lour verdit il dit que 'quecunque
lenquest voet dire jeo sue clerk et pria mon clergie', en quell cas si lenquest trove
quil soit culpable, il perder sez bienz et chateux come devaunt est dit, et serra
commicte al ordinarie. Et si trove soit per lenquest quil nest my culpable, il alera
quiete et ne serra my commicte al ordinarie, neque forfeter sez chateux ou bienz.

Le tercie est lou un home est endite de felony et sur ceo arreign et pled de
rien culpable, et sur ceo mitter soy sur le pays et trove est per lenquest quil est
culpable, et mayntenant devaunt jugement done il pria son clergie, en quell cas
il forfeter forsque sez bienz et chateux come en le prochein cas devaunt, et serra
committe al ordinarie.

Et issint nota le diversite lou il pria sa clergie devaunt jugement et lou il pria
apres jugement done. Et auxi lou il pled directment al felony et lou il pled al
jurisdicion del court et <quil>[d]. Ascunz ount dit que lou il pria son clergie et ne
pled rienz al felony que il serra [Le quarte est lou un felon est arreign et il soy
tynt mute et trove est <quil ceo f>[d] per un enquest doffice quil ceo fist de malice
perpense et apres il pria son clergie, quar ceo nest quun [commutation][1] en quel
cas il ne forfera forsque sez chateux pur que etc. il avera son clergie en tant quil
averoit sil fuit atteynt etc.][2] [fo. 117v] committer al prison forte [et] dure si come
[il][3] serroit un home mute, pur ceo que il ne respondera al felony, mez ceo nest
ley, quar il ad pled tiel plee mitter le court hors de jurisdiction, le court ne ferra
autrement forsque de luy committer al ordenarye etc.

Et nota que clerke atteynt ne clerk convicte mayntenera ascun action <mere-
ment personell>[i] envers ascun home, ne ascun home envers eux, et ceo est graunt
mischief, quar si un soit oblige a moy en xx li. et puis il fait felony, pur que il est
clerke convicte jeo sue saunz remedy coment que il apres fait son purgation, quar
toutz actions envers luy pur ascun dewte devaunt le purgation sont extient en luy,
et auxi toutz dewtes a luy accrewe, come de bien ou chateux sont extientez en
meme le manner etc. per que lez plusours homes sont sovent foitz defraudez etc.

Donquez est a voyer en queux casez home avera son clergie et en queux nemi.
Home avera son clergie en toutz casez lou il est daver jugement de vie et de
member, sil ne soit haute treson ou tielx que sont prohibitez per lestatut, quar
en felony, murder, robberie, ou rape il avera son clergie, mez sil soit endite
que il avoit emble felonice vj d., ou avoit occist un home per misaventour, il
navera son clergie pur ceo que il ne perdre son vie coment que il soit atteynt
de ceo. Auxi in petit treson home avera son clergie, come si un home tua son
master, ou un monke tua <son soveraigne>[i], <meister>[d] scilicet labbot, il avera
son clergie pur ceo que cest en effecte que felony. Et nient contristreant que le
monke avoit fait [forfeit][4] al eglis, scilicet tua son maister, il avera son clergie,
quar est un text en le pleez de le Crown quod [nemini redeunti clausit ecclesia

---

[1] MS. reads comution.
[2] Omitted from the end of the paragraph above and added at the bottom of the page in a different hand.
See translation for correct text.
[3] MS. reads fe.
[4] MS. reads surfeit.

It is otherwise where he is arraigned on the felony and he pleads not guilty and upon this puts himself on the country, and before the inquest gives its verdict he says that 'whatever the inquest says, I am a clerk and pray my clergy', in which case if the inquest finds that he is guilty, he shall lose his goods and chattels as is said before, and shall be committed to the ordinary. And if it is found by the inquest that he is not guilty at all, he shall go quit and shall not be committed to the ordinary, nor shall he forfeit his chattels or goods.

The third is where a man is indicted of felony and arraigned on this and pleads not guilty, and on this puts himself on the country, and it is found by the inquest that he is guilty, and now before judgment is given he prays his clergy, in which case he forfeits only his goods and chattels as in the case before, and shall be committed to the ordinary.

The fourth is where a felon is arraigned and he stays mute and it is found by an inquest of office that he did this by malice aforethought, and afterwards he prays his clergy, for this is only a commutation, in which case he shall only forfeit his chattels, because etc., [and] he shall have his clergy as he would have it if he were attaint etc.

And thus note the diversity where he prays his clergy before judgment, and where he prays after judgment is given. And also where he pleads directly to the felony, and where he pleads to the jurisdiction of the court. Some say that where he prays his clergy and does not plead anything to the felony that he shall be committed to prison *forte [et] dure* as if he were a mute man, because he did not respond to the felony, but this is not law for he has pleaded such a plea which puts the court out of jurisdiction, [and so] the court shall not do otherwise, except commit him to the ordinary etc.

And note that [neither] a clerk attaint nor a clerk convict may maintain any purely personal action against any man, nor any man against them, and this is a great mischief, for if one is obliged to me in £20 and then he commits a felony, because he is a clerk convict I am without remedy even if he makes his purgation afterwards, for all actions against him for any duty before the purgation are extinguished in him, and also all duties accrued to him, such as for goods or chattels, are extinguished in the same manner etc., by which many men are often defrauded etc.

Now we must see in which cases a man shall have his clergy, and in which cases not. A man shall have his clergy in all cases where he shall have judgment of life and limb, if it is not high treason or something prohibited by statute, for in felony, murder, robbery or rape he shall have his clergy, but if he is indicted that he had feloniously stolen 6d. or had killed a man by misadventure, he shall not have his clergy, because he shall not lose his life even if he is attainted for this. Also, in petty treason a man shall have his clergy, as when a man kills his master, or a monk kills his superior (that is, the abbot), he shall have his clergy because this is a felony in effect. And notwithstanding that the monk had made a forfeit to the church, that is to say, killed his master, he shall have his clergy, for it is a text in the pleas of the Crown that 'the church closes her bosom to no-one

gremium].[1] En meme le manner serra fait de un que avoit fait un offence en un eglis et fua en un auter, en quel cas il averoit le beneficez. Auxi si un home soit endite de felony et sur ceo arreign et pled de rienz culpable et mitter luy sur le pays et per lenquest est trove culpable, sur que inquest [verdict] est done, scilicet quil serroit pendu etc., et le viconte commaundez de faire execution, si apres <l>^d eux que ont luy en gard de fair execution voillent luy reducer devaunt lez justices, il peut luy prender a son clergie quar nemi[ni] redeunti etc. Et auxi si un home abjure le roialme, si come pur felony ou petit treson, il avera son clergie sil revient et prist un eglis, pur ceo quil peut aver adevaunt, et auxi pur ceo que nemi[ni] etc. Mez pur haute treson sil revient il navera, pur ceo quil ne purront aver adevaunt. Auxi si un home fait felony et prent leglise et demande le privilege de leglise et apres confesse, nient obstante cell confession il avera son clergie en favorem vite.

Et nota que si un home soit bigamus, scilicet espouse ij virgines ou un wedowe, il navera son clergie, quar il ne peut estre prist ne minister le sacraments de leglise. Et coment que levesque certifia quil est bigamus, unquor il ne serra regular pur ceo.

En ascun cas un certificat serra directe al vicar generall et en ascun cas al metropolitan: al vicar generall come si levesque soit de ouster le mere, et si le vicar generall certifia quil est bastard ou bigamus lentre serra que lordinarie ceo certifia, pur ceo quil nest sinon servaunt al ordinarie et pur ceo etc. Et il serra direct al metropolitan come si levesque soit mort et issint le see est voide etc.

En cas que un home dit devaunt lez justices que il ne voet luy prender a son clergie et puis il est trove culpable, il peut luy prender a son clergie nient contristeant que il avera refuse adevaunt, pur ceo que nemi[ni] redeunti etc. Si home soit <clerk>^i convicte ou atteint et il eschapa et prist un eglis, fuit dit que son [fo. 118] keper peut luy prender hors de leglise, pur ceo que le ley suppose quil est toutz temps deinz le kepyng de le clergie et pur ceo etc. Mez sil fait un felony apres leschape et prist un eglise il avera le benefitez de leglicez pur ceo quil pur cell felony serroit mort, nient contristeant quil averoit le benefitez de son clergie adevaunt, et null luy peut prender hors de leglise.

Si un home soit provour et il tua un home il ne serra prist saunz dispenser de la pape, mez nient contristeant il avera son clergie, et le case est pur ceo que home avera son clergie lou il ne avera tonsure etc., pur ceo quil peut estre prist nient contristeant que il ad cest wayve. Unquor null peut estre dit clerke properment sil navoit tonsour quar Quia littera[tura] non facit clericum nec habetus

---

[1] MS. reads nemi re<un>^ddeunti clausit ecclesia contre action.

returning'.[1] It shall be done in the same manner for one who had committed an offence in a church and fled to another, in which case he shall have the benefit. Also, if a man is indicted of felony and arraigned on this, and pleads not guilty and puts himself on the country, and is found guilty by the inquest, on which a verdict is given, that is, that he shall be hanged etc., and the sheriff is commanded to execute the verdict, if afterwards those who have him in custody to execute the verdict wish to bring him before the justices again he may take his clergy, for 'to no-one returning' etc. And also if a man abjures the realm as for felony or petty treason, he shall have his clergy if he returns and takes a church, because he could have it before and also because 'to no-one' etc. But for high treason, if he returns he shall not have it, because he could not have it before. Also, if a man commits a felony and takes the church, and demands the privilege of the church and confesses afterwards, notwithstanding this confession he shall have his clergy *in favorem vitae*.

And note that if a man is a bigamist, that is, he marries two virgins or a widow, he shall not have his clergy, for he cannot be a priest or minister the sacraments of the church. And even if the bishop certifies that he is a bigamist, still he shall not be regular for this.[2]

In some cases [the request for] a certificate shall be directed to the vicar general, and in some cases to the metropolitan: to the vicar general when the bishop is out of the country, and if the vicar general certifies that he is a bastard or a bigamist the entry shall be that the ordinary certified this, because he is only a servant to the ordinary, and because etc. And it shall be directed to the metropolitan if the bishop is dead and thus the see is vacant etc.

In the case where a man says before the justices that he does not wish to take his clergy and then he is found guilty, he may take his clergy notwithstanding that he refused it before, because 'to no-one returning' etc. If a man is a clerk convict or attaint and he escapes and takes sanctuary, it was said that his keeper could take him out of the church, because the law supposes that he is always within the keeping of the clergy, and therefore etc. But if he commits a felony after the escape and takes sanctuary he shall have the benefit of the church, because he should be put to death for this felony, notwithstanding that he could have had the benefit of his clergy before, and no-one can take him out of the church.

If a man is an approver and he kills a man he shall not be a priest without the pope's dispensation, but notwithstanding he shall have his clergy, and the reason is because a man shall have his clergy where he does not have a tonsure etc., because he may be a priest notwithstanding that he has waived this. Yet no-one may properly be called a clerk if he does not have a tonsure, for 'literacy does not

[1] This tag probably comes from the *Codex* 1.1.8.35 'quia gremium suum numquam redeuntibus claudit ecclesia'. A version of it also appears in YB Mich. 9 Hen. V, p. 23, pl. 29. Ralph V. Rogers, *Year Books of the Reign of King Henry the Fifth* (Würzburg, 1948). It also appears in Reading A, p. 2, above.
[2] This seems to mean 'irregular' in the sense of being out of conformity with Church doctrine or ineligible for ordination. It consistently appears as 'regular' in the readings. See above Reading A, p. 2, Reading C, p. 16, and below Reading E, p. 38, Reading G, p. 53, Reading Two, p. 75, and Reading Seven, pp. 113, 124. Cf. Baker, *OHLE*, pp. 533–534.

monachum set tonsura etc. Quar si un home porter bref de trespass ou de dett
envers un auter per addition de clerke lou il ne aver tonsour, le bref abatera pur
ceo que cest faux addition. Et si <ele>^d <il>^i navera tonsour per le riguster de
ley sil fuit endite de felony et trove culpable il serroit mort. Mez est use a cest
jour, et issint fuit de temps dont memorye ne courge, per prescription, que un
clerk, coment il navera tonsour, quil avera le benefite de son clergie et quil ne
serra mort etc. Auxi si un home quest endite soit un prist et ne aver tonsour, per
le rigourstour de le ley il serra mort nient contristeant quil est prist et luy prist
a son clergie, mez pur ceo que le custom est auter lestatut dit *si lordinarie luy
demanda quil serra delivere si come il fuist use en auncien temps*, mez ceo ne
serra entenduz si non que cestui que lordinarie demanda demanda son clergie, et
cest le cause pur ceo que invito non datur beneficium ubi petenti etc.

Donquez jeo pose quun soit arreign de felony et prist luy a son clergie et est
entenduz per lez justicez quil est bon clerk et lordinarie ne voet luy resceyvor, en
cest cas lez justices facent luy estre reprie tanque al prochein sessionz, et grievous fyn serra cesse sur lordinarie, et al procheyn sessions sil luy refuser il ferra
auter fyn et reprie serra fait come devaunt et toutz ceo <est>^i en favourem vite.
Auxi fuit dit que en cest [cas], solonk loppinion de plusourz, que lordinarie serra
regular pur ceo quil voilet aver cest home mort lou il ne devoit estre mort per le
ley etc. Auxi fuit dit que si un home soit arreign de felony et pria son clergie et
lordinarie ne soit present il serra reprie et lordinarie serra amercy, scilicet son
temporaltez serra seisiez en le mayn del roy tanque il ad fait fyn al roy pur son
default. Et si devaunt le prochyn sessionz il soit endite de treson, unquore il ne
respondra al treson, mez avera son clergie pur ceo que ne fuit nul default en luy
etc.

Et lordinarie peut per sez lettrez fair son depute, mez son depute ne peut my
faire depute. Donquez si un depute soit fait et home pria son clergie et demanda
lordinarie et per lez lettrez lordinarie est entenduz quil fait ij deputees conjunctim et devisim et lun voet luy accepter et lauter nemi, cestui que voet luy rescey-
vour avera luy et lauter serra amercy etc.

Donquez jeo pose que home soit atteynt de felony et demanda coroner et
devient provour pur le roy et appell ij homez, et ils veign et lun joyne bataill
ove luy et lauter soy metter sur le pays, en cest cas si lappellour graunt le
jour de bataille, soit non sue ou face defaut, ambideux aleront quiete, ou si

make a clerk, nor habit a monk, but the tonsure' etc.[1] For if a man brings a writ of trespass or of debt against another by the addition of 'clerk' where he does not have a tonsure, the writ shall abate because this is a false addition. And if he does not have a tonsure, by the rigour of the law if he was indicted of felony and found guilty he would be put to death. But it is the use today, and it was thus since the time before which memory does not run, by prescription, that a clerk shall have the benefit of his clergy even if he does not have a tonsure, and that he shall not be put to death etc. Also, if a man who is indicted is a priest and does not have a tonsure, by the rigour of the law he shall be put to death notwithstanding that he is a priest and takes his clergy, but because the custom is otherwise the statute says *if the ordinary demands him, that he shall be delivered as it was done in olden days*, but this shall not be understood unless the one the ordinary demands [also] demands his clergy, and the reason is because 'a benefit cannot be conferred on someone who is unwilling'etc.[2]

Now suppose that one is arraigned of felony and takes his clergy and it is understood by the justices that he is a good clerk, and the ordinary does not wish to receive him, in this case the justices shall have him reprieved until the next sessions, and a grievous fine shall be assessed on the ordinary, and at the next sessions if [the ordinary] refuses him he shall make another fine and a reprieve shall be made as before, and all of this is *in favorem vitae*.[3] Also it was said that in this case, according to the opinion of many, the ordinary shall be regular because he wished to have this man put to death where he should not have been put to death by the law etc.[4] Also it was said that if a man is arraigned of felony and prays his clergy and the ordinary is not present, he shall be reprieved and the ordinary shall be amerced, that is, his temporalities shall be seized into the king's hands until he has made a fine to the king for his default. And if before the next sessions he is indicted for treason, still he shall not answer to the treason, but shall have his clergy because there was no default in him etc.

And the ordinary may make his deputy by his letters, but his deputy may not make a deputy. Then if a deputy is made and a man prays his clergy and demands the ordinary, and by the ordinary's letters it is understood that he made two deputies, jointly and severally, and the one wishes to accept him and the other not, the one who wishes to receive him shall have him, and the other shall be amerced etc.

Now, suppose that a man is attainted of felony and demands the coroner, and becomes an approver for the king and appeals two men, and they come and the one joins battle with him and the other puts himself on the country, in this case if the appellor grants the day of battle, if he is non-suited, or defaults, or if the

---

[1] A version of this maxim appears in 26 Lib. Ass., fo. 122, pl. 19, 'literatura non facit Clericum, nisi haberet sacram tonsuram'. It may have developed from a statement in the *Liber Extra*, 3.31.13: 'monachum non faciat habitus, sed professio regularis'. Another version appears in YB Mich. 11 Hen. IV, fo. 31, pl. [57] 'quia habitus non facit monachum' per Thirning, and YB Mich. 11 Edw. IV, *Exchequer Chamber* 2: 190 per Catesby. It also appears in Reading A, p. 1, above, and Reading F, p. 49, below.

[2] *Dig.* 50.17.69. This also appears in Reading A, p. 1, above, and Reading F, p. 49, below.

[3] Cf. YB Trin. 34 Hen. VI, fo. 49, pl. 16.

[4] See p. 37, n. 2, above, for use of 'regular'.

lappellor aver charter de pardon, pur ceo que le ley entend que son appell fuit faux etc. Et si un home appell ij ou [*fo. 118v*] iij et ils joynent bataill et lun soiet vencuz il avera reasonable jour et pugnera ove lez auterz, mez si un deux vencuz lappellor, donquez toutz aleront quietez. Auxi si home devient provour et appell un auter est bon plee pur lappelle adire que lappellour est utlage de felony ou disablent de son person.

Et auxi si bigamy soit allege et bref [issist][1] al evesque pur certifier et levesque ne certifia, il serra amercye. Et lestatut est que lordinarie avera sil voet sub suo periculo etc.

Et le court avera un assaye sil soit clerk ou non, et le ordinarie peut luy res-ceiver nient contristeant quil nest clerk. Mez sil luy receiva lou il nest my clerk et cest trove devaunt lez justices de bank le roy, ou devaunt justicez de oyre et determiner, lordinarie peut aver travers a cell office et si cest office soit trove encounter lordinarie il perdre sez temporalitez, et seux justicez ont power aux-ibien denquerer de tielx faitz come lez justicez en eyre averont <silz>[i] fuerent deinz le terre.

Si un home soit arreign et il dit quil est clerk et lordinarie nest present et lez jugges mettont devaunt luy un liver et il ne saver legere, le court ne agard que execution serra fait de luy mez ils mettont process pur lordinarie jesque lordi-narie vient. Quar si lordinarie voet luy resceiver il avera sub suo periculo etc.

Si un home avoit pris un eglise pur certen felony et est pris hors del eglise et arraign devaunt lez justicez, est bon plee pur luy adire que il avoit pris un eglise et fuit pris hors et fuit en tiel viell et en tiel counte et pledra ouster a le felony, et pria que il peut estre restore al eglise. Et donquez lez justicez agardent un venire facias a le vill lou il dit quil fuit pris. Et si trove soit per lenquest quil fuit pris hors il serra restore, et si nemi ils agardent un venire facias pur enquerrer sil soit culpable ou nemi, et sil soit trove culpable execution serra fait sur luy sil ne soit quil est clerk. Et le felony et le pris hors del eglise serra enquer per xij homez etc. Et si le partie que est arreign en un counte dit quil fuit pris hors dun eglise en auter counte lez justicez agardera venire facias en lauter counte lou leglise est, si come quil fuit en meme le counte etc.

Lestat va ouster *Et le roy eux amonester quilz ne serra deliverez saunce dewe purgation* etc. *seux que sont convictes* etc. Donquez en cas que lordinarie suffre un quest clerke atteynt que ne peut fair son purgation defair son purgation, quel remedy envers lordinarie? Jeo entenk quil serra adjuge un eschape pur que il doit ferra fyn al roy, scilicet de c li. si il soit trove issint, le quell fine lordinarie devoit paier al roy pur <chescun>[i] eschape de clerk atteint etc. Et auxi si un clerke convicte eschapa saunz dewe purgation le roy avera meme cell fyn del ordinarie scilicet c li. etc.

Si un quest appelle luy prist a son clergie il ne serra deliver al ordinarie devant quun enquest <soit trove>[d] doffice soit pris, et si un enquest doffice soit pris et luy trove nient coulpable il alera quiete et ne serra delivere all ordinarie, et sil

---

[1] MS. reads issint.

appellor has a charter of pardon, both shall go quit because the law understands that his appeal was false etc. And if a man appeals two or three and they join battle and the one is defeated, he shall have a reasonable day and shall fight with the others, but if one of them defeats the appellor, then all shall go quit. Also, if a man becomes an approver and appeals another, it is a good plea for the appellee to say that the appellor is outlawed of felony or disabled in his person.

And also if bigamy is alleged, and a writ issues to the bishop to certify and the bishop does not certify, he shall be amerced. And the statute is that the ordinary shall have him at his peril etc. if he wishes.

And the court shall test whether he is a clerk or not, and the ordinary may receive him notwithstanding that he is not a clerk. But if he receives him where he is not a clerk at all, and this is found before the justices of King's Bench or before the justices of oyer and terminer, the ordinary may traverse this office, and if this office is found against the ordinary he shall lose his temporalities, and these justices [also] have the power to enquire of such things as the justices in eyre would have if they were in the land.

If a man is arraigned and he says that he is a clerk, and the ordinary is not present and the judges put a book before him and he does not know how to read, the court shall not award execution against him, but they shall hold the process for the ordinary until the ordinary comes. For if the ordinary wishes to receive him, he shall have him at his peril etc.

If a man has taken sanctuary for a certain felony and is taken out of the church and arraigned before the justices, it is a good plea for him to say that he had taken sanctuary and was taken out, and it was in such a vill and such a county, and to plead over to the felony, and to ask that he might be restored to the church. And then the justices shall award a *venire facias* to the vill where he says that he was taken. And if it is found by the inquest that he was taken out he shall be restored, and if not, they shall award a *venire facias* to enquire if he is guilty or not, and if he is found guilty execution shall be made on him, unless he is a clerk. And the felony and the taking out of sanctuary shall be enquired of by a jury etc. And if the party who is arraigned in one county says that he was taken out of a church in another county, the justices shall award a *venire facias* in the other county where the church is, as if it were in the same county etc.

The statute says further, *and the king admonishes them that they shall not be delivered without due purgation* etc., *those who are convicted* etc. Now, in the case that an ordinary suffers one who is a clerk attaint (who may not make his purgation) to make his purgation, what remedy against the ordinary? I understand that it shall be judged an escape for which he must make a fine to the king, that is, £100 if it is found thus, which fine the ordinary must pay to the king for each escape of a clerk attaint etc. And also if a clerk convict escapes without due purgation the king shall have the same fine from the ordinary, that is £100 etc.

If one who is appealed takes his clergy he shall not be delivered to the ordinary before an inquest of office is taken, and if an inquest of office is taken and he is found not guilty he shall go quit and shall not be delivered to the ordinary, and if

soit trove coulpable il serra deliver al ordinarie et toutz sez bienz serra forfaitez al roy.

Lestatut est *en nul manner eux delivere<nt>^d saunz due purgation* etc. Dewe purgation est que proclamation serra fait en iiij countees ou v counteez adjoinantez et si ascun voet vener et dire quil tua son auncestor et cest il entend de averer per xij proves de xij prodes homez, il avera cest averment. Et si [*fo. 119*] un home soit convicte ou atteint lou il ne dever fair purgation, si lordinarie luy suffre luy de fair son purgation il ne serra enquerr si le purgation fuit due ou non, quar per le metropolitan il ne serra certifia, et lenquest de laiez homez nenquerra nul auter si non que sil ad fait purgation ou non, mez ilz nenquerrent si le purgation soit due ou nemi, quar il ne gist en lour notice etc.

Et coment que, solonk mon opinion devaunt, scilicet que si lordinarie suffre un clerk atteynt de fair son purgation que ne devoit per le ley, que ceo serra adjuge un eschape pur que il ferr fyn al roy etc., ascunz teign que cest un voluntarie eschape pur que, solonk lour resonz et oppinionz, il averoit jugement vi et de membre si come <un>^i viconte averoit que avoit suffre un laron deschaper voluntary etc., le quel est adjuge felony etc. Mez solonk plusours auterz, il ne serra issint ajuge en lordinarie pur ceo que le fyn que il ferra pur clerk atteint ou convicte que eschapa est de cy haut et graund value etc., ideo quere.

En cas que clerk convicte soit seisi de certen terrez ove son feme et soit disseisi, lassize serra port en <le>^d son nom et en le nom de son feme, et nemi en le nom de son feme soull, pur ceo que per cell conviction il nad perdu null terre, et cest action trenchz en le realte etc. Clerk atteint perdre toutz sez terrez auxibien come sez chateux, et le roy avera a <lun>^i sez terrez come sez chateux si ne soit de terrez de son feme, quar le feme peut prender de le roy et tener de luy per fee ferm, et si ele soit disseisi ele avera action en son nom tamen pur ceo que per le atteynder son baron ad perduz tout etc. Ecce modo mirum quod femina etc.

Si un home soit clerk atteynt, nient contristeant quil soit atteint sur un faux suerment, il navera atteint pur ceo que lez jurrors diont [perecos]¹ et nient sur lour conscience etc. Si un home soit atteint per erroneous process de utlage de felony et est mort, son heir avera bref derror pur ceo que il est aperdre son enheritaunce, et sil reverse cest process il avera sez terrez hors del mayn le roy etc. Et si le roy pardon un quest clerk convicte ou atteint, et lordinarie luy suffre deschaper, le roy navera eschape pur ceo quil ad luy pardon per sez lettrez pattentez, et lordinarie peut monstre lez letters pattentez. Et nota que si un clerk quest livere al

¹ MS. reads precise.

he is found guilty he shall be delivered to the ordinary and all his goods shall be forfeit to the king.

The statute is *in no manner to deliver them without due purgation* etc. Due purgation is that a proclamation shall be made in four or five adjoining counties and if anyone wishes to come and say that [the clerk] killed his ancestor and that he intends to aver this by twelve proofs of twelve good men, he shall have this averment. And if a man is convicted or attainted so that he should not make purgation if the ordinary allows him to make his purgation it shall not be enquired whether the purgation was due or not for it shall not be certified by the metropolitan, and the inquest of lay men shall only enquire whether he made purgation or not but they shall not enquire whether the purgation was due or not, for this does not lie in their notice etc.

And even though, according to my opinion above, namely that if the ordinary allows a clerk attaint to make his purgation when he should not do it according to the law that this shall be judged an escape for which he shall make a fine to the king etc.: some hold that this is a voluntary escape, so that according to their reasons and opinions he should have judgment of life and limb, as a sheriff would have who had allowed a thief to escape voluntarily etc. which is adjudged a felony etc. But according to many others, it shall not be judged thus in the ordinary, because the fine that he shall make for the clerk attaint or convict who escapes is of such a high and great value etc., but query this.

In the case where a clerk convict is seised of certain lands with his wife and is disseised, the assize shall be brought in his name and in the name of his wife, and not in the name of his wife alone, because by this conviction he has not lost any land, and this action affects realty etc. A clerk attaint shall lose all his lands as well as his chattels and the king shall have his lands as well as his chattels if they are not his wife's lands, for the wife may take them from the king and hold them of him in fee farm and if she is disseised she shall have an action in her name, even though by the attainder her husband has lost everything etc. 'Look, indeed it is a wonder that a woman' etc.[1]

If a man is a clerk attaint notwithstanding that he was attainted on a false oath he shall not be attainted, for the jurors spoke negligently and not according to their conscience etc. If a man is attainted by an erroneous process of outlawry for felony and is put to death, his heir shall have a writ of error because he has lost his inheritance and if he reverses this process he shall have his lands out of the king's hands etc. And if the king pardons one who is a clerk convict or attaint and the ordinary allows him to escape, the king shall not have an escape because he has pardoned him by his letters patent and the ordinary may show the letters

---

[1] 'Look, indeed, it is a wonder that a woman brings the king's writ without naming her husband, who by law is united to her.' It is reported in YB Mich. 1 Hen. IV, fo. 1, pl. 2 that the king sued Sibyl Belknap in the Common Pleas without naming her husband, who was then in exile in Gascony, and Gascoigne C.J.K.B. accepted the suit. This verse is not there, but per Markham when the case is cited in YB Mich. 2 Hen. IV, fo. 7, pl. 26. It appears other times through the fifteenth century: YB Mich. 11 Hen. IV, fo. 7, pl. 16; YB Pas. 5 Edw. IV, Long Quinto fo. 17; YB Mich. 5 Edw. IV, Long Quinto fo. 68, and is cited by Coke: Co. Litt. 132b. It also appears in YB Reading A, p. 4, above, and Reading F, p. 49, below.

ordinarie debrusa le prison, il serra encore arrein de cest felony, unquor il peut prender son clergie arermayn.[1]

Auxi fuit dit quil est graunt diversite lou lordinarie refus un clerke generaly et lou il luy refus pur ceo quil ne savoit lier, quar sil luy refus generaly, coment que cestui quest arreign soit prist, il serra mys a execution, sicome fuit jades un prest devant Magister Litilton, et unquor lordinarie ne ferra fyn all roy pur son refusell, quar peut estre quil luy refus per case pur ceo quil est bigamus, lollard, ou excommenge, dez queux casez le court nest tenuz davoir notice. Mez sil luy refusa especialy pur ceo quil ne savoit lier lou en fait il savoit bien lier, et le justicez ceo entre de record, il ferra fyn au roy pur son refusell et sic vide diversite.

Auxi fuit tenuz per toutz lez justices jades que si bigamye soit allegg en le person dascun que demanda lordinarie, coment que cestui que demande lordinarie confessa devant lez justicez quil avoit ij femes, que lez justicez sur son confession demesne ne doner jugement sur luy einz manderont al ordinarie deux certifier sil soit bigamus ou nemi, et solonk son certificate de proceder al jugement, quar il nest my semblable a bastardie, quest in divers casez port destre trie per le pays, et issint le court peut sur luy prender notice etc.

[CHAPTER 3]

[fo. 119v] Purveu est ensement que nul rienz soit demande, pris, ne leve per viconte etc. Per le comen ley le viconte avoit power en son tournz denquerrer deschapes, mez le viconte en son counte mez le viconte [*sic*] naver nul power de agarder null process vers null home pur enquerrer de cest eschape, mez il devoit, per le comen ley, quaunt un presentement fuit fait devant luy, il devoit metter devant lez justicez en eyre et eux agard process et enquirent si cest fuite eschape come il fuit presente ou nemi, et sil fuit trove devant eux un eschape, le viconte le dever lever cest eschape. Mez lez viconte voilent prender un enquest sicome lez justices en eyre, nient contrestreaunt quil fuit encontre le comen ley, et auxi agarde proces envers lez jurrours pur enquerrer de cell eschape en lour tournez ou en lour counteez, et sur cest eschape trove devant eux ils vouderont prender fyn del partie a lour volunte, scilicet dascuns graunt fyn pur malice, et dascuns petit fyn pur favour, issint sur ceo le roy avoit graunt prejudice pur que cest estatut remedy et voet que le viconte ne nul auter ne devoit lever eschape devant que il soit trove et trie devant justicez errauntes. Mez a cest jour ne sont ascuns justicez errauntes et cest *que desormez le viconte* etc.

Le segnior de un segnior dun segniorie [*sic*] aver power al comen ley pur enquerr, et a cest jour ad en son lete de eschapes, mez il navoit power al comen ley ne a cest jour pur trier leschapez etc.

Lestatut voet que le viconte ne nul auter ad power de lever eschape etc. devant quil soit trie devant justices errauntes etc. Sont auterz justicez que avoyent

---

[1] New hand from 'de cest felony …' to end of folio.

patent. And note that if a clerk who is delivered to the ordinary breaks the prison, he shall be arraigned again for this felony, but he may still take his clergy again.

Also, it was said that there is a great difference where the ordinary refuses a clerk generally, and where he refuses him because he does not know how to read, for if he refuses him generally, even if the one who is arraigned is a priest, he shall be put to execution, just as a priest was recently before Master Littleton, and still the ordinary shall not make a fine to the king for his refusal, for perhaps he refused him because he was a bigamist, Lollard, or excommunicated, of which cases the court is not bound to take notice.[1] But if he refuses him specially because he did not know how to read when in fact he read well, and the justices entered this on the record, he shall make a fine to the king for his refusal, and thus see the difference.

Also, it was held by all the justices recently that if bigamy is alleged in the person of anyone who demands the ordinary, then even if the one who demands the ordinary confesses before the justices that he had two wives, the justices shall not give judgment on his own confession but shall send him to the ordinary to have it certified whether he is a bigamist or not, and shall proceed to judgment according to his certificate, for it is not at all like bastardy, which is in many cases brought to be tried by jury, and thus the court may take notice of it etc.[2]

CHAPTER 3

It is provided also that nothing shall be demanded, taken, nor levied by the sheriff etc. By the common law the sheriff has the power in his tourns to enquire concerning escapes, but the sheriff has no power in his county to award process against any man to enquire concerning this escape, but by the common law when a presentment is made before him he must send it before the justices in eyre and they award process and enquire if this was an escape as it was presented or not, and if it was found to be an escape before them, the sheriff should levy [a fine] on this escape. But the sheriffs wanted to take an inquest like the justices in eyre, notwithstanding that it was against the common law, and also award process against the jurors to enquire concerning this escape in their tourns or in their counties, and on this escape found before them they wanted to take a fine from the party at their will, that is, from some a great fine for malice, and from others a small fine for favour, and this was greatly prejudicial to the king: so this statute remedies this and wills that neither the sheriff nor any other should levy [a fine for] an escape before it is found and tried before justices in eyre. But nowadays there are no justices in eyre and thus it is *that henceforth the sheriff* etc.

The lord of a lordship has power at the common law to inquire and nowadays has escapes in his leet, but he did not and does not have power at the common law to try escapes etc.

The statute wills that neither the sheriff nor any other has the power to levy [fines for] escape etc. before they are tried before the justices in eyre etc. There

---

[1] Littleton makes this point in YB Trin. 9 Edw. IV, fo. 28, pl. 41.
[2] Perhaps part of the discussion in YB Mich. 21 Edw. IV, fos 72–73, pl. 57.

power al comen ley de trier un eschape si bien come justicez en eyre, et ont auxi graunt power in tout a cest jour, scilicet justicez de bank le roy et justicez de oire et determiner. Mez a cest jour ne sont justices en eyre, mez nous avomus en leu deux justices dassize, et devaunt eux il serra <trie et>ᵈ enquer et trie. Et si <rienz soit>ᵈ ascun fin soit pris dascon home pur un eschape per le viconte ou ascun auter lou leschape nest trie devaunt justicez de bank le roy, queux avoient power denquerr de eschapes in le counte de Middlesex ou quecunque counte que le dit bank est, ou devaunt justices de oire et determiner, justiceez dassize, justiceez de gaole delivere, ou justicez per especiall commission, le partie de que leschape fuit pris navera pas generall action de trespass, mez il avera son action de trespass sur cell estatut, pur ceo que le statut est un prohibition en luy meme et pur ceo etc. Et si le viconte soit convicte de cell indroitrell pris, il rendre al partie leschape arermayn et auxi sez damagez nient contristeant que son damagez ne sont my expressez deinz lestatut, pur ceo que <home>ⁱ recoveroit damagez al comen ley en action de trespass. Et ouster ceo scire facias issera vers le viconte a responder al roy de taunt quil avoit reson etc.

Donquez est a voire dez queux personz ilz devoient enquerr etc. (jeo entenk come de <vicontez>ⁱ, constablez, gardeynz de gailez, et auters tielx semblables etc.) et de quel eschape, scilicet sil soit voluntare eschape ou nemi. Quar si home soit atteynt de treson ou atteynt de felony et le viconte ou cestui que avoit luy en gard suffra luy deschap voluntary, il avera jugement de vie et de membre. Et auxi sil ne soit que endite de treson ou de felony et cestui que avoit luy engard suffra luy deschaper voluntary, il est felony et sil de ceo <soit>ⁱ atteynt, il avera jugement de vie et de membre. Mez sil eschape et nient voluntary, le viconte ou gailor que avoit luy en gard ferra fyn al roy pur leschape etc.

Donquez jeo entenk que sont ij manerz dez fynez, scilicet un quest en certen et un auter que nest en certent mez arbitrable solonk le [*fo. 120*] le discrescion dez justices. Le fyn deschap que est encerten est <si come est>ᵈ si come home soit enprison et atteint de felony et il eschape en defaut del viconte: il ferra fyn al roy pur cest eschape scilicet c li. Et sil soit pris pur suspecion de felony et sur ceo imprison, ou soit endite de felony et sur ceo imprison, et eschapa in defaut del viconte, il ferra fyn de c s. Et si soit un provour et eschapa, le fyn serra a x li. Auxi si clerk atteynt <escha>ᵈ ou clerk convicte eschapa lordinarie il ferra fyn al roy a c li. come il est a use a cest jour etc.

Mez en ascun cas home peut estre arestar pur suspecion de felony et coment quil apres eschapa cestui que avoit luy en gard suffre luy a departer, come jeo entenk il nest eschap, ne il ne ferra fyn al roy pur cest departer: come si un home soit pris pur suppecion de felony lou cestui que luy arrester navoit nul chose de luy ducer a luy arester, coment quil suffre luy a departer apres le rest il nest eschap, quar le partie que fuist areste avera envers luy bon action de faux emprison, et la cestui que luy arrester ne peut my cest arrest justifier, et pur ceo etc. Mez si ascun choce soit

are other justices who have power at the common law to try an escape as well as justices in eyre, namely justices of the King's Bench and justices of oyer and terminer, and they have as much power today. But nowadays there are no justices in eyre, but in place of them we have justices of assize, and it shall be inquired and tried before them. And if any fine is taken from any man for an escape by the sheriff or anyone else, where the escape is not tried before justices of the King's Bench (who have power to enquire of escapes in the county of Middlesex or any county where the said Bench is), or before justices of oyer and terminer, justices of assize, justices of gaol delivery, or justices by a special commission, the party from whom the [fine for the] escape was taken shall not have a general action of trespass but he shall have his action of trespass on this statute, because the statute is a prohibition on him and therefore etc. And if the sheriff is convicted of taking this unlawfully he shall render the [fine for the] escape to the party again and also his damages, notwithstanding that his damages are not expressed in the statute, because one would recover damages at the common law in an action of trespass. And beyond this a *scire facias* shall issue against the sheriff to respond to the king for what reason etc.

Now, we must see concerning which persons they must inquire etc. (I believe of sheriffs, constables, keepers of gaols, and other such etc.) and of which escapes, that is, whether they were voluntary escapes or not. For if a man is attainted of treason or attainted of felony and the sheriff, or whoever had him in custody, allowed him to escape voluntarily, he shall have judgment of life and limb. And also if he is only indicted of treason or of felony, and the one who has him in custody allows him to escape voluntarily it is a felony, and if he is attainted of this he shall have judgment of life and limb. But if he escapes and it is not voluntary, the sheriff or the gaoler who had him in custody shall make a fine to the king for the escape etc.

Now, I understand that there are two types of fines, namely one which is certain and another which is not certain, but variable according to the justices' discretion. The fine for an escape which is certain is where a man is imprisoned and attainted of felony and he escapes by the sheriff's fault: he shall make a fine to the king for this escape, that is £100. And if he is taken on suspicion of felony and imprisoned on this, or is indicted for felony and imprisoned on this, and escapes by the sheriff's fault, he shall make a fine of 100s. And if there is an approver and he escapes the fine shall be £10. Also if a clerk attaint or a clerk convict escapes from the ordinary, he shall make a fine to the king of £100, as it is done today etc.

But in any case a man may be arrested on suspicion of felony, and even if he escapes afterwards [and] the one who had him in custody allowed him to go, as I understand it is not an escape, and he shall not make a fine to the king for this departure: for example, if a man was taken on suspicion of felony where the one who arrested him had nothing to justify his arrest, even if he allowed him to leave after the arrest it is not an escape, for the party who was arrested will have a good action of false imprisonment against him, and there the one who arrested him could not justify the arrest at all, and therefore etc. But if there was anything

de luy ducer al arester un pur suspecion un, come jeo oire quun home est occise et un auter vient incontinenter de meme le lieu et cez vestuez sont blodye ou il port son swerd drawe ou autiel auter chose que moy purr ducer quil est suppesious, ore si jeo luy areste sur cest suppecion et apres il eschapa a moy, jeo ferra fyn all roy <et coment que lauter apres>[d] pur cest eschape, scilicet c s., et si le partie que fuit issint arreste voile apres de porter envers moy un bref de faux emprisonment, coment quil fuit acquite de cest felony, jeo justifia le arrest assez bien.

Auxi si un home soit robbe issint que opyn crye est fait et le pays arer, si cestui que luy robbe eschape le fyn serra cesse sur tout le hundred. Et si un tiel felon prist leglise et demanda le privilege et puis abjure le roialme, il avera space de xl jours a aller hors del roialme, et sil face eschape en cest cas le vill serra amercye a c s. etc.

Le fine que serra arbitrable serra en tielx casez, come jeo entenk, scilicet come si un home soit endite de felony ou arrecter de felony et en le gard del viconte et le viconte lessa luy all maynpris et all jour del delivery ou auter jour quest done a luy dapper le felon nappert: en cest il ne peut estre dit properment <quaunt>[i] defaut en le viconte pur ceo quil prender suerte et ne tend pas mez quil voilet aver serva son jour, unquor le viconte ferra fyn al roy le quell serra solonk le discrescion dez justicez. Auxi si un soit endite de trespass et en le gard del viconte, sil eschapa il serra cesse solonk le discrescion dez jugges.

Mez si un home soit condempn en action de dett ou covenaunt al suyte del partie et sur ceo soit en gard, le gardein ne ferra fyn, mez le partie avera bref de dett vers luy sur lestatut etc. Et en cas que un home soit endite de trespass et auxi de felony al suyte de ij homez et il eschapa, en cest cas le viconte ne ferra mez un generall fyn, et sil soit endite al suyte de xx homez le fyn serra generall.

Donquez le letter del estatut est que *nul fyn soit demande ne leve per viconte dauter* etc. Sur cest parolz si home eschape en ascun segniorie dascun segnior que ad pit et galowe de graunt le roy, et un home soit atteynt de felony que duist aver jugement en meme le segniorie, le segnior avera le fyn et en cest cas le seneschall sessera le fyn. Et en meme le maner serra fait en counte palantynes come Derham et Chester.

Donquez en ascun cas lez justicez cesser le fyn saunz enquerrer et en ascun cas per enquerr, come lez justicez veign a un lieu etc., et le clerk dassise voile fair un calendre de toutz lez prisoners que sont en le gayle. Et si apres quaunt ils sont demandez le gailor ou le viconte voile sustrete un, en cest cas il ferra fyn saunz enquerr. Et sil ne metter un en le calendar que est en le [*fo. 120v*] gayle, ceo serra enquerr per pays et il ferra fyn.

Si labbe de Westm' suffer un home quest clerk atteynt de faire eschape, en cest cas scire facias issera vers labbe et il nest respons pur labbe a dire quil navoit tiel prisoner, mez il purr dire null tiel record, ou quil nest eschape.

which led him to arrest one on suspicion, such as that I hear that a man has been killed and another man comes immediately from the same place and his clothes are bloody, or he carries his sword drawn, or some other thing that leads me to think that he is suspicious, now if I arrest him on this suspicion and afterwards he escapes from me I shall make a fine to the king for this escape, that is 100s., and if the party who was thus arrested wishes to bring a writ of false imprisonment against me afterwards, even though he was acquitted of the felony I shall justify the arrest well enough.

Also, if a man is robbed so that an open cry is made and the country is raised, if the one who robbed him escapes the fine shall be assessed on the entire hundred. And if such a felon takes sanctuary and demands the privilege and then abjures the realm, he shall have 40 days to go out of the realm, and if he escapes in this case the vill shall be amerced 100s. etc.

The fine shall be variable in these kinds of cases, as I understand, that is for example when a man is indicted of felony or arrested for felony and in the sheriff's custody and the sheriff lets him go by mainprise and at the day of delivery or on another day given to him to appear, the felon does not appear: this cannot properly be called a fault in the sheriff, because he took surety and it cannot be held but that he did his duty, but the sheriff shall make a fine to the king according to the discretion of the justices. Also if one is indicted of trespass and in the sheriff's custody, if he escapes he shall be assessed according to the discretion of the judges.

But if a man is condemned in an action of debt or of covenant at the suit of the party and is in custody on this, the keeper shall not make a fine, but the party shall have a writ of debt against him on the statute etc. And in the case that a man is indicted of trespass, and also of felony, at the suit of two men and he escapes, in this case the sheriff shall only make a general fine, and if he is indicted at the suit of twenty men the fine shall be general.

Now the letter of the statute is that *no fine shall be demanded or levied on another by the sheriff* etc. On these words if a man escapes in any lordship from any lord who has a pit and gallows by the king's grant, and a man is attainted of felony who ought to have judgment in the same lordship, the lord shall have the fine, and in this case the steward shall assess the fine. And it shall be done in the same way in counties palatine such as Durham and Chester.

Now in some cases the justices shall assess the fine without inquiry, and in other cases by inquiry, as when the justices come to a place etc. and the clerk of the assize will make a calendar of all the prisoners who are in the gaol. And if afterwards when they are demanded the gaoler or the sheriff wishes to withdraw one, in this case he shall make a fine without enquiry. And if he does not put one in the calendar who is in the gaol, this shall be enquired of by the country and he shall make a fine.

If the abbot of Westminster allows a man who is a clerk attaint to make an escape, in this case a *scire facias* shall issue against the abbot, and it is not an answer for the abbot to say that he did not have such a prisoner, but he may say

Mez si le viconte del Middlesex suffre un home de fair eschape bref issera al coroners de certifier sil soit emprison ou nemi etc. Auxi si ascun constable arrester home pur suspecion de felony et ove le maynoure, le viconte est oblige pur resceyver tiel home a son prison, quar sil luy refuser il serra ajuge un eschape auxi bien come il avoit luy resceiver et puis luy lesser deschape etc.

Si un prisoner soit en le calendre del justicez et le viconte ou le gailor soit demande pur porter son prisoner sur payne, le viconte peut luy excuser que le prisoner est enfirmite, ou quil fuit prist de luy per fort mayne dez homez darmez, et ceo serra enquer per le pays, ou quil est remova per certiorari al bank le roy et sic luy excuser. Mez sil ne peut luy excuser lez justicez cesseront fyn sur luy mayntenaunt, saunz enquerr.

Et si si [sic] un home soit utlage de felony la viconte est oblige al garder luy en le gaile, mez sil soit arrester pur dett ou trespas al suyte del partie il purra prisoner luy en son chambour. Donquez si le viconte suffre un que nest maynpernable aler al bayle sil soit endite sur lespeciall mater il ferra fyn etc. Auxi fuit dit que coment le viconte suffre un defair eschape, sil avoit luy prist al temps quil devoit luy aver, quil nest eschape. Mez solonk ascunz, et come jeo entenk destre dentend que ceo serra <entend>ⁱ lou le viconte ou gailor suffre un deschape et puis fait fresch suyt et luy reprent, que adonquez sil luy avoit quaunt deveroit que <a>^d ceo ne serra ajuge eschape, <Mez sil ne face fresch>^d quar la il serra adjuge tout temps en son gard. Mez si un eschapa et le gailor ne face fresch suyte <scilicet quil soit tout temps en son vewe>ⁱ, coment quil est pris apres arermayn ceo serra ajuge un eschape <et issint cociens que nociens>ⁱ etc.

Donquez si un gaylor lessa un que est atteynt de felony de fair voluntary eschape, en cest cas il avera jugement de vi et de membre et nemi le viconte, in favorem vite, pur ceo quil nest son faut et ne serra punysh pur auter fait. Mez peraventour auterment serra si le viconte bien savoit que son gailor devoit tiel favore a felon queux il avoit en son gard quil voilet suffre eux deschaper, quar la <lec>^d il peut estre ajuge le <felon>^d folie del viconte daccepter tiel home pur garder le gaile, le quel il bien savoit quil devoit tiel favour as felon, en quel cas le viconte averoit jugement de vi et de membre si tiel eschape fuert trove envers luy etc.

Et si le viconte fait un gayler que suffre home fair eschape, mez nemi voluntary, sil ne soit sufficient pur fair fyn all roy, le viconte ferr fyn pur ceo quil est oblige de trover un que est sufficient, come il bien appert per lez parolz del estatut queux sont tielx W[estminster] ij capitulo xij^{me} Et si custos gaole non sit sufficient respondeat eius superior etc. Mez si soit gayler en fee il meme ferra fyn et nemi le viconte etc.

Donquez <son>^d en cas que sont ij viconte en un fraunchise, come en Londrez, et lun avoit un prisoner en son gard le quell suffre luy deschape, si le

'no such record', or that he is not escaped. But if the sheriff of Middlesex allows a man to make an escape, a writ shall issue to the coroners to certify if he was imprisoned or not etc. Also, if any constable arrests a man on suspicion of felony and [comes] with the mainour, the sheriff is obliged to receive such a man in his prison, for if he refuses him it shall be adjudged an escape, just as if he had received him and then allowed him to escape etc.

If a prisoner is in the justices' calendar and the sheriff or the gaoler is required to bring his prisoner on a penalty, the sheriff may excuse himself because the prisoner is unwell, or [may say] that he was taken from him by main force by armed men, and this shall be enquired of by the country, or that he is removed by *certiorari* to the King's Bench, and thus he may excuse himself. But if he cannot excuse himself the justices shall assess a fine on him immediately without an enquiry.

And if a man is outlawed for felony, the sheriff is obliged to keep him in the gaol, but if he is arrested for debt or trespass at the suit of the party he may imprison him in his chamber. Now, if the sheriff allows one who is not mainpernable to go on bail, if he is indicted on the special matter he shall make a fine etc. Also it was said that even if the sheriff allows one to make an escape, if he had taken him [again] by the time that he ought to have had him, then it is not an escape. But according to others, and as I conceive it to be understood that this shall be understood, where the sheriff or gaoler allows one to escape and then makes fresh suit and takes him again, that then if he has him when he should this shall not be adjudged an escape, for there it shall be adjudged that he was always in his custody. But if one escapes and the gaoler does not make fresh suit, that is, so that he was always in his view, even if he is taken again afterwards this shall be judged an escape, and the same for the innocent and the guilty etc.

Now if a gaoler allows one who is attainted of felony to make a voluntary escape, in this case [the gaoler] shall have judgment of life and limb and not the sheriff, *in favorem vitae*, because it was not [the sheriff's] fault and he shall not be punished for another's fault. But perhaps it shall be otherwise if the sheriff knew that the gaoler owed such favour to the felon whom he had in his custody that he might allow him to escape, for there it might be judged the sheriff's folly to accept such a man to keep the gaol whom he well knew owed such favour to the felon, in which case the sheriff shall have judgment of life and limb if such an escape should be found against him etc.

And if the sheriff makes a gaoler who allows a man to make an escape but not voluntarily, if he is not sufficient to make a fine to the king the sheriff shall make the fine, because he is obliged to find one who is sufficient, as it appears clearly in the words of the statute which are thus: (Westminster II, c. 12) *and if the keeper of the gaol is not sufficient let his superior answer* etc.[1] But if he is a gaoler in fee he shall make the fine himself and not the sheriff.

Now, in the case that there are two sheriffs in one franchise, as in London, and one has a prisoner in his custody, which prisoner he allows to escape, shall the

---

[1] Westminster II, c. 11 (*SR*, i. 80–81).

fyn serra charge auxi bien sur son companyon que nest <suffre>[d] pas culpable en leschape ou nemi. Et dicitur quil serra charge auxi bien come son companyon mez ils ne ferront forsque un fyn. Mez sil fuerit un voluntarie eschape le quel require jugement de vi et de membre, que adonquez cestui viconte que navoit luy en gard naveroit jugement de son vie et membre en defaut de son companyon, mez taunt solement cestui que luy lessa deschaper causa supradictus.

Auxi fuit dit que lez justicez del bank le roy ne ont power, [fo. 121] ne nuls justices, pur arrainer un quest pris pur felony saunz ceo quil est devaunt eux per originall en le record de le coroner.

Si un home soit emprison pur haut treson et il eschapa, leschape nest my haut treson nient contristeant quil est einz per haut treson. Mez il est felony, et sil soit acquite de le treson il serra arrain de le felony.

Si un soit committe al prison et le gailor suffra luy daler sur un de lez kepers, auxi long quil ad animum eundi et redeundi nest eschape et ne serra dit felony pur ceo que le ley supposa luy destre tout temps en gard. Mez sil eschapa voluntary et le gailor luy suffra, cest felony et si ceo soit trove le gailer serra mort. Et meme la ley est dez borouz dun felon ut dicitur.

Si un home macter [sic] un auter et est mys a prison pur ceo, sil eschapa en le vie le home et le home morust apres, il serra ajuge sur le gailor un eschape pur ceo quil avera relation a le jour que le partie fuit <f>[d] macter [sic] etc. Si un home eschapa a un keper il peut luy arrestar, et sil ne voet estre a son arrest il peut luy macter et ne serra ajuge felony, unquore solonk ma entent il ne peut justifier mez il pledre de rien culpable et metter luy sur le pays etc., et monstra a lenquest lespeciall mater etc.

Auxi fuit dit que si un home que nest constable ne auter officer arester un home pur suspecion de felony et apres luy suffre deschape, que ceo ne serra dit eschape pur ceo quil naver null power de luy arester en taunt quil ne fuit un officer. Mez jeo crey que ceo nest pas ley, quar jeo entenk que chescun home en defaut del presence dun officer purra loialment arrester un felon, et pur le roy a cest temps serra ajuge un officer etc., ideo quere.

Donquez en cas que un home soit emprison pur felony et sur ceo arrain, et il dit quil est clerk et pria son clerge, et lordinarie nest present de luy receyver ou refuser per que il est repri, et proces fait envers lordinarie et devaunt que lordinarie vient le felon est eschape.

Auxi fuit dit que si home soit comdepne et in garde pur cest condempnation, coment quil soit apres <ul>[d] utlage de felony et per cas le roy luy pardon, ceo ne dischargera luy envers le partie de cest condempnation, sicome il fuit jades adjuge in le cas dun Turwhit cy en Londrez etc.[1] Auxi fuit dit que si le gailor suffre un deschap quest condempne come in dett ou damagez envers un auter, coment

---

[1] From the beginning of this paragraph to the end of the text is an addition, in the same hand as the addition on p. 41 above.

fine be charged also on his companion who is not guilty in the escape or not? And it was said that he shall be charged as well as his companion but they shall only make one fine. But if it was a voluntary escape which requires judgment of life and limb, that then the sheriff who did not have him in custody shall not have the judgment of life and limb for the fault of his companion, but only the one who allowed him to escape for the reasons above.

Also it was said that the justices of King's Bench do not have power, nor do any justices, to arraign one who is taken for felony unless he is before them by an original [writ] in the coroner's record.

If a man is imprisoned for high treason and he escapes, the escape is not high treason, notwithstanding that he is in for high treason. But it is felony and if he is acquitted of the treason he shall be arraigned on the felony.[1]

If one is committed to prison and the gaoler allows him to go with one of the keepers, so long as he has intention to go and return this is not an escape and shall not be called a felony, because the law supposes that he is always in custody. But if he escapes voluntarily and the gaoler allows him, this is a felony, and if this is found the gaoler shall be put to death. And the law is the same of the pledges of a felon, as is said.

If one man beats another and is put in prison for this, if he escapes in the life of the man and the man dies afterwards it shall be adjudged an escape in the gaoler, because it relates to the day that the party was beaten etc. If a man escapes from a keeper he may arrest him, and if he will not be arrested the keeper may beat him and it shall not be adjudged a felony, yet according to my understanding he may not justify it, but he shall plead not guilty and put himself on the country etc. and show the special matter to the inquest etc.

Also it was said that if a man who is not a constable or other officer arrests a man on suspicion of felony and afterwards allows him to escape, this shall not be called an escape because he had no power to arrest him inasmuch as he was not an officer. But I believe that this is not law, for I understand that every man, in default of the presence of an officer, may lawfully arrest a felon and shall be adjudged an officer for the king at that time etc., therefore query.

Now in the case where a man is imprisoned for felony and arraigned on this, and he says that he is a clerk and prays his clergy, and the ordinary is not present to receive him or refuse him, he shall thereupon be held again and process made against the ordinary, and before the ordinary comes the felon has escaped.

Also it was said that if a man is condemned and in custody for this condemnation, even if he is afterwards outlawed for felony, and perhaps the king pardons him, this shall not discharge him against the party for this condemnation, just as it was recently adjudged in the case of one Tyrwhit here in London etc.[2] Also it was said that if the gaoler allows one to escape who is condemned in debt or damages against another, that even if he retakes him again he shall be

---

[1] 2 Hen. VI, c. 21 made an escape for high treason, treason (*SR*, ii. 226–227).

[2] Perhaps YB Mich. 8 Hen. V, fos 7–8, pl. 2, or YB Mich. 6 Edw. IV, fo. 4, pl. 11. Tyrwhit is not mentioned, but the discussion fits.

quil luy reprist areremayn, il serra charge a le partie etc. Et il ne serra discharge envers le partie coment quun estrange debrusa le prison per quun tiel prisoner quest condempne eschape si cestui que debrusa le prison soit de south le legiance le roy, sicome il fuit adjuge cy en Londrez en le cas de Jak Cade. Mez auterment serra si lez enemyes le roy, come escootes ou auterz tielx aliens que ne sont de south le legiance le roy, debruser le prison per que tielx prisoners eschapont, en quel cas le gailors ne serra my charge devers le roy nient pluis envers le partie, <S>^d nient plus que lou tielx aliens entront le roialme denglitere et per cas font wast sur le tenours de tenant a terme danz ou a terme de vie etc. Ceux <tenaunts>ⁱ ne serront charge per action de wast envers ceux en le revercion sur le mater monstre etc.

Auxi fuit dit que en ascun cas lou un home suffre un felon deschaper voluntary il ne serra dit felony, sicome un home ferust un auter et le constable per cas luy arrester et suffre luy de aler a large, pensant en son mynde que cestui quest feru devoit viver et nemi morer sur cest ferr. Coment que cestui que luy ferust eschapa, et lauter per cas morust, il ne serra dit felony en le person del constable, coment quil soit felony en cestui que luy ferr, entaunt quil nentend que lome morereit quaunt il luy less daler alarge, mez auterment serra sil entend quil moreroit etc.

charged by the party etc. And he shall not be discharged against the party even if a stranger breaks the prison by which such a condemned prisoner escapes, if the one who breaks the prison is under the allegiance of the king, just as it was adjudged here in London in the case of Jack Cade. But it shall be otherwise if the king's enemies, such as the Scots or other such aliens who are not under the king's allegiance, break the prison by which such prisoners escape, in which case the gaolers shall not be charged against the king at all any more than against the party, any more than where such aliens enter the realm of England and perhaps commit waste on the tenure of a tenant for term of years or for term of life etc.[1] Such tenants shall not be charged by action of waste against those in the reversion on the matter shown etc.

Also it was said that in some cases when a man voluntarily allows a felon to escape it shall not be called a felony, as when a man struck another and the constable perhaps arrested him and allowed him to go at large, thinking in his mind that the one who had been struck would live and not die from this blow. Even if the one who struck him escaped, and the other perhaps died, it shall not be called a felony in the person of the constable, when he let him go at large even if it is a felony in the one who struck him (even if he did not intend to kill the man), but it shall be otherwise if he intended to kill him etc.

---

[1] YB Hil. 33 Hen. VI, fo. 1, pl. 3. Cade is not mentioned by name.

READING F

WESTMINSTER PRIMER, C. 2

LECTURE SUR LE STATUT WESTMINSTER PRIMER EDIT ANNO 3 E[DW.] PRIMO

[*fo. 92*] *Purveu est ensement que quant clerk est pris pur rette de felonie.*[1] All comen ley devaunt le fesaunz de cest estatut si un home ust estre endite de felonie et arreine sur cell, il purroit aver son privilege de seynt esglyse et unquore est meme la ley, mez le myschieff fuit que lez ordinariez voillent all comen leye delyver tielz clerkez convictez saunz due purgation pur le quell vient cest estatut que voet quilz ne serra delyverez saunz due purgation etc.: vide le paroll.[2] Nota que cest estatut est prohibition envers lordinarie et sur ceo gist un contempt. Auxint cest estatut est intenduz dez clerkez convictez et nemi de clerkez atteintyz.

Le lettre est *et sil soit demaunde per cest ordinarie.* Ceo ne serra pris auxi generall, quar si home soit arrein pur felonie luy covient pur responder all felonie, et donquez il avera le privilege. Auxint si home voill prender lesglyse pur fait de felonie luy covient pur conustre le felonie et demande un coroner.[3] Nota que si cestui que est arreine ad fait sacrilege ou oscist home desglyse ou soit bigamus, feme, ou carnifex etc., il navera le privilege dell esglyse etc. Et propriment ceux que ne purront minister le sacriment etc.[4]

Nota que lordinarie serra demande en chescun cessionz generall et sil ne soit mye la ne son comissioner il serra amercye, quar de tielz cessionz due proclamation serra fait. Auter est dun especiall session. Si un ordinarie eit ij comissioners et lun accept un lautre et lauter [*sic*] luy refusa, unquore il serra committe a lour prison pur ceo que ley est in favorem vite etc. Si ij comissioners soient, lun deigne date eit commission que lauter, ici le darrein serra allowe pur ceo quil est revocation dell primer.

Si un home soit arrein pur felonie il navera son clerge devaunt quil respoign all felonie pur ceo que de ceo il fuit arrein.

Si un home soit trove coulpable quil ad furtive pris x d. ou tiell somme que est deins xij d. sterling, icy il navera son clerge pur ceo que son vie nest en jupertie. Mez auter est dun d pris per voy de robberye etc.

---

[1] In margin: Ca iij.
[2] In margin: Vide que levesque ne peut deliver clerk convict saunz due purgation.
[3] In margin: Tempus quant serra delyver (hand 2, later, maybe late sixteenth century).
[4] In margin: queux aver le benefit en la clergy (hand 2).

READING F

WESTMINSTER I, CHAPTER 2

LECTURE ON THE STATUTE OF WESTMINSTER I
MADE 3 EDW. I

It is provided also that when a clerk is taken for guilty of felony. At the common law, before the making of this statute, if a man had been indicted of felony and arraigned on this, he could have his privilege of the Holy Church and this is still the law, but the mischief was that the ordinaries wished at the common law to deliver such clerks convict without due purgation, for which reason this statute was made, which wills that they shall not be delivered without due purgation etc.: see the words [of the statute]. Note that this statute is a prohibition against the ordinary and a contempt lies on this. Also, this statute is understood of clerks convict and not of clerks attaint.

The letter is *and if he is demanded by the ordinary.* This shall not be taken so generally, for if a man is arraigned for felony he must respond to the felony and then he shall have the privilege. Also, if a man wishes to take sanctuary for committing a felony he must confess the felony and ask for a coroner. Note that if the one who is arraigned has committed sacrilege or killed a man of the church, or is a bigamist, a woman, or an executioner etc., he shall not have the privilege of the church etc.[1] And properly those who cannot minister the sacrament etc.

Note that the ordinary shall be demanded in each general sessions and if he is not there, nor his commissioner, he shall be amerced, for due proclamation is made of such sessions. It is otherwise of a special session. If an ordinary has two commissioners and one accepts a [clerk] and the other refuses him, still he shall be committed to their prison because the law is in favour of life etc. If there are two commissioners, one of an earlier date than the other, here the later shall be allowed because it is a revocation of the first [commission].

If a man is arraigned for felony he shall not have his clergy before he answers to the felony, because he was arraigned on this.

If a man is found guilty of furtively stealing 10d. or such a sum less than 12d. sterling, here he shall not have his clergy because his life is not in jeopardy. But it is otherwise of one penny taken by way of robbery etc.

---

[1] *Carnifex* is ordinarily a butcher, but the less-common meaning of executioner makes more sense in this context. Snede, however, makes the point that a butcher's son shall have his clergy, suggesting that there may have been some discussion of the ability of butchers to claim the privilege. See below Reading 7, p. 115.

Nota que cestui que est clerk convicte perdra cez bienz mez cez terrez ne serra forfaitz. Auter est de clerk attaint quar le roy avera cez terrez per an et iour, et apres le segnior dell fee. Meme la ley est de petit treson, scilicet lou un home occist son master, ou un moigne oscist son soveraigne etc.[1]

Si un home soit endite de felonie et est committee all ordinarie il ne serra mye apres arrein pur treson pur ceo quil morter en ley. Auxint si un home soit utlage de felonie et apres est pris, il peut aver son clergie apres il ne serra arrein pur treson.

Nota que levesque ne peut mye delyver tiell clerk convict saunz due purgation. Et purgation et nient purgation serra trie per le pays quar de ceo proclamation serra fait etc. Auter est de due purgation quar ceo attient all espirituell ley.

Nota que lou home est arrein pur felonie et soy pris a son clergie devaunt jugement don sur luy il est clerk convict et si jugement soit done sur luy donquez il est clerk atteint.[2] Si un home soit utlage de felonie et apres est pris et luy prendre a son clerge il est clerk atteint pur ceo quun jugement fuit done sur luy. Auxint si un home abjur le [royalme][3] et apres est trove deinz le [royalme][4] et soy prendre a son clergye il est clerk atteint [fo. 92v] quar sur labjuration fuith un jugement done sur luy etc. Lentre de clerk convict serra commissus est ordinarie, et lentre de clerk attaint serra comissus est ordinarie sine purgatione et issint clerk attaint est saunz remedie.[5] Si un home soit endite de felonie et confesse le felonie et prend luy a son clergie il est clerk convict pur ceo que null jugement fuit done sur luy. Auxint si le defendent en appell gage bataill et soit vayncuz et soy prend a son clergie, il est clerk convicte pur ceo que null jugement fuit done sur luy.

Si un home soit endite de felonie et sur ceo est arrein et trove coulpable, il perdra toutz cez terrez, bienz, et chateux queux il avoit al temps dell fesaunz dell felonie suppose etc. Le contrarie ley est lou home est utlage de felonie: il avera relation all temps dell utlage pronounce quar ceo nest que contempnecye quil ne voill appier etc. Si un home fait felonie et enfeoff un auter etc., et puis est arrein etc., sur que leschetor entre, il avera action et in son title il monstra etc. et concluder 'saunz ceo quil fut coulpable', pur ceo quil ne peut aver bref derror.[6] Auxint meme la ley serra envers le segnior en bref deschete etc. Auxint si un home soit utlage de felonie et aliene etc. sur que le segnior port bref deschete, laliene peut assigner error en le proces per voye de plee quar il nad auter remedie etc.

Si home soit clerke attaynt per faux serement il navera attaynt pur ceo que lez jurours diont [precise][7] et eient sur lour conshience.[8] Si home soit attaynt per erronynos proces per utlagary del felony et il mort, son heire avera bref derrour

---

[1] In margin: petit treason (hand 3).
[2] In margin: diversite perenter clerk convicte et clerk atteint (hand 1).
[3] MS. reads royngne.
[4] MS. reads royngne.
[5] In margin: Diversite perenter lentre de clerk convict et clerk atteint.
[6] In margin: vide lou inquisition serra ij foitz ou home soit coulpable ou nemi.
[7] MS. reads prestice.
[8] Space between paragraphs, beginning of hand 3.

Note that one who is a clerk convict shall lose his goods, but his lands shall not be forfeit. It is otherwise of a clerk attaint, for the king shall have his lands for a year and a day, and afterwards the lord of the fee. The law is the same for petty treason, that is where a man kills his master, or a monk kills his superior etc.

If a man is indicted of felony and is committed to the ordinary, he shall not afterwards be arraigned for treason because he is dead in law. Also if a man is outlawed for felony and afterwards is taken, he may have his clergy and afterwards he shall not be arraigned for treason.

Note that the bishop may never deliver such a clerk convict without due purgation. And purgation and no purgation shall be tried by the country, for a proclamation shall be made of this etc. It is otherwise of due purgation for this belongs to the spiritual law.

Note that when a man is arraigned for felony and takes his clergy before judgment is given on him, he is a clerk convict, and if judgment is given on him, then he is a clerk attaint. If a man is outlawed for felony and afterwards is taken and takes his clergy, he is a clerk attaint, because a judgment was given on him. Also if a man abjures the realm and afterwards is found within the realm and takes his clergy, he is a clerk attaint, for a judgment was given on him upon the abjuration etc. The entry ⌊in the court roll⌋ for a clerk convict shall be 'he is committed to the ordinary', and the entry for a clerk attaint shall be 'he is committed to the ordinary without purgation', and thus the clerk attaint is without remedy. If a man is indicted of felony and confesses the felony and takes his clergy, he is a clerk convict because no judgment was given on him. Also if a defendant in an appeal wages his battle and is defeated and takes his clergy, he is a clerk convict because no judgment was given on him.

If a man is indicted of felony and is arraigned on this and found guilty, he shall lose all his lands, goods and chattels which he had at the time of the committing of the supposed felony etc. The law is contrary when a man is outlawed of felony: it shall refer to the time when the outlawry was pronounced, for this is only a contempt that he did not appear etc. If a man commits a felony and enfeoffs another etc., and then is arraigned etc. for which the escheator enters, he shall have an action, and in his title he shall show etc. and conclude 'without that he was guilty' because he may not have a writ of error. Also the law shall be the same against the lord in a writ of escheat etc. Also if a man is outlawed for felony and aliens etc. on which the lord brings a writ of escheat, the alienee may assign error in the process by way of plea, for he has no other remedy etc.

If a man is a clerk attaint by false oath he shall not have an [action of] attaint because the jurors spoke negligently and they have it on their conscience. If a man is attainted by an erroneous process by outlawry of felony and he dies, his heir shall have a writ of error because there he shall lose his inheritance,

pur ceo que il la perdera son enheritaunce, et sil recover il avera sez terres hors del maygne del roy etc. Si le roy pardon un que est clerk convict ou attaynt, et lordinarie luy suffer de escape, le roy navera le escape pur ceo que le roy aver luy pardon per sez letterz patentz et le ordinarie puit monstre lez letterz pattentz etc.

Home ne puit aver son clergy sinon il demaund son clerge pur ceo que [invito][1] non datur beneficium nisi petenti etc.[2]

Lestat est ewe *quaunt un que serra dit clerke* et null puit estre dit clerke si non que aver tonsure quia litteratuera non facit clericus nec [h]abbitus monachum sed tonsura etc.

Si un soit appel de felony et luy prist a son clergye il ne serra deliver al ordinarie devant que un enquest de office soit prise, et si trove nient culpable il [alera][3] quyte si non il serra deliver al ordinarie: sur la sez byens serra forfyet al roye.

Clerk convict[4] perdra toutez sez biens et nemi sez terres et si soit seisi de certen terres ou son feme est seisi et diseisi, lassise serra port en son nosmez et le nosme le feme et nemi en le feme sole, pur ceo que per cell conviction il nad perd ascun terre, et pur ceo que cest action est en le ryaltie. Clerke attaynt[5] perdra tout, le roye avera annum diem et wastum etc., mez nemy dez terres de son feme quar le feme puit prender del roye et tener en fee ferme et sil soit diseisi el avera assise en son nosme demesne pur ceo que per le attender le baron a perde tout.

Ecce modo mirum quod femina fert breve regis
non nominando virum conjuctim robore legis

[CHAPTER 3]

[*fo. 93*][6] *Purveu est ensement que null fyn* [*sic*] *desormez soit demande pris <ne>*[i] *leve*. All comen ley devaunt le fesaunz de cest estatut, si un laron ust estre en gard de gaillour et ust escape enconter le voluntee le gaillour, lez viconte voill aver pris dell gaillour pur leschape un fyn, et apres si leschape ust estre trove devant lez justices il serra auterfoitz charge, le quell fut myscheff, que home serra ij foitz charge pur un meme chose, et auxint que le viconte aver tiell jugement saunz ley, pur le quell vient cest estatut que voet: vide le letter dell estatut etc.

---

[1] MS. reads In lite.
[2] Hand 3. Space above this entry. In margin: M[b].
[3] MS. reads abiera.
[4] In margin: Clerk <atteynt>[d] <convict>[i].
[5] In margin: Clerk attaynt vide Marlebrige c. 27.
[6] In margin: Capitulo predict.

and if he recovers he shall have his lands out of the king's hands etc. If the king pardons one who is a clerk convict or attaint and the ordinary allows him to escape, the king shall not have the escape because the king pardoned him by his letters patent and the ordinary may show the letters patent etc.

A man cannot have his clergy unless he demands it, because 'a benefit cannot be conferred on someone who is unwilling'[1] etc.

The statute is taken *when one shall be called a clerk*, and no one can be called a clerk unless he has a tonsure, 'because literacy does not make a clerk nor habit a monk, but the tonsure' etc.[2]

If one is appealed of felony and takes his clergy he shall not be delivered to the ordinary before an inquest of office is held, and if he is found not guilty he shall go quit unless he is delivered to the ordinary: for this, his goods shall be forfeit to the king.

A clerk convict shall lose all his goods and not his lands, and if he is seised of certain lands, or his wife is seised and disseised, the assize shall be brought in his name and the name of his wife, and not in the name of his wife alone, because by this conviction he has not lost any lands, and because this action has to do with realty. A clerk attaint shall lose everything [and] the king shall have year, day and waste etc., but not of the lands of his wife, for the wife may take from the king and hold in fee farm, and if she is disseised she shall have an assize in her own name, because by the attainder the husband lost everything.

Look, indeed, it is a wonder that a woman brings the king's writ without naming her husband, who by law is united to her.[3]

CHAPTER 3

It is provided also that no fine shall henceforth be demanded, taken or levied. At the common law, before the making of this statute, if a thief had been in the custody of a gaoler and had escaped against the will of the gaoler, the sheriff was able to fine the gaoler for the escape, and afterwards if the escape was found before the justices he would be charged again, which was a mischief, that a man would be charged twice for one same thing and also that the sheriff should have such a judgment without law, for which reason this statute was made which wills: see the letter of the statute etc.

---

[1] *Dig.* 50.17.69. This also appears in Reading A, p. 1, and Reading E, p. 38, above.

[2] A version of this maxim appears in 26 Lib. Ass., fo. 122, pl. 19, 'literatura non facit Clericum, nisi haberet sacram tonsuram'. It may have developed from a statement in the *Liber Extra*, 3.31.13: 'monachum non faciat habitus, sed professio regularis'. Another version appears in YB Mich. 11 Hen. IV, fo. 31, pl. [57] 'quia habitus non facit monachum', per Thirning, and Mich. 11 Edw. IV, *Exchequer Chamber* 2: 190 per Catesby. It also appears in Reading A, p. 1, and Reading E, pp. 37–38, above.

[3] It is reported in YB Mich. 1 Hen. IV, fo. 1, pl. 2 that the king sued Sibyl Belknap in the Common Pleas without naming her husband, who was then in exile in Gascony, and Gascoigne C.J.K.B. accepted the suit. This verse is not there, but per Markham when the case is cited in YB Mich. 2 Hen. IV, fo. 7, pl. 26. It appears other times through the fifteenth century: YB Mich. 11 Hen. IV, fo. 7, pl. 16; YB Pas. 5 Edw. IV, Long Quinto fo. 17; YB Mich. 5 Edw. IV, Long Quinto fo. 68, and is cited by Coke: Co. Litt. 132b. It also appears in Reading A, p. 4, and Reading E, p. 40, above.

Nota que si un home que est pris pur suspecion de felonie eschape encounter le volunte le gaillour le fyn serra de c s., et si cestui que eschape soit atteint de felonie le gaillour perdre c li. Mez si le gaillour suffer tielz pur felonie prisez voluntare eschaper, cest felonie en luy meme et de ceo le gaillour avera jugement de vie et de member etc.

Lez justices de bank le roye et de gaoll delivery enquire de tielz eschapez. Auxint lez justices dell peas purront enquerer dell voluntarie eschape pur ceo que cest felonie. Si un home soit endite de <un>[i] voluntare eschape lespeciall mater serra monstre, et sil soit jure que un tiell fut en son gard que fuit pris pur suspecion de felonie, il peut dire 'null tiell felonie' ou 'null tiell gard' pur ceo quil nappiert pas de recorde.[1] Auxint si un home soit pris pur suspecion de felonie etc. il peut aver laverment pur dire 'null tiell felonie' pur ceo quil nappiert de recorde. Le contrarie ley serra si un home soit endite de felonie et sur ceo arrein, il navera laverment scilicet 'null tiell felonie' pur ceo quil appiert per le record de enditement.

Si un eschape soit trove devaunt lez justices le viconte saunz commawndment ne peut lever lez devers pur ceo quil nest que officer de ceo etc. Si un laron eschape et le gaillour freshment pursue pur luy et luy pris areremayn, ceo ne serra dit eschape etc. Nota quil est le comen use dez justices de gaill delivery pur aver un kalendare dez nosmez dez laronz a chescun sessionz queux remaignont en prison, et si ascun soit absent son eschape, mez ceo serra inquis per due forme quar le gaillour avera responz a ceo et le forme est pur rehers lenditement etc., et le gaillour peut luy excuser pur dire quil fuit remove per habeas corpus.[2] Auxint il peut dire quil fuit deliver per corpus cum causa all chauncery. Auxint il peut dire que especiall commission issist as certeyn pars pur seyer sur luy etc. Auxint il peut dire quil est languident in prisona ou quil est morte etc.

Si un voluntarie eschape de felonie soit, lenditement serra quod felonice et voluntarie permisit un tiell etc. evadere. Auxint dun accessarie de resceit de felonie lenditement serra quod ipsum scilicet tiell recepit et scivit ipsum feloniam [fecisse].[3] Si un constabill arest un home pur suspecion de felonie et apres il vient ovesque le prisoner per mye un town<e>[i]schip et demande eide de eux et ilz ne luy eider per que le laron eschape, le towneschyp serra charge de son eschape quar ilz sont tenuz de assister ovesque le constable. Auxint si un home soit robbe et va sur un towneschip apres le felon et face un hwe, si le towneschip ne face lour pouer pur prendre le laron ilz ferront fyn au roy etc.

Auxint eschape peut estre lou [fo. 93v] un laron prist le gree desglyse et apres eschape, le paroche ou le paroche ajoinantz ferront le fyn.

Si un home soit en prison pur petit larcenye, et le gaillour luy lesser voluntarie, ceo nest mye felonie pur ceo que cestui que fuit en prison ne duist aver devi pur le case de cest enprisonmente etc.

---

[1] In margin: vide quant home serra re[n] all averment pur dir null tiell felonie.
[2] In margin: vide coment le gaillour peut luy excuser sur le kalender etc.
[3] MS. reads facere.

Note that if a man who is taken on suspicion of felony escapes against the will of the gaoler the fine shall be 100s, and if the one who escapes is attainted of felony the gaoler shall lose £100. But if the gaoler allows such a one taken for felony to escape voluntarily, this is a felony in him himself, and for this the gaoler shall have a judgment of life and limb etc.

The justices of the King's Bench and of gaol delivery shall inquire of such escapes. Also the justices of the peace may enquire of a voluntary escape because this is a felony. If a man is indicted for a voluntary escape the special matter shall be shown, and if it is sworn that such a one was in his custody who was taken on suspicion of felony, he may say 'no such felony' or 'no such custody' because it does not appear of record. Also if a man is taken on suspicion of felony etc. he may have the averment to say 'no such felony', because it does not appear of record. The law shall be contrary if a man is indicted of felony and arraigned on this, he shall not have the averment, that is, 'no such felony', because it appears by the record of the indictment.

If an escape is found before the justices, the sheriff without commandment cannot levy the fines because he is not the officer for this etc. If a thief escapes and the gaoler immediately pursues him and takes him again, this shall not be called an escape etc. Note that it is the common use of the justices of gaol delivery to have a calendar of the names of thieves at each sessions who remain in prison, and if anyone is absent, of his escape, but this shall be inquired into by due form, for the gaoler shall have a response to this and the form is to rehearse the indictment etc., and the gaoler may excuse himself by saying that he was removed by *habeas corpus*. Also he may say that he was delivered by *corpus cum causa* to the Chancery. Also he may say that a special commission issued from a certain part to sit on him etc. Also he may say that he is languishing in prison or that he is dead etc.

If a felon voluntarily escapes, the indictment shall be 'that he feloniously and voluntarily allowed such a one etc. to escape', also the indictment of an accessory who receives a felon shall be that 'such a one received him knowing him to have committed a felony.' If a constable arrests a man on suspicion of felony, and afterwards he comes with the prisoner into a township and demands aid of them and they do not help him, by which the thief escapes, the township shall be charged for his escape for they are bound to assist the constable. Also if a man is robbed and goes to a township after the felon and raises a hue [and cry], if the township does not do everything in their power to take the thief they shall make a fine to the king etc.

Also an escape may be where a thief takes the peace of the church and afterwards escapes, the parish or the parish adjoining shall make the fine.

If a man is in prison for petty larceny and the gaoler lets him go voluntarily, this is not a felony because the one who was in prison should not have died for this imprisonment etc.

Nota que si ascun gaillour soit greve encontre le forme de cest estatut per le viconte il avera son remedie per bref de dette envers luy. Et le roy per voy de presentement etc.

<Si un escape de un keper il luy prist arrer et sil ne voile obbeier ceo areste il puit tuer et justifier ceo mort etc.>[1]

---

[1] Hand 3.

Note that if any gaoler is aggrieved against the form of this statute by the sheriff, he shall have his remedy by writ of debt against him. And the king by way of presentment etc.

If one escapes from a keeper, he takes him again, and if [the felon] will not obey this arrest [the keeper] may kill him and justify this death etc.

READING G

WESTMINSTER PRIMO CAPITULO IJ^{DO} que commence

[*fo. 92*] *Purveu est ensement que quaunt clerke est pris pur rete de felony et sil face demande per lordynarye* etc. En cest estatut soient conteyner ij braunches: le primer est que reherce le comen ley, quar al comen ley si un home este arayne pur felonye et il demande le lyver, il ceo averoit et issint cest branche afferme le comen ley. Le mischef devaunt le fesaunce de le ij^{de} branche fuit que quant un felon ust delyver al ordinare per le privelege de son clergie et le ordenarie luy ust delyver et lesse alarge saunz purgation, le ordenarie fuit dispunyshable, le quell fuit mischevous et conforte al felonz, pur que cest estat voiet que tiell home ne serra lesse alarge saunz due purgation. Et covynt estre entendue de clerke convicte, quar clerke atteynt navera unques son purgation, quar le jugement est que il est delyver al ordenarie absque purgatione facienda. Il semble que le comen ley ne fuit si come est reherce per le primer braunche.

Si un home soit endite ou arrayne de felonye, le quell aperist al court destre clerk per lenditement, si come il serra endite per nome de prester ou per le nome de clerke et tiellez semblez, et si le ordinarie luy demande pur ceo que il est clerk, il navera luy si non que il demande le lyver. Et sil demande le lyver saunz responder al felonye il navera ceo, quar lez justicez demandra luy que il dit al felonye, et sil demande le lyver ceo nest sufficient si non que il dit que il est culpable, et dit que quecunque que le enquest dit, il demande et pria le lyver, et donques il avera etc.

En graunt treson null avera avantage de le lyvere et en null petit treson touchaunt le roy meme, si come en fesaunce de money, ou en [occider]¹ de lez justices le roy, mez en autrez petits treasons, si come servaunt [occider]² son master, ou moygne son abbe, icy il avera avauntage de son lyver.

Home navera avauntage si non lou il est en perell de mort, quar si un home ust demurdur [*sic*] se defendendo, il navera jugement de vi et de membres, mez il perdra sez bienz. Si soit arayne pur petit larsonye il navera son clergie pur ceo que il ne morera pur ceo, mez ferra fyn al roy et serra punye per le discretion dez justicez, si come destre [batue]³ ove whippis et ove auterz tiellez.

Home que est blynde mayme ou feme naveront avantage de clergie pur ceo que per le comen presumption il ne peut estre prester.⁴

Si un home demande son lyver il est bon replication adire que il est bigamus, mez il covynt estre jure especiallment coment il espousa tiell feme a per nome,

---

¹ MS. reads occide.
² MS. reads occide.
³ MS. reads bache.
⁴ In margin: nota.

READING G

WESTMINSTER I, c. 2, which begins:

It is provided also that when a clerk is taken for guilty of felony and if he is demanded by the ordinary etc. In this statute there are two branches: the first rehearses the common law, for at the common law if a man is arraigned for felony and he demands the book he shall have it, and thus this branch affirms the common law. The mischief before the making of the second branch was that when a felon was delivered to the ordinary by the privilege of his clergy, and the ordinary delivered him and let him go without purgation, the ordinary was not punishable, which was mischievous and a comfort to felons, for which reason this statute wills that such a man shall not be let go without due purgation. And it must be understood [to refer] to a clerk convict, for a clerk attaint shall never have his purgation, for the judgment is that he is delivered to the ordinary 'without making purgation'. It seems that the common law was not as is rehearsed in the first branch.

If a man is indicted or arraigned for felony and by the indictment he appears to the court to be a clerk, such as if he shall be indicted by the name of priest or by the name of clerk or some such, and if the ordinary demands him because he is a clerk, he shall not have him unless [the defendant] asks for the book. And if he asks for the book without answering to the felony he shall not have it, for the justices shall ask him what he says to the felony, and if he asks for the book this is not sufficient unless he says that he is guilty, and says that whatever the inquest says, he asks and prays the book, and then he shall have it etc.

No-one shall have advantage of the book in high treason or in petty treason touching the king himself, such as in counterfeiting money or killing the king's justices, but in other petty treasons, such as a servant killing his master, or a monk his abbot, here he shall have the advantage of his book.

A man shall only have advantage where he is in peril of death, for if a man has murdered in self-defence he shall not have judgment of life and limbs, but he shall lose his goods. If he is arraigned for petty larceny he shall not have his clergy because he shall not die for this, but he shall make a fine to the king and be punished at the discretion of the justices, such as to be beaten with whips and other such things.

A man who is blind [or] maimed shall not have advantage of clergy (nor [shall] a woman) because by the common presumption he cannot be a priest.

If a man asks for his book it is a good replication to say that he is a bigamist, but it must be judged specially how he married such a woman who was a widow (by name, in which county, in which diocese), or to say that he married such a woman

en tiell countee, en tiell diocis, le quell fuit wedowe, ou adire que il espousa tiell feme le quell deviast apres quell mort il ad espouse un autre feme, le quell serra trie per levesque de meme le diocise lou lez espousellez soit allegez. Et issint est de chescun bygame generall, mez especiall bigamye serra trie per le pays, si come il confesse le bigamye mez il dit que al temps dez espousellez de primer feme il fuit deinz age de xiiij ans et coment que il ad refuse meme le feme a son age de xiiij ans: ceo est bon plee pur avoyder le bigamye et serra trie per le pays et nemie per levesque. Et issint est lou il dit que al temps de espousellez de ij^{de} feme il avoit un auter en vie, et ceo serra trie per le pays.

Bastardis [et] villeynz ne purront estre prestrez saunz licence, et unquore il nest replication a dire que il est bastard ou villeyn. Meme le [*fo. 92v*][1] ley est de home irregular, mez sil soit bigame il est autre. Et unquore il puit estre prester ove licence, mez ceo est don per lestatut de Bigamis.

Le ordinarie est tenuz de apparre devaunt lez justicez de gaiole delyverer ou de bank le roy sil soit demande, sur payn de grevows fyn, mez devaunt lez justicez de peez la il nest tenuz de apparer. Si ij ordenarez apper et chescun claym destre ordenarie lez justicez ne doient prendre ascun de eux, mez ilz doient scriberi al metropolitan et il certifia ceo que est ordenarie et donques serra delyver a luy que est certifie ordenarie. Si ij abbez claymer destre ordenarez, chescun a per luy, lez justicez scriberont al evesque de meme le diocis etc., mez si abbe et evesque chescun claymer destre ordenarie lez justicez prendre le evesque pur ceo que le evesque est ordenarie immediate al court, et il prendra credence a luy et nemie al abbe, quar le court ne voet escrier al abbe en chescun cas si come al evesque, si come si home plede excomengement en ascun action, le quell excomengement fuist fait per un deane ou abbe ou tiell que ad power de excomenger, ceo nest apropos. Le ordinarie puet faier son depute et il covient al depute de mister lez letterz. Levesque face ij destre son depute et le un apperust et lauter nemie, ceo serra defaute de ambideux et il nest force le quell lez justicez assigner le lyver al prisoner ou le ordenarie. Et si ij deputez apper et le un voit receyver le prisoner pur ceo que il est clerk et lautre nemie, unquore il serra accepte a eux in favorem vite.

Si le prisoner, quant le lyver est assigner a luy, ne sache rien lier sur le lyver, mez il dit un verse hors de lyver per roote et le ordenerye voill accepte luy, unquore il navera luy pur ceo que il est a toller le court le roy hors de juris-diction. Mez sil liast si come un clerk devoit et le ordenarie nient obstante luy refuce, unquore lez justicez compeller luy de resceyver sur payn etc. Et sil liast un parolle in le verse bien et un autre male, ore est en le election le ordenarie sil voit accepter luy ou nemie.

---

[1] Westminster Primer capitulo secundo is a header across the page.

who died [and] after whose death he has married another woman, [and] it shall be tried by the bishop of the same diocese where the marriage is alleged. And it is thus for every general bigamy, but special bigamy shall be tried by the country, as when he confesses the bigamy but says that at the time he married the first woman he was within the age of 14 years, and how he had refused the same woman when he reached 14 years: this is a good plea to avoid the bigamy and shall be tried by the country and not by the bishop. And it is thus when he says that at the time he married the second woman he had another [wife] alive, and this shall be tried by the country.

Bastards and villeins cannot be priests without licence, and yet it is not a replication to say that he is a bastard or a villein. The law is the same of an irregular man, but if he is a bigamist it is otherwise.[1] And yet he may be a priest with a licence, but this is given by the statute *De Bigamis*.[2]

The ordinary is bound to appear before the justices of gaol delivery or of the King's Bench if he is called, on pain of grievous fine, but he is not bound to appear before the justices of the peace. If two ordinaries appear and each claims to be the ordinary the justices may not take either of them, but they must write to the metropolitan and he shall certify the one who is the ordinary, and then [the clerk] shall be delivered to the one who is certified to be the ordinary. If two abbots claim to be ordinaries, each by himself, the justices shall write to the bishop of the same diocese etc., but if an abbot and bishop each claim to be the ordinary the justices shall take the bishop, because the bishop is the immediate ordinary to the court and it shall take credence of him and not the abbot, for the court will not write to the abbot in each case as to the bishop, as when a man pleads excommunication in any action, which excommunication was made by a dean or abbot or such a one who has power to excommunicate, this is not appropriate. The ordinary may make his deputy and the deputy must present the letters. The bishop makes two [men] his deputy and one appears and the other does not, this shall be a default in both, and it does not matter whether the justices assign the book to the prisoner or the ordinary. And if two deputies appear and one will receive the prisoner because he is a clerk and the other will not, still he shall be accepted by them *in favorem vitae*.

If the prisoner cannot read from the book when it is assigned to him but he says a verse from the book by rote and the ordinary wishes to accept him, still he shall not have him because this is to put the king's court out of jurisdiction. But if he reads as a clerk should and the ordinary refuses him notwithstanding, now the justices shall compel him to receive [the convict] on penalty etc. And if he reads one word in the verse well and another badly, now it is the ordinary's choice if he wishes to accept him or not.[3]

---

[1] This seems to mean 'irregular' in the sense of being out of conformity with Church doctrine or ineligible for ordination. It consistently appears as 'regular' in the readings. See Reading A, p. 2, Reading C, p. 16, and Reading E, pp. 37, 38, above, and Reading Two, p. 75 and Reading Seven, pp. 113, 124, below. Cf. Baker, *OHLE*, pp. 533–534.

[2] 4 Edw. I, c. 5 (*SR*, i. 43).

[3] This may be a reference to YB Trin. 9 Edw. IV, fo. 28, pl. 41.

Il est dyversite perentre clerk convycte et clerk atteynt. Clerk convicte est quaunt il demande le lyver devaunt jugement si soit apres verdit ou devaunt. Et en ceo cas il ne perdra bienz ne terrez et il serra aprez delyver per purgation. Mez clerk atteynt est quaunt il demande le lyver aprez le jugment et icy il perdra sez terrez et bienz et ne serra delyver per purgation. Et il est dit que per le ley de seynt esglise que si home confesse felonye et demande le lyver que il ne serra delyver per purgation, mez per nostre il nest que clerk convicte en quell cas il puit estre delyver per purgation.

Le ij^{de} branche est que il ne serra lessa a large saunz due purgation. Le payn de ordenarie sil lessa prisoner escape sil soit clerk atteynt est que il paya c li. al roy et ceo est expresse per le estatute. Mez si clerk convicte escape le ordenarie ne payera que c marc., come semble, quar il nest expresse per lestatute.

Si home soit convicte et puis il enfreynt le prison et auterfoitz il est arrayn devaunt lez justicez, [fo. 93] sil appert a eux quil est meme le person ilz recorder un fyn sur le ordenare. Et nest plee pur cestui que est dereymer a dire que il ad enfreynt le prison levesque et pria quil soit restor, mez il peut demander son lyver auterfoitz. Et issint est sil soit delyver per purgation et auterfoitz est derayme devaunt lez justicez. Et il nest plee pur luy adire que auterfoitz il demander le lyver et avoit et pria que il puit estre restor, mez sil demander le lyver et ait xx foitz, puit il aver le lyver.

Si un prisoner escape hors de prison levesque ceo est felonye en luy meme. Et si le gardeyn lessa le prisoner aler de bon gree ceo est felonye auxi.

Si home soit convicte etc. et puis un appelle est sue vers luy il ne respondra a cell appelle quar il ne peut apper en gard, mez contrarie est ou prisoner en le fleet ou en le counter ou en ascun tiel prison pur dette etc., la il apperera et puis il serra remande a le prison areremayn etc.

WESTMINSTER PRIMER CA^O IIJ^{CIO} que commence

Purveu est ensement que nul rien desormez soit demande ne pris ne leve per le viconte etc. All comen ley devaunt le fesaunz de cest estatut lez vicontes en lour tournez voillent enquerer de escapez de felonz et voillent aver assesser fyn pur lez escapez et ceo leve le quell fuist mischef pur le partie quar ilz fuerent auterfoitz chargez davaunt lez justices de en heyr ou devaunt auters justices que avont power. Et auxi lez vicontes queux ne fuerent appris en le ley ne savont dire que serra dit escape ne quell fyn serra ajuge pur escape. Pur que cest estatut don action al partie vers le viconte pur recoverer ceo quil ad leve et auxi quil rendra taunt al roy.

There is a distinction between a clerk convict and a clerk attaint. A clerk convict is when he asks for the book before judgment, whether it is after the verdict or before. And in this case he shall not lose goods or lands and he shall afterwards be delivered by purgation. But a clerk attaint is when he asks for the book after judgment, and here he shall lose his lands and goods and shall not be delivered by purgation. And it is said that by the law of Holy Church if a man confesses a felony and demands the book that he shall not be delivered by purgation, but by our [law] he is only a clerk convict, in which case he may be delivered by purgation.

The second branch is that he shall not be let at large without due purgation. The ordinary's penalty if he lets a prisoner escape who is a clerk attaint is that he shall pay £100 to the king, and this is expressed by the statute. But if a clerk convict escapes the ordinary shall only pay 100 marks, as it seems, for this is not expressed by the statute.[1]

If a man is convicted and then he breaks out of prison and later he is arraigned before the justices, if it seems to them that he is the same person they shall record a fine against the ordinary. And it is not a plea for the one who is [arraigned] to say that he has broken the bishop's prison and to pray that he be restored, but he may demand his book again. And it is the same if he is delivered by purgation and another time is [arraigned] before the justices. And it is not a plea for him to say that another time he asked for the book and had it and to pray that he shall be restored, but even if he asks for the book twenty times he may have the book.

If a prisoner escapes from the bishop's prison this is a felony in himself. And if the keeper lets the prisoner go willingly this is a felony also.

If a man is convicted etc. and then an appeal is sued against him, he shall not answer to this appeal because he cannot appear in custody, but it is the contrary when a prisoner [is] in the Fleet, or in the Counter, or in any other such prison for debt etc., there he shall appear and then he shall be returned into the prison again etc.

WESTMINSTER I, c. 3, which begins:

It is provided also that nothing shall henceforth be demanded or taken or levied by the sheriff. At the common law, before the making of this statute, the sheriffs in their tourns wished to enquire concerning the escapes of felons, and wished to assess and levy fines for the escapes, which was a mischief for the party because they were charged again before the justices in eyre or before other justices who had power [to assess and levy fines for escapes]. And also the sheriffs, who were not learned in the law, did not know what was an escape or what fine should be ajudged for an escape. For this reason this statute gives an action to the party against the sheriff to recover whatever he has levied, and also for [the sheriff] to render as much to the king.

---

[1] This seems to be based on 25 Edw. III, stat. 6, c. 6 *Pro Clero* (*SR*, i. 326), though no amounts are mentioned in the statute.

Le letter est *tanque que lescapez soient jugez per justices errauntez*. A cest jour ne soient ne sont ascunz tiellz justicez mez en lieu de eux soient justices de gaiolle deliverer de queux cell letter serra entende ou de ascunz auterz que ount power per le commycion le roy.

Cell letter serra entende dez necligentz escapez et nemi dez escapez voluntariez quar voluntarie escape est felonye en ceo meme nient obstante que le prisoner ne soit coulpable al felonye don pur le quell il fuit en prison. Si un gayllour lessa un prisoner escape le quell est atteynt de felonye il payera c li. mez devaunt le atteynder c s. Si home prist auter que est utlage de felonye ou que ad [abjure]¹ le realme et luy lessa escape il paiera al roy c li.

Si le gardein de prison lessa un home daler alarge ou descaper le quell est einz pur trespass il nest que trespassur et fist fin al roy et ceo serra per le discretion dez justicez.

Chescun home ad power pur prendre home pur suspecion de felonye et quant il est areste sil lessa luy de escaper necligenter il serra endite de ceo et rendra c s. al roy.

En ascun cas lescape ne serra enquis mez serra ajuge et en ascun cas il serra enquis per le enquest. Si un soit prisoner de record scilicet il fuit un foitz amesne devaunt lez justices ...²

---

¹ MS. reads perjure.
² Fo. 93v blank, the reading tails off.

The letter is *until the escapes are judged by the justices in eyre*. Today there are no such justices but in their place are justices of gaol delivery, and this statute shall be understood to apply to them or to any others who have power by the king's commission.

This letter shall be understood of negligent escapes and not voluntary escapes, for a voluntary escape is a felony in itself notwithstanding that the prisoner is not guilty of the felony for which he is in prison. If a gaoler allows a prisoner who is attaint for felony to escape he shall pay £100, but before the attainder [he would pay 100s.]. If a man takes another who is outlawed for felony or who has abjured the realm, and [then] allows him to escape, he shall pay the king £100.

If the keeper of a prison allows a man to go at large or to escape who is in [the prison] for trespass, he is only a trespasser and shall make a fine to the king, and this shall be at the discretion of the justices.

Every man has power to take a man on suspicion of felony, and when he is arrested if he allows him to escape negligently he shall be indicted on this, and shall pay 100s. to the king.

In some cases the escape shall not be enquired of but shall be adjudged, and in other cases it shall be inquired of by the inquest. If one is a prisoner of record, that is, he was once brought before the justices ….

READING H

WESTMINSTER PRIMER CAPITULO PRIMO

[*fo. 60v*] *En primez voille le roy et comande que le peas du royalme et seint esglis* etc. Al comen ley devaunt le fesaunz de cest estatut lez segniorz et chivalers et tielx graundez homez voil aver vener a un abbey saunz licence de labbe de meme le lieu et auxi voillent aver estre la tout le noet encontre le volunte de labbe et voillent aver pris lour boeffz etc., et ore cest estatut voiet que null home doet vener a null abbey saunz licence de labbe ou del prior, et sil face labbe peut suer action sur lestatut et labbe recover double damages auxi il ferra fyn <aux>^d all roy. Et sil soit tiel home que labbe ne osa pas suer, donques il serra enditte al suyt le roy. Et le process en le action de cest estatut est attach et distrein et all distreint serra iij semaygnez enter le dit distreint purchace et le retorne et sil ne voet apperrer donques auter distreint <issera>ⁱ, proclamation serra fait, et serra vj semaignez enter le bref purchace et le retorne, et sil et sil [*sic*] ne vient adonques labbe eslera le quel il voiet aver capias ad satisfaciendum ou un elegit daver le moite de sez terrez, ou <fe>^d fieri facias, et il recover double damages et le partie ferra fyn al roy. Et quaunt il est enditte al suyt le roy un capias issera envers luy pro fine et serra en garde et donques labbe peut suer un fieri facias et le partie ne viendra hors del gard tanque labbe soit satisfie del double damages.

Ore est avoyr lou le graunt labbe est bon et lou le acte labbe liera son successor et ou nemi etc. Si un abbe graunt a moy et a mez heirz per son seale que a ascun temps que jeo veign jeo avera harboreght et tielx vitelx que il ad etc., ore durant la vie labbe cel <charg>^d graunt est bon, et durant la vie labbe cest graunt liera le meason. Mez si labbe devie son successor ne serra charge sil ne fuit per le comen seall. Meme le ley est si labbe <S>^d graunt a moy harboroght etc. et puis est cree en evesque, cest graunt ne liera le meason et unquore il est ore en plein vie quar il nest labbe de meme le lieu.

Nota si le roy soit foundor dun meason [*fo. 61*] per son prerogatiff il avera un <cr>^d corodie, mez si un auter person <ad>^d est foundor il navera corodie sil nad especialte. Mez si le roy voille graunte cel corodie que il ad per son <c>^d prerogatif a un autre per sez lettrez patentz, le meason nest pas tenuz de payer le corodie all graunte pur ceo que est done a luy per son prerogatyff. Meme le ley est si un abbe graunte a moy de viendre a son meason ove x chivalx ou xx a ma plesure, et puis jeo voille graunte meme le graunte oustre a un autre cest ijd graunte est voide.

READING H

WESTMINSTER I, CHAPTER 1

First the king wills and commands that the peace of the kingdom and Holy Church etc. At the common law, before the making of this statute, the lords and knights and other great men might wish to go to an abbey without the licence of the abbot of the same place, and also to stay there through the night against the will of the abbot, and they might wish to take the abbey's cattle etc., and now this statute wills that no man should come to any abbey without the licence of the abbot or of the prior, and if he does the abbot may sue an action on the statute, and the abbot shall recover double damages, and [the party] shall make a fine to the king. If [the party] is such a man that the abbot dare not sue, then he shall be indicted at the king's suit. And the process in the action of this statute is to attach and distrain, and at the distraint there shall be three weeks between the purchase of the said [writ of] distraint and the return, and if he does not wish to appear then another distraint shall issue, a proclamation shall be made, and there shall be six weeks between the purchase of the writ and the return, and if he does not come then the abbot shall choose whether he wishes to have a *capias ad satis-faciendum* or an *elegit* to have the half of his lands, or *fieri facias*, and he shall recover double damages and the party shall make a fine to the king. And when he is indicted at the king's suit a *capias* shall issue against him for a fine and he shall be in custody, and then the abbot may sue a *fieri facias* and the party shall not go out of custody until the abbot is satisfied of the double damages.

Now we must see where the abbot's grant is good and where the abbot's act binds his successor, and where not etc. If an abbot grants to me and my heirs by his seal that any time that I go [to the house] I shall have lodging and such food as he has etc., now during the abbot's life this grant is good, and during the abbot's life this grant binds the house. But if the abbot dies, his successor shall not be charged if it was not by the common seal. The law is the same if the abbot grants lodging etc. to me and is then made a bishop, this grant shall not bind the house even though he is still alive, for he is not abbot of the same place.

Note that if the king is the founder of a house, by his prerogative he shall have a corody, but if another person is founder he shall not have a corody if he does not have it by deed. But if the king wishes to grant this corody that he has by his prerogative to another by his letters patent, the house is not bound to pay the corody to the grantee, because it is given to [the king] by his prerogative. The law is the same if an abbot grants to me to come to his house with ten horses or twenty at my pleasure, and then I wish to grant the same grant over to another, this second grant is void.

Nota si un abbe graunte a moy per son convent seale de vener a ma volunte cest graunte liera son successor. Mez si un abbe soit et toutz cez monkes sont mortz forsquez luy meme, et puis il soy oblige per le convent seale a payer a moy c li. et puis il face plusourz moncques et devie, en ceo cas lez monkes ne serront chargez. Vide lou labbe liera son successor saunz le convent seale: si un abbe soit oblige a moy per son fait demesne en x li. et puis jeo port action de dette vers luy et labbe morust, en ceo cas javera <aco>ᵈ action envers son successor pur ceo que il appiert per mater de record. Meme le ley serra si un abbe achate xx boefez et puis il est cre en evesque, javera action envers son successors pur ceo que il averent al oeps del meason. Nota si in tempore vacationis lez moncques graunt a moy de vener a le meason a mon plesure <ce>ᵈ etc., cest graunt est voide pur ceo que ilz sont come mort personz en ley.

Auxi, si home soit foundor dun meason del moncques eslier enter eux memez et luy stalle saunz lassent cestui que est foundor, en cest cas le foundor avera quare impedit vers toutz lez monques et il nosmer eux en son bref moncque et il ne nosmer cestui que est stalle abbe pur ceo que il est [*fo. 61v*] que serra encontre luy meme et auxi encontre son action et issint viez que le meason poyet eslier un abbe, mez ilz ne poient luy stall saunz lassent cesty que est foundor.

Viez le diversite enter fyn, rannsome et amerciement: fyn est si come home porte bref de dette sur un obligation et le fait et trove est sur fait, il ferra fyn. Meme le ley est en action de trespass: si le defendant pled nient coupable et il est trove culpable il ferra fyn all roy. Amercyament est sicome home porte bref de dette et soit nonsue il serra amercye. Et meme le ley serra si home porte bref de dette et le defendant morust avaunt accquittal et le plaintiff confesse que il est son fait demesne, il serra amersye. Rannsome est ceo quaunt home vient ou plusors auterz en un countie ou lez justicez du peas sont ou justicez del deliveraunce et ilz ne suffre eux de proceder en lour jugment donques il ferra raunsome solonque la quantite de lour bienz. Et auxi nota que en ascun cas home serra amercye et auxi cez plegges et en ascun cas cez plegges <et luy meme>ᵈ serront amercye et nient luy meme. Et en ascun cas il serra amercie et nient cez plegges etc. quere inde.

Note that if an abbot grants to me by his convent seal to come at my will this grant shall bind his successor. But if there is an abbot and all his monks are dead except him, and then he obliges himself by the convent seal to pay me £100 and then he makes more monks and dies, in this case the monks shall not be charged. Let us see where an abbot shall bind his successor without the convent seal: if an abbot is obliged to me by his own deed in £10, and then I bring an action of debt against him and the abbot dies, in this case I shall have an action against his successor because it appears by matter of record. The law shall be the same if an abbot buys twenty cows and then he is made bishop, I shall have an action against his successors because he had them to the use of the house. Note that if during a vacancy the monks grant to me to come to the house at my pleasure etc., this grant is void, because they are as dead persons in the law.

Also, if a man is the founder of a house of monks [and the monks] elect [an abbot] among themselves and install him without the assent of the founder, in this case the founder shall have a *quare impedit* against all the monks, and he shall name them 'monks' in his writ, and he shall not name the one who is installed 'abbot' because he is the one who is against him and also against his action, and thus see that the house may elect an abbot but they may not install him without the assent of the founder.

Let us see the difference between a fine, ransom, and amercement: a fine is when a man brings a writ of debt on an obligation and the deed and it is found on the deed, he shall make a fine. The law is the same in an action of trespass: if the defendant pleads not guilty and he is found guilty he shall make a fine to the king. Amercement is as when a man brings a writ of debt and is non-suited, he shall be amerced. And the law shall be the same if a man brings a writ of debt, and the defendant dies before acquittal, and the plaintiff confesses that it is his own deed, he shall be amerced. Ransom is when one man or many others come into a county where the justices of the peace or justices of [gaol] delivery are, and they do not allow them to proceed in their judgment, then they shall make a ransom according to the quantity of their goods. And also note that in some cases a man shall be amerced and also his pledges, and in other cases his pledges shall be amerced and not himself. And in some cases he shall be amerced and not his pledges etc., query why.

READING J

WESTMINSTER I CHALONER ROBERTO

{CHAPTER 1}

[*fo. 121*] *En primes voet le roy et comaund que le peas de sanct esglis…*[1]

{CHAPTER 2}

[*fo. 123*] *Purvue est ensement que quant clerk est pris pur rect de felone* etc.[2]
Si un soit atteint per suit de partie il ne ferra purgation: 12 R[ic.] 2 f. v.
Si ordinare challenge un que nest clerk le court seisire cez temporalte, quar lex-amination est al court et nemi al ordinare.[3]
A un moote fuit dit que clerk convicte ne forfator ascun teres mez durant le [conviction][4] et devant purgation il forfetor totz cez bienz et profets veignant del terre, si come utlage en action personell ferra quar qui committitur ordinario est bon jugement, et nest semble a home que est en exigent al felone: il forfet toutz cez bienz al exigent agard, mez dez bienz que ad puis nemi.[5] Et meme ley si soit trove culpable devant jugement, quel est forfeter, ne sil confese le felonie, uncore devant jugement ne forfetera et jeo prove que cest … ordinare en ‹lez›[i] jugement et attendre etc.
Home abjure et return, aver son liver mez ne ferra purgation.
Et si un enfrent le prison le evesque ceo nest mater allege devant que ad fait son purgation.
Fuit tenuz siun confese le felone ou utlage ou abjure le realm et revient ou soit approver, en cex casez sil soit suffer defair purgation est escape: 27 H[en.] 6 f. 7.
Un avera son liver sur le galos et si lordinar luy refuse a un temps et apres luy resceve il ferra fyn: 34 H[en.] 6 f. 64.
Clerk convict ne forfeter cez profetts de son ter 29 E[dw.] 4 f. 4.
Home navera son livere pur petit treson … vide cases 8 M[ich.] H[en.] 6.

---

[1] In margin: Ca 1. The entire chapter of the statute is quoted, but there is no discussion. Three pages following are left blank.
[2] In margin: Ca 2. The entire chapter of the statute is quoted.
[3] In margin: 7 H[en.] 4 f. 35.
[4] MS. reads convorson.
[5] In margin: meme ley dun que fe pur felonie.

READING J

WESTMINSTER I: ROBERT CHALONER

CHAPTER 1

First the king wills and commands that the peace of the holy Church …

CHAPTER 2

It is provided also that when a clerk is taken for guilty of felony etc.

If one is attainted by the suit of the party he shall not make purgation: 12 Ric. II, fo. 5.[1]

If the ordinary challenges one who is not a clerk, the court shall seize his temporalities, for the examination is for the court and not the ordinary.[2]

At a moot it was said that a clerk convict would only forfeit lands during the conviction, and before purgation he would forfeit all his goods and the profits from the land, as in outlawry in a personal action, for 'to be committed to the ordinary' is a good judgment, and it is not like a man who is in exigent for a felony: he shall forfeit all his goods when the exigent is awarded, but not the goods he has afterwards. The law is the same if he is found guilty before judgment (which is forfeiture), or if he confesses the felony, still before judgment there is no forfeiture and I shall prove that … ordinary in the judgment and attainder etc.

A man abjures and returns, he shall have his book but shall not make purgation. And if one breaks the bishop's prison this is not a matter alleged before he has made his purgation.

It was held that if one confesses the felony or outlawry, or abjures the realm and returns, or is an approver, in these cases if he is allowed to make purgation it is an escape: 27 Hen. VI, fo. 7.[3]

One may have his book on the gallows, and if the ordinary refuses him at one time and afterwards receives him he shall make a fine: 34 Hen. VI, fo. 64.[4]

A clerk convict shall not forfeit the profits from his lands: 29 Edw. IV, fo. 4.[5]

A man shall not have his book for petty treason: cf. the cases Mich. [19] Hen. VI.[6]

---

[1] YB Mich. 12 Ric. II. Fitzherbert, *Corone*, 109.
[2] YB Pas. 7 Hen. IV, pl. 6, fo. 41.
[3] YB Hil. 27 Hen VI, fo. 7, pl. 4; Statham, *Processe*, 60; Fitzherbert, *Scire Facias*, 37, *Corone*, 16; Brooke, *Scire Facias*, 8, *Corone*, 4, *Escape*, 3, *Ordinary*, 18.
[4] YB Trin. 34 Hen. VI, fo. 49, pl. 16.
[5] YB Trin. 20 Edw. IV, fo. 5, pl. 3.
[6] YB Mich. 19 Hen. VI, fo. 47, pl. 103.

Un none navera son livere ne auter que soit profese si soit apres que ad unfois fait purgation si [non] un soit infra sacros. Quere, si un demande son liver si soit bon conterple adire que est bastard, quar donquez ne peut estre prist saunz licens et issint peut un que est begamus ove licens. Mez nest semble, quar est ouster lestatut de bigamez causa quar devant cest estatute begamus et auterz navera son [liver] et nul est ouster … lays .. [1]

{CHAPTER 3}

[*fo. 124*] *Purveu est ensement que nul rien soit demande desormes ne pris ne leve per viconte* etc.[2] Quod priscon fragenter.[3]
Un fuit pris pur suspecion de felonie et ne fuit endict, et puis ilz luy lest aler arer et puis il fuit endict et tout ceo fuit present en bank le roy et ajuge que fuit escape.[4]
Si un resceit auter et puis luy less escape ceo nest escape sil ne luy arestt devaunt.[5]
Si home soit endict descape il serra sur ceo arreign en bank le roy nient obstante de cest estatute …[6]
Si bank de roy veign en un counte est pluys haut que justices en eir quar donquez leir cessera en cest counte et ils maund as toutz justicez in eir quils maund devaunt eux totz lour dictes etc.[7]

---

[1] Fo. 123v blank.
[2] In margin: Ca. 3. The entire chapter is quoted.
[3] In margin: f. 130
[4] In margin: 43 f. 20.
[5] In margin: 9 h[en.] 4 f. 1
[6] In margin: 21 Ass 12.
[7] In margin: 27 Ass 1.

A nun shall not have her book, nor any other who is professed after he has once made purgation unless he is in holy orders.[1] Query, if one demands his book whether it is a good counter-plea to say that he is a bastard, for then he may not be a priest without licence and thus one who is a bigamist may [be a priest] with licence. But it is not the same, for it is outside the statute *De Bigamis*, for before this statute bigamists and others did not have their [book] and nothing is further … [2] laymen …

CHAPTER 3

It is provided also that nothing shall be demanded henceforth or taken or levied by the sheriff etc. Who broke prison.

One was taken on suspicion of felony and was not indicted, and then they let him go again and then he was indicted, and all this was presented in the King's Bench and adjudged that it was an escape.

If one receives another and then allows him to escape, this is not an escape if he did not arrest him before.[3]

If a man is indicted for escape he shall be arraigned on this in the King's Bench, notwithstanding this statute ….[4]

If the King's Bench comes into a county it is higher than the justices in eyre, for then the eyre ceases in this county and they shall send to all the justices in eyre that they shall send before them all their indictments etc.[5]

---

[1] See 4 Hen. VII c. 13 (*SR*, ii. 538).
[2] 4 Edw. I, c. 5 (*SR*, i. 43).
[3] YB Mich. 9 Hen. IV, fo. 24, pl. 3.
[4] YB 21 *Lib. Ass* fo. 79, pl. 12.
[5] YB 27 *Lib. Ass* fo. 133, pl. 1.

READING K

STATUTE WESTMINSTER I ANNO 3⁰ EDW. 1[1]

[*fo. 1*] *En primis voet le roy* etc. *que le peace de seint Esglise* etc. This estatute is not but thaffirmance of the comen lawe and was made in tyme of warr and to thintente to make the people the more tymerouse to breake the peace. And thestatute speakethe of the peace of the Holly Churche. The busshopes are conservators of the peace and alwayes hathe ben sins the tyme of Kinge Edward the saint, but it was otherwise before as appereth in the <booke>,[2] in which tyme if a man had made an offence to a spirituall person or on a spirituall possession they that were judges wolde award aswell amendes to the Church as to the partye.[3]

If a man do a trespas with violence to [*fo. 1v*] a spirituall possession, as to breake the churchdores or digge in the soyle, in this case the parson shall have for the temporall possession and for the temporall wronge <an action by the comen lawe>,[4] and for the sainctification he shall have proces by the sperituall lawe.

If a parson be putt out of his parsonage he is driven to sue his spoliation but if they howlde it with laye powre after the puttinge out the busshopp shall make proces against them <and if he cannot remove them>[5] then he shall make certificate into the chauncery and uppon that a writt of vi laica removenda shall goe oute to the sherif for to remove them etc.

Ther are ij maners of breakinge [*fo. 2*] of the peace of the Churche viz. violence done to a spirituall possession sanctificate and violence made to a spirituall person sanctificate. Touchinge the breaking of the peace of a spirituall possession of the Holly Church, it is to be noted that by the writt of vi laica removenda the sheryf hathe powre to remove the laye powre but not sperituall persons[6] nor a man in sainctuary. But yf the sherif fynde anye ther that fayne them selves to be clerkes by fraude, as by puttinge on or weringe surplises etc., he shall remove them. But if the sherif by color put the partie out that entered and put in others, then the partie shall have a specyall writ for to be restored [*fo. 2v*], and the certificate shalbe made by the bushopp him self or by the archbysshopp or by the gardein of the speritualties in tyme of vacation.[7]

---

[1] *Hg* fo. 262 has the heading 'De pace terre et ecclesie et conservatione eiusdem etc. Marowe lector anno regis Henrici <octam>ᵈ vij xviij vacatione quadragesima'. In the margin is 'Westminster primer capitulo primo lectura prima'.

[2] leys Kunite *Hg* fo. 262.

[3] *Hg* fo. 262 adds 'et cell ley fuit deveyd per lavauntdit Roy Edward seynt que ceo que appertyent all esprituaItye all esprituaIty [*sic*] et ceo que touch le temporaIty as temporelI persons sicome a cest jour'.

[4] action de trespas ou auter action per nostre ley *Hg* fo. 262.

[5] mez ill ne peut recover mez sill ceo contynue *Hg* fo. 262.

[6] *Hg* fo. 262 adds 'come reclusez et auterz <…>ᵈ huius'.

[7] *Hg* fo. 262 adds 'mez auterment est dell <pape>ᵈ <evesque de Rome>ⁱ quar ill ne ferra'.

READING K[: MAROWE]

THE STATUTE OF WESTMINSTER I 3 EDWARD I[1]

First the king wills etc. *that the peace of the holy Church* etc. This statute is only an affirmation of the common law, and was made in time of war with the intention of making the people more fearful of breaking the peace. And the statute speaks of the peace of the Holy Church. The bishops are conservators of the peace and always have been, ever since the time of Edward the Confessor, but it was otherwise before then as appears in the <book>[2], when if a man committed an offence against a spiritual person or a spiritual possession, the judges would award amends to the Church as well as to the party.[3]

If a man commits a trespass with violence against a spiritual possession, such as breaking the church doors or digging in the soil, the parson shall have an action by the common law for the temporal possession and the temporal wrong, and process by the spiritual law for the spiritual wrong.

If a parson is put out of his parsonage he is driven to sue his spoliation, but if they hold it with lay power after he is put out the bishop shall make process against them, and if he cannot remove them then he shall send a certificate into the Chancery, and upon that a writ of *vi laica removenda* shall go out to the sheriff to remove them etc.

There are two manners of breaking the peace of the Church, namely violence done to a spiritual possession, and violence committed against a spiritual person.

Touching the breaking of the peace of a spiritual possession of Holy Church, it is to be noted that by the writ of *vi laica removenda* the sheriff has power to remove the lay power, but not spiritual persons[4] or a man in sanctuary. But if the sheriff should find any there that fraudulently pretend to be clerks, such as by putting on or wearing surplices etc., he shall remove them. But if the sheriff by colour [of the writ] should put out the party that entered and put in others, then the party shall have a special writ to be restored, and the certificate shall be made by the bishop himself or by the archbishop, or by the guardian of the spiritualities during a vacancy.[5]

---

[1] *Hg* fo. 262 has the heading: Concerning the peace of the land and the Church and the conservation of the same. Marowe, Reader, Lent 18 Henry VII.

[2] laws of Canute *Hg* fo. 262.

[3] *Hg* fo. 262 adds 'and this law was changed by the aforesaid King Edward the Confessor so that that which pertained to the spirituality [would belong] to the spirituality, and that which pertained to the temporality [would belong] to the temporality, as it is today'.

[4] *Hg* fo. 262 adds 'such as recluses and other <...>[d] such'.

[5] *Hg* fo. 262 adds 'but it is otherwise of the <pope>[d] <bishop of Rome>[j] for he shall not do it'.

And this certificate is not peremptorye to the title as a certificate of basterdye or bygamy is, for it is not here but of office and he shall have a traverse to it. But if suche certyficate be and the partie is exempte of ordinary jurisdiction he may come into the chauncery and ther showe it and estopp the partie of a vi laica etc., or if the writt be passed he may have a supersedeas to the sherif. But in this case the sherif cannot retorne that they are exempt for he cannot take notice of it, and in the same maner is if the partie have title he [*fo. 3*] maye come into the chauncery and estopp the writt <of>[1] supersedeas.

The writ of supersedeas is of 3 natures, wherof 2 are originall and thother judiciall, but to every one ther ought to be a certificate.

1. The first is generall uppon spirituall possession executed, as a church, and that is in possession. The same lawe is of a churche yarde. Otherwise it is of glebe lande: if it be holden with laye powre ther lieth not this writt for it is not mere speritualt but annexed to the speritualtie, nor of anye pywe in the churche lieth this writt but of a tombe it is otherwise. If ther be a waye, as the procession waye, and is estopt and howlden with laye powre this writt lieth not, nether [*fo. 3v*] liethe it for a free chappell onles it be joyned to a churche, then it liethe, for then the ordinarye hathe jurisdiction ther and so [it] is become spirituall.

If a churche be builded uppon my lande and sainctificate no writt of vi laica lieth against me but otherwise it is betwene parsons for parcell of ther churcheyarde.

If a parson do infeff me in his churche and after howldeth it with laye powre, no writt lieth for me against him, for the feffement was voyde as it semethe. But otherwise it is if he let unto me his parsonage for terme of yeres for then <it lieth against him>[2].

If a parson graunt unto me a certen rent with clause of distres [oute][3] [*fo. 4*] of his churche the graunte is voyd <and therfore no writt liethe for me against him>.[4]

Also this writt lieth not for x[thes] for they be temporall annexed etc.

If an abbye be dissolved[5] and no monke ther the founder shall howlde it and no writt <liethe etc.>[6]

2. The seconde is executorie and also grounded uppon matter in dede and that is not generall but especiall viz. ad requisitionem venerabilis episcopi. And if this writt be once executed it lieth not afterwarde, as if induction be once don. But if the ordinarye hathe a newe <cause>[7] then he shall have a new writt. And it liethe where a churche fallethe voyde and the patron presentithe and the ordinarye wolde make induction, and resistans is made with laye powre. It ought

---

[1] ou aver *Hg* fo. 262v.
[2] mez autermest est *Hg* fo. 262v.
[3] MS. reads 'unte'.
[4] *Om. Hg* fo. 262v.
[5] *Hg* fo. 262v adds 'sur toutes …'.
[6] de vi laica removenda vers luy. Le convicte prisoner devesque est tenus ove lay power null bref gist. *Hg* fo. 262v.
[7] title *Hg* fo. 262v.

And this certificate is not peremptory to the title as a certificate of bastardy or bigamy is, for here it is only of office and he shall have a traverse to it. But if there is such a certificate and the party is exempt from ordinary jurisdiction, he may come into the Chancery and show it there and stop the party from a *vi laica* etc., or if the writ is passed, he may have a *supersedeas* to the sheriff. But in this case the sheriff cannot return that they are exempt for he cannot take notice of it, and in the same manner if the party has title he may come into the Chancery and stop the writ of *supersedeas*.

The writ of *supersedeas* is of three natures, of which two are original and the other judicial, but for every one there ought to be a certificate.

1. The first [writ] is general upon spiritual possession executed, as a church, and that is in possession. The law is the same of a churchyard. It is otherwise of glebe land: if it is held with lay power this writ does not lie, for it is not purely spiritual but is annexed to the spirituality. This writ does not lie for any pew in the church, but it is otherwise for a tomb. If there is a way, such as a procession way, and it is blocked and held with lay power this writ does not lie, nor does it lie for a free chapel unless it is joined to a church; then it lies, for then the ordinary has jurisdiction there and so it becomes spiritual.

If a church is built upon my land and sanctified, no writ of *vi laica* lies against me, but it is otherwise between parsons for parcel of their churchyard.

If a parson enfeoffs me in his church and afterwards holds it with lay power, no writ lies for me against him for the feoffment was void, as it seems. But it is otherwise if he let his parsonage to me for term of years, for then it lies against him.

If a parson grants me a certain rent with a distress clause out of his church the grant is void, and therefore no writ lies against him for me.

Also this writ does not lie for tithes for they are temporal annexed etc.

If an abbey is dissolved and there is no monk there, the founder shall hold it and no writ <lies> etc.[1]

2. The second [writ] is executory and also grounded upon matter in deed, and that is not general but special, namely *ad requisitionem venerabilis episcopi*. And if this writ is executed once it does not lie afterwards, just as if induction is done once. But if the ordinary has a new cause then he shall have a new writ. And it lies where a church falls void and the patron presents, and the ordinary would make the induction and resistance is made with lay power. The act

---

[1] of *vi laica removenda* against him. A bishop's convicted prisoner is held with lay power, no writ lies. *Hg* fo. 262v.

[*fo. 4v*] that <thacte>[1] of thordinarye be touchinge sperituall possession, <for if it be for x^thes>[2] or for distresses for the first fruites,[3] thoughe that resistance be made, no writ liethe.[4]

If a bushopp will make induction of a prebend donatyf <althoughe that resistans be made no writ liethe, but if suche a prebend donatyf>[5] be annexed to a parsonage, and he wolde inducte the parson in the donatyf then the writ lieth quia transmutatur per annexionem. Also if thordinary wolde inducte hym in the glebe lande the writt lieth not, but otherwise it is of parcell of that glebe lande geven in augmentation to the <parson or>[6] the vicar or econtra for by that it is translate etc.

Also yf a churche be ruinous and a newe [church] is made uppon the [*fo. 5*] glebe lande of an other seynt, the which fallethe voyde and the patron presentithe a clerk to that, reservinge to him tholde churche, and the busshopp wolde inducte the clerk in tholde churche and the patron resistethe with laye powre, the writt liethe, as it semethe.

If a churche be suspended by effusion of blood and so fallythe voyde, and thordinarie will make induction before that it be sainctefied and resistans is made, he shal have this writt.

If a churche be appropriate to an abbye to holde in perpetual use and after an other will present and the ordinary will make induction and the abbet reciste the writt doth not lie, for by thappropriation the <matter of induction>[7] is gon. But if he have judgment of it to be disappropriated and then will make induction the writt [*fo. 5v*] lieth if recistaunce be made to him. But in this case if he will putt oute the vicar the writt doth not lie if the vicar doth reciste.

Also if a manour with an avowson appendant be appropriated to holde in proper use and the abbet maketh a feffment of the manour togiuther with thadvouson, the feffe presentyth to thordinarye and he wolde inducte his clerk, if the abbet recisteth no writt liethe ageinst hym.

Also if an avowson be appropriate to an abbeye to howlde in proper use and afterward the abbet him selfe presentythe and his clerk is in and dieth and thabbet entreth and holdeth in proper use and after the vj monethes thordinary wolde make collation, yf the abbet recist with laye powre the writ lieth. But if the abbet in the lief of [*fo. 6*] the incumbent will purchase a newe licence, then the writt dothe not lie.

Also if ij joinctenantes are of an avowson, thon geveth that that to him belongethe to an abbot to hold in proper use and thother present to the ordinary that wolde make induction, and the abbot<h>[d] holdeth him oute with laye powre, the writt lieth.

---

[1] auctorite *Hg* fo. 263.

[2] *Om. Hg* fo. 263.

[3] *Hg* fo. 263 adds 'ou de suer fieri facias'.

[4] *Hg* fo. 263 adds 'Item coment que cest act ne puit aylour estre fait, coment que ceo comence lespirituell possession, come induction, visitation, installation, et elecion: mez de admissyon, institution ou de prendre jur p[at]ronatus auter est quar ceo puit estre fait ayllourz que sur lespirituell possession.'

[5] *Om. Hg* fo. 263.

[6] *Om. Hg* fo. 263 sic.

[7] lenducion levesque *Hg* fo. 263.

of the ordinary ought to be [for matters] touching spiritual possession, for if it is for tithes or for distress for first fruits[1] no writ lies, even though resistance is made [with lay power].[2]

If a bishop makes induction of a prebend donative no writ lies even if resistance is made, but if such a prebend donative is annexed to a parsonage, and he would induct the parson in the [prebend] donative, then the writ lies because it is transformed by the annexation. Also if the ordinary would induct him in the glebe lands the writ does not lie, but it is otherwise of a parcel of that glebe land given in augmentation to the parson or the vicar or the contrary, for by that it is translated etc.

Also, if a church is ruinous and a new church is made upon the glebe land of another saint, [and the new church] falls void, and the patron presents a clerk to that reserving the old church to himself, and the bishop would induct the clerk in the old church and the patron resists with lay power, the writ lies, as it seems.

If a church is suspended by effusion of blood and so falls vacant, and the ordinary will make induction before it is sanctified and resistance is made, he shall have this writ.

If a church is appropriated to an abbey to hold in perpetual use, and afterwards another will present and the ordinary will make induction and the abbot resists, the writ does not lie, for by the appropriation the matter of induction is gone. But if he had judgment of it to be disappropriated and then will make induction, the writ lies if resistance is made to him. But in this case if he will put out the vicar the writ does not lie if the vicar resists.

Also if a manor with an advowson appendant is appropriated to hold in proper use, and the abbot makes a feoffment of the manor together with the advowson, [and] the feoffee presents to the ordinary and he would induct his clerk, if the abbot resists, no writ lies against him.

Also if an advowson is appropriated to an abbey to hold in proper use, and afterwards the abbot himself presents and his clerk is in and dies, and the abbot enters and holds in proper use, and after the six months the ordinary would make collation, if the abbot resists with lay power the writ lies. But if the abbot will purchase a new licence in the life of the incumbent then the writ does not lie.

Also if there are two joint-tenants of an advowson [and] the one gives that [part] that belongs to him to an abbot to hold in proper use, and the other presents to the ordinary who would make induction, and the abbot holds [the ordinary] out with lay power, the writ lies.

---

[1] *Hg* fo. 263 adds 'or to sue *fieri facias*'.

[2] *Hg* fo. 263 adds 'Item, even though this act cannot be done otherwise, even though this begins the spiritual possession, such as induction, visitation, installation and election: but of admission, institution or to take the right of patronage is another thing, for this may be done otherwise than on spiritual possession.'

If thordinary will inducte an abbot or prior that is electif and recistaunce is made with force the writt dothe not lie, but otherwise it is wher he is electif and presentable.

If the founder will present one that was not chosen wher he is elegible and presentable, if thordinarye will induct hym and recistaunce is made the writt liethe. But if that the founder may so present and [*fo. 6v*] release to the abbot, nowe is the <induction of th<abbot>[d] ordinarye>[1] gon and no writt lieth yf[2] etc.

If the founder present one that was not elegible and [he] is inducted by thordinarye they shall chose an other abbot without induction, and if the ordinarye will make induction and be recisted with laye powre the writt lieth not, but if they chose one that is not <able>[3], and thordinarye refuse hym and <they chose a newe ordinarye that makethe collation by lapse, and if he be recisteth the writt lieth>.[4]

3. The iij[de] writt that is executorye is uppon matter of recorde as uppon judgment in a quare impedit or darren presentment but otherwise it is in a writt of right of advowson, but in some case he [*fo. 7*] shall have this writt uppon recovere in a writt of right,[5] as if he swe a scire facias against him against whome he recoverd and hathe judgment in the scire facias and after thincombent dyethe, nowe he maye present, and if recistaunce be made[6] the writt liethe, but if he take execution bye the sherif without scire facias and recistaunce is made, no writt liethe and this writt shalbe especiall and shall resite the recoverye.

Also this writt lieth wher a [clerk][7] is to be removed by the ordinarie, as where one is to be inducted <and if recistaunce be made to him where thordinarye him self hath don that>,[8] yet he shall do the contrarye to that and he hym selfe shall avoide it, as if <hanginge>[9] a writt of quare impedit he dothe <it>[10] the partie that recover shall have [*fo. 7v*] a quare[11] incumbravit and uppon a speciall writt for to discumber the churche, and in that case he hym self shall avoyde the same presente to which he made collation and if recistaunce be made to hym with force the writt[12] liethe agenst his owne dede. And the same lawe is in a quare non admisit: if he admitt the clerk etc., he ought to avoyde and remove the clerk and here this writt of vi laica lieth, but quere if he be excused in a quare <impedit>[13] or not.

---

[1] lenterest lordinarie *Hg* fo. 263v.

[2] *Hg* fo. 263v adds 'resistans soit fait'.

[3] labbot *Hg* fo. 263v.

[4] The Tanner translator seems to have missed the sense of this passage. The *Hg* French suggests that it should be rather: 'and they elect a new [abbot], the ordinary shall make collation by lapse, etc. and if resistance is made, the writ lies'. *Hg* fo. 263v.

[5] *Hg* fo. 263v adds 'de advowson'.

[6] *Hg* fo. 263v adds 'ove force all ordynary'.

[7] *Hg* fo. 263v. MS reads writt.

[8] En ceo lou lordinary que ad fait collation *Hg* fo. 263v.

[9] pendaunte *Hg* fo. 263v.

[10] fait collation *Hg* fo. 263v.

[11] *Hg* fo. 263v adds 'juris'.

[12] *Hg* fo. 263v adds 'de vi laica removenda'.

[13] non admittas *Hg* fo. 263v.

If the ordinary will induct an abbot or prior that is elective, and resistance is made with force, the writ does not lie, but it is otherwise where he is elective and presentable.

If the founder will present one that was not chosen where he is eligible and presentable, if the ordinary will induct him and resistance is made, the writ lies. But if the founder may thus present and [he] should release to the abbot, now the induction of the ordinary is gone and no writ lies if [resistance is made][1] [with lay power].

If the founder should present one that was not eligible and he is inducted by the ordinary, they shall choose another abbot without induction, and if the ordinary will make induction and is resisted with lay power the writ does not lie, but if they choose one that is not able, and the ordinary refuses him and they choose a new ordinary that makes collation by lapse, and if he is resisted the writ lies.

3. The third writ that is executory is upon matter of record, such as upon judgment in a *quare impedit* or *darrein presentment*, but it is otherwise in a writ of right of advowson, but in some cases he shall have this writ upon recovery in a writ of right [of advowson], [such as] if he should sue a *scire facias* against him against whom he recovered and has judgment in the *scire facias* and after the incumbent dies, now he may present, and if resistance is made[2] the writ lies (but if he takes execution by the sheriff without *scire facias* and resistance is made no writ lies), and the writ shall be special and shall recite the recovery.

Also, this writ lies where a clerk is to be removed by the ordinary, as where one is to be inducted [where the ordinary had made collation],[3] yet he shall do the contrary to that and he him self shall void it, as if [for example] [pending][4] a writ of *quare impedit* he [makes collation],[5] the party that recovers shall have a *quare incumbravit* and a special writ to discumber the church, and in that case [the ordinary] himself shall void the presentee to whom he made collation, and if resistance is made to him by force, the writ lies against his own deed. And the law is the same in a *quare non admisit*: if he admits the clerk etc., he ought to void and remove the clerk, and here this writ of *vi laica* lies, but query if he is excused in a *quare impedit* or not.

---

[1] *Hg* fo. 263v adds 'resistance is made'.
[2] *Hg* fo. 263v adds 'with the force of the ordinary'.
[3] *Hg* fo. 263v.
[4] *Hg* fo. 263v.
[5] *Hg* fo. 263v.

DE CONSERVATIONE PACIS SPIRITALIUM
PERSONARUM ECCLESIE:
<STAT RIC. 2 ANNO 1º CAPITULO ULTIMO>[1]

At the comen lawe if a man had with <u>[d] violence put his handes uppon a clerk
he had remedy but none otherwise then a comen [*fo. 8*] person by our lawe. But
by the comen lawe for <arestementes>[2] made uppon them entendinge divine service he hathe no remedye the which was violence in the sperituall lawe, and that
was <aided>[3] by the statute of anno 50 Edw. 3 capitulo ultimo that geveth that no
priest <bearinge the ewcarist>[4], or their clerkes, or other persones of the Hollye
Churche when they are entendinge devine service within the churche or and [*sic*]
churcheyarde shall not be arrested uppon payne of greate forfeiture, the whiche
estatute is in the negatif, and yet no forfeture <that is not but an especiall negatif
and doth not geve any payne certen>[5], for the which the estatute of anno 1º Ric.
2[6] geveth a payne by action as appereth by the writt.

The estatute is *gentz de seint* [*fo. 8v*] *esglise benefitez come auters* etc. This
worde *auters* shalbe entended people of the Hollye Churche as prestes,[7] que-
risters, clerkes and other ministers as[8] sextens[9] etc., as they be arrested beinge
aboute devine service they shall have an action uppon this estatute <and so of
wardens of churches, though that they be temporall persones, if they be arrested,
they shall have the benefit of this estatute>.[10] But otherwise it is of other temporall persones that are attendant to devine service,[11] but prystes and their ministers
<that go for to minister etc. shall have the benefite of this estatute if theye be
arrested.>[12] And this arrest is to be intended by the body for of a garnishment,
<distres,>[13] or attachment by goodes, thoughe they be within the churche, it is
[*fo. 9*] oute of the case of thestatute. A habeas corpora is oute of the case of the
statute and the same lawe is of a writt of ravishment of warde, the sherif may take
the warde.

And this arrest is as well intended in writtes of execution as others, as a capias
ad satisfaciendum, but of a writt of excommunicato capiendo shalbe sued and
none other.

---

[1] *Hg* fo. 264 omits the statute reference and adds 'Marowe lector'. It also has 'Westminster primer capitulo primo lectura secunda' in the margin.
[2] distres *Hg* fo. 264.
[3] ordeyn *Hg* fo. 264.
[4] *Om. Hg* fo. 264.
[5] quar nest quun especiall estatut negatyve et ne don null peyn certen *Hg* fo. 264.
[6] *Hg* fo. 264 adds 'ultimo capitulo'.
[7] *Hg* fo. 264 adds 'in son esglises silz sont intendaunts as devyns services ou non. Item toutz lez'.
[8] *Hg* fo. 264 adds 'ryngers'.
[9] *Hg* fo. 264 adds 'ou que port le cruce'.
[10] *Om. Hg* fo. 264.
[11] *Hg* fo. 264 adds 'come in oyer le service ou alaunt in processyon quar ilz naideront de cest estatut'.
[12] et lour clerkes aver sils alaunt ove le corps Jhesu etc. Et meme le ley est sillz alant pur mynister aschun
sacrement come confessyon, euchariste, matrimone, extreme uncion ou tielx sils sont in lestrete ove
surpluse etc. *Hg* fo. 264.
[13] *Om. Hg* fo. 264.

CONCERNING THE CONSERVATION OF THE PEACE OF SPIRITUAL PERSONS OF THE CHURCH: STATUTE 1 RIC. II, LAST CHAPTER[1]

At the common law if a man had put his hands upon a clerk with violence [the clerk] had remedy, but only the same as a common person by our law. But by the common law he has no remedy for arrests made upon those attending to divine service, which was a violence in the spiritual law, and that was helped by the statute of 50 Edw. III, final chapter, that provides that no priest bearing the eucharist, or their clerks, or other persons of Holy Church, shall be arrested when they are attending to divine service within the church or the churchyard upon pain of great forfeiture.[2] This statute is in the negative and yet [there has been] no forfeiture, for it is only a special negative statute and does not give any certain penalty, for which the statute of 1 Ric. II gives a penalty by action, as appears by the writ.

The statute is *beneficed persons of Holy Church as well as others* etc. This word *others* shall be understood as people of the Holy Church such as priests,[3] choristers, clerks and other ministers such as[4] sextons[5] etc.: if they are arrested while they are about divine service they shall have an action upon this statute, and likewise churchwardens, even though they are temporal persons, shall have the benefit of this statute if they are arrested [while they are attending to divine service]. But it is otherwise of other temporal persons who are attending to divine service,[6] but priests and their ministers <who go to minister etc. shall have the benefit of this statute if they are arrested.>[7] And this arrest is to be understood of the body, for a garnishment, distress or attachment by goods, even if they are within the church, is out of the case of the statute. A *habeas corpus* is out of the case of the statute, and the law is the same of a writ of ravishment of ward; the sheriff may take the ward.

And this arrest is understood as well of writs of execution as others, such as a *capias ad satisfaciendum*, but of a writ of *excommunicato capiendo* shall be sued and no other.

---

[1] 1 Ric. II, c. 15 (*SR*, ii. 5).

[2] 50 Edw. III, c. 5 (*SR*, i. 398).

[3] *Hg* fo. 264 adds 'in their churches whether they are intending divines services or not. Item all the'.

[4] *Hg* fo. 264 adds 'ringers'.

[5] *Hg* fo. 264 adds 'or the one who carries the cross'.

[6] *Hg* fo. 264 adds 'such as hearing the service or going in procession, for they are not helped by this statute'.

[7] and their clerks have [the benefit] if they go with the body of Jesus etc. And the law is the same if they go to minister any sacrament, such as confession, eucharist, matrimony, extreme unction or such like if they are in the street with surplices etc. *Hg* fo. 264.

Also a capias ageinst an apostate if he be arrested he shall not have an action. Also a capias for a laborer uppon thestatute shal be served and no action lyeth.

Also a preist that is endited of heresy before the justices of peace and is taken by a capias etc. shall have an action, for by thinditement is not [*fo. 9v*] proved that he is an heretike, nor that he is convicte nor <dissolved>[1] by thordinary.

Also a priest shalbe taken in the churche for suerty of peace and shall not have anye action. In all cases where he shall have an action uppon this estatute he ought to be arrested by proces, for otherwise he shall have a writt of faux imprisonment and not this action.

And a capias for the kinge shall not be served, no more than for an other person, for that that his ministers be prohibited.

A preist may be arrested for felonye and shall not have an action though that he be taken out of the churche.

All maner of seysors by matter in dede are oute of the case of this estatute,[2] as of my [*fo. 10*] servaunt, villyn, or my warde. But if my villyn enter into religion and I wolde sease him in the churche, thaction lyeth.

If my villyn be presented by me to a churche it is no enfraunchisment so no action lyeth for him. But if my villyn be made abbot yet if I sease him he shall have a writt of false emprisonment.

Also I am sherif and a precept cometh to me at an other mans suite to take my villen and I take him within the churche, he shall have an action by this statute and by it he is enfraunchised.

Also if I have a priest to my baylie and I take him in the churche no action liethe, for he shalbe entended alwayes in my custodye. Otherwise it is of mayneprise, for in thone case the wordes are traditur in balium [*fo. 10v*] the which suppose him to be in warde but of mayneprise otherwise.

Also if a priest go into a churche by covin he shall not have avauntage by this estatute. Also if j<ugyment to>[i] arrest one preist out of a churche and he fliethe into the churche before tharrest made I maye not pursue and take him, but if I arrest him and then he fliethe into that churche I may pursue and take him.

If a priest be arrested in the churche for suertye of peace, if he fynde suertie ther he shall not be taken out and if he be he is within the case of the statute. And the same lawe is where he hathe a supersedeas and is arrested, but otherwise it is of an eschape, for ther thother may pursue him and take him for that he was arrested before, so he is judged in his custodye. But where he maketh rescous and fliethe to the [*fo. 11*] churche he shall not be taken etc., for that that he was not arrested.

If a priest be arrested within the churche and eschapeth and flieth into an other churche and the other pursuethe him and takyth him, ther he shall not have the action for the first arrest nor for thother.

---

[1] disable *Hg* fo. 264.
[2] *Hg* fo. 264v adds 'si sont per matter in fait'.

Also, [in the case of] a *capias* against an apostate, if he is arrested he shall not have an action. Also, a *capias* for a labourer on the statute shall be served and no action lies.

Also, a priest who is indicted of heresy before the justices of the peace and is taken by a *capias* etc. shall have an action, for the indictment does not prove that he is a heretic, nor that he is [a clerk] convict nor dissolved by the ordinary.

Also, a priest shall be taken in the church for a surety of the peace and shall not have any action. In all cases where he shall have an action upon this statute he ought to be arrested by process, for otherwise he shall have a writ of false imprisonment and not this action.

And a *capias* for the king shall not be served, no more than for any other person, because his ministers are prohibited.

A priest may be arrested for felony and shall not have an action even if he is taken out of the church.

All manner of seizures by matter in deed are out of the case of this statute,[1] such as of my servant, villein, or ward. But if my villein enters into religion and I would seize him in the church, the action lies.

If my villein is presented to a church by me it is not an enfranchisement so no action lies for him. But if my villein is made abbot and I seize him he shall have a writ of false imprisonment.

Also, [if] I am sheriff and a precept comes to me at another man's suit to take my villein and I take him within the church, he shall have an action by this statute and he is enfranchised by it.

Also, if I have a priest as my bailee and I take him in the church no action lies, for he shall be understood [to be] always in my custody. It is otherwise of mainprise, for in the one case the words are *traditur in ballium*, which suppose him to be in ward, but of mainprise otherwise.

Also, if a priest should go into a church by covin he shall not have advantage by this statute. Also, if [there is a] judgment to arrest one priest [while he is] outside of a church and he flees into the church before the arrest is made, I may not pursue and take him, but if I arrest him and then he flees into that church I may pursue and take him.

If a priest is arrested in the church for surety of the peace, if he finds surety there he shall not be taken out, and if he is [taken out], he is within the case of the statute. And the law is the same where he has a *supersedeas* and is arrested, but it is otherwise of an escape, for there the other may pursue him and take him: because he was arrested before, so he is judged [to be] in his custody. But where he is rescued and flees to the church he shall not be taken etc., because he was not arrested.

If a priest is arrested within the church and escapes and flees into another church, and the other pursues him and takes him, there he shall not have the action for the first arrest or the other.

---

[1] *Hg* fo. 264v adds 'if it is by matter in fact'.

If a priest be arrested in the churche and knowlegeth [felony][1] he <shall not>[2] have an action upon this estatute, but otherwyse it is of sainctuarye.

Also if one takythe the churche for felonye, and afterwarde will not confesse it before the coroner, and is taken out, he shall not have an action uppon this estatute.

Also if a pryest license an officer to arrest him he shall [*fo. 11v*] not have an action, the same lawe is if he make a fray in the churche.[3]

[*null*][4] *minister ou auters*. This worde shalbe taken for them that make tharrest and those that come with him.

If the sherif make his precept to his baylie or servaunt to make an arrest, and he dothe it in the churche thaction lyethe ageinst the bayly or servaunt, and not against the sherif, <but it lieth against him if he make his precept to arrest in the churche>.[5]

Also if ij sherifes be and thone maketh tharrest, the action lieth against him alone. If one come with an officer into the churche and showethe him the person whome he wolde have arrested and prayeth him to arrest him ther no action liethe against the partie, but if he [*fo. 12*] showe one person for an other then liethe an action of false emprisonment against them and not this action.

Also if the sherif arrest a priest within the churche and an other officer by an other precept cometh and taketh him from the sherif within the churche, he shall have an action upon this estatute against the sherif that did arrest him first, and against thother he shall have a writt of false emprisonment.

Also if a preist be arrested by severall proces at severall tymes he shall have an action and recover damages for all. If a joint capias be against ij priestes and they are arrested in the churche they shall have severall actions <uppon this estatute>.[6] Also if the sherif arrest a priest in the churche by 4 capias at one tyme he shall not have but one action and shall not recover more damages but as for one arrest.

[*fo. 12v*] Also if the sherif arrest a priest in the churche without writt or precept he shall not have an action uppon this estatute, but a writt of false emprisonment. The same lawe is if the capias be awarded and the sherif arresteth him before that he hathe the writt. But if the capias come where no originall was yet thaction liethe uppon this estatute.

Also if the sherif arrest a priest within the churche and after retorne non est inventus or no writt, ther he may chose to have a writt uppon this estatute or a writt of false emprisonment but he cannot have bothe, for thone is contrary to thother.

Also if a sherif make a precept to his baily and he arresteth a priest in the churche and after the sherif dothe not retorne the writt, the priest shall have an action uppon this estatute and not a false emprisonment.

---

[1] *Hg* fo. 264v.
[2] avera *Hg* fo. 264v.
[3] *Hg* fo. 265 adds 'il serra trete hors et null action gist'.
[4] MS. reads vell. 1 Ric. II, c. 15 (*SR*, II. 5). Added in a different hand between the paragraphs.
[5] mez si le vicont ove son baylly luy arrest in lesglise laction gist vers ambideux *Hg* fo. 265.
[6] *Om. Hg* fo. 265.

If a priest is arrested in the church and acknowledges [committing a] felony he shall not have an action upon this statute, but it is otherwise of sanctuary.

Also, if one takes sanctuary for felony and afterwards will not confess [the felony] before the coroner and is taken out, he shall not have an action upon this statute.

Also, if a priest should license an officer to arrest him he shall not have an action: the law is the same if he makes an affray in the church.[1]

No minister [of the king] or others. These words shall be taken to refer to the one that makes the arrest and those that come with him.

If the sheriff should make a precept to his bailiff or servant to make an arrest and he does it in the church, the action lies against the bailiff or servant and not against the sheriff, <but it lies against him if he made his precept to arrest in the church>.[2]

Also, if there are two sheriffs and one of them makes an arrest, the action lies against him alone. If one comes with an officer into the church and shows him the person he would have arrested and asks [the officer] to arrest him, there no action lies against the party, but if he shows one person for another then an action of false imprisonment lies against them and not this action.

Also, if the sheriff arrests a priest within the church and another officer by another precept comes and takes [the priest] from the sheriff within the church, [the priest] shall have an action upon this statute against the sheriff that arrested him first, and against the other he shall have a writ of false imprisonment.

Also, if a priest is arrested by several processes at several times he shall have an action and recover damages for all. If there is a joint *capias* against two priests and they are arrested in the church, they shall have several actions upon this statute. Also, if the sheriff arrests a priest in the church by four *capias* at one time, [the priest] shall have only one action and shall not recover more damages than for one arrest.

Also, if the sheriff arrests a priest in the church without writ or precept [the priest] shall not have an action upon this statute, but a writ of false imprisonment. The law is the same if the *capias* is awarded and the sheriff arrests him before he has the writ. But if the *capias* comes where there was no original [writ] the action lies on this statute.

Also, if the sheriff arrests a priest within the church and afterwards returns *non est inventus* or 'no writ', there [the priest] may choose to have a writ upon this statute or a writ of false imprisonment but he cannot have both, for the one is contrary to the other.

Also, if a sheriff makes a precept to his bailiff and [the bailiff] arrests a priest in the church, and afterwards the sheriff does not return the writ, the priest shall have an action upon the statute and not a [writ of] false imprisonment.

---

[1] *Hg* fo. 265 adds 'he shall be drawn out and no action lies'.
[2] but if the sheriff or his bailiff arrested him the church, the action lies against both *Hg* fo. 265.

[*fo. 13*] If the sherif make a precept to his bailye to take a priest where he hathe not anye writt, and the bailye arrestethe him in the churche he shall have a writt of false emprisonment against the bailye and not uppon this estatute.

Also if the sherif make a precept to the baylie to arrrest him and he arrestethe him and dothe not retorne his proces to the sherif, the partie may chose to have an action uppon this estatute or a writt of false emprisonment.

If the sherif make a precept to his servaunt, and he makethe the arrest and the sherif dothe not not [*sic*] retorne the writt he maye chose to have this action ageinst the servaunt, or an action of false emprisonment ageinst the sherif and his servaunt.

Also if an originall be brought [*fo. 13v*] ageinst J. S. and a capias goeth out ageinst W. S.[1] and the sherif arrestethe J. S.[2] in the churche and after the capias is amended accordinge to thoriginall, he shall have an action uppon the estatute.

Also if a capias go oute ageinst one and ther are ij of the same name, and the sherif arrestethe thone for thother in the churche, he shall have an action uppon this estatute. But otherwise it is if a capias ad satisfaciendum in suche case, for ther he shall have an action of false emprisonment or an action <of>[d] uppon this estatute.

Also if ther be ij priestes of one name and a capias goeth out ageinst one of them and the sherif arrestethe <bothe>,[3] he that ought not to be arrested may have an action uppon this estatute or a writt of false emprisonment. <Et face agreement etc.>[i]

This agrement entendid onely to [*fo. 14*] to the partie hym self for if the priest should have a master that had losse by this arrest of his service, yet he shall not have thaction nor amende for it. But if a woman coverte be a servaunt[4] and be arrested in the churche, the husband and wief shall joyne in action.[5]

Also if a capias go out ageinst an abbot and a monk and the monke is arrested in the churche, thabbot shall have an action without naminge the monke. But if the monke be dereigned before the action brought none shall have thaction. But if the monke be arrested and before anye action brought he is made abbot he shall have thaction. But if thabbot be arrrested within the churche and after is deposed or resigne his successor shall not have thaction, but if he be chosen ageine he shall have the action aswell as before. And the same lawe is if he be made abbot of an other place after [*fo. 14v*] tharrest,[6] he shall not have thaction without his abbot and yet he is able to sue a lone for thinges touching his benyfise. The statute is *per fraudem vel per collucionem*, that shalbe tryed in this action.[7]

---

[1]   WA *Hg* fo. 265v.
[2]   JA *Hg* fo. 265v.
[3]   un deux ambideux *Hg* fo. 265v.
[4]   *Hg* fo. 265v adds 'come enter mynchyns'.
[5]   *Hg* fo. 265v adds 'mez si ambideux sont servaunts in lesglise et sont arrest ilz averont severalls actions sur lun in le baron sole et lauter etc.'
[6]   *Hg* fo. 265v adds 'Siun moygn purchace lycens de prendre benefice et est present a ceo et come ill est chauntaunt in lesglise est arrest.'
[7]   The conclusion of 1 Ric. II, c. 15 (*SR*, ii. 5).

If the sheriff makes a precept to his bailiff to take a priest where he has no writ and the bailiff arrests him in the church, [the priest] shall have a writ of false imprisonment against the bailiff and not upon this statute.

Also, if the sheriff makes a precept to the bailiff to arrest him and he arrests him and does not return his process to the sheriff, the party may choose to have an action upon this statute or a writ of false imprisonment.

If the sheriff makes a precept to his servant, and he makes the arrest and the sheriff does not return the writ, [the priest] may choose to have this action against the servant, or an action of false imprisonment against the sheriff and his servant.

Also, if an original [writ] is brought against J. S., and a *capias* goes out against W. S., and the sheriff arrests J. S. in the church and afterwards the *capias* is amended according to the original [writ], [J. S.] shall have an action upon the statute.

Also, if a *capias* goes out against one and there are two of the same name, and the sheriff arrests the one for the other in the church, he shall have an action upon the statute. But it is otherwise if it is a *capias ad satisfaciendum* in such a case, for there he shall have an action of false imprisonment or an action upon this statute.

Also, if there are two priests of one name, and a *capias* goes out against one of them and the sheriff arrests both, he that ought not to be arrested may have an action upon this statute or a writ of false imprisonment. And this was agreed etc.

This agreement is directed only to the party himself, for if the priest has a master that lost his service by the arrest, still [the master] shall not have the action or amends for [the loss of service]. But if a woman covert is a servant[1] and is arrested in the church, the husband and wife shall join in action.[2]

Also, if a *capias* goes out against an abbot and a monk, and the monk is arrested in the church, the abbot shall have an action without naming the monk. But if the monk is dereigned before the action [is] brought none shall have the action. But if the monk is arrested, and before any action [is] brought he is made abbot, he shall have the action. But if the abbot is arrested within the church and afterwards is deposed or resigns, his successor shall not have the action, but if he is chosen again he shall have the action as well as before. And the law is the same if he is made abbot of another place after the arrest:[3] he shall not have the action without his abbot, and yet he is able to sue alone for things touching his benefice. The statute is *by fraud or by collusion*, that shall be tried in this action.

---

[1] *Hg* fo. 265v adds 'as among the servant girls [meschines].'

[2] *Hg* fo. 265v adds 'but if both are servants in the church and are arrested they shall have several actions; one for the husband alone and the other etc.'.

[3] *Hg* fo. 265v adds 'If a monk purchases a licence to take a benefice and is presented to it and when he is singing in the church he is arrested.'

PART II

READINGS ON MAGNA CARTA, c. 1

READING ONE

[*fo. 1*] Magna Carta

In primis concessimus [*deo*][1] etc. Cest parol *deo* [en][2] cest estatut est voyde <al entent destatut>[3] quar per lez primer parolez destatut le Roy ad graunt a dieu et Seint Eglise toutz sez droitz et libertees et dieu nest pas corps acceptable de tiels libertees et droitours, et pur ceo [tiel paroll deo est voyde.][4]

Nota diversite perentre droitz et libertez:[5] droit de Seint Eglise est come si clerk atteint ou convicte et auxi pur [aver] conusauns de plees apurtenant a Seint Eglise. Liberte de Seint Eglise est si come erchevesque, evesque ou parson <ad mercatt>[6] ou autre chose graunt per patent le Roy. Et auxi cest estatut graunt a toutz frank homez [et a lour heires toutz ceux liberties ensuantes][7] etc. [Item, nota quod ecclesia non est persona capax etc. Item ius cimitorie dividitur in duo etc., ius scriptum et non scriptum secundum ....][8]

Droit desglise est si come quant home prent a sa clerge ou que ascun home fua a Seint Esglise pur ascun felonie etc. Questio:[9] si un home soit abjur le reign et en alaina vers son passage il est pris hors de chymyn et est mesner al prison et puis il enfreint le prison et il fua a Seint Esglise ou il purra auterfoith fair abjuration ou non, pur ceo quant il enfreint prison il refusa le benefit de restitution a son chymyn, quar sil ust demure en prison tanque il ust estre amesner al barr per le mater ut supra il serra restitut a son chymyn en meme le degre ci come il fuit quant il fuit pris etc. Mez ore ceo ad il refuse per que il semble quil navera avantage de abjuration etc.

<Posito ci home prist mez benz et offer cel benz je poy priser cel arere. Item un alians in le temps que nul warre est icy mez peez ilz averunt le libertie scilicet de estre su et serra sue. Mez ci home occise home in tempore guarri il nest ...>[10]

---

[1] *T.*
[2] *T.*
[3] *Om. T.*
[4] *T: RA* cest estatut parol est voide.
[5] In margin: Diversitie perenter droit et libertes.
[6] *T* a avera marchaiz.
[7] *T.*
[8] *T.*
[9] In margin: Questio.
[10] New hand, same as marginal note.

READING ONE

Magna Carta

In the first place we have granted to God etc. This word *God* in this statute is void with regard to the statute, for by the first words of the statute the king granted to God and the Holy Church all their rights and liberties, and God is not a body capable of accepting such liberties and rights so this word *God* is void.

Note the distinction between rights and liberties: the right of Holy Church is as when a clerk is attainted or convicted, and also to have cognizance of pleas pertaining to the Holy Church. Liberty of the Holy Church is as when an archbishop, bishop or parson has a market or other thing granted by the king's patent. And also this statute grants to all free men and to their heirs all these liberties following etc. Item, note that the Church is not a capable person etc. Item, the law of the churchyard is divided in two etc.: written and unwritten law, according to ....

The right of the Church is as when a man pleads his clergy, or when any man flees to Holy Church for any felony etc. Question: if a man is abjured from the realm and going on his way he is taken off the road and is sent to prison, and then he breaks the prison and he flees to Holy Church, may he make an abjuration again or not? For when he broke the prison he refused the benefit of being restored to his way, for if he had remained in prison until he was brought to the bar for the matter as above, he would be restored to his way in the same place as he was when he was taken, etc.[1] But now this shall be refused because it seems that he shall not have advantage of the abjuration etc.

Suppose someone takes my goods and offers these goods [in a church], I may take them back. Item, an alien at a time when there is no war here, but peace, shall have the liberty of [suing] and may be sued. But if a man slays someone in time of war, he is not [...].

---

[1] This may be relying on Statham, *Corone*, 27, though there is no escape in that case.

READING TWO

[*fo. 1*] Assit principio sancte Mari a meo
Magna Carta
<*In primis concessimus deo* etc.: sur cest estat est>[1] reherce coment le Roy Henry
le terce, progenitor le Roy Edward, fist <cest>[2] graunt chartre a honour de dieu[3]
et de Seinte Esglise et pur amendement de royalme, devant quell <chartre>[4] ne
fuist use forsque comen ley et un trete que est <fait a>[5] Roundemede. Et cest
graunt chartre fuist le primer chartre [le roy][6] <que unques fuist fait,[7] <en>[8] quel
chartre>[9] le roy graunte <en primez a dieu et per le <dit>[10]>[11] chartre ad conferme
pur luy et pur cez heirz a touts jours *quod ecclesia anglicana sit libera et habeat
omnia iura sua integra et omnes libertates suas illesas* etc.

[LECTURE ONE]

Mes <vide que>[12] cest parol *deo* [en cest estatut][13] est voide [al entent de lestatute][14]
quar per lez primerz parolx destatut le Roy ad graunte a dieu et Seint Eglise toutz
son droitz et libertiez, et dieu nest pas corps acceptable de tielx <...>[d] libertiez et
droitz, et pur ceo cest parol *deo* est voide.[15] <Nota diversite enter droit et libertie
de Seint Esglise.>[16]

[LECTURE TWO]

<Et lestat voet [ouster][17] <quod ecl>[d] *quod ecclesia* <*libera*>[18] *sit* etc.:[19] ceo est
entendre a ij ententez, scilicet a un entent quil soit frank en luy meme de tout
seculers chargez, a un autre entent que null <nief home ne prendre null ordre de
Seint Esglise>[20]>[21] et [lez parols *libera sit* serront a entendre que null home que ne
soit de franc estat ne soy entermettera de Seint Esglise].[22]

---

[1] Item que sur cest estatut que commence *concessimus deo* etc. fuit *I*.   [2] son *E, H, Ga*.
[3] In margin: Nota que devant le fesaunz de cest charter per Henry primer ne fuit auter ley que comen ley
    (hand 1) *H*.
[4] heure *Ga*.   [5] *E*. appelle *PA* and *I*.   [6] *E*.
[7] In margin: Parke[n]s 12 f *G*.   [8] est *Ga*.   [9] *Om. E*.   [10] grand *PA*.
[11] come avant est dit *I*.   [12] *Om. E*.   [13] *PA*.   [14] *E*.
[15] In margin: voyde parols del estatut (hand 2) *H*. In margin: Deo (later hand; hand 1) *E*.
[16] In margin: nota *I*. This paragraph begins the reading in *I*.   [17] *I*.   [18] *Om. Ga*.
[19] In margin: ecclesia sit libera (hand 1) *E*.
[20] prender order de seynt eglise si non quil soit frank home et legittimus *E*.
[21] Item cest parol *libera* est a entendra a deux ententz: scilicet a un entent quil frank en luy meme de
    toutz secular chargez; a un autre entente que null nief home ne prendra null ordre de seint eglise *PA*. Et
    lestatut voet ouster *quod ecclesia anglicana libera sit* etc. Cest clause est entende en cest maner que nul
    serra fait prest si noun quil soit fraunkhome et legitimus etc. *I*.
[22] *E, H*.

READING TWO

St Mary help me in my beginning.
Magna Carta

In the first place we have granted to God etc.: on this statute it was rehearsed how King Henry III, progenitor of King Edward, made this great charter to the honour of God and the Holy Church and for the amendment of the realm, before which charter only common law was used, and a treaty which was made at Runnymede. And this great charter was the first charter the king ever made, in which charter the king granted first to God and by the said charter confirmed for him and his heirs forever *that the English church shall be free and shall have her rights entire, and all her liberties inviolate.*[1]

[LECTURE ONE]

But see that these words *to God* are void for the purpose of the statute, for by the first words of the statute the king has granted to God and the Holy Church all their rights and liberties and God is not a body capable of accepting such liberties and rights, and for this [reason] these words *to God* are void. Note the distinction between right and liberty of the Holy Church.

[LECTURE TWO]

And the statute wills further *that the church shall be free* etc.: this is to be understood to two intents, namely to one intent that it shall be free in itself of all secular charges, and to another intent that no unfree man shall take any orders in the Holy Church. And the words *shall be free* are to be understood that no man who is not of free estate shall enter Holy Church.

---

[1] In margin *G*: Parke[n]s 12 f. Perkins, *Profitable Booke*, fo. 12v discusses grants to the church, though there is no explicit mention of Magna Carta.

Donques en <le>[1] cas quun villen dun segnior soit fait prest,[2] nient obstante cell, le segnior luy peut seisier[3] <de luy servir en quecunque service quil soit, et sil ne peut luy seisier>[4], il avera bref de nativo habendo. Mez le segnior ne peut luy metter a <ascun>[5] occupation mez a tiel occuppation que est honest pur un prest affeir. Et sil purchase le segnior seisera, ou si rien luy discend etc.

[DISPUTATION TWO]

En cas quil soit fait un parson [questio si][6] le segnior poet luy prendre a son meason ou nemi etc.[7]; dicitur que non, quar il ad pris charge de cur et <il>[8] ne peut luy prendre de cell etc. Questio si le segnior peut <luy>[9] seisier cez bienz: dicitur que non, quar il doit estre pur sustiner et maintener le cure; quere etc. Et en cas quil soit deprive ou mys a son benefice, donques le segnior peut luy <seise>[d] <reseise>[10] <si>[11] come <il purroit>[12] devant etc. Et un tiel prist ne peut meintener action vers son segnior nient <pluis>[13] que auter <villeyn>[14] etc.

<Dicitur que si mone villeyn entre en religion que devant le profession <que>[15] <la>[i] je peut luy seisier, ou avera bref de nativo habendo. Mes sil soit professe, jeo navera auter [remedy][16] forsque bref de trespass et recover mes damages vers labbe, sicome home prent mon <villein>[17] a feme etc.[18] En meme le maner serra fait dun feme quest villen si ele entre en religion etc.

Et auxi dicitur que si <un>[19] villen soit fait prest, et il ad un prebend [fo. 1v] ou auter benefice per quell il na cur et [que le][20] segnior luy peut seisir assetz bien.[21]

[LECTURE THREE]

Nota [quil est][22] diversite enter droit [de Seynt Eglise][23] et libertie <de Seynt Eglise>[24] >[25] <Droit <de Seynt Eglise>[26]>[i] est sicome de saver [un][27] clerk atteint [ou convicte],[28] et auxint pur aver conusance dez <plez>[i] [29] appurtenauntz a Seint Eglise.[30] Et libertez de Seynt Esglise est sicome archevesque, evesque, <ou>[31] parson [de Seint Esglise][32] etc. ount market ou autrez chosez grauntez per

---

[1] cest *I.*

[2] In margin: Coment un villein fait prist uncore le segnior sesie (damaged; hand 3), *H.* In margin: villenage (hand 2) *E.*

[3] In margin: Villen prestre *Ga.*

[4] *Om. I.*   [5] auter *I.*   [6] *I;* le quel *U, Ga.*

[7] In margin: generaltie pluis … que particuleratie (faded, later; hand 4) *H.*

[8] le segnior *I.*   [9] *Om. E.*   [10] seiser *E.*   [11] *Om. E.*   [12] *Om. E.*

[13] *Om. I.*   [14] *Om. Ga.*   [15] *Om. Ga.*   [16] *G;* recovery *U.*   [17] neif *H, Ga.*

[18] In margin: un home peut seiser lez bienz dun abbe ou prest mez nemi dun parson son villein etc. (hand 1) *H.* In margin: 4 E[dw.] 4 25 1 *G.*

[19] mon *Ga.*   [20] *E;* son *U, Ga.*

[21] In margin: vide diversitatem enter droiture et liberte (hand 1) *H.*

[22] *E.*   [23] *E, Ga.*   [24] *Om. Ga.*

[25] *Om. I* (from 'Dicitur que' two paragraphs before).

[26] *Om. Ga.*   [27] *E.*   [28] *E, H, Ga, I.*   [29] *Om. H.*

[30] In margin: Dicitur del esglise liberte (hand 1 to esglise, hand 2 for liberte) *E.*

[31] aulter *Ga.*   [32] *Ga.*

Then in the case that the villein of a lord is made a priest, this notwithstanding the lord may seize him to serve him in whatever service he may, and if he cannot seize him he shall have a writ *de nativo habendo*.[1] But the lord cannot put him to any occupation except an occupation which is reputable for a priest. And if [the villein priest] purchases, the lord shall seize [the thing purchased], or if anything descends to him etc.

[Disputation Two]

In the case where he is made a parson, it was asked if the lord may take him to his house or not etc.: it was said not, for he has taken charge of the cure and [the lord] may not take him from this etc. It was asked if the lord may seize his goods and it was said not, for they are for sustaining and maintaining the cure: query etc. And in the case where he is deprived or put out of his benefice, then the lord may reseize him as he could before etc. And such a priest may not maintain an action against his lord any more than any other villein etc.

It was said that if my villein enters in religion that I may seize him before the profession or have a writ *de nativo habendo*. But if he is professed I shall have no other remedy except a writ of trespass, and to recover my damages against the abbot, just as when a man takes my villein to wife etc.[2] It shall be done in the same way with a woman who is a villein if she enters in religion etc.

And also it was said that if a villein is made priest, and he has a prebend or another benefice with which he does not have cure [of souls], that the lord may seize him well enough.

[Lecture Three]

Note that there is a distinction between the right of Holy Church and the liberty of Holy Church. The right of Holy Church is such as to save a clerk attaint or convict, and also to have cognizance of pleas belonging to Holy Church. And the liberties of Holy Church are as when an archbishop, bishop, or parson of Holy Church etc. has a market or other things granted by the king's [letters]

---

[1] *Register*, 87.
[2] In margin *G*: 4 E[dw.] 4 25 1: YB Mich. 4 Edw. IV, fos 24–25, pl. 2.

patentz le roy etc. Auxint cest estatut graunt a toutz <frankez homez touts lez>[1] libertiez <ensuantez>.[2]

[DISPUTATION ONE?]

Et nota[3] quil semble que le graunt de ceux parolez quant il dit *in primis conces-simus deo* etc. [sont][4] voide come est avaunt dit, pur ceo que dieu nest <pas>[5] person capax. Mez le grant <est>[6] assetz bon pur ceo que le ley fuist a cell jour de fair graunt <per>[7] tielx generalx parolx.[8] Mes a cest jour tiel graunt serra voide, pur ceo que le ley est chaunge a cel entent etc.,[9] <quar>[10] a cest jour si un home done terrez a un esglise per ceo parols [deo et][11] ecclesie beate marie, sil ne nomer ascun home, le don est voide pur ceo que leglise nest <person>[12] capax. Mes si le don soit fait al parson de tiell esglise et a son successors imperpetuum, donques le don est bon, pur ceo que le parson est person capax etc.[13]

En cas quun don soit fait a un convent ou a un abbey saunz nosmer le abbot, le don est voide, <quar>[14] le convent ne labbey ne sont [pas][15] personz capax etc. Mes sil soit fait al abbot et al convent <issint quil ad un person capax>[16] le don est bon[17] etc. En cas quun don soit fait a un abbot et al convent <imperpetuum>[18], quere quel estat ils ont. Dicitur quils ne ont que estat a terme de vie labbe, quar ceux parolx ne done ascun enheritaunce a meason <nient>[19] pluis que <si>[20] ten-ementz soient donez <a un home>[21] imperpetuum: [per cest don][22] il nad que estat <a terme de>[23] vie[24], <pur ceo quil ne peut aver estat en fee saunz parolz denheri-taunce, scilicet a luy et a sez heirz. Issint dun don fait a un abbot et al convent imperpetuum, <il nest don etc.,>[25] saunz ceo que le don soit a luy et a son suc-cessors etc.>[26]

Nota que [si][27] un don fait a un abbot et a son successors, <<cest>[i] [don][28] [est] si bon enheritaunce al meason sicome un don fait al abbot, convent, et a ses suc-cessors etc.>[29] Et nota quun don fait a un comonaltie dun vill lou ils ount maire ou baillif, saunz nosmer le meir etc., <cest done>[30] <ne vaut riene>[31] causa patet. Et nota quun don fait a un comonaltie lou ils nount maier [ou baillif][32] est assetz bon, et en meme le maner un don fait a un fraternite etc.[33]

---

[1] *Om. Ga.*   [2] et frauncheez *I.*

[3] In margin: donez (hand 2) *E.* In margin: nota *I.*

[4] *E*; Que il est *U, Ga, I.*   [5] *Om. E.*   [6] nest *Ga.*   [7] a *Ga.*

[8] In margin: dones (hand 1), *E.*

[9] In margin: Nota de rent graunt gardians ou … laminis ou fraternite en un Esglise nient corporat le graunt est voide mez le parsone ou vicar peut prescriber pur eux (hand 1) *H.*

[10] Item nota *I.*   [11] *E.*   [12] *Om. Ga.*

[13] In margin: corporation (hand 2) *H.*

[14] et *Ga.*   [15] *I.*   [16] et lour successors *I.*

[17] In margin: 10 E[dw.] 4 153 (hand 2) *H.*

[18] *Om. Ga.*   [19] *Om. Ga.*   [20] *Om. E.*   [21] *Om. I.*

[22] *Ga.*   [23] pur *Ga.*

[24] 11 H[en.] 7 12 acc, 11 H[en.] 4 83 contra in margin *Ga.*

[25] *Om. E.*   [26] *Om. Ga* (from 'pur ceo quil').

[27] *Ga, I.*   [28] *E.*   [29] *Om. H, Ga.*

[30] *I.*   [31] est voide *E.*   [32] *I.*

[33] In margin: 21 E[dw.] 4 90 & 39 H[en.] 6 14 per Prisot (hand 2) *H.* In margin: Nota *I.*

patent etc. Also this statute grants to all free men all the liberties following.

[DISPUTATION ONE?]

And note that it seems that the grant by these words, when it says *in the first place we have granted to God*, are void as is said above, because God is not a capable person. But the grant is good enough because the law was in those days to make a grant by such general words. But today such a grant shall be void because the law is changed to this intent etc., for today if a man gives lands to a church by these words 'to God and the church of St Mary', if he does not name any man the grant is void, because the church is not a capable person. But if the grant was made to the parson of such a church and to his successors in perpetuity then the grant is good, because the parson is a capable person etc.

In the case where a grant is made to a convent or to an abbey without naming the abbot, the grant is void, for neither the convent nor the abbey are capable persons. But if it is made to the abbot and the convent, so that there is a capable person, the grant is good etc.[1] In the case where a grant is made to an abbot and to the convent in perpetuity, query what estate they have. It was said that they only have an estate for term of life of the abbot, for those words do not give any inheritance to the house any more than if lands were given to a man in perpetuity: by this gift he only has an estate for term of life,[2] because he cannot have an estate in fee without words of inheritance, namely, 'to him and to his heirs'. Likewise of a grant made to an abbot and convent in perpetuity; it is not a grant etc., unless the grant is to him and his successors etc.

Note that if a grant is made to an abbot and to his successors, this grant is as good an inheritance to the house as a grant made to the abbot, convent, and their successors etc. And note that a grant made to the commonalty of a vill where there is a mayor or bailiff, which does not name the mayor etc., is worth nothing, *causa patet*. And note that a grant made to a commonalty where there is no mayor or bailiff is good enough, and in the same manner a grant made to a fraternity.[3]

---

[1] In margin *H*: 10 E[dw.] 4 153 (hand 2).
[2] In margin *G*: 11 H[en.] 7 12 acc, 11 H[en.] 4 83 *contra* in margin. YB Mich. 11 Hen. VII, fo. 12, pl. 36; YB Trin. 11 Hen. IV, fo. 83, pl. 31.
[3] In margin *H*: 21 E[dw.] 4 90 et 39 H[en.] 6 14 per Prisot (hand 2). YB Mich. 21 Edw. IV, fos 12–15, pl. 4; YB Mich. 39 Hen. VI, fo. 13, pl. 17.

[LECTURE THREE, VERSION TWO]

Item le estatut <parle>[1] ouster <*quod ecclesia*>[2] *habeat omnia iura sua* [*fo. 2*] *integra* etc.[3]: cest entendre que lez jugges de Seynt Eglise eiaunt <conusaunce>[4] <de toutz maners de>[5] punisses et determinations dez pleez que touch matrimony ou testament, [et des][6] dismez, oblations, mortuary, [et huiusmodi],[7] et auxint de toutz [ceux][8] [auters][9] maners de pointz que touchent le correcion de alme: ceux sount iura ecclesie etc.[10]

Et ceux parolx *libertates illoque* sount a entendre si come divers esglises ount divers libertiez, sicome Westm' et auterz <lieus>[11] privileges semble.

Et <auxint privilege>[12] de Seint Esglise est [daver un clerke save per son clergie][13] [et il, per le privilage de Seynt Eglise],[14] <quil>[15] serra livere al ordinare,[16] et unquor en ceo cas le ley dengleterre est pluis favorable a luy que <est>[17] le ley de Seynt Eglise, quar tout soit quil nad mye tonsure ne vestment come clerke [devoiet aver][18] unquore il serra livere al ordinarie.

Et auxint si home soit endite de felonie et soy fewe a Seint Esglise, il demura illoques per xl jours et adonques il prendre son chymyn hors de royalme et ceux et tielx <semble>[19] sont lez privilegez de Seynt Eglise.

[DISPUTATION THREE]

Et nota que lordinarie doit estre prist a chescun deliveraunce a demander cez clerks.[20] Donques en cas quun soy prent a son clergie et lordinarie ne soit prist a luy demander, quere que serra fait le quell lez justicez proceder a fair <examination>[21] ou nemi. Dicitur que le clerk serra [committe sur][22] remys al prison et un bref agard <vers lordinarie>.[23] <Quere quel bref afair lordinarie venir>[24] sur le pene dun contempt, et sil ne venit etc. touts son temporalties serra seisiez en le mayn le roy etc.

Et si un ordinary soit [prist le][25] present quant un clerk luy prent a son clergie, il est en election [de][26] lordinarie le quel il luy voet aver ou non, et si lordinarie luy voill aver quaunt il nest able, si lez justicez veient quil nest <my>[27] sufficient lettere daver benefite de son clergie il navera benefite etc.[28] [Et nota que per lestatut de Westminster primer capitulo primo lordinarie peut luy prendre a son parel.][29]

---

[1] dit *I*.   [2] et *PA, I*.

[3] In margin: iura (hand 1) *H*. In margin: iura ecclesia (hand 1) *E*. In margin: Nota *I*.

[4] causez *I*.   [5] *Om. PA, I*.   [6] *PA, I*.   [7] *E*.   [8] *E*.   [9] *H, PA, I*.

[10] In margin: Iura *U*. Passage on writ of trespass for tithe corn is here in *E* see p. 76, n. 28.

[11] *Om. H*; villez *E*.

[12] le droit *E; auxint nota il est le droit I*.

[13] *E, I*. At end of chapter *U*.   [14] *E*.   [15] *Om. E*.

[16] In margin: privilege *U*. In margin: droit del eglise (hand 2) *E*; privileges clarke (hand 1) *E*. In margin: Privelege (hand 1) *H*.

[17] nest, *U*.   [18] *E, H, PA*.   [19] *Om. E*.

[20] In margin: Vide lordinar doit estre prist etc. *H*.

[21] execution *I*.   [22] *E*.

[23] *I*, admetter sur le peyne dun contempt et sil ne veign *E*.

[24] *Om. I*.   [25] *I*.   [26] *E*.   [27] *Om. I*.

[28] In margin: vide statutum *I*.   [29] *I*.

[LECTURE THREE, VERSION TWO]

And the statute says further *that the church shall have all her rights entire* etc.: this is to be understood that the judges of Holy Church shall have cognizance of all manners of punishment and determination of pleas which touch matrimony or testament, and of tithes, oblations, mortuaries and such things, and also of all those other things which touch the correction of the soul: these are the Church's rights.

And these words *and her liberties* are to be understood that various churches have various liberties, such as Westminster and other similar privileged places.

And also the privilege of Holy Church is to have a clerk saved by his clergy and he, by the privilege of Holy Church, shall be delivered to the ordinary, and also in this case the law of England is more favourable to him than is the law of Holy Church, for even if he had neither tonsure nor vesture as a clerk ought to have, still he shall be delivered to the ordinary.

And also if a man is indicted of felony and flees to Holy Church he shall remain there for forty days, and then he shall make his way out of the realm, and these and things like them are the privileges of Holy Church.

[DISPUTATION THREE]

And note that the ordinary must be ready at every [gaol] delivery to demand his clerks. Then in the case where one takes his clergy and the ordinary is not there to demand him, query what shall be done: should the judges proceed to make an examination or not? It was said that the clerk shall be sent back to the prison and a writ granted against the ordinary. Query what writ to make the ordinary come on pain of a contempt, and if he does not come etc. all his temporalities shall be seized into the king's hand etc.

And if the ordinary is present when a clerk takes his clergy it is the ordinary's choice whether he wishes to have him or not, and if the ordinary wishes to have him when he is not able, if the judges see that he is not sufficiently lettered to have benefit of his clergy, he shall not have benefit. And note that by the statute of Westminster, I c. 1, the ordinary may take him at his peril.[1]

---

[1] Westminster I *rectius* c. 2 (*SR*, i. 28).

Et nota[1] quil est droit de Seint Eglise de salver un home que ad fait felon sil demander le grith <de Seint Esglise>.[2] <Sicome un home occist un auter et prent [le gerth de][3] Seint Eglise il doit estre salve per le privilege et droit de Seint Esglise>,[4] et durant xl jours chescun home et feme poierent don a luy manger ou boier <ou ascun auter refreschement>,[5] et il ne serra empeche de ceo. Mes apris lez xl jours sils donent a eux manger ou boyer, ou ascun auter refreshment, ilz serra punys come resceyttours ou supportours dez felons [*fo. 2v*] le roy [serra][6] etc.[7]

Et nota si apris lez xl jours il ale hors de greth et occist un auter home et <reprent>[8] eglise arermayn, il avera le privilege per xl jours, et chescun home [peut][9] done a luy maunger et boyer etc. saunz enpechement <durant lez xl jours>,[10] mes nemi apris, et sil fait issint xx foitz il avera <le>[11] privilege apris chescun foitz etc. Et <nota>[i] si un home occist un auter en semytory <ou un>[12] eglise, <unquore>[13] il avera le privilege de cel eglise etc. Mes si un home <esteant sur le greth dun esglise>[14] occise un <auter>[15] deinz meme legles,[16] il navera le privilege [de meme lesglise, mez sil prent auter esglise quere sil aver ou noun etc.][17] <quere le cause de le diversite etc.>[18]

Et nota si un home prent le <g>[d] greth de Seint Esglise et soy tient de deinz per xl jours il soi peut tenir einz per si long temps apris si come il voiet, et lez officers le roy ne poient entre de luy prendre hors etc., ne ceux del eglise ne poient luy metter hors del boundes del eglise, quar sils fount cell et <il soit pris mort>,[19] ils serra dit regulers. Et pur ceo en cell cas lez officers le roy [et ceux del ville que ount charge de luy][20] poyent luy murer etc.

Et si [un][21] tiell felon quest deinz le greth voet abjure le royalme, il peut demanda un coroner,[22] et le coroner doit vener a luy et le felon doit conustre le felone et le coroner donera a luy <son>[23] jurament, et il luy don un sign de la cruse [en son mayn],[24] et <doit>[25] assigner a luy a quell port il doit passer oustre le mer, et doit maundre luy al [prochein][26] constablez de le prochein vill, et il luy maunder al constable de le prochein vill, [et sic de singulis][27] etc. Et issint chescun constable a auter tanque il vient a le porte etc. Et <sill ne ale>[28] le plus prochein voie a le porte, <et>[29] quant il vient a le port [il ne aler][30] ouster le mer <einz resortera>[31] en le terre scilicet per ascun auter voie, sil peut estre pris, il <serra>[32] arreigne sur ceo et morter etc.[33]

---

[1] In margin: droit del Eglise (hand 2) *H.* In margin: sanctuary (hand 1) *E.*
[2] *Om. I.*   [3] *I.*   [4] *Om. H.*   [5] *Om. H, I.*
[6] *E;* serreunt *I.*
[7] In margin: Senctuary (hand 2) *H.*
[8] revient al *I.*   [9] *E, H, I.*   [10] *Om. E.*   [11] ceo *E.*
[12] de un *H;* dun *I.*   [13] nient contreteant *I.*
[14] quad prent le privilege de Seint Esglise *I.*   [15] home *I.*
[16] In margin: Nota diversitatem *I.*   [17] *I.*   [18] *Om. I.*
[19] apris il est mort *I.*   [20] *E.*   [21] *E.*
[22] In margin: Abjuration (hand 2) *H.*
[23] *Om. E.*   [24] *I.*   [25] auxint *I.*   [26] *I.*
[27] *E;* que est prochein etc. *I.*   [28] il alera *H.*   [29] ou *I.*   [30] *I;* aler *U.*
[31] mez revient *I.*   [32] *Om. I.*   [33] In margin: Nota *I.*

And note that it is the right of Holy Church to save a man who has committed a felony if he demands the grith of Holy Church.[1] Thus if a man killed another and took the grith of Holy Church, he may be saved by the privilege and right of Holy Church, and for forty days any man and woman may give him food and drink, or any other refreshment, and he shall not be hindered from this. But after the forty days if they give [him] food and drink or any other refreshment, they shall be punished as receivers or supporters of the king's felons etc.

And note that if after the forty days he goes out of the grith and kills another man and takes to the church again, he shall have the privilege for forty days, and every man may give him food and drink etc. without hindrance during the forty days, but not afterwards, and if the felon does this twenty times he shall have this privilege afterwards each time etc. And note that if a man kills another in a churchyard or a church, still he shall have the privilege of this church etc. But if a man in the grith of Holy Church kills another within the same church he shall not have the privilege of the same church, but if he takes another church, query if he shall have it or not etc.: query the reason for this distinction etc.

And note that if a man takes the grith of Holy Church and stays within for forty days, he may stay within for as long time afterwards as he wishes, and the king's officers may not enter to take him out etc., nor may those of the church send him out of the bounds of the church, for if they do this and he is killed afterwards they shall be called regulars[2] etc. And for this reason in this case the king's officers and those of the vill who have charge of him may immure him etc.

And if such a felon who is within the grith wishes to abjure the realm he may demand a coroner, and the coroner must come to him, and the felon must confess the felony, and the coroner shall give to him his oath, and he shall give him a sign of the cross in his hand, and must assign him a port from which he must pass over the sea, and he must send him to the constable of the next vill who shall send him to the constable of the next vill, and thus from one to the next. And thus from each constable to the next until he comes to the port etc. And if he does not go the nearest way to the port, and when he comes to the port does not go over the sea but returns to the land, that is, by another way, if he is taken he shall be arraigned thereupon and put to death etc.

---

[1] Grith: an Old English word originally meaning domicile or home, but by the later Middle Ages effectively meaning sanctuary.

[2] This seems to mean 'irregular' in the sense of being out of conformity with Church doctrine or ineligible for ordination. It consistently appears as 'regular' in the readings. See Reading A, p. 2, Reading C, p. 16, Reading E, pp. 37, 38, and Reading G, p. 53, above, and Reading Seven, pp. 113, 124, below.

[Disputation Four]

Et nota que liberte de Seint Esglise est pur aver feir <oue>[1] market ou ascun auter franchise et ceux veign de graunt le roy et nemi de lour droit demesne.[2] Et en tiels liberties le roy peut [enter][3] et metter eux hors sils <soient misse use etc.>[4]

Et auxi ascun auters esglise ount autres libertiez, si come Westm', Seynt Martyn, et <auterz etc.>[5] <ount libertes que>[6] <si>[7] ascun felon ou home que est endite ou que ad fait ascun trespas [ou][8] treason ou ascun autre, quil serra salve durant le temps quil est deinz le seintwarie etc.[9] Et auxint [en][10] Beverley, si un home occist [fo. 3] un alter et prent le sentwerie de Beverley il serra salve, mez il ne serra salve <deinz le sentwerie Beverley>[11] pur <null>[12] felonie ne trespas mes soulement pur mort de home etc.[13]

Et si ascun esglise que ad tiel libertie mysse use lour libertie[14] le roy ne peut [luy][15] seisier, et le cas est pur ceo que le roy ne peut [my][16] entre <mes>[17] en ceux liberties quex fuerent grauntes a Seint Esglise per luy ou per son progenitors [il peut entre et][18] tiels liberties ne poient estre graunt per eux mez per le pope per que etc. Et sic vide diversitatem <quere etc.>[19]

<Et [nota que][20] en cas[21] que bref de trespass soit port en court le roy de <cez>[22] bleez emporter et le defendant dit quilz fuerent cez dismez, saunz ceo quils fuer-ent [sez bleez][23] etc., et le plaintiff dit meintenant quils fuerent son dismez, saunz ceo etc., la le court ne tiendre plee, mez ilz serra maundez a court Christien etc., pur ceo quil est afferm dez ambedeux partiez que le plee est de [droit de][24] Seynt Eglise. Mes si le <plaintiff>[25] dit quil prist sez bleez etc., et le defendant dit quilz sount son dismez etc., et le plaintiff mayntener quils fuerent [son ley][26] chateux, saunz ceo quilz furent son dismez etc., <la>[27] il serra trie en le court le roy: vide diversitatem etc.>[28]

[Lecture Five]

Et lestatut parle oustre *concessimus etiam omnibus liberis hominibus* etc.: cest entendre que ceux libertiez <southscriptis>[29] extende a toutz homez del roialme, auxibien as niefes come as frankes [homes][30] <forpris>[31] lez niefes le roy, quar chescun niefe home est franc et person able duser action vers chescun home fors-que son segnior a que il est villeyn.

---

[1] *Om. I.*   [2] In margin: liberte (hand 2) *E.*   [3] *E, H, I.*
[4] disusent lour fraunches *E.*   [5] huiusmodi *I.*   [6] *Om. E.*   [7] lou *E.*   [8] *I.*
[9] In margin: sanctuary (hand 1), *E.*   [10] *I.*   [11] *Om. I.*   [12] *Om. I.*
[13] In margin: dyversite ou le libertyes misuse quel fuit grant per le roy ou son progenitors et ou le liberty ne deryve del roy mez del pape et apres ceo est mysuse (hand 3) *H.*
[14] In margin: Exposition … pape … peut graunt … le Roy (mostly illegible, hand 4) *H.*
[15] *E.*   [16] *E.*   [17] *Om. I.*   [18] *E.*   [19] *Om. I.*   [20] *I.*
[21] In margin: Vide bon diversite en bref de trespass (hand 1) *H.*
[22] *Om. I.*   [23] *I.*   [24] *E, H;* le *I.*   [25] *Om. I.*   [26] *I;* ces ley *U;* les *E.*
[27] *Om. E.*
[28] This passage at fos 25–25v in *I:* fo. 18v in *E.* See p. 74, n. 10, above.
[29] *Om. I.*   [30] *I.*   [31] forsque *I.*

[DISPUTATION FOUR]

And note that liberty of Holy Church is to have a fair or market or any other franchise, and this comes from the king's grant and not of their own right. And in such liberties the king may enter and put them out if they are misused etc.

And also some other churches have other liberties: for example Westminster, St Martin's and others etc. have liberties that any felon or man who is indicted or who has committed any trespass or treason or any other [felony] shall be safe during the time he is in the sanctuary etc. And also in Beverley, if a man kills another and takes sanctuary in Beverley he shall be safe, but he shall not be safe within the sanctuary of Beverley for any felony or trespass but only for the death of a man etc.

And if any church which has such a liberty misuses their liberty the king cannot seize them, and the reason is because the king may only enter on those liberties which were granted to the Holy Church by him or his progenitors, [and] these liberties could not be granted by them but by the pope, by which etc. And thus see the distinction: query etc.

And note that in the case where a writ of trespass is brought in the king's court for his corn which has been removed and the defendant says that they were his tithes, without that they were his corn etc., and the plaintiff says now that they were his tithes, without that etc., there the court shall not hear the plea, but they shall be sent to the court Christian etc., because it is affirmed by both parties that the plea is in the right of Holy Church. But if the plaintiff says that he took his corn and the defendant says that they are his tithes, and the plaintiff maintains that they were his lay chattels, without that they were his tithes etc., there it shall be tried in the king's court: see the distinction etc.

[LECTURE FIVE]

And the statute says further *we have also granted to all freemen* etc.: this is understood that those liberties written below extend to all men of the realm, to bondmen as well as free men except the king's bondmen, for every bondman is free and a person able to have an action against every man except his lord to whom he is villein.

Et pur ceo chescun villein dauter segnior est franc devers le roy. Cest le cas que ceux liberties ce extendent auxi as villeins come as auters homez, mez ne extend my as villeins le roy quar <son villeinz ne>[1] purront estre franc devers luy meme.[2]

Et auxi si le roy voile aver graunte en ceo manere a sez villeinz demesne, ilz serra enfraunchise per son graunt, que serra prejudical al roy; quar si ascun home graunt ascun chose a son villeyn, <ou <soy>[3] oblige a son villein>,[4] il serra enfraunchise per ceo etc.[5]

[MISCELLANEOUS]

En quel cas <home>[6] luy savera per son clergie vide statut anno xxv° Edward iij capitulo <v^{to}>[7] de clerico, scilicet que sil soit convicte pur quecunque felone ou treason si ne touche le person le roy ou son roial mageste etc.

[Item dicitur [que][8] si jeo enfeffe un comoign en certein terrez que le chieff seignor ne peut my enter, quar il nest persone capax en que un feffement peut veste, quar il est mort en ley: issint le feffement est voide etc.][9]

---

[1] *Om. PA.*

[2] In margin: vide folio precedent ad tale … (hand 2) *I.*

[3] moy *PA.*

[4] *Om. E.*

[5] In margin: Enfranchisment de villeyn (hand 3) *H.*

[6] *Om. PA.*

[7] *Om. E.*

[8] *I.*

[9] *PA, I.*

And therefore every villein of every lord is free against the king. It is the case that these liberties extend also to villeins as to other men, but they do not extend to the king's villeins, for his villeins cannot be free against him.

And also if the king wishes to grant in this manner to his own villeins, they shall be enfranchised by his grant, which would be prejudicial to the king: for if any man grants anything to his villein, or obliges himself to his villein, he shall be enfranchised by this etc.

[MISCELLANEOUS]

In what case a man may save himself by his clergy, see the statute of 25 Edw. III, c. 5, *of Clerks*, namely that [he may have benefit of clergy] if he is convicted for any felony or treason, as long as it does not touch the king's person or his royal majesty etc.[1]

Item, it was said that if I enfeoff a monk in certain lands that the chief lord may not enter, for [the monk] is not a capable person in whom a feoffment may vest, for he is dead in the law: thus the feoffment is void etc.

---

[1] 25 Edw. III, stat. 6, *rectius* c. 4, *Pro Clero* (*SR*, i. 325).

READING THREE

[*fo. 1*] Edwardus dei gracia etc.[1] In le primes de cest estatut est reherce coment le Roy Henry le iij[e], progenitour le [Roy] Edward le primer, fist son graund chartre all honour <et>[d] de due et de Seint Esglise et pur amendment del royalme, devaunt quel chartre ne fuit use forsque comen ley. Et le graund chartre fuit le primer chartre que unquez fuit fet, en quel chartre il graunt an primez a dieu, et per le dit chartre conferma, pur luy et pur cez heirez a touts jours *quod Anglicana ecclesia libera sit et habeat omnia iura sua integra et omnes libertates suas illesas etc.*

[LECTURE ONE]

In primis concessimus deo etc.: ceo paroll *deo* en cest estatut est voyd al entent de lestatut, quar in le primez il graunt a dieu et seynt esglise tout son droitz et libertez, et dieu nest persone capax de tiel <il>[d] libertez et droitz et pur ceo cest paroll *deo* est voyd. Et auxi quaunt il doner etc. *deo et ecclesie* cest paroll *ecclesie* est void, quar lesglise nest capax, et il ne peut estre entendre que le don fuit fet propermet as corps de leglise, come as murez et fenestres etc. <etc.>[d] Et pur ceo cest don serra entendre servientibus et ministris ecclesie divina selebrantibus. Et auxi lesglise est le parson et son parochiens, oue auterment, sil soit de religion, labbe et le convent, et le prior et le convent font lesglise. Et sic <pur>[d] proponitur continens pro contento et issint [cest][2] paroll *ecclesie* serra pris a cel entent in celle estatut. Mez tile don a ceo jour ne vaut riens, quar covient que en chescun done que soit donour et done et que eux soient persone capacez si le don prendre effect. Et auxi si terre soit done a ascun person et il refuce le done, le don ne vaut <si>[d] et sil port action de son don ceo refucell viendre in debat.

Ore est a veyer queux donz soyent bonz et <qx>[d] queux nemi.[3] Si terre soit don a un cominalte le done ne vaut quar il nest person capax.[4] Meme le ley si terre soit don a un convent. Nota quun cominalte ne peut estre corporat daver ascun possessions <si non per>[i] le patent le roy <et ceo oue auter person come mayor etc.>[i] Mez contrarie est si jeo don terre burgencibus de tile burgh oue citesenz dun citie, pur ceo que chescun home de cest vile burgh est burgher et de cite citsen sil soit faytez corporat per le roy. Et per meme le reson est dit bon <don>[i] estre fet deo et monachis, tamen quere. Et auxi si le roy done terre a un alien en fee le don est bon, mez il nest pas fet denysyn per le don quar sil devie son feme ne serra endowe ne sez heirez enheritez, nient constristiant quil soit fet denisynt

---

[1] In margin: Capitulum primum.
[2] Supplying deletion in MS.
[3] In margin: Que don est bon et que nemi.
[4] In margin: Et auxi le don fait a cominalte ne vaut [pur] ceo qun cominalte ne peut estre sever et pur ceo le roy ne peut fayre un corporation solment de cominalte.

READING THREE

Edward by the grace of God etc. In the beginning of this statute it is rehearsed how King Henry III, progenitor of King Edward I, made his great charter to the honour of God and the Holy Church and for the amendment of the realm, before which charter only common law was used. And the great charter was the first charter ever made, in which charter he granted first to God, and by the said charter confirmed for him and for his heirs forever *that the English Church shall be free and shall have all her rights entire and all her liberties inviolate* etc.

[LECTURE ONE]

In the first place we have granted to God etc.: this word *God* in this statute is void to the intent of the statute, for in the beginning it grants to God and the Holy Church all its right and liberties, and God is not a person capable of such liberties and rights, and for this [reason] this word *God* is void. And also when it gives etc. *to God and the Church*, this word *Church* is void, for the Church is not capable, and it may not be understood that the gift was properly made to the body of the church, such as the walls and the windows etc. And for this [reason] this gift shall be understood to be to the servants and ministers of the Church performing divine services. And also the Church is the parson and his parishioners, or otherwise, if he is in religion, the abbot and the convent, and the prior and the convent make the Church. And thus it is declared *continens pro contento*, and thus the word *Church* shall be taken to this intent in this statute. But such a gift today is not worth anything, for it is necessary that in each gift there should be a donor and donee, and they should be capable persons if the gift is to take effect. And also if land is given to any person and he refuses the gift, the gift is worth nothing, and if he brings an action for this gift the refusal shall come into question.

Now it is to be seen which gifts are good and which are not. If land is given to a commonalty the gift is worth nothing for it is not a capable person. The law is the same if land is given to a convent. Note that a commonalty cannot be corporate to have any possessions except by the king's patent, and this with another person such as a mayor etc. But it is the contrary if I give land to the burgesses of such a borough or the citizens of a city, because each man of such a borough town is a burgess and of [such a] city a citizen, if they are made corporate by the king. And for the same reason it is said to be a good gift made 'to God and the monks', however query. And also if the king gives lands to an alien in fee the gift is good, but he is not made a denizen by the gift, for if he dies his wife shall not be endowed nor shall his heirs inherit, even if he was made a denizen

apris le don le roy. Et si terre soit done deo et monachis de tile lieu est tenuz bon,
pur ceo que tout ne fuit labbe nom per expresse paroll, unquore il est moygne et
issint nom in ceo paroll monachis, mez il nest pas <…>ᵈ un de convent. Et ascuns
diont quil est un de convent per cel reson, ill avera le don fet deo et conventui
assez bon. Et auxi un mayre nest un de cominalte, mez sovereign et governour et
le cominalte [sugget]¹ a luy. Et pur ceo quaunt tile corporation est fet per le roy,
<abe do>ᵈ scilicet meire et cominalte de tile vile, done fet al cominalte ne vaut
saunz nomer le sovereygn. Mez si corporation soit fet per nomer de <mayre et
<citisens>ᵈ>ⁱ Citesens <f>ᵈ, don fet a eux saunz nomer le meyre est assez bon,
quar le meyr est un de eux.

En ascun cas un don peut estre in parcell bon et in parcell nemi,² come si don
soit fet deo et abbatui et successoribus suis de tile lue, quar vers due est voyd et
vers labbe est bon. Meme le ley de don fet un tile moygne et un seculier person.
Et nota que le roy peut graunte terre a son royne oue a un moyne per patent et il
peut <s>ᵈ user action et action devers luy de meme le terres et issint ne peut null
auter vide aᵒ xiiij H[en.] iiijᵗⁱ. Et auxi si le roy don conge a un home de faire un
chauntrie a iij pristez, [fo. 1v] le cause est pur ceo que nest pas limite in serten
com bien de terre il voudre son chauntre estre faire.

[LECTURE TWO]

Lestatut reherce et voyle *quod ecclesia anglicana libera sit* etc.: cest paroll *libera*
peut estre pris a ij ententz, scilicet a un entent que soit frank in luy meme de touts
seculirs chargez, a auter entent que null nef home prendre null order de Seynt
Eglise. Et auxi lestatut parle uster et *habeat omnia iura sua integra* come est a
entendre que lez jugez de Seynt Esglise eient conusance, punition, et determination dez plez que touchent matrymoyn, testament, dez dimez et dez oblacionz,
et <obvencionz>ⁱ <obencionz>ᵈ et auxi de touts auter poyntes quex touchent le
correction de lalme: ceux sont iura ecclesia.

Ore est a voyer oue lesglise avera le jurisdiction de le cort le roy et oue nemi.³
In primez est ordeygne per lestatut anno 8ᵒ E[dw.] 3 pro cleris, capitulo ultima,
que <que>⁴ scire facias ne soit fet in le Chauncerie pur rendre dez dimez in meme
le lue. Si un parson port bref de trespass vers un auter et lauter justefie come
sez dimez et demand jugement, si le cort voyle conuster le cort serra mys hors
de jurisdiction, et le cause est pur ceo que in taunt per le comencement de laction inter parson et parson il est intend que est in droit dez dimez, et le droit dez
dimez ne peut estre trie cienz, einz in cort Cristien; aᵒ xxxviijᵒ E[dw.] 3 termino
Hil. in trespass. Si un parson port bref de covenaunt vers un auter sur composition fet perenter eux que le plaintiff demesne terrez ne serra dimabelez, la ad le

---

¹ MS reads sigget.
² In margin: Le done est in parcell bon et in parcell nemi.
³ In margin: Oue le cort le roy aver jurisdicion et oue nemi.
⁴ Written twice in MS.

after the king's gift. And if land is given 'to God and the monks' of such a place it is held good, because although the abbot was not named by express words, still he is a monk and is thus named in these words ' to the monks', but he is not one of the convent. And others say that he is one of the convent for this reason, he shall have the gift made 'to God and the convent' well enough. And also a mayor is not one of the commonalty, but superior and governor and the commonalty is subjected to him. And for this [reason] when such a corporation is made by the king, namely mayor and commonalty of such a town, a gift made to the commonalty is worth nothing without naming the superior. But if a corporation is made by the name of mayor and citizens, a gift made to them without naming the mayor is good enough, for the mayor is one of them.

In some cases a gift may be in part good and in part not, as if a gift is made 'to God and the abbot and his successors' of such a place, for to God it is void and to the abbot it is good. The law is the same of a gift made to such a monk and a secular person. And note that the king may grant land to his queen or to a monk by patent and he may sue an action against him of the same lands which no other may do: see the year 14 Hen. IV.[1] And also if the king gives permission to a man to make a chantry of three priests, the reason is because it is not limited for certain of how much land he wishes his chantry to be made.

[LECTURE TWO]

The statute rehearses and wills *that the English church shall be free* etc.: this word *free* may be taken to two intents, namely in one way that it should be free in itself of all secular charges, to another intent that no bondman should take any orders in Holy Church. And also the statute says further that *she shall have all her rights entire*, by which should be understood that the judges of Holy Church shall have cognizance, punishment, and determination of pleas which touch marriage, wills, tithes, oblations, obventions, and also all other points which touch the correction of the soul: these are the rights of the Church.

Now it is to be seen where the Church shall have the jurisdiction of the king's court and where not. To begin with, it is ordained by the statute of 8 Edw. III *Pro Cleris*, the last chapter, that *scire facias* should not be brought in Chancery to render tithes there.[2] If a parson brings a writ of trespass against another and the other justifies [them] as his tithes and demands judgment, if the court wishes to acknowledge it shall be put out of jurisdiction, and the reason is because by the commencement of the action between parson and parson it is understood that it is in right of tithes, and the right of tithes may not be tried here [in this court] but in the court Christian: Hil. 38 Edw. III in trespass.[3] If a parson brings a writ of covenant against another on a composition made between them that the plaintiff's demesne lands shall not be tithable, there

---

[1] YB Mich. 14 Hen. IV, fo. 10, pl. 8.
[2] *Articuli Cleri, rectius* 9 Edw. II, stat. 1, c. 1 (*SR*, i. 171).
[3] YB Hil. 38 Edw. III, fo. 5.

defendant eux prist a cort etc., in ceo cas le pouer de le cort le roy fuit affirme, nient obstante que le plaintiff meme jure que son action fuit pur dimez. Et le cas fuit pur ceo quil ad pris son action sur un covenant tayle per son fet demesne et il ne peut null dimez recover in ceo <p>ᵈ bref aᵒ xxxviijᵒ termino Pasc. E[dw.] 3 <t>ᵈ in trespass. Si un comen person port bref de trespass vers un parson et declare dun charete iij chivals oue garbez inportes etc. et le parson justefie le pris dez garbez come sez dimez <et domures>ⁱ et a charet et iij chivalx in taunt quil ad use son suite oue lez blez quex sont nos dimez, de quex ceo cort ne peut conusaunz aver in un bref: jugment de bref. Et le cort ne fuit mys hors de jurisdiction pur ceo que son plee ne fuit forsque travers de son bref et auxi le plaintiff clavm come ley chatell aᵒ xxxviij E[dw.] 3 termino Pasc. in trespass.

Auxi in bref de trespass port per un abbe vers un prior dez blez in garbez et le defendant dit que composition ce fit perenter eux <aver dismez>ᵈ que null deux aver dimez dez auterz demenz terrez, et dit que le lue oue il suppose le trespass estre fet fuit de glebe le defendant, et demand jugment si le cort etc. Et ne fuit pas ajuge, mez jeo entendre que le cort aver son pouer pur ceo que son ple est travers del bref, quar pur son plee il suppose quil nenporter: aᵒ xxxviijᵒ E[dw.] 3 termino Trin. En action de trespass porter quant ij parsons et le defendant justefie come dimez et dit que le lue oue le plaintiff ad suppose etc. est deinz son parocch et lauter dit que le lue nest deinz son paroch, lissue fuit responde le cause fuit pur ceo intaunt quil aver travers il ad afferm le jurisdiction; aᵒ xxxixᵒ E[dw.] 3 termino Mich. in trespass. Meme le ley anno vᵗᵒ Hen. vᵗⁱ in trespass.

En bref de trespass port per parson dun lue vers le vicar de meme le lue, dun schivall pris, le defendant justefie come mortuary et demand jugment et ne fuit my ouste, le cas fuit pur ce que lestatut parle riens forsque dez dimez: anno ijᵒ H[en.] vᵗⁱ termino Hil. in trespass. Un fermor <que fuit>ⁱ <...>ᵈ parson port bref de trespas vers un vicar et il justefie come dimez et le cort afferme, le cause fuit pur ceo que le plaintiff fuit fermor dun prior et issint ley chatell: anno xliij E[dw.] 3 termino Mich. in trespass.

En ascun cas loue lun ad aferme le jurdiction le cort, in meme le ple ad estre reson de disaferm, come in action de trespass per un abbe dez blez inportez vers un prior, et le prior justefie come cez dimez severez de le ix parte: jugment si cort. Et puis labbe jura composisstion perenter labbe et prior que sez demesne terrez ne serra dimeablez. Et sur cest matter jure le defendant demand jugment si le cort voyle conuster, et le cort fuit oute, et le cause fuit pur ceo que le droit dez

if the defendant has taken them to court etc., in this case the power of the king's court was affirmed notwithstanding that the plaintiff himself swore that his action was for tithes. And the reason was because he [the plaintiff] has taken his action on a covenant drawn up by his [the defendant's] own action, and he could not recover any tithes on this writ: Pas. 38 Edw. III in trespass.[1] If a common person brings a writ of trespass against a parson for a wagon and three horses carried off with grain etc., and the parson justifies the seizure of the grain as his tithes, and demurs for both the wagon and three horses that they were part of his suit with the corn which was [his][2] tithes, which this court may not have cognizance of on this writ: judgment of the writ. And the court was not put out of jurisdiction because his plea was only a traverse of his writ, and also the plaintiff claimed as a lay chattel: Pas. 38 Edw. III in trespass.[3]

Also in a writ of trespass brought by an abbot against a prior for grain in sheaves, the defendant says that a composition was made between them that neither of them would have tithes of the other's demesne lands, and says that the place where he supposed that the trespass was committed was the defendant's glebe, and demands judgment if the court [has cognizance] etc. And it was not adjudged, but I understand that the court has its power because his plea is a traverse of the writ, for by his plea he assumes that he did not carry [the grain away]: Trin. 38 Edw. III.[4] In an action of trespass brought when there are two parsons, and the defendant justifies [the trespass] as tithes and says that the place where the plaintiff has supposed [the trespass occurred] is within his parish, and the other says that the place is not within his parish, the issue was answered because having traversed he has affirmed the jurisdiction: Mich. 39 Edw. III in trespass.[5] The law is the same 5 Hen. V in trespass.[6]

In a writ of trespass for a horse taken, brought by a parson of a place against the vicar of the same place, the defendant justifies as mortuary and demands judgment and was not put out, because the statute only speaks of tithes: Hil. 2 Hen. V in trespass.[7] A farmer who was a parson brings a writ of trespass against a vicar and he justifies as tithes, and the court affirms because the plaintiff was the farmer of a prior and thus it was a lay chattel: Mich 43 Edw. III in trespass.[8]

In some cases where one has affirmed the court's jurisdiction he has reason to disaffirm in the same plea, as in an action of trespass by an abbot against a prior for corn carried away, and the prior justifies this as his tithes severed from the ninth part: judgment whether the court [has jurisdiction]; and then the abbot swears a composition between the abbot and prior that his demesne lands will not be titheable; and on this sworn matter the defendant demands judgment if the court wishes to take cognizance, and the court was ousted, and the reason was

---

[1] YB Pas. 38 Edw. III, fo. 8, *rectius* in covenant. From 'And the reason ...' is a close paraphrase of Thorp C.J.C.P. in the case.
[2] The reading text is taken from the year book where 'nos' refers to the defendant and Serjeant Belknap.
[3] YB Pas. 38 Edw. III, fos 8–9.   [4] YB Trin. 38 Edw. III, fo. 19.
[5] YB Mich. 39 Edw. III, fos 23–24.   [6] YB Hil. 5 Hen. V, fo. 10, pl. 23.
[7] YB Trin. 2 Hen. V, fo. 10, pl. 9.   [8] YB Mich. 43 Edw. III, fo. 34, pl. 44.

dimez viendre in debat, [*fo. 2*] le quel ne peut estre trie sienz, nient obstant quil avoit fet un justification etc.

Si dimez passent le iij[e] oue iiij[e] parti de lesglise de quel il est demande, le cort le roy aver le jurisdiction de ceux.

Posito que si in bref de trespass dez blez inportez le defendant justefie come cez dimez, le plaintiff navera generall averment que laye chattell, mez il aver speciall mater que ceo prove pur afermer le power de le cort, et ceo per lestatut le Roy Richard [II] anno primo ca° xiiij et xv° quod nota.

[LECTURE THREE]

Et auxi per meme le charter le roy graunt *libertates suas illesas*:[1] per cest paroll *libertates* est intende sez libertez, si come un felon fue al esglise et est pris hors et amesne devaunt justice et arreyne sur enditment, et il jure cest mater et pria destre restore al esglise: si soit trove pur luy il serra restore, et si ne soit trove pur luy il serra pende, mez credo quil peut apris prendre soy meme a son clergie mez a le felonye il ne peut pledre apris.

Et nota que null ne peut fair seyntwar forsque le pape, mez si un felon fue a un seyntwar et est pris hors ove fort mayn et est arreyn et il jure ceo mater et pria destre restore: question oue le felon aver bref sur son parol de faire vener le record de seyntwar <provant quil fuit pris hors de ceo>[i] oue que lez justices ferra bref all segnior de <son>[d] seyntwar de fayre vener le record de seyntwar, oue auterment que le segnior viendre et clamera son seyntwar. En le cas de William Wad, selon lez justices fuerent un bref al abbe de Bello Loco oue il fuit pris de jure quil avoit de son seyntwar etc.

En quel cas home luy <luy>[2] salvera per son clergy, vide statut anno xxv° E[dw.] 3 capitulo v[to] de cleris: scilicet sil soit convicte pur quequque felonye ou treison si ne soit touche le person oue son royal majeste etc.

---

[1] In margin: 2 que est liberte.
[2] Written twice in MS.

because the right of tithes are in question which may not be tried here [in this court], notwithstanding that he had made a justification etc.

If tithes exceed the third or fourth part of the church for which they are demanded the king's court shall have the jurisdiction of those.

Suppose that in a writ of trespass for corn carried away the defendant justifies it as his tithes, the plaintiff shall not have general averment as a lay chattel, but he shall aver special matter that proves this to affirm the power of the court, and this by the statute of 1 Richard II cc 14 and 15, which note.[1]

[LECTURE THREE]

And also by the same charter the king grants *her liberties inviolate*: by this word *liberties* is understood her liberties, as when a felon flees to a church and is taken out and is brought before a justice and arraigned on indictment, and he swears this matter and prays to be restored to the church: if it is found for him he shall be restored, and if it is not found for him he shall be hanged, but I believe that he may afterwards take himself to his clergy, but for the felony he may not plead afterwards.

And note that no-one may make a sanctuary except the pope, but if a felon flees to a sanctuary and is taken out with main force and is arraigned, and he swears this matter and prays to be restored, it is a question whether the felon shall have a writ on his word to cause the record of sanctuary to be brought, proving that he was taken out of it, or whether the justices shall send a writ to the lord of the sanctuary to bring the record of sanctuary, or otherwise that the lord should come and claim his sanctuary. In the case of William Wad, according to the justices, there was a writ to the abbot of Beaulieu where it was taken *de jure* that he had his sanctuary etc.[2]

In which case a man shall save himself by his clergy, see the statute 25 Edw. III, c. 5 *De Cleris*:[3] namely, if he is convicted for any felony or treason, if it does not touch the person [of the king] or his royal majesty etc.

---

[1] 1 Ric. II, c. 14 (*SR*, ii. 5). See also the discussion in Mich. 13 Ric. II (Ames ser.) pp. 32–34, pl. 2. This case also appears in Reading Six below, p. 92.

[2] The case is discussed by Serjeant Newton in YB Pas. 7 Hen. VI, fo. 33, pl. 27; by Hussey C.J. in Port, *Notebook*, 32; and by Fyneux C.J. in Caryll, *Reports*, ii. 708; and mentioned in YB Pas. 1 Hen VII, fo. 23, pl. 15. Wad's crime occurred in 1425 and is discussed in YB Trin. 7 Hen. VI, fos 42–43, pl. 18 under the name William Waw. The record is copied in BL MS. Add. 25168, fo. 393.

[3] *Pro Clero*, *rectius* 25 Edw. III, stat. 6, c. 4 (*SR*, i. 325).

READING FOUR

REPORTES DE MAGNA CARTA: *In primis concessimus deo*

[*p. 7*] Devant[1] le fesaunt de cest estatut null ley fuit mez tout solment custum et comen ley, sicome un home ust devi son heir deinz age le segnior avera le garde per le comen ley. Et pur ceo que cest ley fuit fait per lez roys et fuit custum, le Roy John voilet distruier lay et avera sa volunte demesne. Et pur <cest>[i] cause cez lordis de terres voilent luy depoiser et myschevier et pur dowte de cez barons et auters lordes il fit cet ley in writing. Et apres ceo le roy H[en.] le iij[de] conferme cest ley ove sa bon volunte saunz coherciun, et fuit seale ovesque sa gret seale. Et cez evesques et toutez cez barons fuerint juris a cet ley issint que cestui que enfreyt serroit excomenger. Et apres ceo le Roy E[dw.], fitz le Roy H[en.] le iij, inspiciendo Magnam Cartam patris suis fit [c]est cherter estatut et issint lez estatutes fuerint faitz per perlement etc.

Letter: Le letter est *in primis concessimus deo* etc. Cest est voide, quar graunt ne peut estre fait saunz iij chosez: un est que <ascun>[d] <sont>[i] person <ss a>[d] <que poient>[i] graunt; auter est que le grantee capacite de accepter le grant; le tre est que le chos que est graunt gisera in graunte. Mez in ce cas le grantee person acceptabil.

Casus: Omnia posito que graunt est al dieu et esglise et monachis de Westm', le graunte est voide pur ceo que le grantee nad capacite daccepter le graunt, quar lez monchez sont mortes in ley.

Casus: Posito que graunt est fait al abbot et cez monkes, le abbot avera astate pur terme de sa vie pur ceo que il est person acceptabill.

Casus: Posito que graunt soit fait al abbot et cez successores, est bon grant et inurera al meason.

Casus: Posito que graunt soit fait al abbot et successores, et toutz le monkys sount mortes excep le abbot, unquis cel graunt inurera al huis si soient monkes faites apres, ils averont en droit de meason. Mes le contrary l[ey] lou toutz les monkes sount mortes et labbe voit fair graunt: cest graunt nest pas bon mez durant le vie del abbot, pur ceo que rienz peut passer saunz convent seall etc.

Casus: Posito que terres sount grauntes a dean et chapter ou al meir et cominalte: cest graunte est bon pur ceo que le dean et chapter sont cors et avoient capacite de accepter tiell graunt. Mez le contray [*sic*] ley est que si graunt soit fait al maier ou dean sole, luy nomant meier et nul auter nome, cest graunt est voide et est defetid pur ceo que est incerteyn quell home est meir ou dean. Mez si le graunt soit al John at Style, meier de Loundre, cest grant inurera a luy mesme John at Style. Et auxi destre chos que gist in graunt.

---

[1] Small space left for an initial, not filled in.

READING FOUR

REPORTS ON MAGNA CARTA: *In the first place we have granted to God*

Before the making of this statute there was no law except custom and common law, so that when a man died with his heir under age the lord had the wardship by the common law. And because this law was made by the kings and was custom, King John wanted to destroy the law and have his own will. And for this reason the lords of the lands wished to depose him and make a mischief, and because of the fear of these barons and other lords he made this law in writing. And after this King Henry III confirmed this law of his good will without coercion and it was sealed with his great seal. And his bishops and all his barons were sworn to this law, so that any one who broke it would be excommunicated. And after this King Edward, son of King Henry III, having inspected his father's Magna Carta, made this charter a statute and thus the statutes were made by Parliament etc.[1]

Letter: The letter is *in the first place we have granted to God* etc. This [word] is void, for a grant cannot be made without three things: one is that there is a person who may grant; another is that the grantee [has] the capacity to accept the grant; the third is that the thing which is granted lies in grant. But in this case the grantee [is not] an acceptable person.

Case: Suppose that a grant is 'to God and the Church and the monks of Westminster': the grant is void because the grantee does not have the capacity to accept the grant, for the monks are dead in law.

Case: Suppose that a grant is made to the abbot and his monks: the abbot will have the estate for term of his life because he is an acceptable person.

Case: Suppose that a grant is made to the abbot and his successors: it is a good grant and operates for the house.

Case: Suppose that a grant is made to the abbot and his successors, and all the monks are dead except the abbot: this grant shall operate for the house if monks are made afterwards, they shall have it in right of the house. But the contrary law where all the monks are dead and the abbot wishes to make a grant: this grant is only good during the life of the abbot, because nothing can pass without the convent seal etc.

Case: Suppose that lands were granted to the dean and chapter or to the mayor and commonalty: this grant is good because the dean and chapter are bodies and have the capacity to accept such a grant. But the law is contrary if the grant was made to the mayor or dean alone, naming him only as 'the mayor' and by no other name: this grant is void and is defeated because it is uncertain what man is mayor or dean. But if the grant is 'to John at Style, mayor of London', this grant operates for the same John at Style. And also it must be for a thing which is grantable.

---

[1] 25 Edw. I (*SR*, i. 114–119).

Casus: Posito que le roy graunte un gard que nest pas in sa possession, cest grant est void pur ceo quil ne unquis fuit possesse. Mez le contrarie ley est lou il fuit possesse de garde: il peut graunt, come appert. Et auxi le roy puit graunt lez amentes dascun cort ou wreke de mere et catalla felonum fugitivorum.

Lettere: Et le letter est *anglicana ecclesia* etc. Cest entendre dez spirituelz homez come pristes.

Casus: Posito que moune villeyn soit fait prist, nynte obstante jeo peut seser sez bonz, mez jeo navera ocupation de son cors, mez tile < mez tiellz>ᵈ occupation que un priste peut fair en le service de <dieu>ᵈ dieu.

Casus: Posito que mon villeyn soit monk, nient obstant que il soit fait abbote jeo ne sesera luy ne cez bons pur ceo que son depose il est mort aderere si come il fuit monk. Mesme le ley de feme durant le covertur quar le segnior ad sa remedy vers labbot del meason lou son villeyn fuit fait monke, ou vers le baron le feme per action dun trespass.

Auxi devant cest estatut, si action ust est port devers un parson desglise et issint issera distres al vicont et voilet enter en lez glebez landys le parson et distreyner, mez apres cet letter fait le vicont returna le bref del que le clericus beneficiatus et donquez issera distress al evesque et issint <leg>ⁱ lesglise *habeat libertates suas*.

Letter: Le letter est *et habeat omnia jura sua integra* etc.

Posito que un felon enter in lesglise et lez officers veignent a luy et il ne voet my monter ascun cause pur que il accedit, ilz purrount accepter luy hors de lesglise et aver luy al prochyn prison. Mez si il jura cause et nul coroner mesme le lieu, il demura taunque le coroner vient la.

Et mesme le ley de un prist quaunt il est in esglise en diavin [*sic*] service: nul officer luy distreniera. Mez sil ust prolonger le temps pur ceo que le officer fuit la, donquez le bayliff luy [*p. 8*] arester et ceo est don per estatut.

Casus: Posito que un felon veint devant le coroner, luy covynt de fair sa enditement acordyng al ley, et donquez le coroner abjura luy et luy assynera un port, et issint il avera spasse convenient daler al port et si il soit accept et imprison apres, il serra restitut a sa port. Et coment que le felon jur un certeyn jour al coroner quant le felon fuit fait ou autrement, le coroner ne serra luy abjure de royalme mez le felon serra accepte hors del esglise et mysse al prison.

Letter: Le letter est *liberis hominibus*.

Casus: Posito que le roy voit grant ascun chos al homes de Islyngton, le graunt est voide pur ceo que lez homez de Islyngton non sunt corporat, quar coment que le roy grant eux son cherter et issint eux incorpora et issint adeprimez vinent toutz lez vilz privelegez cum Loundres et ou Caunterbury ou Oxforde etc.

Case: Suppose that the king grants a ward who is not in his possession: this grant is void because he was never possessed. But the law is contrary where he was possessed of the ward: he can grant [him], as it appears. And also the king may grant the fines of any court or wreck of the sea, and the chattels of fugitive felons.

Letter: And the letter is *the English Church* etc. This is understood [to refer to] spiritual men such as priests.

Case: Suppose that my villein is made a priest: notwithstanding I may seize his goods, but I shall not have the use of his body except in such an occupation as a priest may do in the service of God.

Case: Suppose that my villein is a monk: even if he should be made abbot I shall not seize him or his goods because [despite] his [election][1] he is still dead, just as if he were a monk. The law is the same of a woman during coverture, for the lord has his remedy against the abbot of the house where his villein was made a monk, or against the husband of the woman by an action of trespass.

Also, before this statute, if an action had been brought against a parson of a church and as a result a distress issued to the sheriff, he could enter into the glebe lands of the parson and distrain, but after this letter was made the sheriff returned the writ by which the clerk was beneficed and then a distress issued to the bishop, and thus the church *shall have her liberties.*

Letter: The letter is *and shall have all her rights entire* etc.

Suppose that a felon enters into the church and the officers go to him and he does not at all wish to show any cause for which he came, they can take him out of the church and have him at the nearest prison. But if he swears cause and there is no coroner there, he shall remain until the coroner goes there.

And the law is the same of a priest when he is in the church in divine service: no officer may distrain him. But if he had prolonged the time [of the service] because the officer was there, then the bailiff shall arrest him and this is given by the statute.[2]

Case: Suppose that a felon came before the coroner it behoves him to make his indictment according to the law, and then the coroner shall abjure him and assign him a port: he shall have enough time to go to the port and if he is taken and imprisoned afterwards, he shall be restored to his port.[3] And unless the felon swears a certain day to the coroner when the felony was done or otherwise, the coroner shall not abjure him of the realm but the felon shall be taken out of the church and put in prison.

The letter is *free men.*

Case: Suppose that the king should grant anything to the men of Islington: the grant is void because the men of Islington are not incorporated, even though the king granted them his charter and thus incorporated them, and this is how all the privileged vills came into being in the first place, such as London, Canterbury, or Oxford etc.

---

[1] Conjectural emendation.
[2] 50 Edw. III, c. 5 (*SR*, i. 398), repeated in 1 Ric. II, c. 15 (*SR*, ii. 5).
[3] Perhaps Statham, *Corone*, 27.

READING FIVE

MAGNA CARTA CAPITULO 1

[LECTURE ONE]

[*p. 379*] Lestatute est *quod ecclesia anglicana libera sit*. Ore est a voier que serra dit *ecclesia anglicana*. Et moy semble evechiez, abbez, priories, moynes, freres <le prior de sent John>[d] et toutz auterz quex ount corporation pur feir divine servicez serra dit *ecclesia anglicana* et parsons et vicarez quex ount auctorite pur fair divine servicez. Sont auterz que povent estre et serra dit *ecclesia anglicana*, et uncore ilz ne font divine servicez, come le prior de Seint John et cez chivalers, mez ilz ount lour corparation pur defender lez sarazines que voillent distroier nostre foy. Auxi fraternitez dez gyldes lou ilz ount corporation et paier pur [lauder][1] de dieu, ilz poient estre dit *ecclesia anglicana* et uncore eux nount poier de fair divine servicez, mez sont supervisorz que divine servicez serra fait, et issint de gardeinz desglise lou ilz ount corporation.

[LECTURE TWO]

Lestatut est *libera sit*. Jentend que est entend per cez parolz que lou avant cest estatute le ley ne fuit mys en certeyn que si mon villein ou le villein le roy aver entre en religion ou ad fait un preste, fuit en doute si le segnior le villein peut seisier luy ou nemi, ascun foitz ils fier le seisier. Et pur ceo que <ad>[i] fait certen, est ore per ceo estatut mys en certein que si le villein dun home entre entre [*sic*] en religion, que son segnior <le>[d] ne luy seisiera et issint dun preste, quar nest reson que home que ferr tile honorable servicez que serra demesner com vile person etc. Mez uncore ceo serra toutz foitz entend <lou>[d] de tielz que seront professe en religion et de tielz quex seront infra sacros, quar si issint soit quun villein entre en religion <et>[d] avant son profession sil ne soit infra sacros est loiall pur son segnior de luy prender quar il nest sur obedience avant profession. Quar si action soit use vers un tile que est entre en religion, ou per un tile, nest ple a dire que il est entre en religion mez covient dire que il est entre en religion et professe et south obedience un tile, et lissue serra sur le profession et nemi sur lentre etc. Et issint est de ceux quex sont appelle lewde monkes ou lewde freres et font servicez en lesglise: uncore lour segnior peut eux prender quar nemi en profession uncore ilz feit divine servicez. Et issint de gardenz desglise ou magisters de gyldes et huiusmodi etc., et issint de avowes.

---

[1] MS. reads 'louder'.

READING FIVE

MAGNA CARTA C. 1

[LECTURE ONE]

The statute is *that the English Church shall be free*. Now we must see what will be called the *English Church*. And it seems to me that bishops, abbeys, priories, monks, friars, and all others who are incorporated to perform divine services shall be called *the English Church*, as well as parsons and vicars who have authority to perform divine services. There are others who can be and shall be called *the English Church* even though they do not perform divine services, such as the prior of St John and his knights, but they have their corporation to defend [us from] the Saracens who wish to destroy our faith. Also fraternities of guilds, where they are incorporated and pay for God to be praised, may be called *the English Church*, and yet they do not have the power to perform divine services, but they ensure that divine services shall be performed, and the same of churchwardens where they are incorporated.

[LECTURE TWO]

The statute is *shall be free*. I think that by these words it is to be understood that before this statute the law was not certain: that if my villein or the king's villein had entered in religion or was made a priest, it was in doubt whether the villein's lord could seize him or not, and sometimes he could seize him. And to make this certain, now by this statute it is made certain that if the villein of a man enters in religion, his lord may not seize him and the same of a priest, for it is not reasonable that a man who performs such an honourable service shall be treated as a vile person etc. But yet this shall be always understood of those who are professed in religion and of those who are in holy orders, for if it should happen that a villein enters into religion before his profession (if he is not in orders) it is lawful for his lord to take him, for he is not upon obedience before profession. For if an action is used against such a one who is entered in religion, or by such a one, it is not a plea to say that he is entered in religion, but he must say that he is entered in religion and professed and is under obedience to such a one, and the issue shall be on the profession and not on the entry etc. And thus it is of those who are called 'lay monks' or 'lay brothers' and perform services in the church: still their lord may take them for they are not professed although they perform divine services. The same is true of churchwardens or the masters of guilds and such things etc., and of avowesses.

[LECTURE THREE]

[p. 380] Lestatut est outer *et habeat omnia iura sua integra.* Ceux parolz ne poient estre pris en tile maner que ilz aver toutz lour leyes entierment quar auter plusors cases en lour ley quex ne tiendr lieu en nostre ley. Quar ilz ount un ley que null spirituell home serra arreyn devant un temporall juge pur ascun cryme mez nostre ley est contrary, quar il avera punishment pur un temporall tort fait come temporall home serra, et chescun maner daction gist vers luy come vers temporall home. Auxi en lour ley, si un home aver un fitz per feme avant cover-tor et apres marie mesme le feme il est legittamus, mez le contrary est en nostre ley come appert per lestatut de Merton: ad bref [den]¹ Register de bastardy. Auxi le ley de Seint Esglise est que si un feme deinz lez espouselz demur en avoutry et aver issue en son aueutrer ceo est bastard. Mez nostre ley est auter quar il est mulier si son baron sont infra iiij^or maria et hors de prison etc. Et issint en plu-sors auterz casez lour ley et nostre ley varie, et nota en cell point ne serra rule per lour ley.

Mez ceo estatut entend de toutz chosez quex sont espirituell, que ilz averont *jura sua,* come de toutz chosez que concernont nostre foy come examination dez heretikez, et en causes testamentary, et en matrimonye, et mortuaries, et huius-modi quex sont espirituelz causez. Et auxi pur droit dez dismes sil ne soit en disadvantage dascun et outer le value de 4^e partie dez dismez, mez donquez le primer avera bref de \<ada>^d advocatione decimarum etc. Et auxi en trespass enter ij parsons si le droit dez dismez viendre en debate le spirituell court avera jurisdiction, mez si soit enter un parson et un lay home donquez le court ne serra mys hors de jurisdiction etc.

[LECTURE FOUR]

Lestatut est auter *et libertates suas illesas.* Jentend per cez parolz que ilz averont toutz cez reasonable liberteez, scilicet que quant un est convicte de felonie que il avera son privilege de son clergie quell privilage covient estre demande accord a le ley use ou autrement il navera ceo. Quar sil voill ceo demander avant lenquest aver don lour verdit il navera ceo, quar il nest demandable tanque il soit en jeopardie de son vie. Mez il peut ceo aver apres verdit et avant jugement et donquez est il clerk convict, et il peut ceo aver apres jugement et donquez est il clerk atteint. Et quant il est issint delivere all ordinary il covient estre demesner accord a \<lour>^d nostre ley ou autrement lordinary serra punisch, quar sil suffer luy deschaper il perdra c li. all roy, et sil suffer un de fair purgation que de droit ne *[p. 381]* doit faire purgation

---

¹ MS. reads 'den'.

[Lecture Three]

The statute is further *and shall have all her rights entire*. These words may not be taken in such a way that they shall have all their laws entirely, for there are many other cases in their law which shall not hold in our law. They have a law that no spiritual man shall be arraigned before a temporal judge for any crime, but our law is contrary, for he shall have punishment for committing a temporal injury, as a temporal man shall, and each manner of action lies against him as against a temporal man. Also in their law if a man has a son by a woman before coverture and after marries the same woman, [the son] is legitimate, but the contrary is in our law as appears by the statute of Merton: there is a writ of bastardy in the *Register*.[1] Also the law of Holy Church is that if a woman within the marriage remains in adultery and has issue in her adultery, this is a bastard. But our law is otherwise, for he is legitimate if her husband was within the four seas and out of prison etc. And thus in many other cases their law and our law vary, and note in this point we shall not be ruled by their law.

But this statute is understood of all things which are spiritual, that she shall have *her rights*, as of all things which concern our faith, such as the examination of heretics, and in testamentary causes, and in marriage, and mortuaries, and such things which are spiritual causes. And also for the right to tithes if it is not to the disadvantage of any, or beyond the value of a fourth part of the tithes, [the Church shall have jurisdiction], but then it shall begin with a writ *de advocatione decimarum* etc.[2] And also in trespass between two parsons, if the right to tithes comes in question the spiritual court shall have jurisdiction, but if it is between a parson and a lay man then the court shall not be put out of jurisdiction etc.

[Lecture Four]

The statute is also *and her liberties inviolate*. I understand by these words that they shall have all these reasonable liberties, namely that when one is convicted of a felony that he shall have the privilege of his clergy which privilege must be demanded according to the law used, or otherwise he shall not have this. For if he wishes to demand this before the inquest has given their verdict he shall not have this, for it is not demandable until he is in jeopardy of his life.[3] But he may have this after the verdict and before judgment, and then he is a clerk convict, or he may have it after judgment and then he is a clerk attaint. And when he is thus delivered to the ordinary he must be treated according to our law or otherwise the ordinary shall be punished, for if [the ordinary] allows the felon to escape he shall lose £100 to the king, and if he allows one to make purgation when

---

[1] Merton, 20 Hen. III, c. 9 (*SR*, i. 4). The writ of bastardy is given in *Bracton*, iv. 303.
[2] *Register*, 29v.
[3] This position seems to have been associated with Prysot C.J.C.P. by the end of the fifteenth century. See Mich. 3 Hen. VII, fo. 12, pl. 10, per Bryan.

ceo est auxi eschaper en lordinary, pur que est a voier quell felon feer son purgation et quell nemi.

Cestui que est atteint per verdit et juge don vers luy il peut fair son purgation,
et issint peut cestui que porter son clergy apres verdit et avant jugement quar peut
esteier que uncore il est nient culpable et pur ceo enquestez de clerke luy peut
acquiter. Mez cestui que confesse le felony, et cestui que abjure, et cestui que est
utlage ne unques poient fair lour purgation, et silz font, lordinarie fait auterment
que est le privilege de Seint Esglise et serra demy en luy eschapor etc.

Auxi ilz averont lour liberties de lour seintwariez accord lour grauntez et que
null felon ne tretor serra pris hors deux. Auxi si un felon fue a un esglise sil
demesne luy accord a le ley il avera le privilege de Seint Esglise quell demenyny
covient destre tile: il primez covient demander un coroner et sil soit demande de
luy pur que il prender lesglise il covient dire pur felony mez nemi le certeinte
come il ferra a le coroner. Quar quant le coroner vie, il covient confesse un felonie (quell jour, quell an, et quell lieu il ceo fist) a son paroll de feir un sufficient
confession, et sil ne fait il est loiable pur luy prender hors desglise. Et sil confesse
sufficientment il forjurer le terre et port serra a luy assigne per le coroner etc.

[Disputation Four]

Donquez jeo pose que le felon apres le port assigne ne voill aler a son port mez
demurer en lesglise outer xl jourz, que serra fait? Moy semble que il serra penduz quar il ad misuse son privilege et quant il aver libertie daler et ne voill aler,
donquez est son folie et serra en mesme le case sicome il navera fait sufficient
confession etc. Donquez sil ala a son port et ne soit aver nief pur isser le realme,
jentend que lez constable reameneront luy arrer a lesglise et donquez per le coroner auter port serra luy assign etc.

of right he should not make purgation this is also an escape in the ordinary, for which [reason] it is to be seen what felon shall make this purgation and what not.[1]

One is attainted by verdict and judgment is given against him: he may make his purgation, and so may one who brings his clergy after the verdict and before judgment; for it may be that still he is not guilty and therefore the inquest of clerks may acquit him. But one who confesses the felony, and one who abjures, and one who is outlawed may never make their purgation, and if they do, the ordinary does otherwise than is the privilege of the Holy Church, and it shall be considered an escape in him etc.

Also they shall have their liberties of their sanctuaries according to their grants, and that no felon or traitor shall be taken out of them. Also if a felon flees to a church if he behaves himself according to the law, he shall have the privilege of Holy Church, which must be done this way: first he must ask for a coroner and if he is asked why he took sanctuary he must say for felony, but not the certainty as he shall for the coroner. For when the coroner comes, he must confess a felony (what day, what year, and what place he did it) on his oath to make a sufficient confession, and if he does not make it it is lawful to take him out of the church. And if he confesses sufficiently he shall forswear the land and a port shall be assigned to him by the coroner etc.

[DISPUTATION FOUR]

Then suppose that after the port is assigned the felon will not go to his port but remains in the church beyond forty days, what shall be done? It seems to me that he shall be hanged, for he has misused his privilege and when he has liberty to go and will not go, then it is his folly, and it shall be the same way as if he had not made a sufficient confession etc. Then if he goes to his port and cannot find a ship to leave the realm, I understand that the constable shall bring him back again to the church, and then another port shall be assigned to him by the coroner etc.

---

[1] This is a reference to *Pro Clero* though the statute does not specify the penalties. 25 Edw. III, stat. 6, c. 6 (*SR*, i. 326).

READING SIX

MAGNA CARTA: CAPITULO 1[1]

[*fo. 195*] *In primis concessimus deo et hac presenti carta nostra confirmavimus pro nobis et heredibus nostris imperpetuum* etc. Ceux ordinaunces fueront primerment faytes en temps le roy John etc. et puis furent grauntes per patent per Henry son fitz etc. Lestatute de Marlebrige fist cest destre un estatut etc. Tielx grauntes scilicet *concessimus deo*, a cest jour ne vaylent mez in auncien temps furent bon et William Conqueror dona all abbe de Bury viij hides et di per ceux parolx 'adjaceat monasterio Sancti Edmundi de Bury' etc. Labbe de Glastonbury per ceux parols omnia jura regalia use darreyner felons etc. Labbe de Battell anno xxx <31 nota>[i] in le liver dassisarum per mesme lez parolx avoyt conusance de plee etc. Don fuit fayt in auncien temps a un moygn, sexton, et monasterio etc.: vide pur ceo Belknap xlix [Edw. III][2] in un scire facias etc.

   In primis concessimus deo etc. Deuz ne peut estre graunte [pur ceo quil est donor de toutz choses][3] et in chescun graunt covient estre [grauntor et][4] graunte per que semble avowier que purront estre grauntes etc. Un feme ne peut estre grauntee a son baron etc., mez le royn peut estre graunte all roy etc. Philipa regina suist un scire facias en son nosme demesne xxj [Edw. III] in liver dassisarum etc. Item <iij H[en.] 6>[5] bref de faux jugement fuit abatus pur ceo quill fuist in Curia Regis lou ill serroyt in Curia Regine etc. Devyse per le baron fayt a son feme est bon [et le caus est que il ne prist effecte tanque apres le mort le baron et donsque nest son feme][6]: vide pur ceo lassise Chrystyan Culbere xxviij [Edw. III] in liver dassisarum etc. Item home seisi dona terre per fayt a un estranger et a son feme demesne et fayt liverie all estranger, semble destre bon. Item home seisi fayt lese a term de vie le remainder a son <feme>[i] demesne, est bon etc. Item home seisie leve un fyn a un estranger pur term de vie le remainder a luy mesme in le tayll, ceo ne peut estre: 42 [Edw. III][7] in un scire facias etc.

   Item home done terre a un moign [professe pur terme de vie][8] le remainder outer, ceo est voyd. Mez sill devise terre a un moign, le remainder outer a un <moign>[d] <auter>,[9] ceo est bon: vide pur ceo [semblablez][10] casez mis per Prisott xxxvij H[en.] 6 in un sub pena etc. Home done terre a un moign professe pur terme de son vie, le quell ad licens dell pape daver benefice et ceo que appent a un esglise

[1] In margin: Hervye *HLSa*.
[2] *HLSa, Pb*.
[3] *HLSa*.
[4] *Hg*.
[5] 2 Hen. IV *HLSa*.
[6] *Pb*.
[7] *Pb*.
[8] *Pb*.
[9] estranger *Pb*; *om. HLSa*.
[10] *Pb*; blank in *Hg*.

READING SIX

MAGNA CARTA: CHAPTER ONE

In the first place we have granted to God and by this our present charter confirmed for ourselves and our heirs for ever etc. These ordinances were first made in the time of King John etc., and then were granted by patent by Henry his son etc. The statute of Marlborough made this a statute etc.[1] Such grants namely, *we have granted to God*, are worthless today but in ancient times they were good, and William the Conqueror gave the abbot of Bury eight and a half hides by these words, 'let there be to the monastery of St Edmund of Bury' etc.[2] The abbot of Glastonbury by these words *omnia jura regalia* is accustomed to arraign felons etc. The abbot of Battle in the thirtieth year of [Edw. III in] the *Liber Assisarum* had cognizance of pleas by the same words.[3] A gift was made in ancient times to a monk, sexton and monastery etc.: see for this Belknap in 49 Edw. III in a *scire facias* etc.[4]

    In the first place we have granted to God etc. God cannot be a grantee because he is the giver of all things, and in every grant there must be a grantor and a grantee, by which it appears that we must see who may be grantees etc. A woman may not be a grantee from her husband etc., but the queen may be a grantee from the king etc. Queen Philippa sued a *scire facias* in her own name in 21 Edw. III in the *Liber Assisarum* etc.[5] Item, in 3 Hen. VI a writ of false judgment was abated because it was in the king's court when it should have been in the queen's etc.[6] A devise by the husband made to his wife is good, and the reason is that it does not take effect until after the death of the husband, and then she is not his wife: see for this the assize of Christian Culbere 28 [Edw. III] in the *Liber Assisarum* etc.[7] Item, a man seised gives land by deed to a stranger and to his own wife and makes livery to the stranger, it seems that it is good. Item, a man seised makes a lease for term of life, the remainder to his own wife, it is good. Item, a man seised levies a fine to a stranger for term of life the remainder to himself in tail, this cannot be: 42 Edw. III in a *scire facias* etc.[8]

    Item, a man gives land to a professed monk for term of life the remainder over, this is void. But if he devises land to a monk, the remainder over to another, this is good: see for this like cases put by Prysot, 37 Hen. VI in a *subpoena*.[9] A man gives land to a professed monk for term of his life, [the monk] has a licence from the pope to have a benefice and those things which belong to a church

---

[1] 52 Hen. III, c. 5 (*SR*, i. 20).

[2] D. C. Douglas ed., *Feudal Documents from the Abbey of Bury St. Edmunds* (1932), pp. 48–49. The charter says nine and a half rather than eight and a half. See also Reading Seven below, p. 96, n. 5.

[3] YB 30 Lib. Ass., fos 178–179, pl. 31.

[4] YB 49 Lib. Ass., fos 320–321, pl. 8.

[5] YB 21 Lib. Ass., fo.79, pl. 13.

[6] YB Hil. 3 Hen. VI, fo. 26, pl. 7.

[7] YB 27 Lib. Ass. fos 141–142, pl. 90 (*rectius* 60).

[8] YB Pas. 42 Edw. III, fos 9–10, pl. 11.

[9] Probably YB Trin. 37 Hen. VI, fos 35–36, pl. 23, though Prysot does not speak in the report.

et, sill resign (que bien lirroyt a luy), de prendre un auter benefice xxv H[en.] 6.
Et la est dit quill nyad power de purchacer a luy et cez heires: semble que ceo
estre bon, quere etc. Bulles dexcommengement dell pape ne serront alowes: anno
xxx [Edw. III] in liver dassisarum. Vide ergo diversite dez bullez que enabelent
aschun parson de purchaser etc. et bullez de excommengement etc.

Item le roy fayt un moygn son fermor <pur term danz>[1] ceo est bon et ill avera
action [sans son sovereign][2] [etc. come devant etc.][3] <coment que ceo bref soyt
especiall quar tielx parolx seroit in le bref quo minus debitum domini regis sol-
vere non poterit <saunz son soverayn>[4] etc. Mez si aschun les a luy soyt fayt [fo.
195v] durant cell lees per un estranger, ceo est voyd etc.>[5]

Un abbe parson imparsonee de temps dont etc. que avoit toutz ditz vicar south
luy et labbe a chescun temps davoydance etc., devaunt lestatute Hen. iiij, ad don
ceo a un de cez commoignez et ilz (per tiell nome) ount estre pled et enpledablez
etc. a cell temps: terre done a tiell vicar pur term de vie fuit bon 44 [Edw. III en]
quare impedit.

Item si home don terre all roy saunz matter de record ou fayt in roll est voyd,
mez sill infeffe le roy et un estranger per fayt in fee et delivera seisin a lestranger
semble que le roy avera avayll de ceo, mez saunz fayt ceo ne vault etc. Item si
le roy dona terre etc. a un home utlage de felony le don est voyd etc. Mez si un
comen person fayt feffement a un home <issint>[6] utlage ceo est bon. Mesme
le ley dun home atteynt et commyse all ordinary le quell luy suffre aler a large
per purgation etc. Item [si][7] le roy seisi dell maner de Dale a quell villens soynt
regardant, dona a un dez villens mesme le maner ceo est voyd etc., [quar nest
enfraunches per cest don: autre est de comen person].[8]

Item John att Style ad issue ij fitz, terre est done a le pere pur term de vie le
remainder a cestui <de lez ij>[9] fitz que primez vient a Powlys, semble que ceo
est bon: vide pur ceo le case de M. Geny a⁰ ... E 4ᵗⁱˢ etc. Item les fayt a term de
vie le remainder a lez droit heires John att Style et nul John att Style in rerum
natura est a cell temps mez puis est un tiell John att Style etc., le remainder est
voyd etc.

Mich 11 H[en.] 4ᵗⁱ, Thyrning dit que si terre soyt don a un home et a cestui que serra son primer feme [en le taile][10] tout soyt quill nyad feme all temps
dell don, que le don est bon all <feff>ᵈ feme quar la ill dit que ceo est bon
tayll: quere quar semble que non etc. Item lees fayt a un home a term de vie
le remainder parochyaunce all opps dun esglise etc., le remainder est voyd

---

1   Om. Pb.
2   HLSa, Pb.
3   Pb.
4   Om. HLSa.
5   Om. Pb.
6   Om. Pb.
7   Pb.
8   Pb.
9   Om. HLSa.
10   HLSa, Pb.

and if he resigns (which is certainly permissible for him), to take another benefice: 25 Hen. VI.[1] And there it is said that [the monk] does not have power to
purchase to himself and his heirs: it seems that this is good, query etc. Bulls
of excommunication from the pope are not allowed: 30 [Edw. III] in the *Liber
Assisarum*.[2] See therefore the distinction between bulls which enable some persons to purchase etc. and bulls of excommunication etc.

Item, the king makes a monk his farmer for term of years this is good, and he
shall have an action without his superior etc., as before etc., even if this writ is
special, for such words should be in the writ *quo minus debitum domini regis sol-
vere non poterit*.[3] But if any lease is made to him during this lease by a stranger,
this is void etc.

[There is] an abbot [who has been] parson imparsonate since time immemorial
[and] who has always had a vicar under him, and every time the vicarage became
vacant etc. the abbot (before the statute of Hen. IV)[4] had given it to one of his
co-monks, and they had been pleaded and pleadable etc. (by such a name) for
all that time: land given to such a vicar for term of life was good 44 Edw. III in
quare impedit.[5]

Item, if a man gives lands to the king without matter of record or an enrolled
deed it is void, but if he enfeoffs the king and a stranger by deed in fee and delivers seisin to the stranger, it seems that the king may take advantage of this, but
without a deed it is worthless. Item, if the king gives land etc. to a man outlawed
for felony the gift is void etc. But if a common person makes a feoffment to a
man thus outlawed, it is good. The law is the same of a man attainted and committed to the ordinary who allows him to go at large by purgation etc. Item if the
king [who is] seised of the manor of Dale to which villeins belong gives the same
manor to one of the villeins this is void, for he is not enfranchised by this gift: it
is otherwise of a common person.

Item John at Style has issue two sons, land is given to the father for term of life
the remainder to whichever of the two sons first comes to St Paul's, it seems that
this is good: see for this the case of Mr Jenney ... Edw. IV[6] etc. Item, a lease is
made for term of life the remainder to the right heirs of John at Style and there
is no John at Style alive at that time, but afterwards there is a John at Style etc.,
the remainder is void etc.

Mich. 11 Hen. IV, Thirning says that if land is given in tail to a man and to the
one who shall be his first wife, the gift is good to the woman even though he does
not have a wife at the time of the gift, for there he says that this is a good tail:
query, for it seems not etc.[7] Item, a lease is made to a man for term of life, the
remainder to the parishioners to the use of a church etc., the remainder is void

---

[1] No reported cases for this year.
[2] YB 30 Lib. Ass., fo. 177, pl. 19.
[3] Cf. YB Hil. 8 Hen. V, fo. 6, pl. 23, *rectius* 24.
[4] 4 Hen. IV, c. 12 (*SR*, ii. 136–137). It confirms 15 Ric. II, c. 6 (*SR*, ii, 80).
[5] YB Hil. 44 Edw. III, fo. 4, pl. 17.
[6] Not found.
[7] This point is made in passing in YB Hil. 11 Hen. IV, fo. 40, pl. 5.

etc. <d>ᵈ Mez don fayt parochyeins etc. all opps dell esglise dun mesebook, chales, <greyll, vestyments>¹ et similia ceo est bon: vide pur ceo Prisoyt xxxvij H[en.] vj en trespass [port]² per [deux] gard [de esglise]³ etc. Item les fayt etc. le remainder outer all ij de meliors de tiell fraternyte corporat le remainder est bon: 49 [Edw. III] etc. Cyte corporatt per nome dell mayr, bayly et cominalty: si lez soyt fayt ut supra le remainder all baylly et commynalty etc. le remainder est voyd etc. Mez tiell remainder graunt <comunibus>⁴ ceo est bon si soyt aschun mayr all temps dell lees: <quere si null meir all temps <de lees>ᵈ etc.>⁵ Item lees ut supra le remainder conventivis ceo est voyd etc., mez tiell remainder monachis est bon si soyt aschun abbe all temps dell lees etc.

Item don fayt deo abbe et conventivis ceo est bon a toutz jourz saunz rien parler de lour successors: per Hankeford [*fo. 196*] <11 H[en.] 4ᵗⁱˢ>⁶ etc., mez semble que ceo nest bon forsque pur term de vie labbe tamen [quere] etc. Item si un aprist all covent tempore vacationis xx li., le successor serra charge: per Hanckford <in un scire facias 2 Hen.] 6>.⁷ Donques posito que bienz ou chatelx a eux sont dones tempore vacationis semble le don est bon etc. Item le roy dona le manor de Dale probis hominibus ville de Islyngton riens reservaunt le don est voyd, mez sil reserva aschun rent auter est: <7 E[dw.] 4 en un nota>⁸ etc. Et donques posito que le roy dona ut supra reservaunt certen rent et lees est fayt a term de vie <le remainder>⁹ probis hominibus etc. esteant le patent in son fors si tiell remainder soyt [graunte oustre si ceo soit]¹⁰ bon etc.? Semble que non etc. [Tamen quere].¹¹

Lestatut parle outer et dit quod *anglicana ecclesia libera sit* etc. Ceux parols afferment le comen ley etc.

Mon villein fayt moign ou chanon professe etc. jeo ne luy [puisse]¹² seisera, mez sill soyt darrein auter est etc. Mesme le ley si un soyt enhable per le pape daver benefice [quar donsque]¹³ jeo luy seisera etc. Mesme le ley sill soyt fayt soverayn dun meason, come abbe ou priour, ou soyt cree in evesque: ill serra seisi, ill [forfetera]¹⁴ sez bienz sill soyt utlage, et in temps E[dw.] 4ᵗⁱ ill fyst graund fyn etc. Item villenes esspouse <esspouse>¹⁵ a fraunk home ell ne serra seisi mez si devors soyt ewe ou si le baron devy auter est etc.: [vide Magister Litilton en son lyver de villenage].¹⁶

Item devaunt lestat de Marlebrige archeveques, abbates et huiusmodi fuerent compelles de <vener>¹⁷ all view de fraunkplege: vide pur ceo brevia de statuto in registro etc. <uncore>ᵈ Et uncore ilz ne furent compelles la destre myse in jury pur le roy etc., quar semble a moy que la le ley ne eux compell a fayr ceo que est contrary merement a [lour]¹⁸ ordre, come dentyter aschun home de felony etc.

---

¹ *Om. HLSa; Om. Pb* vestments.   ² *HLSa*; parle *Hg*.   ³ Both additions in *HLSa*.
⁴ civibus *HLSa, Pb*.   ⁵ *Om. Pb*.   ⁶ In margin *HLSa*.   ⁷ In margin *HLSa*.
⁸ In margin *HLSa*.   ⁹ *Om. Pb*.   ¹⁰ *Pb*.
¹¹ *Pb* in very faded ink (a number of additions are made to the text in the same faded ink).
¹² *HLSa*.   ¹³ *Pb*.
¹⁴ *HLSa*; forfera *Hg*.
¹⁵ Written twice in MS.
¹⁶ *HLSa*. In margin: C ixº ixº.
¹⁷ densue interlineated *Pb*.
¹⁸ *HLSa, Pb*; un *Hg*.

etc. But a gift made to the parishioners etc. to the use of the church of a mass book, chalice, grail, vestments and similar things is good: see for this Prysot 37 Hen. VI in trespass brought by two churchwardens etc.[1] Item, a lease is made etc. the remainder over to two of the best of such a corporate fraternity, the remainder is good: 49 Edw. III etc.[2] A city is incorporated in the name of the mayor, bailiff and commonalty: if a lease is made as above [with] the remainder to the bailiff and commonalty etc., the remainder is void etc. But such a remainder granted 'to the commonalty' is good if there is any mayor at the time of the lease: query if there is no mayor at the time etc. Item, a lease as above, the remainder to 'the members of the convent', this is void etc., but such a remainder 'to the monks' is good if there is any abbot at the time of the lease etc.

Item, a gift is made 'to God, the abbot and the members of the convent', this is good for ever without saying anything of their successors: Hankford 11 Hen. IV etc., but it seems that it is only good for term of life of the abbot, so query etc.[3] Item, if one lends £20 to a convent during a vacancy, the successor shall be charged: by Hankford in a *scire facias* 2 Hen. VI.[4] Now suppose that goods or chattels are given to them during a vacancy, it seems the gift is good etc. Item, the king gives the manor of Dale 'to the good men of the vill of Islington' reserving nothing, the gift is void, but if he reserves any rent it is otherwise: 7 Edw. IV in a note etc.[5] And then suppose the king gives as above reserving certain rent, and a lease is made for term of life the remainder 'to the good men etc.', [and] with the patent in force a further remainder is granted over, would this be good? It seems not etc. However query.

The statute speaks further and says *that the English Church shall be free* etc. These words affirm the common law etc.

My villein is made a professed monk or canon etc. I may not seize him, but if he is deraigned it is otherwise etc. The law is the same if one is enabled by the pope to have a benefice, for then I may seize him. The law is the same if he is made superior of a house, such as abbot or prior, or is created a bishop: he shall be seized, he shall forfeit his goods if he is outlawed, and in the time of Edward IV he made a great fine etc. Item, a bondwoman married to a free man shall not be seized, but if she is divorced, or if the husband dies, it is otherwise etc.: see Master Littleton in his book of villenage.[6]

Item, before the statute of Marlborough archbishops, abbots and suchlike were compelled to come to the view of frankpledge: for this see writs on the statues in the *Register* etc.[7] And yet they were not compelled there to be put on the jury for the king etc., for it seems to me that the law does not compel them to do that which is absolutely contrary to their order, as to indict any one of felony etc.

[1] YB Trin. 37 Hen. VI, fo. 30–31, pl. 11, though Moyle J.C.P. makes the point rather than Prysot C.J.C.P.
[2] YB Hil. 49 Edw. III, fo. 3, pl. 7.
[3] YB Trin. 11 Hen. IV, fo. 83, pl. 31.
[4] YB Pas. 2 Hen. VI, fos 9–10, pl. 6.
[5] YB Trin. 7 Edw. IV, fo. 14, pl. 7.
[6] Littleton, *Tenures*, 95 § 202.
[7] *Register*, fo. 175.

Item abbe ou priour tesmoigner in fayt dedit peut estre jur sur ceo etc. Item par-son dun esglyse que ad terre per discent peut estre mys in panell en assise etc.: vide registrum inter brevia de statut. <Parson, vicar ne null home infra sacros serra compell destre [biduall][1] etc.: vide registrum inter brevia de statut>.[2]

Cest paroll *libera* nest solement a entendre pur lez persons dez ministre de Seynct Esglyse mez est a estre intendue que lesglyse serra fraunk dez xv[me] et taxez et auters seculer demandez, quar semble que <nul>[i] labbe, priour ou hui-usmodi serront charge all xv graunt per parlement <per reson daschun chatell quill ad per reson de son esglise, come offrynges, tythynges, et huiusmodi, ou per reson de son glebe et de ces provenauntes, ceo est adir per reson daschun terre apperteynaunt a son esglyse: le xx an E[dw.] le primer. Mez pur chatuex [et profeitz]>[3] etc. provenauntes daschuns terres annex all esglyse puis le dit xx an etc. ilz serront charges: vide pur ceo registrum inter brevia de statut etc. Item in aschun hundred[s] ilz payent pur le terre et nemi pur lez binz: donquez posito quun abbe ou priour purchace tiell terre etc. semble que ilz payent pur cell terre etc.

Secunda Lectura

[*fo. 196v*] *Et habeat omnia sua jura integra* etc. Ceux parolx affirmant le comen ley etc. per cell paroll jura est intendue que ceux de Seynt Esglyse averont toutes plees que a lour court appent etc. per que est avoyer queux manerz dez plees appent a lour court et queux nemi etc. Si debate soyt perenter ij clerkes de Seynt Esglyse dez dysmez que namount dell valu de iiij part dell esglyse indicavit ne gist etc. Donques posito que auter debate soyt perenter mesmez lez parsons de mesme leglise issint que le value dez ambideux dissmez ensemblement amoun-tont all value dell iiij parte etc. <Si un intyer duyte que passe passe [*sic*] le som de xl s. soyt sever in ij partes etc. et sur ceo jugement in court baron don <sur tout le matter gist bref>[d] sur tout le matter gist bref de faux jugement: vide pur ceo in liver [assissarum en][4] bref derror port in Chester anno < >[5] et a ma conceyt ceo cas est semble a lauter quaunt a leffect>[6]; le patron dell clerk avera severalles libelles etc. et sur ceo un indicavit etc.

Item si aschun debate soyt pur desmez dell forest de Inglewood ou de Rockyngham, soyt ill pluis ou mynez ceo appent all court le roy [come appert][7] <xxij libro assisarum>[8] etc., et lez dismez dez ditz forest appertey-nont all roy etc. Item ij parsons etc. lun claym le very value dell moyte de lauter esglyse, auter nad remydy <<sinon>[9] in court Christian etc.>[10] quar quantyte de dysmez entre parson ne viendra en debate etc. Null bref de tres-pass dez dismez per [nosm][11] [de dismes si non en court Christien etc.

---

[1] MS reads viduall.   [2] *Om. Pb.*
[3] *Pb*, also changes the order of the clauses.
[4] *HLSa.*
[5] Left blank in *Hg, HLSa.*
[6] *Om. Pb.*   [7] *Pb.*   [8] In margin *HLSa.*
[9] *Om. Pb.*   [10] *Om. HLSa.*   [11] *HLSa*; nonsuy *Hg.*

Item, an abbot or prior who is a witness to a deed which is denied may be sworn on this etc. Item, the parson of a church who has land by descent may be put on a panel in an assize etc.: see the *Register* in the writs on the statutes.[1] [A] parson, vicar or any one in holy orders may not be compelled to be a bedell etc.: see the *Register* in the writs on the statutes.[2]

This word *free* is not only to be understood as the persons of the ministers of Holy Church, but is to be understood that the Church shall be free of fifteenths and taxes and other secular demands, for it seems that no abbot, prior or suchlike shall be charged for the fifteenth granted by Parliament by reason of any chattel he has by reason of his church, such as offerings, tithes and such things, or by reason of his glebe and of his provenances, that is to say by reason of any land belonging to his church: 20 Edw. I.[3] But for chattels and profits etc. coming from any land annexed to the church after the said twentieth year etc. they shall be charged: see for this the *Register* in the writs on the statutes etc.[4] Item in some hundreds they pay for the land and not for the goods: suppose that an abbot or prior purchases such land etc. it seems that they shall pay for such land etc.

SECOND LECTURE

And shall have all her rights entire etc. These words affirm the common law etc. [and] by this word *rights* it is to be understood that those of Holy Church shall have all pleas which belong to their court etc., therefore we must see what kinds of plea belong to their court and what do not etc. If there is a dispute between two clerks of Holy Church over tithes which do not amount to the value of a fourth part of the church *indicavit* does not lie etc. Now suppose there is another dispute between the same parsons over the same church so that the value of both tithes altogether amounts to the value of a fourth part etc? If an entire debt which exceeds the sum of 40s. is severed in two parts etc., and judgment is given thereupon in court baron a writ of false judgment lies on all the matter: see for this the *Liber Assisarum* in a writ of error brought in Chester in the year [20 Edw. III], and in my view this case is like the other as to its effect: the patron of the clerk shall have several libels etc. and an *indicavit* lies on this etc.[5]

Item, if there is any dispute over tithes of the forest of Inglewood or Rockingham, whether they are more or less [than a fourth], this belongs in the king's court, as appears in 22 *Liber Assisarum* etc.,[6] and the tithes of the said forest belong to the king etc. Item, [there are] two parsons etc. the one claims the true value of the moiety of the other church, the other only has remedy in court Christian etc., for the quantity of tithes between parsons does not come into dispute etc. No writ of trespass [lies] for tithes under the name of tithes except in court Christian etc.

[1] *Register*, fo. 184v has a parson amerced according to his lay fee.
[2] *Register*, fo. 187v.
[3] 20 Edw. I (*SR*, i. 111).
[4] *Register*, fo. 188.
[5] Trin. 20 Edw. III pt. 2 (Rolls Ser.) pp. 147–149, pl. 68; *Register*, fo. 36.
[6] YB 22 Lib. Ass., fos 101–102, pl. 75.

Auxi quant en bref de droit de dismes le droit del dismes est termyn le judge del court Christien donera judgment, per que semble (ut supra) null avera bref de droit des dismes si non le patron.][1]

<Item ij parsons sont le servant lun prent lez dismez lauter, ceo appent all court le roy: vide bref de trespass 44 [Edw. III] term Mich. et H[il.] 6 E[dw.] iiij[tis] etc.>[2] Item deux parsons sont le servant lun prent lez dismez lauter le quell port bref de trespass etc. le servant justyfy etc. <come servant etc.>[3] pur ceo que lez parsonagez furent adjoynantes et le lieu ou il suppose etc. est [deinz][4] le parish etc. et don color all plaintiff, a que le plaintiff fait son title pur ceo quill et toutz ceux que estat etc. come parsons ount use de temps dont etc. de aver lez dismes in le lieu ou etc. saunz ceo quilz fuer lez [dismes][5] de son <mass>[d] master: ceo appent all cort le roy etc.[6] Quere si tiel prescription soyt title sufficient pur le plaintiff ou nemi: vide H[il.] xx H[en.] vj et [Mich. xxxj H[en.] vj][7] quar droit de dismez, come semble, ne serra trie in court le roy mez la possession. [Tamen vide le contrarie de ceo xxij E[dw.] iiij tenduz clerement][8] etc.

Item si ij fermors de ij parsons soynt a variauns ceo appent all court le roy etc. Mesme le ley perenter un parson et le fermor dun auter parson: 35 H[en.] 6 et <Mich. 43 E[dw.] 3>.[9] Contrary vij° H[en.] iiij etc. <Nota que le ley a cest jour est en lez ij cases avantditz que ceo appent al court Cristien etc.>[10]

Item si un home don a un parson un acre de terre a luy et cez successorez per fayt indent, pur le quell mesme le parson oue lassent dell patron et ordinary per mesme le fayt graunta pur luy et cez successorez que lauter et cez heires et sez assignez serront dischargez dez dismes de tiell maner etc., si le successor le parson luy vexa in court spirituell ill puit aver action sur son cas pur tiell [fo. 197] vexation et sur ceo prohibition: vide pur ceo bref in registro inter brevia de prohibition et vide 8 Edw. IV etc. Item si un parson graunt per indentur ut supra a un de cez parisshens destre dischargez dez dismes etc. et ceo nient obstant il luy vexa in court Christian, null prohibition gist, mez lauter peut aver bref de covenant etc. Item home peut prescribe in modo decimandi, come adire quill et toutz ceux que estate etc. de temps etc. ont use de dismer meinz que le x partye, come le xij parte ou le xx parte etc., mez in non decimando null peut prescriber come adire quill et toutz ceux etc. de temps ut supra nount use de payer dismez. Et issint diversite etc.

Item si jeo et un auter sumus fayt executorz etc. et puis jeo graunt per indentur a mon compagnon que jeo ne prendre charge dell administration et ceo nient

[1] *HLSa.*
[2] *Om. Pb.*
[3] *Om. Pb.*
[4] *HLSa, Pb*; de *Hg.*
[5] *HLSa, Pb*; demesne *Hg.*
[6] In margin: lou droit des dismes serra trespass et lou poss *HLSa.*
[7] *HLSa, Pb*; 30 H[en.] 6 *Hg.*
[8] *Pb.*
[9] 44 E[dw.] 3 *HLSa.*
[10] *Pb.*

Also when in a writ of right to tithes the right to tithes is determined the judge of the court Christian shall give judgment, whereby it seems (as above) that no-one shall have a writ of right of tithes except the patron.

Item, there are two parsons [and] the servant of one of them takes the tithes of the other, this belongs in the king's court: see the writ of trespass Mich. 44 Edw. III and Hil. 6 Edw. IV etc.[1] Item, there are two parsons [and] the servant of the one takes the tithes of the other who brings a writ of trespass etc. the servant justifies etc. as servant etc. because the parsonages were adjoining and the place where he supposes [the trespass to have been committed] etc. is within the parish etc. and gives colour to the plaintiff, whereupon the plaintiff makes his title on the grounds that he and all those whose estate [he has] etc. as parsons have been used from time immemorial to have the tithes in the place where etc. without that they were the tithes of his master: this belongs in the king's court etc. Query if such a prescription is a sufficient title for the plaintiff or not: see Hil. 20 Hen. VI and Mich. 31 Hen VI,[2] for the right to tithes, as it seems, shall not be tried in the king's court whereas the possession [shall be]. However see the contrary of this held clearly in 22 Edw. IV etc.[3]

Item, if two farmers of two parsons are at variance this belongs in the king's court etc. The law is the same between a parson and the farmer of another parson: 35 Hen. VI and Mich 43 Edw. III.[4] [See] 7 Hen. IV to the contrary.[5] Note that the law at this day in the two cases aforesaid is that this belongs in the court Christian etc.

Item, if a man gives an acre of land to a parson to him and his successors by a deed indented, whereby the same parson, with the assent of the patron and the ordinary, by the same deed grants for him and his successors that the other and his heirs and assigns shall be discharged of the tithes of such a manor etc.: if the parson's successor vexes him in the spiritual court he may have an action on his case for such vexation, and a prohibition thereon: see for this the writ in the *Register* in the writs of prohibition and see 8 Edw. IV etc.[6] Item, if a parson grants by indenture as above to one of his parishioners to be discharged of tithes etc. and this notwithstanding he vexes him in court Christian, no prohibition lies, but the other may have a writ of covenant etc. Item, a man may prescribe *in modo decimandi*, for instance by saying that he and all those whose estate [he has] etc. from time immemorial have been accustomed to tithe less than the tenth part, such as the twelfth part or the twentieth part etc., but no-one may prescribe in *non decimandi* such as to say that he and all those etc. from time immemorial, as above, are not accustomed to pay tithes. Thus there is a distinction etc.

Item, if I and another are made executors etc. and then I grant by indenture to my companion that I shall not take charge of the administration and this

[1] YB Mich. 44 Edw. III, fo. 39, pl. 38; YB Mich. 6 Edw. IV, fo. 3, pl. 7.
[2] YB Hil. 20 Hen. VI, fo.17, pl. 8; YB Mich. 31 Hen. VI, fo. 11, pl. 7.
[3] YB Mich. 22 Edw. IV, fos 23–24, pl. 3.
[4] YB Mich. 35 Hen. VI, fos 39–40, pl. 47; YB Mich. 43 Edw. III, fo. 34, pl. 44.
[5] YB Hil. 7 Hen. IV, fo. 35, pl. 2.
[6] *Register*, fos 38v-39; YB Mich. 8 Edw. IV, fos 13–14, pl. 13.

obstant jeo luy vex in court Christian daver administration ovesque luy et ill port bref de covenant ale comen ley (come [bien peut][1] etc.), null prohibition gist etc.

Item le parsonage de Dale vault per an xx li. et un que de droit doit dismer per an garbez et auterz chosez a le value de x li. etc. soyt in arrerage de payment de certen dismez: soyt il plus ou meynz est all court Christian. <Item est diversite perenter dismez et un portion>[2] et uncore ambideux soynt le x partye etc. Desmez soynt deinz le parisshe ou le parsonage [est][3] proprement mez portions sont [properment][4] tielx quun parson ad deinz auter parsonage etc.[5]

Item le punysshment pur defamation ou slaunder, come de nosmer un home un avowtrour ou fornicatour, gist in court Christian etc. mez auter si un nosme un auter son villein ou dit quill ad luy robbe ou quill ad robb un auter etc., quar cell purgation gist a le comen ley, come per bref de nativo habendo ou per appell ou acquittell sur indytement. Ceo suffist pur lez inditors etc. Mez si null tiell suyt soyt vers le party a le comen ley, [quere][6] si aschun punysshment soyt in court Christian et semble que non. Et prohibition in le registrum quando quis trahitur etc. [eo quod asseront se counter][7] fecisse sigillum etc. inter brevia de prohibition etc.

Item si un parson soyt oute de glebe de son esglise ill avera assize et sill re-entre sur le disseisor ill avera bref de trespass pur le mesne trespass: 43 <E[dw.]>[d] [III][8] in liver dassisarum etc.

Item si le cimitorie soyt noun clause le punishment appent a court Christian. Item dez herbez pues in un cimitore le parson avera bref de trespass etc. [Quere en que][9] le franktenement de ceo est? In nullis: <vide Wad M[ich.] 13 <R[ic.] 2>[10]>.[11]

Item si un home face surment a un auter de luy infeffer en certen terre per un certen jour et all jour etc. ill ne luy infeff pas lauter luy vex in court Christian pur le surment infreynt ill avera prohibition: per Hankford 11 H[en.] 4 in un attach-ment sur un prohibition. <M[ich.]>[12] 2 H[en.] 4 in un consultation accord etc. Item si un confesse devant un ordinarie quill ad iff infrent [sic] son foy de ceo quill ad fayt surment [fo. 197v] a un auter de luy aver pay x li. etc. et ill ne paya pas, lordinarye peut luy injoyn corporall penaunce mez ill ne peut luy injoyn de payer le dett etc.: per Thorp <<22>[13] [Edw. III] en le liver dassissarum in le fyn dun nota>[14] etc. Donques si cestui que ad infreynt son surment a un auter, ut supra, de son offer <voyr>[d] demesne voyll fayr promyse de payer all partye a que ill fist surment certen som dargent pur son redemption scilicet pur estre discharge

---

[1] bon plee (conj.) Pb.
[2] Item dismez deffer dun portion Pb.
[3] HLSa, Pb.   [4] HLSa.
[5] In margin: diversitie enter dismes et portions HLSa.
[6] Pb.
[7] Pb; HLSa has a blank space in the MS. followed by conter.
[8] In margin: 44° libr ass HLSa.
[9] Pb.   [10] E[dw.] 2 HLSa.
[11] Om. Pb.   [12] Om. HLSa, Pb.   [13] Om. Pb.
[14] Om. HLSa. In margin: 22 libr ass.

notwithstanding I vex him in the court Christian [in order] to have administration with him, and he brings a writ of covenant at the common law (as he may well do etc.), no prohibition lies etc.

Item, the parsonage of Dale is worth £20 a year, and someone who by right ought to tithe yearly in grain and other things to the value of £10 etc. is in arrears of payment of certain tithes: whether it is more or less, this belongs in court Christian. Item, there is a distinction between tithes and a portion, and yet both are the tenth part etc. Tithes are properly within the parish where the parsonage is, but portions are properly those things which a parson has within another parsonage etc.

Item, the punishment for defamation or slander, such as calling a man an adulterer or fornicator, lies in court Christian etc., but it is otherwise if one calls another his villein, or says that he has robbed him or that he has robbed another etc., since purgation for this lies at the common law, as by a writ *de nativo habendo* or by appeal or acquittal on indictment.[1] This suffices for the indictors etc. But if there is no such suit against the party at common law, query if there can be any punishment in court Christian, and it seems not. And there is a prohibition in the *Register quando quis trahitur* etc. in the writs of prohibition etc.,[2] because they assert that it is done against the seal etc.

Item, if a parson is ousted from the glebe of his church he shall have an assize, and if he re-enters on the disseisor he shall have a writ of trespass for the mesne trespass: 43 Edw. III in the *Liber Assisarum* etc.[3]

Item, if the churchyard is not enclosed, the punishment belongs to court Christian. Item, for grass growing in a churchyard the parson shall have a writ of trespass etc. But query in whom the freehold is? In no-one: see Wad Mich. 13 Ric. II.[4]

Item, if a man makes an oath to another to enfeoff him of certain land by a certain day, and on the day etc. he does not enfeoff him, [and] the other vexes him in court Christian for the broken oath, he shall have a prohibition: by Hankford 11 Hen. IV in an attachment on a prohibition.[5] Mich. 2 Hen. IV agrees, in a consultation etc.[6] Item, if someone confesses before an ordinary that he has broken his faith, in that he has made an oath to another to pay him £10 etc. and he has not paid, the ordinary may enjoin him to corporal penance, but he may not enjoin him to pay the debt etc.: by Thorpe, 22 Edw. III in the *Liber Assisarum*, at the end of a note etc.[7] Now if someone who has broken his oath to another (as above), of his own free will makes a promise to pay a certain sum of money to the party to whom he made the oath for his redemption, namely to be discharged

---

[1] *Register*, fo. 87.
[2] *Register*, fo. 42.
[3] YB 43 *Lib. Ass.*, fo. 269, pl. 13.
[4] Mich. 13 Ric. II (Ames Ser.), p. 34, pl. 2. There is no Wad mentioned in this report, though John Wadham was a justice of the Common Pleas at the time.
[5] YB Trin. 11 Hen. IV, fo. 88, pl. 40.
[6] YB Mich. 2 Hen. IV, fos 9–10, pl. 45.
[7] YB 22 *Lib. Ass.*, fo. 101, pl. 70.

dell dit penaunce, et sill ne paya [pas][1] cell som accordaunt a son promise, soyt le promyse [fayt all party][2] devaunt lordinarye ou perenter lez partyez, mesme le partye avera bon action de cell some pur son <son>^d redemption en court Christian etc.

Item si feme inherit <prent baron le quell alien etc., le feme>³ fait suerment <all aliene quell ne voet luy trubill pur le terre issint alyen, et ceo nient obstant>⁴ el port cui in vita: [si] laliene luy vex pur son suerment enfrent in court Christian, el avera prohibition, soit le suerment <fait durant le coverture>⁵ ou apres: <vide regestrum inter brevia de prohibition>.⁶

Item si un apprompte de un <u>^d auter x li. arender a luy all fyne dell an xx li., le jour occure, action est port pur lez xx li. etc. et cety a quy la apprompte ceo fist luy sua en court Christian, le suyt nest mayntenable a <ma conceyte: et unquore en le regester il <…>^d ad un consultation en tiel case etc.>⁷

Item si benes <sont>⁸ divysez a un John fitz et heir B et il sue lez executours en court Christian daver lez biens etc. et lez executors diont que il nest fitz et heire [B]⁹ nient obstaunt que ceo soit temporall matter de ple, unquore le court tiendra <avant le>¹⁰ ple, quar <le>^d cest triall depend sure <le primez>¹¹ matter <que est>¹² spirituall <et pur cell il ne poet aver [son]¹³ action all comen ley>¹⁴ etc. Item si un parson sua un [home]¹⁵ pur mortuary etc. et <ilz>¹⁶ sont a issue sur le properte, nient obstant que lissue soit pris sur matter temporall unquor le court Christian tiendra le ple avaunt etc. cause supra.

Item dez terres et tenements divisablez: ceo est toutz ditz a le comen ley etc.

Item si contract ceo prist perenter ij scilicet que lun esspousa le file lauter et le pere le feme donera ove son file en mariage a lauter c li., silz pursuount pur le mariage ceo appent all court Christian et pur le money action de dett <gist>¹⁷ all comen ley: per Thorp <xxij [Edw. III] in le liver dassissarum>¹⁸ etc. Mez xlv <[Edw. III] term Michelis>¹⁹ si le dett commensera per fayt ceo est in court le roy, mez si le dett soyt saunz fayt ceo appent a court Christian: mez [come]²⁰ semble soyt le dett per fayt ou saunz ceo appent all court le roy 31 E[dw.] 3. [Vide xxxvij H[en.] vj bon cas de ceo matter]²¹ etc.

Donques lez parolx destatut soynt outer et *habeat omnes libertates suas illesas* etc. Si home²² fua un esglise pur felony pur quell son vie est in jeopardy ill avera tuition, [*fo. 198*] et auterment nemi etc. Thorp en appell xxij in liver dassissarum: pur felony que amount a xij d. home avera tuition dun esglise etc. Item siun home soy indyte de felony dun berb precij de xij d. et sur ceo arreyn et trove culpable

---

[1] *Pb.*   [2] *Om. HLSa, Pb.*   [3] *Om. Pb.*
[4] Item si feme enherit fist serement al disconue le baron dez cez terrez que ele ne lui troblera aprez le mort son baron et puis *Pb.*
[5] devante le mort le baron *Pb.*   [6] *Om. Pb.*
[7] come semble tamen vide consultation en tiel cas en le registre etc. *Pb.*
[8] soient *Pb.*   [9] *Pb.*   [10] *Om. HLSa.*   [11] *Om. Pb.*
[12] *Om. Pb.*   [13] *Om. HLSa.*
[14] dl que answer nest pas al comen ley *Pb.*
[15] *HLSa.*   [16] lez parties *Pb.*   [17] *Om. HLSa, Pb.*
[18] *Om. HLSa.* In margin: 22 libr ass.
[19] *Om. HLSa.*   [20] *Pb.*   [21] *Pb.*   [22] *Pb*; feme *Hg*; un *HLSa.*

of the said penance, and he does not pay this sum according to his promise; whether the promise was made to the party before the ordinary or between the parties the same party shall have a good action on this sum for his redemption in court Christian etc.

Item, if a woman inherits [and] takes a husband who aliens etc., [and] the woman makes an oath to the alienee that she will not trouble him for the land thus alienated, and this notwithstanding she brings *cui in vita*: if the alienee vexes her for her broken oath in court Christian she shall have prohibition, whether the oath was made during coverture or after: see the *Register* in the writs of prohibition.[1]

Item, if someone borrows £10 from another to render £20 to him at the end of the year, when the day comes an action is brought for the £20 and the one by whom the loan was made sues him in court Christian, the suit is not maintainable in my understanding: nevertheless, in the *Register* there is a consultation in such a case etc.[2]

Item, if goods are devised to one John, son and heir of B, and he sues the executors in court Christian to have the goods etc., and the executors say that he is not the son and heir of B, notwithstanding that this plea is a temporal matter yet the court shall continue to entertain the plea, for the trial depends on the first matter, which is spiritual, and thereby he may not have his action at the common law etc. Item, if a parson sues a man for a mortuary etc. and they are at issue on the property, notwithstanding that the issue was taken on a temporal matter, the court Christian shall nevertheless continue to entertain the plea etc. for the reasons above.

Item, of lands and tenements devisable: this is always at the common law etc.

Item, if a contract takes place between two, namely that the one shall marry the daughter of the other, and that the father of the woman shall give £100 with his daughter in marriage to the other, if they sue [him] for the marriage this belongs in court Christian, but for the money an action of debt lies at the common law: by Thorpe 22 [Edw. III] in the *Liber Assisarum* etc.[3] But in Mich 45 Edw. III[4] if the debt begins by deed it is in the king's court, but if the debt is without a deed it belongs to the court Christian: but as it seems, whether the debt is with or without a deed, this belongs to the king's court: 31 Edw. III. See 37 Hen. VI for a good case on this matter etc.[5]

Then the words of the statute are further *and she shall have all her liberties inviolate* etc. If a man flees to a church for felony whereby his life is in jeopardy he shall have sanctuary, but not otherwise etc. Thorpe in an appeal 22 [Edw. III] in the *Liber Assisarum*: for a felony which amounts to 12d. a man shall have sanctuary of a church etc.[6] Item, if a man is indicted of felony for a sheep worth 12d. and arraigned on this and found guilty etc., but it is found that the sheep is

[1] *Register*, fo. 43.   [2] Ibid., fos 49–49v.
[3] YB 22 Lib. Ass., fo. 101, pl. 70.
[4] *Rectius* YB Trin. 45 Edw. III, fo. 24, pl. 30. Dated Mich. in Fitzherbert, *Execucion*, 40, and *Dette*, 131.
[5] *Rectius* YB Pas. 38 Hen. VI, fo. 29, pl.11.
[6] YB 22 Lib. Ass., fo. 94, pl. 39. Thorpe does not mention sanctuary, but the amount for which a man shall be hanged.

etc. mez que le berb ne vault forsque x d., ill ne serra pendu mez ill serra punis per discrestion dez justices etc. Donques sill fua a un esglise pur felony que amount a iiij d., sill confesse le felony dez iiij d. nient parlaunt de lauter matter ut supra, [semble qu][1] ill navera tuition: mez sill jure ambideux <felonyez>[2] all coroner, semble quill avera tuition etc.

Item siun [home][3] ferist un auter <pur quill>[4] ill prist un esglise etc. le quell est prise hors dell esglise pur ceo que leom est in vie: si lem morust apres lauter serra restore etc. Item si un prent esglise pur chos que nest felony ale comen ley all temps dell fayt ne all temps quill est prise hors dell esglise, mez puis per auctorite de parliament cell act est fayt felony, et sur ceo ill est <indite et>[5] arreyn, semble quill serra restore etc.

Item suffist a cestui que fua all esglise adire a lez comen gents adire general-ment quill ad fayt felony saunz [plus],[6] mez all coroner ill covient de jurer esspe-cialment le felony etc. mez dez circumstuncez dell fayt come lan, jour et lieu le coroner luy ayda <p>[d] per examination etc. Mez si le coroner demande de luy lan et jour et lieu et ill ne voyll luy <jurer>[7] ill serra prise hors dell esglise etc., et sill voyll auterfoytz en apres <jurer>[8] le lan, jour et lieu ceo nest a purpose. Item ill ad estre adjuge en temps le roy E[dw.] le iiij que lou home fuit pris hors dun esglise que le juge nest tenuz de luy ayder dez circumstaunces. Et ceo fuit le cas de Thomas Phyllyp a Newgate in Londrez etc.

Item si un herityck soyt commyse as lays gentz per lordinary pur aver execu-tion sill escape et fua a un esglise il avera tuition, quar le privelege va all lieu et nemi all person <come daver son clergye, quar herityck navera son clergy>[9] quar ceo va all person.[10] [Et issint le diversite, tamen][11] quere etc.

Item si un fua all esglise et conust quill ad fayt felony covient all vill de luy garder per xl jours etc. Et sill deinz lez xl jours fua in auter esglise ill aver tuition <in lauter esglise>[12] per xl jours. Item si un fue a un esglise lou <le>[d] ne soynt <aschunz parisshens>[13] inhabitants si le lieu devaunt consecratt ill avera tuition mez si lesglise soyt susspend per effusyon de sank ou en auter maner. [Mesme le ley, come semble, sil fua a lesgles quel il avoit robbe adevante pur mesme le robberie quia auxilium legis habere non debet qui in legem committit][14] <Auter est etc.>[15]

Item si home abjure fua a un esglise ill navera son liberty per xl jours mez ill serra mur mayntenant etc. Mesme le ley de home atteynt per verdict ou per utla-gary de felony [lou][16] le jugement est que ilz serront penduez per que etc. [Tamen quere: semble moy devante lez xl jours home ne serra mure etc.][17]

---

[1] Pb. [2] matterz Pb. [3] Pb.
[4] et pur dowte que lauter serra mort de ceo Pb.
[5] Om. HLSa. [6] HLSA, Pb. [7] monstre HLSa.
[8] monstre HLSa.
[9] auterment est sil claime son clergy Pb.
[10] In margin: privilege va al lieu et nemy al person HLSa.
[11] Pb. [12] Om. Pb. [13] Om. Pb.
[14] Pb. [15] Om. HLSa. [16] Pb. [8] Pb.

worth only 10d., he shall not be hanged but he shall be punished by the discretion of the justices etc. Then, if he flees to a church for a felony worth 4d., if he confesses the felony of 4d. saying nothing of the other matter as above it seems that he shall not have sanctuary, but if he swears both felonies to the coroner, it seems that he shall have sanctuary etc.

Item, a man strikes another for which he takes sanctuary etc., and he is taken out of the church because the man is alive: if the man dies afterwards the other shall be restored etc. Item, [if a] man takes sanctuary for something which is not a felony at the common law at the time of the deed nor at the time that he is taken out of the church, but afterwards by the authority of Parliament this thing is made a felony, and on this he is indicted and arraigned, it seems that he shall be restored etc.

Item, it suffices for one who flees to a church to say to the common people generally that he has committed a felony without more, but to the coroner he must swear the felony specially etc. but for the circumstances of the deed, such as the year, the day and place, the coroner shall help him by examination etc. But if the coroner asks him the year, day and place and he will not swear to him he shall be taken from the church etc., and if he wishes afterwards to swear the year, day and place, this does not matter. Item, it was adjudged in the time of King Edward IV that where a man was taken out of a church the judge is not bound to help him with the circumstances. And this was the case of Thomas Phillips at Newgate in London etc.

Item, if a heretic is committed to the laity by the ordinary to be executed and he escapes and flees to a church, he shall have sanctuary, for the privilege goes with the place and not with the person, as in having his clergy, for a heretic shall not have his clergy for that goes with the person. So there is a distinction, however query etc.

Item, if one flees to the church and confesses that he has committed a felony, the vill must guard him for forty days etc. And if within the forty days he flees to another church he shall have sanctuary in the other church for forty days. Item, if one flees to a church where there are no parishioners inhabiting, if the place was consecrated before he shall have sanctuary, but [not] if the church is suspended on account of bloodshed or in some other manner. The law is the same, as it seems, if he flees to the church which he had previously robbed for the same robbery, because 'he who goes against the law should not have its help'.[1] It is otherwise etc.

Item, if an abjured man flees to a church he shall not have his liberty for forty days, but he shall be immured forthwith etc. The law is the same of a man attainted by verdict or outlawed of felony, where the judgment is that he be hanged whereby etc. However, query: it seems to me before the 40 days the man shall not be immured etc.

---

[1] This saying seems to be the reader's (or note-taker's) version of a familiar saying, 'Frustra legis auxilium querit qui in legem committit.' Attributed to 2 Hale P.C. 386 in Broom's *Legal Maxims*.

Auxi auterz liberties isont touchaunts lez parsons [de Saint Esgles]:[1] come per launcyent custom de royalm null espirituell [*fo. 198v*] home serra mys in temporall office come baylye, constable, \<bayle\>[2] bedyll et huiusmodi etc.: vide de ceo registrum. \<I\>ᵈ

Item aschuns liberties sont done a eux per divers statutes, come per lestatut de Marlebridge ilz ne serra compelles de venir a aschun lete etc. Item per un estat Edw. III null preest serra arrestue durant le temps quill intend all devyn service, ne dehors lesglise durant le temps quill alast ove le Eucharist sill ne ceo face per covyn.

---

[1] *Pb.*
[2] *Om. HLSa, Pb.*

Also there are other liberties touching the persons of Holy Church: for instance, by ancient custom of the realm no spiritual man shall be placed in a temporal office such as bailiff, constable, bedell and such like etc.: see the *Register* for this etc.[1]

Item, other liberties are given to them by various statutes, as by the statute of Marlborough they are not compelled to come to any leet etc.[2] Item, by a statute of Edward III[3] no priest shall be arrested during the time that he attends to divine service, nor outside the church during the time that he goes with the eucharist unless he does this by covin etc.

---

[1] *Register*, fo. 187v.
[2] 52 Hen. III, c. 10 (*SR*, i. 22).
[3] 50 Edw. III, c. 5 (*SR*, i. 398).

READING SEVEN

Lectura M Snede in quadragesima a° 2° Henry viij[1]

[*fo. 56*] *In primis concessimus deo*: ca° j° Magna Carta

Cest statut en tout nest mezque affermans de comen ley et ceo est prove per cest paroll *habeat jura sua* et issint fuit use en temps le Roy Edward le seynt et en temps William conqueror. Mez puis, scilicet en temps le Roy Henry le ij[d], molt contention fuit enter ly et le royalm pur mesmez lez lybertees sur que debatys Seynt Tomas morust, et puis en temps le Roy John debat fuit et le Roy John per son charter portant [date] … grant mesmez lez lybertees et granta oster que si il enfreynt ascun artycul de ceo que bien lerra a certen de mesme lez barons de oppungner conter luy, et puis pur lenfreynder de ce ils issint fesont. Mez il fuit eyd per le roy de Escoce <que a ly fyst homag>[i] <…>[d] et pur ce ne fuit redres. Et puis le Roy Henry le tyers grant cest chartor arer le ix an de son reyng, et apres <…>[d] pur certens enfreynders de part le dyst Roy Henry contention fuit, et a darren pur … de cel la xxxviij levesque assembles banneront tout queux enfreyndront et puis lan 10 meme le roy fuit conferm per <le pape ovesque cur et puis en temps>[d] meme le roy en Marlybryg capitulo lj°. Et puis en temps le Roy Edward le <tyers>[d] j fuit conferm per un charter que portant dat quant il fuit oster le meer et puis en son temps conferm per act de parliament scilicet per articuli super cartas.

Concessimus deo: cest grant est voyd a ceo jour entant que nest ascun que poet prender de mon don, quar a chescun don est recquisite abylyte en donor et en done et le choce don. Mez en launcyun temps fuit bon si lentent appyert, et pur ceo le Roy Edgar grant a eux de Beverlay 'to be as fre as hart can thynk or y can see' et per ceo ils claymont daver <sent>[d] sentuary a felons [et] traytors. Et issint William conqueror dyst 'adjaceat monasterio Sancti Edmundi de Bury un hyde' ce fuit accept pur bon. Et issint si en eyne temps home don a un 'habendum sebi imperpetuum' il avoyt fe.

Ore est a voyr queux persons poyent fayr don. Feme covert ne poet fayr feffment ne don mez est cleerment voyd non obstant lyvere et non obstant que soyt devorce apres quar a temps fuit covert. Mez si el soyt executryce el poet [vender] lez biens le testator ou vendur ter si son volunte soyt que ter serra vendus et issint poet un moyng. Mez semble que feme ne poet doner biens ne auter choce fayr si non en payr lez bequestes ou dettes et si le vend ne soyt a tyel purpos est voyd …

READING SEVEN

The reading of Master Snede in Lent 2 Hen. VIII

In the first place we have granted to God: chapter 1 of Magna Carta.
All of this statute is only an affirmation of the common law, and this is proved
by these words *shall have her rights*, and it was thus in the time of King Edward
the [Confessor] and William the Conqueror. But then, namely in the time of King
Henry II, there was much contention between him and the realm over the same
liberties, in which debates St Thomas died, and then in the time of King John there
was debate and King John by his charter dated [1215] … granted the same liberties, and it was further granted that if he broke any article of this that certain of the
same barons could oppose him, and then for breaking the charter they did so. But
he was helped by the king of Scotland who did homage to him, and for this there
was no redress. And then King Henry III granted this charter again in the ninth
year of his reign,[1] and afterwards there was contention because of certain infringe-
ments on the part of the said King Henry, and at last thirty-eight bishops together
banned all those who had broken it, and then in the tenth year [of his reign] it was
confirmed by the same king in Marlborough, c. 51.[2] And then in the time of King
Edward I it was confirmed by a charter dated when he was overseas,[3] and then in
his time it was confirmed by an act of Parliament, namely by *articuli super cartas*.[4]

We have granted to God: this grant is void today inasmuch as there is no-one
who can take my gift, for each gift requires ability in the donor and in the donee
and in the thing given. But in olden times it was good if the intent appeared, and
for this King Edgar granted to those of Beverley 'to be as free as heart can think
or eye can see', and because of this they claim to have sanctuary for felons and
traitors. And similarly William the Conqueror said 'let a hide be to the monastery
of St Edmund of Bury', and this was accepted as good.[5] And thus if in olden
times a man gave to one 'to have unto him in perpetuity' he had a fee.

Now it is to be seen what persons may make a gift. A feme covert may not
make a feoffment or a gift, as it is clearly void notwithstanding livery and notwithstanding that she is divorced afterwards, for at the time she was covert. But
if she is an executrix she may sell the goods or lands of the testator if his will is
that the land shall be sold, and so may a monk. But it seems that a woman may
not give goods or do any other thing unless paying bequests or debts, and if the
sale is not for this purpose it is void ….

[1] *SR*, i. 22.
[2] 52 Hen. III, *rectius* c. 5 (*SR*, i. 20). This may mean in the fifty-first year of his reign, or may be an error
in copying 5.
[3] 25 Edw. I (*SR*, i. 114–119): 5 November 1297 when he was in Ghent.
[4] 28 Edw. I (*SR*, i. 136–141).
[5] This example is also given in Reading Six above, p. 87, n.2.

Enfantes act per lyvere est voydabul mez en ceux chosis que ne passont per lyvere est voyd … <et non obstant>^d mez le lyvere discharge le done en trespass. Son les pur ans est voyd si ne l… per cas ad profyst et nul disprofyst.

Le don ou feffment per mayr sans <cony>^d comynalte [est] voyd et issint de don de biens per go… deen sans chapyter. Mez labbe poet don biens entant que le propurte est soolment a ly et il … casys devant bosoyn si le mayr et cominalte enfeff que le garr datterney se… fayt … en cas dabbe quar la fuit nota est a ly en possession tamen [quere].

En touts casis lou le roy ad interest en le possession le feffment cestui que ad franktenement est voyd come lo… ou le roy [ses] le gard le feffment voyd devant lyvere quar le roy ne poet estre hors de possession … poet enfeff <deva>^d apres offys, mez cestui que est insan per lucyda intervalla poet quar en lun cas … per prerogatyf, mez en lauter cas nemi mez lordynary <…>^d. Et issint est lou le tenant le roy fuyst … apres offys trove le feffment est voyd, pur ce que le roy devoyt sesyr et preyng lez profytes tanque fyn … lyvere. <Meme le ley de heretyk quar le roy>^d Meme le le [sic] ley de alien, villen le roy ou br … feffment nest bon, non obstant que le roy [navoit ses], quar en ceux casys le roy est daver … en fe … avera relation ab initio. Et meme le ley si home soyt atteynt en preminire ou lou le ter ad estre seisi de ….

Mez dauter part en toutes casys lou le roy nad interest en le ter … m… quar la livere de seisin poet estre fayt entant que le roy nest oster de ch…, [fo. 56v] come lou home est utlage en action personel ou <qu>^d clerk convict, heretyk, ou abjure, ou estoy mut per que il ad me…, <la for>^d en ceux casys le feffment le party est bon pur lour vys, quar le roy nad possession en lez ters mez soolment pernor dez profytes et ne poet manur le ter, et pur ceo per feffment riens est <depart hors>^d plok hors de roy, quar en cas de heretyk et clerk convyct et mut, le heyr apres lour mort devoyt enter sans lyvere. Mes semble a moy que abjure devoyt a toutes jours perder son ter et issint ceo est le diversite de ground.

Mez auters casys sont, scilicet si le heretyk escap ou ascun dez auters que devoyent de perder lour vys per statut de frangentibus prisonam ust felony en escap, et donques si de [ceo] soyt atteynt en appres covient daver relation ad primes et pur ceo le feffment voyd.

Le roy ne poet doner biens sans fayt mez le royng poet per lauctoryte de parliament.

Home mut poet enfeoff auter per fayt mez nemi auterment, <ne il>^d mez per fayt il poet si deliver le fayt et le reson de ce est pur ce que le certente de <ce>^d <son mynd>ⁱ ne poet appereer sans fayt. Mez si soyt deff per fayt nest bon si non que il mesme poet escryer et escria le fayt ou auterment copy de son mynd. Mez come semble, si soyt bien voyer et soyt understand que il meme poet leer et

Acts of an infant by livery are voidable but in those things which do not pass by livery they are void [from the beginning], but the livery discharges the donee in trespass. His lease for years is void unless … because he has profit and no loss.

The gift or feoffment by a mayor without the commonalty is void, and the same of a gift of goods … [by a] dean without the chapter. But an abbot may give goods inasmuch as the property is solely in him and he … [in the] cases above if the mayor and commonalty enfeoff they need a warrant [of] attorney … [It is otherwise] in the case of the abbot, for there it was noted that it is in him in possession, however query.

In all cases where the king has an interest in the possession, the feoffment of the one who has the freehold is void, as where … or the king seizes the wardship the feoffment is void before livery because the king cannot be out of possession … [An idiot] may [not] enfeoff after office, but one who is insane with lucid intervals may, for in the one case … by prerogative, but in the other case not, but the ordinary [power]. And likewise where the king's tenant was [within age] … after office found the feoffment is void, because the king must remain seised and take the profits until the end [of the wardship after] … livery. The law is the same of an alien, the king's villein or … feoffment is not good, notwithstanding that the king has not seized, for in these cases the king is to have … in fee … with relation from the beginning. And the same law if a man is attainted in *praemunire* or where the land was seized of ….

But on the other hand, in all cases where the king does not have an interest in the land … for there livery of seisin can be made so that the king is not ousted from …, as when a man is outlawed in a personal action or a clerk convict, heretic or abjured or mute, by which he has …, in those cases the party's feoffment is good for their lives, for the king does not have possession in the lands but is only the pernor of the profits and may not cultivate the land, and because of this nothing is plucked from the king by the feoffment, for in the case of a heretic and a clerk convict and a mute the heir ought to enter without livery after their death. But it seems to me that an abjurer ought to lose his lands always and thus this is the diversity of principles.

But there are other cases, such as if the heretic escapes or any of the others who ought to lose their lives by the statute of *de frangentibus prisonam*[1] committed a felony in escaping, and then if they are attainted of this afterwards it must relate back to the beginning, and by this the feoffment is void.

The king may not give goods without a deed, but the queen may by the authority of Parliament.

A mute man may enfeoff another by deed but not otherwise, but by deed he may if he delivers the deed, and the reason for this is because the certainty of his mind cannot appear without a deed. But if he is deaf [a feoffment] by deed is not good unless he can write himself and he writes the deed or otherwise copies his mind. But as it seems, if he can see well and it is understood that he can read and

[1] 23 Edw. I (*SR*, i. 113).

si apres voyl deliver seisin et le fayt semble que ce est bien fayt. Auxi mut poet vender biens mez nemi doner entaunt que per le vend son mynd appyert plus pleynment.

Le roy exempt homes de toutes jurres est bon mez ce ne serra allow en atteyntes ne pur temoyns. Mez pur temoyns <est cleer>d ou atteyntes est cleerment voyd, mez semble que non si non que 'sine eis justicia exibere non potest' ce est pur defaut dez auters.

Ij grant revercion per fyn dont lun riens ad est bon pur toutes pur ce que ore ad per conclucion, mez auter si soyt sans fayt. Mez si 20x enfef dont lun riens ad ovesque garr en fayt de feffment, unquore le garr voyd vers cestui que riens avoyt <...>d pur ceo que riens passa de ly per le feffment. Mez ce covient estre entend, come semble, lou est nul parol de confirmavi issint que poet estre come confirmation de cestui que rienz ad, come si cestui en le revercion voyl fayr tyel fayt a tenant pur term de vie ovesque confirmation serra pris come confirmation.

Ij joyntenants, lun poet grant rent ou leve fyn <a>i auter pur ce que nul livere. Ij grant annuite chescun several annuite pur ce que charge le person. Mez si rent charge et lun riens ad en le ter unquor bon, mez si il avoy pur rent <le primer>d cestui que riens ad est discharge pur ce que le ter est charge.

Les pur vi sur condition que si il graunt le revercion que donques il avera fe et il <alien>d grant le reversion per fyn, ore le tenant ad fe. Et a ce cas fuit repli, mez pur melior opinion de tout le bench fuit agre, entant que tout werk a un instant et pur ce le fe per le condition <...> serra primer operation. Nest semble a cas home don en tayl que si il alien que donques remainera a puny fytes quar la le puny fytes ...t aver ... ..re et donque ne poet enter pur le fe presedent le quel est discontinuans, mez icy ne bosoyng entre .... Et mesme le ley de les pur ans si livere soyt fayt.

... son feme <fyst>d a que avoyson [est] les pur term de vie et puis est devors, le tenant pur term de vie surrender <lease>d al baron ... quant le prochen voydans pur ce que le discontynuans est purge et semble a ce poynt, mez semble que covient primes enter entant que el poet present et per ce recontynu le possession. Mez unquore devant recontynuans semble le grant voyd et mesme ... ...isler de tyel maner.

... granter le prochen voydans de avowson que son tenant pur term de vie avoyt, ce nest que voyd <devant>d ... son tenant pur term de vie morust devant le voydans, mez si il dyst le prochen voydans apres le mort de tenant pur term de vie ... quar donques est bon. <Mes semble tout un quar>d Et le reson pur ceo que lun enpli li mesme estre en possession, mez semble nul ... ...en le revercion poet grant rent charge, et ce ne prendera effect tanque apres son mort.

if afterwards he wishes to deliver seisin and the deed it seems that this is well done. Also a mute may sell goods but not give them, inasmuch as by the sale his mind appears more plainly.

The king exempts a man from all juries it is good, but this shall not be allowed in attaints or for witnesses. But for witnesses or attaints it is clearly void, but it seems that [it is] not [void] unless 'without them justice cannot be done', that is for default of others.

Two grant a reversion by fine whereof one of them has nothing: this is good for all because now he has it by conclusion, but it is otherwise if it is without a deed. But if twenty enfeoff whereof one [of them] has nothing with a warranty in the deed of feoffment, still the warranty is void against the one who has nothing because nothing passes from him by the feoffment. But this must be understood, as it seems, where there is no word *confirmavimi* so that it is like a confirmation by someone who has nothing; for instance, if the reversioner wishes to make such a deed to a tenant for term of life with confirmation it shall be taken as a confirmation.

[If there are] two joint-tenants, the one may grant a rent or levy a fine to the other because [there is] no livery. Two [joint-tenants] grant an annuity, each is a separate annuity because it charges the person. But if [there is a] rent charge and the one has nothing in the land it is still good, but if he has rent the one who has nothing is discharged because the land is charged.

[If there is] a lease for life on condition that if he grants the reversion that then he shall have fee, and he grants the reversion by fine, now the tenant has the fee. And to this case it was replied, but [by the] better opinion of all the bench it was agreed, inasmuch as all works at one instant and therefore the fee by the condition shall be the first operation. It is not like the case where a man gives in tail that if he aliens that then the remainder goes to the younger son, for there the younger son … to have… and then he cannot enter for the preceding fee which is a discontinuance, but here there is no need to enter …. And the law is the same of a lease for years if livery is made.

… his wife from whom an advowson is leased for term of life and then they are divorced, the tenant for term of life surrenders to the husband … when the next vacancy because the discontinuance is purged and it seems on this point, but it seems that they must first enter so that she may present and in this way recontinue the possession. But still before the recontinuance it seems that the grant is void and the [law is the] same … of such a manner.

… to grant the next vacancy of an advowson which his tenant for term of life has, this is only void [if] his tenant for term of life dies before the vacancy, but if he says the next vacancy after the death of the tenant for term of life [it is not void] for then it is good. And the reason is because the one implies the same is in possession, but it seems not … in the reversion can grant a rent charge, and this shall not take effect until after his death.

LE SECOND LECTURE

[*fo. 57*] Or est a voyer de disabilite de done:

Un moyng ne poet accepter feffment, les, ne don et si les soyt a ly remainder oster tout voyd quar debile fundamentum [fallit opus] etc. Mes si le roy granta <pur ans>[i] reservando rent bon, mez nemi pur term de vie ne sans reserve rent, quar il nest abul de prender franktenement. Feffment a feme le baron poet disagre, et donques <nest>[d] si auter soyt joynt enfeff tout vest en ly non obstant livere de seisin soolment a feme. Mez en lauter cas de moyng, si le moyng accept le livere tout voyd pur ce que le livere est voyd. Mez en lauter cas bon tanque …

En ascun casis le baron ne poet disagre, come si soyt alien, utlage, ou atteynt, quar le roy ad tytl a les profytes enconter el; ne si soyt deins age; ne si les soyt pur vi et le feme ad fayt wast pur ce que nest reson mez que ce serra punise et selonque le natur de wast; ne si le grant le revercion oster per fyn devant disagrement quar la serra accompt de temps de fyn leve entant que fuit tenant al primes; ne si les soyt <p>[d] a baron pur term de vie remainder a son feme, le baron ne unquez avoyt temps a disagre ne assent si le remainder ne estut en vie le baron; ou chescun remainder tayll a feme.

Home lessa remainder ad heyrs John at Style bon non obstant que John at Style soyt en vy, si soyt mort quant …. Mez si soyt nul tyel John at Style en estre a temps, ou que John at Style soyt moyng profes, ou si soyt a cominalte et eux ne sont incorporates a ce temps, non obstant dereyngment ou corporation en apres, quar la ly mynd de donor ne poet estre pris effectuel. Home lessa remainder a wysyst man ou le best man ce est cleerment voyd pur ce que ne poet estre discus mez remainder a le plus aunycien en Dal bon.

Home lessa remainder a cominalte <…>[d] lou sont incorporates per tyel nosm bon, mez si per nosm mayr et cominalte remainder a cominalte est voyd, quar le meyr nest impli. Mez si a burges est bon quar le mayr est burges. Et issint est si home <don>[i] ter capitulo et ils avoyt deen a temps bon, come est agre, pur ce que le deen est emply. Home don ter <a abbe et>[d] monachis est bon <fe>[i] sans successoribus mez nemi si a convent: tamen quere, labbe est emply en primer.

Home don ter remainder as heyrs dalien: si lalien morust non obstant que ad issu ne denis[en] unquor ne poet prender per nom de heyr, mez poet per cas come heyr a myer. Mez si alien devant son mort soyt fayt denezen…[d]onque lissue ne devant … avera le ter, quar come semble nest corruption de sank come utlary de felony.

The Second Lecture

Now we must look at the disability of the donee:

A monk may not accept a feoffment, lease, or gift, and if a lease is made to him with a remainder over it is void because where there is a weak foundation, the work falls. But if the king grants [to a monk] for years reserving rent it is good, but not for term of life, nor without reserving rent, for he is not able to take the freehold. [If there is a] feoffment to a wife the husband may disagree, and then if another is jointly enfeoffed everything vests in him, notwithstanding that the livery of seisin was solely to the woman. But in the other case of the monk, if the monk accepts the livery it is all void because the livery is void. But in the other case it is good until [the husband disagrees] ….

In some cases the husband may not disagree, as when he is an alien, outlawed or attaint, for the king has title to the profits against her; nor if he is within age; nor if the lease is for life and the woman has committed waste, because there it is only reasonable that this should be punished according to the nature of waste; nor if the grant with the reversion over was by fine before disagreement, for there it shall be accounted from the time the fine was levied inasmuch as he was tenant from the beginning; nor if the lease is made to the husband for term of life remainder to his wife (the husband never had time to disagree nor assent if the remainder was not in the life of the husband); or each remainder entailed to the wife.

A man makes a lease with the remainder to the heirs of John at Style, [this is good] notwithstanding that John at Style is alive, if he is dead when [the remainder falls in]. But if there is no John at Style alive at the time [of the lease], or if John at Style is a professed monk, or if it is to the commonalty and they are not incorporated at the time (notwithstanding deraignment or incorporation afterwards) [it is void], for there the mind of the donor cannot be understood effectively. A man leases with the remainder to the wisest man or the best man, this is clearly void because it cannot be determined; but a remainder to the oldest [man] in Dale is good.

A man leases [with the] remainder to a commonalty which is incorporated by such a name it is good, but if by the name of the mayor and commonalty with the remainder to the commonalty it is void, for the mayor is not implied. But if it is to the burgesses it is good, for the mayor is a burgess. And similarly if a man gives land 'to the chapter', and they have a dean at the time [it is] good, as is agreed, because the dean is implied. A man gives land 'to the monks' it is a good fee without 'to their successors', but not if it is 'to the convent': however query, the abbot is implied in the former.

A man gives land [with the] remainder to the heirs of an alien: if the alien dies, notwithstanding that he has issue nor [that he was] denizen, still his issue cannot take it as heir, though he may perhaps as heir to his mother. But if an alien before his death is made denizen, then the issue born before [his death] shall have the land, for as it seems it is not a corruption of blood such as outlawry for felony.

Le roy ne poet don a home utlage ou atteynt quar ce devoyt donque enur pur profy… serra desseypt. Ne le roy ne poet don a son villen quar donques il serra enfranchys per … Si le roy grant probis hominibus ville de Dalle ce serra corporation deins luy mesme, quar la est … de prender effect.

Le roy ne poet estre enfeff sans fayt enrowl mez le royng poet per prescription, unquor … de parliament. Mez home poet les remainder a roy sans fayt enroll et issint home poit … feff … livere de seisin a auter, mez livere de seisin a roy tout voyd, come en cas de monk et en le cas de … et lauter serra mys a peticion.

Le roy grant ters al abbe et priori et conventui ita quod le prior et le convent prendera lez prof*ytes issint* … soyt pur ferm le roy ou auterment que ils sont issint exemptes per le pape de le medullyng labbe … ou per parliament come ceex de Westm' per cas.

Ore est a voyer de le maner destates:
Ter est don a un et a sequelis suis il ad fe mez si don a ly et exitibus suis … proxima … ce est tayll ou de carne sua exeuntibus mez semble que de sanguine il ad fe. Ter est done a un et heredibus non obstant que le garr soyt et heredibus suis unquor il nad que franktenement …. Mez fe soyt soyt [*sic*] don a un habendum sibi et heredibus il ad fe quar <…>^{d} nul estranger poet … le habendum ne per voy de remainder ne auterment. Mez si en le primer cas il va oster et dyst quod si … [*fo. 57v*] sans heyr de son corpes que ce remainder a sez droit heyrs, ore il ad tayl et issint si as heyrs le donor. Mez si ters soyt don sibi et heredibus suis quod si contyngat ut supra a lez heyrs de ly mesme est bon, mez nemi as heyrs le donor ne de estranger.

Ter est don a un en tayll, remainder a auter in simili modo ut in forma predicta ce est voyd, quar ne poet remainder in forma predecta. Mez si un don un acur de ter et per mesme le fayt don auter acur habendum in forma predicta sive simili modo ce est bon, quar ambydeux sont <un>^{d} de un natur.

Ter est don al pier et heyrs de corps de <…>^{id} fytes le pier en tayl, et si le fytes que est nosm soyt son puny fytes il ad tayl condytionalment scilicet si <…>^{d} son freer eyne morust. Mez si ter soyt don al pier et fytes et lour heyrs de corps le fytes, la le pier <ad>^{d} <ambideux ont>^{i} stat tayll, <et le fytes se port le parol a lour heyrs, et heyr le fytes poet estre engender de corps le pier>^{d} mez si soyt don a pier et fytes et <lor>^{i} heyrs de corps le pier, la le pier ad tayl et le fytz fe. Si don soyt a B et C et as heyrs de C de corps de B engendurs, la C ad fe et lauter fe condytionel, scilicet si leyr C soyt de corps B. Si soyt don a fytes et heyres de corps le pier il ad stat en fe, mez semble que stat tayll.

The king may not give to an outlawed or attainted man because this must then operate for … shall be deceit. The king also may not give to his villein, for then he would be enfranchised by [the grant]. … If the king grants 'to the good men of the vill of Dale' this shall be an incorporation in itself, for there it [it is necessary for it] to take effect.

The king may not be enfeoffed without an enrolled deed, but the queen may [be enfeoffed], by prescription, and yet [the king may by an act] of Parliament. But a man may lease [with the] remainder to the king without a deed enrolled and similarly a man may [make a] feoffment ... [with] livery of seisin to another, but livery of seisin to the king [is] completely void, as in the case of a monk and in the case of [a feme covert] ... and the other shall be put to petition.

The king grants lands to the abbot and 'to the prior and convent so that' the prior and convent shall take the profits … for the king's farm or otherwise that they are thus exempted by the pope from the meddling of the abbot … or by parliament, such as those of Westminster, for example.

Now we must look at the manner of estates:[1]

[If] land is given to one and 'to his successors' he has fee, but, if it is given to him … this is tail and his issue … next or 'to the issue of his flesh', but it seems that [if it is] 'of his blood' he has fee. Land is given to one and 'the heirs', notwithstanding that the warranty is 'and to his heirs' still he only has freehold …. But [if a] fee is given to one 'to hold to him and the heirs' he has fee for no stranger may … the *habendum* by way of remainder or otherwise. But if in the former case he goes further and says that if [he dies] without heir of his body or this remainder [shall go] to his right heirs, now he has tail and similarly if it is to the heirs of the donor. But if lands are given 'to him and his heirs' on the condition, as above, it is good to his own heirs, but not to the heirs of the donor or of a stranger.

Land is given to one in tail, remainder to another 'in the same way and in the form aforesaid' this is void, for a remainder may not be 'in the form aforesaid'. But if one gives an acre of land and by the same deed gives another acre 'to hold in the form aforesaid or in the same way' this is good, for both are of the same nature.

Land is given to the father and to the heirs of the body of the father's son in tail, and if the son who is named is his younger son he has a conditional tail, namely if his elder son dies. But if land is given to the father and sons and the heirs of the bodies of the sons, there both have an estate tail, but if it is given to the father and sons and the heirs of the father's body, there the father has tail and the son fee. If a gift is to B and C and to the heirs of C begotten on the body of B, there C has the fee and the other a conditional fee, namely if the heir of C is from the body of B. If there is a gift to the sons and heirs of the body of the father he has an estate in fee, but it seems that it is an estate tail.

---

[1] Cf. Spelman, *Quo Warranto*, pp. 81–83.

3[D] LECTURA

Ore est a voyer quex chosys pusoyent estre grant:

Chos poet commens per grant, come comen, rent, et chos ne estre poet pas per grant come rent etc. Rent <ne>[d] grant de comenz a roy est bon et issint si hors de rent, pur ce que limitation de distreint a roy est plus que bosoyng, quar le roy poet distrein en chescun lew pur anuite ou det etc. Et si le roy grant oster ce est bon, mez le grante ne poet distrein forsque … bestes le comyner. Et issint semble que poet si rent soyt grant hors de comen en estranger, mez semble en cas de rent que le grant … rent sek et poet pas de roy entant que est plus tost a benefyst le tenant que disprofyst …ment a roy per son prerogatyf etc.

Malat dyst que est agre si le roy ad obligation per … grant oster et le grante suera ovesque speciall count mez si un patron grant rent hors davowson … a roy si un que soyt parson en parsony. Mez semble que ce cas ne vary de cas de rent grant hors.

… poet estre grant pur hurt de tenant ne grant de comenz engros non certen et <fees non br>[i] <ne ceez appendant>[d] quinsmo[i] … nul auter certente si non a le parson, mez auter est le comenz certen, comenz appendant, ne … si grant soyt de comenz pur term de vie le tenant quant le revercion le grant est voyd et issint de … que ad nul revercion. Mez si il grant mesme le rent ou <…>[d] comenz pas come novel comenz.

… annuite <& grant>[d] ou rent charge et grant oster un rent de recever de le mesme per mayn le tenant ce est voyd. … si rent de recever de costom come le cas fuit ix° H[en.] vj[i]. Mez auter est si soyt grant parcel de ce rent dee …ey que … si pur term <de vie>[d] dans reservando rent, et puis grant oster cel rent al un auter et a sez heyrs, ce est bon: semble que serra per ceo come rent sek apres term. Mez en cas le roy est nul pur ceo que cst un chos per conclusion … patronag serront le procheyn avoydans ce est voyd entant que est parcel de mesme le chos depart ne si le … foundar et il grant le nomination de corody a un estranger, ce est voyd pur ce que ne poet estre sever … *fun*dation. Mez si granta le corody <et>[d] a un et sez heyrs <semble que>[d] est bon, pur ce que ce afferm le fundation … [Si] … soyt patron dun abbe savont a ly le denomination a corody, le reservation est voyd.

… bon et issint en ce cas le roy nest favor plus que comen person.

… de toutes ters, tenementes, pastures, [ne] unques comenz, ne pasture: le cas est agre en liver dassissarum.

THIRD LECTURE

Now we must see what things may be granted:

Something may begin by a grant, such as common [or a] rent, and some things cannot pass by a grant, such as rent etc. Rent granted out of common to the king is good, and similarly if it is out of rent, because the limitation of distraint to the king is more than necessary, for the king may distrain everywhere for annuity or debt etc. And if the king grants this over it is good, but the grantee may only distrain ... the commoner's beasts. And it seems that he may do this if a rent is granted out of a common to a stranger, but it seems in the case of rent that the grant ... rent seck and may pass to the king, inasmuch as it should rather be to the benefit of the tenant than loss ... to the king by his prerogative etc.

Malat said that it was agreed that if the king has a bond by ... [with a] grant over and the grantee shall sue with a special count, but if a patron grants rent out of an advowson ... to the king if one who is a parson imparsonate ... but it seems that this case does not differ from the case of a rent granted out.[1]

... may [not] be granted for the hurt of the tenant, nor an uncertain grant of common in gross and fees not br... no other certainty except to the parson, but it is otherwise with common certain, common appendant, nor ... if grant is of common for term of life of the tenant as to the reversion the grant is void and similarly of ... which has no reversion. But if he grants the same rent or common it is not like a new common. ... annuity or rent charge and grants further a rent to be received of the same by the hand of the tenant, this is void. ... if rent to be received from the customs as the case was in 9 Hen. VI.[2] But it is otherwise if it was granted as parcel of this rent to be ... that ... if for term of years reserving rent, and then grant over this rent to another and to his heirs, this is good: it seems that this shall be like rent seck after the term. But in the case of the king it is null because it is a thing by conclusion ... patronage they shall have the next vacancy this is void inasmuch as it is parcel of the same departed thing nor if the ... founder and he grants the nomination of the corrody to a stranger, this is void because it cannot be severed [from the] foundation. But if he grants the corrody to one and his heirs it is good, because this affirms the foundation ... if ... there is a patron of an abbey saving to him the nomination of the corrody, the reservation is void.

... good and similarly in this case the king is not more favoured than a common person.

... of all lands, tenements, pastures, never commons, nor pasture: the case is agreed in the *Liber Assisarum*.

---

[1] Presumably Baldwin Malet, reader in the Inner Temple in Autumn 1512 (Magna Carta, cc. 18–23) and Lent 1519 (Westminster II, c. 1). *Readers and Readings*, pp. 75–76; Baker, *Men of Court*, pp. 1052–1053.

[2] YB Trin. 9 Hen. VI, fo.12, pl. 1. In this case the claimed annuity was to be paid from the London customs, part of the queen's dower. A similar case appears in YB Mich. 9 Hen. VI, fo. 53, pl. 36, where the annuity is to be paid from money paid annually to Henry V by the abbot of Bury and also assigned to the queen's dower.

[*fo. 58*] Feme fyt les et puis grant le revercion et devant atturnment prist le grante a baron, apres le tenant atturn: latturnment est bon enter il que el ad pris, meme le grante, a baron, et issint ore ne serra accompt come novel don denterest. Mez <le ley>[d] si prist lestranger a baron, come fuit cleerment agre, latturnment est nul et allege mesme rul xiij R[ic.] ij.[1] Auxi si el prist le lesse latturnment est bon, et a ce cas fuit repli et ne faytes <fort conqueter le reder quar>[d] et le reson entant que le baron poet elyer destre seisi de catel en son droit demesne, ou de franktenement en auter droit, et quant il ad atturn serra pris come agrement a les.

Home grant un manor una cum manerio de Dall que nest parcel de primer maner: le grant est bon et issint dacur et issint una cum advocatione quel avouson nest apurtenant. Mez si il dyst semul cum manerio ce est voyd, quar ne poet tener simul si non que fuit apurtynant devant.

Vestura terre ne peut estre grant sans fayt, quar est interest en rialte, et livere de seisin ne peut estre fayt. Mez si lez perfytes [*sic*] de ter sont grantes, ce poet estre per livere et tout est un come de grant le <rent>[d] ter. Et issint home grant le mariage denfant ou le costody ce nest bon sans fayt, mez si il ad le gard come catel et il grant le gard est bon sans fayt.

Tenant en tayll fayt les reservind rent et morust, son heyr grant meme le rent et puis <grant meme le rent>[d] recover le ter per formedon, ore le rent est determyn quar a son purpos ce grant ne conturvaut aceptans et grant, mez ceo est a voyer.

Senior et tenant, le senior grant son segniory a tenant en tayll ce est voyd, mez semble cler que serra per voy de discharge envers le tayll. Mez si soyt don a home et heyr femels de corps ou as heyrs de corps le second feme, ou a un que est tenant en borowenglis issint que apres son mort leyre per comen ley avera, en ceex casys le seniory est en suspens et <devi>[d] devoyt revyv per several dissentes come rent et revertion poyent, et si le ter soyt en gawelkynd apres partytion le seniory serra reviv <pur moyte>[i], et issint en cas de parceners si un purchas le seniory. Mez quere quar semble en lez casys <deveyt>[d] devant que leyr poet avera le seniory auxi.

Le roy grant a un que quant <son heyr>[d] il morust que son heyr ne suera livere, le grant nest bon entant que <leyr n>[d] ex... a heyr <nul>[d] ne si soyt a ly et sez heyrs quar <d>[d] ne poet estre sever de coron. Grant a un lez biens queux serront forfetes ou le doty que serra pay de reconusans ce est voyd, quar ne poet enure per voy de grant entant que navoyt nul tyel a temps et covenant le roy ne unques serra pris come grant. Mez le roy grant wayff, strey, et huiusmodi ... est bon entant que lenherytans de ceex chosys est en ly a temps de grant. <...>[d] Auxi le roy grant a un ... ce est voyd, pur ce que nest en ly de granter. Mez le roy grant a un que quant il alien ... et come semble serra pris come licens. Issint le roy grant a un lez perquisytes de tyel coort ce ... enheritans.

---

[1] Nota in margin.

A woman makes a lease and then grants the reversion, and before attornment takes the grantee as her husband, and afterwards the tenant attorns: the attornment is good between him whom she has taken as husband (the same grantee), and thus it shall not now be counted as a new gift of interest. But it was clearly agreed that if she takes a stranger as husband, the attornment is null and the same rule is given in 13 Ric II.[1] Also, if she marries the lessee the attornment is good, and on this case it was replied that it was not done [this way], and the reason was that the husband may elect to be seised of chattels in his own right, or of freehold in right of another, and when he has attorned it shall be taken as agreement to the lease.

A man grants a manor 'together with the manor' of Dale which is not parcel of the first manor: the grant is good, and the same of an acre, and the same 'together with the advowson', which advowson is not appurtenant. But if it says 'together with the manor' this is void, for he cannot hold them together unless they were appurtenant before.

Growing crops cannot be granted without a deed, for it is an interest in realty, and livery of seisin cannot be made. But if the profits of the land are granted, this may be by livery and it is the same as a grant of land. And similarly if a man grants the marriage of an infant or the custody, this is not good without a deed, but if he has the wardship as a chattel and he grants the wardship it is good without a deed.

A tenant in tail makes a lease reserving rent and dies, his heir grants the same rent and then recovers the land by formedon, now the rent is determined for in his view this grant does not imply aceptance and grant, but this is to be seen.

Lord and tenant, the lord grants his lordship to the tenant in tail this is void, but it seems clear that this shall be by way of discharge against the tail. But if there is a gift to a man and the heirs female of his body, or to the heirs of the body of the second wife, or to one who is a tenant in borough English so that after his death the heir by common law shall have [the land], in these cases the lordship is suspended and must be revived by several descents as rent and reversion may, and if the land is in gavelkind, after partition the lordship shall be revived for the moiety, and similarly in the case of parceners if one purchases the lordship. But query, for it seems in the cases before that the heir could have the lordship also.

The king grants to one that when he dies his heir shall not sue livery, the grant is not good inasmuch as … to the heir, nor if it is to him and his heirs for it cannot be severed from the Crown. A grant to one [of] goods which shall be forfeit, or the duty which shall be paid for acknowlegment, is void, for it may not operate by way of grant, inasmuch as he does not have any such thing at the time [of the grant], and the king's agreement shall never be taken as a grant. But if the king grants waif, stray, and such [things] this is good, inasmuch as the inheritance of these things is in him at the time of the grant. Also if the king grants to one … this is void, because it is not in him to grant. But if the king grants to one that when he aliens … and as it seems it shall be taken as a licence. Similarly if the king grants to one the perquisites of such a court this … inheritance.

---

[1] *Maxstoke* v. *Martyn*. Trin. 2 Ric. II (Ames Ser.), pp. 21–22, pl. 6; Statham, *Attournement*, 11; Fitzherbert, *Attournement*, 8.

4ᴬ LECTURA

Ore est a voyer de grant le roy, tamen:

\<Catells\>ᵈ per tytl a catelis pas de roy, non obstant que ad cause daver ex jure corone come wayf, strey, infangthyf, outfangthyf, catalla felonum et huiusmodi, mez le roy ne peut grant que le grante avera annum, diem et vastum, ne ters de traytors ne dez aliens …. Et non obstant le grant le roy, unquor le grante navera tyels privylagis come si le maner soyt tenus in capite … le maner et un des tenants alien \<v\>ᵈ a estranger unquore ne payera fyn, ne si le seniory soyt en le r… il grant a auter il navera tyel \<priver\>ᵈ privelage daver le gard de corps.

Le roy ne poet grant en prejudys dauter come waren en auter ter ou que fera en extorcio come si il … avera \<certe le\>ᵈ metyng de chescun … et que il avera pur chescun meet tyel som, ce est voyd. Mez auter est … ou feyrs et que il avera pur chescun viage ou stall, \<el\>ᵈ ce est pur comen well. Mez si il grant apres que il prend … extorcio, quere, quar semble que ce est come sender de eyne patent et le grant issint fayt all primes pur … ad ….

Le grant le roy ne serra \<pt'\>ᵈ bon si soyt generall si soyt de franctenement mez auter est de catels … en Dall ce est voyd ou touts oks cressentes en \<da\>ᵈ boys de Dalle, mez auter est de toutes biens un tyel … [fo. 58v] auxi si leyr sut special livere durant le \<…\>ᵈ non age, le livere covient estre certen et fayr [apres]¹ in … de avowson et huiusmodi et a toutes purposys come grant. Et meme le ley si levesque, devant que est consecrat, su daver lez temporaltes de roy a ferm, quar \<le m\>ᵈ en ceex cases le roy nest ly de droit de restor et pur ce serra pris come grant.

Le grant le roy ne serra pris per implication, scilicet un chos per reson de auter, et \<pur ceo si\>ᵈ come villen \<et wrekes vewe de frank\>ᵈ et tyels chosis profytabuls. Et pur ceo revercion ne pas de un que est tenant pur term de vie \<de\>ᵈ de ters: lc mancr nc rcnt nc pas, mcz all comen ley avouson pas pur ce que ne fuit valuabul ne de profyst. Mez si le roy \<…\>ᵈ pris notys cn ccrtcntc cn cccx casys est bon, come si il voyl resyt que lou un tyel est tenant de mon les et grant le maner le revercion pas et rent si resyt le rent, et issint semble a cas davouson si il dyst habendum simul cum advocacione etc. Auxi en cas davouson si il grant auxi largment come John at Style que fuit atteynt \<avoyd\>ᵈ avoyt ce est bon pur ce que est refer a certente, mez toutes ters en tyel maner est voyd.

Auxi si le roy \<grant\>ⁱ en auxi ampul maner unquor vew de frankplege ne pas ne wrek de meer ne offys appendant, ne libertes ne passont quar sont en le roy en auter natur etc., scilicet en droit de son coron et pur ceo \<sont detere\>ᵈ ce maner \<est\>ᵈ doccupyng est determyn. \<que\>ᵈ Meme le ley de infangthyff.

Pikage stallage ne pas quant le roy grant feyr si non que soyent expres pur ce que poyent estre severes. Mez auter est de chosys queux ne poyent

---

¹ MS. reads agpres.

Fourth Lecture

Now we must see concerning the king's grant, however:
[Chattels] under the title of chattels [may] pass from the king, notwithstanding
that he has cause to have them in right of the Crown, such as waif, stray, infangthief, outfangthief, the chattels of felons and such things, but the king may not
grant that the grantee shall have year, day and waste, nor the lands of traitors nor
of aliens .... And notwithstanding the king's grant, still the grantee shall not have
such privileges, as for instance if the manor is held in chief ... the manor and one
of the tenants aliens to a stranger, still he shall not pay a fine, nor if the lordship
is in the ... he grants to another, he shall not have such a privilege to have the
wardship of the body.

The king may not grant in prejudice of another, such as a warren in another's
land, or which would be done by extortion: for instance if he ... shall have the
weighing of each ... and that he shall have such a sum for each weighing, this is
void. But it is otherwise [of markets] or fairs [where he grants] what he shall have
for each road or stall, this is for the common weal. But if he grants afterwards
what he may take ... by extortion, query, for it seems that this is like rescinding
an older patent and the grant thus made in the beginning for ....

The king's grant shall not be good if it is general if it is of freehold, but it is
otherwise of chattels ... in Dale this is void, or all oaks growing in the woods of
Dale, but it is otherwise of all the goods of such ... also if the heir sues special
livery during the nonage, the livery must be certain and made after ... advowson
and such things and to all purposes like a grant. And the law is the same if the
bishop, before he is consecrated, sues to have the king's temporalities to farm, for
in these cases the king is not bound by right to restore [them] and for this reason
it shall be taken as a grant.

The king's grant shall not be taken by implication, that is, one thing by reason
of another, such as a villein and such profitable things. And because of this a
reversion does not pass from one who is a tenant for term of life of lands: neither
the manor nor the rent shall pass, but at the common law an advowson shall pass
because it was not valuable nor profitable. But if the king takes notice in certainty
in these cases it is good, as if he wishes to recite that where such a one is tenant
of my lease and grants the manor the reversion passes, and the rent if he recites
the rent, and it seems the same in the case of an advowson if he says 'having it
together with the advowson' etc. Also in the case of an advowson if he grants
broadly, such as that John at Style, who was attainted, should have it, this is good
because it refers to a certainty, but 'all lands' in this manner is void.

Also if the king grants in as ample a manner still a view of frankpledge does
not pass, neither wreck of the sea, nor office appendant, nor liberties pass, for
they are in the king in another nature etc., namely in the right of his Crown, and
for this [reason] this manner of occupying is determined. The law is the same of
infangthief.

Pickage [and] stallage do not pass when the king grants a fair unless they are
expressed, because they can be severed. But it is otherwise of things which cannot

estre severes, come comenz appendant,<p>ᵈ ou cort baron, ou pypouders a feyr toutes pas et issint si le roy grant le patronage dabbe.

Le grant le roy serra pris stricte et pur ceo si il grant advocationes ecclesiarum le grante navera advocationes abathiarum, ne si le roy grant conusauns dez ples le party navera conusans de pleynt dassyses, ne de pleyntes in custodia mareschalli, ne si grant catalla felonum et dampnatorum, il navera lez biens de convicts esteants felo de se ne dez traytors haut mez de petit il avera pur ce que felony: mez semble que non entant que stricte. Mez il dy oster <et alia>ᵈ catalla felonum qualitercumque forisfacta ou confiscate toutes catels de eux convictes passont et huiusmodi.

Le grant de costodia quam diu in manibus nostris fore contigerit le grante navera mez durant le non age <mez>ᵈ et non tanque ad su livere, mez semble que non, quar est diversite durante minore etate et lauter etc.

Le roy <nad>ᵈ navera corody si non que soyt <soy>ᵈ founder en droit de son coron et nemi en droit de dochi princypalite, si non que il ad ce per voy de conclucion, scilicet que labbe ad accept <ce home>ᵈ un de presentment le roy et donque pur ce que est maund a ly per mater de record et il ad fayt un convend seel, serra conclus a toutes jours et est cleer si labbe devy et bref de corodia habenda … il accept et return en le chauncery et la est record que il serra conclus, et vide que ce est le form … bosyng ascun bref mez soolment le patent.

…es pertant dates un jour ambydeex sont voyd, quar leffect de patent ne prist effect per livere …et pur ce que sont tout un, pur le weroste tout sont voyd.

…lx verdyst ou erroneos jugement, le roy seisit et grant a estranger, nul remedy pur cestui enconter que le …le bref derror ou atteynt fayll mez semble que est, et que bref derror gyst vers alien et scire facias vers … recovery per de[fault] et oster, com devant, que il ad bon remedy per bref de droit.

… tant un consyderation quel est faulx, tout est voyd sı ce resytall soyt cause materyall, come ıl resyt lou … <a ly b>ᵈ su son baylle de tyel maner, il grant a moy tyel fe, quar est ore pur cel cause, mez si il resyt …t deen de pouls ou un poor home il grant a ly tyels ters ou tyel fe ore le cause de grant … de doty, mez de pyte et pur cheryte et pur ce bon: quod nota que issint semble ley devant statut de grauntes de … felony non obstant le surmys faulx.

LECTURA 5ᴬ

[*fo. 59*] Ore serra monster en queux casys le patente monstrera le patent le roy, et en queux casys le patent serra forfayt per mater en fayt, et en queux casys per mater de record:

be severed, such as commons appendant, or court baron, or piepowders at a fair [which] all pass, and similarly if the king grants the patronage of an abbey.

The king's grant shall be taken strictly and for this reason if he grants the advowsons of churches the grantee shall not have the advowsons of abbeys, and if the king grants cognizance of pleas the party shall not have cognizance of plaints of assize, nor of plaints in the custody of the marshal, and if he grants the chattels of felons and the condemned, he shall not have the goods of convicts being suicides nor of high traitors, but he shall have the goods of petty [traitors], for that is a felony: but it seems not, since it should be taken strictly. But [if] it says further 'the chattels of felons however they are forfeited or confiscated' [then] all the chattels and so forth of those convicted pass.

By the grant of custody 'so long as he shall be in our hands', the grantee shall only have him during the nonage and not until he has sued livery, but it seems not for there is a distinction between 'during his minority' and the other.[1]

The king does not have a corrody unless he was the founder in the right of his Crown and not in right of the duchy [or] principality, unless he has this by way of conclusion, that is that the abbot has accepted one by the king's presentation and then because he is sent to him by matter of record and the abbot has made a convent seal, he shall be concluded for always; and it is clear that if the abbot dies and a writ *de corodia habenda* [issues which] he accepts and returns in the Chancery and it is there recorded he shall be concluded, and see that this is the form [and there is no] need for any writ but only the patent.

[A grant and letter patent] dated on one day, both are void, for the effect of the patent does not take effect by livery ... and because they are both one, because of the doubt both are void.

[Land forfeit by false] verdict or erroneous judgment, the king seizes and grants to a stranger, there is no remedy for him against whom the ... the writ of error or attaint fails; but it seems that there is, and that writ of error lies against an alien and *scire facias* against ... recovery by default and further, as above, that he has a good remedy by a writ of right.

... a consideration which is false, all is void if this recital is material cause, as if it recites that whereas I am his bailiff of such a manor, he grants to me such a fee, for it is now for that cause, but if it recites [that whereas he is] dean of St Paul's or a poor man, he grants to him such lands or such a fee, now the cause of the grant [is not] out of duty, but of pity and for charity and therefore it is good: which note, that it seems that the law was thus before the statute of grants of ... felony, notwithstanding the false surmise.

LECTURE FIVE

Now we shall see in what cases the patentee shall show the king's patent, and in what cases the patent shall be forfeit by matter of fact, and in what cases by matter of record:

---

[1] Spelman makes a similar distinction in his reading on *Prerogativa Regis*, see McGlynn, *Royal Prerogative*, p. 170.

En toutes casys lou le roy est party covient de monster lez patents come en quo warranto, non obstant que il soyt assyne, come semble il clayme wayf et strey et huiusmodi.

En ascun casys ne bosoyng de monster lez patents vers le roy lou de presumption ne remayn en son costody, come sy le roy granta maner a que avowson est appendent et puis port quare impedit vers le patron et encombent, lencombent pledera lez patentes sans monster. Et meme le ley si tenant le roy lez ters pur vi le remainder oster et cestui en le remainder vient sur le ter de voyer le wast et soyt endyt de trespass: il justifier per les le roy sans monster, quar per cas ne serra aret son foly que il navoyt endentur come en cas de comenz person. Meme le ley si le roy face vicount per patent le quel fayt souzthvicount, il justyfyera en endytment <en executant>[i] son offys sans monster lez patentes quar le patent apres tyent soolment a <roy>[d] vicount. Mesme le ley si toln soyt grant a bayllef de vyll, un baylle[f] prist tolut sur endytment, il justyfie sans monster pur ce que lez patentes apurteynont a le novel baylle. Auxi ne bosoyn monster vers estranger si il mesme ad estre en possession de meme le chos come pur wayff enport ou …. Mesme le ley si le roy grant seniory et le grante est en possession. Mez auter est si le <roy>[d] <grante>[i] navoyt estre unquez seisi, quar latturnment nest a purpos en cas lou le <grante>[d] roy grant.

Auxi pur trespas fayt en chas ne bosoyng de monster patentes pur ce que nest de recover meme le chace et est en possession. Mes en avower conseu sur cel covient de monster lez patentes, come en formedon en dissender sur don en tayl fayt a pier, quod quere quar semble que ne <…>[d] <bosoyng>[i] nient plus que grant de chace quar le pier pusoyt aver perd le fayt.

Ore serra dyst dez forfeturs per mater en fayt, come lou le roy licens dalien en mortmayn ou auterment dieux acres et il alyn iiij, tout est forfayt pur le non cert-ente que est ce que pas per licens. Mez auter est si le roy licens dalien le maner de Dalle et il alien le maner de Dalle et de Sale: voyd solement quant a Salle, pur ce que est certen que est misuse. Meme le ley de licens demporter, si le <roy>[d] licens le roy soyt un foytes execut le power de licens est determyn, come le roy licens enfant deins age daliener et il alien et puis a pleyn age enter et alien arere, ce est sans licens pur ce que le licens fuit un foytes execut et voyd. Mez auter est lou il fayt per duras demprisonment ou si <le baron et le feme>[d] licens soyt a feme dalien et el prist baron et ils alien, le baron recover per cui in vita ore si le feme alien en apres el peut per primer licens, quar le licens ne fuit unques execut un reson que le baron et feme <ne unques>[d] alien et ce fuit voyd quant a licens. Auter reson quar per le cui in vita el cleer… a feffment fayt u… et pur ceo lentre ne serra suppose en cui in vita si non per baron. Mez en don fait infra etatem il … suppose son entre per luy [meme] et pur ce, si le baron <et feme>[i] avoyt fayt feffment sur condition

In all cases where the king is party the patents must be shown, as in *quo warranto*, notwithstanding that it is assigned: as for example if he claims waif, stray and such things.

In some cases there is no need to show the patents against the king where by presumption it does not remain in his custody, as if the king grants a manor to which an advowson is appendant, and then brings *quare impedit* against the patron and incumbent, the incumbent shall plead the [letters] patent without showing them. And the law is the same if the king's tenant leases lands for life the remainder over, and the remainderman comes on the land to see the waste and is indicted for trespass: he shall justify by the king's lease without showing it, for it will be accounted his foolishness that he did not have an indenture as in the case of a common person. The law is the same if the king makes a sheriff by letters patent who makes an under-sheriff: [the under-sheriff] shall justify the execution of his office without showing the letters patent, for the patent is held solely by the sheriff. The law is the same if a toll is granted to the bailiff of a vill, a bailiff takes toll on indictment, [the bailiff] justifies without showing because the patents pertain to the new bailiff. Also they need not be shown against a stranger if he himself was in possession of the same thing, such as waif, carrier away …. The law is the same if the king grants a lordship and the grantee is in possession. But it is otherwise if the grantee was never seised, for the attornment is to no purpose in the case where the king grants.

Also for a trespass committed in a chase there is no need to show patents because it is not to recover in the chase and it is in possession. But in an avowry conceived thereon the patents must be shown, as in formedon in the descender on a gift made in tail to the father, which query, for it seems that it is not necessary any more than with a grant of a chase for the father could have lost the deed.

Now we must talk of forfeitures by matter of fact, as where the king licenses to alien two acres in mortmain or otherwise and he aliens four: all is forfeit for the uncertainty of what was not covered by the licence. But it is otherwise if the king licenses to alien the manor of Dale, and he aliens the manor of Dale and of Sale: this is void only for Sale, because it is certain what was misused. The law is the same of a licence to import: if the king's licence is once executed the power of the licence is determined, as when the king licenses an infant within age to alien and he aliens, and then at full age he enters and aliens again, this is without licence because the licence was once executed and void. But it is otherwise where he aliened under duress of imprisonment or if the licence is to a woman to alien and she takes a husband and they alien [and] the husband recovers by *cui in vita*, now if the woman aliens afterwards she may by the first licence, for the licence was never executed because the husband and wife aliened and this was void by the licence. [There is] another reason, for by the *cui in vita* she clearly … feoffment made … and by this the entry shall only be supposed in *cui in vita* by the husband. But in a grant made within age he … suppose his entry by himself, and for this [reason] if the husband and wife have made a feoffment on condition

le condition est enfre*nt* ... el afferm sa act mez si el port cui in vita et recover, el est remyt sicome nul tyel aucyt e*stre*. ... son memory et a sez heyrs dalien quel alien leyr recover en don non fuit compos mentis si ...entant que afferm le feffment per le pier pur meme le reson que est denfant. le committee de ydeot est utlage en .... Mez feme nul ley quar il ad frankt...[1]

Le licens le roy ne exedera lez parolis, come si le roy licens un abbe de purchas toutes ters que John at *Style* ... et John at Dale tenont joint: John at Dale morust, John at Style fyst lestat de tout ... ce est sans licens, et le ... temps de licens John at St*yle* tenoyt joint et pur ce le licens avera relation a temps de licens. Et pur ce le roy ... toutes ters que tyel home ad issint que nexed le valu de x li. et apres le licens le meson est edefy ou ... valu xx li. unquor labbe peut purchas. Mez, come semble, auter est si le licens nenepli a toutes ters <tyel licens>[i] mez sol... mez si le roy licens a un prior de purchas, le quel apres est fayt abbe, le licens est unquor bon quar ... devant. <issint si le>[d] Si le roy licens un de purchas ters en tyel vyll tenus de roy et en mesme ... per service de chyvaleer et auters per socage, le licens ne extend forque a socage pur le plus perfect ...

Lyberty misuse est unques forfayt mez non use est fynabul, come si home ad market le lundy ...ce est non use, mez si il tyent le lundy et le mercredy nest forfeytur ne fynabul pur le market ... pur usurper dauter, mez si il misus come en leet al covert le punisment de pyllory en fyn ou e... teyng ples de faictes dehors le feyr ceux sont misuses et forfayturs, mez semble le ground ... forfaytur mysus fynabul pur ce que non use est le plus prejudys a comenz weel. Mez si conusans de ... forfaytur ne fynabul, mez solment pur le mater que pend entant que nest lyberty pur comen ....

[*fo. 59v*] Ore serra a voyer de forfayturs et determyntions per mater de record: Si le roy grant le gard <durante>[d] quam diu in manibus nostris fore contygerit et puis grant patent a auter le primer patent est determyn. Mez auter est si le primer patent ust estre durante minore etate. Mez semble que le primer cas nest ley, mez le diversite est si le roy en le primer cas suffer leyr de suer speciall lyvere le patent est determyn, mez nemi en le darren cas.

Le roy grant un patent a un et puis grant meme le chos a auter, le primer patente su sire facias pur repeller <le 2e est voyd envers le Roy>[i] le 2e et est nonsu, ambydeux sont voyd: le primer entant que il est nonsu. Et pur ce si home travers un foytes et soyt nonsu il ne unques arere travers en apres. Et meme le ley de petytion, et issint si home purchas lycens et ad ad quod dampnum et soyt nonso del *p*... return en le chauncery il ne unques avera auter. Et meme le ley si le roy sesy per <fay>[d] faulx offys et fayt patent ... estranger: cestui que est oste tend travers et ad scire facias et le patente fayt default, ore son patent serra voyd et lez ters sont convy a cestui que tend le travers en ferm don... discussu

---

[1] This last sentence off-set on the page.

[and] the condition is broken … she affirms her act, but if she brings *cui in vita* and recovers, she is restored as if there had been no such act. [The king licenses one who has lost] his memory and his heirs to alien and he aliens, the heir recovers in a grant *non fuit compos mentis* if … inasmuch as it affirms the feoffment by the father for the same reason as the infant. The idiot's committee is outlawed in … But woman; no law for he has freehold ….

The king's licence shall not exceed the words, as if the king licenses an abbot to purchase all the lands which John at Style … and John at Dale held jointly: John at Dale dies, John at Style makes an estate of the whole, this is without licence, and the … time of the licence John at Style held jointly and therefore the licence shall have relation to the time of the licence. And for this the king … all lands which such a man has as long as they do not exceed the value of £10, and after the licence the house is built or … value of £20 still the abbot may purchase. But, as it seems, it is otherwise if the licence does not [extend to] all lands such licence but only …. But if the king licenses a prior to purchase, who is afterwards made abbot, the licence is still good for … before. If the king licenses one to purchase lands in such a vill held of the king and in the same … by knight service and others by socage, the licence only extends to socage for the more perfect ….

Liberty misused is always forfeited, but non-use is finable, as if a man has a market [on] Monday [and does not hold it]… this is non-use, but if he holds it [on] Monday and Wednesday this is not forfeiture or finable for the market … for usurping the other, but if he misuses, as in a leet to convert the punishment of pillory to a fine or … holding pleas of actions outside the fair, these are misuses and forfeitures, but it seems that the ground … forfeiture misuse finable because non-use is the most prejudicial to the common weal. But if the cognisance of … forfeiture nor finable, but only for the matter pending, inasmuch as it is not a liberty for common ….

Now we must see concerning forfeitures and determination by matter of record: If the king grants the wardship 'for as long as it remains in our hands' and then grants the patent to another, the first patent is determined. But it is otherwise if the first patent was 'during his minority'. But it seems that the first case is not law, but the difference is if the king in the first case allowed the heir to sue special livery the patent is determined, but not in the latter case.

The king grants a patent to one and then grants the same thing to another, the first patentee sues *scire facias* to rescind, the second is void against the king, the second is non-suited, both are void: the first inasmuch as he is non-suited. And for this reason if a man traverses once and is non-suited he shall never traverse again after. And the same law of petition, and thus if a man purchases a licence and has *ad quod dampnum* and is non-suited of the … return in the Chancery he shall never have another. And the law is the same if the king is seised by false office and makes a patent [to] a stranger: the one who is ousted tenders a traverse and has a *scire facias* and the patentee defaults, now his patent shall be void and the lands are conveyed to the one who tendered the traverse in farm … discussion

fuerit il est nonsu, son patent est voyd quar le descusson est ore determyn per son act. Mez si le roy grant market en Dale et meme le jour grant market en Sall que est adjoynat, si sont dun teste unquor ambydeux bon quar nest prejudycyal al roy etc. Mez si le darren patent soyt apres le primer, et le primer sut scire facias de repeller ce entant que est icy prochen adjoynant et est nonsu ambydeux bon, quar le scire facias la est soolment sut pur linterest de party et come semble scire facias ne gyst entant que est de several chosys.

Le roy commyt ters de home utlage al auter, le quel port bref derror pur utlage et <et ad scire facias vers patente>[i] reverse lutlage, unquor il avera auter scire facias en apres pur repeel le patent <mez semble que pur cyrcumstanz>[d] quar est nul garrante a ce purpos. Si le roy commyt ters en Irland a un home ou en counte palantyn et puis commyt mesme lez ters a auter, le primer patente avera scire facias vers le 2[e] en Irland ou Chester et nemi en chauncery pur ce que lez breffs le roy ne curront la.

Lectura vj[A]

Ore serra monster ... prescriptions, queux chosys home peut prescryber et en quel maner:
Home peut prescryb tyels chosys queux atteyn a roy queux le roy meme poet aver per mater en <wayff>[d] fayt come wayff, strey, feyr, ... de ce chose que napurteyn a roy, si non per mater de record: en ceo nul home peut prescryb com catalla felonium fugit ... biens de mut, ou de clerk convyct, quar ceex ne atteynct a roy si non per meens de record. Meme le ley ... et amersements.

...costom et prescription. Costom est que lextend a toutes le inhabytans de pays ou deins vyl come gavel kind, borowenglis <diversite>[d] diviser dez ters et huiusmodi: <mez donques coment si>[d] ce costom ne poet estre grant per roy quar serra ...tyels person ...nques reser... synguler person ou privat ou polytyk et ce covient unques destre en laffyrmatyff scilicet que il ad estre discharg ... que il devoy pay nul toln, quar ce ne poet gyser en conusans come mater issuabul serra tend en affyr... ...a volunte poyent prescryber mez donquez covient prescryber en droit de le tenant de franktenement, scilicet que il ad use daver tyel comenz a ly et touts sez ... ne poyent prescryber per que estat. <Mes>[d] Mesme le ley si home voyl <prescryber>[i] que le tenant de maner et toutes lez inhabytants ont su ...t ce que eux fueront tenant a volunte et nest reson que lour act lyera, mez il covient va oster et dyr que estat le defendant ad ou h... ... de comenz place ou le chauncery poyont prescryber de doner offyce ou benefycye souzht le som de xx s.

... commenser a roy entant que il ne unquez dona mez ce prescriptio est ...r le roy

...ez ley est voyd et dobul come pur rent servis ou ... feffment a ...

was he is non-suited [and] his patent is void, for the discussion is now determined by his act. But if the king grants a market in Dale and the same day grants a market in Sale which is adjoining, if they are by one *teste*, still both are good, for it is not prejudicial to the king etc. But if the latter patent was after the former, and the former sued *scire facias* to rescind this, inasmuch as they are here adjoining and [he] is non-suited both are good, for there the *scire facias* is solely sued for the interest of the party, and as it seems *scire facias* does not lie inasmuch as there are several things.

The king commits land of an outlawed man to another, the outlaw brings a writ of error for outlawry and has a *scire facias* against the patentee to reverse the outlawry, still he shall have another *scire facias* afterwards to repeal the patent, for there is no warrant for this purpose. If the king commits lands in Ireland or in a county palatine to a man and then commits the same lands to another, the first patentee shall have *scire facias* against the second in Ireland or Chester and not in the Chancery, because the king's writs do not run there.

LECTURE SIX

Now we shall see [concerning] prescriptions, for what things one may prescribe and in what manner:

[One] may prescribe [for] things which belong to the king which the king himself may have by matter in fact, such as waif, stray, fair, …. [It is otherwise] of the things which do not belong to the king except by matter of record: in them no-one may prescribe, such as the chattels of fugitive felons, … the goods of a mute, or a clerk convict, for these only fall to the king by means of record. The law is the same [of fines] and amercements.

[Now we must see the difference between] custom and prescription. Custom is that which extends to all the inhabitants of the region or within a vill, such as gavelkind, borough English, devising lands and suchlike: this custom cannot be granted by the king because it is … such person …singular or private person or [body] politic, and it must always be in the affirmative, that is that he has been discharged [from toll, for if he prescribes that] he ought to pay no toll, this cannot lie in knowledge [of the jury] as an issuable matter, so it shall be tendered in the affir[mative]. [Tenant] at will may prescribe, but then he must prescribe in right of the freehold tenant, namely that he is accustomed to have such commons to him and to all his [tenants, for a tenant at will] cannot prescribe in the *que estate*. The law is the same if a man wishes to prescribe that the tenant of the manor and all the inhabitants have … so that they were tenants at will, and it is not reasonable that their acts should bind, but he must go further and say what estate the defendant has or … of Common Pleas or the Chancery may prescribe to give office or benefice under the sum of 20s.

… begins with the king to the extent that he never gives but this prescription is … the king.

… law is void and double as for rent-service or … feoffment to …

… extorcio et ne peut commens per resonabul meen est voyd come lou vicount voyl prescryber daver xij d. de rent … tyel vyl pur son exscuse de vener a torn, ce est voyd quar ne pusoyt commens loyalment. Mesme le ley si home prescrybe daver … quar ce ne pusoyt commens sinon per usurpation, quar le temps nest a saveyr mez il poet bien prescryber daver toln travers … unquez enpeyry. Mesme le ley si le segnior voyl claym xij d. de chescun que vient a devier deins son maner: ce est voyd [*fo. 60*] quar ne peut comens forsque per usurpation. Mez si il voyl prescryber daver heriot apres le mort le tenant ce est bon, quar poet commens per reservation. Meme le ley si home prescrybe de reteynger distress tanque fyn a son plesyr, ce est voyd. Mesme le ley si eux de London voyl presc-ryber de reteyner auter biens a eux pleges tanque le doty soyt pay. Mez auter est <si>^d dez biens le roy si le roy grant a eux de fayr issint, ne si home voyl prescry-ber de bater transgressor en mon ter. Mez come semble, ce puis ly … de ter per batery ou econtrary que *il avoydera* prescription est voyd si non que le corps que prescrybe ad ce contynuans, come de vyl, si non que ils ont estre incorporates devant temps [etc.]: mez semble que le costom en tyel vyl est bon. Mez unquor nest ple de pleder que le vyl ad estre fount puis temps [etc.] quar auterment et covient de travers <especialment>^d generalment que nad estre seisi. Mez est bon ple si soyt de rent de pleder que mon auncestur leve fyn de meme le rent <ter>^d deins temps [etc.] mez semble cleer que ce est nul ley vide xlvj^o [Edw. III] quar ce est argumentyff.

Prescription de choce que nest en profyst de tenant nest bon, come si il voyl prescryber de reteynur distress dieux jours sans lyvere, ce nest bon ple nest en profyst de tenant. Mesme le ley si home voyl prescryber que ils et toutes que estat en mece ont dyg en soyl le plaintiff pur reparer le h… nest bon mez auter si soyt ly per tenur de issint fayr et donquez covient de commensera ce prescrip-tion. Mez si soyt son privat voy ou … de ce lou per cas si ils decayont peut hurt le soyl ce prescription est bon ou si home prescryb per que estat de reparation de son meason ce est bon et issint daver acquitel. Mez si home prescrybe vers un abbe que ly et sez predecessors ont use de temps etc. de ly acquite, ce nest bon si non que il dy oster que estat en seniory. Mez semble que ce est eyant regard a bref dentre mez aver action sur le cas semble que ce priscription est bon quar bref dentre ne gyst mez vers mesn. Mez si home <prescryber que>ⁱ predecessors que estat ont use <en ter>ⁱ de scowrer un dych ce est nul mez come alleger que il et sez predecessors: quere quar semble cleer nul ley, quar tout est un de abbe et de auter tenant en fe a ce purpos.

Home ne poet prescrybe contrary a statut, come tenant en tayll de dyvyser ou daver dysms de silva sedua quar ce ne poet commens loalment de prescryp-tion consernant maters de record. Si home prescryb que le petit jurre serra amersy si lour verdyst soyt trove faulx ce est nul, quar ce soolment conferme le

… extortion and may not commence by reasonable means is void, as when a sheriff wishes to prescribe to have 12d. of rent … such a vill for his excuse from coming to a tourn, this is void because it cannot begin legally. The law is the same if one prescribes to have … for this can only commence by usurpation, for the time … is not to be known, but he can well prescribe to have a toll-traverse … never made worse. The law is the same if the lord wishes to claim 12d. of everyone who comes to die within his manor: this is void for it can only begin by usurpation. But if he wishes to prescribe to have a heriot after the tenant's death this is good, for it can commence by reservation. The law is the same if a man prescribes to retain distress until fine at his pleasure, this is void. The law is the same if those of London wish to prescribe to retain other goods pledged to them until the duty is paid. But it is otherwise of the king's goods if the king grants to them to do this, or if a man wishes to prescribe to beat a trespasser in my lands. But as it seems, this may … him … by battery or otherwise that he shall avoid, the prescription is void unless the body who prescribes has this continuance, as of a vill, unless they were incorporated before time [immemorial]: but it seems that the custom in such a vill is good. But still it is not a plea to plead that the vill was made since time [immemorial], for otherwise [etc.], and he must traverse generally that he has not been seised. But it is a good plea if it is of rent, to plead that my ancestor levied a fine for the same rent within the time [of memory], but it seems clear that this is no law, see 46 [Edw. III] for this is argumentative.[1]

Prescription of something which is not profitable to the tenant is not good, as if he wishes to prescribe to retain distress for two days without livery, this is not a good plea [and] is not to the tenant's profit. The law is the same if a man wishes to prescribe that they and all those whose estate is in the messuage have dug in the plaintiff's soil to repair the h[ighway], [it] is not good, but it is otherwise if he was bound by tenure to do this and then it must begin this prescription. But if there is a private way or [road] in this place which, if they perhaps decayed might hurt the soil, this prescription is good, or if a man prescribes by *que estate* for the repair of his house this is good, and likewise to have acquittal. But if a man prescribes against an abbot that he and his predecessors have been accustomed from time [immemorial] to acquit him, this is not good unless he says further 'whose estate in the lordship [he has]'. But it seems that this is with regard to a writ of entry, but to have an action on the case it seems that this prescription is good, for a writ of entry only lies against the mesne. But if a man prescribes that [his] predecessors whose estate [he has] have used to scour a ditch in land this is null, but like alleging that he and his predecessors: query, for it seems clearly no law, for an abbot and another tenant in fee are all the same for this purpose.

A man may not prescribe contrary to a statute, as for a tenant in tail to devise or have tithes of *silva caedua*, for this cannot commence legally for a prescription concerning matters of record. If a man prescribes that the petty jury shall be amerced if their verdict is found false this is null, for this only confirms the

---

[1] YB Hil. 46 Edw. III, fo. 28, pl. 1.

coron est si hut en natur et issint de faulx jugement mez pur amersyer pur concelmentes ce est bon.

Auxi en London est tyel prescription que <de>ᵈ chescun pleynt que est afferm devant le vicount devant issu joyn, le mayr ad power de remover devant ly et si poyent appeer per examination et per provs que le defendent est vex sans caus, ils dimytterent le cas sans auter chos fayr. Et a ce fuit reply un si ils poyent remov ce quar ce est jurisdicion royall, mez entant que ont come un power non obstant severall ... unquor chescun poyent eydur auter et all commensement lez lybertys ne fuer grantes mez as cytezyns et puis quant ils ont enter eex meme ... tyel ordur et unquor lour power nest mez un et le mayr poyent reverser jugement don devant vicount mez ce est ... grant de roy et .... Mez come semble que il ne poet tryer ce per provs quar va en bar et pur ce le costom hors de comen <person>ᵈ reson et ... ou fuit en coort devant lou le tryell serra plus hut et pur ce a superiore ad suum inferius non est decidendum. Mez unquor le reder dyst que fuit rul x° ... que tyel costom fuit bon. Auxi sur denyer de costom issint fuit certyfy per recorder ore tenus. Auxi le costom de London est que ils poyent dyvyser ters en mortmayn et ore comment poyent: semble que ne poet estre si non per grant ... est contrary a statut.

Auxi un vikar que est datyf et nient removabul per prescription poet suer action mez un tyel vykary ne poet estre ... de prescryb puis le temps le roy Ryc. [I] le quel est temps de prescription. Labbe prescryb destre discharg de corody lou le roy est founder nest bon entant que jugdment a ce que contynu. Si parson ou abbe prescryb en rent covient dalleger seisin expresment et ce est traverssabul pur ce que est choce en possession, mez si soyt un foytes interupt de son possession le prescription est distroy. Mez ce covient destre prys si il agrea a cel prescryption come per acceptans de darren rent.

En ascun cas covient de monster patent auxi prescription come lou <_>ᵈ eyne grant est fayt per parolys obscur, come le roy grant ... justiciam si ils voyllent demander conusans covient surmetter que ce ad unques estre allow pur meme cel cause. Et meme le ley en prol... .... Meme le ley si home de <bien dure>ᵈ voyllent prescryber daver comenz <per travers>ⁱ <de monster comment>ᵈ bien dure covient de monster charter de ...: semble que prescription serve ambiydeux quar home peut aver ... per prescryption.

Per costom mals et femals poyent enheryt quar non obstant que ne poet commens per loyall ... ascun reson issint que ce darren est le ground si estoy ovesque reson et en ly meme nest emply o... ...: ce est bon prescryption.

VIJᴬ LECTURA

[*fo. 60v*] Ore serra monster sur cest parols *ecclesia anglicana* et en ce sont quarters maters incluses scilicet lesglis materyel, lespyrytuel persons, lez lays persons, et le spyrytuell persons.

Et primez est a voyer de ecclesia et de privelag dicel, scilicet de imunite et tuition. En primez sont troys maner de de [*sic*] privelagys, scilicet privat come

Crown is so high in nature and likewise of false judgments, but for amercements for concealments this is good.

Also in London there is a prescription that the mayor has power to remove before him each plaint that is affirmed before the sheriff before issue is joined, and if it should appear by examination and by witnesses that the defendant is vexed without cause, to dismiss the case without doing anything else. And to this it was replied [to ask] if they can remove this for this is a royal jurisdiction, but inasmuch as they have as a power notwithstanding several ... still each can help the other, and at the beginning the liberties were only granted to the citizens, and then when they had among themselves ... such order and yet their power was only one and the mayor could reverse judgment given before the sheriff, but this is ... the king's grant and .... But it seems that he cannot try this by witnesses, for it goes in bar and for this reason the custom is outside common reason and ... or was in court before, where the trial shall be higher, and therefore a decision may not go downward from a superior to his inferior. But still the reader said that it was ruled in 10 ... that such a custom was good. Also on denying the custom it was certified by the recorder by word of mouth. Also the custom of London is that they can devise lands in mortmain: but how may they? It seems that it can only be by grant [since] it is contrary to the statute.

Also a vicar who is endowed and not removable may sue an action by prescription, but such a vicarage cannot ... prescribe since the time of King Richard [I], which is the time of prescription. The abbot prescribes to be discharged of a corody where the king is founder: this is not good inasmuch as [there is] judgment for this which continues. If a parson or an abbot prescribes in rent he must allege seisin expressly, and this is traversable because it is a thing in possession, but if he is once interrupted of his possession the prescription is destroyed. But this must be taken to mean, if he agrees to this prescription, as by the acceptance of the last rent.

In some cases he must show a patent [and] also prescription, as where the older grant is made by obscure words, as where the king grants ... justice, if they wish to demand cognisance they must submit that this has always been allowed for the same cause. And the law is the same in .... The law is the same if a man wishes to prescribe to have common by traverse ... he must show a charter of ...: it seems that a prescription serves for both for a man may have ... by prescription.

By custom males and females may inherit, for notwithstanding that it cannot commence by legal ... any reason, so that this latter is the ground [why], if it is reasonable and in itself does not imply ...: this is a good prescription.

SEVENTH LECTURE

Now we must see on these words *the English Church*, and on this there are four matters included, namely the material church, the spiritual persons, the lay persons, and the spiritual persons:

And first we must see about *the Church* and its privileges, namely immunity and sanctuary. First there are three types of privileges, namely private, such as

Westmenster [et] Seynt Marten lez quewx serve durant le vy de home pur chescun cause et ceux sont issint privelages per le pape; church gre come en chescun
eglis de comenz droit et issint fuit puis le commensement de crystyn pur caus que
homs averont melyor favor al Eglys; leus privelages come seynt John et toutes
tenementes et lez sytes de ycel mez ne lez feeldes ne lez barns ne schephous, mez
semble cleer contrary si sont deins le syte. Et [un] que prist church gre covient
confes felony a chescun que ly examyn ou auter bien lyst de ly traher hors. Mez
covient soolment[1] confes le felony ad coroner certen, scilicet le jour, lan, et toutes
lez cyrcumstancys et ce covient de fayr ou auter nest a purpos. <mes>[d] Et donques apres durant lez xl jours apres le confessyon il soy advysera si voyl abjure
<et si le>[d] mez semble per argument que est en discressyon le coroner quar si
ly plest poet ly constrayn sur son confessyon de abjure ou auterment nest tenus
de vener puis aly. Et si en ce cas ne soyt harrand theff conus le coroner peut de
discressyon ly ayder en le certente de son confessyon.

Lez xl jours serront accomptes de temps de confessyon et pur ceo si le coroner ne vient a ly xx ans il avera le privelag. Si contynu la oster les xl jours per
launcyn ley ils voyllent ly murer mez ce est nul ley, mez que est felony si ascun
don a ly viand apres lez xl jours et semble a Reder que peut estre tre hors apres
mez ne peut.

Toutes ceux queux ne sont en juperdy <de vy>[i] naveront le privelag, come
clerk atteynt, clerk convyct si eux escapont, quar lour vy est pardon. Meme le ley
de mut si ne soyt escryer, <mez unquor ce devoyt et donquez per cas>[d] <mez la
ne>[i] peut abjure mez doom <ne unques>[d] navera <ne>[d]. Mez ne serra abjure pur
ceo que ne <…>[i] poyet oyer le jugement. Mez semble que nul de[2] eux averont
le privelag quar nul de lour vys serront en juperdy unques. Mez come semble
per enquest doffys si soyent troves coupable ils averont perpetuel enprisonment,
atteynt avera, mez ne serra abjure entant que jugement est don vers ly de meme
le felony.

Accessory ne prend sanctuary apres que le princypall ust abjur si non que voyl
confes. Auxi ceux naveront privelag queux ne poyent confes <le felony quar son
vy nest en juperdy>[i] come ydeot [ou] lynatyk durant le temps que est lynatyk,
et pur ce serra tret hors et puis quant ad arer son wyt il serra restor. Mez enfant
de discression peut a… semble avera privelag de cel pur ce que est indifferent as
clers et nient. Et pur ce en vy le roy Henry … fyn averont le privelag si eex fuent
a ce entant que ont confydens a ce.

Mez si … soyt apech de heresy ou treson serra tret quar pur ceux le sentuary
pur fault a deu ou roy que est chef de le soyl privelagys. Mez si prist sentuary
pur felony et est tret pur heresy ou treson et abjure le heresy ou trove nient coupable il serra restor. Meme le ley si prist sentuary pur un chose que nest felony,

---

[1] In margin: … si soyt … ycy confes … y tout reson unquor … est a purpos … le … coroner nest per ce pris
   … al endytment mez … come semble auter est si soyt … endyt devaunte le … coronir meme.
[2] In margin: ne si home voyll comist felony en gals … vi nest en juperdy … engliter.

Westminster and St Martin's, which serve during the life of a man for every cause and they are thus privileged by the pope; church grith, as in each church by common right and it was thus since the beginning of Christianity so that men might have greater favour for the Church; and privileged places, as St John's and all its tenements and sites, but not the fields nor the barns, nor sheepfolds – but it seems clearly the contrary if they are within the site.[1] And one who takes church grith must confess felony to everyone who examines him, or otherwise it is good to drag him out. But he need only confess the felony with certainty to the coroner, namely the day, the year and all the circumstances, and he must do this or otherwise it is ineffective. And then afterwards during the forty days after the confession he shall consider if he wishes to abjure, but it seems upon argument that it is in the coroner's discretion, for if it pleases him [the coroner] may constrain him on his confession to abjure or otherwise he is not bound to go. And if in this case he is not known as an arrant thief the coroner, at his discretion, may help him in the certainty of his confession.

The forty days are counted from the time of confession, and therefore if the coroner does not come to him for twenty years, he shall have the privilege [for that time]. If he remains there beyond the forty days by the old law they may immure him but this is no law, although it is a felony if someone gives him food after the forty days. And it seems to the reader that he could be taken out afterwards, but he cannot.

All those who are not in jeopardy of their life cannot have the privilege, such as a clerk attaint or clerk convict if they escape, for their life is pardoned. The law is the same of a mute if he cannot write, but there he cannot abjure but shall not have judgment. But he shall not abjure because he cannot hear the judgment. But it seems that none of them shall have the privilege, for none of their lives shall ever be in jeopardy. But as it seems, if they are found guilty by the inquest of office they shall have perpetual imprisonment, [and] they shall be attainted, but they shall not abjure even though judgment is given against them of the same felony.

An accessory shall not take sanctuary after the principal has abjured unless he wishes to confess. Also, those who cannot confess the felony because their life is not in jeopardy [shall not have the privilege], such as an idiot, [or] a lunatic during the time he is lunatic, and therefore he shall be taken out and then when he has his wits again he shall be restored [to sanctuary]. But it seems that a child of the age of discretion may have the privilege because it is indifferent as to clerks and non-clerks. And for this in the life of King Henry ... shall have the privilege if they flee to this inasmuch as they have confidence in it.

But if [one] is impeached of heresy or treason he shall be taken out, since for these the sanctuary [fails] for a fault against God or the king who is the lord of the privileged soil. But if he takes sanctuary for felony and is taken out for heresy or treason and abjures the heresy, or is found not guilty, he shall be restored. The law is the same if he takes sanctuary for something which is not a felony,

---

[1] YB Hil. 9 Hen. VII, fo. 20, pl. 15.

<et puis ce>[d] ore serra tret si puis ce soyt fayt felony per statut il serra restore admyt que lestatut extend a offencys devant, quar donques ce fuit come felony a commensement. Meme le ley si streek un home et puis est tret puis meme le home morust il serra restore. Issint si prist <sen>[d] church gre et puis ce est fayt sentuary pur vi il serra restor et avera le pryvelag pur son vye.

Si ... home confes felony devant le coroner et puis escap al auter egles la il avera le privelag et <ne besoyn>[d] per auter xl jours. Et meme le ley si cel egles soyt est per le cost de meer, il serra restor a auter esglis, mez ne bosoyn ... ... auter confessyon si soyt deins le <jus>[d] jurisdicion de cel coroner et si abjure sur primer confessyon. Unquor si escap il avera le privelag, mez ne unquor serra abjure en apres <ne>[d] pur <cel>[i] felony ne pur auter fyst devant quar toutes sont determyns ... jugment a ce purpos. Mez si fyst felony en apres poet abjur auter-foytes come home atteynt peut estre areyng pur cel ...t auxi conuster toutes felo-nys dez queux il voyl aver privelag al coroner et pur ce si soyt trey et areyng sur ... ne serra restor. Unquor vide que quant il pray destre restor devant ascun juge il ne dirra le certente [*fo. 61*] de felony mez pro quadam felonia per ipsum prius perpetrata <..>[d] mez covient de monster expres le jour et an de pris de centuary, ou auterment nest a purpos si non que soyt en discressyon de justys de ly ayder et assyner ysel si ne soyt harrand theff come fuit en cas de Huet. Isint per ceo semble que le certente de felony ne unques viend pur que le felony il confist mez per cas le coron peut estre examyn.

Si en cel cas home voyl pled que il ad pris esglis en Gales et pray destre restor ne serra restor pur ceo que le plee ne poet estre try per nul meen quar nos ne mandermus unques en Gales a tryer issu come serromus en Chester et Durram, quar eex sont come parcel de royalm et pur ce la serra maund et remaund arer mez en Galis est auter si ne soit ... en cas <destatut>[d] de quare impedit serra port desglis en Galys <pur ce>[d] en le prochein paroche en adjoynant: le reson, come semble, quar nul est de sy haut power la de maunder bref al evesque et pur ceo covient a suer a coort le roy. Auxi ter[res] de cheff segniors marchers ser-ront determyn icy pur ce que ne <souȝth>[d] sont souȝth lobediens de prynce. Mez auterment nul mater serra determyn pled en Gales mez toutes serra voyd ple. Mez come Schefeld dyst, que si contract fyt fayt en Galys de payer lez deners en Engleter entant que ce est un entyer contract que extend en part en Engliter tout serra determyn icy et issint si en Frauns. Mez si de payer en Fraunce nul remedy mez tryer ce per ley marchand en vyll marchandes per provs ou en le chauncery per sub pena quod nota.

Si <leglis soy>[d] home sur un endytment est arreang et pled nient coup-able et pray destre restor il ad surces son temps, mez sur auter endytment il

now he shall be taken out, but if this is then made a felony by statute he shall be restored, as long as the statute extends to offences [committed] before [the statute], for then this was a felony from the beginning. The law is the same if [someone] strikes a man and then is taken out and then the same man dies, he shall be restored. Thus if he takes church grith and then this is made a sanctuary for life, he shall be restored and shall have the privilege for his life.

If a man confesses a felony before the coroner and then escapes to another church, he shall have the privilege there for another forty days. And the law is the same if this church is by the sea coast: he shall be restored to another church, but there is no need [to make] another confession if he is within the jurisdiction of this coroner and if he abjures on the first confession. Still, if he escapes he shall have the privilege, but [he shall] now not be abjured afterwards for this felony nor for another committed before, for all is determined [by a] judgment to this purpose. But if he commits a felony afterwards he may abjure again, as an attainted man can be arraigned for this … also confess all felonies for which he wishes to have the privilege to the coroner, and for this if he is tried and arraigned on [these felonies] he shall not be restored. Yet see that when he asks to be restored before any judge he need not specify the [certainty of the] felony, but [say only] 'for a certain felony previously perpetrated by him', but he must show expressly the day and year that he took sanctuary, or otherwise it is useless unless it is in the discretion of the justice to help him and assign it, if he is not an arrant thief as it was in the case of Huet. By this it seems that the certainty of the felony never comes by the felony he confesses, but from the case the coroner may examine.

If in this case a man wishes to plead that he has taken to a church in Wales and asks to be restored, he shall not be restored because the plea cannot be tried by any means, for we never send into Wales to try an issue as we shall in Chester and Durham, for they are as a parcel of the realm and therefore things shall be sent and re-sent there, but in Wales it is otherwise, except in a case of *quare impedit* it shall be brought of a church in Wales in the next adjoining [English] parish: the reason, as it seems, is that no-one is of so high power there to send a writ to the bishop, and therefore he must sue to the king's court. Also, lands of chief marcher lords shall be determined here because they are not under the obedience of the prince [of Wales]. But otherwise no matter shall be determined [which was] pleaded in Wales, but all such shall be void pleas. But as Sheffield said, if a contract is made in Wales to pay the money in England, inasmuch as this is an entire contract which extends in part into England all shall be determined here; and likewise if it is in France.[1] But if it is to pay in France there is no remedy but to try this by the law merchant in a mercantile town by witnesses, or in the Chancery by *subpoena*, which note.

If a man is arraigned on an indictment and pleads not guilty and prays to be restored, he has passed his time, but he may ask [for his time again] on another

---

[1] This is Sir Robert Sheffield, who became a governor of the Inner Temple in 1511. Julian Lock, 'Sheffield, Sir Robert (b. before 1462, d. 1518)', *Oxford Dictionary of National Biography*, online ed., (Oxford, Sept 2004); Baker, *Men of Court*, p. 1389.

peut prayer si soyt trovenient coupable sur le primer. Mez auter est si devient approver sur le primer et est non su, quar donques serra mort sur le primer.

Si le esglis soyt suspend per sank espandu le prevylag est determyn tanque novelment .... Mez si soyt un foytes en sentuary et puis est suspend et nient per son act il <nav>[d] avera le privelag, mez auter est si soyt per son act. Mez si leglis soyt enterdyt pur temps pur fayt de enormyng de esglis ou tyel caus unquore le lyberty demurt pur ce que poet estre en meme le cours come devant sans novel consecration. Meme le ley si soyt surond per eu ou en dekay, mez auter est si novel esglis soyt edyfy ou que esglis soyt remov, donque bosoyng novel conse-cration mez unquor, come semble, le cymetery lyberty demurt.

Si un feme soyt enseint que prist lesglis per lann el avera privelag.

Si rob meme lesglis ou fyst felony quant il est .. lesglis unquor il nad perdu le privelony, mez si soyt tyra hors et puis fyst felony et arreyng sur ce il ne serra restore: .. que est fayt puis que vient hors de centuary.

Home peut confes felony devant coroner et deveyng approver, mez semble cleer que ne poet entant que le coroner nest juge si non all entent ... abjuration. Mez si le felon confes le felony et ne voyl abjure sur certyfication de coroner, <entant>[d] si le felon soyt prys ... il devoy moryr et ne travessera entant que le coroner avoyt jurisdicion de le meme et est come juge de record.

Si vient hors ly meme ne unques serra restore si non en speciall casys come pro pondere natural deponendo, ou pur feer de son vy per caus de feu en lesglis, ou pur dowt de ere, ou pur cause de assaut sur ly fayt. Mez si ceux feers commens per son act donques est auter, come si il meme commens lassaut ou set lesglis en few. Mez si vient hors pur auter caus nessessary a quel il nest compel, come pur depertyer 2[x] homs ou help de sclake le fyr dans un hous adjoynant a esglis, quar en ceux casys nest compellabul de fayr tyelx chosys. Mez si soyt pur ce que il voy le person le roy en juperdy il peut bien entant que per ce son person le quel est come nebur le roy serra en juperdy.

V<small>IIJ</small>^A L<small>ECTURA</small>

[fo. 61v] Ore serra monster que privelag lespyretuel persons averont plus que lays:

Le quel privelag est ordeyn per lestatut a° 10 E[dw.] iij ca° v° le quel nest penall mez en negatyff et lestatut de Ric. le ij[d] a° j° ca° l quel <don>[d] est penall et leffect

indictment if he is found not guilty on the first. But it is otherwise if he becomes an approver on the first and is non-suited, for there he shall be dead on the first.[1]

If a church is suspended for spilt blood the privilege is ended until a new [consecration].[2] But if he was once in a sanctuary and then it is suspended and not by his act he shall have the privilege, but otherwise if it was by his own act. But if the church is interdicted for a time because of the doing of an enormous crime in the church or some such reason, nevertheless the liberty remains, because it may be in the same course as before without a new consecration. The law is the same if it was flooded by water or in decay, but it is otherwise if a new church is built or the church is removed: then there must be a new consecration but still, as it seems, the churchyard's liberty shall remain.

If a pregnant woman takes sanctuary for a year she shall have the privilege.

If [one] robs the same church or commits a felony when he is [within] the church, still he shall not lose the privilege, but if he is taken [out of the church] and then commits a felony and is arraigned on this he shall not be restored: [query] what is done after he comes out of sanctuary.

A man can confess a felony before the coroner and become an approver, but it seems clear that he may not inasmuch as the coroner is not a judge except for the purposes of abjuration.[3] But if the felon confesses the felony and does not wish to abjure on the coroner's certification, if the felon is taken … he must be put to death and shall not traverse, inasmuch as the coroner has jurisdiction of the same and is like a judge of record.

If he comes out by himself he shall never be restored except in special cases, such as '*pro pondere naturale deponendo*', or for fear of his life because of a fire in the church, or for doubt of air, or because of an assault committed on him. But if these fears commence by his own act then it is otherwise, as if [for example] he himself began the assault or set the church on fire. But [it is otherwise] if he comes out for another necessary reason by which he is not compelled, such as to separate two men or to help slake a fire in a house adjoining the church, for in these cases it is not compellable to do such things. But if it is because he saw the king's person in jeopardy he may well do it, inasmuch as by this his person, which is like the king's neighbour, shall be in jeopardy.

Eighth Lecture

Now we shall see what privileges spiritual persons shall have more than lay persons:

These privileges are ordained by the statute 10 Edw. III, c. 5 which is not penal but in the negative and the statute of 1 Ric. II, c. 1 which is penal and the effect

---

[1] The classic case on this is YB Hil. 21 Edw. III, fo. 17, pl. 21, and it appears in Statham, *Corone*, 24 and Fitzherbert, *Corone*, 447.

[2] Brooke, *Sanctuarie*, 11. Brooke has a note at the end of this case that it came from the reading of W. N.

[3] Perhaps thinking of YB Mich. 9 Hen. IV, fo. 24, pl. 1, where the felon confessed before the justices of the peace. Also in Statham, *Corone*, 46; Brooke, *Corone*, 25; and Fitzherbert, *Corone*, 457.

de ambydeux estatuts est que nul person de Seynt Esglis soyt arrestu en fesant divyn servys. Mez lez parollis de lestatut de E[dw. III] extend a parych clerk per expres resytall, et si nemi unquor serra constru benefycyally pur ce que est en negatyffes nest penal, mez le statut de Ric. [II] est penal et pur ce nextendera a nul forsque a persons de Seynt Esglis. Le penalte per statut de Ric. [II] est imprisonment per un an et reynt et gre all party, mez all comen ley devant cel estatut fuit action sur le cas, et issint a ce jour, et ce est prov per parolis de statut de Ric. [II] enconter le fraunchys de seynt esglis.

Toutes casys de felony ou lour vy estre destre perd per comen ley ou per statut est hors de purve de cest statut pur ce que ne bosoyng pur ce ascun estat mez le remedy fuit all comen ley devant: scilicet de pray le privelag de Seynt Esglis et ce est indifferent a toutes. Et pur ce si soyt arest pur felony en fesant divyn servys est hors de purve de lestatut pur action. Mez vide que lestatut est generall que nul soyt arestu per auctoryte royall etc. et per cas le prest ne voyl pray le privelag entant que nest coupable de le felony et pur ce ne voyl conuster: mez unquor come semble <est hors de>[d] peut aver action.

Auxi en toutes casys lou est enmy le roy ou hors de protection le roy navera cest privelag, entant que ce est privelag al person et ce ne peut aver et issint nest semble lou il claym privelag per caus de lew et sur ceux groundes: vide lestatut de premynyre que est hors de protection et que nient.

Cest dyvyn servys covient destre entend comen servys en lesglis, come matens, mase, mez nemi quant il dyst per ly meme ambulant en churchyard. Mez burryyng, visytyng lez ynfyrms ovesques le corps de Jhesus, duryge, auxi, coment que soy servys a que il est ly, come prosessyons en rogation week, mez nemi le scynners prosessyon. Mez ce fayt petit diversyte, quar home nest tenus de dyser mas chescun jour, mez come semble, en toutes comyns servys avera le privelag mez nemi en privat, come lou home est prayant et en contemplation soyt moyng ou auter, mez en fesaunt devine servys et en alant a ce deins lesglis mez peut estre arest per le voy.

Reguler ou apostata ou si soyt prest et ad feme en vy, quar donques chescun home poet aver notys, mez auter est sy ne soyt mez contractyd: en ceux casys navera le privelag, pur ce que il de son tort dyst sez servys. Meme le ley si le ordynary ad interdyst lesglis pur ennormyng quar donque ne devoyt sauf la. Mez auter est si lesglis soyt suspendu per sank <mes semble>[d] quar

of both statutes is that no-one of the Holy Church shall be arrested while performing divine service.[1] But the words of the statute of Edward [III] extend to parish clerks by express recital, and if not, still it would be construed beneficially because it is in negatives [and] not penal, but the statute of Richard II is penal and therefore does not extend to anyone except to the persons of the Holy Church. The penalty by the statute of Richard II is imprisonment for a year and punishment and satisfaction to the party, but at the common law before this statute there was an action on the case and the same today, and this is proved by the words of the statute of Richard II 'against the liberty of Holy Church'.[2]

All cases of felony where their life is to be lost by common law or by statute are outside the purview of this statute, because there is no need for any statute but the remedy was at the common law before: namely to ask for the privilege of Holy Church and this is the same for all. And therefore if one is arrested for felony while performing divine service it is out of the purview of the statute for the action. But see that the statute is general that no-one shall be arrested by royal authority etc., and perhaps the priest does not wish to ask for the privilege inasmuch as he is not guilty of the felony, and therefore he does not wish to confess: but still, as it seems, he may have the action.

Also in all cases where he is the king's enemy or outside the king's protection he shall not have this privilege, inasmuch as this is a privilege for the person and this he cannot have, and thus it is not like where he claims privilege because of the place and on these grounds: see the statute of *praemunire* who is out of protection and who not.[3]

This divine service must be understood [as] common service in the church, such as matins [or] mass, but not when he says [prayers] by himself walking in the churchyard. But burying, visiting the infirm with the body of Jesus, *dirige* [and] other things [are divine service] even if they are services to which he is bound, such as processions in rogation week, but not the Skinners' procession. But this makes little difference, for a man is not bound to say mass every day, but as it seems he shall have the privilege in all common services but not in private (as when a man is praying and in contemplation, whether he is a monk or another), but while performing divine services and in going to them within the church, but he may be arrested on the way.

[If one is] regular or apostate, or if he is a priest and has a wife alive for then everyone may have notice (but it is otherwise if he is only contracted): in those cases he shall not have the privilege, because he says his services wrongfully.[4] The law is the same if the ordinary has interdicted the church for an enormous crime, for then he shall not be safe there. But it is otherwise if the church is

---

[1] *Rectius* 50 Edw. III, c. 5 (*SR*, i. 398); 1 Ric. II, c. 15 (*SR*, i. 5).

[2] 1 Ric. II, c. 15 (*SR*, ii. 5), though the punishment is imprisonment at the king's pleasure.

[3] 16 Ric. II, c. 5 (*SR*, ii. 84–86). The exceptions are on p. 85.

[4] This seems to mean 'irregular' in the sense of being out of conformity with Church doctrine or ineligible for ordination. It consistently appears as 'regular' in the readings. See Reading A, p. 2, Reading C, p. 16, Reading E, pp. 37, 38, Reading G, p. 53, Reading Two, p. 75, above, and Reading Seven, pp. 113, 124, below.

donque non obstant avera le privelag, mez semble que ce est nul ley et que ce est pluis fort cas que lauter: et vide le darren lecture. Auxi si soyt heretyk navera le privelag. Meme le ley si soyt excommeng en excommunicato capiendo, et issint en vi layca removenda, soyt ce pur ce que il ne voyl suffer levesque de visyter le quel nest returnabul ou que [ne] voyl suffer le parson desglis docupyer le quel est returnabul, quar en ceex casys il de son tort kep lesglis.

Levesque q*uant* se en vysytyng navera le privelag quar nest dyvyn servys mez auter est si soyt en halowyng.

Auters privelages sont hors de letter de ceux statuts: scilicet le senyor ne peut sese son vyllen que est profes moyng, mez si soyt fayt parson de parych, abbe ou erchevesque le senyor peut ly sese, quar donque lobedyens a auter soverayn est determyn. Mez le senyor ne peut eux compel de fayr auter servys mez dyvyn servys, et issint de prest, et si il soyt, semble a moy que ce est mysbeaver come mayhn et <feffment>[d] manumission.

Evesque ou abbe ou prest ne serront en gard sur execution de statut marchand sur lexpres parol de statut et si ils sont grev ils averont <lex>[d] non molestando. Mez sur statut stapul ils poyent pur ce que ne sont exeptes ... reson que sont prestes ils averont pluis privelag que le roy peut grant, quar ils serront discharges de toutes ... ...andes assise, atteyntes, et de toutes auters, si non que sont temoyns et la ils serront compelys de [veign].[1] Issint ils sont discharg de offys de vicount, eschetor, et huiusmodi. Auxi si ils teynont per servys de chivaler et sont deins age et ens per dissent ne serront en gard. Mez semble que pur ter serront.

Si ils teynont de le roy per grant serjanty pur eux meme aler, le servis serra en suspens pur lour vys mez auter est ... lez. Mez si teynont per convenient servys nest issint come destre karver ou cupberer etc.

Ix[A] Lectura

[*fo. 62*] Ore serra monster quel privelag lay persons averont per lesglis, scilicet le clergye ou le lyver:

En toutes casys de haut treson home navera son clergy lez queux sont espesyfy per lestatut de a° xxv° E[dw.] iij ca° ij° de proditonibus et auters estatuts sur ce faytes come de tonsur, lotur de coyng, ou de amesner quoyn counterfet dauter royalm ou conterfetur mez nemi pur tonsur ou lotur de ce qoyn quar ce est hors de purve de statut.

Mez en toutes casys lou le treson extend as partyculer persons serra dyst felony ou treson <al plesur de roy>[d], come sy soyt endyt proditorie est treson. Mez si leyr port appeel de mort son pyer justys et le <def soyt>[d] appele soyt

---

[1] MS. reads voyn.

suspended for blood[shed], for then notwithstanding he shall have the privilege, but it seems that this is no law and that this is a harder case than the other: see the last lecture. Also if he is a heretic he shall not have the privilege. The law is the same if he is excommunicated in *excommunicato capiendo*, and the same in *vi laica removenda*, whether this is because he did not wish to allow the bishop to visit, which is not returnable, or that he [did not] wish to allow the parson of the church to occupy it, which is returnable, for in these cases he kept the church wrongfully.[1]

The bishop [while] visiting shall not have the privilege for it is not divine service, but it is otherwise if he is hallowing.

Other privileges are outside the letter of these statutes: namely the lord cannot seize his villein who is a professed monk, but if he is made parson of a parish, abbot or archbishop the lord may seize him, for then the obedience to another superior is determined. But the lord may not compel him to perform service other than divine service, and the same of a priest, and if he does [compel him to perform other service] it seems to me that this is misbehaviour like maiming and [effects a] manumission.

A bishop or abbot or priest shall not be in custody on execution of a statute merchant by the express words of the statute, and if they are grieved they shall have *non molestando*.[2] But on a statute staple they may because this is not excepted … reason who are priests, they shall have more privilege than the king can grant, for they are discharged of all … assizes, attaints, and of all others, unless they are witnesses and there they are compelled to come. Similarly, they are discharged from the office of sheriff, escheator, and such things. Also, if they hold by knight service and are within age and in by descent they shall not be in ward. But it seems that for land they shall be [in ward].

If they hold land of the king by grand serjeanty to go themselves the service shall be in suspense for their lives, but it is otherwise …. But if they hold by a suitable service it is not so, such as to be a carver or cupbearer etc.

Ninth Lecture

Now we shall see what privileges lay persons shall have through the Church, namely the clergy or the book:

In all cases of high treason a man shall not have his clergy, which is specified by the statute of 25 Edw. III, c. 2 'on treason', and other statutes on these things such as clipping, washing of coin, or to bring counterfeit coin from another realm, or to counterfeit, but not for clipping or washing of this [counterfeit] coin, for this is out of the purview of the statute.[3]

But in all cases where the treason extends to particular persons it shall be called felony or treason, as if he was indicted 'traitorously' it is treason. But if the heir brings an appeal for the death of his father [to the] justices and the appellee

---

[1] *Register*, fos 65, 59–60.
[2] *Register*, fo. 24.
[3] 25 Edw. III, stat. 5, c. 2 (*SR*, i. 319–320) deals with treason, but not benefit of clergy.

atteynt il avera son clergy. Et sy home soyt endyt justys de pees ou nisi prius ou <gar>^d gaol delyvere ce nest treson, quar sont hors de parolys de statut avantdyst et lestatut, come semble, quant a ce poynt fayt ley.

Cestui que tu ou rob un que ad saufcondyst, le quel nest nessessary a nul si non a envy le roy, mez ce est fayt treson haut per lestatut a° ij° H[en.] vⁱ ca° vj°. Mez si le questyon soyt demande de ly sy avoyt saufcondyst et il ce deny, si home ly occyst nest felony, quar lengloys ne pusoyt aver notys si non per monstrans. Meme le ley si il commens assaut.

Forgyng de coyn que ne cort en cest royalm come scottys grotes ou huiusmodi, mez auter est de yrys coyn, quar ce poet estre a hurt de yrys <pep>^d pepul lez queux sont leges le roy.

Sont haut tresons per comen ley queux ne sont espesyfys per statut come de ymagyn de depoce le roy ou de [re]fus rend son homage, le quel fuit issint fayt en temps R[ic.] ijⁱ mez puis repel. Mez non obstant cest treson all comen ley et issint en toutes casys al comen ley queux extend en impediment de le royal power, come si interupt le roy en fesant sez justys, ou ly causer scuer parliament enconter son volunte ou de dissolver ou huiusmodi come vide lez questyons demande de justys a° xxj° R[ic.] ijⁱ ca° xij° et lour repons. En meme le maner si un tu un purssyvant en servant un prive seel ou letter myssyv ou sub pena ce est auxy haut treson xxij° liver assysarum et semble ley entant que est come resyst de le royall power le roy. Mez come semble, en toutes ceux casys lez jugges ne poyent doner jugement tanque advys soyt per parlyament come appyert a° xxv° devant et auxi per respons Thyrning enter lez questyons devant dytes.

Home abjur, basterd, home mayhn, ou bocher son ou huiusmodi unquor averont lour clergy, mez bygamus navera et cest solment per <lestatut>^d lact le pope en consel de [Lugdunum]¹ et puis conferm per lestatut de <...>^d bigamis. Et pur ce que ce dispensation est solment per constytution le pape ad power de dispence ovesque et pur ce si le pape ly lycens destre prest que ne soyt unqor prest unquor avera clergy et per ce il avoydera le ple de bygamy en pledant.

Bigamus est que mary ij femes ou wydou et non obstant que soyt devorce de primer, unquor nest materyall entant que [il fuit] un foytes corrupt. Et pur ce si mary strumpet le ley dyst que il est bigamus pur le corruption mez si mary un le quel disagre et il mari auter, la nest bigamus entant que ne fuit corrupt et

---

¹ MS. reads Logdon.

is attainted he shall have his clergy. And if a man is indicted [by a] justice of the peace or at *nisi prius* or gaol delivery this is not treason, for it is out of the words of the aforesaid statute and the statute, as it seems, makes law on this point.

If someone kills or robs one who has a safe-conduct, which is not necessary for anyone except the king's envoy, this is made high treason by the statute of 2 Hen. V, c. 6.[1] But if he was asked if he had a safe-conduct and he denied it, if a man kills him it is not felony, for the Englishman cannot have notice except by showing it. The law is the same if he commences an assault.

Forging of coin which does not circulate in this realm such as Scottish groats or suchlike [is not felony], but it is otherwise of Irish coin, for that can be a hurt to the Irish people who are the king's lieges.

There are high treasons by the common law which are not specified by statute, such as imagining the deposition of the king or refusing to render homage, which was made [treason] in the time of Richard II but then repealed.[2] But notwithstanding, this [is] treason at the common law, and similarly in all cases at the common law which extend to an impediment of the royal power, as if they interrupt the king in carrying out his justice, or cause him to prorogue Parliament against his will or to dissolve it or suchlike: see the questions asked of the justices 21 Ric. II, c. 12 and their response.[3] In the same manner if one kills a pursuivant serving a privy seal, or letter missive or subpoena, this is also high treason, 22 *Liber Assisarum*, and it seems to be law inasmuch as it is like resisting the royal power of the king.[4] But as it seems, in all those cases the judges cannot give judgment until advised by Parliament as appears 25 [Edw III] above, and also from Thirning's response among the questions aforesaid.[5]

An abjured man, a bastard, a maimed man, or a butcher's son or suchlike shall still have his clergy, but a bigamist shall not, and this is only by the pope's act in the council of Lyons which was then confirmed by the statute *De Bigamis*.[6] And because this dispensation is solely by constitution the pope has power to dispense with it, and therefore if the pope licenses one to be a priest who never was a priest still he shall have his clergy, and by this he shall avoid the plea of bigamy in pleading.[7]

A bigamist is one who marries two women or a widow, and notwithstanding that he is divorced from the first, still it is not material inasmuch as [he] was once corrupted. And thus if he marries a strumpet the law says that he is a bigamist for the corruption, but if he marries one who disagrees [with the marriage] and he marries another, there he is not a bigamist inasmuch as he was not corrupted

---

[1] 2 Hen. V, stat. 1, c. 6 (*SR*, ii. 178–181).

[2] 21 Ric. II, c. 3 (*SR*, ii. 98–99). 21 Ric. II, c. 4 (*SR*, ii. 99) declared any attempt to repeal any statutes from this parliament treason. 1 Hen. IV, c. 10 (*SR*, ii. 114) repealed all treasons other than those in the statute 25 Edw. III, stat. 5, c. 2 (*SR*, i. 320).

[3] 21 Ric. II, c. 12 (*SR*, ii. 101–104).   [4] 22 *Lib. Ass* fos 95–96, pl. 49.

[5] 25 Edw. III, stat. 5, c. 2 (*SR*, i. 320); 21 Ric. II, c. 12 (*SR*, ii. 104).

[6] Reading F, above p. 47, states that a 'carnifex', there translated as executioner, shall not have the privilege. Snede is the only one to raise the question of a butcher's son.

[7] The Second Council of Lyons, const. 2, 16 deals with bigamy. 4 Edw. I, c. 5 (*SR*, i. 43) makes reference to the council.

ce matrimony est ore voyd a toutes entants. Et si le baron discontynu le feme poet enter. Meme le ley si apres le mariag et devant que ly togedurs el morust, issint que tout le reson de bygamy est pur corruption. Si soyt enfant bigamus unquor est ly per lact.

Si home soyt perjurd et trove coupable le quel nest que petit larcyne, mez si puis devant memez lez justys soyt endyt pur auters vj d. ou devant auter justys et certyfi il perdera son vy et avera son clergy: mez en robory pur un j d. sufys.

Si home ad estre mark en mayn et puis pray son clergy il navera si <so>^{d} non que soyt infra ordines, ce est a dyr subdccon, et donque avera jour de porter ens le letter lordinary lou fuit fayt prest pur ce prover: a° ij° H[en.] vij.

Home que devient approver avera <soy>^{d} son clergy si soyt vencus et issint cestui que est appeel et home ne unques devoyt ses … en … de liver et pur ce si il pray under le galows le vicount poet ly repriver al gaol si il voyl mez justys ly mez le … ly comyt all ordynary entant que nest jug de ly.

Home praya son clergy devant que est trove coupable est voyd <et p>^{d} si non que voyl confes le felony et si vj^x sont en … et pray son lyver lauter dyst que <nest>^{d} tyel home est en vi quest suppose destre murjur ou si soyt de felony … fuit mez vj d, unquor lauter serra <…>^{d} clerk atteynt et, come semble, devoyt estre pendus si ne fuit pur clergy … si il pled ple et nient confes, mez ore ne unques peut prender avantage nient plus que en cas que accessory confes …

[fo. 62v] Al comen ley si home fuit endyt come insydiator viarum et depopulator agrorum et trove coupable il a avera son clergy mez ce ore est repeel al sut de clergy a° iiij° H[en.] iiij° que tyels parols serront voyds.

Si un pray son clergy lordinary peut ly refus generalment sans caus monster entant que sont plusors causys de queux le temporal jugges ne devoyent prender notyce come excommengement, ou que il est heretyk, mez ne que il ad rob church ou tu un preste pur ce que ce privelag est annex al person. Auxi nest cause de refuser Jue, Sarazyn mez eux averont le benefyt de clergy entant que poyent amend. En toutes ceux casys si il monster caus <il>^{d} nient suffycyent lez justys ne devoyent, come adyr que il est basterd ou <non b>^{d} huiusmodi, quar eux sont memburs desglis et ne poyent a coort mez que poyent estre preestes et si non unquor nest materyal. Et meme le ley a dyr quod non habet tonsuram etc. Mez feme, come semble, navera lyver quar el ne peut estre nul membre desglis, mez lauter pusoyent enter en religion et issint estre prestes: quere. Issint nest cause de refuser pur ce que est <by>^{d} bigamus entant que ce mater

and this marriage is now void to all intents. And if the husband discontinues, the wife may enter. The law is the same if after the marriage, and before they lie together, she dies, since the whole reason for bigamy is corruption. If an infant is a bigamist still he is bound by the act.

If a man is perjured and found guilty [of an offence] which is only petty larceny, but if then before the same justice he is indicted for another 6d., or before another justice and certified, he shall lose his life and have his clergy: but robbery for 1d. suffices [for the death penalty].

If a man has been marked on the hand and then prays his clergy he shall not have it unless he is in orders (that is to say subdeacon), and then he shall have a day to bring the letter from the ordinary who ordained him priest to prove this: 2 Hen. VII.[1]

A man who becomes approver shall have his clergy if he is vanquished, and the same for one who is appealed, and a man can never become … book and for this if he prays under the gallows the sheriff may reprieve him to the gaol if he wills it, but the [judge must] … commit him to the ordinary, inasmuch as he is not a judge of him.

[If] a man prays his clergy before he is found guilty, it is void unless he wishes to confess the felony, and if six are in … and he prays his book, the other says that such a man is alive who is supposedly murdered, or if it is for felony … [for an object worth] only 6d., still the other shall be a clerk attaint and, as it seems, would be hanged if it was not for his clergy … if he pleads a plea and does not confess, but now he may never take advantage any more than in the case where an accessory confesses …

At the common law if a man was indicted as a 'highway robber and pillager of fields' and found guilty he should have his clergy, but this is now repealed at the suit of the clergy in 4 Hen. IV, that such words shall be void.[2]

If one prays his clergy the ordinary may refuse him generally without showing cause inasmuch as there are many causes of which the temporal judge should not take notice, such as excommunication, or that he is a heretic, but not that he has robbed a church or killed a priest because the privilege is annexed to the person. Also there is no cause to refuse a Jew or Saracen, but they have the benefit of clergy inasmuch as they may amend. In all these cases if he shows insufficient cause the justices do not have to [give judgment] as to say that he is bastard or such a thing, for [felons] are members of the Church and do not have to go to court if they can be priests, and even if they are not still it is not material.[3] And it is the same law to say that he does not have the tonsure etc. (But a woman, as it seems, shall not have the book, for she cannot be a member of the Church, but the others may enter in religion and thus may be priests: query.) Thus there is no cause to refuse because he is a bigamist inasmuch as this matter

---

[1] *Rectius* 4 Hen. VII, c. 13 (*SR*, ii. 538).

[2] 4 Hen. IV, c. 2 (*SR*, ii. 132–133). The phrase comes from *Decretales Gregorii IX*, 3.49.6. See Helmholz, *Ius Commune*, p. 34. This point is also raised in Reading D, p. 26, n. 8, above, and Reading Nine, p. 136, n. 22, below.

[3] This translation does not follow the grammar of the passage, but probably represents the sense.

ne poet apper a ly come jugement mez covient daver le circumstans try per proves. Mez auter de excommengement ou heretyk atteynt.

Un blynd home avera clergy per dyr un vers que de discressyon dez justys serra assyng a ly: unquor ne peut estre prest mez quant il ly pusoyt estre prest. Auxi un Grek ou Indyan averont lour clergy et devera leer en lour langag per ynterpretor scilicet …

Un abbe serra ordynary a son moyng, levesque al abbe, metropolyton al evesque, labbe de Crychurch al metropolyton, et <le metropolitan>ᵈ son evesque a ly, sy ne soyt tempore vacationis et donque le collector le pape.

Et nota que home abjure, home utlage de felony, entant que ne poet ly prayer la de caus de son conviction, clerk atteynt per confessyon, meme le reson de abjure et comen laron, le quel fuit le reson que al comen ley insidiator viarum navera clergy. Auxi home atteynt de petit treson, tout ceux navera lour clergy per constytutions provincyals: vide aᵒ iiijᵒ H[en.] iiijⁱ caᵒ iijᵒ.

Xᴬ Lectura

Ore serra monster de privelag de lour persons:

Toutes ters queux fueront en mayns de spyrytuel persons en temps Edward le primer sont <…>ᵈ le xxj an sont charchabul a dismes quant dysmes sont grauntes per parlyament come appyert …[1] <mez>ᵈ et fuit <g>ᵈ agre sur certen debates perenter le roy et le spyrytualte, quar ils voyllent que le roy ne sez leys <…>ᵈ ne temporalls gentes eux chargeront et donques <checn>ᵈ le roy ordgna que chescun que eux fayt tort serra dispunissabul per comenz ley et donques home fesoyent a eux molt tort et ne curont pur excommengement sur que ils fueront faynes de agre que le temporall ley currera sur eux et que lour voudront obeyir le proces de ley et oster pur cest discharg de xvᵐᵉ que ils voudront estre charge le xᵐˢ Mez ce nappeyert en ascun estatut et pur ce de veresimily fuit per grant de convocation composition ovesque le roy issint que a ore le ley est que toutes ters purchas per lespyrytualte puis ce temps serront charchabul a <dysmes>ᵈ quyndysmes et toutes devant serront charg a dysmes.

Si ils alienont et reprondont estat ore al xvˢ mez auter est si sur condytion <…>ᵈ et il entront pur enfreyndur ou que ils alienont lour ter devant statut de quia [emptores] <et puis le compotion com puseyent>ᵈ et puis le ter eschet. Et meme le ley si a ce jour le done … de lour don morust sans issu, en toutes ceux le ter est charchabul a dismes arer discharg de xvˢ. Et meme le [ley ou un] lessont pur term de vie et le lesse alien ou fayt wast et ils entront ou recover, ore est charchabull a dismes …t ens come devant et nest semble lou lesse pur vie quant rent charg: la labbe tyendra charg mez icy le charg … si non per grant et a ce temps lez possessions fueront en mayn labbe.

---

[1] Blank in MS.

cannot appear as a judgment but he must have the circumstances tried by witnesses. But it is otherwise of excommunication or an attainted heretic.

A blind man shall have his clergy by saying a verse which shall be assigned to him at the discretion of the judges: still he may not be a priest, but when he reads he is able to be a priest. Also, a Greek or an Indian shall have their clergy and ought to read in their language through an interpreter, namely ....

An abbot shall be ordinary to his monk, the bishop to the abbot, the metropolitan to the bishop, the abbot of Christ Church to the metropolitan, and his bishop to him, unless it is a vacancy, and then the papal collector [shall be ordinary].

And note that an abjured man, a man outlawed for felony (inasmuch as he cannot pray there [for himself] because of his conviction), and a clerk attainted by confession [have] the same reason to abjure as a common thief, which was the reason that at common law a highwayman could not have clergy. Also a man attainted of petty treason, all those shall not have their clergy by provincial constitutions: see 4 Hen. IV, c. 3.[1]

TENTH LECTURE

Now we shall show the privilege of their persons:

All the lands which were in the hands of spiritual persons in the time of Edward I (the 21st year) are chargeable for tenths when tenths are granted by Parliament as appears [ ][2], and it was agreed in certain debates between the king and the spirituality, for they wished that neither the king, nor his laws, nor temporal men should charge them and then the king ordained that anyone who did them wrong would not be punishable at common law, and then men did many wrongs to them and were not bound by excommunication, on which [the spirituality] were fain to agree that the temporal law should bind them and that they wished to obey the process of the law, and further for this discharge of fifteenths that they wished to be charged a tenth. But this does not appear in any statute, and therefore it was probably compounded by a grant of convocation with the king so that now the law is that all lands purchased by the spirituality since that time shall be chargable for fifteenths, and all [purchased] before shall be charged for tenths.

If they alien and re-take the estate [they shall pay] the fifteenth, but it is otherwise if it is on condition and he enters for the breaking [of the condition] or if they alien their land before the statute of *Quia Emptores* and then the land escheats.[3] And the law is the same if today the donee [in tail] of their gift dies without issue: in all these [cases] the land is chargeable for tenths again [and] discharged of fifteenths. And the law is the same where one leases for term of life, and the lessee aliens or commits waste and they enter or recover, now it is chargable for tenths ... as before, and it is not like a lessee for term of life when there is a rent charge: there the abbot shall have the charge but here the charge ... except by grant, and at that time the possessions were in the abbot's hands.

---

[1] 4 Hen. IV, c. 3 (*SR*, ii. 133).   [2] Blank in MS.
[3] *Quia Emptores*, 18 Edw. I (*SR*, i. 106).

… nest plusors casis lou lentre labbe soyt loyal <et ou>ᵈ arer de recontynuer choce en eyne cours et ou … de plusors conditions queux bons et queux nient, et queux enfreynt et queux nient. … aᵒ ijᵒ R[ic.] ijⁱ que don trebul dam*ages* vers le purveers le roy queux prynont ascun choce de homes de esglis.

Xjᴬ Lectura

[*fo. 63*] Lestatut est *quod ecclesia anglicana libera sit et habeat sua jura et libertates suas illesas*:

Sur ceux troys troys [*sic*] chosys sont a declarer, scilicet privilegium ecclesiasticum le quel est declar en lez quarters redynges devant; jus ecclesiasticum le quel serra ore declar; et libertas ecclesiastica le quel remayn a declarer.

Et fuit nota per Bracton quod 'a justicia quasi a quosdam fonte omnia jura emanant et quod vult justicia idem jus prosequitur'.[1] Et selonque cest diffinitio jus ecclesiasticum est a tener ple, fayr droytes, ministur justys de chosis spyrytuelx pur que et entant que a chescun apurteyn a determyn choce de que il est juge. Est a voyer queux ples sont terminabuls en cort Crystyan et queux nient et pur ce vide lestatut de prohibitione, articuli cleri, et circumspecte agatis et auters novels statutes.

Et prims ore est a voyer de decimis entant que toutes lautors statutes parlont que ceux sont determinabuls, et sont 2ˣ maner de disms, scilicet decime prediales et majores queux surdont per reson de ter personales, sive minores queux surdont per reson de perse… <mann>ⁱ opere. De ambydeux est a voyer mez de darren unques est determinabul per ley espyrytuel.

Si lez dysms sont en debate queux amount al valu de quart party perenter 2ˣ parsons, le patron le clerk le defendant avera indicavit per lestatut Wij cᵃ vjᵒ in fine vers le parson plaintiff le quel est en ley un prohibition et quant cel coort est prohibyt le patron le clerk plaintiff poet aver bref de droyt de dysms. Mez ce bref de indicavit gyst vers nul forsque vers le parson plaintiff et nient vers plusors iiijᵒ E[dw.] ij.

Mez general prohibition poet bien gyser vers plusors et sur ce auxi le patron poet aver bref de droit de disms, le quel bref de droit il poet aver sans indicavit auxi bien le patron, clerk plaintiff ou defendant, pur ce que autrement ils poyent perder lour … per collucion quar, come semble, si ce soyt un foytes discus en coort cristyan serra conclucion a toutes jours. Auxi nota que <cest>ᵈ nul auter avera cest bref de indicavit mez le patron le clerk defendant mez le patron

---

[1] *Bracton*, ii. 22 *rectius* 'quia a iustitia quasi a quodam fonte omnia iura emanant, et quod vult iustitia ius idem prosequitur.'

... are not more cases where the abbot's entry is lawful again to recontinue something in the later course and where ... of more conditions which are good and which are not, and which are broken and which not. [See the statute of] 2 Ric. II which gives triple damages against the king's purveyors who take anything from churchmen.[1]

ELEVENTH LECTURE

The statute is *that the English Church shall be free and shall have her rights and liberties inviolate*:

On this three things have to be explained, namely the privileges of the Church which were explained in the four lectures above; the rights of the Church, which shall now be explained; and the liberties of the Church which remain to be explained.

And it was noted by Bracton that 'since from justice, as from a fountain-head, all rights arise and what justice commands right provides'.[2] And according to this definition the rights of the Church are to hold pleas, do right, and administer justice for spiritual things, wherefore and inasmuch as pertains to each to determine the thing of which he is the judge. Now we must see which pleas are determinable in the court Christian and which are not, and for this see the statute of prohibition, *Articuli Cleri*, *Circumspecte Agatis* and other recent statutes.[3]

And first we have to see concerning tithes, inasmuch as all the other statutes say that these are determinable, and there are two kinds of tithes, namely praedial tithes and greater tithes which arise by reason of personal land, or smaller tithes which arise by reason of personal manual work. We must look at both, but the latter is always determinable by spiritual law.

If the tithes in dispute amount to the value of the fourth part between two parsons, the patron of the defendant clerk shall have *indicavit* by the statute of Westminster II, c. 6 (at the end) against the plaintiff parson which is a prohibition in law, and when this court is prohibited the patron of the plaintiff clerk may have a writ of right of tithes.[4] But this writ of *indicavit* only lies against the plaintiff parson and not against others: 4 Edw. II.

But a general prohibition may well lie against others and on this also the patron may have a writ of right of tithes, which writ of right he may have without *indicavit*, as well [as] the patron, the clerk, plaintiff or defendant, because otherwise they may lose their [right] by collusion for, as it seems, if this is once discussed in the court Christian it shall be concluded forever. Also note that no-one else shall have this writ of *indicavit* except the patron of the defendant clerk, but the patron

[1] *Rectius* 1 Ric. II, c. 3 (*SR*, ii. 1–2).
[2] *Bracton* ii. 22. From Azo, *Summa Inst.* 1.1, pr.; Cortese, ii. 24 ff.
[3] 50 Edw. III, c. 4 (*SR*, i. 398); 9 Edw. II, stat. 1 *Articuli Cleri* (*SR*, i. 171–174); 13 Edw. I *Circumspecte Agatis* (*SR*, i. 101–102).
[4] Westminster II, 13 Edw. I, c. 6 (*SR*, i. 77) does not seem to be relevant. Snede may be thinking of the Statute of Joint-Tenants, 34 Edw. I (*SR*, i. 145), which does have a paragraph on *indicavit* at the end. *Register*, fos 35–36.

le plaintiff poet aver generall prohibition. Auxi nota que cest bref ne serra unques grant en le chauncery si non per inspexion de lybel. Si soyt souȝht le valu indicavit ne gist mez si pendant cel auter sut est commens per meme le parson plaintiff et ambydeux amount al quart partye indicavit gyst. Mez auter est si le pere defendant soyt soyt [*sic*] plaintiff en darren, quar donques ambydeux serront discus en cort crystyan, mez semble que non.

Mez indicavit ne gyst mez generall prohibition pur cestui que <patron>[d] voet suer. En ce cas si le sut soyt oster le valu de quart party unquor priminire [*sic*] ne gyst, quar est nul que poet aver laction, quar le patron ne poet aver entant que nest vex, <entant>[d] ne le parson entant que eyant regard a ly le mater est determinabul per le spyrytuel coort, mez semble pusoyt estre punys per endytment al sut le roy.

En ascun cas dysms souȝht le valu de iiij partye serra determinabul per comenz ley et en ascun cas oster le valu serra determine en ley spyrytuel. En primer cas, come <fy>[d] si debat soyt enter 2[x] parsons en quel parych le lew ou le prys … est ce serra determinabul per noster ley xxxix° E[dw.] iij[i]. Et meme le ley enter parson et fermor, et parson et servant … si soyt sut enter eux en cort crystyan nul indicavit gyst mez prohibition. Mez <le ley>[d] <quaunt>[i] … auxi lou debat est enter 2[x] parsons dun patron quar la <est un>[d] le patron est a nul mischeff que deux avera et est nul vers que il poet suer bref *de* … de dysms.

Meme le ley de toutes ceux chosys queux sont lay fe dependant sur spyrytuel fe come rent grant pur estre discharg dez disms, ou annuite, ou lou vend est pur le mony de barbeyn: en ceux casis ceux chosys sont temporall auxi bien come lez dysms meme quar per vendi comez res temporales fiont temporales.

Meme le ley auxi <fou>[d] lou le lew est en nul parysch, come forest de Ingylwod et Wyndsor en queux le roy avera le profyst (mez quere quel profyst): en ceux casys le mater serra determinabul al comenz ley. Mez <le ley>[d] <auter est>[i] lou un person est spoyll dez sez dysms come cleerment este per ascun parson le quel claym tytul en meme le parsonage. Mez en ce cas si le parson soyt parson en parsony prohibiton gyst, come est dem xlv° [Edw. III] et xiiij° H[en.] iij[i].

Meme le ley auxint en cas lou en Chester est tyel costom que si home morust apres le fest de Seynt Chad que lexecutors averont lenbleymentes si le … parson soyt a demander vers eux covient de demaund al comenz ley, unquor vers home que ne voyl tytht serra punysh en spyrytuel cort, mez icy <nest >[d] le <_>[d] ils ne devoyent tyther de ce come de lour ter quar ils nont interest mez soolment claymont purpurty. Meme le ley auxi lou le parson est seisi <…>[d] ou si sont severes et <le per>[d] un oster … enport. Mez si le tenant meme eux emport apres severans et devant collection <habbe>[d] le parson l… vers le tenant meme en spyrytuel ley. Mez come semble que est a son lyberty quar est a

of the plaintiff may have a general prohibition. Also note that this writ shall never be granted in the Chancery except by an inspection of the libel. If it is under the value [of the fourth part] *indicavit* does not lie, but if during this another suit is begun by the same plaintiff parson and both amount to a fourth part, *indicavit* lies. But it is otherwise if the defendant priest is a plaintiff in the latter, for then both shall be discussed in the court Christian, but it seems not.

But *indicavit* does not lie for the one who wishes to sue [in court Christian], but general prohibition. In this case if the suit is above the value of a fourth part still *praemunire* does not lie, for there is no-one who can have the action: the patron cannot have it because he is not vexed, nor the parson because with regard to him the matter is determinable by the spiritual court, but it seems that he can be punished by indictment at the king's suit.

In some cases tithes under the value of the fourth part shall be determinable by common law, and in some cases [tithes] over the value shall be determined in spiritual law. In the first case, when there is a dispute between two parsons in which parish the place where the [tithes were taken] is, this shall be determined by our law: 39 Edw. III.[1] And the law is the same between a parson and a farmer, and a parson and a servant … if there is a suit between them in the court Christian no *indicavit* lies but prohibition. But [it is otherwise] when there is a dispute between two parsons of the same patron, for there there is no mischief to the patron whichever one has [the tithes] and there is no-one against whom he can sue a writ of [right] of tithes.

The law is the same of all those things which are lay fee dependent on a spiritual fee, such as rent granted to be discharged of tithes, or an annuity, or where sheep are sold for money: in these cases these things are temporal as well as the tithes themselves, for by selling them as temporal things they become temporal.

The law is also the same where the place is in no parish, such as the forest of Inglewood and Windsor in which the king has the profit (but query what profit): in those cases the matter shall be determinable at common law. But it is otherwise where a parson is spoiled of his tithes, as he clearly is by any parson who claims title in the same parsonage. But in this case if the parson is a parson imparsonate prohibition lies, as is shown in 45 [Edw. III] and 14 Hen. IV.[2]

The law is also the same where in Chester there is a custom that if a man dies after the feast of St Chad the executors shall have the emblements if the … parson demands against them he must demand at common law, yet against a man who does not wish to tithe he shall be punished in the spiritual court, but here they do not have to tithe of this as of their land, for they do not have an interest but only claim a share. The law is the same also where the parson is seised or if [the tithes] are severed and another carries [them] away. But if the tenant himself carries them away after severance and before collection the parson … against the same tenant in spiritual law. But as it seems that is at his choice, for he has a

---

[1] YB Mich. 39 Edw. III, fos 23–24.
[2] YB Trin. 45 Edw. III, fo. 17, pl. 8; YB Hil. 14 Hen. IV, fo. 17, pl. 14.

son lyberty de pren … ly vers le tenant ou nient. Mez si il vient la a coyller et le tenant voyl preyng son chyvall de son charue… distorb en cel maner il est transgresser et punissabul en noster ley, entant que il fayt nul act en disag… severans pur entant dez dysms …

[*fo. 63v*] Si debat soyt enter mon parson et eux de Cysteux lez queux claymont destre quytes de dysm, en ce cas prohibition ne gyst pur le patron entant que nul tytl de patronag est en debat ne de droit de parsonag. Meme le ley est lou lez ters ou dysms le parson sont assyng all vykary ou econtra per lordinary ovesque lassent le patron: en ce cas enter eux deux serra unques determynabul per ley spyrytuel. Mez auter est si soyt de ter purchas per vykary quar lassyngment <ne>[d] est voyd, quar le patron nad interest tanque son yncombent est present a ce et come semble, per cas le parson ne poet prender ter a ly et sez successors quar il nad estat mez pur term de vi et si issint donques cel ground tyent lew en nul cas … lou lesglise est issint endowe all commensment.

Le parson covenand ovesque un que il serra discharg de disms et action de covenant est port, ne serra determynabul en noster ley, <quar>[d] xxxviijº E[dw.] iij[i] en covenant. Le reson, come semble, quar est endout sy le covenant per lour ley soyt voyd ou nient, quar home ne poet prescryb en non decimando sed in modo decimandi come a doner checun xij scheff.

En ascun casys le tort le parson nest punissabul per noster ley ne per lour ley, come lou il nad droit daver tythes, come lou le tenant meme distru son gras ou corn ou ne voyl mouer, ou lou <son>[d] ne sont severes, et un estranger eux enport devant severans. Mez si le tenant port bref de trespass et recover damages, le parson conpellera ly de tyȝth en cort crystyan, mez si un estranger [fourche][1] et succyde et emport non obstant que il port bref de trespass et recover, unquor nul remedy pur le parson quar ce <f>[d] parcel del franktenement al temps de faucher pur quel caus lez damages sont auxi taxes: quere.

Si le parson su pur tyȝht pur *silva sedua* prohibition gyst per statut xlvº E[dw.] iij[i] et fuit comenz ley auxi devant, pur ce que il <avera>[d] sont de reperer franctenement et pur nul auter reson. Et pur ce le parson avera tyȝht de auters arburs, scilicet hasels et huiusmodi non obstant que sont dage de xx ans.

Si le parson soyt distorb de son chymyn quant il ayl a coyller sez dysms le remedy est per spyrytuel cort come vide le regyster enter consultations.

Si debat soyt en cort crystyan pur chose nient dismabul prohibition gyst, come de col pyt, quarrey, quar naver tyȝth de eux pur ce que ne cressont et il avera tyȝht de gras cressantes sur le meme. Mez semble unquor que ce serra determinabul en cort crystyan si soyt dismabul ou nient: quere.

---

[1] MS. reads furuch.

choice whether to take … against the tenant or not. But if he goes there to collect and the tenant wishes to take his horse from his plough … disturb in this manner he is the transgressor and is punishable in our law, inasmuch as he did no act in [disagreement] … severance in connection to tithes ….

If there is a dispute between my parson and the Cistercians who claim to be quit of tithes, in this case prohibition does not lie for the patron, inasmuch as no title of patronage is in dispute nor any right of parsonage. The law is the same where lands or tithes of the parson are assigned to the vicarage (or the contrary) by the ordinary with the assent of the patron: in this case between the two it shall always be determinable by the spiritual law. But it is otherwise if it is of land purchased for the vicarage, for the assignment is void, for the patron has no interest until his incumbent is presented to it and as it seems, perhaps the parson cannot take land to him and his successors for he has no estate except for term of life and if it is so then this ground holds in no case … where the church is thus endowed at the beginning.

The parson covenants with another that he shall be discharged of tithes and an action of covenant is brought, it shall not be determinable in our law: 38 Edw. III in covenant.[1] The reason, as it seems, is that it is in doubt if the covenant is void in their law or not, for a man cannot prescribe in *non decimando* but in *modo decimandi* such as to give every twelfth sheaf.

In other cases the parson's injury is not punishable by our law or by their law, as where he does not have the right to have tithes, such as where the tenant himself destroyed his grass or corn or will not mow it, or where it is not severed and a stranger carries it away before severance. But if the tenant brings a writ of trespass and recovers damages, the parson shall compel him to tithe in court Christian, but if a stranger divides it and cuts it down and carries it away, notwithstanding that he brings a writ of trespass and recovers, still there is no remedy for the parson for this was parcel of the freehold at the time of the reaping for which reason the damages are also taxes: query.

If the parson sues for tithe for *silva caedua* prohibition lies by the statute of 45 Edw. III, and it was also common law before, because it is to repair the freehold and for no other reason.[2] And therefore the parson shall have tithe of other trees, namely hazels and suchlike notwithstanding that they are twenty years old.

If the parson is disturbed on his way when he goes to collect his tithes the remedy is by the spiritual court: see the *Register* among the 'Consultations'.[3]

If there is dispute in the court Christian for things not titheable, such as a coal pit or quarry, prohibition lies, for he shall not have tithe of them because they are not growing, [but] he shall have tithe of the grass growing on them. But still it seems that this shall be determinable in court Christian whether it is titheable or not: query.

---

[1] YB Pas. 38 Edw. III, fo. 8.
[2] 45 Edw. III, c. 3 (*SR*, i. 393).
[3] *Register*, fos 44–44v.

Xɪⱼᴬ Lectura

Ore serra monster de oblations, obventions, et mortuaris, lou le parson avera et per quel remedy:

Oblations sont dutys certen come iiij foytes en an ou auterment come lusag est et pur ceux atteyng le remedy est per spyrytuel ley. Obventions sont de charyte et devotion et nient de duty, come al fest de puryfycation ou al <fne>ᵈ funeralles ou al weddynges, ou tapurs ou auter chosys offres a seynt: en ceux casys nul remedy pur compel homes de payer. Mez si un foytes pay et soyt reprys le remedy est en temporall cort et meme le ley a ce purpos en primer cas. Mes si un lyver, vestyment, chalys, pax soyt affer et sont enport nul remedy pur le pere mez pur lez parochyens quar apurtyent a eux entant que ils sont compelys de trover meme le chos sans que le servys de Dewe ne peut estre fayt et issint de grand campoans. Mez auter est de cor de seynt, schous de sylver, ou huiusmodi, quar ceux sont al parson et le parson peut eux prender, ce est a dyr come semble, sy soyt mys la come offeryng, mez si soyt mys la come un tokun et rembraunce et nient pur offeryng auter est, come coot armor etc.

Offeryng <alter>ᵈ ne lyera cestui que est proprietaryus come sal en open market mez que il purroyt eux reprender non obstant lopynyon Prisot xxxiiijᵒ H[en] vj, quar nest fayt de cheryte de offer auters biens et pur ce si ijˣ joyntenants lun offer lauter poet enporter <ft>ᵈ. Mez auter est … execucion et pur ce offeryng de toutes biens forfaytes est nul. Et issint si ad properte en biens condytionally et le condytion enfreynt.

Si distorbans soyt fayt a un en eglis … le parson ly suera en cort crystyan pur le contempt spyrytuel en lesglis et issont … pur chescun auter distorbans ou ryot et le party meme suera en temporall cort, mez si distorbans soyt hors de holy ter nul *rem*edy pur le parson <entant unquor quere quar>ᵈ quar nest semble lou home est distorb de vener a mon market, quar la est distorb de fayr temporal mez ɪcy est distorb de fayr spyrytuel act et en spirytuel cort nul remedy pur ce que nest fayt en ter sanctyfy. Et a distorbans … esglis nest diversite enter farmor de parson, patron, et auters come devant.

[*fo. 64*] Si un ad propurte condytionel en ley et offer eux sont ales a toutes jours, come si le plaintiff en repl*evin* ad auter biens en whythernam et eux offer <et cestui que>ᵈ quar veggnont en lew de sez biens demesn, avera encres come de sez demesne. Mez auter est de lauter part, si le defendant en repl*evin* ad auter biens en whyternam et cestui que lez own offer le rent, il poet eux arer reprender entant que le defendant navoyt eux mez en lew de plege. Si le baron offer non obstant devors, unquor le feme navera issint, come semble, si ne unques devorce.

TWELFTH LECTURE

Now we shall see concerning oblations, obventions and mortuaries, where the parson shall have them and by what remedy:

Oblations are duties which are certain, such as four times in the year or otherwise as the usage is and to get them the remedy is by spiritual law. Obventions are from charity and devotion and not duty, as at the feast of the Purification or at funerals or weddings, or tapers or other things offered to a saint: in these cases there is no remedy to compel someone to pay them. But if they are paid once and then repeated, the remedy is in the temporal court, and the law is the same for this purpose in the first case. But if a book, vestment, chalice [or] pax are offered and are taken away [there is] no remedy for the priest but only for the parishioners, for they belong to them inasmuch as they are compelled to find those same things without which God's service cannot be done, and the same of the great bells. But it is otherwise of a body of a saint, silver shoes, or such things, for these are the parson's and the parson may take them, that is to say as it seems, if it is placed there as an offering, but if it is put there as a token and remembrance and not as an offering, it is otherwise, such as coat armour etc.[1]

An offering does not bind the owner, as with a sale in a market overt, but he may take it again notwithstanding Prysot's opinion in 34 Hen. VI, for it is not a deed of charity to offer the goods of another, and therefore if there are two joint-tenants and one makes an offering the other can take it back.[2] But it is otherwise [after] execution, and therefore the offering of all forfeited goods is null. And the same if he has property in goods conditionally and the condition is broken.

If a disturbance is made by one in a church … the parson shall sue him in court Christian for the spiritual contempt in the church, and … for every other disturbance or riot, and the party himself shall sue in the temporal court, but if the disturbance is outside holy ground there is no remedy for the parson, for it is not like where a man is disturbed while selling in my market, for there he is disturbed from performing a temporal [act], but here he is disturbed from performing a spiritual act, and in the spiritual court there is no remedy because it was not done on sanctified ground. And [for] a disturbance [in] church there is no difference between the parson's farmer, patron and others as above.

If one has property conditional in law and offers them they are gone forever, as if the plaintiff in replevin has other goods in withernam and offers them (for they come in place of his own goods), he shall have increase as if they were his own. But it is otherwise on the other side, if the defendant in replevin has other goods in withernam, and the one who has them offers the rent, he may take them again inasmuch as the defendant only had them as a pledge. If the husband offers notwithstanding a divorce, still the wife shall not have it, as it seems, if they were not yet divorced.

---

[1] YB Trin. 9 Edw. IV, fo. 14, pl. 8. The case is discussed in J. H. Baker, 'Funeral Monuments and the Heir', *The Common Law Tradition: Lawyers, Books and the Law* (2000), p. 358.
[2] YB Mich. 34 Hen. VI, fos 10–11, pl. 21.

Ore serra dyst de mortuary:

Mortuary serra dyst unques le melior best de quyk catel que le mort avoyt et si il navoyt de quyk catel le melior dez auters biens come de chayn, jewel, ou huiusmodi, si non que soyt selonque lespecial costom come en London: la nul mortuary serra don.

Et mortuary nest don pur buryel quar ce serra dyst extortion mez pur oblationibus et obventionibus obletis et non debito non solutis et pur ce home que ne poet estre bury payera mortuary come excommeng, pheylo de se, ou cestui que est merg en le se: ce ne serront burys, et unquor payer mortuary. Mez quere de ceux que ne unques fuer demurantes en parych, si eux encor nyant muryer ils payer mortuary unquor ne fuer unquor demurantes la. Mez come semble, le generall reson est pur ce que il morust la le parson avera de…eter… <pur ly>[d] fayr orysons pur ly. Le reson de phylo de se non obstant que le roy en <mold>[d] molt casys est prefer, est le tytal icy faielt a un temps, scilicet le forfaytur a roy et le mortuary a parson, et pur ce le parson serra prefer en droit desglis. Meme le ley si home que navoyt que un chyvall, le quel ly occys: le chyval ne serra deodand mez mortuary et ce pur 2[x] resons, un pur le reson avandyst, auter pur ce que le roy nest daver a son profyst demesne mez al auter ops. Mez si cestui que morust avoyt ij chyvals le roy avera le deodand et lauter serra al parson quar toutes interests pusoyent estre salves, mez semble que non, que poet que lauter est le melyor best. Auxi le parson serra prefer devant le heyr lou il est daver melior best per costom, auxi le senyor pur haryot.

Un Ju ou heretyk ne payer mortuary quar pur toutes purposys serra come don en vayn, ne pur oryson, ne pur prayer.

Meme le ley auxi de toutes ceux que nont propurte en biens per atteyndur devant ou utlagary de felony. Meme le ley de <jurror que est atteynt pur>[d] vyllen apres que le senyor ad fayt general seisir. Meme le ley sy home soyt <atteynt>[i] de murdur soy defend ou per misaventur, <…>[d] ou <de suffer>[d] ou jurror atteynt ou convict en preminire [sic] ou auterment face defendant al proces issint que il perd sez biens et est hors de protection. En ceux casys il ne payera mortuary de ceux biens mez de biens atteyngs apres ils payerent, quar ils ne forfessont mez biens a temps <unquor>[d]. Mez auter est si soyt clerk atteynt quar la son person serra disabul tanque ad purchas chartor, come en cas de utlage en action personel.

Si un envy le roy morust il payera mortuary unquor toutes sez biens sont al roy et son vend ou don est voyd: quar nest semble al cas de home utlage, quar come semble si un estranger prist ovesque fors de ly serra ajuge come choce gayg[n] per batel mez envers le vende ou done ne serra pris si come le propurte fuit a roy quar le vendor est party et come agreant a son possession.

Si le fermor dun parson morust il payera nul mortuary quar il meme ad le cause daver et non obstant que ore son interest soyt determyn … term

Now we shall speak of mortuaries:

A mortuary is always called the best beast of the live cattle that the dead man had, and if he did not have live cattle the best of his other goods, such as a chain, jewel or suchlike unless it is according to a special custom, such as in London: there no mortuary shall be given.

And mortuary is not given for burial for this would be called extortion, but for forgotten and unpaid oblations and obventions and offerings, and therefore a man who cannot be buried shall pay a mortuary, such as an excommunicate, suicide, or one who has drowned in the sea: these people shall not be buried and still they shall pay a mortuary. But query concerning those who never lived in the parish – if they die there they pay mortuary even if they never lived there. But as it seems, the general reason is that because he dies there the parson shall have [an obligation] to intercede for him. The reason suicides [pay mortuary to the parson first] notwithstanding that the king is preferred in many cases, is that the title here failed at one time, namely the forfeiture to the king, and the mortuary to the parson, and therefore the parson shall be preferred in right of the Church. The law is the same of a man who only has one horse, which kills him: the horse shall not be a deodand but a mortuary, and this for two reasons, one for the reason aforesaid, the other because the king does not have it for his own profit but to another use. But if the one who died had two horses, the king shall have the deodand and the parson shall have the other, for all interests could be saved: but it seems not, for it is possible that the other is the best beast. Also the parson shall be preferred before the heir where he is to have the best beast by custom, [and] also [preferred] to the lord for heriot.

A Jew or a heretic shall not pay mortuary since for all purposes it would be given in vain, whether for intercession or for prayer.

The law is the same also of all those who have no property in goods because of a previous attainder or outlawry for felony. The law is the same for a villein after his lord has made a general seizure. The law is the same if a man is attainted of murder in self-defence or by misadventure, or a juror is attainted or convicted in *praemunire* or otherwise made a defendant in the process, so that he lost his goods and is out of protection. In these cases he shall not pay mortuary from these goods but from goods acquired afterwards they shall pay, for they only forfeit the goods [they held] at the time. But it is otherwise if he is an attainted clerk, for there his person shall be disabled until he has purchased a charter, as in the case of an outlawry in a personal action.

If an envoy of the king is killed he shall pay a mortuary, yet all his goods go to the king and his sales or gifts are void: it does not seem to be the case for an outlawed man, for as it seems if a stranger takes from him with force it shall be adjudged as a thing gained by battle, but against the vendee or donee it shall not be taken as if the property was the king's, for the vendor is party and it agrees with his possession.

If the farmer of a parson dies he shall pay no mortuary for he himself has reason to have it, and notwithstanding that his interest is now determined ... term

expyr come per cas il ad interest pur vy, unqor le parson ne poet claym de temps son mort. Ij joyntenants possessors dun chyval lun morust le parson navera mortuary ne le moyte: si tenant en comenz le reson appyert. Mez si divers heyrs per costom ont certen biens lun morust devant severans le parson avera le melior best et si lauter morust apres le melior de toutes, quar le mort serra devision en ley et lexecutors averont le part de chescun et issint ne sont joynt et est lour foly que ne voudont fayr partytion.

Si <lexecutors>[d] parochyens fayt le parson executor le quel ad un boeff et soyt enport il peut suer en cort Crystyan pur le haryot et refuser droit que il avoyt come executor ou il peut aver action per detenu ou trespas come executor. Mez si il port ce action il ne unquor peut claym ce come mortuary: quod quere. Si le mortuary soyt mys en le cymytory et devant actuel seisin enport, remedy en lun cort ou en auter, mez auter si navoyt que cel boeff quar donques covient defors de prender ce pur le possession et covient suer en temporal cort. Et issint en toutes casys lou nest que un boeff et le parson ad ascun actuel possession ou indifferent come lou fuit … a parson en vy le mort et lexecutors offer le mony et prist et issint lou le parson avoyt distr pur rent a ly … ore per le mort il ad propurte et covient defors de suer a noster ley entant que nest chang dez bestes. Meme le le*y* … le boeff fuit les a ly pur compastur son ter mez auter [est] lou il navoyt mez de agystur quar la il ad … de possession parson meme. Auter est lou estranger avoyt pris en vi le testator ou de lez executors, la le parson suera vers lestranger en cort …

Si le mort navoyt possession en le catel al temps de mort le parson navera mortuary come <si un>[d] … <ad ce en port ou>[d] le parson meme <ad ce enport>[i]. Si lexecutors recover en trespass ou detenu unquor le parson navera pur mortu*ary*. Mez si lez testators avoyt propurte en ly a toutes ententes auter, come il ad bayll a un auter. Mez si le testator avoyt pleg auter ou que senior ad distrein le parson ne poet fes mez compellera lez <tenants>[d] executors per spyrytuel de <fayr repl>[d] payer le mo*ny* replevu

[*fo. 64v*] Le parson avera le best <en>[d] pur mortuary que est pris en whyternam de part le plaintiff si ne soyt auter best mez de part le defendant auter est, mez compellera lez executors de plaintiff de payer le rent et prender cest bestes arer come devant ales dyst. Mez semble que le primer cas nest ley et nest semble lou il voyll fayr don en faytes…

Si un que soyt ly en stat stapul morust le parson avera mortuary quar lez biens ne sont lyers tanque execution soyt sue.

Xiij[A] Lectura

[*fo. 65*] Ore serra monster dez auter chosys dont le spyrytuel coort ad conusans et ou nient sur le statut de <m>[d] circumspecte agatis et auter estatuts:

expired as perhaps he has an interest for life, still the parson cannot claim at the time of his death. [If] two joint-tenants are possessors of one horse and one dies, the parson shall not have a mortuary or the moiety: if they are tenants in common the reason is apparent. But if different heirs by custom have certain goods [and] one dies before severance, the parson shall have the best beast, and if the other dies after the best of all, for the death shall be a division in law and the executors shall have the part of each and thus they are not joint, and it is their folly who did not wish to make partition.

If parishioners who have an ox make the parson their executor and the ox is carried away, he may sue in court Christian for the heriot and refuse the right he has as executor, or he may have an action of detinue or trespass as executor. But if he brings this action he may never claim this as mortuary: query. If the mortuary is put in the churchyard and carried away before actual seisin, remedy is in one court or the other, [but it] is otherwise if [the deceased] only had this ox, for then [the parson] had necessarily to take possession of it and he must sue in the temporal court. And thus in all cases where there is only one ox and the parson has any actual or indifferent possession, as where it was … to the parson in the life of the dead man, and the executors offer the money and he takes it, and thus where the parson has distrained for rent to … now by the death he has property and he must sue at our law inasmuch as there is no change of beasts. The law is the same … the ox was leased to him to manure his land, but it is otherwise where he only had them to agist for there he has … of possession the same parson. It is otherwise where a stranger has taken [the ox] in the life of the testator or of the executors, there the parson shall sue against the stranger in court [Christian].

If the deceased did not have possession in the cattle at the time of his death the parson shall not have mortuary as … the parson himself had carried it away. If the executors recover in trespass or detinue still the parson shall not have it for a mortuary. But if the testators have property in it to all intents [it is] otherwise, as when he has bailed to another. But if the testator had pledged [to an]other, or the lord had distrained, the parson can only compel the executors by spiritual [law] to pay the replevied money.

The parson shall have as a mortuary the beast which is taken in withernam on the part of the plaintiff if there is no other beast, but on the part of the defendant it is otherwise, but he shall compel the executors of the plaintiff to pay the rent and take the beasts again as said before. But it seems that the first case is not law and it is not like where he wishes to make a gift by deed…

If one who is bound in a statute staple dies the parson shall have a mortuary, for the goods are not bound until execution is sued.

THIRTEENTH LECTURE

Now we shall see about other things where the spiritual court has cognizance and where it does not according to the statute *Circumspecte Agatis* and other statutes:[1]

---

[1] 13 Edw. I (*SR*, i. 101–102).

Primis de redemption de penance: si cestui que ad penance a ly enjoyn et voyl redemer le redemption serra demande en coort crystyan mez auter est[1] si lordinary voyl enjoyn le party de fayr amendes. Si lordinary enjoyn un de offer un tapur ou torsh, vestyment ou chales a un eglis quar ceux sont chosys per queux le servys est susteyn, mez si lordinary voyl enjoyn un de fayr un fenester ou de founder un hospytall le prohibition gyst: <quar ce>ᵈ quere son reson, quar semble tout un. Mez lordinary peut enjoyn un de vyver en wyldurness <quar>ᵈ per space dun an etc., quar ce est corporall penance. Mez <lordy>ᵈ lordinary ne poet donera un home penance de enter en religion quar a ce fayr nul serra constrayn et si il fayt prohibition gyst. Mez semble que il ly ground sur nul ground quar non obstant la soyt <enloyall ou ce>ᵈ justys ordur a mys:[*sic*] unquor le correction de ce apurteyng a metropolyton et nient en noster cort.

Si un clerk [est] infra ordurs de subdekon il peut suer al coort crystyan pur excommengement mez nemi pur amendes. <si un>ᵈ Mez <sill>ᵈ je puis bat le clerk en mon defens ou en defens de mez biens per ley espyrytuel, auxi en executyng precept de ley come capias si il voyl rescu et la si il su per cas prohibition gyst. Mez si le clerk soyt reguler ou apostata nul remedy, mez auter est si soyt suspend.

Si le esglise ne soyt susteyn le peryse serront compel de susteyn le corps desglis et le parson le chauncel mez pur toutes enorment queux sont nessassarys a dyvyn servys le paryse est tenus a sustenger come lyver, chaleys, grand campans, mez nemi pelur, salur, ryngbels, ne tapurs, si non un pur le mas, et ils ne sont tenus de trover ascun choce quel nest nessessary mez en honor come lampes et huiusmodi. Ceux maters apurteyng meerment a coort speyrytuel et ne sont arguumentabul per noster ley.

Pencion est lou un abbe ou auter spyrytuel patron ad estre seisi de temps etc. de rent de meme lesglice: ce serra demande en coort chrystyan. Mez auter est lou est per composition puis temps ou, come semble, annuite pay a auter parson pur dysms, quar ceux serront demandez en noster ley. Si le patron morust lexecutor averont action de det quar ils ne sont spyrytuel patron.

Si un soyt defam en cause meer spyrytuel come lechery, avowtry, apostacy, usury, symony et huiusmodi pur ce il peut suer en cort crystyan mez auter est si soyt en cause temporal come thef, murdur, forgyng de faytes ou forgyng de testament, quar ceux sont punissabul per temporall ley. Mez ascun defamation poet estre en cause determynabul per comenz ley come en rape si il defam home de ravishment, quar pur le avowtry il serra punyse en cort crystyan et pur le auter en temporall cort. Mez come semble que tout le defamation est myxt et issint ne serra punys en spyrytuel cort, mez si le sclaunder fuit de avowtry auter serra.

---

[1] Marginal note: [illegible].

First concerning redemption of penance: if one has penance enjoined to him and wishes to redeem it the redemption shall be demanded in court Christian, but it is otherwise if the ordinary wishes to enjoin the party to make amends. The ordinary may enjoin one to offer a taper or a torch, a vestment or a chalice to a church, for those are things by which the service is supported, but if the ordinary wishes to enjoin one to make a window or to found a hospital prohibition lies: query his reason, for it all seems to be the same. But the ordinary may enjoin one to live in the wilderness for the space of a year, etc., for this is a corporal penance. But the ordinary may not give a man a penance of entering in religion for no-one shall be constrained to do this, and if [the ordinary] does prohibition lies. But it seems that he grounds himself on no grounds, for notwithstanding justice shall be ordered to be done there: still, the correction of this belongs to the metropolitan and not in our court.

If a clerk is in the orders of subdeacon he may sue to the court Christian for excommunication but not for amends. But I may beat the clerk in self-defence, or in defence of my goods, by spiritual law, also in executing a precept of the law such as *capias* if he wishes to rescue, and there if he sues perhaps prohibition lies. But if the clerk is regular or apostate there is no remedy, but it is otherwise if he is suspended.[1]

If the church is not maintained the parish shall be compelled to maintain the body of the church and the parson [shall maintain] the chancel, but for all objects which are necessary for divine service the parish is bound to maintain them, such as the book, chalice, great bell, but not the basin, the salt, ring-bells or tapers, except one for the Mass, and they are not bound to find anything which is not necessary but honourable such as lamps and suchlike. These matters belong purely in the spiritual court and are not arguable at our law.

A pension is where an abbot or other spiritual patron has been seised from time immemorial of a rent from the same church: this shall be demanded in court Christian. But it is otherwise where it is by composition after time [immemorial] or, as it seems, an annuity paid to another parson for tithes, for those shall be demanded at our law. If the patron dies the executor[s] shall have action of debt for they are not the spiritual patron.

If one is defamed in a purely spiritual cause such as lechery, adultery, apostacy, usury, simony and suchlike, he may sue in court Christian, but it is otherwise if it is in a temporal cause, such as theft, murder, forging of deeds or forging of wills, for those are punishable by temporal law. But some defamation can be in a cause determinable by common law, as in rape if he defames a man for ravishment, since for adultery he shall be punished in court Christian and for the other in the temporal court. But it seems that all defamation is mixed and thus shall not be punished in spiritual court, but if the slander was for adultery it shall be otherwise.

---

[1] This seems to mean 'irregular' in the sense of being out of conformity with Church doctrine or ineligible for ordination. It consistently appears as 'regular' in the readings. See Reading A, p. 2, Reading C, p. 16, Reading E, pp. 37, 38, Reading G, p. 53, Reading Two, p. 75 and p. 113, above.

Auxi cestui que don evydens, come en elopment de baron en dower ou en appeel de rape, nest punissabul quar est pur enform le cort. Ne tyel perjury serra punys en cort crystyan, scilicet doner devydens en appeel de rap ou pur pleder ou doner devydens en cas lou le feme alop de son baron, ne en toutes lez casys devaunt tochant le <speyrytualte>[d] <temporalte>[i]. Mez auter est lou home est jurre de mary tyel feme ou <dely>[d] executor jurre a delyver le legacy, quar leffect de cel mater conferme le spyrytuel jurisdicion. Auterment que lou home est jurre denfeff un tyel ou de ly payer tant de mony, mez come semble si il soyt su en coort crystyan pro lesione fidei: tamen quere come je perceu per levidenz dez rouls un foytes a tabul de evesques de Exetur que fuer 2[x] sutes, scilicet pro lesione fidei tantum et pur ambydeux et en primer cas prohibiction ne gyst. Mez en cas de sclaunder ly covient a fyn force de fayr son purgation et ce ne poet en ce cort.

Usury et symony est <en cas>[d] punissabul per spyrytuel ley si non que soyt en casys destatuts, scilicet Marton, a[o] xj[o] H[en.] vij[i] et auters. Unquor vide que ce est offens spyrytuel come rap, unquor entent que tout le mater est punissabul per <spyrytuel cort>[d] temporal cort.

De choce que toch matrymony serra determyn en lespyrytuel cort. Si home promys xx l. pur maryer son fyl et il marya, il peut su pur le mony en cort crystyan, <que>[d] mez auter est sur catel pur cel caus, scilicet per endentur ou auterment, come semble, quar donques son remedy est en temperall cort. Quar contract covient cest agrement a cel <part>[d] temps de chescun part, mez si soyt forsque promys de un party ce soun en covenant et non obstant que le choce soyt fayt en apres <dauter party>[i] unquor ce ne face contract que ne unques fuit contract.

Si le feme dun home soyt prys de ly il peut aver action de trespass en noster ley de <muliere>[d] <uxore>[i] abducta ou en spyrytuel cort de uxore spoliata le quel gyst en le droit et ne poet estre mayteyn si non que le feme soyt feme en droit quar la ils voyllent ce tryer.

Si home soyt mary a un feme et ad issu et morust le freer <ne>[d] de baron ne peut suer devors apres son mort pur basterder lissu et si il fayt prohibition gyst quar entent que lespousels contynuer sans devorce serra unquor pris come lauful. Mez si home mary <fem et>[d] ij femes et ad issu per le second et le primer feme fuit de ly devorce le frer peut suer pur anuller le dyst devorce et issint de basterder lissu quar ore nest forsque de undo un spyrytuel jugement. Et meme le ley si home enter en religion et est dereyng per precontract et ad issu et morust, son frer peut suer reversel de cest dereygnment.

De chosys que toch testament: le divise dez biens ne poet prender si non en speciall casys, come lou le testator dyvice son term le divise peut enter et il alleg ce destre agre deins les ij terms en comenz place, et unquor que ce term serra charg a dettes et serra come possession de lez executors. Mez come semble a moy, ce nest possybul destre constru en cel form et meme le ley de rent charg pur ans ou annuite

Also someone who gives evidence (as in the elopment of the husband in dower or in appeal of rape) is not punishable, for [the evidence] is to inform the court. No such perjury shall be punished in court Christian, namely to give evidence in an appeal of rape, or to plead or give evidence in the case where a woman elopes from her husband, nor in all the cases above touching the temporality. But it is otherwise where the man is sworn to marry such a woman or an executor is sworn to deliver the legacy, for the effect of this matter confirms the spiritual jurisdiction. [It is] otherwise where a man is sworn to enfeoff such a one or to pay him so much money unless, as it seems, he is sued in court Christian *pro laesione fidei*: however query as I once perceived by the evidence … of the rolls at the table of the bishops of Exeter that there were two suits, namely *pro laesione fidei* alone and for both, and in the first case prohibition does not lie. But in the case of slander he must by absolute necessity make his purgation and this may not be in this court.

Usury and simony are punishable by the spiritual law unless they are within the case of the statutes, namely Merton, 11 Hen. VII [c. 8] and others.[1] Nevertheless see that there may be a spiritual offence such as rape, where the whole matter is punishable by the temporal court.

Things touching matrimony shall be determined in the spiritual court. If a man promises [one] £20 to marry his daughter and he marries her, [the husband] may sue for the money in court Christian, but it is otherwise of chattels for this cause, namely by indenture or otherwise, as it seems, for then his remedy is in temporal court. For a contract must be an agreement at [one] time on each side, but if it was only a promise by one party, it sounds in covenant, and notwithstanding that the thing was done afterwards by the other party still this does not make something a contract which never was a contract.

If a man's wife is taken from him he can have an action of trespass *de uxore abducta* in our law or *de uxore spoliata* in the spiritual court, which lies in the right and cannot be maintained unless the woman was a wife in right, for there they will try this.

If a man is married to a woman and has issue and dies, the husband's brother cannot sue divorce after his death to bastardise the issue, and if he does prohibition lies, for inasmuch as the spousals continued without divorce they shall still be taken as lawful. But if a man marries two women and has issue by the second, and the first woman was divorced from him, the brother can sue to annul the said divorce and thus to bastardise the issue for now it is only to undo a spiritual judgment. And the law is the same if a man enters religion and is deraigned for precontract and has issue and dies, his brother can sue for reversal of the deraignment.

Concerning matters which touch testaments: the devisee of goods can only take them in special cases, as where the testator devises his term, the devisee can enter – and he alleges this to be agreed within the [last] two terms in the common place – and still this term shall be charged for debts and shall be as a possession of the executors.[2] But as it seems to me, this cannot be construed in this form and

---

[1] 20 Hen. III, c. 5 (*SR*, i. 3); 11 Hen. VII, c. 8 (*SR*, ii. 574).
[2] Cf. *Reports, Hen. VIII*, i. 108, pl. 57 (Roger Yorke's notebook).

pur ans, semble <molt plus ley quar ce>[d] tout un. Meme le ley est en toutes casys lou le dyvise ad possession de meme le choce dyvys en vy le testator, come lou le testator baylla a ly meme lez biens ou que il est senior et eux distrayn ore serra constru executor pur favor de possession, come semble a lez groundes de remitter.

[fo. 65v] Si un soyt en det al testator et le testator dyvice a ly meme le det ore le dutye est extyent si soyt contract. Mez si soyt sur obligation non que nest mez mater en fayt mez covient ly de suer en cort Christian pur compeller lexecutors de release a luy. Si un dyvyce que sez executors devoyent vender le ter a un tyel et ils veyllont ou vendont a un auter nul remedy pur cestui que devoyt aver quar en legacy de ter ils ne mellont ne per noster ley, quar nad nul remedy mez denter et ce ne poet. Mez semble que si soyt ascun remedy est per sub pena.

Si le roy divice lez juels de son coron est voyd, come le coron, le cepter. Meme le ley si master dospytal devyce <de>[d] biens de son hoos le dyvyce est voyd quar <il ne unquor avoyt propurte en ce>[d] leyne propurte avera preferment scilicet le meson: quere donques que est diversite en reson enter le cas de baron et feme.

Le feme poet dyvyser bona paraphanalia per spyrytuel ley ce est a dyr sa weryng ger, mez si el ce face sans assent le baron et le divise sua pur atteygnur cel prohibition gyst entant que est voyd per noster ley. Mez auter est si feme covert face divyce per licens son baron, mez en ce cas lexecutors devoyent monster le lycens le baron en mayntener de lour action et ce, come semble, covient destre per fayt entant que est choce depend sur mayntenans dobligation. Mez quere de ce quar home pledera lycens en plusors casys sans monster. Si feme covert soyt detect de defamation en cort cristian et charg ovesque costes, come poet bien, le feme morust le baron en lour ley serra charg.

Si home dyvice biens a son fytes et heyr et basterd eyne su pur cel dyvyce prohbition gyst. <Mez auter est lou le>[d] Mez unquor nul priminire [sic] quar le mater est spyrytuel mez <si>[d] le cause que voyllet suer la est pur ce que il est mulier per lour ley et avera jugement en cel cort, mez si le puny fytes su pur le legacy prohibition ne gyst non obstant que soyt en debat si soyt heyr ou non per Pygot xxij° E[dw.] iiij[i].

Si un divice biens per son testament porter dat en Fraunce le dyvyce suera devaunt le metropolyton quar peut estre try per provs et issint le testament serra prov devant ly et pur meme le reson si un dyvice biens et ne face sez executors ou face sez executors et ils disagreont issint que administration est commyt unquor le dyvyse suera vers ladministrators et si lordynary ne commyt ladministration le ordynary serra su en coort le metropolyton. Mez quere si ce soyt spyrytuel ley entant que nul testament serra prov, mez per cas poet aver ce per provys.

the law is the same of rent charged for years or an annuity for years, it seems it is all the same. The law is the same in all cases where the devisee has possession of the thing devised during the testator's lifetime, as where the testator delivers the same goods to him, or where he is the lord and distrains them, now he shall be construed as executor in favour of possession, similarly to the principles of remitter.

If one is in debt to the testator and the testator devises the [same] debt to him now the duty is extinguished if it was a contract. But if it was on an obligation it is not, for it is only a matter in fact, but he must sue in court Christian to compel the executors to release to him. If one devises that his executors must sell the land to such a one and they convey or sell it to another, there is no remedy for the one who ought to have it, for in a legacy of land they must not meddle in our law, for he has no remedy but to enter and he cannot. But it seems that if there is any remedy it is by *subpoena*.

If the king devises the crown jewels, such as the crown [or] the sceptre, it is void. The law is the same if a master of a hospital devises the goods of his house, the devise is void for the earlier property shall have preference, namely the house: query then what is the reason for the difference in the case of husband and wife.

The wife can devise *bona paraphernalia* (that is to say her 'wearing gear') by the spiritual law, but if she does this without the assent of her husband and the devisee sues to have this, prohibition lies, inasmuch as it is void by our law. But it is otherwise if a feme covert makes a devise with her husband's licence, but in this case the executors must show the husband's licence in maintaining their action and this, as it seems, must be by deed, inasmuch as it depends on the maintenance of an obligation. But query this, for a man may plead a licence in many cases without showing it. If a feme covert is convicted of defamation in court Christian and charged with costs, as she may well be, and the wife dies, the husband shall be charged in their law.

If a man devises goods to his son and heir and the bastard eigné sues for this devise prohibition lies. But still there is no *praemunire* for the matter is spiritual but the cause that he wishes to sue there is because he is legitimate in their law and shall have the judgment in that court, but if the younger son sues for the legacy prohibition shall not lie, notwithstanding that it is in debate whether he is heir or not: by Pygot 22 Edw. IV.[1]

If one devises goods by his will bearing date in France the devisee shall sue before the metropolitan for it may be tried by witnesses, and thus the testament shall be proved before him, and for the same reason if one devises goods and does not make his executors, or makes his executors and they refuse so that the administration is committed, still the devisee shall sue the administrators and if the ordinary does not commit the administration the ordinary shall be sued in the metropolitan's court. But query if this is spiritual law inasmuch as no testament is to be proved, but perhaps he may aver it by witnesses.

---

[1] Fitzherbert, *Consultacion*, 5.

Al comenz ley fuit prohibition infenyt mez ore ce est repel per statut aᵒ 10
E[dw.] iijⁱ caᵒ iiijᵒ que ils procederont non obstant prohibition a eux direct apres
consultation mez cest consultation ne serra grant devant le chaunceler et le chef
justys ont ynspect le lybel que soyt la nul cause que toch le coron.

Fuerunt <tres>ᵈ duo lecture plus: una ubi processus exiera ad episcopu ratione
basterdie, professionis, institutionis et <hyes similibus>ⁱ etc. sur cest paroll libertates; alia lectura sur cest paroll liberis hominibus <que>ᵈ dez villens ovesque
toutes lez cyrcumstancys <queux>ᵈ quas lecturas non repeti turpedinis causa.

At the common law prohibition was infinite, but now this is repealed by the statute of [50] Edw. III, c. 4 that they should proceed notwithstanding a prohibition directed to them after consultation, but this consultation shall not be granted before the chancellor and the chief justice have inspected the libel to ensure that there is nothing in the cause which touches the crown.[1]

There were two more lectures: one on when process goes to the bishop by reason of bastardy, profession, institution and such things etc. on this word *libertates*; the other lecture on this word *liberis hominibus* concerning villeins with all their circumstances, which lectures I shall not repeat because of their turpitude.

---

[1] 50 Edw. III, c. 4 (*SR*, i. 398).

READING EIGHT

[*fo. 20*] Assit principio beata Maria meo Jhesus foy lady helpe.
Magna carta fuit fait per ...[1] Roy John et a round mede per compulson ad ...
h... aprez est dit que fuit, tamen quere le roy H[en.] iij^d et conferm 29 ...
per luy.

MAGNA CARTA   ROBERT CHALONER

[LECTURE ONE]

Lestatut est *concessimus deo*: en chescun don devoet estre abilite del donour
et capacite del done et auter nest bon. Nonabilite est ou le donor est deinz age,
quar poet avoid son don a son plein age. Auxi disabilite est quant le donor est
hors de son memory et son heir peut avoid cest don apres son mort. Nonabilite
est en chescun cominalite sils nont corporation, et issint chescun esglise ou
chose espirituell, et pur ceo ascuns diont que cest Esglise cest estatut nest able
de prend et ascuns diont per cest act de parlement lesglise est fait able coment
que ne fuit able devant, quar lestatut peut fair corporation et corps nient able,
able.

[LECTURE TWO]

Lestatut est *libera*: cest peut estre entend ou ascun villen est fait prest, il sera
pluys frank que si ne fuit priste uncore son segnior peut luy prend pur luy server
come prister et ne don a luy forsque vesture et maunger. Mesme le ley sil ait
prebend, jeo puis luy prend, mez sil ad cure dez almes nemi. Mez si <soit>^{i}
deprive de son benefice donquez puise arer <prend>^{i} et sil enter en relegion,
devant profession le segnior luy peut prinde mez apres profession il est mys a son
action de trespass vers le abbot ou prior etc.

Auxi *libera* peut estre entend que ne serra mys en enquisition ascun charge per
reason de lour glebe terre come auterz homez serra per reason de lour tenourz, ou
que rienz est pair per reason de tax ou auter charge grant per parlement per roy,
ou que don en frankalmoign rent rendre.

Et peut estre pris que null esteant en esglise pur senctuary serra pris hors per
xl jourz, et que chescun home peut luy porter maunger et boier saunz prejudice
dascun, et si al fyn dez xl jours il ne voet mitter pur un coroner il serra mure en

---

[1] Corner damaged.

READING EIGHT

Blessed Mary be with my beginning, Jesus faith, lady help.
Magna Carta was made by ... King John and at Runnymede by compulsion ...
afterwards it is said that it was, however query, King Henry III and confirmed
29 ... by him.[1]

MAGNA CARTA   ROBERT CHALONER

[LECTURE ONE]

The statute is *we have granted to God*: in each grant there must be the ability of
the donor and the capacity of the donee, and otherwise it is not good. Non-ability
is where the donor is within age, [and he] may avoid his grant at his full age. Also
disability is when the donor is out of his mind and his heir may avoid this grant
after his death. Non-ability is in every commonalty if they are not a corporation, and likewise in every church or spiritual thing, and therefore some say that
the Church [in] this statute is not able to take, and some say that by this act of
Parliament the Church is made able even though it was not able before, because
a statute may make a corporation and body which is not able, able.

[LECTURE TWO]

The statute is *free*: this may be understood where any villein is made a priest,
he shall be more free than if he were not a priest, but still his lord may take him
to serve him as priest and give him nothing but clothes and food. The law is the
same if he has a prebend, I may take him, but not if he has a cure of souls. But if
he is deprived of his benefice then afterwards takes it again, and if he enters in
religion, before profession the lord may take him, but after profession [the lord]
is put to his action of trespass against the abbot or prior etc.

Also *free* may be understood that he shall not be put on an inquisition [or pay]
any charge by reason of their glebe land as other men shall by reason of their
tenures, or that [he should not]² pay by reason of tax or other charge granted by
the king's Parliament, or that a grant in free alms shall render rent.

And it may be taken that no-one being in a church for sanctuary shall be taken
out for forty days, and that every man may bring him food and drink without
prejudice of anyone, and if at the end of the forty days he does not wish to send

---

[1] Magna Carta was not confirmed in 29 Henry III, though it was confirmed in 21 and 36 Hen. III (*SR*, i.
28).
[2] Conjectural.

un petit meason, et si ascun va hors desglise et fist felonie et revient il serra la pur
auterz xl jours: quere sil ils serra accompt de jour de prinder deglise ou de jour
de confession de felonie. Et lez espirituell homez sont toutz estrange a cest grant
fait deo et ecclesie et pur ceo navont avantage: quere. <Lestatut est *quod habeat
omnia iura sua integra et>*[d] Si ascun clerk fue al esglise, sil ne demande un coroner il ne doit aver le benefice desglise, mez ne list a ascun lay home de luy traher
hors.

[LECTURE THREE]

Lestatut est *quod habeat omnia iura sua integra*: scilicet toutz plees que touchent
matrimonie ou testament ou ascun cremenall action. Mez si ij parsons font
debate pur dismez que amount al iiij[ter] partie lez parsons sueront al comen ley,
quar auterment lenherit[ans] dun dex peut estre empere.

[LECTURE FOUR: BENEFIT OF CLERGY]

Item *libertate* etc. peut estre entend que felons clerkes averont lour liverz, mez
si le ordinarie luy recu un que nest clerk lordinarie forfetera sez temperalties
a roy per W ij ca° […][1] et sil die que est clerk et ne responde al felone il avera
payn fort et dur, et si <soit>[i] begamuss naver son clerge: quere si lordenary
ne voill unques certifie etc., et home avera lesglise auxi pur treason come pur
felonie.

Hales, lector tempore quadragesime anno xj H viij, dit quod ecclesia Anglicana
ad plusours privilegez que ascun auter Esglise in le mond ad, quar en null terre
forsque ceo si un clerke ne soit [prist][2] soit deinz tonsure come nad benet al
meyns quil ne avera privilege de<sglise>[d] son liver.

[LECTURE FOUR: SANCTUARY]

Auxi un que occist auter per malice prepence navera benefice desglise et ceo fuit
le ley de dieu ut patet genesis. Et auxi comen laron navera esglise ut patet.

Auxi ceo covient estre esglise et nemi chapell, quar in lesglise chescun peut
venir a son plesor mez jeo ne bosign suffer ascun home de venir in mon chapell
forsque a mon plesour coment que jeo bury et baptize in ceo: tamen quere si un
peut estre evele de ceo ou nemi si le sacrament soit la present. Et fuit dit que si

---

[1] Blank in MS.
[2] Conjectural reading.

for a coroner he shall be immured in a small house. And if anyone goes out of the church and commits a felony and returns, he shall be there for another forty days: query if they shall be accounted from the day of taking sanctuary or the day of confessing the felony. And the spiritual men are strangers to this grant made *to God and the Church* and therefore they cannot take advantage [of it]: query. If any clerk flees to a church, and he does not demand a coroner he may not have the benefit of the church, but it does not lie to any lay man to draw him out.

[LECTURE THREE]

The statute is *that [the Church] shall have all her rights entire*: namely all pleas which touch matrimony or wills or any criminal action [on the part of a clerk]. But if two parsons dispute tithes which amount to the fourth part, the parsons shall sue at the common law, for otherwise the inheritance of one of them may be impaired.

[LECTURE FOUR: BENEFIT OF CLERGY]

Item *liberty* etc. may be understood that felonious clerks shall have their books, but if the ordinary receives someone who is not a clerk, he shall forfeit his temporalities to the king by Westminster II, c. [2], and if he says that he is a clerk and is [indicted] for felony he shall have *peine fort et dure*, and if he is a bigamist he shall not have his clergy: query if the ordinary does not wish to certify etc., and one shall have the church as well for treason as for felony.[1]

[John] Hales, reader in Lent 11 Hen. VIII,[2] says that the English Church has more privileges than any other Church in the world has, for in any land except this if a clerk is not a priest with a tonsure, as even an exorcist has, he shall not have the privilege of his book.[3]

[LECTURE FOUR: SANCTUARY]

Also one who killed another with malice aforethought shall not have the benefit of the church, and this was the law of God as it appears in Genesis.[4] And also a common thief shall not have the church as it seems.[5]

Also this must be a church and not a chapel, for in a church everyone may come at his pleasure but I do not have to allow any man to come into my chapel except at my pleasure, even though I bury and baptise there: however query if one may avail [himself] of this or not if the sacrament is present there. And it was said

---

[1] Chaloner is probably thinking of Westminster I, 3 Edw. I, c. 2 (*SR*, i. 28) though it does not discuss temporalities. *De Bigamis* 4 Edw. I, c. 5 (*SR*, i. 43).

[2] This was Hales's second reading in Gray's Inn in Lent 1520. See *Readers and Readings*, p. 32.

[3] A benet, or exorcist, was effectively the lowest of the seven clerical orders and the first to have a tonsure.

[4] Genesis 4: 12–14.

[5] See Helmholz, *Ius Commune*, pp. 34, 42, 67, 75–76.

ne soit tiel esglise ou chescun sacrament est minister que ne servera pur sanctuary, quar si soit dedicat saunz plus nad tiel privilege de sentuary. Et fuit dit que
leez walles del church3erd fuerent faits si lowe que chescun peut venir in ceo a
son plesour et al commencement lez grants dez privilegez fuerent pur corrager
homes esteant christen.[1]

Si un segnior licens son tenant de fair un cemetere de terres tenu de luy, quant
est fait le segnior navera ascun service, mez cest <rel>[d] [licence][2] est auxi fort
come reles per segnior al tenant del terre, et si apres lesglise soit dissolve, lordinary avera le terre et nemi le segnior: tamen quere et cest case est pris per cex
parollx *ecclesia anglicana libera sit* etc.

Si un home soit attaint de felonie et puis hape esglise il forjurera mez si [home][3]
soit atteint per verdit ou unfois abjure et revient il unquez <forjure>[d] abjure, quar
il ne abjura pur mesme le felone pur ceo quil unfois ad ceo confese et pur ceo il
ne peut ceo confese arer, et home unquez abjur sinon quil peut confese le felone
et pur auter felone il ne unquez abjure la quar unfois aient le benefite [*fo. 20v*]
benefite [*sic*] de Sanct Esglise et in lez casez ne list a home de luy traher hors
desglise. Mez est un bref in le regester que nul home don a eux maunger apres et
ceo est le murynge, come jeo entend, quar per Dominus Fenex ceux casez fueront
agre. Uncore home utlage de felonie et auxi feme utlage abjur[eront] quar la ils
purront confese le felonie, quar rienz est fait a ceo devaunt: issint dun …, quod
nota. Et auxi feme ne avera son clergye et uncore el abjur[era], quod nota. Mez
pur grand treson, heretik, Jue, ou home excommenge navera privilege desglise.
Mez pur petit [treson][4] home avera benefite desglise.

Et chescun home deinz le terre santify come charnel howys, frater, dortor,
ou tielx lieux queux sont occupy ove bons chosez avera mesme mesme [*sic*]
le privilege come lesglise ad. Mez si taveren, schope a vender merchandisez
ou meason de bordell hows et tielx que sont occupy oue peche etc., est per ceo
devenuz profayn arer, issint que in <eux>[i] <est>[d] nul avera sanctuary. Auxi
home avera sentury in lesstepel et sur lesglise, quar [cujus][5] est solum [eius][6]
est usque ad summum [vel][7] celum etc. Si un esglise soit suspend et ne soit santify deinz dex ans apres uncore ne peut prendre sentuary la, et ceo est le cause
que si un tavern etc. soit edify deinz le terre que fuit unfois sanctify, si con-
tenue ouster dex ans il est suspend a toutz entents espiritellx, uncore nest disolve
etc.: quod nota bien comen erudition, tamen quere si le donor donquez nentra in
ceo etc.

Dominus Fenex dit in toutz casez ou mort insue issint que est in juperde de
son vie, il forjurera, auter nemi, et que un demurera in lesglise tanquez coroner
vient, coment que ne vient per demi an ou entter an et que nest null muryinge etc.

---

[1] From here to bottom of page damaged.
[2] MS. reads lve or lue.
[3] Conjectural reading.
[4] MS. reads home.
[5] MS. reads cause.
[6] MS. reads eiusdem.
[7] MS. reads le.

that unless it is such a church where every sacrament is administered it does not serve as a sanctuary for if it is dedicated, without more, it has no such privilege of sanctuary. And it was said that the walls of the churchyard were made so low that everyone could go in it at his pleasure, and from the beginning the grants of privilege were to encourage Christian men.

If a lord licenses his tenant to make a churchyard of lands held of him, when it is made the lord shall not have any service, but this livery is as strong as a release for the lord to the tenant of the land, and if afterwards the church is dissolved, the ordinary shall have the land and not the lord: however query, and this case is taken by these words *the English church shall be free* etc.

If a man is attainted of felony and then gets hold of a church he shall forswear. But if he is attainted by verdict or once abjures and returns, he cannot abjure again, for he cannot abjure for the same felony because he had once confessed this, and therefore he may not confess it again, and a man never abjures unless he may confess the felony, and for another felony he never abjures, for he has once had the benefit of the Holy Church, and in these cases it does not lie to a man to draw him out of the church. But there is a writ in the *Register* that no man should give him food afterwards and this is the immuring, as I understand, for these cases were agreed by Lord Fyneux.[1] Still, a man outlawed for felony, and also an outlawed woman, [may] abjure, for there they may confess the felony, for nothing is made of this before: the same of a ..., which note. And also a woman shall not have her clergy and yet she shall abjure, which note. But for high treason, a heretic, a Jew, or an excommunicated man shall not have the privilege of the church. But for petty treason a man shall have the benefit of the church.

And every man within sanctified land, as a charnel house, frater, dorter or such places which are occupied with good things, shall have the same privilege as the church has. But if [sanctified lands are used for] a tavern, a shop to sell merchandise, or a bawdy house, and such places which are occupied with sin etc. [and] are by this become profane again, no-one shall have sanctuary in them. Also a man shall have sanctuary in the steeple and on the church, 'for whoever owns it, it is his to the highest or to heaven'. If a church is suspended and is not sanctified within two years afterwards, one cannot take sanctuary there, and this is the reason why if a tavern etc. is built within the land which was once sanctified, if it continues beyond two years it is suspended for all spiritual purposes, yet it is not dissolved etc.: which note well as common learning, however query if the donor then does not enter in it etc.

Lord Fyneux says in all cases where death follows so that he is jeopardy of his life he may forswear, otherwise not, and that one must remain in the church until the coroner comes, even if he does not come for a half year or an entire year, and that there is no immuring etc.

---

[1] Fyneux C.J. seems to be speaking at the reading. There is an extensive discussion of sanctuary dominated by Fyneux in *Pauncefote v. Savage*, Easter 1519 (Caryll, reports, ii. pp. 704–713).

[INTRODUCTION]

Quant le terre fuit estable apres le conquest le roy et son counsell veir que grandes misheifes fueront all comens lez queux lez grand homes recollier[ont] in un liver et donquez compele le roy deux granter sur son comen seall, quar a cest temps ne fuit ascun parlement. Et pur ceo que toutz lez segniors agre a ceo, coment que nc fuit forsque sur le seall le roy tantum uncore fuit tenuz que toutz homez fueront fueront [sic] liez a eux gerder. Mez donquez apres fuit consele que ne fuit reason que le roy mesme ou le roy et cez segniors fera actes que liera lez comens dell realme. Fuit ordene que parlement serra et que a cest viendra le roy, lez segniors, ij de chescun contie et deux de chescun borowe: lez queux ij de contie serra eslieu per lez comens del contie et lez ij del burghes, que fueront somons del contie, serra eslieu per lez comens del burght. Et le primer estatut fuit [52]¹ H[en.] 3 donques per Marlbrige fuit enact que magna carta serra estatut. Et si ne issint ust est fait ne fuit estatute a cest jour, quar coment que le roy et son counsel purrunt fair ordenauncez a lier chescun home uncore ceux ne sont estatutz, quar nul home nad remedi sil soit order encontre lordenaunce. Mez pur enforcer cest mesme carter fuit excomengment pronounce vers eux que offend etc. et ceo prove que ne fuit estatute,² quar a un estatut sont v chosez requisit ou auter nest estatut, scilicet que soit court le roy; le ijᵈ que soit pur le comen well; le 3 est lassent le roy; le 4 est lassent lez segniors; le vᵗ est lassent de comens, et si ascun de lez v choses faut nest estatut. Et pur ceo que magna carter faut ceux choses ne fuit estatut tanque marlbrige ceo fait estatut.

Donquez si estatut soit fait et est obscur serra construe per iiijᵒʳ voies, scilicet per le letter si ad sufficient in ceo; et si nad sufficient parolx donquez serra construe solonque lentenles dez fesours de ceo, quar si un estatut soit obscure et le parlement endure serra construe solonque lentent dez fesors et si soit dissolve donquez serra construe per lez justicez; auxi serra construe come ad este use coment que est contrariaunt as parolx come gerrante et assez in formdon est per equite de [statute]³; issint semble que per lexecution de ceo que lentents dez fesors de W2 fuerent que gerrantes et assez serra bar.

Donquez est a voir que fuit le mischeif devant le fesaunce destatut et queux chosez sont remedi per lestatut et queux chosez sont prisez per lequitie destatut et queux chosez remayn nient remedi per lestatut.

---

¹ MS. reads 50.
² In margin: 5 choses d… a fair estatute et coment estatut serra contrue. In a later hand.
³ MS. reading unclear.

[INTRODUCTION]

When the land was established after the conquest, and the king and his council saw that great mischiefs came to the commons, which the great men collected in one book and then compelled the king to grant them [a remedy] under his common seal, for at that time there was no parliament. And because all the lords agreed to this, even though it was only under the king's seal, still it was agreed that all men were bound to keep it. But then afterwards it was advised that it was not right that the king himself, or the king and his lords, should make acts which would bind the commons of the realm. It was [therefore] ordained that there should be a parliament and that the king, the lords, two of each county and two of each borough should come to it: the two of the county should be elected by the commons of the county and the two of the borough, who were summoned from the county, should be elected by the commons of the borough. And the first statute was 52 Hen. III, [when] by Marlborough it was enacted that Magna Carta should be a statute.[1] And if it had not been so made it would not be a statute today, for even though the king and his council could make ordinances to bind every man still these were not statutes, for no man had a remedy if things occurred against the ordinance. But to enforce this same charter excommunication was pronounced against those who offended etc., and this proves that it was not a statute, for in a statute five things are needed or otherwise it is not a statute, namely that it is the king's court; the second, that it should be for the common weal; the third is the king's assent; the fourth is the assent of the lords; the fifth is the assent of the commons: and if any of these five things are missing, it is not a statute. And because Magna Carta lacks these things it was not a statute until Marlborough made it a statute.

Then if a statute is made and it is unclear, it shall be construed in four ways, namely by the letter if it has sufficient [matter] in it; and if it does not have sufficient words then it shall be construed according to the intents of the makers of it, for if a statute is unclear and the parliament is still in session it shall be construed according to the intent of the makers, and if it is dissolved then it shall be construed by the judges; also it shall be construed as it has been used, even if this is contrary to the words, such as warranty and assets in formedon, [this] is by the equity of the statute: thus it seems by the execution of this that the intents of the makers of Westminster [I] were that warranties and assets should be a bar.[2]

Now we need to see what the mischief was before the making of the statute, and what things are remedied by the statute, and what things are taken by the equity of the statute, and what things remain without remedy by the statute.

---

[1] Marlborough, 52 Hen. III, c. 5 (*SR*, i. 20).

[2] Chaloner may be thinking of Westminster I, 3 Edw. I, c. 40 (*SR*, i. 36). Roger Yorke's Notebook has a version of this with three methods of construction where it is attributed to Fyneux C.J.K.B., as do Chaloner's Reports where it is also attributed to Fyneux and dated to 1516. *Reports, Hen. VIII*, i. 114, pl. 73 (Roger Yorke's notebook); *Reports, Hen. VIII*, ii. 278, pl. 1 (reports by Robert Chaloner). See Baker, *OHLE*, pp. 76–81 for a broader discussion of construction in this period and Fyneux's position.

[LECTURE TWO, VERSION TWO]

Et entent que lestatut dit *Ecclesia Anglicana* quere de chapel desglise de Irland, Cales, Galys etc.

Et coment que le roy grant pur luy et cez heires, uncore leirez le roy que adonquez fuit sont liez per plusors articlez in cest estatut, come dirra apres, et uncore ils ne sont nome per exprese parolx del heirez etc.

[Lecture Two, Version Two]

And even though the statute says *the English Church*, query of a chapel, of the church of Ireland, Calais, Wales etc.

And even though the king grants for him and his heirs, still the heirs of the king who then were bound by many articles in this statute, as I shall say afterwards, even though they are not named by express words as 'heirs' etc.

READING NINE

Magna Carta

[*fo. 14*] Il est bien conus a ceux que rien sache en croniquois que le Roy Johan fuit envie de ses subjectes pur son tirannie et cowardize en gwere, et auxi accursa de le Pope Innocentius pur ceo que il, de son auctoritie demeasne, ordena John, evesque de Norwiche, archevesque de Cauterbury et refuse Stephen Lancton que fuit appointe et electe per le pope[1] et per les [monks][2] del lew avandit. Durant quel perplexities nient sachant que de faire il ad darren submit luy mesme a les claves de Seint Esglise, et sur son absolucion il promis per son serement ceux trois choses: lun, que voilet restorer le clergie a lor estate et dignitie; secondment, il voilet restorer a le people les auncient liees [*sic*] et especyalment les leyes de St. Edwarde, que eux fuerit per eux especialment requises; et finalment, sil avoit fait injurie a ascun home[3] que il voloet recompencer et amender ceo. Mes apres, quaunt fuit require pur deliver les auncient leyes il ceo dedit, affirmant que le le [*sic*] promise et serement que [il][4] [a][5] fesoit adevaunt fuit pur dowt et duresse de gwere. Per cause de quel les piers move civill gwere encounter le roy et all darrein luy compella a Runnie meade en Oxon de condescende al peax lan 13 de son reigne, lou, al request de toute le realme, il escria un charter et appella ceo lestatut de <Roun>[d] Rownndade [*sic*].

Cest charter jeo mesme aye view et il differ en multes lewes de ca Magna Carta, eyant en ascuns [lewes][6] pluis et en ascuns mesme les choses et in auters lez choses que sont icy performer ne furent la forsque promis. Quar la restitution de les pledges de Scotland al Alexander, le Scottishe roy, que fuit la [purveiu][7] est icy omitte, et la promeshe concernant le disaforestation des terres, et que le roy naver prerogatyve des terres que il ad per reason descheat que fuit la forsque [promise][8] destre fait apres son pilgranage [*sic*] (quell il la apella susceptionem crucis) sue estre ore performe, et le estate que feme navera apelle dauter que son baron, que est contenus in cest estat, fuit auxi contenus la.

Pur le plus suer observans de cest estate il granta a la fyne de dit estatute que 25 barons serront eslies et sil face encounter eux que ilz aver ponishment del cause et distreignera ses chastellz, le quell issint que peut pluis melior apperer jee recita les parolx:

> Cum autem pro deo et ad emendationem regni nostri et ad melius sopiendam discordiam inter nos et barones nostros ortam hec omnia concessimus, volentes ea integra et firma stabilitate imperpetuum gaudere facimus et concedimus eis securitatem subscriptam: videlicet quod

---

[1] In margin: 166/3/*G*. [2] *G*. [3] In margin: 275/33 *G*. [4] *G*. [5] *Om. G*.
[6] *G. Gb* reads leves. [7] *G. Gb* reads prove. [8] *G. Gb* reads prius.

READING NINE

MAGNA CARTA

It is well known to those who know nothing from chronicles, that King John was disliked by his subjects for his tyranny and cowardice in war, and also cursed by Pope Innocent because he ordained John, bishop of Norwich, archbishop of Canterbury of his own authority and refused Stephen Langton, who was appointed and elected by the pope and by the monks of the aforesaid place. During these complexities, not knowing what to do, he at last submitted himself to the keys of the Holy Church, and on his absolution he promised by his oath these three things: first, that he would restore the clergy to their estate and dignity; secondly, he would restore to the people the ancient laws and especially the laws of St Edward, which were especially requested by them; and finally, if he had done injury to any man that he would make recompense and amend this. But afterwards, when he was required to deliver the ancient laws he refused, affirming that the promise and oath which he had made before was by doubt and duress of war. Because of this the peers moved civil war against the king, and in the end they compelled him at Runnymede in Oxfordshire [sic] to agree to peace in the thirteenth year of his reign, where, at the request of all the realm, he wrote a charter and called this the statute of Runnymede.

I have seen this charter myself and it differs in many places from Magna Carta, having in some places more and in others the same things, and in other places the things which are performed here were only promised there; for the restitution of the pledges of Scotland to Alexander (the Scottish king) which was provided there is omitted here; and the promise concerning the disafforestation of lands; and that the king would not have prerogative of lands that he has by reason of escheats, which there was only promised to be done after his pilgrimage (which he there called taking the cross), is now performed, and the statute that a woman shall not have an appeal for anyone except her husband, which is contained in this statute, was also contained there.

For the surer observance of this statute it grants at the end of the said statute that twenty-five barons shall be elected, and if [the king] acts against them that they shall have punishment of the cause and distrain his chattels. I shall recite the words so that it may appear more clearly:

> Since for God and for the improvement of our kingdom and to better allay the discord which has arisen between us and our barons we have granted all these concessions, wishing them to be enjoyed in their entirety with firm endurance for ever, we give and grant to [the barons] the following security: namely, that the barons shall choose any twenty-five barons of the

barones eligant 25 barones de regno quos voluerint qui debeant pro totis viribus suis observare tenere et facere observari pacem et libertates quas eis concessimus et presenti [*fo. 14v*] charta nostra confirmamus. Ita scilicet quod si nos vel iusticiarius vel ballivi nostri vel aliquis de ministris nostris in aliquo erga aliquem deliquerimus vel aliquem articulorum pacis aut securitatis transgressi fuerimus et dilectum ostensum fuerit quator de viginti quinque baronibus illi quatuor barones accedant ad nos vel iusticiarium nostrum si fuerimus extra regnum proponentes nobis excessum petent ut excessum illum sine delatione faciat emendari. Et si nos excessum illum non emendaverimus vel si fuerimus extra regnum et justiciarius non emendaverit infra tempus quadraginta dierum a tempore quo monstratum fuerit nobis vel justiciario nostro si extra regnum fuerimus predicti quatuor barones referant causam illam ad residuos de illis viginti quinque baronibus et illi viginti quinque barones cum communitate totius terrae nos distringent et contra nos ibunt omnibus modis quibus poterunt: scilicet per captionem castrorum nostrum terrarum et possessionum et aliis modis quibus poterunt donec fuerit emendatum per arbitrium eorum, salva persona nostra et reginae nostrae et liberorum nostrorum. Et cum fuerit emendatum intendent nobis sicut prius fecerunt. Et quicunque de terra voluerit juret quod ad omnia predicta exequenda parebit mandatis predictorum 25 baronum et quod gravabit nos pro posse cum ipsis. Et nos publice et libere damus licentiam jurandi unicumque jurare volenti.

Mes toute ceo [nient <obstant>[i]][1] il obteina de pope immunite de cest promis fait [<et morust>[i]][2] issint que le [people][3], dowtant ne cest chartes ne continua desier [que][4] le Roy Henry [<le tierce>[i]][5] ceo confirma. Per que [il][6] anno regni sui nono corrige, confirme, et amplifie ceo et done ceo de south le graund seale sur quel fuit apell [le][7] graund charter. Et puis al intent que peut estre in memorie[8] et mitte in usse, il fuit confirme per Roy Edward le i an de son reigne [25][9] per ladvise de son counsall adonsque a Lincolne, e a luy fuit quiunzun[10] [*sic*] graunte que est resite en le fine de cest estatute pur [son][11] confirmation et ouster graunte que celuy que enfreint cest estatute serroit excommenge. Finalment, per lestatut de Articuli super cartas et per 1, 2, 4, 5, 10, 14, [28,][12] 31, 36, 37, 38, [42,][13] 45,

---

[1] *G. Gb* reads mater.
[2] *G.*
[3] *G. Gb* reads pope.
[4] *Gb.*
[5] *G.*
[6] *G.*
[7] *G.*
[8] In margin: 338/20 *Gb.*
[9] *Om. G.*
[10] In margin: 338/20 *G.*
[11] *G.* reads ceo.
[12] *G.*
[13] *G. Gb* reads 48.

kingdom they wish who should with all their might observe and hold and cause to be observed the peace and liberties we have granted to them and confirmed by this our present charter. Then, if we or our justiciar, our bailiffs or any of our officials, offend in any respect against any man or break any of the articles of the peace or of this security and the offence is shown to four of the said twenty-five barons, those four barons shall come to us (or to our justiciar if we are outside the realm) to declare the transgression and petition that we make amends without delay. And if we have not corrected that transgression (or our justiciar if we are outside the realm) within forty days from the time at which the offence was shown to us (or to the justiciar if we are outside the realm), the aforesaid four barons shall refer the matter to the rest of the twenty-five barons and those twenty-five barons, together with the community of the whole land, shall then distrain us and go against us in every possible way: namely by seizing our castles, lands, and possessions, and in every other way they can until the offence has been corrected, in their judgment, saving only our own person and those of our queen and our children. And when it has been corrected they shall obey us as before. And anyone in the country who wishes to may take an oath to obey the orders of the twenty-five barons for the execution of all the previously mentioned matters and, with the barons, to distress us to the utmost of his power. And we publicly and freely give licence to swear to every one who wishes to take this oath.[1]

But notwithstanding all this, King John obtained immunity from this promise made, and died, so that the people, doubting that this charter should continue, desired King Henry III to confirm it. For which [reason] in the ninth year of his reign he corrected, confirmed, and amplified this and gave it under the great seal, for which reason it was called the great charter.[2] And then to the intent that it might be remembered and used, it was confirmed by King Edward I in the twenty-fifth year of his reign by the advice of his council, then at Lincoln, and he granted everything which is recited in the end of this statute in his confirmation, and further granted that anyone who breaks this statute shall be excommunicated.[3] Finally, by the statute of *Articuli super cartas*[4] and by 1,[5] 2, 4, 5, 10, 14, 28,

---

[1] Magna Carta (*SR*, i. 9–13). There are some small differences from the printed version.

[2] 1225 version: (*SR*, i. 22–25).

[3] 1297 version: (SR, i. 114–119). There is no mention of excommunication in the 1297 statute, but the bishops had issued a sentence of excommunication in 1225 against those who broke the reissue of that year (F. M. Powicke and C. R. Cheney eds., *Councils and Synods*, ii. part 1(Oxford, 1964), p. 138), as a possible alternative enforcement mechanism to the repugnant security clause. This was repeated in 1237 (Powicke and Cheney, *Councils*, p. 206), and intensified in 1253 (Powicke and Cheney, *Councils*, p. 477). The 1253 sentence of excommunication was republished through the second half of the century and took on the status of a statute: 37 Hen. III, (*SR*, i. 6). The reader seems to be drawing on this tradition rather than the text of the 1297 Magna Carta.

[4] 28 Edw. I (*SR*, i. 136).

[5] Actually 1 Edw. III, stat. 2, c. 1 (*SR*, i. 255).

et 50 <E[dw.] 2>[d] <E[dw.] 3>[i] cap. 1, et per 1, 2, stat 2, 5, 6, stat 1, stat 2, 7 et 12 R[ic.] 2. 1, 2, 4, 7, 9, 13 H[en.] 4 cap. 1, 4 H[en.] 5 ca 1° cest estatut est confirme et per lestat fait 42 E[dw.] 3 ca. 2 ordeigne est <ch>[d] que chescun acte de parliament fait enconter cest estat serroit voide si mult fuit le dit estat en observacon.

Capitulo 1: Magna Carta

[fo. 16] Concessimus deo: Ascuns entende que a cest jour tielx grauntes ne valt, quar a lour entent cest paroll *deo* nest person able a prender chose graunted:[1] 12 H[en.] 8, 10, Brudnell; 33 H[en.] 6, 22 Prisoit. Mes savant correction est a voier en nostre lyvers un paroll destre mise pur auter, et le done bon, come done fait fabrice talis acclesie [*sic*] est bone: 10 H[en.] 4, 19 4; Parkes 98g, et union fait collegio est bon [<par intendment mes nest argue sur cest parol>[i]]:[2] 6 H[en.] 7, 13; 10 H[en.] 7, 20; 12 R[ic.] 2, devise 27. Devise ecclesie Sant Andru de Holborne [et][3] le parson porte ex gravi <que non>[d] querela de ceo et recover. Et in auncient grauntes le sence fuit pluis toste consider que les parolz, et un paroll avott plus sens in luy a cest temps que 20 a ore. Et ici auxi notes que les parolx in estates que ne sont le substance de ceo ne <sss>[d] serront observes pro regula <ceo>[d] <come>[i] icy. Si les parolz de *concessimus deo* serront observes il seroit confirmation de tielx grauntes contrarie de quel est la ley. Et si viscount return mandamus ballivo ducatus il est bone[4] et cibien, come en tote ceux cases leglishe serra prise pur les parrishioners, le college pur les scollers, et le duchie pur le duke, cybien auxi en cest case *deo* peut estre prise pur divinis hominibus et deo servientibus.

Pro nobis et heredibus: sur ceo est de [estre][5] notez que si come quant comen person graunt anyute que il convient graunte ceo pur luy et ses heires (3 H[en.] 4 [fo.][6]) issint quant le roy graunt ascun chose il covient estre pur luy et ses heires (2 H[en.] 7 [fo.],[7] 10) mes quod serra dit intant que les sucessors sont omis et uncore serra [bone vers] les successors, quar coment que soit usurpor le graunte de le auter luy liera: 9 E[dw.] 4 [fo.][8] 5.

---

[1] Illegible marginal note and interlineation: *G.*
[2] *G.*
[3] *G. Gb* reads el.
[4] Illegible marginal note: *G.*
[5] *G.*
[6] *G.*
[7] *G.*
[8] *G. Gb* reads baners.

31, 36, 37, 38, 42, 45, and 50 Edw. III cap. 1,[1] and by 1, 2 stat. 2, 5, 6 stat. 1, 7 stat. 2, and 12 Ric. II[2] [and] 1, 2, 4, 7, 9, 13 Hen. IV, c. 1,[3] and 4 Hen. V, c. 1[4] this statute was confirmed and by the statute made 42 Edw. III, c. 2 it is ordained that every act of Parliament made against this statute shall be void as much as the said statute is being observed.[5]

CHAPTER 1: MAGNA CARTA

We have granted to God: Some argue that at this day such grants are worthless, for to their understanding this word *God* is not a person able to take a thing granted: 12 Hen. VIII, 10, Brudenell; 33 Hen. VI, 22, Prysot.[6] But, saving correction, it can be seen in our books that one word can be taken for another, and the grant is good, as a grant made 'to the fabric of such a church' is good: 10 Hen. IV, 19, 4; Parkes 98g,[7] and a union made 'with a college' is good by intention, but it is not argued on this word: 6 Hen. VII, 13; 10 Hen. VII, 20; 12 Ric. II, *devise* 27.[8] A devise to the church of St Andrew of Holborn and the parson brings *ex gravi querela* on this and recovers.[9] And in old grants the sense was sooner considered than the words, and one word had more sense in it at that time than twenty [words] now. And here also note that the words 'in estates', which are not the substance of this, are not observed as rules as here. If the words *we have granted to God* are observed it would be confirmation of such grants contrary to the law. And if the sheriff returns a *mandamus* to the bailiff of the duchy it is good and just as in all those cases the Church shall be taken for the parishioners, the college for the scholars, and the duchy for the duke, so also in this case *God* may be taken for the holy men and servants of God.

For us and our heirs: on this it is to be noted that just as when a common person grants an annuity, he must grant this for him and his heirs (3 Hen. IV fo.), in the same way when the king grants anything it must be for him and his heirs (2 Hen. VII, fo. 10), but that it shall be said even though the successors are omitted and yet it shall be good against the successors for even if there is a usurper, the grant of the other binds him: 9 Edw. IV, fo. 5.

---

[1] *SR*, i. 257, 261, 265, 275, 281, 349, 371, 378, 383, 388, 393, 396. The reader excludes 15 Edw. III (*SR*, i. 295) which also confirms Magna Carta.

[2] *SR*, ii. 1, 12, 17, 26, 32, 55. The reader excludes 3, 9 and 15 Ric. II (*SR*, ii. 13, 38, 78), which do not refer explicitly to Magna Carta but simply confirm statutes, and 8 Ric. II (*SR,* ii. 36) which does confirm Magna Carta.

[3] *SR*, ii. 111, 120, 132, 150, 159, 166.

[4] *SR*, ii. 196. This is the only time Henry V confirmed Magna Carta, and subsequent kings dropped the practice.

[5] 42 Edw. III, *rectius* c. 1 (*SR*, i. 388).

[6] Mich. 12 Hen. VIII (119 Selden Soc.), p. 37, pl. 1; YB Pas. 33 Hen. VI, fo. 22, pl. 22, though Littleton makes the point rather than Prysot.

[7] YB Mich. 10 Hen. IV, fo. 3, pl. 5: Perkins, *Profitable Booke*, fo. 98.

[8] YB Hil. 6 Hen. VII, fo. 13, pl. 2; YB Pas. 10 Hen. VII, fo. 19, pl. 7; fo. 20, pl. 12; Fitzherbert, *Devise*, 27 cited as Pas. 21 Ric. II.

[9] *Register*, fo. 244v. This is the case from Pas. 21 Ric. II cited above.

Ecclesia Anglicana libera sit. Liberum ad double entendment: un que null excomenge, [atteint,][1] utlage, ne villen serra receyve a les sacred orders. Et sur ceo ascuns ont prise occasion adire que si le segnior fait son villen prist que il serroit enfranchise (Britton fo. 79b): que le favour de libertie, le dignitie de Seint Esglish, et les parolz destatut sont cy fortes que solonsque ascuns est un villayne adire que membre de Sainte Esglise peut estre villin. Mes, come semble, il nest absurde que un villen soit priste: Littelton 37r. Et le segnior peut teuts foitz luy prinder si non que il soit al devine service ou en presence le Roye: 27 Fitzher p. 49. Mes quant fuit present lordinarie peut luy refuser: 14 H[en.] 7, 36. Et donsque quant le segnior ad luy fait daver cure, il nad luy enable de provider chose mes tant solement al opus le segnior quar il luy present solement et est lordinarie que done a luy le chose.

<Lauter signification de *liberum* est que ilz ne serra taxes ne mise en enquestes ne prist a les guerres ne chargable al wacches et gardes et que ilz aller tolle free et aver lor election franke.>[2] Mez uncore ilz paier dismes et primer profettes et lour temporalties serra en garde quar per generalz parolz chose [*fo. 16v*] que est de comon droit ne passa.[3]

[Il yad un][4] semble figure de speche in cel paroll *ecclesia*, si come fuit avant in le paroll *deo*, quar come Rolfe dit, il ne mise icy pro muris domo aut huiusmody, mes pur lentier esperituell Esglise: 8 H[en.] 5 execution 166, et pro ecclesiastic hominibus, et coment que un done al esglise de Saint Peters a Westm', ad estre bon pur ceo que labbot et convent prist, mes al paroche churche [nemi][5] pur ceo que nad corporation, si non pur personell choses: 12 H[en.] 7 fo. ultimo Fyneux. Uncore icye [est][6] myse [chescun][7] tiell esglise, issint que tout ceo que estre parle de senctuaries et tielz [serra][8] intend del esglise <soit metropolis cathedralis, conventualis, collegiates, hospitalis, parochialis, et capelle, mes oratorie ou chappell nient endowe ove sufficient living nest entend.

Quant a les homes de le Churche le priviledge personell extende a touts sont ilz deins [minores][9] [ordres] come hostianus, lector, exorcista, accolitus, ou [maiores][10] [ordres] come Subdiaconus, diaconus, presbiter.>[11] Illud auxi nota in ceo que il dit *Ecclesia Anglicana* coment lesglise Engliter differ des auters[12] quar le pollace [*sic*] devesque est sainctuarie in auters esglises icy, vel per auters esglises comen un misfesor et robber per le waye naver sanctuarie [Exod decret de immunitate][13] icy aver, et ilz accompt lan de dew de temp de novell mes nos de jour de nostre dame in Lent.[14]

---

[1] *G.*   [2] MS. reads sacerd.
[3] Underlined *G*. In margin: Libertas ecclesis quod sit: *G*.
[4] *G. Gb* reads Je jades.   [5] *G. Gb* reads nest.   [6] *G. Gb* reads que.
[7] MSS read prochun.
[8] *G. Gb* reads sans.
[9] MSS read maiores.   [10] MSS read minores.
[11] Underlined, *G*. In margin: ecclesis quod[?] modis intelligi potest de intentione huius statute[?] & modis, *G*.
[12] In margin: lou de ... ferra accompt per ecclesiam anglicanam, *G*.
[13] *G. Gb* reads ... decretal de Innocente.
[14] In margin: ... jus et libertas qualiter different, *G*.

The English church shall be free. Free has a double meaning: one, that no-one excommunicated, attainted, outlawed, or unfree shall be received in sacred orders. And on this some have taken occasion to say that if the lord makes his villein a priest that he shall be enfranchised (Britton f. 79b),[1] that the favour of liberty, the dignity of the Holy Church, and the words of the statute are so strong that according to some it is a villainy to say that a member of the Holy Church may be a villein. But, as it seems, it is not absurd that a villein may be a priest: Littleton 37r.[2] And the lord may always take him unless he is at divine service or in the king's presence: 27 Fitzherbert, p. 49.[3] But when he was presented the ordinary could refuse him: 14 Hen. VII, 36.[4] And then when the lord has caused him to have a cure, he has only enabled him to provide a thing to the use solely of the lord, for only he presents him, and it is the ordinary who gives him the thing.

The other meaning of *free* is that they shall not be taxed nor put on an inquest nor taken to war nor chargeable for watches and wards and that they shall go toll free and have their free election. But still they shall pay tithes and first fruits and their temporalities shall be in ward, for a thing which is of common right shall not pass by general words.[5]

This is a similar figure of speech in this word *Church*, just as it was before in the word *God*, for as Rolf said, it does not stand here for the walls of the building or such things, but for the entire spiritual Church (8 Hen. V, *execution* 166),[6] and for ecclesiastical men, and even though one gives to the church of St Peter's at Westminster, it is good because the abbot and convent took, but [a grant] to the parish church [is] not [good] because it is not a corporation, except for personal things: 12 Hen. VII, last folio, Fyneux.[7] Again here all such churches are meant, so that all those things which are said of sanctuaries and such things shall be understood of the church whether it is a metropolitan cathedral, conventual, collegiate, hospital, parish [or] chapel, but an oratory or a chapel not endowed with a sufficient living is not meant.

As for the men of the Church, the personal privilege extends to all of them whether they are within minor orders, such as doorkeeper, reader, exorcist, acolyte, or major orders such as sub-deacon, deacon, priest.[8] Also note there that it says *the English Church* even though the English Church differs from others, the palace of the bishop is a sanctuary in other churches and here it is not, in other churches a common misdoer and highway robber shall not have sanctuary [according to] the decretal of [Pope] Innocent, [but] here they have it, and they account the year of God[9] from the time of New [Year] but we [count it] from the day of Our Lady in Lent.[10]

---

[1] *Britton*, F. M. Nichols ed. (Washington, D.C., 1901), pp. 165–166.

[2] Sir Thomas Littleton, *Littelton tenures neuly imprinted in the yere of our Lord God, M.ccccc.xxxix* (London, 1539) [STC/1900:13] is the first edition I have found where the section on villeinage begins on fo. 37r. The passage in question is on fo. 42v (Book 2). Littleton, *Tenures*, 94.

[3] YB 27 Edw. III, Lib. Ass. fo. 140, pl. 49; Fitzherbert, *Villenage*, 18.   [4] YB Trin. 14 Hen. VII, fo. 28, pl. 2.

[5] This may be a reference to 26 Hen. VIII, c. 3 (*SR*, iii. 493–499), which moved the payments of first fruits and tenths to the crown rather than the papacy.

[6] YB Hil. 8 Hen. V, fo. 4, pl. 15; Fitzherbert, *Execucion*, 166.   [7] YB Trin. 12 Hen. VII, fo. 29, pl. 7.

[8] This issue comes up a number of times in *Standish's Case*: Caryll, reports, ii. 683–692.

[9] That is, *anno domini*.

[10] See *Decretales Gregorii IX*, 3.49.6, and Helmholz, *Ius Commune*, p. 34. This point is also raised in Readings D and Seven above, p. 26, n. 8 and p. 116, n. 32.

Jura integra et libertates illesas: *iura integra* et *libertates* differ que jus icy est prist pur esperitule jurisdiction come a tener ple de mariage, de dismes, de testamentes, de diffamation, de lesione fidei. De sembles liberties de Eglise sount in deux maner ou a lour terres ou a lour persons. *Libertates* sont sount [*sic*] prise pur le prerogative et dignitie de Saint Eglise, come que lour seyntuarie serra inviolate, que ilz avera le benefite de clergie que pust. Et toutz lour auters comodities et preemynances quelcunque soit des queux serra treit pluis playment sur lestatut articulie cleri.

Omnibus liberis hominibus: le signification de *liberum* ne icy prise cy stricte que il serra solement entend pur celuy que ne bound, mes il serra auxi prise cy stricte que est villen et nest de franke estate que il est enheritable a les loies et franke envers touts forsque son segnior et pur ceo nul foitz en ceux estatutes le sence de *liberum* est intend pur un ledge subiecte et pur ceo villen peut avers avantage de eux.

Has libertates. Multes choses sount recites apres in le estatut les queux ne sont liberties, come lou est dit que null alienera en mortmayne, [ou][1] que feme ne suera apele de auter mort que de son baron ou le roy navera les terres de home attaine ouster lan et jour: ceux ne sont liberties eins plustors un restreint de libertie. Sed quid dicemus serra liberties solement grauntes pur ceo que eux [sont solement nosmes ou ne serra lez autres choses graunte per ceo que eux][2] ne sont liberties.

Nest certes que especiall amble ne restreignera les generalz parolz en le bodie dun fait et pur ceo si jeo graunt a vous toutes les chattells que sont apres mentione[3] en mon fait et apres cibien enheritans est mise en le fait come chattellz ambideux passera quar coment il dit chattellz il ne dit chattellz solement et pur ceo ceux solement ne passera.

[1] *G.*
[2] *G.*
[3] In margin: nota cest counceypt ... ut ... forsque councept ... et nul ley, *G.*

Her rights entire and liberties inviolate: *her rights entire* and *liberties* differ, because right here is taken for spiritual jurisdiction, such as to hold pleas of marriage, of tithes, of testaments, of defamation, of *laesio fidei*. There are two such kinds of liberties of the Church, either for their lands or for their persons. *Liberties* are taken for the prerogative and dignity of the Holy Church, such as that their sanctuary shall be inviolate, or that they shall have the benefit of clergy, which they may. And all their other commodities and pre-eminences whatsoever are those which are treated more fully in the statute *Articuli Cleri*.[1]

To all freemen: the meaning of *free* is not here taken so strictly that it shall be solely understood as those who are not bound, but it shall be taken so strictly that if there is a villein not of free estate that he is inheritable by the laws and free against everyone but his lord, and for this reason at no time in these statutes is the sense of *free* understood for a liege subject, and therefore a villein may have advantage of it.

These liberties. Many things are recited after in the statute which are not liberties, as when it is said that no-one shall alien in mortmain, that a woman shall only sue an appeal of death for her husband, or the king shall not have the lands of an attainted man beyond a year and a day: these are not liberties, but rather a restraint on liberty. But what we shall call liberties are solely granted because they are solely named or shall not be the other things granted because they are not liberties.

[It is] not certain that a special preamble shall not restrain the general words in the body of a deed, and therefore if I grant to you all the chattels which are after mentioned in my deed and afterwards as well an inheritance is put in the deed as chattels both shall pass, for even though it says chattels it does not say only chattels and therefore not only chattels shall pass.

---

[1] 9 Edw. II (*SR*, i. 171–174).

READING TEN

INTRODUCTION

[*fo. 146*] The Commonwelthe of everye Contrie consisteth and dependethe upon three thinges: upon the kinge, the lawe and the people. Upon the kinge as the cheif governor; upon the lawe by the whiche the kinge doth governe; and upon the people which under the kinge, by the lawe, are rewled and governed. Which comonaltye being a bodye politique may verie fittlie be compared unto the naturall bodye of a man, viz. the kinge unto the heade, the lawe unto the hart, and the people unto all the rest of the partes of the bodie. Soe as the hart which is called *primum vivens*, the first that liveth, and hathe in it blod which it distributith emongst all the other members of the bodie whereby they are quickned and alive; even so in this bodie politique the lawe is *primum vivens*, the first liveinge thinge, havinge within it politique provision for the welth and profett of the people, which it importith aswell to the head as to the other members of the same bodie, whereby the whole bodie is nurished and mainteined. And even by sinewes the bodie of man is joined and knitt together, even so by the lawe, which takethe his name *a ligandi*, that is of buyndinge togather, the commonaltye beinge a politique bodie is tied and bound togather. And as a naturall bodie lackinge a hart is a deade bodie and not able to move or lyve, even so the comon welthe beinge a bodie politique without lawe cannot aptelie be called a bodie but is deade, being not able of it self orderlie to move or stirre.

Which thinge to prove unto youe at this time by storyes of forrene contryes I meane not forasmuch as our awne stories do plente fullie declare the same and especiallie seeing the statute of Magna Carta, which I meane by your patience and favours to read upon, doth give me occasion to speake thereof. And for your better understandinge herein I have thought good to shewe unto yow what disorder doth growe by the lacke of lawe and dewe execution of the same, and howe that for lacke of good lawes, great warres and discencion did growe within this realme betwext the kinge and his subjectes which was the onelie cause of the makinge of the foresaid statute. And therefore as concerninge the lacke of lawes in the comonaltie yt cannot be denyed but that contrie or comon wealthe that is not ruled by certaine lawes and provisions can never continewe any time in peace and order but shall always remaine [*fo. 146v*] from time to time in discorde and discention.

READING TEN

INTRODUCTION

The commonwealth of every country consists of and depends upon three things: upon the king, the law, and the people. [It depends upon] the king as the chief governor; upon the law by which the king governs; and upon the people who are ruled and governed by the law under the king. This commonalty, as a body politic, may very appropriately be compared to the natural body of a man, that is, the king [may be compared to] the head, the law to the heart, and the people to all the rest of the parts of the body. <So as the heart, which is called *primum vivens*, the first that lives, has within it blood which it distributes among all the other parts of the body, whereby they are quickened and alive, in the same way in this body politic <the law>[1] is *primum vivens*, the first living thing, having within it politic provision for the wealth and profit of the people, which it imparts to the head as well as to the other parts of the same body, whereby the whole is nourished and maintained. And just as by sinews the body of man is joined and knit together, so by the law (which takes its name *a ligandi*, that is of binding together) the commonalty, as a body politic, is tied and bound together.>[2] And as a natural body lacking a heart is a dead body and not able to move or live, so the commonwealth, as a body politic, without law cannot aptly be called a body but is dead, being unable to move or stir by itself in an orderly fashion.

   I do not mean to prove this to you at this time with stories of foreign countries, for our own stories do plentifully declare the same, and especially considering that the statute of Magna Carta, which I mean by your patience and favour to read upon, gives me occasion to speak of it. And for your better understanding of this I have thought it good to show to you what disorder grows by the lack of law and the due execution of the same, and how that, for lack of good laws, great wars and dissension grew within this realm between the king and his subjects, which was the single cause of the making of the aforesaid statute. And therefore, as concerning the lack of laws in the commonalty, it cannot be denied but that that country or commonwealth which is not ruled by certain laws and provisions can never continue [for] any [length of] time in peace and order, but shall always be periodically in discord and dissent.

---

[1] In Fortecue's text this is 'intentio populi'.

[2] This is an adapted translation of a section of Sir John Fortescue, *De Laudibus Legum Angliae*, ch. 13, originally published as *Prenobilis militis, cognomento Forescu [sic], qui temporibus Henrici sexti floruit, de politica administratione, et legibus ciuilibus florentissimi regni Anglie, commentaries* (*c*.1545), fo. 16r-v. The sentence which follows is quite different from Fortescue, and the paragraph as a whole is less coherent as the reader casts the law as both the heart and the sinews of the body, while Fortescue has the *intentio populi* as the heart, the law as the sinews, and the king as the head who cannot change the sinews.

For althoughe good men (which are but fewe in nombre in comparison to the wicked) would live orderlie and in quiet one with an other, yet those which are wicked and ungodlie would not do so, for that which doth bridle and stay wicked men for doinge amisse is onelie the lawe and the feare of punishment, accordinge to the sayinge of Horace: 'oderunt peccare mali formidine pene'. And therefore if correction be taken from the scholemaster what rule is like to be amongst the scholers; if punishment be taken from the maister what disorder is like to growe emongst the servantes; if lawe be taken from the prince, what tormoyle is like to growe emongst the subjectes. So that if yow once remove and take away the lawes, see (I beseiche yow) what doth streight steppe into the place thereof: surelie nothinge els but discorde, discention, breache of peace, lacke of justice, warres, bludsheade, and in the end the utter rewynne and subvertion of the comon welthe, so that without lawe we have nothinge but discorde and discention and by the meanes of lawes we have quyetnes and peace. For to make quyetnes and peace emongst men, lawes were first made and inventid and therefore Tullie in treatinge of lawes saithe 'a maioribus nostris nulla alia de causa leges sunt inventur, nisi ut suos cives in pace conservant.' Furthermore, Bracton, seeinge howe nedfull a thinge lawes are in a comon wealthe saithe 'si autem deceterunt leges, extreminabuntur iusticia nec erit qui justum faciat judicium.'

But to come nearer unto the matter and to shewe unto yow the particuler causes of the makeinge of this statute, first you shall understande that althoughe the lawes of this realme had contynued in this Iland many yeares before this statute was made (some of which lawes were made by Lucius sometyme kinge of this realme, some by Canutus, some by [*fo. 147*] St Edward the confessor, some by William Conquere and some by others) yet were the same lawes so out of use that as it semithe in the time of Kinge John, in whose time this statute of Magna Carta was made, there were almost none of the said aunctient lawes of this realme putt in use whereby the noubles and subjectes of this realme did fynd them selves much greivad, and did thinke that the kinge had thereby not onelie incrotched upon the libertyes of the Churche but also had otherwise done many wronges and iniuryes unto diverse of his subjectes contrarie to the said aunctient lawes of this realme. By the reason whereof great warres and discentyion did growe in this realme betwixt the foresaid kinge and his subjectes, which warrs in our croncules are called the barons warres. In which warres the kinge, beinge driven to great distresse, did desire to knowe what his said subjectes did require to have graunted of him unto them. Wherupon the nobilitie and others the subjectes of this realme, required of the said kinge three thinges: *1.* the first was that he would restore unto the clargie of this realme all suche dignetyes and priviledges as he had taken from them. *2.* Secondarelie that he would

For although good men (which are but few in number in comparison to the wicked) would live in an orderly way and in quietness with one another, yet those who are wicked and ungodly would not do so, for it is only the law and the fear of punishment which bridles and stays wicked men from doing amiss, according to the saying of Horace: 'bad men hate to sin out of fear of punishment'.[1] And therefore if correction be taken from the schoolmaster, what rule is likely to be among the scholars? If punishment be taken from the master, what disorder is likely to grow amongst the servants? If law be taken from the prince, what turmoil is likely to grow among the subjects? So that if you once remove and take away the laws, see (I beseech you) what immediately steps into their place: surely nothing else but discord, dissent, breach of the peace, lack of justice, wars, bloodshed, and in the end the utter ruin and subversion of the commonwealth, so that without law we have nothing but discord and dissent, and by the means of laws we have quietness and peace. For laws were first made and invented to make quietness and peace among men, and therefore Tully [Cicero] in treating of laws says 'laws were invented by our ancestors for no other reason than to keep their people in peace'.[2] Furthermore, Bracton, seeing how necessary laws are in a commonwealth, says ' if, however, laws fail, justice will be extirpated nor will there be any man to render just judgment'.[3]

But to come nearer to the matter and to show you the particular causes of the making of this statute, first you should understand that although the laws of this realm had continued in this island for many years before this statute was made (some of which laws were made by Lucius, sometime king of this realm, some by Canute, some by St Edward the Confessor, some by William the Conqueror and some by others), yet the same laws were so out of use that as it seems, in the time of King John, when this statute of Magna Carta was made, there were almost none of the said ancient laws of this realm put in use, whereby the nobles and subjects of this realm found themselves much aggrieved, and thought that the king had thereby not only encroached on the liberties of the Church but had otherwise done many wrongs and injuries to various of his subjects contrary to the said ancient laws of this realm. For this reason great wars and dissents grew in this realm between the aforesaid king and his subjects, which wars in our chronicles are called 'the baron's wars'. In which wars the king, being driven to great distress, desired to know what his said subjects required him to grant to them, whereupon the nobility and other subjects of this realm required three things of the king: *1*. the first was that he would restore to the clergy of this realm all such dignities and privileges as he had taken from them. *2*. Secondly, that he would

---

[1] Correctly 'Oderunt peccare boni virtutis amore, Oderunt peccare mali formidine poenae': Good men hate to sin out of love of virtue; bad men hate to sin out of fear of punishment. The first line is Horace, *Epistulae* i. xvi. 52. The second line seems to be a medieval addition, but the couplet is quoted in *Bracton*, ii. 20.

[2] This appears to be a rough paraphrase of Cicero, *De Inventione*, i. 68.

[3] Correctly 'Si autem arma defecerint contra hostes rebelles et indomitos, sic erit regnum indefensum: si autem leges, sic exterminabitur iustitia, nec erit qui iustum faciat iudicium': 'If arms fail against hostile and unsubdued enemies, then will the realm be without defence; if laws fail, justice will be extirpated nor will there be any man to render just judgment.' *Bracton*, ii. 19.

restore unto the people there auncient lawes and customes, and especially the lawes of St Edward the Confessor, who was the last kinge but one before the conquest. *3.* Thirdlie that whereas he had done diverse injuries unto diverse of his subjectes that he would speidelie reforme and redresse the same and give unto everye one of them recompence for the wronges done unto them. Wherupon the kinge did make unto his subjectes a charter at a place which is called Rounde Meade in the countye of Oxforde [*sic*], calleinge at that tyme the charter of Rownd maide, in which [some] of the auncient lawes of this realme were mentioned, and diverse of them augmented and inlarged, as by the same charter maye appeare.

And after that the said charter in the lij yeare of Kinge Henrye the third was made a statute and a generall lawe to contynue for ever as may appeare by the statute of Marlebridge cap. quinto made in the tyme of the said [*fo. 147v*] kinge. The like maye appeare in the tyme of Edward the <sixte>ᵈ first and Edward the thirde and in the tyme of other kinges that have lived sythence that tyme. Furthermore, this charter was thought so necessarie for the comonwelth of this realme that in the tyme of Kinge Edward the first a generall curse was pronownced by all the bushopps of England against such as should breake the great charter.

I haveinge more shortlie showid unto you the cause of the making of this charter, I will (as it were by the waye, before I come to the exposition and opneinge of the same) note unto you one thinge in the makinge thereof to the which as it semeth our forfathers have had great regard in tymes past: that is that they in all there statutes and provisions have have [*sic*] first sought principallie to provide for those thinges which are for the glorie of God and after that to provide for the comonwelth accordinge to the sayeinge of our saviour Christ 'Inprimis querite regnum dei, et hec omnia adijcientur vobis': first seke the kingdome of God, and then all thinges nedefull shalbe given unto you. Which matter (that it maye more manefestlie appeare unto you) I will shewe you what I do fynde in the auncient lawse of this realme concerninge the same Kinge Canutus in his parliament holden at Winchester. After sondrie lawes and ordynances made towchinge the faithe (receveinge of the comunion, the forme of baptisme, fastinge, and <saith>ᵈ suche like matters of religion), in the ende thereof saithe this 'jam sequitur institutio legum secularum': nowe followeth an order for temporall lawes. Also in a parliament holden by William Conquerer it is wrytten thus: 'rex quia vicarius summi regis est ad hoc constituitur ut regnum et populum domini, et super omnia sanctam ecclesiam regat et defendat': the kinge, for that he is the vicarr of the hiest kinge, is therefore appointed to this [*fo. 148*] purpose, that he should rule and defend the kingdome and people of the lord and first and above all thinges the Holie Churche.

restore to the people their ancient laws and customs, and especially the laws of
St Edward the Confessor, who was the last king but one before the conquest. *3.*
Thirdly, that since he had done various injuries to various of his subjects, that he
would speedily reform and redress the same, and give every one of them recompense for the wrongs done to them. Whereupon the king made a charter for his
subjects at a place called Runnymede in the county of Oxford [*sic*], calling [the
charter] at that time the charter of Runnymede, in which some of the ancient laws
of this realm were mentioned, and various of them augmented and enlarged, as
appears in the same charter.

And afterwards, in the fifty-second year of King Henry III, the said charter was
made a statute and a general law to continue forever, as appears by the statute of
Marlborough, c. 5, made in the time of the said king.[1] A similar [confirmation]
appears in the time of Edward I and Edward III, and in the time of other kings
that have lived since then.[2] Furthermore, this charter was thought so necessary
for the commonwealth of this realm that in the time of King Edward I a general
curse was pronounced by all the bishops of England against such as should break
the great charter.[3]

Having more briefly showed you the cause of the making of this charter, I will
(by the way as it were, before I come to the exposition and beginning of the same)
note one thing in the making of it for you, to which, as it seems, our forefathers
have had great regard in times past: that is that they, in all their statutes and provisions, have first sought principally to provide for those things which are for the
glory of God, and after that to provide for the commonwealth, according to the
saying of our saviour Christ '*Inprimis querite regnum dei, et hec omnia adjicien-
tur vobis*': first seek the kingdom of God and then all necessary things shall be
given unto you.[4] [Concerning] which matter (that it may more clearly appear to
you) I will show you what I find in the ancient laws of this realm concerning the
same King Canute in his parliament held at Winchester. After sundry laws and
ordinances made touching the faith (receiving of the communion, the form of bap-
tism, fasting, and suchlike matters of religion), at the end it says this: '*jam sequitur institutio legum secularum*': now follows an order for temporal laws.[5] Also, in
a parliament held by William the Conqueror it is written thus: '*rex quia vicarius
summi regis est ad hoc constituitur ut regnum et populum domini, et super omnia
sanctam ecclesiam regat et defendat*': the king, because he is the vicar of the highest king, is therefore appointed to this purpose, that he should rule and defend the
kingdom and people of the lord, and first and above all things the Holy Church.[6]

---

[1] Marlborough, 52 Hen. III, c. 5 (*SR*, i. 20).
[2] See the Table of Statutes, below, for later confirmations.
[3] 37. Hen. III (*SR*, i. 6).
[4] Matthew 6: 33.
[5] *The Laws of the Kings of England from Edmund to Henry I*, A. J. Robertson ed. and trans. (Cambridge, 1925), p. 175.
[6] *Leges Edwardi Confessoris* c. 17, Bruce O'Brien ed., in Bruce O'Brien, *God's Peace and King's Peace: The Laws of Edward the Confessor* (Philadelphia, 1999), p. 174. *Rectius* 'Rex autem, quia uicarius summi Regis est, ad hoc constitutus est, ut regnum et populum Domini, et super omnia sanctam eccle-siam regat et defendat.'

Furthermore you shall understande that as everye man ether is or ought by the lawes of this realme, after he be of the age of xij yeares, be sworne unto the prince, so the prince in his coronation is sworne unto his people, in which othe the prince is first sworne to see unto and provide for those thinges that are for the glorie of God before any thinge towchinge the comon welth, theffecte of which othe is conteyned in theis wordes followinge: 'debet enim rex in coronatione sua in nomine Jesu Christi prestito sacramento hec tria promittere populo sibi subjecto: In primis se esse precepturum et pro viribus operem impensurum, ut ecclesie dei et omni populo Christiano vera pax, omni suo tempore observetur: Secundo ut rapacitates et omnes iniquitates omnibus gradibus interdicat: Tertio ut in omnibus judicijs equitatem precipiat et misericordiam, ut indulgeat ei suam misericordiam clemens, et misericors deus; et ut per justitiam suam firma gaudeant pace universi.' By which it maye appeare that the first thinge that the kinge by his othe is bound unto is to manteyne the peace of the Churche; seconderelie, to punishe oppressions and wronges emongst all degrees, and thirdlie and lastlie, that he do justice with mercye.

And as by their examples which I have here rehearsed unto you it maye appeare that our forfathers have in all theire doinges had a cheif regard to prefarr matters concerninge God and the Churche before any other thinge which towched or concerned the comonwelth, so in this estatute of Magna Carta the Churche of God was first remembred and provided for before any other thinge which did concerne the Comonwelth, as may appeare by the wordes of the said statute: 'In primis concessimus deo et hac presenti charta nostra confirmavimus pro nobis et heredibus nostris imperpetuum quod Ecclesia Anglica libera sit et habeat omnia jura sua integra et libertates suas illesas': first we have granted to God, and by this our present charter have confirmed for us and our heires forevermore, that the Churche of England shalbe free and shall have all her hole rightes and liberties inviolable. And this muche as concerninge the makinge of this statute etc.

Lecture One

[fo. 148v] Inprimis concessimus deo. 1. Sur ceux parols, per vostre patience, jeo entende a cest temps a monstre a vous coment en ancient temps ceux parols fuerent bone nosme de purchaise en grauntes faitz per le roy ou en grauntes faitz per comen persons, coment que nul certene person a que le graunt serra fait fuit nosme en le graunte. Si a ceo temps le roy ad graunte per ses lettres patentz un maner *deo*, sans auter certayntye de nosme, et lez ditz lettres pattentz ount estre deliver a un prior, per ceo il et ses successorres averont fee symple en ceo maner. Issint si soit un parson de Dale et a ceo temps le roy ad graunte terre ou tenementz deo et ecclesie de Dale, ceo fuit un bon graunte al parson et a ses successors.

Si a ceo temps un ad devise terre deo et ecclesie de Dale, a que temps fuit un parson la, et puis un viccar est endowe et le parsonage <ap>[i] <im>[u]propriat a

Furthermore you shall understand that as every man either is or ought by the laws of this realm to be sworn to the prince once he is 12 years old, so the prince in his coronation is sworn to his people, in which oath the prince is first sworn to see to and provide for those things which are for the glory of God before anything touching the commonwealth, the effect of which oath is contained in these words following: *debet enim rex in coronatione sua in nomine Jesu Christi prestito sacramento hec tria promittere populo sibi subjecto: In primis se esse precepturum et pro viribus operem impensurum, ut ecclesiae dei et omni populo Christiano vera pax, omni suo tempore observetur: Secundo ut rapacitates et omnes iniquitates omnibus gradibus interdicat: Tertio ut in omnibus judiciis aequitatem praecipiat et misericordiam, ut indulgeat ei suam misericordiam clemens, et misericors deus; et ut per justitiam suam firma gaudeant pace universi.*[1] By which it appears that the first thing that the king is bound to by his oath is to maintain the peace of the Church; secondly, to punish oppressions and wrongs amongst all degrees, and thirdly and lastly, that he should do justice with mercy.

And as by their examples which I have here rehearsed to you it may appear that our forefathers have had in all their doings a chief regard to prefer matters concerning God and the Church before any other thing which touched or concerned the commonwealth, so in this statute of Magna Carta the Church of God was first remembered and provided for before any other thing which concerned the commonwealth, as may appear by the words of the said statute: '*In primis concessimus deo et hac presenti charta nostra confirmavimus pro nobis et heredibus nostris imperpetuum quod Ecclesia Anglica libera sit et habeat omnia jura sua integra et libertates suas illesas*': first we have granted to God, and by this our present charter have confirmed for us and our heirs forevermore, that the Church of England shall be free and shall have all her whole rights and liberties inviolable. And this much concerning the making of this statute etc.

LECTURE ONE

First we have granted to God. 1. On these words, by your patience, I intend at this time to show to you how in olden times these words were a good name of purchase in grants made by the king, or in grants made by common persons, even though no certain person to whom the grant is to be made was named in the grant. If in those times the king granted a manor *to God* by his letters patent, without any other certainty of name, and the said letters patent were delivered to a prior, he and his successors should thereby have fee simple in this manor. Likewise if there is a parson of Dale and at that time the king granted lands or tenements 'to God and the church of Dale', this was a good grant to the parson and his successors.

If at that time one had devised land 'to God and the church of Dale', at which time there was a parson there, and then a vicar was endowed and the parsonage

---

[1] *Bracton*, ii. 304.

un abbey, et puis le devisor moruste, le abbot et ces successors averont ceo terres come parson et nemi le viccar. Mes si en ceo caise avant le mort le devisor le parsonage impropriat ad estre graunt a un comen person et a ses heires, le parson <nemi>ᵈ ne le viccar prenderont riens pur ceo devise. Mes si le devise ad estre fait apres le appropriation, le viccar et ses successors prenderont per force de ceo devise et nemy le parson.

Un seisi del moitie de un manor en Dale a ceo temps devisa toutz ses terres et toutes en Dale deo et ecclesie de Dale, puis il purchaset lauter moitie del maner et morust: per ceo le parson de Dale avera forsque le moitie de ceo maner et le heire le devisor avera le auter moitie. Mes si puis le devise fait en ceo cense et avant le moitie le devisor, le devisor ad estre disseissi del entire manner et morust avant reentree, le parson navera ascun parte de ceo per force de ceo devise. [*fo. 149*] Si a ceo temps graunt ad estre fait deo et ecclesie de Dale et al temps del graunte nest tiel ecclesie mes puis est fait, taile graunt est voide.

Le parson de un esglise morust et en temps de vaccation graunt est fait deo et ecclesie de Dale, et puis un parson est fait, le graunt est voide et le parson et ses successors prenderont reins [*sic*] per ceo. Mesme le ley est <se>ᵈ si parson fait admit et institut et avante induction grant est fait deo et ecclesie de Dale et puis il est induct, cest grant est voide. Mes si a ceo temps devise ad estre fait deo et ecclesie de Dale et al temps del devise nest tiel ecclesia, mes avant le mort le devisor tiel ecclesia est fait, ceo devise est bone. Si a ceo temps un ad fait grant del terre deo et ecclesie de Dale et al temps del graunt lesglise est en edefyinge, le graunt est bone si fuit un parson de Dale a ceo temps. Si a ceo temps ad estre un parson de esglise de Dale et le esglise eschewe per tempest et avant quil est reedefie graunt est fait deo et ecclesie de Dale, ceo est bone graunte al parson et a ses <he>ᵈ successors. Si a ceo temps un que ad 100 acres de terre en Dale grauntest deo et ecclesie 10 acres de terre en Dale, cestye que est parson en Dale a ceo temps morust avant quil ad fait elleccion que x acres il voit aver, le successor del parson aver reins per force de ceo graunte. Mes si en ceo cause liverye et seisin ad estre fait al parson en un parte des ditz terre en Dale, le parson avera x acres en ceo lewe ou liverye fuit fait.

Lecture Two

2. Jeo avis monstre a vous en mon darren lecture coment en auncient temps ceux parols *concessimus deo* fueront bon nosme de purchase et en tant que eux parols done occasion daver plus parle deux que fuit parle en le darren lecture ore jeo monstre a vous, per vostre patiens, ottre sur mesm les parols et sur auters parols a mesm le effecte: que maner de graunte faite en auncient temps fueront tenus pur bone et que nemy.

impropriated to an abbey, and then the devisor died, the abbot and his successors shall have these lands as parson and not the vicar. But if in this case before the death of the devisor the impropriated parsonage had been granted to a common person and to his heirs, neither the parson nor the vicar should take anything by this devise. But if the devise had been made after the appropriation, the vicar and his successors would take by force of this devise and not the parson.

One seised of the moiety of a manor in Dale at this time devised all his lands and all in Dale 'to God and the church of Dale', then he purchases the other half of the manor and dies: by this the parson of Dale shall only have the half of this manor, and the devisor's heir shall have the other half. But if after the devise made in this sense and before the moiety of the devisor, the devisor was disseised of the entire manor and died before re-entry, the parson shall not have any part of this by force of this devise. If at this time a grant is made 'to God and the church of Dale', and at the time of the grant there is no such church, but then it is built, such a grant is void.

The parson of a church dies and during the vacancy a grant is made 'to God and the church of Dale', and then a parson is made, the grant is void and the parson and his successors shall take nothing by this. The law is the same if the parson is admitted and instituted, and before induction a grant is made 'to God and the church of Dale' and then he is inducted, this grant is void. But if at that time a devise is made 'to God and the church of Dale', and at the time of the devise there is no such church, but before the death of the devisor such a church is built, this devise is good. If at that time one had made a grant of land 'to God and the church of Dale', and at the time of the grant the church was being built, the grant is good if there was a parson of Dale at that time. If at that time there was a parson of the church of Dale and the church fell down in a storm, and before it was re-built a grant was made 'to God and the church of Dale', this is a good grant to the parson and to his successors.[1] If at that time someone who has 100 acres of land in Dale grants 'to God and the church' ten acres of land in Dale [and] the parson of Dale at that time dies before he had chosen which ten acres he wished to have, the successor of the parson shall have nothing by force of this grant. But if in this case livery and seisin had been made to the parson in a part of the said lands in Dale, the parson shall have ten acres in that place where livery was made.

Lecture Two

2. I have shown you in my last lecture how in olden times these words *we have granted to God* were a good name of purchase, and inasmuch as these words give occasion to speak more about them than was said in the last lecture, now I shall show you, with your patience, more on the same words and on other words to the same effect: what kind of grant made in ancient times was held good and what was not.

---

[1] Damage done by a storm is a standard example: see Reading D, p. 28, above, for its use in an escape from prison, and *Combe* v. *Gargrave* (1455): *The Case of the Marshalsea. Baker and Milsom*, pp. 261–262.

Si a ceo temps le roy ad graunte terre deo et ecclesie de Dale ou sont ij esglisez de Dale et le roy est patron de nul de eux, le parson de ceo esglise prendera per le graunt a quele entent le roy fuit a graunter et ceo gist in averment. [fo. 149v] Mes si en ceo case le roy fuit patron del un esglise et nul tiel speciall averment poit estre fait, ceo esglise prender de que il mesm est patron.

Si a ceo temps le roy ad fait lease pur vie per ses lettres patentes rendront rent deo et ecclesie de Dale, pur ceo le parson de Dale poit distreyne pur ceo rent. Mes si un comen person ad fait tiel lease et reservation le parson de Dale prendra nemi per ceo.

Si a ceo temps le roy ad grante a un prior quil serra cye free en son meson come il fuit en son crowne, ceo dischargera le prior de corodies et pencions coment que le meson soit del fundation le roy. Issint si a ceo temps le roy ad graunt a un prior quil serra cye free en son meson 'as herte can think or tongue can speake', ceo dischargera le prior de pencions et corodies coment que ils ne sont especialment nosme en le pattentes.

Si a ceo temps graunt des terres ad estre fait fabrice tils ecclesie ceo serra bon graunt ad parson et a ces successores. Si a ceo temps done ad estre fait des terres al parishoners de tiel parishe ceo graunt ad estre voide. Mes si a ceo temps done des biens ad estre fait al parisheoners de Dale ceo ad esse un bone done. Si a ceo temps graunt de terre ad estre fait deo et ecclesie de Dale, donques la etient un parson de Dale, et liverye est fait al John at Style pur ans et John at Style ad entre durant le vie le parson, donques le successor le parson prendera per force de ceo graunte.

Si a ceo temps un parson de [Dale] disseize John at Style de un carewe de terre et puis John at Style per fait ad release al parson tout son droit, le parson et ses successors averont ceo terre et nemy le parson et ses heires. Mes si en ceo cayse le parson al temps del disseizen ad clayme ceo terre a luy et a ses heires et puis tiel release est fait a luy, le parson et ses heires averont ceo terre et nemy ses successors.

[fo. 150] Si a ceo temps terre ad estre devise al John at Style pur vie le remayndre ecclesia sancti Clementes des danes, ceo fuit un bon devise en remaynder al parson de saint Clementes et a ses successors si le parson soit en vie al temps del mort del devisor, coment quil ne soit en vie al temps del morte le tenaunte pur vie.

LECTURE THREE

3. Jeo avis monstre a vous en mon daren lecture coment en auncient temps eux parolx, *concessimus deo*, fueront bone nosme de purchase. Et ore jeo monstra a vous, per vostre patience, que coment que tiels graunts faits en auncient temps sont destre alowe si sont pleade a cest jour uncore si tiels graunts fueront faitz a cest jour ils fueront voide, et ottre jeo monstra a vous quex choses sont necessaire en grauntes a cest jour.

If at that time the king granted lands 'to God and the church of Dale' where there are two churches of Dale and the king is patron of neither of them, the parson of that church shall take by the grant what the king intended to grant, and this lies in averment. But if in this case the king was patron of one of the churches and no such special averment could be made, that church shall take of which he himself is patron.

If at that time the king had made a lease for life by his letters patent rendering rent 'to God and the church of Dale', by this the parson of Dale may distrain for this rent. But if a common person had made such a lease and reservation the parson of Dale should take nothing by this.

If at that time the king had granted to a prior that he shall be as free in his house as [the king] was in his crown, this shall discharge the prior of corrodies and pensions, even if the house is of the king's foundation. Thus if at that time the king had granted to a prior that he shall be as free in his house 'as heart can think or tongue can speak', this shall discharge the prior of pensions and corrodies even if they are not specially named in the [letters] patent.

If at that time a grant of lands was made to the fabric of such a church, this shall be a good grant to the parson and his successors. If at that time a grant was made of lands to the parishioners of such a parish this grant was void. But if at that time a grant of goods was made to the parishioners of Dale this would have been a good grant. If at that time a grant of land had been made 'to God and the church of Dale', there being then a parson of Dale, and livery is made to John at Style for years, and John at Style had entered during the life of the parson, then the parson's successor shall take by force of this grant.

If at that time a parson of Dale disseised John at Style of a hide of land, and then John at Style by deed had released all his right to the parson, the parson and his successors shall have this land and not the parson and his heirs. But if in this case the parson at the time of the disseisin had claimed this land to him and to his heirs and then such a release was made to him, the parson and his heirs shall have this land and not his successors.

If at that time land had been devised to John at Style for life the remainder 'to the church of St Clement Danes', this was a good devise in remainder to the parson of St Clement's and to his successors if the parson is alive at the time of death of the devisor, even if he is not alive at the time of death of the tenant for life.

Lecture Three

3. I have shown you in my last lecture how in ancient times these words, *we have granted to God*, were a good name for purchasing. And now I shall show you, with your patience, that even though such grants made in ancient times are allowed if they are pleaded today, still if such grants were made today they would be void, and furthermore I shall show you what things are necessary in grants today.

Si a cest jour graunte soit fait deo et ecclesie de Dale tiel graunte est voide et le parson de Dale prendra riens per ceo, et uncore en auncient temps ceo fuit un bone graunte. En grauntes destre faits a cest jour iiij choses sont requisit a feere ceo un perfecte graunt, sestasaviour: <1>ⁱ grauntor, <2>ⁱ graunte, chose destre graunte, et <4>ⁱ parolx a feere un graunt: et si ascun deux faulx le graunt est voide.

Si feme covert ou monke graunt terre al parson de Dale et a ses successors ceo est un void graunt. Issint si un infant ou un que est lunatick graunt rent charge a un parson et a ses successors ceo est un void graunt, car en ceux caises nest sufficient grantor.

Si John at Style graunt terre al John at Dale et a son feme et a lour heires et fist livery al John at Dale et a ceo temps John at Dale nad fem mes prist fem apres, ceo est un void graunt. Si terre sont lesse pur vie, le remaynder al droit heires del John at Style, leassee pur vie morust, John at Style estient en vie et puis John at Style ad issue et morust ceo issue prendera reins per force de ceo graunt, car nest sufficient graunte.

[*fo. 150v*] Le parson de Dale morust et en temps de vacation un entrast come parson sans admission et institution et rent est graunt a luy et a ses <heires>ᵈ successors et il morust, son successor prendra reins per ceo. Mes si le parson de Dale soit disseize et otta del parsonage, et durant le disseizen rent est graunt a luy et a ses successors, ceo est bone graunt et ses successors prenderont pur ceo.

Si soit seignor et tenaunt, le segnor grauntast le garde del fitz son tenaunte durant le vie son tenaunte et puis son tenaunt morust ceo est un void graunte. Issint si jeo lease terre al John at Style pur ans per paroll, et puis jeo purchase les ditz terres, ceo est void lease. Mes si tyel leas fuit fait per fait indent le lesse poit entre puis le purchase.

John at Style est seizee de un rent in fee et il grauntast ceo apres son mort a John at Dale et a ses heires, ceo est void graunte. Mes si John at Style ad graunte rent horse de son terre a comenser apres son mort ceo fuit un bon graunte. John at Style est possesse de certayne terres pur tearme des ans en Dale et grauntast toutes ses terres en Dale a aver et tener al grauntee, son interest et tearme en eux pur tout des ans come seront expende apres le mort le grauntor: ceo est un void graunte car les parols ne sont sufficient a feere graunte. Terre est graunt al John at Style per fait a aver et tener a luy et al John at Dale et a lour heires, et liverye et seizen est fait al John at Style secundum formam carte, ceo est un bone graunte al John at Style et void al John at Dale.

Lecture Four

[*fo. 151*] 4. En mon daren lecture jeo avis monstre a vous coment en auncient temps eux parolx *concessimus deo* fueront bone nosme de purchase et que tielx auncient grauntes sont destre alowe si sont plead a cest jour et que si tielx grauntes sont faites a cest jour que ils sont voide. Et auxi jeo adonquez monstre a vous que choses sont necessaire en grauntes a cest jour. Et ore jeo monstra

If today a grant is made 'to God and the church of Dale' such a grant is void and the parson of Dale shall take nothing by it, and yet in ancient times this was a good grant.

In grants made today four things are requisite to make this a perfect grant, that is to say: 1. a grantor, 2. a grantee, [3.] a thing to be granted, and 4. words to make a grant: and if any of them are missing the grant is void.

If a feme covert or a monk grants land to the parson of Dale and to his successors, this is a void grant. Likewise if a child or a lunatic grants a rent charge to a parson and to his successors, this is a void grant, for in these cases there is not a sufficient grantor.

If John at Style grants lands to John at Dale and to his wife and to their heirs and makes livery to John at Dale, and at this time John at Dale does not have a wife but takes a wife afterwards, this is a void grant. If land is leased for life, the remainder to the right heirs of John at Style, [and the] lessee for life dies with John at Style alive, and then John at Style has issue and dies, this issue shall take nothing by force of this grant, for it is not a sufficient grant.

The parson of Dale dies and during the vacancy one enters as parson without admission and institution, and a rent is granted to him and to his successors and he dies, his successor shall take nothing by this. But if the parson of Dale is disseised and put out of the parsonage, and during the disseisin rent is granted to him and to his successors, this is a good grant and his successors shall take by this.

If there is a lord and tenant, [and] the lord grants the wardship of his tenant's son during the life of his tenant, and then his tenant dies, this is a void grant. Likewise, if I lease land to John at Style for years by word, and then I purchase the said lands, this is a void lease. But if such a lease was made by deed indented the lessee may enter after the purchase.

John at Style is seised of a rent in fee and he grants this after his death to John at Dale and to his heirs, this is a void grant. But if John at Style had granted rent out of his land to begin after his death this would have been a good grant. John at Style is possessed of certain lands for term of years in Dale, and grants all his lands in Dale to have and to hold to the grantee [to have] his interest and term in them for all the years as shall be spent after the grantor's death: this is a void grant for the words are not sufficient to make a grant. Land is granted to John at Style by deed to have and hold to him and to John at Dale and to their heirs, and livery and seisin is made to John at Style according to the form of the charter, this is a good grant to John at Style and void to John at Dale.

LECTURE FOUR

4. In my last lecture I showed to you how in olden times these words *we have granted to God* were a good name of purchasing and that such ancient grants are allowed if they are pleaded today, and that if such grants are made today they are void. I also then showed you what things are necessary in grants today. And now I shall show

a vous, per vostre patience, sur eux parolx *concessimus et confirmavimus* estient mis en cest estatut en le preter present tence quiles fueront prist en cest graunt en le presentence. Et ottre jeo monstra a vous sur mesme les parolx coment parols en faits diverse foits ne serront prist solonque le letter come sont escres mes solonque le entente des partyes.

Et pur ceo en le construcion des faits trois choses sont destre considre. Le primer est que fait serra prist le plus beneficiall pur luy a que il est fait et plus fort vers luy que fist le fait. Le second est que le fait ne unques serra constre destre void ou les parolx ponit estre reduce a ascon intente. Le tierce est que les parolx en un fait seront priste solonque le entente des partyes et ne auturmente.

Les parolx de cest estatute sont *concessimus et confirmavimus* que importe un done precedent. Mes en ley seront prise come si avouit estre conce<ss>^d <d>ⁱimus et confirmamus.

Un que est possesse des biens en Londres dona al John at Style touts ses biens en Londres <que est possess>^d si qui fueront: en cest case, cest paroll 'fueront' serra prist pur le presentence. Un fait graunt de terre al John at Style per eux parolls 'dedi et concessi' eux parolx seront prist pur 'do et concedi' en le presentence. Si terre soit done al John at Style et a son feme et 'heredibus quos ipse aprocreaverit [*sic*]' et John at Style ad issue per le dit A avant le done mes nemi apres, le issue quil avoit per luy avant le done enheriteront ceo terre per force de ceo done.

[*fo. 151v*] Leasse est fait des terre al John at Style pur vie et le fait voit ottre qui apres le morte le ditt John at Style que les ditt terres 'redibunt' al estrange et a ses heires, ceo parol 'redibunt' serra prist come 'remanebunt' et issint il prist per voy de remainder. Lease est fait des terre al John at Style pur vie et que apres son mort les ditz terres 'revertebunt' al John at Dale et a ses heires, ceo serra prist come un remainder.

Si lease pur ans soit fait rendront rente et que si le rent soit arreare a ascun jour de payment en que il doit esstre paye, qui les terres returnerunt al leasor, eux parolx serront prist que si le rent soit areare que le leasour et ses heires point reentre car les terres de eux mesmes ne ponit returne.

Si John at Style soit tenus en un obligation de c li. sur condition que John at Style 'et omnes alii qui fuerint feoffati ad usum dicti Johannis at Dale de manerio de Dale relaxaverunt totum jus suum quod habent quamdiu' en cest case cest paroll 'fuerint' serra prist en le pretertence, et serra entende qui eux qui 'fuerint' ses feoffes releaserunt.

LECTURE FIVE

5. En mon daren lecture jeo avis monstre a vous coment eux parolls *concessimus et confirmavimus* etient en le preter perfectence, serront prist come si avouit estre parle en le presentence et ore jeo intendre a monstra ottre a vous, per vostre patience, sur mesme les parols (pur ceo que le un parol est paroll de graunte et le autre

you, by your patience, upon these words *we have granted and confirmed* being put in this statute in the perfect tense, that they were understood in this grant in the present tense. And further I shall show you upon the same words how words in deeds shall sometimes not be taken according to the letter as they are written, but according to the intent of the parties.

And therefore three things must be considered in the construction of deeds. The first is that a deed shall be taken as the most beneficial for him for whom it is made, and most strongly against him who made the deed. The second is that the deed shall never be construed to be void where the words can be reduced to some intent. The third is that the words in a deed shall be taken according to the intent of the parties and not otherwise.

The words of this statute are *we have granted and confirmed* which implies a preceding grant. But in law it shall be taken as if it were 'we grant and confirm'.

One who is possessed of goods in London gives to John at Style all his goods in London if there were any: in this case this word shall be taken for the present tense. One makes a grant of land to John at Style by these words, 'I have given and granted': these words shall be taken for 'I give and grant' in the present tense. If land is given to John at Style and to his wife and 'to the heirs which he shall have begotten', and John at Style has issue by the said A [his wife] before the grant but not afterwards, the issue which he had by her before the grant shall inherit this land by force of this grant.

A lease of land is made to John at Style for life, and the deed wills further that after the death of the said John at Style the said lands 'shall go back' to a stranger and to his heirs, this word 'shall go back' shall be taken as 'shall remain', and thus it shall be taken by way of remainder. A lease is made of land to John at Style for life and that after his death the said lands 'shall revert' to John at Dale and to his heirs, this shall be taken as a remainder.

If a lease for years is made rendering rent and [providing] that if the rent is in arrears on any day of payment on which it should be paid, that the lands shall return to the lessor, those words shall be taken [to mean] that if the rent is in arrears the lessor and his heirs may re-enter, for the lands themselves cannot return.

If John at Style is bound in a bond of £100 on condition that John at Style 'and all others who were enfeoffed to the use of the said John at Dale of the manor of Dale shall release all their right which they have until', in this case this word 'were' shall be taken in the past tense, and it shall be understood that those who 'were' his feoffees should make the release.

Lecture Five

5. In my last lecture I showed you how these words *we have granted and confirmed* being in the perfect tense shall be taken as if they had been spoken in the present tense, and now I intend to show you further, by your patience, upon the same words (since the one word is a word of grant and the other

est paroll de confirmation) coment seront prist en cest graunt come paroll de
graunte ou come parols de confirmation et coment ascun foites ent [*sic*] tielx
grauntes le grauntee poit eux use come parols de graunte ou comes parols de
confirmation a son election et lou le graunt le roy serra constre a deux ententes
et ou forsque a un entente.

Si le roy graunt a un pasture pur deux bofes en son ter et puis le roy per ses
second lettres pattentes, resitant son primer graunte, ceo confirme et ottree [*fo.
152*] 'damus et concedimus' al primer grauntee pasture pur deux boves en mesme
le terre, eux lettres pattentes enurerunt come confirmation del primer graunte et
auxi come novel graunte de pasture pur deux boves: sic le grauntee avera pasture
pur 4 boves.

Le roy resite per ses lettres pattents qui ou il ad fait John at Style denizin il eux
confirme et ottre graunte quil faire denizin, John at Style ne poit pleade les seconde lettres pattentz pur fere luy denizin sic les seconde lettres pattentes seront
prist pur confirmation et nemy pur un novell graunte. Le roy resitast per ses lettres pattents qui on avant ore ad manumit John at Style son villain il confirmast
son dit manumission et ottre il luy manumise, le villene ne poit pleade manumission per les seconde lettres pattente.

Le roy per ses lettres pattents grauntast al un quil poit done certene terres en
mortmen: sil done en mortmen terres tenus del roy immediat le roy poit entre non
obstant son dit graunte.

Le roy resitast per ses lettres pattents que ou un franches fuit graunte al maior
et comnaltie de Dale il ceo confirmast et ottre 'damus et concedimus' al maior
et comynaltie de Dale mesme les frauncheses: le maior et commaltie de Dale ne
poit pleade eux lettres pattents come un graunte et si ils avoint nul francheses
avant ceo confirmation est voide. Mes si en ceo case le roy ex certa scientia et
mero motu ad resite que lou tiels francheses fueront grauntz al maior et comnaltie de Dale il eux ratefie et confirme, et ottre 'damus et concedimus' mesme
les francheses al maior et comnaltie de Dale, il est conclude a dire mes qui tiel
graunt fuit precedeunte. Mes si en ceo case le roy ad resite per ses lettres patents coment le maior et comynaltie de Dale sont seisi de tiels frauncheses 'ut
informetur' quil eux ratefie et confirme et ottre 'damus et concedimus' memes
les frauncheses al maior et comnaltie de Dale, ne serra conclude a dire que nul
graunt fuit precedent.

John at Style fit feoffament al John at Dale sur condition et puis John at Style
enfeoffe John at Dale per fait sans condition: en action porte vers John at Dale
il poit pleade ceo fait de feoffament come confirmation de son estate. [*fo. 152v*]
Deux jointenants sont et le un fist <fait de>[i] feoffment al auter et fit livery et
seisen accordant, cestie joyntenant a que le fait fuit fait poit pleade ceo come
confirmation si son estate fuit defeizable per luy que fit le fait avant la confirmation fait.

Le <roy>[i] grauntast al un et a ses heires quils seront dukes de Everwicke et
grauntast al luy et ses heires oveque le dukdome certeyne terres: ceo inurera a
creat luy un duke et auxi come un graunte del terre.

is a word of confirmation) how it shall be taken in this grant as a word of grant or as words of confirmation, and how sometimes in such grants the grantee may use them as words of grant or as words of confirmation at his choice, and where the king's grant shall be construed to two intents and where only to one intent.

If the king grants to someone pasture for two cows in his land, and then the king by his second letters patent, reciting his first grant, confirms this and further says 'we give and grant' to the first grantee pasture for two cows in the same land, these letters patent shall operate as confirmation of the first grant and also as a new grant of pasture for two cows: thus the grantee shall have pasture for four cows.

The king recites by his letters patent that whereas he has made John at Style denizen, he confirms them and further grants that he makes [him] denizen, John at Style cannot plead the second letters patent to make him denizen, and so the second letters patent shall be taken as a confirmation and not as a new grant. The king recited by his letters patent that some one before now had manumitted John at Style his villein, [and] he confirmed his said manumission and further manumits him himself, the villein cannot plead manumission by the second letters patent.

The king by his letters patent granted to one that he might give certain lands in mortmain: if he gives lands immediately held of the king in mortmain the king may enter notwithstanding his said grant.

The king recited by his letters patent that where a franchise was granted to the mayor and commonalty of Dale he confirmed this, and further that 'we give and grant' to the mayor and commonalty of Dale the same franchises: the mayor and commonalty of Dale may not plead these letters patent as a grant, and if they had no franchises before this confirmation is void. But if in this case the king *ex certa scientia et mero motu* had recited that whereas such franchises had been granted to the mayor and the commonalty of Dale he ratified and confirmed them and further that 'we give and grant' the same franchises to the mayor and commonalty of Dale, he is estopped from gainsaying that there was such a preceding grant. But if in this case the king had recited by his letters patent how the mayor and commonalty of Dale were seised of such franchises 'as he was informed', [and] he ratifies and confirms them and [says] further that 'we give and grant' the same franchises to the mayor and commonalty of Dale, he shall not be estopped from gainsaying that there was no such preceding grant.

John at Style makes a feoffment to John at Dale on condition, and then John at Style enfeoffs John at Dale by deed without condition: in an action brought against John at Dale he may plead this deed of feoffment as confirmation of his estate. There are two joint-tenants, and one makes a deed of feoffment to the other and makes livery and seisin accordingly, this joint-tenant to whom the deed was made may plead this as confirmation if his estate was defeasible by him who made the deed before the confirmation was made.

The king granted to one and to his heirs that they should be dukes of York, and granted certain lands to him and his heirs with the dukedom: this shall operate to create him a duke and also as a grant of lands.

Lecture Six

6. En mon daren lecture jeo avis monstre a vous coment eux parolx *concessimus et confirmavimus*, le un estient un paroll de graunte et le autre un paroll de confirmation, poit ascun foitz estre use come parols de graunt et ascun foitz come parolx de confirmation. Et pur ceo que les parols en cest estatute sont ottre *pro nobis et heredibus nostris* jeo entende ore a monstre a vous sur les ditz parolls, per vostre patience, ou eux parolls *pro nobis et heredibus nostris* sont requisit et necessarie en graunts destre fait et ou nemy.

John at Style grauntast rent charge horse de son terre oveque clause de distresse et ne dit 'pur luy et ses heires' uncore ceo est bone graunt encountre luy et ses heires. Mes si John at Style grauntast anuytie en fee et ne dit 'pur ley et ses heires' sil morust le graunte est determined et son heire ne serra charge a payer ceo coment que assettes en fee simple discend a luye.

John at Style est seisi de un molne en fee et grauntast ceo all autre en fee et ne dit 'pur luy et ses heires' uncore ceo graunte lyera son heire. Mes si en ceo case John at Style ad covenant per son fait al altre et a ses heires que ils point moler lour blesse al dit moline towle free et ne dit 'pur luy et ses heires' ceo ne lyera son heire.

Si un soit sesisi de un river en fee et grauntast al autre et a ses heires seperalem piscariam en ceo river et ne dit 'pur luy et ses heires' et morust, uncore le grauntee et ses heires averont severall piscarie la.

[*fo. 153*] Si un soit seisi de un parke et graunt al autre et a ses heires anuelment un dame en le dit parke et ne dit 'pur luy et ses heires' et morust, le graunt pur ceo nest determine mes lyera le heire le grauntor.

Un seisie de un bois en fee grauntast al occutie et a ses heires estovers en ceo bois pur ardre en le meson del grauntee en Dale et ne grauntast les estovers 'pur luy et ses heires' et puis le grauntor morust, le grauntee et ses heires point prendre estovers la de ardre en le dit meson. Issint est si un soit seisi de un warren deins ses terre en fee et grauntast ceo al autre et a ses heires et ne dit 'pur luy et ses heires' et puis le grauntor morust: per ceo le graunte est determine.

Un seisi de un markett en fee grauntast ceo markett al autre et a ses heires et ne dit 'pur luy et ses heires' uncore ceo est bone graunte et lyera les heires del grauntor. Mes si un soit seisi de un markett en fee et covenant al autre et a ses heires <et>^{d} qui ils seront quite de towle dans ceo market et ne dit 'pur luy et ses heires' et morust, le heire le grauntor poit prendre towle del grauntee et ses heires nient obstant ceo graunte.

Un fit feoffment de terre et garrant ceo al feoffee et a ses heires et ne dit 'pur luy et ses heires' et morust, <le>^{i} <apres>^{d} heire le feoffor ne serra vouche per force de ceo graunte.

Jeo covenante ovesque John at Style a levye un fine de certeyne terres a luy et ne dit 'pur moy et mes heires' puis jeo morust avant le fine levye, breif de covenenat ne gist vers mon heire. John at Style fit obligation al John at Dale de c li. en que il oblige luy mesme mes nemy ses heires ne executors. Sil morust debt gist vers ses executors mes nemy vers son heire. John at Style enfeofast un auter

Lecture Six

6. In my last lecture I showed to you how these words *we have granted and confirmed*, the one being a word of grant and the other a word of confirmation, may sometimes be used as words of grant and sometimes as words of confirmation. And because the next words in this statute are *for us and our heirs*, I intend now to show you upon the said words, by your patience, where these words *for us and our heirs* are requisite and necessary in making grants and where not.

[If] John at Style granted a rent charge out of his land with a clause of distress and did not say 'for him and his heirs', still this is a good grant as against him and his heirs. But if John at Style granted an annuity in fee and did not say 'for him and his heirs', if he dies the grant is determined and his heir shall not be charged to pay it even though assets in fee simple descend to him.

John at Style is seised of a mill in fee and granted this to another in fee and did not say 'for him and his heirs', still this grant shall bind his heir. But if in this case John at Style had covenanted by his deed to another and to his heirs that they might mill their corn at the said mill toll-free and did not say 'for him and his heirs', this shall not bind his heir.

If one was seised of a river in fee and granted to another and his heirs a several fishery in this river and does not say 'for him and his heirs' and dies, still the grantee and his heirs shall have a several fishery there.

If one was seised of a park and grants to another and to his heirs annually a doe in the said park and does not say 'for him and his heirs' and dies, the grant for this is not determined but shall bind the grantor's heir.

One seised of a wood in fee granted to the occupant and his heirs estovers in this wood to burn in the grantee's house in Dale and did not grant the estovers 'for him and his heirs' and then the grantor dies, the grantee and his heirs may take estovers there to burn in the said house. So it is if one is seised of a warren within his lands in fee and granted this to another and to his heirs and did not say 'for him and his heirs' and then the grantor dies: by this the grant is determined.

One seised of a market in fee granted this market to another and to his heirs and does not say 'for him and his heirs', still this is a good grant and shall bind the heirs of the grantor. But if one was seised of a market in fee and covenanted to another and to his heirs that they shall be quit of toll in this market and does not say 'for him and his heirs' and dies, the heir of the grantor may take toll of the grantee and his heirs notwithstanding this Six.

One makes a feoffment of land and warrants this to the feoffee and to his heirs and does not say 'for him and his heirs' and dies, the feoffor's heir shall not be vouched by force of this grant.

I covenant with John at Style to levy a fine of certain land to him and do not say 'for me and my heirs' then I die before the fine is levied, a writ of covenant does not lie against my heir. John at Style makes a bond to John at Dale of £100 in which he binds himself but not his heirs or executors. If he dies, debt lies against his executors but not against his heir. John at Style enfeoffed another

de certeyne terre sur condition que si ascun de ses heires payast al feoffee xx li. que ils poit reentre, en ceo case John at Style ne prendra ascun advantage de ceo condition, mes son heire poit.

Lecture Seven

[*fo. 153v*] 7. En mon darein lecture jeo avis monstre a vous ou eux parolx *pro nobis et heredibus nostris* sont requesit et necessaire en grauntes et ou nemy. Et ore, per vostre patience, jeo intende a monstre a vous sur eux parolls *ecclesia anglicana* coment seront prist et qui serra dit *ecclesia anglicana* et queux esglises sont include en eux parolx et que nemy.

Primis est considre sur eux parolls *ecclesia anglicana* que maner de chose *le ecclesia* est et coment est comunement prist en les scriptures de Dyeu et en comen parlans. Come jeo entende per les scriptures de dieu, de 'esglise' est entende le congregation de bone et foial gentes soient ils spiritual ou del leitie, mes en comen parlans ascun foites le esglise est prist pur le material temple que est fait per homes come les esglises que sont faite en cyties ou villes. Et ascun foitz est prist pur les revenewes et profyttes qui veignont per le administration en le esglise, come ou le parson grauntast rectoria ou les profettes de son esglise pur ans. Et ascun foitz est prist pur les ecclesiastical persons qui sont en le esglise et issint est prist per cest estatute et cest graunt *deo et ecclesie* est entende a tiels persons et en null de les auters respectes devant rehearse.

Et deins le entendment de ceo paroll *ecclesia* sont prist archevesque, evesque, archedeacons, deacons, parsons, vicares, ministers, et toutz persons conventuales et collegiales et auxi toutz qui sont infra sacros ordines,[1] car les evesques et les persons avant rehearse de southe eux governant lesglise et pur ceo un dit 'episcopi noverint in commune debere se ecclesiam regere' et autre dit 'qui cum episcopo non sunt in ecclesia non sunt'. Eux qui sont deacons ou subdeacons ne sont tiels persons qui sont entende deins le provision de cest estatute.

Et en tant que les parolls del statute avant dit sont *ecclesia anglicana* est avoier queux Esglises seront entende deins eux parolls *ecclesia anglicana* et queux nemy. [*fo. 154*] Les esglises de Irelande ne sont deins le provision de cest estatut car, come jeo avis monstre a vous en mon primer lecture, Irelande ne fuit partie al controversie qui fuit entre le roy et ses subjectes. Les esglises de Gales, come semble, sont deins le provision de cest statute, car al temps de fezante de cest estatute Gales fuit parcell de Angliter mes le roy H[en.] le 3. fit

---

[1] In margin: Deanes.

of certain land on condition that if any of his heirs paid £20 to the feoffee that they might re-enter: in this case John at Style shall not take any advantage of this condition, but his heir may.

LECTURE SEVEN

7. In my last lecture I showed you where these words *for us and our heirs* are requisite and necessary in a grant and where not. And now, by your patience, I intend to show you how these words *the English Church* shall be understood, and what shall be called *the English Church*, and which churches are included in these words and which [are] not.

The first thing to consider on these words *the English Church* is what manner of thing *the Church* is and how it is commonly taken in the scriptures of God and in common parlance. As I understand from the scriptures of God, by *Church* is understood the congregation of good and faithful people, whether they are spiritual or of the laity, but in common parlance sometimes the Church is taken for the material temple which is made by men, such as the churches which are made in cities or towns. And sometimes it is taken for the revenues and profits which come through the administration of the church, such as where the parson granted a rectory or the profits of his church for years. And sometimes it is taken for the ecclesiastical persons who are in the Church, and so it is taken by this statute, and this grant *to God and the Church* is understood of such persons and in none of the other respects rehearsed before.

And within the meaning of this word *Church* are taken archbishop, bishop, archdeacons, deacons, parsons, vicars, ministers and all conventual and collegial persons and also all who are in holy orders, for the bishops and the before-rehearsed persons under them govern the Church, and therefore one says 'let bishops know that they ought to rule the Church together', and another says 'those who are not with the bishop are not in the Church'.[1] Those who are deacons or subdeacons are not such persons who are understood [to be] within the provision[s] of this statute.[2]

And inasmuch as the words of the statute aforesaid are *the English Church*, we must see which churches shall be understood [to be] within these words *the English Church* and which [shall] not. The churches of Ireland are not within the provisions of this statute for, as I have shown you in my first lecture, Ireland was not part of the controversy between the king and his subjects. The churches of Wales, as it seems, are within the provision of this statute, for at the time of the making of this statute Wales was parcel of England, but King Henry III made

---

[1] Jerome, 'Commentary on the Letter to Titus', *Patrologia Latina*, xxvi. col. 0563C. *Rectius* 'episcopi noverint se magis consuetudine, quam dispositionis Dominicae veritate, presbyteris esse majores, et in commune debere Ecclesiam regere'; Cyprian, Epistula 66 in *Sancti Cypriani Episcopi Epistularum*, G. F. Diercks, ed., *Corpus Christianorum* Series Latina, iii. c (Turnholt, 1946), 443. *Rectius* 'qui cum episcopo non sit in ecclesia non esse'.

[2] 23 Hen. VIII, c. 1 (*SR*, iii. 362–363) removed benefit of clergy for major crimes from those in minor orders.

Edward son fitz prince de Gales apres quel temps Gales ad estre southe le gouern-
ment del prince et nemy del roy, et le eigne fitz del roy est toutz [foitz][1] prince
de Gales. Mes le esglises que fueront deins les dominions que le roy adonques
avoit en Normandye ou en auters liewes perde la ne fueront deins le provision de
cest estatute.

Si prius le fesance de cest charter un esglise soit fait per licence le roy et le
evesque et un parson est present a ceo, il aver auxi graunde benefitt et advantage
des provisions et liberties graunte per cest charter come si le esglise ad estre fait
et le parson present a ceo avant que le dit charter fuit fait.

Lecture Eight

8. En mon daren lecture jeo avis monstre a vous sur eux parolx *ecclesia anglicana* coment seront prist et qui serra dit *ecclesia anglicana* et queux esglises sont
enclude en eux parolls et queux nemy. Et ore, per vostre patience, jeo entende
a monstre a vous ottre sur lez ditz parols queux privilege le esglise <deins les
esglises>[d] ad per eux parols et queux persons averont priviledge deins les esglises
per vertue de eux parolls et queux nemye.

Siun esglise soit profaned ou suspended nad ascun priviledge per force et vertue de cest estatute.

John at Style conspier a tuer le roy ou levye guarr vers le roye et puis prist un
esglise et prayia priviledge la per 40 jours, il navera priviledge en ceo case per
force de cest estatute mes poit bien estre prist horse del dit esglise. Mes si John
at Style ad fait pety treason et ad fewe a un esglise et prayast le priviledge la per
40 jours il avera ceo a luy allowe.

Si le roy per ses lettres pattents grauntast al abbott de Dale et a ses successors
tiel priviledge que si ascun fait haute [*fo. 154v*] treason et fewe deins le precincte
de ceo abbey quil avera tiel priviledge la quil ne serra prist horse si un fait treason al dit roy et fewe all dit abbey ne serra prist horse et si soit prist horse serra
<restorte> restorde. Mes si ceo roy que ad fait tiel graunte morust et John at Style
comitt treason encontree ceo roy que luy succeade et fewe al dit abbey, poit estre
prist horse nient contustant ceo graunte.

Si home que est surde fait felonye et fewe al esglise il aver le priviledge la
per 40 jours mes il ne abjurera le realme. Si un que est mute et auxi de non sane
memorye tua John at Style et fewa a un esglise il navera priviledge la per 40
jours. Si un que est deins lage de xxi ans fait felonye et fewa a un esglise il aver
le priviledge la per 40 jours. Un que est lunatike tuast autre et prist un esglise
sera prist horse durant le temps quil est de non sane memory et quand est de sane
memory serra restore et aver 4[0] jours puis le restitution.

---

[1] MS. reads fitz.

Edward his son prince of Wales, after which time Wales was under the government of the prince and not of the king, and the eldest son of the king is always prince of Wales. But the churches which were within the dominions which the king then had in Normandy, or in other places lost there, were not within the provisions of this statute.

If before the making of this charter a church was built by the king's licence and the bishop's and a parson is presented to it [after the charter], he shall have as great a benefit and advantage of the provisions and liberties granted by this charter as if the church had been made and the parson presented to it before the charter was made.

Lecture Eight

8. In my last lecture I showed to you on these words *the English Church* how they shall be taken and what shall be called *the English Church*, and which churches are included in those words and which [are] not. And now, by your patience, I intend to show to you further on the said words which privileges the Church has by these words, and which persons shall have privilege within the churches by virtue of these words and which [shall] not.

If a church is profaned or suspended it has no privilege by force and virtue of this statute.

John at Style conspires to kill the king or levies war against the king and then takes a church and prays privilege there for forty days, he shall not have privilege in this case by force of this statute but may well be taken out of the church. But if John at Style had committed petty treason and had fled to a church and prayed the privilege there for forty days, he shall have this allowed to him.

If the king by his letters patent granted to the abbot of Dale and to his successors such a privilege that if anyone commits high treason and flees within the precinct of this abbey that he shall have such a privilege there that he shall not be taken out, [and] if one commits treason against the said king and flees to the said abbey he shall not be taken out, and if he is taken out he shall be restored. But if the king who had made such a grant dies and John at Style commits treason against the king who succeeds him and flees to the said abbey, he may be taken out notwithstanding this grant.[1]

If a man who is deaf commits a felony and flees to a church he shall have the privilege there for forty days, but he shall not abjure the realm. If one who is mute and also of unsound memory kills John at Style and flees to a church he shall not have privilege there for forty days. If one who is within the age of 21 years commits a felony and flees to a church he shall have the privilege there for forty days. [If] a lunatic kills another and takes a church he shall be taken out during the time in which he is not of sound memory, and when he is of sound memory he shall be restored and shall have forty days after the restitution.

---

[1] YB Trin. 1 Hen. VII, fo. 25, pl. 1.

Apres que un ad prist un esglise ne alera horse mes en case ou son vie est endanger. Un que ad prist un esglise pur felonye deins les 40 jours est assaulter en le esglise per un auter poit aler horse del esglise pur se salvation de son vie si auterment ne poit escape sans danger de son vie de luy que fit le assault sur luy et serra restore all esglise arreare. Issint est si le esglise soit arse ou eschewe, cestuy que est en ceo poit aler horse pur saver son vie et serra restore. Un que ad issint prist un esglise viast deux [enconterment][1] ensemble issint que sont en danger de lour vies ne poit ala horse del esglise de eux departe car si fait ne serra restore. Mes si un que ad issint prist un esglise viast le roy en danger de sone vie poit aler horse a saver le vie le roy et serra restore al esglise arreare.

[*fo. 155*] Le seignor robbast son villayne et fewe a un esglise il navera le priviledge la per 40 jours. John at Style ad un meason qui est covert ovesque leade et John at Dale per le nutt imblea parte de ceo leade et fewa a un esglise, il navera le privilege la per 40 jours. Mes si le leade en ceo caise ad gist prochein al dit meason al entent quil ferra puis ceo coveir ovesque ceo ey avant que le meson soit cover ovesque le dit leade, John at [Dale][2] ad imblee parte de ceo per le nut et fewa a un esglise, il aver le priviledge la per 40 jours.

LECTURE NINE

9. En mon darein lecture jeo avis monstre a vous sur eux parols *ecclesia anglicana* queux priviledge le Esglise avoit per eux parolx, et queux persons averont priviledge deins les Esglises per vertue de eux parols et queux nemy et ore, per vostre patience, jeo intende a monstre a vous pur ceo que les parolz sont ottre *libera sit*, coment per vertue de eux parolx les ministers del Esglise seront franke en lour persons et ou en lour biens et ou en lour terres, trialls, et elections et ou nemy.

Come semble, le clargie al temps de feizance de cest charter avouit trois principall greiffs towchante lour libertyes. Un fuit que ils ne feront adjudge avant temporall judge avant quils fueront disgrade accordant al canons del pape. Autree fuit que ils voint estre franke en lour elections de evesque le autres tiels ecclesiasticall homes, car le deniall de ceo fuit un graunde parte del cause del garr et contention de que jeo perle a vous en mon primer lecture.

Et pur le melior entendment de cest mattre jeo entende destre necessarie primes a considerer quel authorotie la ley de cest terre done al roy ou al pape ottre le spiritualtie en cest terre. Per la course del comen ley le roy est le supreme <heade>[d] governer del spiritualtie et auxi del temporaltie en cest terre et nemy le pape, car come appert per le comen ley et auxi per diverse ancient estatutes ceo authorotie que le pape avoit gayne en cest terre fuit per usurpation et nemy de jure. [*fo. 155v*] Et pur ceo appert per lestatute de Carlell fait en le 35 an del reigne le roy Edwarde le primer, que si le pape presente a ascun evesque ou benefytt deins cest terre que tiels oppressions ne serront suffer.

---

[1] MS. reads emonterment.
[2] MS. reads Style.

After one has taken a church he shall not go out except in the case where his life is in danger. [If] one who has taken a church for felony is assaulted in the church by another within the forty days he may go out of the church to save his life, if he otherwise cannot escape without danger to his life from him who made the assault on him, and he shall be restored to the church again. So it is if the church is burned or falls down: the one who is inside may go out to save his life and shall be restored. One who had thus taken a church sees two fighting together so that they are in danger of their lives, [he] may not go out of the church to separate them for if he does he shall not be restored. But if one who had taken a church sees the king in danger of his life he may go out to save the king's life and he shall be restored to the church again.

The lord robbed his villein and fled to a church he shall not have the privilege there for forty days. John at Style has a house which is covered with lead, and John at Dale by night steals part of this lead and flees to a church, he shall not have the privilege there for forty days. But if the lead in this case had lain next to the said house so that it should later be roofed with this, [and] before the house was covered with the said lead John at Dale had stolen part of this in the night and fled to a church, he shall have the privilege there for forty days.

Lecture Nine

9. In my last lecture I showed to you on these words *the English Church* what privileges the Church had by these words and what persons shall have privilege within the Church by virtue of those words and what shall not and now, by your patience, I intend to show to you, because the next words are *shall be free*, how by virtue of those words the ministers of the Church shall be free in their persons, and where in their goods, and where in their lands, trials, and elections, and where not.

As it seems, the clergy at the time of the making of this charter had three principal grievances touching their liberties. One was that they should not be judged before a temporal judge before they were degraded according to the papal canons. Another was that they wished to be free in their elections of bishops and other such ecclesiastical men, for the denial of this was a large part of the reason for the war and contention of which I spoke to you in my first lecture.

And for the better understanding of this matter I understand it to be necessary first to consider what authority the law of this land gives to the king or to the pope and also to the spirituality in this land. By the course of the common law the king is the supreme governor of the spirituality and also of the temporality in this land and not the pope, for as it appears by the common law and also by various old statutes, this authority which the pope has gained in this land was by usurpation and not by law. And therefore it appears by the statute of Carlisle, made in the thirty-fifth year of the reign of King Edward I, that if the pope presents to any bishopric or benefice within this land that such oppressions shall not be suffered.[1]

---

[1] Statute of Carlisle, 35 Edw. I (*SR*, i. 150–152). The statute does not prohibit papal presentation.

Et que le roye fuit toutz foitz accompte supreme governor del spiritualtie per le comen ley per divers voyes appert, come jeo avis monstre a vous en <un>[i] <le>[d] argument en le comencement de cest vacation.

Et pur ceo per le course del comen ley le roy meme avoit le appointment de toutz evesques et le elecion del evesques per le chapter ne fuit use avant le fesance de cest charter et pur ceo per nostre ley le roy est appell le sovereigne patron de toutz les evesques en Angliter. En auxi apperte en auncient recorde que le roy meme poit feere un evesque, les parols de quel recorde sont come insuit: 'Rex Henricus facit Henricum episcopum London episcopum Cantuariensem et eum investat baculis et anulo'.

Si un esglise deveigne voide et le patron ne present deins vj mois ne le ordi-naire deins autres vj mois ne le metropolitain deins autre vj mois, le roy come supreme governor del spiritualtie presentera per laps per la ley dangliter et nemy le pape.

Le roy per la comen ley de cest terre pur ceo quil est supreme del spiritualtie poit exempte un parson de jurisdiction ordinarie et issint ne poit le pape.

Si terres estient deins un forrest sont sewe ovesque bles les queux sont horse de chescun parishe en que caise les dismes sont dewe a ascun, en ceo case le roy come supreme governor del spiritualtie avera les dismes de eux terres per la comon ley et nemy le pape, car nul auter person poit ferr title a eux.

En le temps le Roy Edward le primer un pleadast excomengment en le court del Rome vers un autre en un sute al Westm' pretendant per ceo que le pape fuit supreme governor del spiritualtie et nemy le roy. Et pur ceo que per ceo il derogat del roy ceo aucthorotie ottre le spiritualtie que la ley del terre luy donast, fuit adjudge haute treason encontre le roy en luy que pleadast le excomunicacon en le court del Rome.

[*fo. 156*] Si un soit excommunicate en le spirituall courte et est prist et imprison et proferast sufficient causion al evesque que ceo refuse, le partye que est inprison avera breffe le roy de cautione admittenda a commande le evesque (avouit prist sufficient causion) de cause luy estree leesse horse de prison et le roy come supreme governor del spiritualtie sera judge si ceo causion que le partie in prison proferast soit sufficient ou nemy.

Si un evesque fait felonye pur que est attaynte et prayast son clergie le metro-politane doit doner a luy son clergie. Et si le metropolitane soit attaynte de felo-nye et prayast son clergie le roy come supreme governor del spiritualtie et nemy le pape comendera a un a doner a luy son clergie.

LECTURE ELEVEN

[*fo. 157*] 11.[1] En mon darren lecture jeo avis monstre a vous sur eux parolx *libera sit* coment per vertue de eux parolx les ministers de Sancte Esglise seront franke

---

[1] Lecture 10 seems to be missing: the bottom two-thirds of fo. 156, all of fo. 156v, and the top third of fo. 157 are blank.

And that the king was always accounted supreme governor of the spirituality by the common law appears in various ways, as I have shown you in an argument in the beginning of this vacation.

And therefore by the course of the common law the king himself had the appointment of all bishops, and the election of bishops by the chapter was not used before the making of this charter, and therefore by our law the king is called the sovereign patron of all the bishops in England. And also it appears in an ancient record that the king himself was able to make a bishop, the words of which record are as follows: 'King Henry makes Henry, bishop of London, bishop of Canterbury and invests him with the staff and ring.'[1]

If a church becomes vacant and the patron does not present within six months nor the ordinary within another six months, nor the metropolitan within another six months, by the law of England the king, as supreme governor of the spirituality, shall present by lapse and not the pope.

The king may exempt a parson from the jurisdiction of the ordinary by the common law of this land because he is supreme [governor] of the spirituality, and this the pope may not do.

If lands within a forest are sown with corn outside of any parish, in which case the tithes are due to someone, in this case the king as supreme governor of the spirituality shall have the tithes of those lands by the common law and not the pope, for no other person may make title to them.

In the time of King Edward I someone pleaded excommunication in the court of Rome against another in a suit at Westminster thereby pretending that the pope was supreme governor of the spirituality and not the king. And because he thereby derogated from the king this authority over the spirituality which the law of the land gave him, it was adjudged high treason against the king in him who pleaded the excommunication in the court of Rome.

If one is excommunicated in the spiritual court and is taken and imprisoned and proffers sufficient cause to the bishop who refuses it, the party who is imprisoned shall have a writ to the king *de cautione admittanda* to command the bishop (having taken a sufficient caution) to cause him to be let out of prison, and the king as supreme governor of the spirituality shall be judge if this cause which the party in prison proffered is sufficient or not.[2]

If a bishop commits a felony for which he is attainted and prays his clergy, the metropolitan must give him his clergy. And if the metropolitan is attainted of felony and prays his clergy the king, as supreme governor of the spirituality, and not the pope shall command someone to give him his clergy.

Lecture Eleven

11. In my last lecture I showed to you on these words *shall be free* how by virtue of these words the ministers of the Holy Church shall be free

---

[1] The only archbishops of Canterbury named Henry during the reign of a King Henry were Chichele and Dean. Neither was bishop of London.

[2] *Register*, fo. 66.

en lour persons, et pur ceo que en le dit darren lecture jeo avis parle forsque solement coment seront franke en lour persons jeo intende a monstre a vous ottre sur
les ditz parols coment les ministre de sancte esglise seront franke en lour persons,
biens, terres, trialls, ellections, et tiels semblabes et ou nemi.

Si un parson soit robbe et porte appeale de robbery le defendent per le reason
de eux parols *libera sit* ne poit joyne battell en le appeale ovesque le parsonne.
Mes si un parson porte breif de droit del seizen son auncestre le tenant poit joyne
le myse per battell et pur ceo serra trie que deux ad melior droit.

Per vertue de eux parolx *libera sit* un spirituall person ne sera compell a server
en le guerr come eux que sont del <laietie>[i] leveitie seronte. Un parson per vertue de eux parols *libera sit* ne serra compell a feere sute a un lete ne al turne del
viconte per le reasons de son resiance, come un auter homme sera.

Si un recoverast debt vers un evesque navera capias ad satisfaciendum vers
luy pur prendre son corps en execution pur ceo debte quar la ley entende quil
est sufficient. Mes capias ad satisfaciendum gist vers un parson de un esglise sur
recoverye en debt vers luy quar nest entende sufficient en ley come un evesque
est. [*fo. 157v*] Mes per vertue de eux parols *libera sit* null spirituall person sera
prist per vertue de ascun *capias* en ascun esglise si les ditz persons ne eux gar-
dent en les ditz esglises per collusion, come appert per lestatut de 50 E[dw.] 3
cap. quinto et per lestatute de primo R[ic.] 2 cap. 15, le quel statute dit que a feere
tielx arreastes [est] contrarie al liberties de Sancte Esglise.

Si un prior perde ishewes al roy et ad biens horse de son sanctuarie et
le vicomte fist precepte a son bailif de levye les ditz issues, le bailif ne poit
entree en le sanctuarie et prendre les biens le prior come distres pur les ditz
issues.

John at Style distreynast son leassee pur rent arreare et impoundast le distresse
deins le rectorie de un esglise, le leasse suist replevine, le vicoune en ceo caise ne
poit fere deliverance del distres et prendre ceo horse del rectorie mes sil returne
le especiall matter un withernam sera agarde des avers John at Style que prist le
distres.

Les avers de un parson ne seront distreyne pur les fees des chevallers que alant
al parlyament.

Si un recoverast debt vers un parson il navera elegit al vicounte dell moitie del
terre que le parson ad en le droit de son esglise car est bone retorne pur le vicont
a dire que le defendent est clericus beneficiatus non habendum laicum feodum.
Mes si un parson soit condempne en debte de x li. et ad terre per discente de
ascun de ses auncesters ou parson purchase demesne, execution poit estre sewe
de eux ters per elegit.

Un parson est tenus en un recognizance que est forfecte, le cognisee navera
sur ceo un levari facias al vicont de levye le some conteyne in le recognizance
des terres et chattells le parson mes avera levari facias agarde al evesque de ceo
diocis ou le esglise de qui le cognisor est parson est [*sic*] de levie le some conteyne en le recognizance des biens le cognisor.

in their persons, and because in the said last lecture I spoke only about how they shall be free in their persons, I intend to show to you further on the said words how the ministers of Holy Church shall be free in their persons, goods, lands, trials, elections, and such things and where not.

If a parson is robbed and brings an appeal of robbery, the defendant by reason of these words *shall be free* may not join battle in the appeal with the parson. But if a parson brings a writ of right of his ancestor's seisin, the tenant may join the mise by battle and by this it shall be tried which of them has better right.

By virtue of these words *shall be free* a spiritual person shall not be compelled to serve in the war as those who are of the laity shall. A parson shall not be compelled to make suit to a leet or to the sheriff's court by reason of his residence by virtue of these words *shall be free*, as another man shall.

If one recovers a debt against a bishop he shall not have a *capias ad satisfaciendum* against him to take his body in execution for this debt for the law presumes that he is sufficient. But a *capias ad satisfaciendum* lies against a parson of a church upon a recovery in debt against him, for he is not presumed to be sufficient in law as a bishop is. But by virtue of these words *shall be free* no spiritual person shall be taken by virtue of any *capias* in any church, provided the said persons do not stay in the said churches by collusion, as appears by the statute of 50 Edward III, c. 5, and by the statute of 1 Richard II, c. 15, which statute says that to make such arrests is contrary to the liberties of the Holy Church.[1]

If a prior loses issues to the king and has goods outside his sanctuary, and the sheriff gives an order to his bailiff to levy the said issues, the bailiff may not enter in the sanctuary and take the prior's goods as distress for the said issues.

[If] John at Style distrained his lessee for rent in arrears and impounded the distress in the rectory of a church [and] the lessee sues replevin, the sheriff in this case may not make delivery of the distress and take this out of the rectory, but if he returns the special matter a withernam shall be awarded for the beasts of John at Style who took the distress.

The beasts of a parson shall not be distrained for the fees of the knights who go to Parliament.

If one recovered debt against a parson he shall not have *elegit* to the sheriff of the moiety of the land which the parson has in the right of his church, for it is a good return for the sheriff to say that the defendant is 'a beneficed cleric not holding lay fee'. But if a parson is condemned in debt of £10 and has land by descent of any of his ancestors, or the parson purchases in demesne, execution may be sued of these lands by *elegit*.

A parson is bound in a recognizance which is forfeit, the conusee shall not have a *levari facias* on this to the sheriff to levy the sum contained in the recognizance from the lands and chattels of the parson, but he shall have *levari facias* awarded to the bishop of this diocese or the church of which the conusor is parson to levy the sum contained in the recognizance from the goods of the conusor.

---

[1] 50 Edw. III, c. 5 (*SR*, i. 398); 1 Ric. II, c. 15 (*SR*, ii. 5).

Si un evesque, deane, ou parson fait felonye ou treason serra indite et arreane sur ceo devant le temporall judge, non obstant eux parols *libera sit*. Et si soit trove culpable serra mis al execution come ascun autre del leytie serra.

Si un que est indebt soit fait monke debte ne gist vers luy, mes si un fait trespas et puis est fait monke trespas gist vers luye. [*fo. 158*] Si un parson tient parte de son gleib de John at Style per certayne rent, si le rent soit arreare John at Style poit distreyne pur ceo non obstant eux parols *libera sit*.

Si un evesque morust le roy avera le temporalties en temps de vacation non obstant eux parols *libera sit*.

Si un parson soit horse del semytorie et viest un vegnont a luy areaster et il fewe al semytorie le autre poit luy pursuer et luy areaster etient deins le semytorie ou deins le esglise.

LECTURE TWELVE

12. En mon darren lecture jeo avis monstre a vous sur eux parols *libera sit* coment per vertue de eux parols les mynisters de Saint Esglise seront franke en lour persons et ou en lour biens et ou en lour terre, trialles, et elections, et ou nemy. Et ore, per vostre patience, jeo intende a monstre a vous sur les prochen parols en cest estatute que sont *et habeat omnia iura sua integra et libertates suas illesas* queux please les spirituall judges point determyne et <les>^d de queux averont conisans per vertue de eux parols et de queux nemye et coment jurisdiction de clergie est restore a eux per vertue de eux parols et queux auters priviledge [ils] ount per vertue de eux parols et queux nemye.

Per ceux parols *omnia jura sua* les spirituall judge ount power de oier et determine pleas towchant matrimonye, testaments, legaces des biens et chateux, dismes et tiells semblables.

Si un promisast a doner al auter c li. en mariage ovesque son file sil voit luy marier et il mariast le file et le c li. nest paye, poit suer pur ceo en le spirituall courte. Mes si un promise un x li. sil voit marie son file, sil mariast le file et lauter ne voit payer le money ne suera luy en court Cristyan pur cell.

Avant le fesance de cest estatute probat de testament apertinast al court le roy et nemy al spirituall court et les spirituall judges <nient>^d nont le probate de eux en auters terres except Angliter et en plousours lieues deins Angliter les seignours des maners ont probate de testament a cest jour devant lour senescalls en lour temperall courte.

[*fo. 158v*] Si home conust en court Christian quil doit a un autre c li. sur un contracte pur certeyne biens a paier a luy a certayne jour et nest paye al jour ne serra sue en le spirituall court pur ceo. Mes si John at Style per le reason de matromonye ou testament conust en court Christian quil doit payer c li. a certayne jour, la sil ne payast al jour poit estre sue en court Christian pur cell.

If a bishop, dean or parson commits felony or treason he shall be indicted and arraigned on this before the temporal judge, notwithstanding these words *shall be free*. And if he is found guilty he shall be sent to execution as anyone else of the laity shall be.[1]

If one who is in debt is made a monk debt does not lie against him, but if one commits trespass and then is made a monk trespass lies against him. If a parson holds part of his glebe of John at Style by certain rent, if the rent is in arrears John at Style may distrain for this notwithstanding these words *shall be free*.

If a bishop dies the king shall have the temporalities in the time of vacancy notwithstanding these words *shall be free*.

If a parson is outside the churchyard and he sees someone coming to arrest him and flees to the churchyard the other may pursue him and arrest him within the churchyard or within the church.

Lecture Twelve

12. In my last lecture I showed to you on these words *shall be free* how by virtue of these words the ministers of Holy Church shall be free in their persons, and where in their goods and where in their lands, trials and elections and where not. And now, by your patience, I intend to show to you on the next words in this statute which are *and shall have all her rights entire and her liberties inviolate*, which pleas the spiritual judges may determine and which they shall have cognizance of by virtue of these words and which not, and how the jurisdiction of the clergy is restored to them by virtue of these words, and what other privilege they have by virtue of these words and what not.

By these words *all her rights*, the spiritual judge has power to hear and determine pleas touching matrimony, testaments, legacies of goods and chattels, tithes and such things.

If one promises to give to another £100 in marriage with his daughter if he will marry her, and he marries the girl and the £100 is not paid, he may sue for it in the spiritual court. But if one promises another £10 if he will marry his daughter, if he marries the girl and the other will not pay the money he shall not sue him in court Christian for this.

Before the making of this statute probate of wills belonged to the king's court and not to the spiritual court, and the spiritual judges did not have the probate of them in other lands except England, and in many places within England the lords of manors have probate of wills today before their stewards in their temporal court.

If a man acknowledges in court Christian that he owes £100 to another on a contract for certain goods to pay to him at a certain day, and it is not paid on the day [he], shall not be sued in the spiritual court for this. But if John at Style by reason of matrimony or testament acknowledges in court Christian that he must pay £100 by a certain day, there if he does not pay on the day [he] may be sued in court Christian for this.

[1] This may refer to Spelman, *Reports*, i. 49, pl. 15; Yorke, *Reports, Hen. VIII*, i. 90, pl. 5.

Si terre sont devise al un pur ans et autres terres a luy pur vie, le devisee poit suer pur les terres devise pur ans en le spirituall court mes nemye pur les terres devise pur vie, issint est si les terres fueront en taile ou en fee.

Concernant dismes, apperte que avant le counsell de Lateran un poit aver done ses dismes a que person spirituall quil voit et per ceo counsell est provide et decree qui nul home de temps a vener grauntast ou donast ses dismes si non a son proper curat, puis quel temps si ascun home ne voit payer ses dismes a son curat demesne le curat poit luy suer pur ses dismes en le spirituall court.

Si le roy ad dismes a un forest en eux graunt a un auter per ses lettres pattents et autre eux prist le pattente poit aver scire facias vers luy que eux prist en le chauncery et seront al issue la et donquez sera maunde en banke le Roy a trier ceo. Mes si cetye que doit payer les dismes ne voit eux payer al pattente, [le patentee] ne poit luy suer en le chancery mes doit luy suer en lespirituall courte.

Si John at Style grauntast a un parson et a ses successors le tenth parte des bles cresant de toutz ses terres ottre les dismes le parson en mesme les terres le parson ne poit suer pur ceo xth parte en lespirituall courte.

Si un que est seisie de certeyne terres en Dale per son industrie trovast carbons deins ceo terre le parson de Dale ne poit luy suer pur les dismes de eux carbones en le spirituall courte. Issint est si un ad quarre des stones deins son terre le parson ne poit suer le owner del soyle pur les dismes de eux stones en le spirituall courte.

[*fo. 159*] Si dismes qui ne amount al quart parte del valewe del esglise sont en debate enter deux parsons ceo serra determyne en le spirituall courte. Mes si dismes sont en debate entre deux persons que excead la quart parte del profett del esglise ceo serra determyne en le court le roy et nemy en le spirituall court.

Un poit prescribe quil et toutez ses auncesters et toutz eux que estate il ad en tiell terre ont use temps dont memorye de homes [ne]^1 curge al contrarie, a payer anuelment un certayne somme de argent en consideration de ses dismes de eux terres et ceo custome serra trie en le court le roye et nemy en le spirituall courte. Mes un ne poit prescribe in non decimando scilicet quil et ses auncesters et eux que estate il ad en tiel terre ont use a payer nul dismes ne ascun chose en consideration de eux.

Lecture Thirteen

13. En mon daren lecture jeo avis monstre a vous sur eux parolx *et habeat omnia jura sua integra et libertates suas illesas* coment les spirituall judge[s] per force de eux parolx ount power de oyer et determyner pleas touchant matrimony, testamentes, legaces des biens et chateux et dismes et ore, per vostre patiens, jeo intende a monstre a vous ottre sur lez ditz parolx coment jurisdiction de clergie est restore

---

^{1} MS. reads en.

If land is devised to one for years and other lands to him for life, the devisee may sue for the lands devised for years in the spiritual court but not for the lands devised for life, [and] it is so if the lands were in tail or in fee.

Concerning tithes, it appears that before the Lateran Council one was able to give his tithes to whatever spiritual person he wished, and by this council it is provided and decreed that no man in time to come should grant or give his tithes except to his own curate, after which time if any man did not wish to pay his tithes to his own curate the curate might sue him for the tithes in the spiritual court.[1]

If the king has tithes in a forest and grants them to another by his letters patent and someone else takes them, the patentee may have a *scire facias* in the Chancery against him who took them and they shall be at issue there and then it shall be sent into the King's Bench for trial there. But if the one who must pay the tithes does not wish to pay them to the patentee, the patentee may not sue him in the Chancery but must sue him in the spiritual court.

If John at Style granted to a parson and to his successors the tenth part of the corn growing on all his lands beyond the parson's tithe in the same lands, the parson may not sue for this tenth part in the spiritual court.

If one who is seised of certain lands in Dale by his industry found coal within this land, the parson of Dale may not sue him for the tithes of that coal in the spiritual court. So it is if one has a quarry of stones within his land, the parson may not sue the owner of the soil for the tithes of those stones in the spiritual court.

If tithes which do not amount to the fourth part of the value of the church are in dispute between two parsons this shall be determined in the spiritual court. But if tithes are in dispute between two parsons which exceed the fourth part of the profit of the church this shall be determined in the king's court, and not in the spiritual court.

One may prescribe that he and all his ancestors and all those whose estate he has in such lands have been used, from the time from which the memory of man does not run to the contrary, to pay annually a certain sum of money in consideration of his tithes in those lands, and this custom shall be tried in the king's court and not in the spiritual court. But one may not prescribe in *non decimando*, namely that he and his ancestors and those whose estate he has in such land have been used to pay no tithes nor any thing in consideration of them.

Lecture Thirteen

13. In my last lecture I showed to you on these words *and shall have all her rights entire and her liberties inviolate* how the spiritual judges by force of these words have the power to hear and determine pleas touching matrimony, testaments, legacies of goods and chattels, and tithes and now, by your patience, I intend to show you further on the said words how jurisdiction over the clergy is restored to

---

[1] Lateran IV, canon 56.

a Saincte Esglise per vertue de eux parolx et queux auters privileges ount per vertue de eux parolx et queux nemi.

'Clergie' est quand un deins holie orders ou autree en que nest ascun imposibilitie destre un ministre est arreigne de felonye devant un seculer judge. Il poit prayer son clergie que est a tant come si il ad praye destre dismes del temporall judge et destre deliver al ordinarie de purge luy mesme de cest offence.

Un villane ou basterd, sil soit arreigne pur felonye, averont lour clergie pur ceo que per dispensation ils point estre faites ministeres de sainct esglise mes un que est blinde ou meighm navera son clergie. Si un feme soit arreigne pur felony il navera son clergie. Si un commit sacrelegie et praiast son clergie [le]¹ ordinarie poit luy refuse ou prayer quel soit deliver a luy a son elecion. Si un tuast autre per misadventure ou seipsum defendendo ou fait petye latrocynye navera son clergie car la nest daver judgment de vie et de membre. [*fo. 159v*] Un que fait haut treason encountre le roy navera son clergie. Un que ad ewe deux femes ou que ad marie un widowe aver son clergie tanque le contrarie soit provide en le counsell de Lyons. Un que conust un felony navera son clergie per cest estatute tanque lestatute de articuli cleri fuit fait, intant que contrarie a son confession demesne ne poit purger luy meme de ceo offence.

Cetye que fit felonye et ad son clergie et fitt felony arreare avera son clergie arreare et issint a chescun temps quil ceo demaunde tanque le contrarie fuit provide per lestatute de 4 H[en.] 7 cap. 13, per que statut est provide que nul aver son clergie forsque un foitz. Si un felone soit condempne et judgment done sur luy et est amesne al gallewes estre pendens et estient southe les gallowes il priast <son>ⁱ clergie et est amesne per le vicont avant les justices, son clergie sera a luy alowe.

Un que est attaint de felonye ne voit prieir son clergie et les justices, savoint quil est clerke, ne doint done judgment sur luy quil sera pendus.

Quand le ordinarie port un livre a vier si la prisoner poit lieer de ceo le court poit prender le liver et appoynt al prisoner un vears a ceo a lier. Si le ordinarie demande un prisoner estre delyver a luy come un clarke et semble a les justices quil ne lyast sufficient come clerke le ordinarie ferra un grand fine et auxi le prisoner sera pendus, car les justices sont judge de son lieer et nemy le ordinarie quar les justices fesoit quil soit entre en le recorde 'quod legit ut clericus et quod deliberatur ordinario' et le ordinarie nest la forsque come un ministre al courte. Si le prisoner lyast sufficient et le ordinarie luye refuse [il] fera fyne et le prisoner ne serra pendus.

Siun infant que est deins lage de 14 ans mariast un widowe, il aver son clergie sil disagre al mariage al 14 ans. Mes si infant ottre lage de 14 ans marast un widowe

---

¹ MS. reads de.

the Holy Church by virtue of those words, and which other privileges they have by virtue of those words and which not.

'Clergy' is when one in holy orders, or someone in whom there is no impossibility of being a minister, is arraigned of felony before a secular judge. He may pray his clergy, which is as much as if he had prayed to be dismissed by the temporal judge and to be delivered to the ordinary to purge himself of this offence.

A villein or bastard shall have his clergy if he is arraigned for felony because by dispensation they may be made ministers of the holy church, but one who is blind or maimed shall not have his clergy. If a woman is arraigned for felony she shall not have her clergy. If one commits sacrilege and prays his clergy the ordinary may refuse him, or pray that he should be delivered to him, at his choice. If one kills another by misadventure, or in self-defence, or commits petty larceny, he shall not have his clergy for there he is not to have judgment of life and limb. One who commits high treason against the king shall not have his clergy. One who has had two wives or who has married a widow had his clergy until the contrary was provided in the council of Lyons.[1] One who confesses a felony shall not have his clergy by this statute until the statute of *Articuli Cleri* was made, inasmuch as he could not purge himself of this offence contrary to his own confession.[2]

One who commits a felony and has his clergy and commits a felony again shall have his clergy again, and likewise every time that he demanded it until the contrary was provided by the statute of 4 Hen. VII, c. 13, by which statute it is provided that one shall only have his clergy once.[3] If a felon is condemned and judgment given on him, and he is brought to the gallows to be hanged, and being below the gallows he prays his clergy and is brought by the sheriff before the justices, his clergy shall be allowed to him.

[If] one who is attainted of felony does not wish to plead his clergy the justices, knowing that he is a clerk, should not give judgment on him that he shall be hanged.

When the ordinary brings a book to see if the prisoner can read from it the court may take the book and appoint a verse from it for the prisoner to read. If the ordinary demands a prisoner to be delivered to him as a clerk and it seems to the justices that he does not read sufficiently well as a clerk, the ordinary shall make a great fine and also the prisoner shall be hanged, for the justices are the judge of his reading and not the ordinary, for the justices cause it to be entered in the record 'that he read as a clerk and that he was delivered to the ordinary', and the ordinary is only there as an officer of the court. If the prisoner reads sufficiently and the ordinary refuses him, [the ordinary] shall make a fine and the prisoner shall not be hanged.

If a child who is within the age of 14 years marries a widow, he shall have his clergy if he disagrees with the marriage at 14 years. But if a child above the

---

[1] This decree was passed in the second council of Lyons of 1274 (Constitution 2.16), but the reader probably has the reference from the statute *De Bigamis*, 4 Edw. I, c. 5 (*SR*, i. 43), which mentions the council.
[2] *Articuli Cleri* 9 Edw. II, c. 16 (*SR*, i. 174).
[3] 4 Hen. VII, c. 13 (*SR*, ii. 538).

il navera son clergie. Si un que ad feme mariast autre feme, le primer feme etient en vie il navera son clergie. [*fo. 160*] Si infant del age de x ans mariast un feme en facie ecclesie et puis quand il est del age de xvj ans et devant ascun assent, in disagrement a ceo mariage il mariast un autre feme que morust et puis est attaint de felonye etc. il avera son clergie sans suer de ascun devorce avante ceo del primer mariage. John at Style prist feme et le feme morust et puis John at Style mariast autre feme et apres ceo John at Style et le seconde feme sont devorce causa precontractus del parte le feme et John at Style est attaint de felonye, il aver son clergie.

LECTURE FOURTEEN

14. En mon daren lecture jeo avis monstre a vous sur eux parolx *et habeat omnia jura sua integra et libertates suas illesas* coment jurisdition de clergie est restore a Saint Esglise per vertue de les ditz parolx. Et ore, per vostre patiens, jeo entende a monstre a vous ottre sur lez ditz parolx que maner de difference est entre cest parolx *jura* et cest parol *libertates* et coment seront entende en cest estatute.

Cest parol *jura* en cest estatute est prist solement pur spirituall jurisdiction et nemy pur temporall jurisdiction, come a tener plea de matromonye, defama-tion, de droit [de][1] dismes si ne excedunter le iiij parte de le value del esglise, de testament, de lesione fidei, de heresie, usurie, et tiels semblables. *Libertates ecclesie* sunt <de>[d] en deux manners, ou concernant lour terre et possessions ou concernant lour persons.

Le entent de eux parols *et habeat omnia jura integra* fuit que Sanct Esglise [ne][2] sera restore a parte de lour droitz mes a toutz et le entent de eux parolx *et libertates suas illesas* sont qui Sanct Esglise aver tout ses libertates que aver droit inviolat sans ascun restreinte. Liberties de Sanct Esglise sont en troies manners, scilicet ou est libertie en grose, ou libertie annex al terre, ou liber-tie annex a lour persons. Liberties en grose sont faires, markettes, lete, toule, infancke theif, outfanke theif, conisaunce de plea, waif, straye, deodant et tiels semblables. Liberties annex a lour terre sont come daver francke garren, parke, chase, ou que lour tenauntes deins lour manners seront franke de towle. [*fo. 160v*] Libertie annex a lour person est come un clarke prayast son clergie ou lou un prist sanctuarie pur salvation de son vie.

Si come trois maner de liberties sont restore al clergie per cest parolx 'liber-ties' issint per trois maner de vois point eux liberties estre forfett, scilicet per non user, mysuser, et disuser. Nonuser est lou le libertie del clarke del markett est graunt a un et il ne unques usat son office, per ceo est forfett car le user de ceo office est pur le bien publick. Issint semble ou viewe de francke pledge est graunte al un a tener deins son manner et il ne use ceo a ascun temps.

---

[1] MS. reads et.
[2] MS. reads en.

age of 14 years marries a widow he shall not have his clergy. If one who has a wife marries another woman while the first wife is still alive he shall not have his clergy. If a child aged 10 years marries a woman *in facie ecclesiae*, and then when he is aged 16 years and before any assent, in disagreement with this marriage he marries another woman who dies, and then is attainted of felony etc., he shall have his clergy without previously suing any divorce in respect of the first marriage. [If] John at Style takes a wife and the wife dies and then John at Style marries another woman, and afterward John at Style and the second wife are divorced for pre-contract on the part of the woman, and John at Style is attainted of felony, he shall have his clergy.

LECTURE FOURTEEN

14. In my last lecture I showed you on these words *and shall have all her rights entire and her liberties inviolate*, how the jurisdiction of the clergy is restored to the Holy Church by virtue of the said words. And now, by your patience, I intend to show you further on the said words what manner of difference there is between this word *rights* and this word *liberties*, and how they are understood in this statute.

This word *rights* in this statute is taken solely for spiritual jurisdiction and not for temporal jurisidiction, such as to hold pleas of matrimony, defamation, of right to tithes if they do not exceed the fourth part of the value of the church, of testaments, of *laesio fidei*, of heresy, usury and such things. The liberties of the Church are of two kinds, either concerning their lands and possessions or concerning their persons.

The intent of those words *and shall have all her rights entire*, was that the Holy Church would not be restored to part of their rights but to all, and the intent of those words *and her liberties inviolate* is that the Holy Church shall have all its liberties which it ought to have inviolate without any restraint. Liberties of the Holy Church are in three manners, namely liberties in gross, or liberties attached to the land, or liberties attached to their persons. Liberties in gross are fairs, markets, leets, tolls, infangthief, outfangthief, cognizance of pleas, waif, stray, deodand and such things. Liberties attached to their land are such as having free warren, park, chase, or that their tenants within their manors shall be free of toll. Liberties attached to their person are as when a clerk prays his clergy or where one takes sanctuary to save his life.

Just as three kinds of liberties are restored to the clergy by this word *liberties*, so by three kinds of ways those liberties may be forfeited, namely by nonuser, misuser and disuser. Nonuser is where the liberty of the clerk of a market is granted to someone and he never uses his office: it is thereby forfeit, for the use of this office is for the public good. Likewise it seems where a view of frankpledge is granted to one to hold within his manor and he does not use this at any time.

Mysuser est ou est use mes en autre manner que il doit estre use, come ou le roy granntast a un a tener markett chescun Friday en le semayne et il tient ceo chescun Friday et chescun Londay en le semayne, ou le roy grantast a un a tener un faire un jour del an et il ceo tient deux jours en le an.

Disuser est en chose graunte est un foitz bien use et puis ceo est omitt et nyent use come en le case del clarke del markett avant mis: ou il usat son office un foitz et puis ne voit use son office ceo est disuser et bon cause a sease son office pur forfete.

Si le roy grauntast al maier et commonaltie de A tenere placita et ne [volurent][1] tener ascun plea devant eux ceo nest ascun forfeture del graunte del libertie. Mes si le roy grauntast al maior et commaltie de A tenere placita in A et que nul home impleadera autre de ascun choise fait en A nisi en mesme le ville et que ne seront impleade en autre liewe forsque ibidem et le maier et commonaltie ne voint tener plea de ascun chose devant eux ceo est un forfaiture del dit libertie. Si le roy grantast conisance de toutz pleas al maior et commonaltie de A et ne voint demaunde conisance de ascun plea en ascun des courtes de roy ceo nest forfaiture del dit libertie.

[fo. 161] Si un que est convicte de felony prayast son clergie et le ordinarie luy refusat sans cause il perdera les franches de chalenger clerkes et auxi ses temporalties seront seisie en les maynes le roy.

Si le roy grauntast a un abbott franches de aver gaile et pur ceo que le abott ne voit estre al costage pur aver deliverance il detient gentz per longe temps en prison que sont prist pur suspicion de felonye, le roy pur ceo cause poit seise le francheses pur forfaite.

---

[1] MS. reads vonerit.

Misuser is where it is used but in another manner than it should have been used, as where the king grants to one to hold a market each Friday in the week and he holds it each Friday and each Monday in the week, or the king grants to one to hold a fair one day in the year and he holds it two days in the year.

Disuser is where the thing granted is once used well and then it is omitted and not used, as in the above case of the clerk of the market: where he used his office once and then would not use his office this is disuser and a good cause to seize his office by forfeiture.

If the king granted to the mayor and commonalty of A to hold pleas and they will not hold any plea before them, this is not any forfeiture of the grant of the liberty. But if the king granted to the mayor and commonalty of A to hold pleas in A, and that no man should implead another of anything done in A except in the same town, and that they shall not be impleaded in another place except there, and the mayor and commonalty will not hold pleas of anything before them this is a forfeiture of the said liberty. If the king granted cognizance of all pleas to the mayor and commonalty of A and they do not wish to demand cognizance of any plea in any of the king's courts this is not a forfeiture of the said liberty.

If one who is convicted of felony prayed his clergy and the ordinary refused him without cause, he shall lose his franchise to challenge clerks and also his temporalities shall be seised into the king's hands.

If the king grants to an abbot a franchise to have a gaol, and because the abbot does not wish to have the cost of a gaol delivery he detains people who are taken on suspicion of felony for a long time in prison, the king for this reason may seize the franchise for forfeit.

PART III

OTHER TEXTS ON THE COMMON LAW AND THE CHURCH

HEN. 8 TIME: CERTEN CONSIDERATIONS WHY THE SPIRITUELL JURISDICTION WOLD BE ABROGATT AND REPELLED OR AT THE LEEST REFORMED.[1]

[*fo. 241*] Fyrst I cannot see but that all suche lawes whiche be called spirituell lawes first commenced ayenst the kinges prerogative for asmuche as the clergy have not ne at any tyme hadd, any power yevyn them immediately of God to make any lawes within this realme ne to execute any lawes but ther lawes, [but they] have ben made and executed by the only usurped power of the bisshup of Rome by the sufferaunce and admittence of the kinges grace and his progenitors kinges of this realme, wherby they have not only lost grett avantage whiche they ought to have hadd by suche sutes which they call spirituell sutes if they hadd byn takyn in ther owne corts as issuez, fines, amerciamentes, and forfetures, with the advantage of all the processe of the law if suche sutes hadd byn takyn after the ordinary corsse of the law of the realme, as of the seale of the originall writtes and judicialles, but also it hathe byn gretly in derogation of his lawes and almost growen to a subversion of them. Wherfore if they weare repelled and set in some good order by the kinges lawes it wold cause the clergy the better to remember ther bounden duty to God and the people, whiche is to edefye the people with good preching and teaching of the trew word of God. And then we shold shortly have more divines then lawyers wher now it is clene contrary.

   Item I take it that albeit a man be convicted in the spirituell court of eny crime and dothe penaunce compulsatory, whiche be ther comenly used, yet he must after that be reconsiled to God by contricion, confession, and penance, and also by making satisfaction to his neibor whom he hathe offended or els he cannot be discharged ayenst God. So that it shold seme the seid spirituell lawes be but ad terrorem, wherfore it were more to reduce them to the kinges courts according to his prerogative. And that for divers consideracions wherof oon is because they juge in many cases upon tithes, oblations, obventions, mortuarys, probatt of testaments, and other thinges for the execution <of them>[i] appon pencions, portions, proccys, simony, and other, whiche be profittes oonly apperteining to the clergy, and therfor by comen prescription they will not always juge indifferently appon them. And if they wold geve any erronyouse jugement none appele lieth

---

[1] Later hand.

(159)

THE TIME OF HENRY VIII: CERTAIN CONSIDERATIONS WHY THE SPIRITUAL JURISDICTION WOULD BE ABROGATED AND REPEALED, OR REFORMED AT LEAST.

First, I cannot see but that all such laws which are called spiritual laws first commenced against the king's prerogative forasmuch as the clergy have not, nor at any time had, any power given to them directly from God to make any laws within this realm nor to execute any laws but their laws, but they have been made and executed by the single usurped power of the bishop of Rome by the sufferance and allowance of the king's grace and his progenitors, kings of this realm, whereby they have not only lost great advantage which they ought to have had by such suits (which they call spiritual suits) if they had been taken in [the royal] courts, [such] as issues, fines, amercements and forfeitures, with the advantage of all the process of the law if such suits had been taken after the ordinary course of the law of the realm, [such] as of the seal of the original and judicial writs, but also it has been greatly in derogation of his laws and almost grown to a subversion of them. For this reason, if they were repealed and set in some good order by the king's laws it would cause the clergy better to remember their bounden duty to God and the people, which is to edify the people with good preaching and teaching of the true word of God. And then we should soon have more divines than lawyers where now it is completely contrary.

Item, I take it that even though a man might be convicted in the spiritual court of any crime and does a compulsory penance, which is commonly used there, yet after that he must be reconciled to God by contrition, confession and penance, and also by making satisfaction to his neighbour whom he has offended, or else he cannot be discharged against God. So that it should seem [that] the said spiritual laws are only for terror, for which reason it would be more [appropriate] to reduce them to the king's court according to his prerogative. And that [is] for several considerations, of which one is because they judge in many cases on tithes, oblations, obventions, mortuaries, probate of testaments, and other things for the execution of them upon pensions, portions, process, simony and others, which are profits pertaining only to the clergy, and therefore by common prescription they will not always judge indifferently upon them. And if they give any erroneous judgment no appeal lies except in certain cases recently

but in certen casez of late ordeined by parlament, whiche be very few in number conserning the residue.

And as towchyng laynge of violent handes appon clerkes and ecclesiastical persons they cannot by comen presumption be so indifferent as the kinges justices, and that may appere by certen priveleges whiche they heretofore have clamed and affermed it to be by the word of God, whiche is that they ought not be araigned before seculer juges for felony ne otherwise whiche they cannot prove to be contrary to the word of God as I thinke. And that pervyth daily experience. And also they cannot be indifferent in that case because it concernyth them selffez and non other.

[fo. 241v] Also for layng of violent handes in clerkes and other ecclesiasticall persons perteyneth not to them to determyn but to the kinges court because it staundeth in trespass, the nature wherof properly apperteyneth to the kinges court to determyne, although they have byn faverd therin by the tretice of circumspecte agatis, articuli cleri, and sub qua forma, as by them it dothe appere. And also they have not ben only faverd by the kinges lawes in that case, but also they have not byn compelled to abjure the realme for felony when they have takyn seyntuary for hit and confessed the facte, as it also apperith in articuli cleri.

And as towchyng reparations of chyrches, chyrche yeardes, dilapidations, ornaments of the chyrche, and accomptes to be made by the chyrchewardens, I thynke they perteyne most properly to the kinges court because they stonde in the nature of an action of waste or accompte, <And like>ᵈ <wherefore>ⁱ remedy wold be provyded by parlament in suche casez. And I thynke they weare first sufferd to have jurisdicion in those casez because they weare matters of litill wyght or else men weare very scrupulouse at those daies.

And as towchynge matrimony, fornication, diffamation, idolatre, and suche other, [these] myght be reduced to the kinges court and ther determyned very well appon lawes therfore to be ordeyned by parlament.

Also if the spirituell jurisdiction shold continue, if any of the kinges subjectes be convicted of any crime or cause whiche they call spirituell it wold be ordeined that they shold not injoine the partye to agre with the party adversaunt, for then they must nedes juge appon temporall causes and so always deface the kinges court. For the party after satisfacion made to the <kinges court>ᵈ party adversaunt cannot sue for the wronge in the kinges court wherby the kinge shall lose all his advantages

ordained by parliament, which are very few in number considering those that remain.[1]

And with regard to laying of violent hands upon clerks and ecclesiastical persons they cannot, by common presumption, be as indifferent as the king's justices, and that may appear by certain privileges which they have heretofore claimed and affirmed it to be by the word of God, which is that they ought not [to] be arraigned before secular judges for felony nor otherwise which they cannot prove to be contrary to the word of God, as I think. And that daily experience proves. And also they cannot be indifferent in that case because it concerns themselves and no others.

Also, laying violent hands by clerks and other ecclesiastical persons does not pertain to them to determine, but to the king's court, because it stands in trespass, the nature of which properly pertains to the king's court to determine, although they have been favoured therein by the treatise[s] of *Circumspecte Agatis*, *Articuli Cleri*, and *sub qua forma*, as by them it appears.[2] And also they have not only been favoured by the king's laws in that case, but also they have not been compelled to abjure the realm for felony when they have taken sanctuary for it and confessed the fact, as also appears in *Articuli Cleri*.[3]

And with regard to [the] repair of churches, churchyards, dilapidations, ornaments of the church, and accounts to be made by the churchwardens, I think they pertain most properly to the king's court because they stand in the nature of an action of waste or account, for which reason remedy would be provided by parliament in such cases. And I think they were first suffered to have jurisdiction in those cases because they were matters of little weight, or else men were very scrupulous in those days.

And as touching matrimony, fornication, defamation, idolatry, and such other [causes], these might be reduced to the king's court and there determined very well upon laws ordained by Parliament for them.

Also, if the spiritual jurisdiction should continue, if any of the king's subjects were convicted of any crime or cause which they call spiritual, it would be ordained that they should not enjoin the party to agree with the party adversant, for then they must needs judge upon temporal causes and so always deface the king's court. For the party cannot sue for wrong in the king's court after making satisfaction to the party adversant, whereby the king shall lose all his advantages

---

[1] 24 Hen. VIII, c. 12, The Act in Restraint of Appeals (*SR*, iii. 427–429) provided for appeals in cases relating to wills, marriage, tithes, oblations and obventions, but though the appeals were kept within England they remained in the hands of the clergy, working their way through the hierarchy to the archbishop of Canterbury, or Convocation if the issue involved the king. 25 Hen. VIII, c. 19, The acte for submission of the clergy (*SR*, iii. 460–461) re-affirmed the Act in Restraint of Appeals (though omitting wills from the list of subjects), but ordered appeals to go to Chancery, which would appoint a commission in the same way as for appeals from the Admiralty Court. Over the course of this year there seems to have been a substantial shift in policy during which the ecclesiastical courts were moving from being church courts without a pope to being integrated into the secular legal system.

[2] 13 Edw. I, *Circumspecte Agatis* (*SR*, i. 101); 9 Edw. II, stat. 1, c. 16 *Articuli Cleri* (*SR*, i. 174); 13 Edw. I, *Circumspecte Agatis* (*SR*, i. 102).

[3] 9 Edw. II, stat. 1, c. 15 *Articuli Cleri* (*SR*, i. 173).

and profittes aforerehersed. And yet per case no justice shold insue appon suche agrement and satisfacion, for that they cannot agre the partyes after the lawez of the realme as they arr bounde for lacke of the trew knowledge of them. And although they weare lerned in bothe lawes, yet if ther lawes shold continue, ther jugements shold be contrary to the kinges lawes, for by the law of the realme if <ij men be>ⁱ <ij tenants in comen or joint jointenants [sic] be of>ᵈ possessed of any goodes <jointly or in common>ⁱ and oon of them maketh a bequest of his part and dieth yet the survivor shall have the hole goodes. And yet the spirituell law will compell the executorz of the ded to yelde the value of those goodes bequethed to the party to whom it was bequethed wherin they do wronge because the law of the realme is contrary. And in those casez if <the>ᵈ any of the said men so possessed geve his part in his liff the survivor shall not have that parte so geven but only his owne parte.

Also by the spirituell law a child <begoten>ᵈ <borne>ⁱ before matrimony is mulier if matrimony folow betwyn the man and the woman and <by>ⁱ the law of the realme that child is basterd. Many other casez might be put wherin the seid lawez be contraryouse, wherfore, and for that yn divers of the articlez aforeseid and other now in debate, sometimez the kinges court hath hadd jurisdicion and sometime the spirituell court, wherby the jugez and others of bothe lawez have divers tymez byn in dowte whiche court shold have jurisdicion, it wold be all brought to oon court. And how the seid jurisdicions be mixt it somewhat apperith afterward.

IN CRIMINIBUS

Heretice Privitates

[*fo. 242*] Herysies have byn always enqured of in leetes by the old customes of the realme, <but>ⁱ the examinacion of heresye hath by custome only ben <exa>ᵈ takyn in this realme <by ordineries>ⁱ and they before the statut of anno xxvᵒ Hen. viij myght take other to be associatt to them. But now sith that statute ordinarys may tak none to them as we take it, but by the kinges commission etc. and it was expedient that no ordinary shold sitt therappon withowte suche commission.

Nota: Also the ordinerye sith the seid statut may arrest none for heresye but he be indited or that too witnes be brought ayenst him. And if he do an action of false imprisonment lieth and etc. and so it doth if the inditment or witnes be not sufficient to prove it heresye.

Nota: Also withowte the kinges <withowte the kinges>ᵈ writ de heretico comburendo none shal be brent ne never shold have byn, but only betwyn the statut of secundo Henrici quarti that is repelled and the seid statut of anno xxvᵒ Rex nunc [Henry VIII]. And the kinge may command the ordinary to shew the processe, and therappon may pardon the party if he so chuse.

and profits rehearsed above. And yet perhaps no justice should ensue upon such [an] agreement and satisfaction [of the suit], because they cannot reconcile the parties according to the laws of the realm as they are bound for lack of [their own] true knowledge of them. And even if they were learned in both laws, yet if their laws should continue, their judgments should be contrary to the king's laws, for by the law of the realm if two men are possessed of any goods jointly or in common and one of them makes a bequest of his part and dies, yet the survivor shall have the whole goods. And yet the spiritual law will compel the executors of the dead to yield the value of those goods bequeathed to the party to whom it was bequeathed wherein they do wrong, because the law of the realm is contrary. And in those cases if any of the said men so possessed gives his part during his life the survivor shall not have that part so given, but only his own part.

Also, by the spiritual law a child born before matrimony is legitimate if matrimony follows between the man and the woman, and by the law of the realm that child is illegitimate. Many other cases might be put wherein the said laws are contrary, for which reason and because in several of the articles aforesaid and others now in debate, sometimes the king's court has had jurisdiction and sometimes the spiritual court, whereby the judges and others of both laws have several times been in doubt which court should have jurisdiction, it would all be brought to one court. And how the said jurisdictions are mixed appears somewhat afterwards.

ON CRIMES

ON PRIVATE HERESIES

Heresies have always been enquired of in leets by the old customs of the realm, but the examination of heresy has by custom only been taken in this realm by ordinaries, and before the statute of 25 Hen. VIII they might take others to be associated with them.[1] But now since that statute ordinaries may take no-one to [be associated with] them, as we understand it, except by the king's commission etc., and it would be better if no ordinary should sit upon this cause without such a commission.

Note: Also, the ordinary, since the said statute, may arrest no-one for heresy unless he is indicted or two witnesses are brought against him. And if [the ordinary] does [arrest someone] an action of false imprisonment lies and etc., and so it does if the indictment or the witness is not sufficient to prove it heresy.

Note: Also, without the king's writ *de heretico comburendo* no-one shall be burnt nor ever should have been, except between the statute of 2 Hen. IV that is repealed and the said statute of 25 the king that now is [Henry VIII].[2] And the king may command the ordinary to show the process and may pardon the party upon this if he so chooses.

---

[1] 25 Hen. VIII, c. 14 (*SR*, iii. 454–455).
[2] 2 Hen. IV, c.15, *De Heretico Comburendo* (*SR*, ii. 125); 25 Hen. VIII, c. 14 (*SR*, iii. 454–455).

Simonie[1]

Simonye by custome belongith to thc spirituell jurisdiction but if it weare brought by parlament to the kinges court we thinke it weare well don, for we never sawe correction don in that behalf and yet many have offended therin as we thinke.

Adulterii, incestus, <Concubinatus>[d]
fornicacionis, and concubinatus

[*fo. 242v*] The examinacion of all thiez by custome perteyne to the clergy, but if a vicyousse housse be kept wherin suche offensis be commynly used it is to be ynquered of as for a comen nuisaunce and to be punished by the kinges lawes.

Nota: Also if a man knowe my servaunt carnally within my howsse <and gett hyr with child>[i] I shall have an action of trespasse ayenst him, quare domum fregit and AB servientem meam carnaliter cognovit <et impregnavit>[i] per quod servicium <eius per magnum tempus>[i] omisi etc.

Nota: Also gret parcialite hathe byn seyn in suche thinges when clerkes in the gretter offences have gon unponnished and pore lay men in the lesse offence have byn grevousely handled.

Pecati contra natura[2]

Sith the statut <was made>[i] wherby this offence was made felonye the clergye may therin take no examination for the cryme, for if they shold ther proffes and sentence therappon might blinde the trouthe upon the triall of the felonye at the kinges lawes and that the kinges lawes will nott suffer. And that is the very cause why that though a man falsly slaunder and say that he murdered such a man, ravyshed suche a woman, or stele suche a horsse, that yet no processe shal be made for punishement of the crime by the clergy.

Usurarum

[*fo. 243*] There arr foure articlez concernynge usurye wherappon gret penaltiez be sett by parlament as appereth <in the>[d] anno vj Henry vij and if some other weare so lykwise it weare well don, so we thynke.

Falcitates[3]

Actions upon false returnes of Shreffes upon deceites in bargainz, forging of dedez, and breking of promisez lye at the kinges cort, and we know no case wher any

---

[1] Six to seven centimetres of space between the paragraphs.
[2] Five centimetres left between sections.
[3] Space left between sections.

ON SIMONY

Simony by custom belongs to the spiritual jurisdiction, but if it were brought by Parliament to the king's court we think it would be well done, for we never saw correction done in that circumstance and yet many have offended therein, as we think.

ON ADULTERY, INCEST,
FORNICATION AND CONCUBINAGE

The examination of all these by custom pertains to the clergy, but if a vicious house is kept wherein such offences are commonly used it is to be enquired of as a common nuisance and to be punished by the king's laws.

Note: Also, if a man shall know my servant carnally within my house and get her with child I shall have an action of trespass against him, 'because he broke into my house' and 'he carnally knew A.B. my servant and impregnated her, for which reason I have lost her service for a long time' etc.

Note: Also, great partiality has been seen in such things when clerks have gone unpunished in their greater offences, and poor men have been greviously handled in lesser offences.

ON SINS AGAINST NATURE

Since the statute was made whereby this offence was made a felony the clergy may take no examination for this crime, for if they should their proofs and sentence upon it might blind the truth upon the trial of the felony at the king's laws, and that the king's laws will not allow.[1] And that is the real reason why even if a man should falsely slander [one] and say that he murdered such a man, ravished such a woman, or stole such a horse, still no process shall be made for punishment of the crime by the clergy.

ON USURY

There are four articles concerning usury upon which great penalties are set by Parliament as appears in 6 Hen. VII, and if some others were similarly [set] it would be well done, so we think.[2]

ON FALSENESS[3]

Actions upon false returns of sheriffs upon deceits in bargains, forging of deeds, and breaking of promises lie at the king's court, and we know no case where any

---

[1] 25 Hen. VIII, c. 6, An acte for the punysshement of the vice of buggerie (*SR*, iii. 441).

[2] *Rectius* 11 Hen. VII, c. 8, An acte agaynst usurye (*SR*, ii. 574).

[3] In the canon law the title 'De crimine falsi' referred to forgery, but this text seems to interpret it more broadly. Cf. Bray, *Tudor Church Reform*, p. 23.

sute shalbe takyn in the spirituell court for any falsenes, but it be for perjury and breking of his faith, wherof ther be other articles folowing in your bill, and if ther be any suche we desire that ye declare them unto usse.

Perjurii et fidei lesionis

For perjury made in the kinges court upon wagers of lawe and geving of false verdictes ne upon othez to make suerte of any temporall thynge that is not performed, no sute liethe in the spirituell court. But if a man make an othe to mary a woman by a day and do not, it may rether stonde with the kinges lawez that a sute may lie for it in the spirituell court, and we desire youe to shewe usse some particler casez wherappon ye thinke that the sute liethe ther upon perjury or breking of faithe.

Secrilegii, divinacionis augurii, Idolatrie, and blasphemacionis

[fo. 243v] We know not that the kinges court hath medled with thez offences, how beyt we wold desire to know the specialteez of them.

Sacrilegii

Iff a chalice, booke, vestyment, or other thing that belongith to the chyrche be stolyn owte of the chyrche, the chyrche wardens shall have appele of robbery or an action of trespass if they will. And so shall the parson if his goodes be takyn owte of the chyrche.

  Also, if a man for savegard of certen goodes that he pretendith to be his and yet be not so in dede bringith them to a chyrche and claymeth it as it were a sentuary for his goodes as he might do in some wise for his body, and after he that hathe right takith them owte of the chyrche, he ought not to be sud for sacrileage. And what other casez ye meyne by that terme sacrilege we desire youe somewhat to declare therof in specialteez.

Diffa[ma]cionis and convitii

[fo. 244] For all diffamationis and reproffez, whiche we take to be ment by the terme convitium, wherby the party defamed or reproved hathe any werldly lose, as lose of goodes, of services, of frendshippe, or other like wherby other lossez arr like to folow, an action upon the case liethe in the kinges writ howbeit if the party will he may take his sute in the spirituell court except it be for a sclaunder of murder, felonye, rape, trespass, or suche other, wherappon actions may be takyn after and tried upon the principall mater in the kynges court. But we thinke it resonable that it be prohibited that none sue in bothe courtes.

suit shall be taken in the spiritual court for any falseness unless it is for perjury and breaking of his faith whereof there are other articles following in your bill, and if there are any such [cases] we desire that you declare them to us.

On perjury and breach of faith

No suit lies in the spiritual court for perjury made in the king's court upon wagers of law and giving of false verdicts, nor upon oaths to make surety of any temporal thing that is not performed. But if a man makes an oath to marry a woman by a [certain] day and does not [do so], it may stand better with the king's laws that a suit may lie for it in the spiritual court, and we desire you to show us some particular cases where you think that the suit lies there upon perjury or breaking of faith.

On sacrilege, divination by augurs, idolatry and blasphemy

We do not know that the king's court has meddled with these offences, even though we would like to know the particular kinds of them.

On sacrilege

If a chalice, book, vestment, or other thing that belongs to the church is stolen out of the church, the churchwardens shall have appeal of robbery or an action of trespass, if they wish it. And so shall the parson if his goods are taken out of the church.

Also, if a man brings certain goods that he pretends are his, which actually are not, to a church to safeguard them and claims it as a sanctuary for his goods, as it were, as he might do in some way for his body, and afterwards the one that has right [in the goods] takes them out of the church, he ought not to be sued for sacrilege. And we would like you to explain further the particular kinds of other cases you mean by that term sacrilege.

On defamation and abuse

An action on the case lies in the king's writ for all defamations and reproofs, which we take to be meant by the term *convitium*, whereby the party defamed or reproved has any worldly loss, [such] as loss of goods, of services, of friendship, or other such things whereby other losses are likely to follow, even though if the party wishes he may take his suit in the spiritual court unless it is a slander of murder, felony, rape, trespass or such things upon which actions may be taken after and tried upon the principal matter in the king's court. But we think it reasonable that it should be prohibited that no-one sues in both courts.

Injectionis manuum violentarum in Clericos et ecclesiasticas personas necnon criminum et excessuum aliorum quorumcunque spiritualium, dummodo ad correctionem animarum et penam canonicam agatur et non petatur principaliter pecunia

The sutes wher a man leyethe violent handez *in Clericos* and *in conversos* is appointed by the \<articlez>[i] \<_\>[d] of *sub qua forma*, but ther is no mention made ther of thiez wordez *ecclesiasticas personas* ne we know redely what persons ye meyne by those wordes. And also the seid articlez of *sub qua forma* arr contrariaunt in it self, for first it seithe that for breking of the peece amendes must be made before the king and for the excommunication before the bisshopp and then it \<ge>[d] seithe forder that if corporall paine be injoined and he will frely redeme it, gevinge to the prelate or to the party greved money that he may do it and no prohibition to lie, and so by that later clause the making an ende before the king is takyn away, wherby the kyng shall lose his finez and so finally the clergy shall judge upon trespasse.

Also treson, murder, rape, felonye, and trespasse in landez and goodez be crimez and excesses yet may not ordynaryez ponishe clerkes that offend in suche crimez: but for advowtry, fornication, and suche other flesheley incontinency they may punishe them by the statut of anno primo Hen. vij. And in suche thinges as the principall mater [*fo. 244v*] therof perteineth to the triall and juydment of the kinges lawez, the ordinaryez shall make no percesse for correcion of the sinne, as is seid before, for if they might, the proves upon that correction, if they weare untrew, wold be a gret blindinge upon the triall of the principall mater in the kinges court, and therfor the ordinariez in suche casez be perhibitt by the kinges lawez to do correction whether they do pretend to do it principally for money or for correction of the sin for the soules helth.

Quere de beneficialibus

But if it be ment for the benevolence of parishens accustomed to be payed by the assent of the parishens for the meyntenaunce of the chyrche or for corne money or any other thing assessed by the parishens and accustomed to be payed time owte of mind, he that will withold it and will not paye it may be distreined for the same and avowr maintenable therfor in the kynges courts. And if ye meyne any other thing we desire yow to declare it to usse.

Matrimonialibus

Many thinges concerninge matrimonye perteine to the triall and jugement of the kinges lawez, as it is of this issue borne before the spouselles or not borne before

ON PLACING VIOLENT HANDS UPON CLERKS AND ECCLESIASTICAL PERSONS
AND ALSO CRIMES AND EXCESSES OF OTHER SPIRITUAL PERSONS WHATSOEVER
AS LONG AS IT WAS DONE FOR THE CORRECTION OF SOULS AND IMPOSITION OF
CANONICAL PENALTIES AND MONEY WAS NOT PRINCIPALLY DEMANDED

The suits whereby a man lays violent hands 'on clerks' and 'on lay brothers' is appointed by the articles of *sub qua forma*, but there is no mention made there of these words 'ecclesiastical persons', nor do we readily know what persons you mean by these words.[1] And also the said articles of *sub qua forma* are internally inconsistent, for first it says that amends for the breaking of the peace must be made before the king and for the excommunication before the bishop, and then it says further that if corporal penance is enjoined and [the defendant] will freely redeem it, giving money to the prelate or to the aggrieved party, that he may do this and no prohibition lies, and so by that later clause [the possibility of] ending [the case] before the king is taken away, whereby the king shall lose his fines and so finally the clergy shall judge upon trespass.

Also, treason, murder, rape, felony, and trespass in lands and goods are crimes and excesses, yet the ordinary may not punish clerks that offend in such crimes: but for adultery, fornication, and other such fleshly incontinency they may punish them by the statute of 1 Hen. VII.[2] And in things like this where the principal matter pertains to the trial and judgment of the king's laws, the ordinaries shall make no process for correction of the sin, as is said before, for if they might, the witnesses upon that correction, if they were untrue, would be a great blinding upon the trial of the principal matter in the king's court, and therefore the ordinaries in such cases are prohibited by the king's laws from doing correction, whether they pretend to do it principally for money or for the correction of sin for the soul's health.

QUERY CONCERNING BENEVOLENCES

But if it is meant for the benevolence of parishioners accustomed to be paid by the assent of the parishioners for the maintenance of the church, or for corn money or any other thing assessed by the parishioners and accustomed to be paid time out of mind, he that will withold it and will not pay it may be distrained for the same and avowry is maintainable for this in the king's courts. And if you mean any other thing we desire you to declare it to us.

ON MATRIMONY

Many things concerning matrimony pertain to the trial and judgment of the king's laws, such as issue born before the spousals or not born before

---

[1] *Sub qua forma* is the second part of *Circumspecte Agatis* 13 Edw. I (*SR*, i. 101–102). Part of the language of the heading comes from earlier in the statute.

[2] 1 Hen. VII, c. 4 (*SR*, ii. 500–501).

the spouselles, and of bastardy aleged in them that be straungerz to the writ, or if bastardy be aleged in personall actiouns, his wiff or not his wiff, he maried hyr or not maryed hyr, and likewise in devorces in some casez, and also the lawez of the realme and the <spirituell>[i] law [fo. 245] vary in some casez upon bastardy, as if a woman alop fro hyr husband and have a child, that child after the lawez cannon is a bastard and after the lawez of the realme if the husband be within the foure seez and owte of prison the childe is mulier and shall inherite his fathers inheritaunce. Likewise the law cannon dothe afferm the child mulier that is borne before the spousells if espousalles after folow betwyn the father and mother of the same child, and by the lawez of the realme the same child is a basterd. But what contract of matrimony is good and what not and at what age matrimonye may be made or at what age they may disagre and within what degreys they may mary, by the old custome of the realme perteineth to the clergye. But if the lawez cannon be contrarye to the statut latly made for degrees of mariage we thinke those lawez ought not to be putt in execution. And if ye understond any thing by the terme *matrimonialibus* but as is touched we desir you to declere it.

DECIMARUM ETIAM SI FUERINT HUIUSMODI DECIMAE SEPARATUR A NONEM PARTIBUS

Iff a parishener will not sever his tithe fro the ix partes the sute, after the custome of the realme, hathe byn takyn alway before the ordinary but if the parishener sever owte his tithe and a straunger takithe it away the curat hathe no remedy but in the kinges court. And like law we thinke to be if the parishener [him]self after he hathe sefferd the tith cary it away that the curat shall have his sute in the kynges court.

Nota: Also if ther be variaunce betwyn ij parsons in whose parishe the ground that the tithe is on liethe, it shalbe tried by the kinges lawe.

Also if the tithez amount to the fourthe part of the benefice <it shall>[d] the right therof shalbe tried in the kinges court. [f. 245v] In an action of trespasse brought by oon parson agenst another parson for corne in sheves, the defendant seithe that they weare in his parishe and he toke them as his tithe severd from the ix[th] parte etc. and the pleyntiff seith that he and his predecessors have always hadd the tithe ther etc. in this wise the kinges court hathe hadd jurisdiction. And <st>[d] ther bese many diversiteez wher the action is brought by a parson agenst the fermor of another parson or his servant, or by a fermor of on parson agenst a fermor of another parson, and wher sometime the plaintif shal be received to averr that it is his lay chatell and wher not, and wher a scire facias liethe for the kyng <or his patentes>[i] for dismez in the chauncerye or in the escheker and wher not, and wher the

the spousals; and of bastardy alleged in those who are strangers to the writ; or if bastardy is alleged in personal actions; his wife or not his wife; he married her or did not marry her; and likewise in divorces in some cases: and also the laws of the realm and the spiritual law vary in some cases upon bastardy, as if a woman elopes from her husband and has a child, that child under the canon law is a bastard, and under the laws of the realm if the husband is within the four seas and out of prison the child is legitimate and shall inherit his father's inheritance. Likewise, the canon law affirms that the child born before the spousals is legitimate if spousals follow afterwards between the father and mother of the same child, and by the laws of the realm the same child is a bastard. But what contract of matrimony is good and what not, and at what age matrimony may be made or at what age they may disagree and within what degrees they may marry, by the old custom of the realm pertains to the clergy. But if the canon laws are contrary to the statute lately made for degrees of marriage we think those laws ought not to be put in execution.[1] And if you understand anything by the term matrimony beyond what is touched [upon], we desire you to declare it.

On tithes, although the tenth will have been separated from the nine parts in this way

If a parishioner will not sever his tithe from the nine parts the suit, by the custom of the realm, has always been taken before the ordinary, but if the parishioner severs out his tithe and a stranger takes it away the curate has no remedy but in the king's court. And we think the law is likewise if the parishioner himself carries the tithe away after he has severed it, that the curate shall have his suit in the king's court.

Note: Also, it shall be tried by the king's law if there is disagreement between two parsons in whose parish the ground that the tithe is on lies.

Also, if the tithes amount to the fourth part of the benefice the right thereof shall be tried in the king's court. In an action of trespass brought by one parson against another parson for corn in sheaves, [where] the defendant says that they were in his parish and he took them as his tithe severed from the ninth part etc., and the plaintiff says that he and his predecessors have always had the tithe there etc., in this instance the king's court has had jurisdiction.[2] And there are many diversities where the action is brought by a parson against the farmer of another parson or his servant, or by a farmer of one parson against a farmer of another parson, and where sometimes the plaintiff shall be received to aver that it is his lay chattel and where not, and where a *scire facias* lies for the king or his patentees for tithes in the Chancery or in the Exchequer and where not, and where the

---

[1] 25 Hen. VIII, c. 22, § 2 (*SR*, iii. 472) repeated and extended to apply to sexual relations as well as marriage in 28 Hen. VIII, c. 7 (*SR*, iii. 658).

[2] YB Hil. 20 Hen. VI, fo.17, pl. 8. There was a complex history of the king's court claiming jurisdiction over tithe cases for a variety of reasons, see for example YB Mich. 39 Edw. III, fos 23–24, and YB Hil. 5 Hen. V, fo. 10, pl. 23.

write of right of dismez liethe and wher not, that it wold aske alonge time to declare the particler casez of hyt.

OBLACIONIS, OBVENCIONIS, DEBITARUM ET CONSUETARUM ECCLESIE ET PERSONIS ECCLESIASTICARUM, MORTUARIORUM, PENCIONUM, PORCIONUM SIVE PRESTACIONEM QUORAMCUNQUE SPIRITUALIUM ET ECCLESIASTICORUM

In thiez we desire to know of youe what jurisdicion <the>^d ye thinke the clergye shold have by reason of thier termez. And then we shall ferder shew our mindez to the as we shall see cause and also to the residue of the articlez.[1]

---

[1] The MS. ends abruptly here.

right of tithes lies and where not, [so] that it would require a long time to declare the particular cases of it.

ON [ALL] OBLATIONS, OBVENTIONS, DUES AND CUSTOMS OF THE CHURCH AND ECCLESIASTICAL PERSONS, MORTUARIES, PENSIONS, PORTIONS OR SURETIES WHATSOEVER, SPIRITUAL OR ECCLESIASTICAL

In these we desire to know of you what jurisdiction you think the clergy should have by reason of their terms. And then we shall further show our minds to thee as we shall see cause, and also to the residue of the articles.

EDWARD HALL'S READING

[*fo.74*] Spiritus sancti gracia sit in omnibus nobis.
Lectio Magistri Hall super le statut de Seint Eglise in vacatione quadragesimali anno regni Henrici octavi dei gratia Anglie et Fraunce rege, fidei defensoris etc. xxxij[do]

Prima Lectura

Anno 2 Hen. 4 ca° primo: le seint Eglise eit ce droit etc. Cest Eglise est ici a intendre le spiritualtie de cest realm et pur ceo que evesques fuerent les primers <de>[d] spirituall persons de cest Eglise et apres eux religious persons est avoyer que est perfist evesque al comen ley et que fuit perfist religious person all comen ley.

Le roy nosme un destre evesque de Londres il nest perfist evesque per le comen ley. Mesme le ley sil nosme un destre evesque de Londres et rendre a luy les temporaltis del evesquerie, uncore il nest pas evesque. Mes si le roy nosme un destre evesque et fait commission a ij evesques <pur>[d] de luy consacrer il est perfist evesque coment que il nad les temporalties.

Le roy escript all dean et chapiter de Powles de eslier John at Style evesque et ilz luy esliont et il est consacrat, il est perfist evesque. Mes si le roy escript pur John at Style et ilz esliount John N[oke] il nest evesque en fait ne elect. Le deane et chapiter <esliont>[il] John at Style come le roy escript et certefiont ceo all roy et le roy fist commission <all archevesque>[2] de consecrater John at Dale, ore John at Style est perfist evesque elect et John at Dale perfist evesque en fait. Issint si le roy escript pur John at Style ou John at Dale et ilz esliont John at Style deinz xij jors et apres esliont John at Dale que est consecrat, il est perfist evesque en fait et John at Style <est perfist>[3] evesque elect. Mes si John at Style soet consecrat evesque il est evesque en fait et John at Dale nest evesque elect.

Le roy escript all chapiter de Powles de eslier levesque de Hertford et ilz luy esliont et certefiont ceo all roy et il lui restore all temporalties, il est perfist evesque sans novell consecration. Quere ley est sil ne fuit consecrat devant. Le roy nosme un destre evesque de Waltham il est evesque nominate et nemi elect, mes si le roy nosme un evesque de Ely et apres escript all chapiter la de luy eslier il est evesque elect et nemi nominater.

Quell persons fuit perfit religious all comen ley.

Home ad enter en meason de religion et use labbit il ne fuit religious mes sil prist labbit et professe obedience il fuit religious. Segnior et tenant, le tenant devi

---

[1] *Om. Hr.*
[2] *Hr: Om. Ha.*
[3] *Om. Hr.*

EDWARD HALL'S READING

May the grace of the holy spirit be within us all.
The reading of Master Hall on the statute of Holy Church in the Lent vacation in the thirty-second year of the reign of King Henry VIII, by the grace of God king of England and France, defender of the faith etc.

First Lecture

2 Hen. IV c.1[1]: *The Holy Church has this right* etc. This Church is here under-stood as the spirituality of this realm, and because the bishops were the first spiritual persons of this Church and after them religious persons, it must be seen what is a perfect bishop by the common law and what is a perfect religious person by the common law.

[If] the king names one to be the bishop of London he is not a perfect bishop by the common law. The law is the same if he names one to be the bishop of London and renders to him the temporalities of the bishopric, still he is not the bishop. Yet if the king names one to be bishop and makes a commission to two bishops to consecrate him, he is a perfect bishop even if he does not have the temporalities.

The king writes to the dean and chapter of St Paul's to elect John at Style bishop and they elect him and he is consecrated, he is a perfect bishop.[2] But if the king writes for John at Style and they elect John [at] Noke he is not bishop in fact nor elect. The dean and chapter elect John at Style as the king writes and certify this to the king, and the king makes a commission to the archbishop to consecrate John at Dale, now John at Style is a perfect bishop-elect and John at Dale a perfect bishop in fact. Thus if the king writes for John at Style or John at Dale and they elect John at Style within twelve days, and afterwards elect John at Dale who is consecrated, he is a perfect bishop in fact and John at Style is a perfect bishop-elect. But if John at Style were consecrated bishop he is bishop in fact and John at Dale is not bishop-elect.

The king writes to the chapter of St Paul's to elect the bishop of Hertford and they elect him and certify this to the king and he restores him to the temporalities, he is a perfect bishop without a new consecration. Query what the law is if he was not consecrated before. [If] the king names one to be the bishop of Waltham he is bishop-nominate and not [bishop]-elect, but if the king names a bishop of Ely and after writes to the chapter there to elect him, he is bishop-elect and not [bishop]-nominate.

What persons were perfect religious at the common law.
If a man entered a house of religion and used the habit he was not a religious but if he took the habit and professed obedience he was a religious. [If] there are

---

[1] 2 Hen. IV, c. 1 (*SR*, ii. 120).   [2] 25 Hen. VIII, c. 20 § 3 (*SR*, iii. 463).

son heir deinz age de xij anz leir est professe, il nest religious et le segnior luy prendra. Issint si villein entre en relligion deinz age il nest religious et le segnior lui seisera: quere sil soet de pleyn age. Mes si apprentisse soit professe deinz age ill nest religious et uncore le magister <...>ᵈ ne luy seisera.

Home espouse apres carnall copulation entre en religion et est professe uncore il nest religious, mes si home espouse devant copulation est professe il est religious.

Home professe ultra le mere et vient en cest realme ill est religious ycy mes si levesque dun dioses professe home en autre diocesse sauns licence del ordinarie il nest religious quar est voyd: 12 Ric. 2.[1]

Les moignes esliont un seculer de estre abbe et il est install, il est abbe a respoindre mes nemi a suer. Mesme ley silz esliont freer ou chanon deestre abbe. Mes silz esliont un de mesme le religion, nient obstant que il ne soet de mesme le lieu, il est abbe.

[*fo. 74v*] Abbay du fondation le roy esliot un abbe sauns licens <le>ᵈ <du>ⁱ roy et levesque ceo certefie il nest abbe, mes si le roy conferme le election donques il est perfist abbe.

Lou religious avera capacite de suer per grant le pope et sauns licens le roy et ou per grant le roy et lou tielles bulles seront voyd per fault de renovation.

Religious person devant anno 20 [Hen. VIII] est fait evesque et le pape dispence evesque son obediens il peut suer saunz licens le roy de chose que touche son evescherie. Mesme le ley si le pape luy licens daver benefice il peut suer etc. Issint sil luy licens de appropriat un benefice ceo est voyd saunz licens le roy. Le pape licens un religious de purchaser terre et devant le statute anno 31° [Hen. VIII] le roy conferme mesme le licens, ambideux <licens>ᵈ licences sont voyde. Le pape licens et dispence ovesque un pur non residence a cest jor et le roy, rechersaunt mesme le licens, dispence ovesque mesme le person le primer est voyd et le second <et>ᵈ <est>[2] bon. <Mesme le licens dispence ovesque mesme le person le primer est void.>ᵈ Mes si le roy <dispens>ᵈ conferme le dispensation donques ambideux sount voide.

Le roy licens un relligious que nest graduat daver ij benefices ill est present al esglise de Dale et apres al eglise de Sale il perdera le primer benefice nient obstant cel licens, mes si fuit doctor ou magister en art il avera ambideux per cell licens.[3] Mes si un doctor ad un benefice et prist auter sauns licens le roy il perdera le 2ᵈ benefice et nemi le primer. Le pape licens un infaunt daver <ijs>ᵈ ij benefices devant le statut anno 21 H[en.] 8 et il ne renovat cell licens devant anno 29 [Hen. VIII]

---

[1] In margin: evesque *Hr*.
[2] *Om. Hr*.
[3] In margin: dyversite *Ha, Hr*.

a lord and tenant [and] the tenant dies with his heir under the age of twelve years and professed, [the heir] is not a religious and the lord shall take him. Thus if a villein enters in religion within age he is not a religious and the lord shall seize him: query if he was of full age. But if an apprentice is professed under age he is not a religious, and yet the master shall not seize him.

A man espoused enters in religion after carnal copulation and is professed still he is not a religious, but a if man espoused is professed before copulation he is a religious.

A man professes beyond the sea and comes into this realm he is a religious here, but if the bishop of a diocese professes a man in another diocese without a licence from the ordinary he is not a religious, for it is void. 12 Ric. II.[1]

[If] the monks elect a secular to be abbot and he is installed, he is abbot to answer but not to sue. The law is the same if they elect a friar or a canon to be abbot. But if they elect one of the same order, notwithstanding that he is not of the same place, he is abbot.

[If] an abbey of the king's foundation elects an abbot without the king's licence, and the bishop certifies this [the abbot-elect] is not the abbot, but if the king confirms the election then he is a perfect abbot.

Where religious shall have capacities to sue by the pope's grant and without the king's licence, and where by the king's grant, and where such bulls shall be void by fault of renovation.

[If] a religious person before 20 Hen. VIII is made a bishop and the pope dispenses the bishop of his obedience, he is able to sue without the king's licence on things which touch his bishopric. The law is the same if the pope licenses him to have a benefice, he is able to sue etc. [However] if he licenses him to appropriate a benefice this is void without a licence from the king. [If] the pope licenses a religious to buy land and the king confirms the same licence before the statute of 31 Hen. VIII, both licences are void.[2] [If] the pope licenses and dispenses one for non-residence today and the king dispenses the same person, rehearsing the same licence, the first is void and the second is good. But if the king confirms the dispensation then both are void.

[If] the king licenses a religious who is not a graduate to have two benefices, [and] he is presented to the church of Dale and after to the church of Sale, he shall lose the first benefice notwithstanding this licence, but if he was a doctor or a master of arts he shall have both by this licence. But if a doctor has a benefice and takes another without the king's licence he shall lose the second benefice and not the first. [If] the pope licenses an infant to have two benefices before the statute of 21 Hen. VIII and he does not renew this licence before 29 Hen. VIII,

[1] 12 Ric. II, c. 15 (*SR*, ii. 60).
[2] 31 Hen. VIII, c. 6, An acte that such as were religious persons may purchace (*SR*, iii. 724–725).

et est present a ij eglises, ambideux sount voyde. Mes sil soit de plein age et ne renovat son licens uncore le primer presentment est solement void. Le pape licens un de marier deins les degrees et il est marier devant anno 28 [Hen. VIII] cest mariage est bon coment que le licens ne soit renovat, mes si home ad tiell licens devant anno 28 [Hen. VIII] et ne renovat ceo devant anno 29 [Hen. VIII] et apres marie cest marriage nest bon. Un deane ad licens dappropriater un benefice devant anno 28 [Hen. VIII] et appropriate et ne emport son bulle cest appropria-tion est solement bon pur un an, mes sil emport son bulles et est renovat ceo est bon a tote jours. Home ad licens de unier un parishe devant anno 28 [Hen. VIII] et unite et ne renovat son bulles cest union est dissolvyd. Mesme le ley si evesque ad un benefice en comendam per bull et ne renovat, il ad perd son benefice.

Quant ceux relligious sount hors de relligion per dereigment ou suppres-sion, quell capacite ilz que sount dereigne ont que ceux que sount suppresse naverount.

Home ad issue ij fits, leigne entre en relligion et est professe, le pere devi, le puisne fitz entre et leigne est dereign, il enheritera come heire. Mes si leigne fitz est professe moign et le abbay est suppresse il ne enheritera come heir. Terre est done < a un a>^d a cest jour a un que fuit moign et derreign et a lauter que fuit moign et suppresse et cestui que fuit derreign devi et cestui que fuit suppresse devi, son heir enheritera. Mes si lees pur term dans ou pur term <dans>^d de vie soet fait a eux et cestui que fuit derreign devi, cestui que fuit suppresse navera le lees. Lees est fait a un moign suppresse sur condition que sil alien il avera fee et il alien et devi, son heir ne enheritera. Terre est don a un moign suppresse et a un que fuit derreign [fo. 75] et a les heires de son corps engendres et cestui que fuit supresse devi, leir dell corps <de>^d cestui que fuit derreign enheritera. Mes si cestui que fuit derreign devi et cestui que fuit supresse devi, null serra heir de son corps. Richard at Style que fuit moign professe et supresse est vouche come heir a John at Style et entre en le garrantie et vouche John at N[oke] que pled et perd, le demandent ad jugement de recovery vers Richard at Style de terre per lui purchase, il suera execution vers John at N[oke] et uncore il ne prendra ryens come heir.

Home seisi dun rent charge graunt ceo a un moign suppresse pur ans ou pur vie ceo est voyd. Mes si un graunt a lui un annuitie ou profitte de son terre ceo est bon graunt. Home entre en relligion et son fite entera et apres il est suppresse, il ne entra sur son fite. Tenaunt en tail fait feoffment en fee et entre en relligion

and he is presented to two churches, both are void.[1] But if he is of full age and does not renew his licence still only the first presentment is void. [If] the pope licenses one to marry within the degrees and he marries before 28 Hen. VIII this marriage is good even though the licence was not renewed, but if a man has such a licence before 28 Hen. VIII and does not renew this before 29 Hen. VIII and afterwards marries, this marriage is not good.[2] [If] a dean has a licence to appropriate a benefice before 28 Hen. VIII and appropriates and does not bring his bull this appropriation is only good for a year, but if he brings his [bull] and it is renewed this is good always. [If] a man has a licence to unite a parish before 28 [Hen. VIII] and unites [it] and does not renew his bulls this union is dissolved. The law is the same if a bishop has a benefice *in commendam* by bull and does not renew, he has lost his benefice.

When these religious are out of religion by deraignment or suppression, what capacity those who are deraigned have which those who are suppressed do not have.

[If] a man has issue two sons, the elder enters into religion and is professed, the father dies, the younger son enters [on the land] and the elder is deraigned, he shall inherit as heir. But if the elder son is a professed monk and the abbey is suppressed he shall not inherit as heir. [If] land is given today to one who was a monk and was deraigned, and to another who was a monk and was suppressed, and the one who was deraigned dies and the one who was suppressed dies, his heir shall inherit. But if a lease for term of years or for term of life was made to them and the one who was deraigned dies, the one who was suppressed shall not have the lease. [If] a lease is made to a suppressed monk on condition that if he aliens he shall have the fee and he aliens and dies, his heir shall not inherit. [If] land is given to a suppressed monk and to one who was deraigned and to the heirs of his body begotten, and the one who was suppressed dies, the heir of the body of the one who was deraigned shall inherit. But if the one who was deraigned dies and the one who was suppressed dies, no-one shall be the heir of his body. [If] Richard at Style, who was a professed monk and is suppressed, is vouched as heir to John at Style and enters in the warranty and vouches John at Noke who pleads and loses, [and] the demandant has a judgment of recovery against Richard at Style of land bought by him, he shall sue execution against John at Noke and still he shall take nothing as heir.

[If] a man seised of a rent charge grants this to a suppressed monk for years or for life this is void. But if one grants an annuity or profit from his land to him this is a good grant. [If] a man enters into religion and his son enters [on the land] and afterwards he is suppressed, he shall not enter on his son. [If] a tenant in tail

---

[1] 21 Hen. VIII, c. 9, An acte that no spirituall persons shall take to ferme of the Kinge ... (*SR*, iii. 293). 28 Hen. VIII, c. 16, An acte for the release of such as have obteyned pretended lycences and dispensacions ... (*SR*, iii. 672–673). The statute allowed dispensations from Rome which could be granted by the archbishop of Canterbury to remain in effect until Michelmas 1537, and provided that all holders of such dispensations could have them confirmed under the great seal during the same period.

[2] The same statute allows that any marriage solemnized under a papal dispensation before 3 November 1534 is valid, assuming that it is not 'prohibited by Goddis lawes', ibid., 672.

et son fite port formedon quia habitum relegiosum assumpsit et le pere est derreigne ou suppresse il ne entra ne le <ff>ᵈ feffe. Mes si home fait feffement en
fee sur condition et entre en relligion et le heir entre pur non performans del
condition et le pere est derreign il <entre>:[1] quere ley sil soet suppresse. Mes si
leir soet attaint et le pere est derreigne il ne reentra. Issint si le seignor ust recover
en cessavit.[2]

Queux de ceux spiritual persons poient marrie per le statuit fait anno 31 [Hen.
VIII] saunz estre felons et queux nemi.
     Home est elect evesque per dean et chapiter de Powles et consecrat evesque
esteant deacon, marrier. Issint si home ou feme professe all age de xij ans et est
fait abbot et nest preist, peut marrier, mes si home de xvj ans per licens du roy est
fait preist, sil marie est felonie. Home entre en relligion all age de xxvj <annz>[3]
et demur la xx ans nient professe, peut marier. Un evesque de son eveschie esteant prist marie, est felonie. Mes si un lay home soet consecrat evesque et depose
il marier et nest felonie.
     Un prist que est disgraded pur heresie ou treason et ad son pardon dell roy
uncore ne peut marier et sil fait est felonie. Mes si home ii foites espouse, esteant bigamus, soit fait prist peut marier et nest felonie. Quere ley si home ii foites
marie est professe en relligion all age de xxi ans et la demur per ascun space fes-
soit divine service et est suppresse, ne peut marier.[4]
     Feme marie apres copulation est professe en relligion et son baron <devi>[5]
et le meason est suppresse si ell marie nest felonie, mes si ell entree en religion
devant carnal copulation et est professe et son baron est en vie et le meason est
suppresse ell ne peut resorter a son baron ne, si son baron soit mort, si ell marie
est felonie.
     Home nient entree infra sacros est fait <m>ᵈ hermyt peut marier saunz licens
et nest fellony. Mesme ley si feme soit fait ancres ou sister de hospitals, mes si
home fuit professe all relligion de St. Johanes esteant dage de xxi ans et la demur
per ascun temps, ne peut marie, quar il vowe chastitie.
     Feme devorce de son baron a mensa et thoro fait vowe de chastitie et prist le
mantell et [annelle][6] et son baron devi, ell peut marier, mes si ell soit devorce per
cause de consanguinite ou precontract et fait vowe et prist le mantell et [annelle][7]
ell ne peut marier <et [annelle][8] ell ne peut marier>[9]. Un widdowe fist vowe de
chastite devant son curat uncore ell peut marier:[10] quere ley si ell fait vowe solem-
ply devant levesque.
     Home relligious esteant apostata ou expulse hors de ceo relligion pur offence
ne peut marier. Un infidell nient christened est fait prist et apres christened peut
marier, mes sil soit christened devant [il][11] ne peut.[12]

---

[1] reentre *Hr.*   [2] In margin: diversitie *Ha, Hr.*
[3] *Om. Hr.*   [4] In margin: contrarie *Ha.*   [5] *Hr.*
[6] *Ha* and *Hr* read ameane.   [7] *Ha* and *Hr* read ameane.   [8] *Ha* and *Hr* read ameane.
[9] Words repeated by dittography.   [10] In margin: contrarie *Ha.*   [11] MS. reads [el].
[12] The bottom quarter of fo. 58 and the following 7 pages (not foliated) are left blank in *Hr*. This passage
     ends at the bottom of fo. 75 in *Ha* and picks up with no gap at the top of fo. 75v.

makes a feoffment in fee and enters in religion and his son brings a formedon *quia habitum religiosum assumpsit* and the father is deraigned or suppressed, he shall not enter nor shall the feoffee. But if a man makes a feoffment in fee on condition and enters in religion, and the heir enters for non-performance of the condition and the father is deraigned, he shall enter [on the land]: query the law if he was suppressed. But if the heir was attainted and the father is deraigned he shall not re-enter. The same if the lord had recovered in *cessavit*.

Which of these spiritual persons may marry by the statute made 31 Hen. VIII without being felons and which may not.[1]

[If] a man is elected bishop by the dean and chapter of St Paul's and consecrated bishop when he is a deacon, [he may] marry. Thus if a man or woman professes at the age of twelve years and is made abbot and is not a priest he may marry, but if a man of sixteen years is made a priest by the licence of the king, if he marries it is a felony. [If] a man enters in religion at the age of twenty-six and remains there unprofessed for twenty years he may marry. [If] a bishop of his bishopric marries, being a priest, it is a felony. But if a layman is consecrated bishop and deposed he may marry and it is not a felony.

A priest who is degraded for heresy or treason and has his pardon from the king still may not marry, and if he does it is felony. But if a man who is twice married is made a priest (being a bigamist) he may marry and it is not a felony. Query the law if a man twice married is professed in religion at the age of twenty-one and remains there for some time performing divine service and is suppressed, [if] he may not marry.

A married woman is professed in religion after copulation and her husband dies and the house is suppressed: if she marries this is not a felony, but if she enters in religion before carnal copulation and is professed and her husband is alive and the house is suppressed, she may not return to her husband, [and] if her husband is dead, if she marries, it is a felony.

[If] a man who has not entered into holy orders is made a hermit he may marry without licence and it is not a felony. The law is the same if a woman is made an anchoress or a sister of the hospitals, but if a man was professed to the order of St John at the age of twenty-one years and remains there for some time he may not marry, for he vowed chastity.

[If] a woman divorced from her husband *a mensa et thoro* makes a vow of chastity and takes the mantle and ring and her husband dies she may marry, but if she is divorced by reason of consanguinity or precontract and makes a vow and takes the mantle and ring she may not marry. [If] a widow makes a vow of chastity before her curate still she may marry: query the law if she makes a vow solemnly before the bishop.

A religious man being apostate or expelled out of his order for an offence may not marry. [If] an infidel who was never christened is made a priest and afterwards [he is] christened [he] may marry, but if he was christened before he may not.

---

[1] 31 Hen. VIII, c. 14, An acte abolishing diversity in opynions (*SR*, iii. 739).

Secunda Lectura

[*fo. 75v*] Devant jeo aye monstre a vous coment le clergie claym come lour droit daver probation del testament si home fait testament et ore jeo monstra a vous si home ne fist testament mes devi intestate come ilz claym de commyter ladministration de ces biens, et pur ceo est avoyer quell person morust intestat.

Home fait volunt et ne fist ascun son executor il devi intestait. Issint sil <fait>[1] John at Style ou John at N[oke] son executor il devi intestait. Mes sil <voil>[d] fait John at Style son executor et voill que syl <John>[d] refuse que John at Dale serra executor il ne devi intestat.

Si home voil que le college de Eton serra son executor il devi intestat. Mesme ley sil voil que le comonaltie de London serra son executor. Mes sil voil que son heir serra son executor et devi son feme esteant grossement enseint ovesque fitz que est nee, il ne devi intestat. Quere ley si lenfant soit nee et nest fait executor, le pere devi intestat ab initio.

Home voil que le magister et confreres de tiel gild incorporat serra son executors il devi intestat. Mes sil voil que John at Style et John at Dale, magisters de tiel gild, serra son executors, <il>[2] ne devi intestat. Mes si le person fait executor il ne devi intestat.[3]

Home voil que le heir de John at Style serra son executor et devi vivant John at Style il devi intestat, mes sil voil que John at Style, heir apparaunt al John at Style, serra son executor il ne devi intestat.

Home fait volunt et fait John at Style et <ou>[d] John at Dale son executors et voil que son volunt ne serra prove devant lordinaire, mes in le chauncerie, il devi intestat per le spirituall ley, mes nemi per le temporall ley.

Home volle que John at Style maria son file quil serra son executor John at Style maria le file et est devorce uncore il ne devi intestait. Mes si John at Style maria le file ayant auter feme vivant, il devi intestait.

Home voile que si son feme <devi>[d] ad issue fitz <que le fitz>[d] que le fitz serra son executor et si ell ad <issue>[4] file que John at Style serra son executor et ell ad issue fitz le fitz <fitz>[d] serra executor et sil devi intestat John at Style ne serra <son>[5] executor mes le testator devi intestat. Si home in extremitie dit que John at Style serra son executor et ne fist ascun volunt il devi <in>[d] intestait.

Ou home devi intestait pur part et pur part nemi.

Home deliver bienz a John at Style et voille per son testament que John at Style ferra tiel chose de <cez>[d] <ceux>[i] bienz pur son alme et devi, il devi <in>[d] testait <pur>[6] ceux bienz et intestat pur le remnant.

Home ad bienz en Dale et <et>[d] Sale et voile que John at Style serra son executor de totes bienz in Dale il devi testait de ceux <bienz>[i] in Dale et intestait de ceux biens in Sale. Mesme ley sil fist John at Style executor de <tote>[d] son

---

[1] *Hr.*   [2] *Om. Hr.*
[3] In margin: Nota ceux cases bien in *Ha* and *Hr.*
[4] *Om. Hr.*   [5] *Om. Hr*   [6] de *Hr.*

Second Lecture

Before I have shown you how the clergy claim as their right to have the probate of the will if a man makes a will, and now I shall show you how, if a man does not make a will but dies intestate, they claim to commit the administration of his goods, and for this we must see what person dies intestate.

[If] a man makes a will and does not make anyone his executor he dies intestate. Thus if he makes John at Style or John at Noke his executor he dies intestate. But if he makes John at Style his executor and wills that if he refuses John at Dale shall be executor he does not die intestate.

If a man wills that the college of Eton shall be his executor he dies intestate. The law is the same if he wills that the commonalty of London shall be his executor. But if he wills that his heir shall be his executor and dies with his wife heavily pregnant with a son who is born, he does not die intestate. Query the law if the infant is born and is not made executor, [does] the father die intestate *ab initio*?

[If] a man wills that the master and brothers of such an incorporated guild shall be his executors he dies intestate. But if he wills that John at Style and John at Dale, masters of such a guild, shall be his executors, he does not die intestate. But if the person makes an executor he does not die intestate.

[If] a man wills that the heir of John at Style shall be his executor and dies with John at Style living he dies intestate, but if he wills that John at Style, heir apparent to John at Style, shall be his executor he does not die intestate.

[If] a man makes a will and makes John at Style and John at Dale his executors and asks that his will shall not be proved before the ordinary, but in the Chancery, he dies intestate by the spiritual law, but not by the temporal law.

[If] a man wills that [if] John at Style marries his daughter he shall be his executor [and] John at Style marries the daughter and is divorced, still he does not die intestate. But if John at Style marries the daughter, having another wife living, he dies intestate.

[If] a man wills that if his wife has issue a son that the son shall be his executor, and if she has issue a daughter that John at Style shall be his executor, and she has issue a son, the son shall be the executor, and if [the son] dies intestate John at Style shall not be his executor but the testator dies intestate. If a man in extremity says that John at Style shall be his executor and does not make any will, he dies intestate.

Where a man dies intestate for a part and not for a part.

[If] a man delivers goods to John at Style and [he] wills by his testament that John at Style shall do such a thing with those goods for his soul and dies, he dies testate for those goods and intestate for the rest.

[If] a man has goods in Dale and Sale and wills that John at Style shall be his executor for all the goods in Dale he dies testate for those goods in Dale, and intestate for those goods in Sale. The law is the same if he makes John at Style the

barbitz ou <de>[1] son plat solement. Mes sil voille que John at Style avera le order de tote sez bienz ne devi intestait. Home fait John at Style son executor de tote sez bienz in Yorke et John at Dale de tote ses bienz in London et devant ascun probait John at Style devi intestait, il devi intestait pur ceo part.

Home ad lease come executor et fist execution de tote ses propre bienz, il devi intestait que ad le lease et testait pur le remnant. Mesme ley si home ad leas in droit son feme et fist execution de son propre bienz et devi et le feme devi, lordinaire sequestra le leas per intestation. Home ad avouson et fait execution de toutz son bienz movables il morust intestait de avouson: mesme ley de leas pur anz ou obligation. Contrarie ley est de gard del corps mes nemi de gard de terre.

Home fait testament devant anno 31 [Hen. VIII] de terres et bienz il devi intestait pur les terres et testait pur les bienz. Mesme ley sil fait volunt de son villein et chivall. Mes sil fait testament de ii partes de profite de son terre a cest jour il devi testait de tot son terre, quar est tot que il peut devise per le statut.

Donques quant home devi intestait quell ordinaire ferra sequestre.

[*fo. 76*] Lordinaire del diocese de fair sequestration est proprement lordinaire del diocese et sede vacante le metropolitain. Et le se metropolitaine esteant void le deane del Christe Churche est ordinaire pur Canterburie et le deane de York pur Yorke et vicegerent de roy pur tout. Home ad bienz en diverses counties et dioces le metropolitaine sequestre et nemi lordinaire. Home ad bienz en ambideux <counties>[d] provinces et devi intestait ambideux primates sequestre. <Mesme le ley sil devi <in>[d] testait, le testament serra prove en ambideux provinces>.[2]

Evesque est excomunicat et un devi intestait, uncore il est ordinairie a sequestre. Mes sil soet deprive ou convict de heresie le metropolitaine sequestre et nemi levesque. Un evesque devi intestait le metropolitaine sequestre et si le metropolitaine devi intestait le deane del lieu est ordinaire a sequestre. Le deanery de York est voyd et le archevesque devi intestait et novell archevesque est elect et apres novell deane, le deane sequestra et nemi larchevesque. Mesme ley si un evesque de son province ust devi sede vacante.

Home ad bienz en diverses dioces sede metropolitani vacante, le deane comit le novell administration a un et devi, auter archevesque est elect et ladministrator devi, le deane comittera novell administration et nemi larchevesque. Mesme le ley si testament soet prove devant le deane et les executors devi intestait et novell evesque est eliew, le deane comittera ladministration et nemi larchevesque. Le metropolitaine sequestre bienz dun que devi intestait et devant administration commit devi intestait, le deane comittera <ld>[d] ladministration de

---

[1] *Om. Hr.*
[2] *Hr.*

executor for only his sheep or his armour. But if he wills that John at Style shall have the ordering of all his goods he does not die intestate. [If] a man makes John at Style his executor for all his goods in York and John at Dale for all his goods in London, and before any probate John at Style dies intestate, he dies intestate for this part.

[If] a man has a lease as executor and makes execution of all his own goods, he dies intestate for the lease and testate for the rest. The law is the same if a man has a lease in right of his wife and makes an execution of his own goods and dies and the wife dies, the ordinary shall sequestrate the lease for intestacy. [If] a man has an advowson and makes an execution of all his moveable goods he dies intestate for the advowson: the law is the same for a lease for years or a bond. The law is the contrary for the wardship of the body but not for the wardship of land.

[If] a man makes a will before [the year] 31 [Hen. VIII] of lands and goods he dies intestate for the lands and testate for the goods. The law is the same if he makes a will of his villein and horse. But if he makes a testament of two parts of the profit of his land at that time he dies testate for all his land, for that is all that he can devise by the statute.[1]

Then when a man dies intestate, what the ordinary shall do to sequestrate.

The ordinary of the diocese for the purpose of making sequestration is properly the ordinary of the diocese, and *sede vacante* the metropolitan. And if the metropolitan see is vacant the dean of Christ Church is the ordinary for Canterbury, and the dean of York for York, and the vicegerent of the king for everything. [If] a man has goods in several counties and dioceses the metropolitan shall sequestrate and not the ordinary. [If] a man has goods in both provinces and dies intestate both primates shall sequestrate. The law is the same if he dies testate, the testament shall be proved in both provinces.

[If] a bishop is excommunicated and one dies intestate, still [the bishop] is the ordinary to sequestrate. But if he is deprived or convicted of heresy the metropolitan shall sequestrate and not the bishop. [If] a bishop dies intestate the metropolitan shall sequestrate, and if the metropolitan dies intestate the dean of the place is the ordinary to sequestrate. [If] the deanery of York is vacant and the archbishop dies intestate and a new archbishop is elected, and afterwards a new dean, the dean shall sequestrate and not the archbishop. The law is the same if a bishop of his province had died *sede vacante*.

[If] a man has goods in several dioceses *sede metropolitani vacante* [and] the dean commits the new administration to one and dies, [and] another archbishop is elected and the administrator dies, the dean shall commit the new administration and not the archbishop. The law is the same if a testament is proved before the dean and the executors die intestate and a new bishop is elected, the dean shall commit the administration and not the archbishop. [If] the metropolitan sequestrates goods of one who died intestate, and before the administration is committed [the metropolitan] dies intestate, the dean shall commit the administration of

---

[1] 32 Hen. VIII, c. 1, An acte that landes may be willed by testament (*SR*, iii. 744–746).

ambideux. Mes si larchevesque ad commit <administration>[1] et devi intestait et ladministrator devi et novell <arch>[i] evesque est elect, il committera ladministration et nemi le deane.

En quell casez home avera action originall vers lordinairie que sequestre et ou il serra charge come ordinaire et ou come executor.

Home est en det per obligation a un et devi intestait, lordinaire sequestre, le dettee avera action vers lordinaire. Mes si evesque sequestre et devi intestait et le metropolitaine sequestre action serra port vers lui et sil devi intestait laction serra port vers le deane come gerden des spiritualties. Mes si evesque sequestre et fist executor et devi, laction serra port vers les executors.

Home ad divers infaunts et devi intestait levesque sequestra, lenfantes averont rationabile parte bonorum vers levesque. Mesme ley si home hire un servant en husbandrie, il avera action vers lordinairie pur son salaire, mes si les wages fuerent pluis que lestatut lymit il navera action.

Lordinaire comit ladministration de part de bienz et reteign part le dette peut aver action envers lordinaire ou vers les administrators a son pleasure. Mes sil comit ladministration de tout les bienz action solement gist vers les administrators.

Home ad fee du roy hors de hanaper et ad liberate currant direct al clerk del hanaper de lui paier et de prendre acquittance, si lez clerkes ad sufficient en <leurs>[d] <son>[i] maines il serra charge et sil devi intestait et lordinaire sequestre laction gist vers lordinaire sil ad possession dez bienz. Contrarie ley sil soet per taile sealed. Home prist distress et devi intestait et lordinaire sequestre le<s>[d] distress, replevin gist vers luy. Segnior et bailee et le bailee est trove en surplusage en laccompt et le segnior devi intestait, le ordinaire sequestre et le [bailee] avera action de det vers lordinaire. Home recover det <vers>[d] sur obligation et le dettor devi intestait et lordinaire sequestre, action gist vers luy. Mes si home recover en action de det sur contract et le dettor devi, null action gist vers lordinaire.

Home ad bienz en divers dioces et devi intestait et lordinaires sequestre et paiont detes, action gist vers eux come executors et nemi come ordinaries, quar le metropolitaine doet sequestre et nemi eux. [fo. 76v] Mesme ley si larchevesque de Canterburie sequestre bienz en dioces de York, mes si levesque administre solement les funeralle null action gist vers lui.

Home est oblige en obligation et entre en relligion ovesque sufficient licens sans fair testament, null action gist vers labbe, ne vers lordinaire, et le partie [est] sauns remedie.

Si home fist son ordinaire son executor et il refuse et sequestre, action gist vers lui come ordinaire et nemi come executor. Mes sil prist possession

---

[1] *Hr.*

both. But if the archbishop has committed the administration and dies intestate and the administrator dies and a new archbishop is elected, he shall commit the administration and not the dean.

In what cases a man shall have an original action against the ordinary who sequestrates, and where he shall be charged as ordinary and where as executor.

[If] a man is in debt by a bond to one and dies intestate [and] the ordinary sequestrates, the creditor shall have action against the ordinary. But if the bishop sequestrates and dies intestate and the metropolitan sequestrates, the action shall be brought against him, and if [the metropolitan] dies intestate the action shall be brought against the dean as guardian of the spiritualities. But if the bishop sequestrates and makes an executor and dies, the action shall brought against the executor.

[If] a man has several children and dies intestate [and] the bishop sequestrates, the children shall have *rationabili parte bonorum* against the bishop. The law is the same if a man hires a servant in husbandry, [the servant] shall have an action against the ordinary for his salary, but if the wages were more than the statute delimits he shall not have an action.

[If] the ordinary commits the administration of part of the goods and retains part the creditor may have an action against the ordinary or against the administrators at his pleasure. But if he commits the administration of all the goods action lies solely against the administrators.

[If] a man has the king's fee out of the hanaper and has a current *liberate* directed to the clerk of the hanaper to pay him and to take acquittance, if the clerk has enough in his hands he shall be charged, and if he dies intestate and the ordinary sequestrates the action lies against the ordinary if he has possession of the goods. The law [is] the contrary if it was by a sealed tally. [If] a man takes distress and dies intestate and the ordinary sequestrates the distress, replevin lies against him. [If there is] a lord and bailiff and the bailiff is found in surplus in the account and the lord dies intestate, the ordinary sequestrates and the bailiff shall have an action of debt against the ordinary. [If] a man recovers a debt on a bond and the debtor dies intestate and the ordinary sequestrates, action lies against him. But if a man recovers in an action of debt on a contract and the debtor dies, no action lies against the ordinary.

[If] a man has goods in several dioceses and dies intestate and the ordinaries sequestrate and pay debts, action lies against them as executors and not as ordinaries, for the metropolitan ought to sequestrate and not them. The law is the same if the archbishop of Canterbury sequestrates goods in the diocese of York, but if the bishop administers only the funeral no action lies against him.

A man is obliged on a bond and enters into religion with sufficient licence without making a testament, no action lies against the abbot nor against the ordinary, and the party is without remedy.

If a man makes his ordinary his executor and he refuses and sequestrates, an action lies against him as ordinary and not as executor. But if he takes possession

des bienz sans refusell il sera charge come executor. Home devant anno 27 [Hen. VIII] voile que son executor vendre son terre et fist levesque son executor et levesque vend le terre devant volunte prove et apres refuse et sequestre, action gist vers lui come executor et nemi come ordinairie.

Home voile que John at Style serra son executor et que levesque de dioces serra son coadjutor pur distributer lez bienz. J[ohn at] S[tyle] refuse et levesque sequestre laction gist vers lui come ordinaire et nemi come come [*sic*] executor. Mes si le volunt fuit que John at Style serra executor una cum levesque de dioces et John at Style refuse, uncore action serra port vers levesque come executor et nemi come ordinaire.

Si lordinaire commit administration pendent le brefe ou executor prove le volunt, lou le brefe abbatera et lou nemi.

Home fist son executor et devi, ilz refuse ladministration et lordinaire sequestre et action est port vers lui et pendent le brefe ilz prove le volunt devant le vicegerent, <le>ᵐ brefe abatera si lordinaire ceo monstra. Mes si home soet executor de son torte demesne et action est port vers lui come executor et pendent laction [il] commit ladministration, uncore le brefe nabbatera.

Si action est port vers levesque de Londres et il est translat a Canterburie, uncore le brefe nabbatera. Ordinaire commit administration et ilz sount empled levesque revoke le administration le brefe abatera, mes si levesque discharge executors pendent le brefe le brefe nabatera. Home port action vers ordinaire et recover et devant execution il commit administration, uncore le brefe nabatera. Home devi intestait et action est port vers ordinaire et il commit administration a un estranger, le brefe ne abatera. Contrarie ley sil commit a prochein del sanque, quar il est en lun case son acte demesne et en lauter il est compellable per lestatut. Si ordinairie commit administration et action est <port>¹ per administrator et pendent le bref levesque reles all defendant, uncore ceo nabatera le brefe. Mes si lordinairie reles a lui devant ladministration ceo est bon barr. Si home prist bienz dun et il devi intestait et lordinaire commit administration et ilz port action et lordinaire reles all defendant, ceo nabatera le brefe. Mes si les bienz fuerent prises hors de son possession demesne et ilz portent action et il reles al defendent ceo est barr vers ladministrator.

Ou ceux a queux legacies sount fait per testament sount sans remedie en le spiritual ley pur ceo que le testament ne fuit prove averont remedie per le comen ley.

Home bequeath un cupp all roy per testament et son executor refuse et ordinaire sequestra, il nad remedie per spiritual ley mes avera action de detinue en

---

¹ *Hr.*

of the goods without refusing he shall be charged as executor. [If] a man before the year 27 [Hen. VIII] wills that his executor should sell his land and makes the bishop his executor, and the bishop sells the land before the will is proved and afterwards refuses and sequestrates, an action lies against him as executor and not as ordinary.[1]

A man wills that John at Style shall be his executor and that the bishop of the diocese shall be his co-adjutor to distribute the goods: [if] John at Style refuses and the bishop sequestrates an action lies against him as ordinary and not as executor. But if the will was that John at Style be executor together with the bishop of the diocese and John at Style refuses, still an action shall be brought against the bishop as executor and not as ordinary.

If the ordinary commits the administration pending the writ or the executor proves the will, where the writ shall abate and where not.

[If] a man makes his executor and dies, they refuse the administration and the ordinary sequestrates and an action is brought against him, and while the writ is pending they prove the will before the vicegerent, the writ shall abate if the ordinary shows this. But if a man is the executor de son tort demesne and an action is brought against him as executor and during the action he commits the administration, still the writ shall not abate.

If an action is brought against the bishop of London and he is translated to Canterbury, still the writ shall not abate. [If] the ordinary commits the administration and they are impleaded, [and] the bishop revokes the administration, the writ shall abate, but if the bishop discharges the executors during the writ, the writ shall not abate. [If] a man brings an action against the ordinary and recovers, and before execution [the ordinary] commits the administration, still the writ shall not abate. [If] a man dies intestate and action is brought against the ordinary and he commits the administration to a stranger, the writ shall not abate. The law [is] the contrary if he commits [it] to the next in blood, for it is in the one case his own act and in the other he is compellable by the statute. If the ordinary commits the administration and an action is brought by the administrator, and during the writ the bishop releases to the defendant, still this shall not abate the writ. But if the ordinary releases to him before the administration, this is a good bar. If a man takes the goods of one and he dies intestate, and the ordinary commits the administration and they bring an action, and the ordinary releases to the defendant, this shall not abate the writ. But if the goods were taken out of his own possession and they brought an action and he released to the defendant, this is a bar against the administrator.

Where those to whom legacies are made by testament are without remedy in the spiritual law because the testament was not proved, [they] shall have remedy by the common law.

[If] a man bequeaths a cup to the king by testament and his executor refuses and the ordinary sequestrates, [the king] has no remedy by the spiritual law

---

[1] 27 Hen. VIII, c. 10, An acte concernyng uses and wylles (*SR*, iii. 539–542).

ascun de son courtes a son pleasure. Mesme ley si le bequest soet per paroll. Issint si un home baille bienz a un auter pur rebailler et fait bequest de ceux etc. a roy et les executors refuse, le roy avera action de detinewe vers le bailie. Si home fait legacie de chien all roy et les executors refuse et lordinaire sequestre et vend le chien pur paier les detes, uncore il rendra al roy le value de son propre bienz.

Home possesse de bienz en citie ou bienz sount deportables fait legacie de son part a son fits, les executors refuse, levesque commit ladministration, le fits avera action de detinewe vers les administrators.[1] [fo. 77] Mes si le custome soet que le fitz avera le principall chose de chescun chose deinz le maner de J et le pier fist fefement del maner et prist <estate>[2] a lui et sa feme et bequeathe le principall chose a son fitz et devi, le fitz navera ascun action durant le vie la feme.[3] Contrarie ley si le feme ust devi devant le baron.

Home possesse dun maner lou heir lomes sount appendent per custome et alien le maner et fist legacie de heir lomes et les executors refuse et lordinaire commit ladministration, leir avera null remedie en espiritual court ne en temporall court. Mes si le pier fist feffment del maner en mortgage et bequeath les heire lomes a son fitz et devi, les executors refuse et lordinaire commit le administration et et [sic] leir redeme le terre, il peut prendre les heire lomes ou si lordinaire avera ceo sequestre il avera action vers lui.

Home fist legacie dun cuppe a un pur terme de vie le remainder a un auter a tote joure, lordinaire commit ladministration et ilz deliveront le cuppe a primer tenant pur terme de vie et il devi et son executor happa le cuppe, cestui en le remainder avera action de detinew. Mes si le cuppe ne fuit deliver a tenant pur terme de vie cestui en le remainder est sans remedie en le comen ley.

Lou home nad remedie pur legacie en le spiritual ne temporall court mes solement en le chauncerie.

Home est oblige pur un auter en c li. et paiera largent cestui pur que il fuit oblige bequeathe a lui c li. et fist son executors et devi et ilz refuse et administration est commit, il ad remedie solement en le chauncerie, quar lordinairie nest charge sur simple contract. Home apprompt argent <solement>[d] de John at N[oke] et deliver obligation a John at Style a deliver a John at N[oke], John at Style voile per testament que ces executors deliveront ceo a John at N[oke], ilz refusent et administration est commit, il nad remedie sinon en le chauncerie.

Home reteigne un servant pur keper son hawke et bequeath a lui x li. pur son gages et fist son executor et devi. Ilz refusent et levesque sequestre null action

---

[1] In margin: P[as.] 39 E[dw.] 3. *Ha, Hr.*
[2] *Hr.*
[3] In margin: H[il.] 39 E[dw.] 3. *Ha, Hr.*

but he shall have an action of detinue in any of his courts at his pleasure. The law is the same if the bequest was by parol. Thus if a man delivers goods to another to return and makes a bequest of them etc. to the king and the executors refuse, the king shall have an action of detinue against the bailee. If a man makes a legacy of a dog to the king and the executors refuse, and the ordinary sequestrates and sells the dog to pay the debts, still he shall render to the king the value from his own goods.

[If] a man possessed of goods in the city or movable goods makes a legacy to his son of his share, the executors refuse [and] the bishop commits the administration, the son shall have an action of detinue against the administrators.[1] But if the custom is that the son shall have the principal thing of each thing within the manor of J, and the father makes a feoffment of the manor and takes back an estate to him and his wife and bequeaths the principal thing to his son and dies, the son shall not have any action during the life of the wife.[2] The law [is] the contrary if the wife had died before the husband.

[If] a man is possessed of a manor to which heirlooms are appendant by custom and [he] aliens the manor and makes a legacy of the heirlooms, and the executors refuse and the ordinary commits the administration, the heir shall have no remedy in a spiritual court or in a temporal court. But if the father makes a feoffment of the manor in mortgage and bequeaths the heirlooms to his son and dies, the executors refuse and the ordinary commits the administration and the heir redeems the land, he can take the heirlooms, or if the ordinary has sequestrated them he shall have an action against him.

[If] a man makes a legacy of a cup to one for term of his life, the remainder to another forever, the ordinary commits the administration and they deliver the cup to the first tenant for term of life and he dies and his executor grabs the cup, the remainderman shall have an action of detinue. But if the cup was not delivered to the tenant for term of life, the remainderman is without remedy in the common law.

Where a man has no remedy for a legacy in the spiritual or the temporal court but only in the Chancery.

[If] a man is obliged for another in [the sum of] £100 and pays the money, [and] the one for whom he was obliged bequeaths £100 to him and makes his executors and dies, and they refuse and the administration is committed, he has remedy solely in the Chancery, for the ordinary is not charged on a simple contract. [If] a man borrows money from John at Noke and delivers a bond to John at Style to deliver to John at Noke, [and] John at Style wills by testament that his executors should deliver this to John at Noke, [if] they refuse and the administration is committed [John at Noke] has no remedy except in Chancery.

A man retains a servant as the keeper of his hawk and bequeaths him £10 for his wages and makes his executor[s] and dies. [If] they refuse and the bishop

---

[1] YB Pas. 39 Edw. III, fos 9–10.
[2] Perhaps YB Hil. 39 Edw. III, fo. 6.

gist mes solement en chauncerie. Mes si fuit bailie en husbandrie il avera action vers lordinairie.

Home appromt argent et voile que son executors paier et ilz refusent et levesque sequestre, null remedie pur le det mes en le chauncerie.

Home est en det a John at Style et John at Dale per severall obligations et voile que John at Style serra primerment paie et les executors refusent et levesque commit ladministration. John at Style port action primerment et apres John at Dale port action, les administrators confesse laction de John at Dale et ne sont plusors bienz, John at Style avera sub pena.

Home fait legacie dun cuppe a un que maria son file et devi et les executors refuse et lordinaire sequestre et il maria le file, il nad remedie en le comen ley mes en le chauncerie.

Home fait legacie de xx li. all eglise de St. Andrew en Holborn et devi et son executors refuse et lordinaire commit ladministration, le parson avera sub pena.[1] Mesme ley sil fuit pur trimer un lampe.

Issint sur droit de administration, deo gratias jeo aie conceive cest lecture.[2]

8 LECTURA: LEIGLISHE EIT SON DROICT.

[fo. 77v] Devant jeo aie monstre de juridiciall droicte et droicte de profettes queux le clergie claime daver. Ore jeo monstra a vous un auter droicte que ils clam de punisher overt sine et ceo est en iij pointes principalles, scilicet usurie, perjurie et diffamation, et pur ceo jeo voile entreate le natures et qualities de ceux iij choses, lou ilz seront punishe en lun ley et en auter et lou en ambideux et lou en null ley. Et primerment est avoyer de usurie.

Appert per Magister Glandvile en son livere des leys dengletere que per le ley del terre devant le conquest usurie fuit prohibite et si home fuit endite de usurie per serement de xij homes il perdera son terre et tenementes et son fitz ne enheritera, que fuit dur ley. Mes apres le Juiffe usent userie et prendront lour auctorite Deutronomin 23, lou est dit 'non feneraberis fratri tuo ergo fenerari cum alienigena est permissible' et per cest voie ilz gaineront grand somes <dargent>[3] des Anglois pur ceo que ilz ne puissent committer usurie forsque ovesque eux. Et pur ceo le Roy Edward le primer anno 4° de son reign fist lestatut de Judeismo que prohibit les Juiffe que ilz ne prendre ryens de terre ou tenements, rents ou auters choses, sur peine deestre punishe all volunt le roy et de rendre le userie et plege au Christian. Uncore per cest estatut, ne per null auter, usurie ne fuit punisheable entre Christian et Christian en le temporall ley mes solement per le spirituall ley tanque all an 3° H[en.] 7 lou fuit enact que chescun home que fist corrupt bargaine que est grounded sur usurie que il forfetera un c li.

---

[1] In margin: P[as.]; R[ic.] 2 *Ha* and *Hr.*
[2] Followed by three and a half blank pages, *Hr.*
[3] *Om. Hr.*

sequestrates, action lies only in the Chancery. But if he were a bailiff in husbandry he would have an action against the ordinary.

[If] a man borrows money and wills that his executors should pay and they refuse and the bishop sequestrates, [there is] no remedy for the debt except in the Chancery.

A man is in debt to John at Style and John at Dale by several bonds, and wills that John at Style be paid first and the executors refuse and the bishop commits the administration. John at Style brings an action first, and afterwards John at Dale brings an action, [if] the administrators confess the action of John at Dale and there are no more goods, John at Style shall have a subpoena.

[If] a man makes a legacy of a cup to whoever shall marry his daughter and dies and the executors refuse, and the ordinary sequestrates and he marries the daughter, he has no remedy by the common law but in the Chancery.

[If] a man makes a legacy of £20 to the church of St Andrew in Holborn and dies, and his executors refuse and the ordinary commits the administration, the parson shall have a subpoena.[1] The law is the same if it was to trim a lamp.

Thus on the law of administration, by the grace of God, I have conceived this lecture.

EIGHTH LECTURE: THE CHURCH SHOULD HAVE ITS RIGHT.

Before I have shown of right of jurisdiction and the right to profits which the clergy claim to have. Now I shall show you another right which they claim to punish overt sin and this is in three principal points, namely usury, perjury and defamation, and for this I wish to treat of the natures and qualities of these three things, where they shall be punished in one law and in the other and where in both and where in no law. And firstly we shall look at usury.

It appears by Master Glanville in his book of the laws of England that by the law of the land before the conquest usury was prohibited, and if a man was indicted of usury by the oath of twelve men he would lose his lands and tenements and his son would not inherit, which was hard law.[2] But afterwards the Jews used usury and took their authority from Deuteronomy 23, where it is said 'you shall not lend money at interest to your brother, but it is permitted to lend at interest to a stranger', and in this way they gained great sums of English money because [the English] were not able to commit usury except with them.[3] And for this King Edward I, in the fourth year of his reign, made the statute of the Jews, which prohibited the Jews from taking anything from lands or tenements, rents or other things, on pain of being punished at the king's will and to render the usury and pledge to a Christian.[4] Still, usury between Christian and Christian was not punishable by this statute or any other in the temporal law, but only by the spiritual law until the year 3 Hen. VII when it was enacted that every man who made a corrupt bargain which is grounded on usury shall forfeit £100,

---

[1] Fitzherbert, *Devise*, 27. [2] *Glanvill*, p. 89.
[3] Deuteronomy 23: 19–20. [4] Temp. Incert. (*SR*, i. 221–222).

savant all spirituall ley lour punishement. Auxi pur les spirituall offences sur cest estatut fuerent divers substantiall persons vexes, entre auters segnior William Capell de Londres, pur ceo que il avoiet deliver plate a un pur lx li. que fuit vend pur l li. et le partie fuit oblige de paier le dit lx li. en estatuit de 80 li. et fist feffement auxi de son terres sur condition que sil ne paie le lx li. que les feoffes serra seisi al use de segnior William Capell: il faiel de paiet, segnior William Capell sua le statut vers lui pur le det et auxi prist les profittes del tere. Ceo fuit adjuge userie et il paia le forfatur, mes pur ceo que cest estatut fuit dure, anno 11° H[en.] 7 novell estatut fuit fait et la fuerent declare iij maners de bargaines deestre usurie.[1] Le primer si ascun home prist ascun chose pur la lone de son argent si ne soet loiall penaltie. Le 2^d lou home vend a un auter esteant en necessitie queux sount vendres pur minor price et le primer vendor ou son factor ou broaker reachate eux deinz iij mois, sachant destre mesme les bienz, et ceo ne fuit usurie all comen ley ne Spirituall ley. Le 3^{ce} lou home pur lone de son monie covenant daver terres et de prendre les profittes tanques all temps de payment oustre le some: ceo est fait usurie per cest estatut et serra punishe en la temporall court quar il ad forfait le moitie dell chose, et auxi avera spirituall punishement.

Cest paroll *usura* per ascuns doctors dicitur de usu rei, scilicet quant home prist profit pur le use del chose.[2] Autors doctors diont que dicitur de usu eris, scilicet quant home prist profite pur le use de monie. Mes totes doctors agreont que usura est quodcunque solucione rei mutate accedit ipsius rei usus gracia pactionis interposita vel hac intentione habita in contractu vel ex occasione habita ex post facto hoc est usury est chescun chose que vient all chose mutate pur le use de mesme le chose ovesque un pact de covenant ou per endentment ewe en le pact ou apres per ascun act. Et sur ceo estatuit est a noter que en userie sount ceux choses: chose appromte, profitt appromte pur le use del chose per pact, expresse ou entended all temps del pact ou per auter by means apres et ceo est a voier.

[*fo. 78*] Quel pact serra dit usurie per le temporall ley et quell per le spirituall ley et lou usurie serra permy en lun ley et nemi en lauter.

Blees sont en Engleterre a xl d. le quarter et a xx s. en Espaigne, home vend a un auter x quarters pur v li. de paier un an apres, ceo nest usurie en lun ley ne en

---

[1] In margin: *iii maners de userie, Hr.*
[2] In margin: *difinitio, Hr.*

saving their punishment to the spiritual law.[1] Also for the spiritual offences on this statute divers substantial persons were vexed, among others Sir William Capell of London, because he had to deliver plate to one for £60 which was sold for £50 and the party was obliged to pay the said £60 in a statute of £80, and he also made a feoffment of his lands on condition that if he did not pay the £60 that the feoffees would be seised to the use of Sir William Capell: he failed to pay [and] Sir William Capell sued the statute against him for the debt and also took the profits of the land.[2] This was adjudged usury and he paid the forfeit, but because this statute was hard a new statute was made in the year 11 Hen. VII and there three types of bargains were declared to be usury.[3] The first [is] if any man takes anything for the loan of his money except a lawful penalty. The second [is] where a man who is in necessity sells [things] to another for a smaller price and the first seller or his factor or broker buys them back within three months knowing that they are the same goods, and this was not usury at the common law or the spiritual law. The third [is] where a man for loan of his money agrees to have lands and to take the profits until the time of payment beyond the sum [originally lent]: this is made usury by this statute and shall be punished in the temporal court for he has forfeited half of the thing, and also he shall have a spiritual punishment.

This word *usura* by some doctors is said to be *usu rei*, namely when a man takes a profit for the use of a thing. Other doctors say that it is *usu aeris*, namely when a man takes a profit for the use of money. But all doctors agree that usura is *quodcunque solutione rei mutuate accedit ipsius rei usus gracia pactionis interposita vel hac intentione habita in contractu vel ex occasione habita ex post facto*, that is, usury is something which comes to the thing borrowed [in return] for the use of that thing with a pact of covenant or by an understanding had in the pact or afterwards by some act. And on this statute it is to be noted that in usury there are these things: a thing borrowed, profit borrowed for the use of the thing by a pact, expressed or understood at the time of the pact or by another by means afterwards, and this is to be seen.

What pact shall be said to be usury by the temporal law and what by the spiritual law, and where usury shall be permitted in the one law and not in the other.

[If] corn is in England at 40d. a quarter and at 20s. in Spain [and] a man sells ten quarters to another for the payment of £5 a year later, this is not usury in the

---

[1] 3 Hen. VII, c. 6, An acte agaynst exchaunge and rechaunge without the kyng's lycence (*SR*, ii. 515). *Rectius* £20.

[2] Sir William Capell's Case is reported in Port, *Notebook*, pp. 13–14, where it is dated to Mich. 1494. In 1495 Capell was charged a fine of £2,743. 3s. for offending 'agayn certayn statutis of the parlement and parlementis by many dayes & yeris passid by which men thowgth shuld nevyr have been callid to myend'. A. Thomas and I. Thornley eds., *The Great Chronicle of London* (1938), p. 258; cf. C.L. Kingsford ed., *Chronicles of London* (Oxford, 1905), p. 205. Capell was in trouble again at the end of Henry's reign, and his offences then seem to have been connected with price fixing, which might also fall under the heading of usury, *Great Chronicle*, p. 331; *Chronicles of London*, p. 262. See also Baker, *OHLE* vi, 833 n. 100.

[3] 11 Hen. VII, c. 8, An acte agaynst usurye (*SR*, ii. 574).

lauter. Issint quant home lone un corne quant blees sont de value de v s. de paier tant le prochein an et donque corne est a x s. et prist tant, ceo nest usurie en ascun ley. Mes si home lone corne cest ann et fist pact daver tant de corne prochein an et un surplusage coment que corne decaie en price, uncore cest usurie quar lentent commence sur le bargaine.

Home prompt xx li. et est oblige en xxx li. et ne paiera le xx li., le oblige prist xxx li., nest usurie per le statut. Mes si home doit xx li. et puis daver longer space fist single obligacion de xxx li. et puis ceo est usurie per ambideux <le ieye>[d] leis.

Home apprompte argent de un auter en hope daver profit pur le lone cest usurie en espiritual ley mes nemi en temporal ley. Mes sil reserve ascun profit per paroll ou escript est usurie en ambideux leyes. Home apprompt dun auter et lui repaia et de son mere mocon dona a lui profit pur le lone sans demaunde, nest usurie <en>[i] ascun ley. Mes sil demaunde profit apres est usurie en le spiritual ley mes nemi en le temporal ley.

Home apprompt milke bestes a un pur an et le apprompter promise de deliver les bestes ou le value et ij d. chescun sepmaine cest usurie per le spiritual mes nemi per le temporall ley. Home apprompt drie vaches de compaster, rendrent rent et les vaches arere, ceo est usurie en ambideux leyes.[1] Contrarie ley est de chivalle.

Home est oblige de paier x li. le primer jour de May et ouster sil ne paiera le dit x li. all jour, il lui oblige de paier xv li. mesme le jour: le oblige[e] sue lobligation ceo nest usurie.

Home vend a un auter esteant en necessite un bale de [wode][2] et apres deinz iij mois son servant achate mesme le balle sachant estre mesme, ceo nest usurie coment que soit deinz iij mois. Mes sil achate ceo all use de son magister et le magister consent, ceo est usurie en le magister.

Home vend un drape a un home que est … riche et apres achata ceo deinz trois mois sachant destre mesme le drap, ceo nest usurie.

Home vend a un auter esteant en necessitie broken argent et il de parte de ceo fait un hanap et vend pur meindre price le primer vendor sciant destre fait de mesme le argent, uncore ceo nest usurie. Mesme le ley si home vend chivall et le vendee ceo fait geldinge. Mes si home vend a un blanke drape et lui dia ruge et il achate mesme le clothe sachans estre mesme le drap, ceo est usurie. Contrarie ley si home vend un pane et le vende fist robe de ceo et apres le primer vendor reachatat sachant estre fait de mesme le pane, ceo nest usurie. Mesme ley si un home vend lether et vende[e] fist boutes ou males.

Home achat<er>[d] un chival de xl s. de paier iiij li. iij ans apres, ceo nest usurie al temporall ley. Mesme ley si home deliver un [annelle][3] de x li. de aver xx li. al jour de son mariage. Home apprompt dun auter x li. de paier xx li. quant tiell shippe vient a tiel porte de London, nest usurie.

---

[1] In margin: H[enry] 8, *Ha* and *Hr*.
[2] *Ha* ode; *Hr* cole.
[3] MS reads annean; amean in *Hr*.

one law or the other. Thus when a man lends corn when grain is [valued] at 5s. to pay as much the next year, and then corn is [valued] at 10s. and [he] takes as much, this is not usury in any law. But if a man lends corn this year and makes a pact to have as much corn the next year, and more even if corn goes down in price, this is usury for the intent begins with the bargain.

[If] a man borrows £20 and is obliged in £30 and does not pay the £20 [and] the obligee takes £30, this is not usury by the statute. But if a man owes £20 and then to have it for a longer time he makes a single bond of £30, then this is usury by both laws.

[If] a man borrows money of another in the hope of having profit for the loan this is usury in the spiritual law but not in the temporal law. But if he reserves any profit by word or writing it is usury in both laws. If a man borrows from another and repays him, and by his free choice gives him a profit for the loan without a demand, this is not usury in any law. But if he demands a profit afterwards this is usury in the spiritual law but not in the temporal law.

[If] a man borrows milk beasts from one for a year and the borrower promises to deliver the beasts or the value and 2d. each week, this is usury by the spiritual law but not by the temporal. If a man borrows dry cows to manure, rendering rent and the cows back again, this is usury in both laws. The law is the contrary for horses.

A man is bound to pay £10 the first day of May, and if he does not pay the said £10 on the day he is further bound to pay £15 the same day: [if] the obligee sues the bond this is not usury.

A man who is in necessity sells a bale of woad to another and within three months afterwards his servant buys the same bale knowing it to be the same, this is not usury even though it is within three months. But if he buys this to the use of his master and the master consents, this is usury in the master.

A man sells a cloth to a man who is … rich and afterwards he buys this within three months knowing it to be the same cloth, this is not usury.

A man who is in necessity sells broken silver to another and the other makes a cup from part of this and sells it for a greater price [to the] first seller knowing it to be made of the same silver, still this is not usury. The law is the same if the man sells a horse and the buyer makes it a gelding. But if the man sells a white cloth and he dyes it red and he buys the same cloth knowing it to be the same cloth, this is usury. The law [is] contrary if a man sells a cloth and the buyer makes a robe of this, and afterwards the first seller buys it back knowing it to be made of the same cloth, this is not usury. The law is the same if a man sells leather and [the] buyer makes boots or bags.

[If] a man buys a horse [worth] 40s. to pay £4 three years afterwards, this is not usury in the temporal law. The law is the same if a man delivers a ring of £10 to have £20 on the day of his marriage. [If] a man borrows £10 of another to pay £20 when such a ship comes to such a port of London, this is not usury.

Home fait feffement en mortgage et le mortgage[e] prist les profites et le mortgager repaie largent sans deducation des profites, ceo nest usurie per lestatut. Mes si home apprompt argent a un auter et le appromptor covenant que le apprompte[e] <avera>^d avera les profites de maner de Dale tanque il soit paie et ij ans apres, sil prist les profites ij ans apres il est usurie per le statut et spirituall ley. [*fo. 78v*] Contrarie ley est si home fist feffement <a un auter>ⁱ reservant certein rent et pur defaut de chescun jour que le feffe forfetera x s., ceo nest usurie en le temporall ley mes per le spiritual ley est. Home apprompt argent de un et le apprompt[or] enfeffe le apprompt[ee] dun manner tanque que il ad prist le some, le some est encourus et ill prist les profittes apres uncore ceo nest usurie per le statut sans covenant.

Quelle serement serra dit perjurie en le spiritual ley et quelle en temporall ley et lou un serement serra dit perjurie en lun ley et nemi en lauter.

Home de son bon gre fait serement quill paier x li. a John at Style tiel jour et ne fait ceo nest perjurie en spirituall ley mes <en>^d il serra sue pro fide laesa. Mes sil jure devant le juge est perjurie en lour ley mes nemi en temporall ley. Home fist serement devant un juge que il aidera John at Style si longe come John at Style lui aidera et John at Style ne lui aida en necessitie et apres ill ne aide John at Style, ceo nest perjurie en lun ley ne en lauter. Mes si home jur devant le chauncelor que il voidra hors de realme <devant>^d per tiel jour et il entre en religion, ceo est perjurie per le temporall ley mes nemi per le spirituall ley.

Home apprompt argent de moi et fait moi jur que jeo ne demaunder largent et jeo demaunde, ceo est perjurie per ambideux leis mes solement punisheable per le spiritual ley. Mes si home robbe moi et fait moi jur que jeo ne lui disclose et jeo disclose ceo, jeo ne suis perjure. Issint si home dit a moi que il voit tuer tiel home et fait moi jur de keper secret.

Si home fist serement en le chauncerie que il maria tiel feme devant tiel jour et ell devant est deforme <ou>ⁱ <et>^d en povertie devant le jour il est perjur en le temporal ley mes nemi en le spiritual ley. Mes sil fist serement a <le>ⁱ feme et <le>ⁱ feme a lui il est perjur en ambideux leis quar est contract. Home fist serement en le chauncerie de non accepter part vers John at Style et apres action est per aunc[estre] discend a lui et il sue John at Style pur son droit il ne perjur en ascun ley. Mes sil soit atturney pur un auter vers lui est perjure en ambideux leys.

Home est jur en le chauncerie a deliver totes les evidence queux il ad en possession mesme le jour et apres auter evidences devient <en>^d <a>ⁱ son main et il[s] ne delivera, il nest perjur. Contrarie ley est sil soit jur que il delivera totes les evidences que sont a viendre a son mains.

Lou home serra perjur al comen ley et nul punishement.

Tenant en assise pled nul tort et son title est un record quell il jura et ilz trovent pur le pleintif, ceo est faux serement et encor nul punishement al comen ley.

ⁱ *Hr.*

[If] a man makes a feoffment in mortgage and the mortgagee takes the profits and the mortgagor repays the money without deducting the profits, this is not usury by the statute. But if a man borrows money from another and the borrower covenants that the lender shall have the profits of the manor of Dale until he is paid and [for] two years afterwards, if he takes the profits [for] two years afterwards it is usury by the statute and spiritual law. The law [is] contrary if a man makes a feoffment to another reserving certain rent and for default of each day the feoffee shall forfeit 10s.: this is not usury in the temporal law but by the spiritual law it is. A man borrows money from one and the borrower enfeoffs the lender of a manor until he has taken the sum: [if] the sum is incurred and he takes the profits afterwards still this is not usury by the statute without a covenant.

What oath shall be called perjury in the spiritual law and what in the temporal law, and where an oath shall be called perjury in the one law and not in the other.

[If] a man of his free will makes an oath that he shall pay £10 to John at Style on such a day and he does not do [this], this is not perjury in the spiritual law but he shall be sued for *fidei laesio*. But if he swears before the judge it is perjury in their law but not in the temporal law. [If] a man makes an oath before a judge that he will help John at Style as long as John at Style helps him, and John at Style does not help him in necessity, and afterwards he does not help John at Style, this is not perjury in the one law or the other. But if a man swears before the chancellor that he shall go out of the realm by such a day and [instead] he enters in religion, this is perjury by the temporal law but not by the spiritual law.

[If] a man borrows money from me and makes me swear that I shall not demand the money and I demand it, this is perjury by both laws but only punishable by the spiritual law. But if a man robs me and makes me swear that I shall not disclose it and I disclose it, I am not perjured. The same if a man says to me that he wishes to kill a man and makes me swear to keep the secret.

If a man makes an oath in the Chancery that he shall marry such a woman before such a day and she is deformed or in poverty before the day, he is perjured in the temporal law but not in the spiritual law. But if he makes an oath to the woman and the woman to him he is perjured in both laws for it is a contract. [If] a man makes an oath in the Chancery not to take part against John at Style, and afterwards an action descends to him through an ancestor and he sues John at Style for his right, he is not perjured in any law. But if he is an attorney for another against [John at Style] he is perjured in both laws.

A man is sworn in Chancery to deliver all the evidence that he has in his possession the same day, and afterwards other evidences come into his hand and he does not deliver them, he is not perjured. The law is contrary if he had sworn to deliver all of the evidences which came into his hands.

Where a man shall be perjured at the common law with no punishment.

[If] a tenant in assize pleads no tort and his title is a record which he swears and they find for the plaintiff, this is a false oath and yet there is no punishment at the common law.

TABLES AND INDEX

TABLE OF CASES

I: Named Cases

II: Cases Cited by Year

III: Undated

IV: Canon and Civil Law

TABLE OF STATUTES

INDEX